AMERICA COMPARED

AMERICA COMPARED

American History in International Perspective

SECOND EDITION

VOLUME II: Since 1865

CARL J. GUARNERI

SAINT MARY'S COLLEGE OF CALIFORNIA

HOUGHTON MIFFLIN COMPANY   BOSTON   NEW YORK

To my parents-in-law, George and Alice Weller

Publisher: Charles Hartford
Editor-in-Chief: Jean Woy
Senior Sponsoring Editor: Sally Constable
Development Editor: Lisa Kalner Williams
Senior Project Editor: Rosemary R. Jaffe
Editorial Assistant: Rachel Zanders
Senior Art and Design Coordinator: Jill Haber
Senior Composition Buyer: Sarah Ambrose
Senior Photo Editor: Jennifer Meyer Dare
Senior Manufacturing Coordinator: Priscilla Bailey
Senior Marketing Manager: Sandra McGuire

Cover image: *Anti-War Protest in Solidarity with India, Pakistan, and the Moslem Community,* by Franklin McMahon, c. 2002. © Franklin McMahon/Corbis.

Printed in the U.S.A.
Library of Congress Control Number: 2002109469
ISBN: 0-618-31857-7
1 2 3 4 5 6 7 8 9-QWF-08 07 06 05 04

CONTENTS

PREFACE

American History in International Perspective

Events have conspired to make the appearance of a second edition of *America Compared* especially timely. The attacks on the World Trade Center and the Pentagon in September 2001 shattered Americans' sense of separateness and awakened feelings of national vulnerability. When American policymakers responded by invading Afghanistan and Iraq and declaring a worldwide war on terrorism, the United States reached its highest level of global intervention since the Cold War. Pondering these developments, many journalists have called upon teachers and scholars to provide a more global context for understanding America's history. Their sense of urgency is understandable, but it is important to remember that this appeal has been voiced many times before. Throughout the twentieth century, including the time after Japan's surprise bombing of Pearl Harbor in December 1941 — an attack to which the events of 9/11 have been widely compared — calls to place American history in international perspective appeared regularly in newspapers and scholarly journals whenever Americans were reminded by momentous events that their nation's fate is entwined with the rest of the world.

If we pull back from the trauma of 9/11 to analyze longer-term trends, we can see that three modern developments have highlighted the international dimension of American history. First, in the twentieth century the United States emerged as an unusually potent world player: a "superpower" that intervened in two world wars, waged a successful cold war against Soviet communism, and undertook foreign policy initiatives that influenced the lives of people everywhere. Charting the rise of the United States from provincial backwater to world power has become an essential task for those studying its history. Second, the linking of the world's people through instant communication, open markets, multinational corporations, and mass entertainment — a phenomenon loosely referred to as "globalization" — has prompted scholars to rethink the American past. Today's global connections have their origins in revolutions begun by printing presses and oceanic sailing ships five centuries ago, when Europeans' expansion began to create an interlinked world economy. The United States, a nation settled in the first stage of globalization, has been implicated in international patterns of trade and migration from its birth. Its story must be told with these connections in mind. Third, beginning in the 1960s, the varying fortunes of America's world position, from the tragedy of the Vietnam War to the triumphant end of the Cold War to the jarring ups and downs of the nation's economy, have spurred a lively debate over America's special uniqueness. American "exceptionalism" is the belief, dating back nearly four hundred years to the era of colonization, that America is a "chosen land" that developed fundamentally apart from the rest of the world and has been exempt from its problems. This faith is so linked to Americans' national identity that it is part of the air they breathe, but in recent decades it has been questioned by many people at home and abroad as they try to examine more objectively America's place in the world.

The commitment to exceptionalism has traditionally produced insular narratives of the American past. But the United States' involvement in the world has become too obvious to ignore, and as its global impact has grown, scholars have increasingly sought larger contexts for describing its history. More and more historians are tying American events to trends elsewhere, pursuing ideas and movements across national boundaries, and analyzing American history comparatively.

America Compared gathers some of the best of these internationally informed writings for assignment in American history courses. This reader is intended for undergraduate survey classes, although it has also been used in high school Advanced Placement courses and served as a text for specialized college courses aimed at upper-division students. The topics covered are synchronized with those of most introductory courses in American history. Thus, *America Compared* takes familiar subjects and tries to see them anew through international contexts and comparisons. The primary focus is, of course, American history, but each reading that I have selected gives its topic a new dimension by relating it to comparable features in other societies or by situating it in a history of transnational contacts and exchanges. In this way, each selection is meant to contribute to the two major aims of this book: to place U.S. history in an international context and to assess the nature and extent of American uniqueness.

The Varieties of Comparative History

To illustrate the different ways that American history can be internationalized, I have used an elastic definition of comparative history. It incorporates **four "c-words"** that help to lead U.S. history outward toward larger frameworks of interpretation. First, and most obviously, there are direct **comparisons** between different national experiences. Most of the selections in *America Compared* offer focused comparisons, sometimes brief but at other times extended, between developments in the United States and elsewhere. A second way to internationalize America's history is to explore transnational **connections.** Many selections included in this reader describe contacts or connections between Americans and other peoples through such experiences as migration, trade, travel, international social movements, the transfer of technology, diplomacy, and wars. A third strategy measures specific features of American history against **concepts** that social scientists have developed to describe processes that go beyond particular societies. In this case, scholars examine overall theories or models concerning such developments as revolutions, nation building, industrialization, or imperialism to determine how well they describe the American version of these processes. Finally, encompassing the first three strategies, there is the search for larger **contexts** for understanding events that took place on American soil. Once we follow the flow of people, ideas, and goods across national borders, we begin to realize that many developments that we think of as uniquely American were not. The American Revolution, religious revivalism, the expanding frontier, and other key features of American history were variants of larger movements that proceeded simultaneously on other continents and were related through economic and cultural ties. Several readings in this collection explore these transnational contexts and systems and discuss America's place in them.

Each of these interpretive strategies expands our appreciation of the international dimensions of American history. There is also much overlap between them. Since all of the "four c's" involve international comparisons in one way or another, the selections that adopt their approaches discuss similarities and differences between America's history and that of other places.

The French historian Marc Bloch once noted that the most illuminating comparisons are those between societies with common influences and substantial basic similarities. Keeping this in mind, most of the selections in this reader relate the United States to one of three reference groups: 1) other European "settler societies" in Latin America, Canada, Australia, and South Africa that were established as colonies, confronted indigenous peoples, and attained their independence; 2) western European nations, such as Great Britain, France, and Germany, that forged transatlantic connections with the early United States and later underwent similar political, social, and industrial trends; and 3) the new political and industrial world powers of the twentieth century, Japan and Russia. The possibilities for making brief and intriguing comparisons across places and times are endless, as opinion pieces in our newspapers' editorial pages demonstrate daily. But the richer rewards that come from more sustained comparisons and deeper engagement with history are what we are after here. These are more likely to surface when focusing our attention on nations with substantial ties or basic similarities to the United States.

The Format and Features of This Book

The topics covered in *America Compared* are divided into periods and themes ranging from the Columbian encounter to Reconstruction (Volume I) and from Reconstruction to the controversy over globalization and American empire (Volume II). Each chapter of the book features two journal articles or book extracts. These **selections** represent the heart of this collection. They are not historical documents from the time period being studied, which historians call "primary sources." Rather they are works of historical interpretation, or "secondary sources," in which historians describe and analyze past events and consider their significance. As noted above, these readings have been chosen because they make fresh contributions to our understanding of American history by examining its features and events in an internationally comparative perspective.

Brief **chapter introductions** announce the topic and set it in an international or comparative context, then note the place of the selections that follow in that context. There is no single theme or approach that links every pair of selections. Some chapters ask students to distinguish between interpretations that stress American uniqueness and those that emphasize transnational similarities. Sometimes the readings offer sharply contrasting interpretations of the same event or era. In other cases, the first selection makes comparative generalizations that can be tested by a specific case study in the second. Often the selections cover different aspects of the chapter's overall topic, and they frequently feature different types of comparative approaches. The chapter introductions help to get students started in characterizing and comparing the selections that follow.

After this overview, **introductions to each selection** set the stage for its specific topic and approach. These introductions describe the broad historical issue or question the selection addresses and suggest the new dimension that comparative or transnational history brings to the topic. Offering a "sneak preview" of the selection to students, they note some ideas or arguments to look for and perhaps to contrast with other selections. When necessary, the introductions also provide basic background information on the foreign event or development that the selection uses as a comparative reference point.

Following each introduction and preceding the selection, a brief **Glossary** includes historical terms, persons, or events that appear in the reading but are not adequately described there. This will allow students to make the most of this reader without resorting to dictionaries, encyclopedias, or even an American history textbook. These glossaries are especially important for terms relating to other countries' histories, which are not likely to be identified in other books assigned in a U.S. history course. Students may want to peruse the glossary before beginning the selection, or they can simply consult it for information as they go along. Either way, the glossaries make it easier for students to grasp international references and comparisons.

At the end of each selection I have provided **Questions to Consider** to help students understand and analyze the reading. These questions are clustered into five numbered groups and are carefully constructed to guide students to increasing levels of historical understanding. The first questions help students comprehend the reading. The next questions encourage students to analyze its ideas and evidence and to relate its findings to important historical issues. The final questions ask students to compare the selection's viewpoint to those of others in the book and to assess the value of its particular kind of comparative method. These study questions are intended to integrate students' understanding of specific topics in America's past, and at the same time they invite them to explore the longer timespans and wider contexts of American history.

What's New in This Edition

This second edition of *America Compared* features **new selections** drawn especially from recent historical writings.

> Volume I includes **seven new selections** that explore the international dimensions of early American history. These cover British colonial "folkways," the Atlantic economy, the Louisiana Purchase, American nationalism, the Second Great Awakening, transatlantic abolitionism, and the international women's rights movement.

> Volume II includes **nine new selections** that place modern American history in comparative perspective. These feature such topics as Indian–white relations, settlement patterns on the frontier, American imperialism in the Philippines, World War I, and jazz music. They also include entirely new chapters on the Cold War and on globalization and American empire.

Consistent with the first edition, many of these readings situate domestic American events in their international context, but the new edition gives substantially increased attention to America's role in the world through diplomacy, war, and economic and cultural influence.

There are other changes that are intended to maximize the selections' impact and to deepen students' understanding of historical interpretation and method.

> **Expanded introductions to chapters and selections** initiate more comparisons and contrasts between the selections and provide insights about the particular kinds of comparative approaches they use.

> **New and revised glossaries** provide succinctly the most accurate and useful information on people, events, and terms found in the selections.

> **Expanded Questions to Consider** consistently encourage students to connect, compare, and contrast different selections in the book.

> **More reference maps** have been provided to clarify the geographic contexts of events in the United States and elsewhere.

I am gratified by the interest that teachers and students showed in the first edition of *America Compared,* and I have incorporated some of their suggestions for revisions. Partly because of their feedback, readers will find this edition more tightly organized, more focused in its approach, and more accessible in its information about events around the world.

Acknowledgments

Although I take sole responsibility for this book's contents, I am pleased to credit its existence to many people, from those who influenced my thinking over decades to others who offered specific assistance more recently. Years ago, my interest in comparative history was stimulated by inspiring teachers in graduate and undergraduate history programs: John Higham, Marcus Cunliffe, Robert Sklar, Robert Rosen, Stuart Samuels, and Jack Reece. Since then, numerous colleagues and friends have sustained our conversation on the global dimensions of American history, leading me to new insights and sources along the way as well as pointing out factual errors in my work. Among them I would like to thank Jonathan Beecher, Robert Blackey, Christopher Clark, Michel Cordillot, George Fredrickson, Jay Gordon, Nancy Green, Michael Kammen, Thomas Osborne, Jacques Portes, Allan Potofsky, Andrew Rotter, David Russo, Peter Stearns, Ian Tyrrell, and Francois Weil. I was fortunate to participate in the La Pietra conferences on Internationalizing United States History that took place from 1997 to 2000 under the joint auspices of New York University and the Organization of American Historians. At these meetings, ably conducted by NYU's Thomas Bender, several dozen scholars and teachers from around the world exchanged ideas about how American history should be rethought for a global age. Their insights profoundly shaped my thinking and are reflected in many ways in this edition of *America Compared*.

In practical terms, my plan for this reader crystallized when a curriculum development grant from the James Irvine Foundation enabled me to design an upper-division course on "United States History in Comparative Perspective" and then to revise my introductory U.S. history survey along similar lines. I am grateful to several groups of my students for testing most of the selections found here as well as others that were not chosen for the book. Saint Mary's College and its faculty have been generous in their support. An Alumni Faculty Fellowship Grant helped defray some of the first edition's permissions expenses, and the Frank J. Filippi Endowment provided some respite from full-time teaching in order to complete revisions for the second edition. My colleagues in the history department have suggested readings to include and offered encouragement for the project from the outset.

Colleagues at other institutions reviewed various drafts of this reader, in whole or in part, and made significant contributions to the final version of the first or second editions. I thank the following teachers and scholars for their thoughtful criticisms and suggestions.

For the second edition:

Amy E. Davis, University of California, Los Angeles
Anthony G. Gulig, University of Wisconsin — Whitewater
Paul A. Kramer, Johns Hopkins University
Victor Silverman, Pomona College

For the first edition:

Thomas A. Brown, Augustana College — Illinois
David B. Castle, Ohio University
Anthony Edmonds, Ball State University
Ellen Eslinger, DePaul University
Lisbeth Haas, University of California, Santa Cruz
Judith M. Ishkanian, University of California, Santa Barbara
Elizabeth A. Kessel, Anne Arundel Community College
Alexander W. Knott, University of Northern Colorado
Michael Kurtz, Southeastern Louisiana University
Everett Long, University of Wisconsin — Whitewater
James I. Matray, New Mexico State University
Elizabeth McKillen, University of Maine
Scott Nelson, College of William and Mary
T. Michael Ruddy, St. Louis University
Bruce J. Schulman, Boston University
Michael W. Schuyler, University of Nebraska at Kearney
Ron Spiller, Stephen F. Austin State University
William W. Stueck, University of Georgia
Thomas Templeton Taylor, Wittenberg University
Sara W. Tucker, Washburn University
William Woodward, Seattle Pacific University

At Houghton Mifflin, Leah Strauss, Christina Lembo, and Lisa Kalner Williams helped develop this edition of *America Compared,* which is sponsored by Sally Constable. Rosemary Jaffe oversaw the production process, while Michael Farmer, Stella Gelboin, Jan Kristiansson, Penny Peters, Lisa Jelly Smith, and Linda Sykes played important roles in various stages of the project. Special thanks again go to Menton Sveen, who got my foot in the door.

C. J. G.

I

Emancipation and Reconstruction

As the Civil War ended, Americans were faced with the dual task of restoring the Union and securing the freedom of the former slaves. The first was a uniquely American problem, but the second was not. When the United States ratified the Thirteenth Amendment abolishing slavery in 1865, it followed an international trend that began with the Haitian Revolution in 1801, continued with British emancipation in the West Indies in 1833, and ended with Brazil finally freeing its slaves in 1888. Wherever emancipation happened, whether it was accomplished by black revolution, legislation, or civil war, it brought controversy over what economic and political role the freedmen would play in the new society. In the case of the United States, emancipation proceeded in the bitter aftermath of the Civil War and was complicated by the same sectional divisions that had caused that conflict. It was also compromised by impatience to restore the Union quickly and especially by the limits of white Americans' commitment to full equality for blacks. As Reconstruction developed, it became a struggle in which the nation briefly took two steps forward, then took one back. During the years of Radical Reconstruction (1867–1871), Republicans imposed sweeping egalitarian social and political changes on the defeated South, but failed to secure them against white southerners' return to power. As a result, although slavery was not reinstated, many of the gains freedmen made immediately after the war were reversed within a decade.

The selections in this chapter model two very different ways to weigh the successes and failures of American Reconstruction in comparative perspective. Eric Foner shows how emancipation in the United States, in a process very similar to that in the British West Indies, resulted in legal restrictions and economic dependency for the ex-slaves. But he also documents the Americans' unique attempt to grant freed slaves political rights. Although this "unfinished

1

revolution" proved temporary, it did leave behind a legal framework that would lend critical support to future struggles for black equality. C. Vann Woodward is less optimistic. Denying that Reconstruction was at all revolutionary, Woodward undertakes a "counterfactual" comparison between what actually happened and what *might* have happened if northerners had been seriously committed to overthrowing the old southern order and achieving racial equality. The outcome of this imaginative experiment leaves Woodward doubtful that radical change was possible, given the pervasive nineteenth-century American commitment to white supremacy.

The issue of how "revolutionary" Reconstruction was should lead you to consider various kinds of revolutions that can provide models to measure Reconstruction against. The two essays in this chapter also give you an opportunity to assess the relative usefulness of "traditional" historical comparisons versus "counterfactual" analysis. What conclusions do Foner's comparisons between emancipation in the United States and in the West Indies support? Is Woodward's "what if" analysis equally reliable as history? Do his speculations about possible alternatives in the American past simply confirm Foner's conclusions, or do they add important new insights?

1

The Politics of Freedom

ERIC FONER

No nineteenth-century change in the Western Hemisphere was as dramatic and far-reaching in its consequences as the abolition of slavery — or as controversial. What system of economic organization and what kind of social relations would replace slavery? Every plantation society undergoing emancipation witnessed bitter conflict over the role of the freedmen. Former slaves wanted control over their lives and ownership of land, while planters demanded a low-cost, disciplined labor force to continue tending and harvesting staple crops for export. In most cases the landed white elite retained the upper hand and used the law to coerce ex-slaves back to work. In Jamaica and Barbados, British colonial policy compensated owners and put the ex-slaves through a six-year system of "apprentice" farmwork. Planters in Trinidad and British Guiana turned instead to the importation of indentured laborers from India under five-to-ten-year contracts. Even Toussaint L'Ouverture, the black liberator of Haiti, conciliated the powerful planters by imposing a rigid system of forced labor upon the freedmen. Such policies did not always succeed. On larger Caribbean islands where land was available, for example, some former slaves managed to evade the system and become landowning peasants growing crops for local, rather than foreign, markets. But throughout the Caribbean the mass of ex-slaves were prevented from wielding political power either by outright exclusion or, in British dominions, by prohibitive property qualifications.

What about the United States? In the Reconstruction-era South, the same struggle took place between planters' prejudices and prerogatives on one side and the freedmen's aspirations on the other. But the United States was unique among postemancipation societies in granting freed slaves equal political rights — at least for a time. Here the struggle was complicated by divisions between slaveholders and non-slaveholders among southern whites and especially by the influence of northern Radical Republicans. Determined to make the South over in the North's free-labor image, these politicians joined with the emancipated slaves to create a unique, though short-lived, experiment in interracial democracy.

In this excerpt from his comparative study of emancipation, Nothing but Freedom, *Eric Foner surveys postwar conflicts in the South over labor laws, property rights, and taxes — all crucial to the future of blacks in the region. He traces the up-and-down fortunes of the freedmen during the three phases of Reconstruction. In 1865 and 1866, President Andrew Johnson pursued a lenient policy that restored ex-Confederates to economic and political power. One result of this "Presidential Reconstruction" was the infamous Black Codes, which reduced the freedmen to near-slave conditions. Outraged by Johnson's actions, Republican congressmen took control of the federal reins in 1867, forced southern states to accept black suffrage and civil rights in the Fourteenth and Fifteenth Amendments, and oversaw the election of biracial Republican regimes in the South. Gradually, however, conservative southern Democrats rallied under the banner of white supremacy and lower taxes and regained control of southern legislatures, ending Radical Reconstruction. These so-called Redemption governments put in place a new version of the South's "old regime" buttressed by repressive legislation that reversed important gains blacks had won. As Reconstruction wound down in the mid-1870s, the federal government, like British authorities in the West Indies, backed away from protecting the freedmen's civil rights and instead left intact a pattern of land distribution and black dependency essentially similar to the days of slavery.*

When the smoke of Reconstruction cleared, the outcome in the United States seemed depressingly similar to the Caribbean debacle. As in other postemancipation societies, slaves had won "nothing but freedom." Nevertheless, Foner points out, the unique U.S. experiment in Radical Reconstruction brought significant temporary advances in southern blacks' social and economic conditions. And — far more important — it put on the books federal laws and constitutional amendments that guaranteed freedom. Once enforced, these would support the struggle for racial equality during the "Second Reconstruction" a century later: the Civil Rights movement of the 1960s.

GLOSSARY

CONVICT LEASE SYSTEM   A legal provision by which the government hired out convicts to employers for low wages. In combination with vagrancy laws and excessive jailing of freedmen, this system was used to provide cheap black labor for planters and railroad companies.

COOLIE   Derived from Tamil and Urdu words for "hireling," a pejorative label for imported contract workers, especially from India or China.

ENCLOSURE   The process of enclosing, with fences, hedges, or other barriers, land formerly subject to common rights. The enclosure movement in eighteenth-century England was linked to the decline of the manorial system and the rise of commercial agriculture.

FOURTEENTH AMENDMENT   Formally adopted in 1868, the constitutional amendment that gave citizenship to all persons born or naturalized in the United States, including ex-slaves, and guaranteed them "the equal protection of the laws." As a key part of Radical Reconstruction, Congress required southern states to ratify this amendment in order to rejoin the Union. It took away congressional representatives from states that denied black males the vote.

FREEDMEN'S BUREAU   An agency of the army created by Congress in 1865 to oversee the condition of ex-slaves by providing food and clothing, establishing schools, and supervising labor contracts. Led by General O. O. Howard, the bureau had its role expanded by Congress in 1866 over President Johnson's veto.

MORANT BAY REBELLION   A freedmen's uprising in Jamaica in October 1865 in which angry blacks stormed a courthouse to protest the punishment of squatters, killing a magistrate and fifteen others. The colonial government retaliated by burning peasant villages, executing over four hundred blacks, and returning control of the colony to Britain.

PEONAGE   A system of involuntary servitude based on the indebtedness of the laborer (peon) to his or her creditor. It replaced slavery after emancipation in several Latin American countries and, for a time, in the United States.

POLL TAX   A uniform tax on adults that was levied in the South as a prerequisite for voting, thereby disfranchising many blacks and poor whites. The Twenty-fourth Amendment to the U.S. Constitution (1964) outlawed poll taxes in federal elections.

SHARECROPPING   A system of tenancy under which landowners gave blacks or poor whites a plot of land to work in return for payment of a share of the crops, usually from one-half to two-thirds, plus their debt to the landlord. In the long run, this system proved disastrous to sharecroppers because of falling cotton prices, high credit rates, and cheating by landowners and creditors.

TOUSSAINT L'OUVERTURE, FRANÇOIS DOMINIQUE (1743–1803)   Leader of the Haitian Revolution. A self-educated freed slave, he joined the rebellion of 1791 to liberate the slaves and played a key role in uniting the colony's blacks first against English and Spanish interference, then in an independence struggle against the French. He died in a French prison a year before the republic of Haiti became a reality.

WOOLSACK   A cloth-covered seat in the British House of Lords, reserved for the use of judges, especially the lord chancellor.

✯ ✯ ✯ ✯ ✯ ✯

At first glance, the scale, manner, and consequences of emancipation in the United States appear historically unique. The nearly four million slaves liberated in this country far outnumbered those in the Caribbean and Latin America. Although no abolition was entirely without violence, only in Haiti and the United States did the end of slavery result from terrible wars in which armed blacks played a crucial part. The economies of the Caribbean islands, tiny outposts of empire, had little in common with the nineteenth-century United States, where slavery existed within a rapidly expanding capitalist economic order.

Politically, the cast of characters in the United States was far more complex than in the West Indies. American blacks were outnumbered, even in the South, by whites, but this white population was divided against itself. There are few parallels in other postemancipation societies to the southern whites who cooperated politically with the freedmen, or the northerners, variously numbered at between twenty and fifty thousand, who moved into the South after the Civil War, carrying with them a triumphant free-labor ideology and, for a time, playing a pivotal role in political affairs. Nor were there counterparts to the Radical Republicans of the North, a group with real if ultimately limited political power, which sought to forge from emancipation a thoroughgoing political and social revolution, supplanting plantation society, as one put it, by "small farms, thrifty villages, free schools, . . . respect for honest labor, and equality of political rights."

Finally and most strikingly, the United States was the only society where the freed slaves, within a few years of emancipation, enjoyed full political rights and a real measure of political power. Limited as its accomplishments may appear in retrospect, Black Reconstruction was a stunning experiment in the nineteenth-century world, the only attempt by an outside power in league with the emancipated slaves to fashion an interracial democracy from the ashes of slavery.

Despite these and other exceptional features of their national experience, nineteenth-century Americans sensed that prior emancipations held lessons for the aftermath of slavery in this country. Their precise significance, however, was a matter of some dispute [for] . . . the experience of Caribbean emancipation was interpreted through the lens of rival American ideologies concerning race and slavery.

. . . To abolitionists, the West Indies revealed the dangers of leaving the fate of the emancipated blacks in the hands of their former owners. If British emancipation was open to criticism, it was for not going far enough. "England," the Boston cotton manufacturer and Republican reformer Edward Atkinson wrote, "after she had caused the negroes to cease to be chattels, stopped far short of making them men, leaving them subject to oppressive laws made entirely under the influence of their former owners."

Eric Foner, "The Politics of Freedom," in *Nothing but Freedom: Emancipation and Its Legacy* (Louisiana State University Press). Reprinted by permission of Louisiana State University Press.

The First Vote: *This lithograph appeared in* Harper's Weekly *in November 1867. It represents the uniquely American — but temporary — postemancipation policy of granting freed slaves equal political rights. Portrayed here are representative African American leaders in the South: an artisan, a member of the middle class, and a Union soldier. (*Harper's Weekly, *November 16, 1867.)*

His Boston colleague, railroad entrepreneur John Murray Forbes, likewise warned that Americans should take heed of "Jamaica's former experience in legislating the blacks back into slavery, by poor laws, vagrant laws, etc." Another abolitionist cited the Morant Bay "rebellion" of 1865 to demonstrate Britain's "grave mistakes" in attempting to create a halfway house between slavery and complete civil and political equality for blacks. Even Toussaint [L'Ouverture] now came in for censure, for what [abolitionist] Lydia Maria Child called "his favorite project of conciliating the old planters."

Toussaint's mistake, Child believed, lay in "a hurry to reconstruct, to restore outward prosperity," rather than attempting radically to transform his society on the basis of free labor principles. The implications of all these writings for American Reconstruction were self-evident.

Not surprisingly, white southerners drew rather different conclusions from the West Indian example. Opponents of Reconstruction seized upon Morant Bay and the demise of local self-government in the islands to illustrate the dangers of black suffrage and rule by "representatives of hordes of ignorant negroes." Democratic newspapers, north and south, were filled during the early days of Reconstruction with lurid reports of West Indian blacks sinking into a "savage state" when liberated from the controlling influence of whites. In Haiti, supposedly, they had reverted to barbarism, paganism, and even human sacrifice, and, said the New York *World,* "intimations of analogous phenomena have already reached us from the region of the lower Mississippi."

Most important, the West Indies demonstrated that plantations could not be maintained with free labor: "the experiments made in Haiti and Jamaica settled that question long ago." J. D. B. De Bow, the South's foremost economic writer, amassed statistics to demonstrate the collapse of the West Indian economies and the indolence of the blacks. Julius J. Fleming, the South Carolina journalist, noted, "It seems to be a conceded fact that in all countries where slavery has existed and been abolished the great difficulty in the way of improvement has been the very subject of labor." Certainly, the Caribbean example reinforced the conviction that American blacks must be prevented from obtaining access to land: otherwise, they would "add nothing to those products which the world especially needs." If the South were to escape the fate of Caribbean societies, it could only be through "some well regulated system of labor, . . . devised by the white man." The emancipated slave, the Louisville *Democrat* concluded after a survey of the West Indies, needed to be taught that "he is *free,* but free only to labor."

Whatever their ultimate conclusions, contemporaries were not wrong to draw parallels between American and Caribbean emancipations. For when viewed in terms of the response of blacks and whites to the end of slavery, the quest of the former slaves for autonomy and the desire of planters for a disciplined labor force, what is remarkable is the similarity between the American experience and that of other societies. As in the Caribbean and, indeed, everywhere else that plantation slavery was abolished, American emancipation raised the interrelated questions of labor control and access to economic resources. The plantation system never dominated the entire South as it did in the islands, yet both before and after emancipation, it helped define the quality of race relations and the nature of economic enterprise in the region as a whole. It was in the plantation black belt that the majority of the emancipated slaves lived, and it was the necessity, as perceived by whites, of maintaining the plantation system, that made labor such an obsession in the aftermath of emancipation. As Christopher G. Memminger, former Confederate secretary of the treasury, observed in 1865, politics, race relations, and the social consequences of abolition all turned "upon the decision which shall be made upon the mode of organizing the labor of the African race."

As in the Caribbean, American freedmen adopted an interpretation of the implications of emancipation rather different from that of their former masters. Sir Frederick Bruce,

the British ambassador to the United States, discerned little difference between the behavior of American and West Indian freedmen: "The negro here seems like his brother
in Jamaica, to object to labour for hire, and to desire to become proprietor of his patch
of land." The desire for land, sometimes judged "irrational" when viewed simply as a
matter of dollars and cents, reflected the recognition that, whatever its limitations, land
ownership ensured the freedmen a degree of control over the time and labor of themselves and their families. Candid observers who complained blacks were lazy and shift-
less had to admit that there was "one motive sufficiently powerful to break this spell, and
that is the *desire to own land*. That will arouse all that is dormant in their natures." Equally
a sign of the desire for autonomy was the widespread withdrawal of women from plantation field labor, a phenomenon to which contemporaries attributed a good part of the
postwar labor shortage.

For the large majority of blacks who did not fulfill the dream of independence
as owners or renters of land, the plantation remained an arena of ongoing conflict.
In postemancipation east Africa, according to Frederick Cooper, "the smallest
question — whether to plant a clove or cashew nut tree — became questions not just of
marginal utility, but of class power." And so it was in the postemancipation South,
where disputes over supervision by overseers, direction of the labor of black women
and children, and work like repairing fences, ditches, and buildings not directly related
to the crop at hand, followed the end of slavery. Emancipation ushered in a period of
what that perceptive South Carolina planter William H. Trescot called "the perpetual
trouble that belongs to a time of social change."

The eventual solution to the labor problem in the post–Civil War cotton South was
the system of sharecropping, which evolved out of an economic struggle in which
planters were able to prevent most blacks from gaining access to land, while the freedmen utilized the labor shortage (and in many cases, the assistance of the Freedmen's
Bureau) to oppose efforts to put them back to work in conditions, especially gang labor,
reminiscent of slavery. A way station between independent farming and wage labor,
sharecropping would later become associated with a credit system that reduced many
tenants to semipeonage. Yet this later development should not obscure the fact that, in
a comparative perspective, sharecropping afforded agricultural laborers more control
over their own time, labor, and family arrangements, and more hope of economic
advancement, than many other modes of labor organization. Sharecroppers were not
"coolie" laborers, not directly supervised wage workers. And whatever its inherent
economic logic, large numbers of planters believed sharecropping did not ensure the
requisite degree of control over the labor force. Sharecropping, complained one planter,
"is wrong policy; it makes the laborer too independent; he becomes a partner, and has
a right to be consulted." Such planters preferred a complete transition to capitalist agriculture, with a closely supervised labor force working for wages. A wage system did in
fact emerge on Louisiana sugar plantations and many Upper South tobacco farms. But
in general, sharecropping became the South's replacement system of labor after the end
of slavery. "To no laboring class," said a southern senator, "has capital — land — ever
made such concessions as have been made to the colored people at the South."

As in the Caribbean, the form of agrarian class relations that succeeded American slavery resulted from a struggle fought out on the plantations themselves. What made the American experience distinct was that the polity as well as the field became an arena of confrontation between former master and former slave. Here, emancipation occurred in a republic. In the British Empire, as one historian notes, "the question, 'does a black man equal a white man?' had little meaning in an age when few thought all white men deserved equality." In America, however, where equality before the law was the foundation of the political culture, emancipation led inexorably to demands for civil and political rights for the former slaves. In contrast to Caribbean peasants, moreover, whose major ambition seems to have been to be left alone, Afro-Americans demanded full participation in the political life of the nation. Nowhere else did blacks achieve a comparable degree of political influence after the end of slavery. "Their civil and political elevation," as a Tennessee congressman put it, "is unparalleled in the history of nations. . . . France and England emancipated their slaves, but the emancipated never dreamed that they should have letters of nobility, or should be elevated to the woolsack."

Black suffrage fundamentally altered the terms of the postemancipation conflict in the United States. Far more than in the Caribbean and Africa, where white planters, farmers, and mine owners monopolized local political power, state and local government in America became a battleground between contending social classes, including the black laborer. Southern planters, initially restored to local power during Presidential Reconstruction, sought to use the state to stabilize the plantation system and secure their control of the labor force. With the advent of Radical Reconstruction, the role of the state was transformed and the freedmen won, in the vote, a form of leverage their counterparts in other societies did not possess. Then, after Redemption, political and economic authority once again coincided in the South. If in the long run, planters, like their counterparts elsewhere, largely succeeded in shaping the political economy of emancipation in their own interests, by the same token Radical Reconstruction stands as a unique moment when local political authority actually sought to advance the interests of the black laborer. Many of the specific issues upon which postemancipation southern politics turned were the same as in the Caribbean and Africa: immigration, labor laws, the definition of property rights, taxation, and fiscal policy. The conflict over these questions, and its eventual outcome, reveal how much of postemancipation politics was defined by the "labor problem."

As in the Caribbean, some American planters advocated in the aftermath of emancipation that the government directly promote "the accumulation of population," to break the bargaining power of black labor. Immigration, said one observer, would solve two problems at once: "If you would control [the freedman's] political power, you must outvote him; and if you would control him as a laborer, you must fill the country with a more congenial and more reliable laborer."

Many southern states established agencies after the Civil War to encourage immigration from Europe, but the results were disappointing. Of the millions of immigrants landing in New York, Boston, and other northern cities, only a handful made their way south, a reflection, in part, of the ambivalent attitude white southerners communicated about their desire for immigration in the first place. Some reformers looked upon immigrants as prospective landholders; they urged planters to break up the large estates and make land available on easy terms to newcomers. Generally, however, immigration was intended not to undermine the plantation system, but to preserve it. A Republican newspaper was not incorrect when it concluded that the appeal for immigration, "when stripped of its verbosity, is about as follows: 'We have lands but can no longer control the niggers; . . . hence we want Northern laborers, Irish laborers, German laborers, to come down and take their places, to work our lands for ten dollars a month and rations of cornmeal and bacon.'"

"Immigration," a prominent North Carolina lawyer wrote in 1865, "would, doubt-less, be a blessing to us, provided we could always control it, and make it entirely subservient to our wants." As in the Caribbean, many planters concluded that inden-tured laborers would admirably meet this need. West Indian experiments with "coolie" labor were widely publicized in the post–Civil War southern press, and Chinese con-tract laborers were known to be at work in mines, railroad construction, and large-scale agriculture in contemporary California. A commercial agency offered to deliver "coolies" under five-to-seven-year contracts to Mississippi planters in 1865, and two years later a few Chinese, dispatched from Cuba by southerners living there, arrived to labor in Louisiana sugar fields. Robert Somers, the traveling British correspondent, encountered a gang of some six hundred Chinese laborers, drawn from California, at work on the Alabama and Chattanooga Railroad in 1871; and a number of Chinese laborers were introduced into the Yazoo-Mississippi delta around the same time. But despite enthusiastic predictions of how the Chinese would transform the labor situa-tion, . . . the total number of Chinese in the South never exceeded a handful. And many who were introduced proved less docile than anticipated, abandoning plantation labor to set up as small-scale merchants and truck farmers.

Compared with the situation in Trinidad and British Guiana, the need for imported laborers was less in the United States, and the obstacles to their introduction greater. Relatively few blacks had been able to abandon the plantations to take up independent farming. There was also the danger that meddling northerners would bestow the vote on the Chinese, further exacerbating political problems in the Reconstruction South. Blacks, moreover, exercising a measure of political power during Reconstruction, opposed the introduction of "coolies." And federal authorities warned that any effort to bring in laborers under long-term indentures would be deemed a violation of the 1862 statute outlawing the "Coolie Trade." During Reconstruction, Commissioner of Immigration A. N. Congar and Secretary of the Treasury George S. Boutwell promised that "all vigilance" would be exercised to suppress "this new modification of the slave trade."

As in the Caribbean, the effort to introduce Chinese labor in the postbellum South formed only one part of a broader effort to use the power of the state to shape the postemancipation economic order and create a dependent plantation labor force. "There must be stringent laws to control the negroes, and require them to fulfill their contracts of labor on the farms," wrote a South Carolina planter in 1865. "No one will venture to engage in agricultural occupations without some guarantee that his labor is to be controlled and continued under penalties and forfeitures." . . . [M]ost Southern whites accepted the fact that slavery was dead. But its dissolution, many believed, need not mean the demise of the plantation. "I am sure we will not be allowed even to contend for gradual emancipation," wrote Texas political leader and railroad promoter J. W. Throckmorton in August, 1865. "But I do believe we will be enabled to adopt a coercive system of labor."

The outcome of such pressures was the Black Codes of 1865 and 1866. Ostensibly, their purpose was to outline the legal rights to be enjoyed by the former slaves. Generally, blacks were accorded the right to acquire and own property, marry, make contracts, sue and be sued, and testify in court in cases involving persons of their own color. But the main focus of the laws was labor. As a New Orleans newspaper put it, with slavery dead, a new labor system must "be prescribed and enforced by the state."

First to rise to the challenge were the legislatures of Mississippi and South Carolina. The Mississippi Code required all blacks to possess, each January, written evidence of employment for the coming year. Laborers leaving their jobs before the contract expired would forfeit all wages up to that time, and the law empowered every white person to arrest any black who deserted the service of his employer. Any person offering work to a laborer already under contract was liable to a fine of five hundred dollars or a prison sentence. Finally, to ensure that no economic opportunities apart from plantation labor remained for the freedmen, they were forbidden to rent land in rural areas.

A vagrancy statute, enacted at the same time, imposed fines or involuntary labor on a bizarre catalog of antisocial types:

> rogues and vagabonds, idle and dissipated persons, beggars, jugglers, or persons practicing unlawful games or plays, runaways, common drunkards, common night-walkers, lewd, wanton, or lascivious persons, . . . common railers and brawlers, persons who neglect their calling or employment, misspend what they earn, or do not provide for the support of themselves or their families, or dependents, and all other idle and disorderly persons, including all who neglect all lawful business, habitually misspend their time by frequenting houses of ill fame, gaming-houses, or tippling shops.

And an apprenticeship law permitted the binding out to white employers of black orphans and children whose parents were unable to support them, with "the former owner of said minors" enjoying "the preference." In case anything had been overlooked, all previous penal codes defining offenses of slaves were declared to remain in force, unless specifically altered by law.

South Carolina's Black Code was, in some respects, even more discriminatory. It did not prohibit blacks from renting land, but barred them from following any occupation other than farmer or servant except by paying an annual tax ranging from ten to one hundred dollars. Blacks were required to sign annual contracts, and there were elaborate provisions regulating such agreements, including labor from sunup to sundown, deductions from wages for time not worked, and a prohibition against leaving the plantation or entertaining guests upon it, without permission. . . .

The uproar created by this legislation led other southern states to modify the language and provisions, if not the underlying intention, of early legislation regarding freedmen. Virtually all the former Confederate states enacted sweeping vagrancy, apprenticeship, labor contract, and antienticement legislation. Florida's code, drawn up by a three-member commission whose report praised slavery as a "benign" institution whose only shortcoming was its inadequate regulation of black sexual behavior, made disobedience, impudence, or even "disrespect" to the employer a crime. Louisiana and Texas, seeking to counteract the withdrawal of black women from field labor, declared that labor contracts "shall embrace the labor of all the members of the family able to work." Apprenticeship laws continued to seize upon the consequences of slavery — the separation of families and the poverty of the freedmen — as the excuse for securing to planters the labor of black minors free of expense. Many localities supplemented these measures with vagrancy ordinances of their own.

The laws of the southern states concerning labor, *De Bow's Review* claimed in 1866, were as "liberal, generous, and altogether as humane and equitable as the legislation of any country in the world under similar circumstances." De Bow was not being entirely disingenuous, for despite their excesses, the Black Codes were not as severe as the *Code Rural* of Haiti or some of the statutes enacted in the British Caribbean after emancipation. Southerners, indeed, insisted that precedents existed even in free labor societies for strict legal regulation of the labor force. "We have been informed by a distinguished jurist, who is a member elect of the Virginia Legislature," reported a South Carolina newspaper, "that the 'labor laws' of England . . . contain just such provisions for the protection of the employer as are now needed . . . at the South." And, it is true, laws subjecting employees, but not employers, to criminal penalties for breach of contract remained on the British statute books until 1875, and were widely enforced. Draconian English vagrancy laws, however, had long since fallen into abeyance. . . .

The Black Codes are worth dwelling upon not because of any long-range practical effect — most provisions were quickly voided by the army or Freedmen's Bureau, or invalidated by the Civil Rights Act of 1866 — but because of their immediate political impact and what they reveal about the likely shape of southern economic relations if left to the undisputed control of the planters. As W. E. B. Du Bois observed, the Codes represented "what the South proposed to do to the emancipated Negro, unless restrained by the nation." The Codes persuaded many in the North that continuing federal intervention was essential if the fundamental rights of the freedmen were to be protected. They convinced southern blacks as well that their former owners could not be entrusted with political power. The "undisputed history" of Presidential Reconstruction, black Congressman Josiah Walls later recalled, explained why southern blacks refused to cast Democratic ballots, and stood as a warning "as to what they will do if they should again obtain control of this Government." But, as quickly as planters attempted to call forth the power of the state in their own interests, their political hegemony was swept away, and a new series of measures regarding labor was placed on the southern statute books.

Radical Reconstruction, in this respect, profoundly if temporarily affected the relationship of the state to the economic order. The remnants of the Black Codes were repealed and laws were passed seeking to protect blacks from arbitrary dismissal and to ensure payment for time worked. "There is a law now in this State," a black state senator from Florida told a congressional committee, "that allows a man to get what he works for." By the same token, planters' pleas for legislation "the more effectually to secure punctually the observance and performance of labor contracts" went unheeded. . . .

Equally important, the machinery of justice had, particularly in the black belt, been wrested from the planter class. As blacks and their white Republican allies took control of local courts, sheriff's offices, and justiceships of the peace, there were increasing complaints that vagrancy laws were unenforced, trespass was left unpunished, and efforts to discipline troublesome laborers enjoyed no support from the state. . . .

With Redemption, the state again stepped forward as an instrument of labor control. Georgia's Redeemer Governor James M. Smith was quite candid about the intention: "We may hold inviolate every law of the United States, and still so legislate upon our labor system as to retain our old plantation system." . . . Not all these measures, of course, were entirely effective. Black efforts to escape the clutches of tenancy and debt peonage persisted, and federal law placed limits on measures forthrightly designed to restrain the freedmen's mobility. The point is not that the law succeeded fully in its aims, but that the state's intervention altered the balance of economic power between black and white.

What one black political leader called "the class legislation of the Democrats against the race" embraced vagrancy laws, restrictions on labor agents, laws against "enticing" a worker to leave his employment, and criminal penalties for breach of contract. Apart from a few remaining enclaves of black political power, moreover, these laws were now administered by white sheriffs and judges who owed no political debt to the black community. Such legislation, as a Tennessee black convention noted in 1875, was calculated "to make personal liberty an utter impossibility and . . . place the race in a condition of servitude scarcely less degrading than that endured before the late civil war." As required by the Fourteenth Amendment, the statutes were, on the surface, color-blind — in this respect they differed from the Black Codes of Presidential Reconstruction. But as the Tennessee blacks commented, "a single instance of punishment of whites under these acts has never occurred, and is not expected." . . .

As far as most southern whites were concerned, the issue of property rights for the former slaves simply did not arise. As General Robert V. Richardson put it in 1865, "The emancipated slaves own nothing, because nothing but freedom has been given to them." Blacks, on the other hand, contended that freedom should carry with it a stake in the soil, a demand reminiscent of the aspirations of Caribbean freedmen, but legitimized in ways distinctively American.

Blacks in the Caribbean . . . had enjoyed under slavery the "right" to extensive provision grounds, the embryo of the postemancipation peasantry. Many American slaveholders also permitted blacks to keep chickens and sometimes hogs, to raise vegetables to supplement their diets, and to sell the products of their "kitchen gardens" to raise spending money. Slaves, Eugene D. Genovese contends, came to view these gardens as a right rather than a privilege, but they were far less extensive than their counterparts in the West Indies, and American slaves tended to market their corn, eggs, vegetables, and pork directly to the planter rather than at town markets as in Jamaica. Only in coastal Georgia and South Carolina, where the task system allowed slaves considerable time to cultivate their own crops and the planters were absent for much of the year, did an extensive system of marketing and property accumulation emerge under American slavery.

Blacks' claim to landed property in the aftermath of American emancipation, then, was not primarily legitimized as a "right" that had been recognized during bondage. Rather, it rested on a claim to compensation for their unrequited toil as slaves. . . .

. . . To blacks the justice of a claim to land based on unrequited labor seemed self-evident. It was not that blacks challenged the notion of private property per se; rather, they viewed the accumulated property of the planters as having been illegitimately acquired. . . .

In its most sophisticated form, this claim to land rested on an appreciation of the role blacks had historically played in the evolution of the American economy. This was the import of the remarkable speech delivered by freedman Bayley Wyat protesting the eviction of blacks from a contraband camp in Virginia in 1866:

> We has a right to the land where we are located. For why? I tell you. Our wives, our children, our husbands, has been sold over and over again to purchase the lands we now locates upon; for that reason we have a divine right to the land. . . . And den didn't we clear the land, and raise de crops ob corn, ob cotton, ob tobacco, ob rice, ob sugar, ob everything. And den didn't dem large cities in de North grow up on de cotton and de sugars and de rice dat we made? . . . I say dey has grown rich, and my people is poor.

Such an appeal, Georgia lawyer Elias Yulee responded, was "mere nonsense." As he informed Georgia blacks in 1868, "as well may the Irish laborer claim New York city, because by his labor all the stores and residences there were constructed. Or claim our railroads because they labored on them with their shovels and wheelbarrows."

Yulee's comment illuminates the paradoxical double quality of free labor. As Marx emphasized, free labor is not bound as serf or slave, but is also "free" in that it enjoys no claim to the means of production. As labor became free, E. P. Thompson has explained in a different context, so "labour's product came to be seen as something totally distinct, the property of landowner or employee." Emancipation thus demanded a sharper demarcation between property and labor than had existed under slavery (since the laborer himself was no longer property). And, while the distribution of land never did materialize, the conflict over the definition of property rights continued on many fronts in the postbellum South. . . .

Like their Caribbean counterparts, southern freedmen did not believe the end of slavery should mean a diminution of either the privileges or level of income they had enjoyed as slaves. The slave, after all, possessed one customary "right" no free laborer could claim — the right to subsistence. . . .

The "right" to subsistence, however, had no place in a free labor society. Indeed, the end of slavery required a complete overhaul of the law; in a wide variety of instances, what had once been "rights" were now redefined as crimes. Under slavery theft of food belonging to the owner had been all but universal. Virtually every planter complained of the killing of poultry and hogs, and the plundering of corn cribs, smoke houses, and kitchens by the slaves. Most planters seem to have taken a lenient attitude, particularly where the theft was for purposes of consumption (selling stolen food was another matter entirely). "I do not think a man ever prosecuted his own slave for a larceny," a South Carolina lawyer remarked after the Civil War. Most masters seem to have assumed that thievery was simply another of those inborn black traits that made slavery necessary in the first place. To slaves, on the other hand, as one freedman later recalled, theft simply followed the Biblical injunction: "Where ye labor there shall ye reap."

Under slavery the boundary between public and private authority had been indefinite; crimes like theft, looked upon as labor troubles, were generally settled by planters themselves. Abolition obviously required a restructuring and strengthening of the enforcement machinery. As George A. Trenholm, a prominent South Carolina merchant, explained soon after the end of the Civil War, " . . . Theft is no longer an offense against his master, but a crime against the State." Thus, in the transition from slavery to freedom, the criminal law emerged as a means of enforcing the property rights and demands for labor discipline of the landowner against the claims of the former slave.

Everywhere, the end of slavery witnessed a determined effort to put down larceny by the former slaves. In the United States as well, planters complained of the widespread depredations committed by the freedmen. No one was able to raise stock in South Carolina, according to one planter, because "the negroes have shot and stolen them all." In Louisiana the "thefts of animals by the 'colored gentlemen' who do not want to work," were described in 1868 as "appalling." . . .

[During the Redemption period], the southern criminal law was transformed to increase sharply the penalty for petty theft (and provide a source of involuntary labor for those leasing convicts from the state). There was precedent for such measures in the early Black Codes. South Carolina's criminal law as amended in 1865 had been, a southern writer noted, "emphatically a bloody code." It made every theft a felony punishable by death, the result of which, critics charged, was that convictions would be impossible to obtain. Severe criminal penalties for theft fell into abeyance during Reconstruction, but were revived by the Redeemers. South Carolina did not go to quite the extreme of 1865, but did increase the penalty for the theft of any livestock to a fine of up to one thousand dollars and a maximum of ten years in prison. In North Carolina and Virginia after Reconstruction, a black spokesman charged, "They send him to the penitentiary if he steals a chicken." Mississippi, in its famous "pig law," defined the theft of any cattle or swine as grand larceny, punishable by five years in prison. . . .

Such legislation made the convict lease system, which had originated on a small scale during Reconstruction, a lucrative business in the Redeemer South. Republicans were not far wrong when they charged of the system in Texas, "The courts of law are employed to re-enslave the colored race." . . .

A further example of the use of law to redefine class and property relations and enhance labor discipline is the evolution of legislation concerning liens and the control of standing crops. Crop liens as a form of agricultural credit had originated soon after the Civil War, but the early statutes made no distinction among suppliers — anyone who made advances could hold a lien on the crop. The Freedmen's Bureau and some military officials superimposed upon the credit system the requirement that laborers enjoy a lien superior to all others for their wages or share of the crop, and several states during Reconstruction enacted the laborer's lien into law. Some went further and prohibited the removal of crops from a plantation until the division and settlement took place before some disinterested party. As a result, control of the crop was somewhat indeterminate during Reconstruction.

As in so many other areas, what was an open question, an arena of conflict during Reconstruction, became a closed issue with Redemption. The right to property and terms of credit — the essence of economic power in the rural South — were redefined in the interest of the planter. Generally, landlords were awarded a lien superior to that of the laborer for wages or merchants for supplies. North Carolina placed the entire crop in the hands of the landlord until rent was fully paid, and allowed no challenge to his decision as to when the tenant's obligation had been fulfilled. In Texas the law prohibited the tenant from selling anything until the landlord received his rent. The law attempted to accomplish what planters by themselves had failed to achieve: the complete separation of the freedmen from the means of production, the creation of a true agricultural proletariat. Beginning with *Appling v. Odum* in Georgia in 1872, a series of court decisions defined the sharecropper simply as a wage worker, with no control of the land during the term of his lease, and no right to a portion of the crop until division. Croppers, said the court, enjoyed "no possession of the premises, . . . only a right to go on the land to plant, work, and gather the crop."

Conflicts over the legal definition of contract rights, liens and tenancy are familiar legacies of emancipation. Less well known, although equally important as an example of the reshaping of property relations, was the matter of fencing, an explosive political issue in parts of the postemancipation South because it directly involved the laborer's access to economic resources and alternative means of subsistence.

. . . The common law doctrine requiring that livestock be confined to the property of its owner, as in New England, did not apply in the slave states. Rather, the farmer, not the stockowner, was required to fence in his holdings. All unenclosed land, even if privately owned, in effect became public commons, on which anyone could graze his livestock. . . .

. . . Blacks, it appears, had a vested interest in existing southern fence laws, which allowed landless freedmen to own animals, grazing them on the property of others. . . .

. . . "All they need," said one writer, "is a little to plant, their diminutive gangs of stock can herd it about over the woods, and are no expense to them." Some freedmen, like the father of Nate Shaw, the protagonist of that classic of oral history, *All God's Dangers,* were able to subsist for a time entirely by hunting and the free ranging of their hogs, thereby avoiding wage labor altogether.

The first tentative steps to close the southern range had been taken during Presidential Reconstruction, directed at the black belt counties where most freedmen lived. Nothing more was done during Reconstruction, but with Redemption the legal offensive resumed. . . . Generally, the battle was fought out first in the black counties, although early efforts to enact local statutes were often defeated by the votes of black tenants and laborers. But fraud, state laws restricting the vote on fence issues to landowners, and statutes simply ending common rights in black counties without a popular vote, succeeded by the mid-eighties in enclosing most of the black belt, a severe blow to the ability of freedmen to earn a living independent of plantation labor. The conflict then shifted to the white upcountry, where bitter struggles were waged between agricultural reformers and poorer yeomen determined to preserve their customary rights. The closing of the open range was a long-drawn-out process; in some states it was not completed until well into the twentieth century. But, as with the analogous English enclosure movement of the eighteenth century, the result was a fundamental redefinition of property rights. Southern small farmers and tenants, black and white alike, might well echo the lament of the English rural laborer who had seen his access to the land legislated out of existence: "Parliament may be tender of property; all I know is I had a cow, and an Act of Parliament has taken it from me."

Much the same demise of customary rights allowing an alternative to plantation labor was reflected in another postwar development, the growth of laws to prohibit hunting and fishing on private property. Here, too, the pattern had been established in eighteenth-century England, where a series of game laws, including the infamous Black Act of 1723 making the hunting or stealing of deer and hares in royal forests capital crimes, redefined traditional practices as criminal offenses. Such laws were resented by those accustomed to hunt on privately owned land, and supported by large landowners who saw them as a means of counteracting the inclination to idleness among the poor, as well as preserving a much-esteemed sport.

In the pre–Civil War South, a sparsely settled region whose extensive woods harbored plentiful supplies of game, there were few restrictions on hunting and fishing by free men. Evidence suggests that a significant number of slaves also had experience hunting, trapping game, and fishing. . . .

Presidential Reconstruction witnessed legislative efforts to restrict blacks' rights to hunt and fish. The Black Codes of several states made it illegal to carry firearms on the premises of any plantation without the permission of the owner, defined hunting or fishing on private property as vagrancy, and imposed taxes on dogs and guns owned by blacks. Georgia in 1866 outlawed hunting on Sundays in counties with large black populations, and forbade the taking of timber, berries, fruit, or anything "of any value whatever" from private property, whether or not fenced. During Reconstruction these laws were repealed or went unenforced, while planter petitions for new trespass and game laws were ignored. . . . Nearly all black families, it seemed, owned shotguns which, as Cyrus Abram, an Alabama freedman, put it, were "a heap of service in shooting squirrels, birds, ducks, and turkeys, etc. That is the way we get a good portion of our meat." In the 1874 election campaign, however, armed whites confiscated the guns belonging to Abram and other freedmen. "My gun was a mighty loss to me," he told a congressional committee, "because it is so hard for a black man to get something to eat."

In the Redeemer period, scores of local ordinances and many state-wide measures were enacted, designed to secure white private property from trespass, thereby discouraging men like Abram from getting "something to eat" without plantation labor.

Georgia once again took the lead, restricting hunting and fishing in black belt counties, establishing hunting seasons for deer and fowl, and limiting the ownership of dogs. As in the case of fence laws, the redefinition of private property at the expense of customary rights provoked dissension, especially in white upcountry counties where the right to vote could not be as easily restricted or manipulated as in the black belt. . . . But those laws which applied in only the black counties faced weaker opposition, and represented a serious restriction on the opportunities for freedmen to earn an independent living.

In one final area, taxation, the relationship between the state and private property was also transformed after the Civil War. Before the war, landed property in the South had gone virtually untaxed, while levies on slaves, commercial activities, luxuries such as carriages, race horses, and gold watches, and licenses on professions provided the bulk of revenue. The result was that white yeomen paid few taxes — their tools, livestock, and personal property were generally exempted — while planters bore a larger burden, but hardly one commensurate with their wealth and income. The tax on slaves and luxury items drew money from the planter class, but the extremely low rate on real estate and the widespread practice of allowing the owner to determine the assessed value of his own land, meant planters could engross large holdings of unimproved land without incurring an added tax burden. . . .

With emancipation, the southern tax system became a battleground where the competing claims of planter and freedmen, as well as yeoman farmers and commercial interests, were fought out. In Presidential Reconstruction, planters, like their counterparts in other parts of the world, looked to taxation as one means of compelling blacks to offer their services in the labor market. Less well known than the Black Codes, the revenue laws of 1865 and 1866 formed part of the same overall attempt to create a dependent labor force. While taxes on landed property remained absurdly low (one-tenth of one percent in Mississippi, for example), heavy poll taxes were levied on freedmen, as well as imposts on the earnings of urban craftsmen. Because so much state revenue derived from taxes on individuals, an inequitable situation existed in which "the man with his two thousand acres paid less tax than any one of the scores of hands he may have had in his employ who owned not a dollar's worth of property." Not surprisingly, blacks resented a revenue system whose incidence was unfair, and from whose proceeds, as a North Carolina Freedmen's Bureau agent reported, "they state, and with truth, that they derive no benefit whatever."

Reconstruction witnessed a fundamental restructuring of the southern tax system. . . . The need to rebuild and expand the social and economic infrastructure of the South, coupled with the sudden growth of the citizenry resulting from emancipation, vastly increased the financial necessities of southern state governments. Moreover, with the fall of property values, tax rates had to rise, simply to produce revenue equivalent to that of the prewar years. But more significant than the overall rate of taxation was the change in its incidence. Every southern state adopted an ad valorem tax on landed and personal property, shifting the burden of taxation to property holders. The result was that planters and poorer white farmers, many for the first time, paid a significant portion of their income as taxes, while propertyless blacks escaped almost scot-free.

Democrats complained that apart from poll taxes, blacks contributed nothing to the support of the state, since generally a certain amount of personal property, tools, and livestock was exempted from the new levies. . . .

In some parts of the Reconstruction South, Republican lawmakers designed the tax laws to force land onto the market and stimulate the breakup of the plantation system. "The reformers complain of taxes being too high," said a South Carolina black leader. "I tell you they are not high enough. I want them taxed until they put these lands back where they belong, into the hands of those who worked for them." In this century a progressive land tax, often employed in the Third World, has proved an inefficient means of promoting a redistribution of landed property. The same seems to have been the case during Reconstruction, although the new tax system did seriously inconvenience those holding large tracts of land for purposes of speculation. One result of Reconstruction fiscal policy, it is true, was that vast acreages — one-fifth of the entire area of Mississippi, to cite one example — fell into the hands of the state for nonpayment of taxes. . . . State law often required that they be sold at auction in 40-acre plots, and there is some evidence of blacks acquiring land in this manner. The title to such holdings, however, was far from secure, since state laws generally allowed the former owner to redeem his property by paying the back taxes plus a penalty. . . . Where tax auctions did take place, the buyers tended to be neighboring white farmers, land speculators, or urban businessmen, who gathered up considerable expanses at a few cents per acre.

After Redemption, the southern tax system was transformed anew. First of all, the level of taxes was sharply reduced. The parsimony of the Redeemer regimes is notorious; in Louisiana, "they were so economical that public education and other state services to the people almost disappeared." But the reduction in taxes and expenditures did not affect all classes equally. Partly due to upcountry pressure, landed property enjoyed the sharpest decline in tax rates, while privilege and license taxes rose. The reduction in land taxes was not passed along to black tenants. As a black Louisiana politician complained, "The landowners get all the benefit and the laborers none from the reduction in taxes." Reconstruction laws exempting a certain value of property from taxation were replaced by exclusions only for specific items, such as machinery and implements utilized on a plantation. The result was that blacks now paid taxes on virtually every piece of property they owned — tools, mules, even furniture — while larger farmers had several thousand dollars exempted from levy. . . . Then, too, poll taxes — the most regressive form of revenue — remained in force. The result was that throughout the post-Reconstruction South, as in the postemancipation Caribbean, the poor bore the heaviest burden of taxation and received the fewest public services.

To reiterate the obvious, no one can claim that the complex structure of labor, property, and tax laws initiated immediately after the war, then dismantled during Reconstruction, and finally, with modifications, reinstated after Redemption, were completely successful in controlling the black laborer or shaping the southern economy. . . . Nor could any statute eliminate the colonial status of the South within the national economy, or counteract the slowdown in the rate of growth of world demand for cotton. But the post-Reconstruction legal system did have profound consequences for

black and white alike, foreclosing economic possibilities for some, and opening opportunities for others. The issue, as Du Bois noted, was not so much whether the South
could produce wealth with free labor — "It was the far more fundamental question of
whom this wealth was to belong to and for whose interests laborers were to work."

In poverty, malnutrition, illiteracy, and a host of other burdens, the freedmen paid
the highest price for the failure of Reconstruction and the economic stagnation of the
plantation South. Even though these hardships were not confined to blacks, the freedmen were caught in a unique web of legal and extralegal coercions which distinguished
their plight from that of the growing number of white sharecroppers. To the architects
of the post-Reconstruction South, black poverty was a small price to pay for political
peace and labor discipline. "I do not think that poverty disturbs their happiness at all,"
a Georgia editor told a congressional committee. Another Georgian took a slightly
different route to the same conclusion: "The Nigger, when poverty stricken . . . will
work well for you — but as soon as you get him up and he begins to be prosperous, he
becomes impudent and unmanageable." For their part, blacks fully understood that their
aspirations were incompatible with those of their former owners. "What motive has he
to see you oppressed and down trodden?" a visiting congressman asked David Graham,
an Edgefield County, South Carolina black leader in 1876. "In case I was rich, and all
colored men was rich . . . ," Graham replied, "how would he get his labor? He could-
n't get it as cheap as he gets it now. . . . His interest is in keeping me poor, so that I will
have to hire to some one else."

Here, in the candid recognition of irreconcilable interests, lay a recipe for continuing conflict. And, indeed, it is the ongoing struggle over the definition of freedom and
the control of labor that unites the experience of the American South with that of
other postemancipation societies. Long after the end of slavery, the conflict would
culminate in the enmeshing of blacks in a comprehensive system of segregation,
disfranchisement, and, in many cases, virtual peonage, and the proletarianization of the
agricultural labor force of the South. Here, as elsewhere, the adjustment to emancipation appears as a saga of persistence rather than change, stagnation rather than progress,
the resiliency of an old ruling class rather than the triumph of a new order.

Yet if the ultimate outcome seems in retrospect depressingly similar to the Caribbean
and South Africa experiences, by the same token it underscores the uniqueness of
Reconstruction in the history of postemancipation societies, and the enduring changes
American emancipation did accomplish. However brief its sway, Reconstruction
allowed scope for a remarkable political and social mobilization of the black community, opening doors of opportunity that could never again be completely closed. If
Reconstruction did not overturn the economic dominance of the planter class, it did
prevent the immediate putting into place of a comprehensive legal and judicial system
meant to define the political economy of emancipation solely in the planters' interests.
Despite Redemption, the complete dispossession and immobilization of the labor force
envisioned in 1865 and 1866 never was achieved, and blacks stubbornly clung to the
measure of autonomy in day-to-day labor relations assured by sharecropping. Nor were
plantation labor controls extended, as in twentieth-century South Africa, into industry,
an outcome of great importance when employment opportunities opened for blacks

in the North. And Reconstruction established a framework of legal rights enshrined in the Constitution that, while flagrantly violated in practice after Redemption, planted the seeds of future struggle and left intact a vehicle for future federal intervention in southern affairs.

Thus, a subtle dialectic of persistence and change, continuity and conflict, shaped America's adjustment to abolition. As in most other societies that experienced the end of slavery, black aspirations were, in large measure, thwarted and plantation agriculture, in modified form, survived. Yet for a moment, American freedmen had enjoyed an unparalleled opportunity to help shape their own destiny. The legacy of Reconstruction would endure as blacks continued to assert their claims, against unequal odds, to economic autonomy, political citizenship, and a voice in determining the consequences of emancipation.

QUESTIONS TO CONSIDER

1. What conclusions did Civil War–era Americans draw from the West Indian emancipation experience of the 1830s? How did their conclusions reflect each group's ideas about slavery and their expectations for the future?

2. How did the political context of emancipation differ in the United States from that in Caribbean societies? In what ways did the American ideal of equality, the granting of black suffrage, and the realities of national politics shape the nature of the conflict between white planters and ex-slaves?

3. Explain how the Black Codes showed what southern economic relations would look like if left completely under the planters' control. Why did the "solution" of importing immigrant plantation laborers not succeed in the South? Why was the former slaves' claim to land not recognized?

4. Planters and freedmen pursued their competing agendas in the southern political arena. Discuss how the two groups' ideas about property and subsistence rights differed. How did southern state laws reflect the victory of each group on these issues at different times? How did southern fence and game laws resemble the eighteenth-century English enclosure legislation? In what ways, according to Foner, did changing tax laws affect planters, independent farmers, and propertyless southerners?

5. In what sense was the system of sharecropping a compromise between the former slaves' desire for independence and the planters' demands for dependent wage laborers? How did landlords manage in the end to control sharecroppers?

Reconstruction:
A Counterfactual Playback

C. Vann Woodward

For a second opinion on Reconstruction, we turn from the hard evidence of Eric Foner's essay to the intriguing speculations of C. Vann Woodward, a distinguished historian looking back upon a half-century of Reconstruction scholarship, including his own. Like Foner, Woodward has compared Reconstruction to emancipations elsewhere and found a general pattern of limited gains for former slaves. But in this essay Woodward suggests a more imaginative and perhaps equally illuminating type of comparative history.

His starting point is the recognition that Reconstruction was a failure and that Americans always have a hard time coming to grips with failure. It will not do, Woodward says, to compensate by exaggerating Radical Reconstruction's partial and fleeting gains for blacks; nor, on the other hand, should Americans continue to berate our ancestors for falling short of the nation's lofty ideals. Instead, to arrive at a realistic assessment of Reconstruction, says Woodward, we need to seek comparative angles. First, understanding that emancipation in other nations did not lead to equality for their former slaves "removes the stigma of uniqueness" and should help Americans to live with their nation's failure. Second, we should dismiss the hyperbole that Reconstruction was a "revolution" and thus lower our expectations for it. Finally — and here Woodward hits his stride — we might ask whether Reconstruction would have succeeded if it had in fact been revolutionary.

What would have happened if the North had been seriously committed to revolutionizing the South and raising the ex-slaves to equality? Woodward is at his witty best when he compares what might have been with what actually happened — an exercise historians call "counterfactual" history. Moving historical figures around like chess pieces, Woodward has Ben Wade (a Radical Republican senator) replace an impeached President Johnson and sign into law a confiscation act that breaks up southern plantations and makes the land available to black homesteaders. As if this were not enough, Woodward next proposes to "liquidate white resistance" in the South down to "the last bed-sheeted Ku Kluxer." Finally, having killed off the planters and their allies, Woodward turns the South over to the Union army and northern reformers.

Would this revolution have succeeded? To address this question with evidence from the same period, Woodward recounts the depressing tale of how speculators undermined white homesteading in the West and how well-intentioned reformers were unable to prevent army violence and the triumph of white supremacy over the Native Americans. What actually happened in the West casts a long shadow over what might have happened in the South. At the essay's end, Woodward confesses himself "overcome with doubts" that even drastic revolutionary steps would have made Reconstruction successful. Reminding us that historians have to work with "human materials" and be true to the context of the past, Woodward seems to be saying — though he denies it — that Radical Reconstruction was doomed.

As you read Woodward's essay, ask yourself whether it demonstrates the usefulness of "counterfactual" analysis by highlighting aspects of the past not found in more conventional historical comparisons. You may find it ironic that Woodward the "armchair revolutionary" ends up more pessimistic than Foner the radical historian about the results of Reconstruction. Woodward, a master of irony, would be delighted. But the differing styles and conclusions of this chapter's two essays ought to challenge you to develop your own explanation of Reconstruction's successes and failures, and your own assessment of its implications for racial democracy today.

GLOSSARY

ARMSTRONG, SAMUEL (1839–1893)   A philanthropist and educator who worked for the Freedmen's Bureau after the Civil War. Armstrong helped establish the Hampton Institute in Virginia in 1868 to provide vocational training for former slaves and headed it until 1893.

CARPETBAGGERS   A derogatory term for northern whites who migrated to the South after the Civil War and became active Republicans. These included Union army veterans, businessmen, politicians, teachers, and missionaries.

COPPERHEADS   A derogatory term for northerners who actively sympathized with the Confederacy during the Civil War.

CROMWELL, OLIVER (1599–1658)   A forceful Puritan leader who emerged victorious in the English Civil War of the 1640s. One of the most controversial figures in English history, Cromwell defeated the Royalist forces of Charles I and Charles II and proclaimed England a republican commonwealth. He led an expedition into Ireland, where he began a policy of dispossessing the Irish. In 1653 he was named Lord Protector, or sole ruler, of England, Scotland, and Ireland, but the monarchy was restored shortly after his death.

DOUGLASS, FREDERICK (1817–1895)   An escaped slave who became an eloquent abolitionist and African American spokesman. In 1845 he published his first autobiography, and two years later he established a newspaper in Rochester, New York, which he edited for seventeen years, urging abolition through political activism. Committed to Radical Reconstruction, Douglass pushed for full black equality after the Civil War.

FREEDMEN'S BUREAU   An agency of the army created by Congress in 1865 to oversee the condition of ex-slaves by providing food and clothing, establishing schools, and supervising labor contracts. Led by General O. O. Howard, the bureau had its role expanded by Congress in 1866 over President Johnson's veto.

GRANT ADMINISTRATIONS (1869–1877)   The two terms of President Ulysses S. Grant. They were characterized by corruption, special-interest legislation, and a gradual retreat from Radical Reconstruction.

HOMESTEAD ACT   The 1862 law that opened millions of acres of western public land to settlers, who could receive ownership of 160 acres after five years of continuous residence or, alternatively, could buy the land after six months' residence at $1.25 an acre.

JACKSON, STONEWALL (THOMAS) (1824–1863)   The Confederate general who became Robert E. Lee's ablest lieutenant. Jackson conducted brilliant campaigns in Virginia during the first half of the Civil War, but was mortally wounded by fire from his own troops at Chancellorsville.

KU KLUX KLAN   The secret society, organized by ex-Confederates and led by Nathan B. Forrest, that terrorized southern blacks and their supporters during Reconstruction to maintain white supremacy and deny rights to the former slaves.

PRATT, RICHARD HENRY (1840–1924)   A Civil War soldier transferred to the West during Reconstruction who became an influential Indian educator. He organized the Indian branch of the Hampton Institute in 1878 and the following year established the Carlisle Indian School, the first nonreservation federal school for Native Americans. Pratt was an advocate of assimilation who sought to root out tribalism and to end Native Americans' separate reservation status.

REDEEMERS   Southern Democrats who rallied to regain control of their state governments and suppress Radical (or "Black") Reconstruction.

SCALAWAGS   A derogatory term for white Southerners who supported the Republicans during Reconstruction. Never more than one-fifth of the South's white voters, they included backcountry farmers, financiers and businessmen, and a few philanthropic ex-planters.

STALIN, JOSEPH (1879–1953)   The Russian communist who ruled the Soviet Union as virtual dictator from 1927 to his death. Stalin sent enormous numbers of citizens to their deaths during the forced collectivization of agriculture and in periodic mass purges of his critics and political foes.

STEVENS, THADDEUS (1792–1868)   A powerful Radical Republican congressman from Pennsylvania. Stevens favored harsher Reconstruction terms than those of Presidents Lincoln and Johnson. He led the movement to impose military Reconstruction on the South in 1867 and was the most outspoken congressional advocate of confiscating Confederates' land.

STUART, J. E. B. (1833–1864)   The Confederate cavalry commander whose information on Union troop movements, gathered on bold raids such as the circling of General McClellan's army in June 1862, proved valuable to General Robert E. Lee. Stuart was killed during the Wilderness Campaign in Virginia in May 1864.

SUMNER, CHARLES (1811–1874)   An abolitionist senator from Massachusetts who was a leader of the Radical Republicans' Reconstruction program and active in the impeachment of President Johnson.

TORIES   Also called Loyalists; American colonists who refused to renounce their allegiance to the British Crown after 1776. Many suffered physical abuse, disfranchisement, or confiscation of property, and about one hundred thousand were forced into exile in Canada, England, or the Caribbean.

WADE, BENJAMIN F. (1800–1878)   An Ohio senator and Radical Republican who led congressional oversight of the Civil War effort and opposed Lincoln's mild Reconstruction terms. As president pro tempore of the Senate, Wade would have succeeded as president had Andrew Johnson been convicted of impeachment charges in 1868.

WASHINGTON, BOOKER T. (1856–1915)   A young slave liberated by the Civil War who studied at Hampton Institute and became an instructor there in 1879. In 1881, he organized Tuskegee Institute in Alabama, which became a leading center for black industrial education. As a public spokesman for southern blacks, Washington advocated self-help and economic independence, but was criticized for accepting racial segregation and political disfranchisement.

★ ★ ★ ★ ★ ★

T he ruins of two great failures dominate the landscape of American history. They stand close together in the middle distance, back to back, but separate and distinct. One is the ruins of the Confederacy, the South's failure to gain independence. The other is the ruins of Reconstruction, the North's failure to solve the problem of the black people's place in American life. The South's failure was the North's success and vice versa. Each can be and, of course, has been described by its opponents as simply the wreckage wrought in preventing acknowledged wrong. But from the standpoint of their supporters and champions there can be no doubt that each of these ruins represents a great American failure.

They stand out all the more conspicuously on the historical landscape because of their unique character. Failures and defeats on the grand scale are notoriously exceptional and uncharacteristic in the American experience. And so far, at least until very recent years, these two stand as the only instances of striking significance. They are surrounded by monuments of success, victory, and continuity, features far more familiar to the American eye. Some of these monuments — the Revolution, the Constitution, the two-party system, the parties themselves, the basic economic institutions, all still live and going concerns — are much older than the two historic ruins. This side of them in the foreground of American history stand more recent monuments in the traditional success style of the American Way, marred only somewhat by late twentieth-century exceptions. But the middle distance is still dominated by the two great historic failures.

The unavoidable responsibility of the historian is to explain these failures. But the strangeness and un-American character of failure seems to have inhibited or warped the fulfillment of the task. One evasive strategy of historians of the Confederacy has been first to acknowledge more or less candidly that the movement was misguided and perhaps destined to fail from the start and even to admit tacitly that it was best for all concerned in the long run that it did fail. But then to dwell at length on the high moments, the ephemeral triumphs, the selfless devotion, the nobility of leadership, and the hardships and suffering of the participants. Essentially romantic, the lost-cause approach emphasized the glory and tragedy without too much attention to causes and consequences. Recent historians of the Confederacy have been addressing themselves more and more to the causes of failure and less to the ephemeral triumphs. But for a long time the South's refusal to face up to its own defeat contributed to the North's failure in accounting for the sequel to Appomattox.

Historians of Reconstruction have played variations on these Confederate themes without exactly duplicating the order or the mood. For a long time they too started with the assumption that the movement was misconceived and doomed to failure from inception and that, all things considered, it was just as well that it did fail. Since failure was regarded as both inevitable and fortunate, the problem of explaining it did not appear very challenging. With these more or less common assumptions, historians of the old school divided mainly on how they distributed their sympathy and admiration among the victims — the humble freedmen, the misguided idealists, the bumbling Presidents, or the long-suffering Southern whites — and on their distribution of blame among villains — Radical Republicans, Carpetbaggers, Scalawags, or black freedmen. They were in substantial agreement, however, in their homage to the tragic muse. Whether the spotlight was focused on the victims or the villains, the overriding preoccupation was with tragedy. The best seller on the subject was entitled *The Tragic Era,* by Claude Bowers. But whether as a cause for satisfaction or lament, there was little equivocation about the verdict of failure.

In the last few decades a shift has occurred in the common assumptions and preoccupations about Reconstruction historians. Failure is no longer regarded as inevitable or complete, the movement as misconceived, or the outcome as fortunate. On all these matters there has occurred a reversal of attitude. The treatment is still fundamentally tragic, but the reading of the tragedy has changed. The tragedy was not that a misguided movement had caused so much unnecessary suffering, but that a noble experiment had come so near fulfillment and failed. Furthermore, the impact of failure itself has been blunted and the historical problem of explanation shelved by a new emphasis on the positive accomplishments of Reconstruction.

Much of the attention of revisionists has been focused on correcting the excessively negative picture painted by the old school and exposing the injustice and crudity of the stereotypes. New studies have pictured the old abolitionists as persevering champions of the freedmen. The collective portrait of the Radical Republican congressmen that emerges from revisionist biographies and monographs is one of high-minded idealists who rose above selfish political and economic interests. Studies of Northern teachers and preachers who went to the South on missionary enterprises stress their seriousness of purpose and the devotion and fearless dedication of their service. Carpetbaggers of vision and courageous statesmanship have been sympathetically portrayed. Scalawags of the new historiography appear to derive either from wealthy Southern aristocrats or from sturdy Jacksonian yeomen, depending on one's school of revisionism or one's technique of quantification. Among black leaders and statesmen revisionists have discovered a gratifying amount of talent, ability, and vision. Swindlers, grafters, and corruption have been discounted by comparison with contemporaneous fraud and graft in Northern states. The result of all this has been a wholesale decimation of stock figures in the demonology of Reconstruction.

Praiseworthy achievements of Radical Reconstruction include not only the legislative and constitutional foundations for black citizenship, franchise, and civil rights, but the training and preparation of freedmen for political action. Radical state governments are also justly credited with framing laudable and often durable state constitutions and law codes, with providing relief and welfare for the distressed, with establishing public schools, and with inaugurating new public services. Scholars have pronounced the freedmen's economic progress during Reconstruction, given their low starting point, a tremendous success and enumerated with pride their gains in land and capital. Others have pointed out the general progress of the South in economic recuperation and growth. The emphasis here, as in so many other areas of revisionist history, is not on failures but on the successes of Reconstruction. . . .

The achievements of the revisionists are impressive. But as a contribution to explaining the failure of Reconstruction they tend rather to complicate than to solve the enigma. For if, as they have demonstrated, the statesmanship of the Radicals was all that inspired and their motivation all that pure, if the freedmen were so responsive and capably led, if government by the Scalawag-Carpetbagger-freedmen coalition was all that constructive, and if the opposition were indeed headed by a misfit in the White House who was out of touch with the electorate, then success would seem more indicated than failure. The paradox reminds me of the first historical problem I confronted as a boy. It went something like this: If Marse Robert [Robert E. Lee] was all that noble and intrepid, if Stonewall [Jackson] was all that indomitable and fast on his feet, if Jeb Stuart was all that gallant and dashing, and if God was on our side, then why the hell did we *lose* that war? . . .

. . . This brings me back to the old problem of failure. As I have remarked earlier, Americans have rather a thing about failure — about confronting it, confessing it, and accepting it, as well as about explaining it. It is noteworthy that the great bulk of work done by the revisionists has been on Andrew Johnson's administration, not on the two Grant administrations, that is, on the period where, paradoxically, the ephemeral successes and triumphs multiplied, not the period of twice that length when the failures piled up or became unavoidably conspicuous. This may be mere coincidence, but my guess is that it is more than that. Another tendency might be called the deferred success approach, the justification (or dismissal) of failure in the First Reconstruction on the ground that it prepared the way for success in the Second Reconstruction, or maybe a Third yet to come. Thus one historian writes that the failures of the First Reconstruction diminish to insignificance in comparison with successes of the Second in advancing equal civil and political rights for blacks and promise of further progress to come. This is a generational shift of the burden of responsibility. But it must be recognized as essentially another strategy of evasion.

One habit of mind that has complicated American ways of dealing with failure, apart from a relative unfamiliarity with the experience, has been the isolation of

American history from comparative reference. Comparisons have indeed been used with regard to Reconstruction, but they have been internalized. Lacking foreign comparisons, or indifferent to them, Americans have turned inward to compare professed ideals with actual practice. This has encouraged a strong moralistic tendency in our historical writing and controversy. Since the nation has advertised a commitment to some very lofty ideals and principles, the contrast between performance and principle has always been painful, and the application of absolute and abstract standards of judgment often sets up moral disturbance that clouds issues and distorts perspectives.

For more realistic perspective on the American experience of Reconstruction we need to turn to comparison with foreign experiences, including but not limited to those of the other twenty-odd slave societies in the New World that went through the post-emancipation ordeal. To avoid repetition [of an earlier essay] . . . I must be content with summarizing conclusions of the best informed authorities. The most important finding is that wherever slavery was widespread, emancipation was invariably followed by resort to drastic measures, including use of force, to put the freedmen back to work. The old masters of the American South were by no means alone in resorting to black codes and chain gangs. Old masters everywhere — West Indies, Latin America, Africa, Asia — took forceable steps to drive the freedmen back to work.

Furthermore, in those lands undergoing emancipation where the process of reconstruction was subject to outside control or supervision, whether from the crown, the mother country, an imperial or metropolitan administration, or as in the South the federal government under Northern control, such authorities proved quite ineffective in protecting the lives and rights of the emancipated. The universality of failure by authorities and oppression by old masters does not excuse or justify either the governments or the masters anywhere — especially not a government that had just fought a bloody civil war in the name of freedom. Reconstruction left a lasting blot on the American conscience and national history and continues to breed moral recrimination between regions and races. But at least the comparative context removes the stigma of uniqueness and places moral issues in a broader setting. That, I believe, is a legitimate use of history — not only to recover the past but to enable us to live with it.

Another type of comparison has often been used in interpreting Reconstruction, but not always with sufficient caution. To place a historical event in a category of events is to make a comparison. Thus, when Reconstruction is spoken of as a revolution, we are compelled to think of it in comparison with other revolutions. If we reserve the term "revolution" for the classic phenomena of England in the seventeenth century, America and France in the eighteenth century, and Russia and China in the twentieth century, then it is certainly misused when applied to the American Reconstruction of the nineteenth century. For in the last instance there were no mass executions, no class liquidations. No heads rolled. There were constitutional changes, to be sure, but they were insignificant compared with those in England, France, Russia, and China, and they were mainly effected through constitutional forms. The South's so-called Bourbons or Redeemers did not become proscribed and outlawed émigrés. They remained at home, retained their estates, took over from the ephemeral radical governments, and after their so-called counter-revolution they did not find it necessary to make very drastic changes in the system left them by the so-called revolution. All things considered, it would be better to abandon both the concept of revolution and that of counter-revolution in writing of Reconstruction as it *was*.

But in writing of what it *might* have been, what many hoped it would be, and of why Reconstruction failed, the concept of revolution seems indispensable. It should be fairly obvious that in order to succeed with the professed aims of full civil rights, equality, and justice for the freedmen, Reconstruction would have had to go much further in the way of revolutionary measures than it ever did. Even then it might have failed, for revolutions are not invariably successful nor are their innovations always lasting. It is not very helpful to prescribe revolution in the abstract without specifying the revolutionary program. Nor is it very realistic to imagine a revolutionary program without regard to the nature of the party and the people who would carry it out and the historical context in which they would have worked. Only by that means can we test the hypothesis that the failure of Reconstruction is to be explained by the lack of revolutionary measures.

One revolutionary measure, a favorite for the speculation over a century, is the confiscation of rebel estates and redistribution of them among the freedmen. This deserves serious consideration for a number of reasons. In the first place such a proposal was seriously made and had an able and powerful advocate in Thaddeus Stevens. The Stevens plan called for the confiscation of all rebel estates over $10,000 or over 200 acres. He estimated that this would result in the taking over of some 394 million out of 465 million acres in the rebel states. The redistribution would give 40 acres to each adult male freedman. This would take 40 million acres, and the remaining 354 million would be sold to the highest bidder and the proceeds allocated to pensions for Union veterans, damages and reparations, and enough left to retire three-quarters of the national debt. The plan was defeated, of course, but it has had later advocates such as W. E. B. Du Bois and various other Marxists.

Americans need no Marxist precedents, however, for there was ample precedent for the wholesale confiscation of the estates of disloyal elements of the population in the treatment of Tories during the American Revolution, and there was a spectacular contemporary example abroad in the distribution of some of the confiscated lands to emancipated serfs by the Czar of All the Russias in 1861. The American freedmen surely had as great a moral claim on the land on which they had toiled for 250 years. Furthermore if the federal government could overcome the legal and constitutional problems of confiscating the slave property of the planters, it surely could have justified confiscating their landed property as well. The planters would have objected strenuously, of course, but they would have been powerless to prevent the action had Congress been determined. Let us assume, then, that the Stevens Land Confiscation bill actually passed, that President Ben Wade signed it in the White House after President Johnson's removal by successful impeachment, and that the Fortieth Congress then brought to bear all its experience and wisdom in refining the legislation and President Wade marshaled the best talents for administering the land act. What would have been the consequences for the outcome of Reconstruction? Would this have converted a failure into a reasonable success?

No one can possibly say for sure, of course. What one *can* describe with some assurance, however, is the record of the same federal government, the same Congresses under the control of the same party in administering and distributing public lands elsewhere. Again we resort to the comparative approach, though this time the comparisons are drawn from domestic rather than foreign instances. The Reconstruction period coincided with the great era of public land distribution by the federal government according to the provisions of the Homestead Act of 1862 and other federal land laws placed on the books between 1862 and 1878. The public domain available for distribution under the Homestead and subsequent acts amounted to some 1,048,000,000 acres, more than half the total area of the nation and more than two and a half times the 394 million acres of confiscated rebel estates that would have been added to the public domain by the Stevens Act. This fabulous opportunity, without precedent in history, appeared to be the fruition of the American dream, the most cherished dream of reformers — free land for those who tilled the land.

What came of that dream in the administration of the Homestead Act is a matter of public record. We know that as things turned out the homesteaders got short shrift and proved to be the least favored of the various groups attracted to the western lands. The land-grant railroads alone got four times as much land as the homesteaders in the first four decades of the Homestead Act. In that period 84 percent of the new farms brought under cultivation were purchased or subdivided from larger holdings. Of the patents actually granted to homesteaders a great number were handed to pawns of speculators and monopolists, so that in all probability little more than one-tenth of the new farms were free in the homestead sense. Furthermore, the bona fide homesteader was typically shunted off into the poorest land and least desirable tracts, while the speculators pre-empted tracts closest to settlement and transportation and held them for resale at prices beyond the means of the class the Homestead Act was presumably designed to help. It is the opinion of Fred Shannon that, "In its operation the Homestead Act could hardly have defeated the hopes of the [land-reform] enthusiasts . . . more completely if the makers had drafted it with that purpose uppermost in mind."

While many of the same people who drafted and administered the Homestead Act for the West would in all probability have drafted and administered the Stevens Act for the South, it is only fair to remember that the Western land problem was complicated by variables absent from the Southern picture — granting that the latter had its own complications. But at least the South lay within the humid, forested longitudes, conditions that were far more familiar to Eastern lawmakers than . . . [the] Great Plains, and also the rebel estates provided a larger proportion of arable land, much more conveniently located in relation to the prospective homesteaders. Because of these advantages and the idealism said to have motivated Radicals in their dealings with freedmen (however inoperative it was in the same men's dealings with Western homesteaders) it is possible that the Stevens Act would have had a happier history than the Homestead Act and that the black freedmen would have actually entered into the promised land, peacefully and cheerfully, each one secure in the possession of his forty acres. And let us throw in an army mule apiece for good measure.

That outcome is conceivable and one would hope even probable. But in calculating the degree of probability one is forced to take into account certain other conditioning and relevant factors in addition to the western homestead experience. For one thing the Stevens Act as detailed by the Pennsylvania Radical set aside nine-tenths of the 394 million acres of confiscated rebel land for sale to the highest bidder — an open invitation to the speculator and monopolist. It is possible that these types might have behaved toward the black homesteaders of the South in much the same way they behaved toward the white homesteader in the West. If so the probability of success for the philanthropic part of the Stevens Act is appreciably diminished.

Prospects of success for the Stevens Act are also illuminated by the history of a Southern Homestead Act that actually *was* adopted by Congress. There were 47,700,000 acres of public land in five of the Confederate states in 1861, more than the amount of rebel estates set aside for freedmen by the hypothetical Stevens Act. In 1866 the Radicals pushed through a drastic bill applying exclusively to these lands, reserving them to homesteaders at 80 acres per holding, and favoring freedmen by excluding ex-Confederates from homesteading privileges. These lands were generally less accessible and less desirable than those of confiscated estates might have been, and as in the case of the Western act no provision was made for furnishing credit and transportation to homesteaders. These conditions probably explain why extremely few blacks seized upon this opportunity to double the elusive 40 acres. In that respect the act was a failure and, at any rate, Congress reversed the policy in 1876 and threw open this rich Southern empire to unrestricted speculation. There ensued a scramble of monopolists that matched any land rush of the Wild West, and the freedmen were thrust aside and forgotten. Admittedly this episode offers further discouragement for the chances of the revolutionary Stevens Act.

Determined revolutionists are not disheartened by reverses, however. They merely press forward with more heroic measures. Perhaps Thaddeus Stevens was not revolutionary enough. There is the problem of the rebel resistance to Radical Reconstruction and federal authority in the defeated states. My own researches have impressed me deeply with the seriousness of this resistance. It was often open, defiant, organized, and effective. White Southerners repeatedly insulted, persecuted, and sometimes murdered federal officials, army officers included. They scoffed at the law and ridiculed the courts. They did everything to black citizens the law forbade their doing and invented mistreatments that [the] law never thought of. How any self-respecting government put up with such defiance unless, indeed, it was at least subliminally sympathetic with the resistance, it is difficult to understand. With overwhelming power in its hands, even an ordinary respectable non-revolutionary government could have done better than this.

Let me remind you, however, that this is a revolutionary program that we are pursuing. Here Thad Stevens lets us down. He raises the question whether any Republican, Senator Charles Sumner included, really deserved the name "Radical." It is true that his rhetoric against the "proud, bloated, and defiant rebels" was violent enough, that he promised to "startle feeble minds and shake weak nerves," that he ridiculed "the prim conservatives, the snobs, and the male waiting maids in Congress," that he asked, "How can republican institutions, free schools, free churches . . . exist in a mingled community of nabobs and serfs," and that he thundered the promise to "drive her nobility into exile," or worse. But when it came right down to it he confessed that he "never desired bloody punishments to any extent." This admission of bourgeois softness proves that Stevens has exhausted his usefulness as a guide to revolutionary solutions.

It is becoming a bit tiresome (and it is entirely unnecessary) to be flanked on the left in speculative audacity. Armchair bloodbaths can be conducted with impunity by any-one, even a professor emeritus. Let us then pursue the logic of the revolutionary process on past Stevens and Sumner, past the Old Left and the New Left, and out to the wild blue — or rather infra-red — yonder. Let us embrace in our revolutionary program, along with the Stevens Act, an act for the liquidation of the enemy class. There is ample precedent for this in the history of revolutions. Even the American Revolution drove the Tories into exile. Mass deportation, considering the merchant marine's state of total disrepair in 1865, is unfortunately not a practicable option. That leaves available only the messier alternatives. It is true that the Alaska purchase from Russia made providentially available an American Siberia in 1867, but that would take care of relatively few, and again there is the tedious problem of transportation. The numbers are formidable, for the counter-revolutionary resistance extended beyond the planter class through a very large percentage of Southern whites. A few hundred thou-sand Northern Copperheads can be handled in concentration camps, but in Dixie harsher measures are indicated. Let no true revolutionary blanch at the implications. Remember that we must be cruel in order to be kind, that we are the social engineers of the future, that we are forestalling future bloodbaths, race riots, and relieving our Northern metropolitan friends of problems that trouble their thoughts and for a time threatened to destroy their cities. If our work is bloody our conscience is clear, and we do all that we do — compassionately.

Having liquidated the white resistance down to the last unregenerate lord of the lash and the last bed-sheeted Ku Kluxer, let us proceed unencumbered to build the true Radical Reconstruction. We will find it expedient to import managerial talent in large numbers to replace the liquidated white resistance, and place them in charge of agri-culture, industry, railroads, and mines. They will doubtless come from the same states the carpetbaggers hailed from, but they must be carefully screened to eliminate the more objectionable types and certified as non-racists and non-Copperheads. We will also es-tablish a permanent Freedmen's Bureau, perhaps modeled on the Indian Bureau, and place in command of it the very finest talent. If not General O. O. Howard, perhaps we can get the nomination of Frederick Douglass through a miraculously radicalized U.S. Senate, after a radicalized U. S. Grant had executed a Pride's Purge of half the members.

After these Draconian, Cromwellian, Stalinist measures had removed all resistance and interference from Southern and Northern racists and Kluxers and nightriders, silenced all Confederate orators, and shut down the last obstructionist press, the revolutionists should have had a perfectly free hand. What then would have been the consequences for fulfillment of Reconstruction purposes? Would these additional measures have con-verted failure into success? One would surely hope so after paying such a bloody price.

But again, no one can say for sure. And again we turn to the comparative method for possible illumination. I hope that I am sufficiently alert to the dangers of these comparisons. I realize that no analogy is complete, that no two historical events are identical, and that the risks of drawing conclusions by such reasoning are most formidable. I have tried to guard against such risks and to be very tentative about drawing conclusions, but I suspect I have already outraged respected historians by mentioning Grant in the same breath with Cromwell or Stalin. Nevertheless I shall take heart and venture one last excursion into the treacherous field of comparative or counterfactual history.

Once again the comparison is close to home and contemporaneous with the Reconstruction period. Moreover, the same electorates, the same congressmen, the identical presidents and judiciary, the same editorial chorus and clerical censors are involved in the one as in the other — one cast for two dramas. The second drama also has as its plot the story of reformers using the federal government to bring justice and rights and decent lives to men of color. This time the theater is in the West instead of the South and the colored minority is red instead of black. Since we have "controlled the variable" (as the quantifiers say) of Confederate slave owners' resistance in the South — with a regrettable amount of bloodshed to be sure — the two theaters are more readily comparable. For while the reformers in the West had their own problems, they were not encumbered by die-hard Confederate reactionaries, former owners and masters of the red people, and not dogged at every step by determined and desperate night-riders. In these respects they had a relatively free hand.

The personnel and policies of the white guardians of the blacks and the white guardians of the reds were often interchangeable. General W. T. Sherman moved from command of the Southern District to command of the Western District in 1867, from the final arbiter of the black freedman's destiny to final arbiter of the redskin's fate. Many other military officers including General O. O. Howard moved back and forth from South to West. While General Howard, who had been head of the Freedmen's Bureau, was serving as president of an all-black Howard University in 1872 he was dispatched by Grant to conclude a treaty with the Apaches; in 1874 he was placed in command of the Department of Columbia, and in 1877 he led a punitive expedition against the Nez Perce Indians. Black regiments served in West and South under the same white officers. In the educational field Samuel Armstrong of Hampton Institute, Booker Washington's mentor and model, took Richard Henry Pratt, the great Indian educator, as disciple and assistant, and the two of them integrated and taught black and red students at Hampton. Later Pratt took the Armstrong–Booker Washington gospel to Indian schools. The same missionaries, preachers, editors, and reformers often concerned themselves with the problems and destinies of both colored minorities.

What can be said, in view of the relatively free hand they had in the West, of the performance of the American reformers toward the Indian, as compared with their performance toward the Negro, when they did not have the free hand I have imagined for them? Was it any better? As a matter of fact the two problems were solved in much the same way. The red man like the black man was given to understand that the white man's will was supreme, that he had few rights the white man was bound to respect. He was promised land and the land was taken away. He was promised integration and then segregated, even more completely than the black man. He was degraded, exploited, humiliated, and because he offered more resistance he was cut down ruthlessly by military force or vigilante action. Idealists like Richard Henry Pratt who operated in both South and West were as frustrated in their efforts for the red man as they were with the black man. White supremacy forces were as triumphant over Eastern "Indian lovers" in Arizona and Colorado as they were over Northern "nigger lovers" in Mississippi and Alabama.

But this comparison is an outrage against established compartmentalizations of historical thought, a preposterous violation of respected conventions. Everyone knows what a "good Indian" was. And what but confusion of the undergraduate mind can possibly come from comparing Colorado and Alabama? I apologize for this travesty against sound canons of the profession. . . .

I owe further apologies. Having invited you to consider the causes of the failure of Reconstruction, I have produced nothing but negative results. While applauding the revisionists for their excellent work, I have questioned the emphasis on the idealism and sincerity of the Radicals and their ephemeral triumphs as an adequate indication of their ultimate failure. In the second place, I have raised doubts about moralistic and uniquely American explanations for post-emancipation failure in the protection of freedmen on the ground that much the same pattern of forced labor occurred everywhere in the world as a sequel to abolition. Thirdly, having embraced the Stevens policy of rebel land confiscation and redistribution, I am forced to admit that contemporaneous experience with federal administration of public lands discourages optimism about the freedman's chances. And finally, after eliminating Confederate resistance with bloody measures I am overcome with doubts, caused by belated reflections on the fate of the poor red man, that even these drastic steps would ensure success. With the candor I have urged upon other historians I am obliged to confess a failure of my own, the failure to find a satisfactory explanation for the failure of Reconstruction.

The problem remains unsolved. The assignment still goes begging. It deserves high priority among the unfinished tasks of American historiography. Those who next undertake the task will not, I hope, rely too uncritically on the received ideas, the shared moral convictions and political values of their own time to sanction their premises. They should give scrupulous attention to uniquely American conditions, but remember that the post-emancipation problem they attack was not unique to America. They may well profit from consideration of allegedly idyllic race relations on happy islands in the Caribbean sun, but remember that their home problem was environed by Protestant Anglo-American institutions of a temperate zone unblessed by Pope or tropical sun. They should give due weight to constitutional issues without fruitlessly pining for an English-type constitution to deal with states' rights, a Russian-type Czar to distribute land among the emancipated, or a Soviet-type commissar of security to liquidate mass resistance.

I hope those who accept this challenge will not take these reflections as the counsel of despair, or as intimation that Reconstruction was doomed to failure, or that our ancestors might not have done better by their experiment than they actually did. Nor should other historians be discouraged from revolutionary speculations by the inconclusive results of my own. Let them be as far-out left as is currently fashionable. But in the transports of revolutionary imaginings, arm-chair edicts, and dreams of glory, they would do well to keep in mind the human materials and the historic context of their problem. If they do this, they will face up to the fact that nineteenth-century Americans (and some in the twentieth century as well) were fatefully stuck with a perverse mystique of squatter sovereignty. The tenets of this perversion of the democratic dogma, this squatter sovereignty, were that whatever the law or the Constitution or the Supreme Court or world opinion or moral codes said to the contrary notwithstanding, the will of the dominant white majority would prevail. And where whites were not in the majority it would prevail anyway. How it was, and how early, we got stuck with a commitment to this caricature of democracy is a long story, a very long story, and the story did not begin in 1865, and the commitment was not confined to the South.

QUESTIONS TO CONSIDER

1. Why, according to Woodward, are interpretations of Reconstruction inadequate unless they see it as tragic? Why is it "a strategy of evasion" to say that the First Reconstruction prepared the way for the Second? What gains did the southern Reconstruction governments and the ex-slaves make, and why does Woodward discount them?

2. To what extent, if any, was Radical Reconstruction revolutionary in its goals or methods? What definition of "revolutionary" should be used in assessing it? How would Woodward and Eric Foner address these questions? How would you choose between their viewpoints?

3. Woodward makes a telling analogy between the treatment of ex-slaves in the South and Native Americans in the West. Why did the federal government (for a time) support black assimilation and enfranchisement, but simultaneously deny Indians citizenship and confine them to reservations? How, in the end, were these two "problems," according to Woodward, "solved in much the same way"?

4. What, at bottom, does Woodward blame for the failure of Reconstruction? human nature? capitalist greed? the sanctity of private property? the ineffectiveness of big government? white racism? Does Woodward's essay leave you with the impression that Reconstruction was doomed and that what happened was inevitable? Why or why not?

5. Has Woodward effectively demonstrated the usefulness of "counterfactual" analysis? Is this method "quackery," as one historian has charged, or are there benefits to speculating about options in the past? Are Woodward's analogies to the Homestead Act and Indian policy appropriate? Would anything have been different had Radical Reconstruction never occurred? What if the Confederacy had won the Civil War? What if Radical Reconstruction had *succeeded* and African Americans had had equal access to land, education, and the vote? How would subsequent American history have been changed?

Conquering and Settling the West

Just over a century ago, the historian Frederick Jackson Turner declared that the western frontier, which was then vanishing, had played a decisive role in making the United States unique. Confronted with the need to survive against the wilderness, frontier settlers, said Turner, developed habits of practicality, individualism, and democracy that indelibly shaped the American character. Whatever the merits of Turner's thesis — and it has been hotly disputed — his image of the frontier as the boundary between "civilization" and "wilderness," settled and unsettled land, was badly distorted. Like nineteenth-century frontiers in Canada, South America, Australia, Russia, and South Africa, the American West was not an empty landscape. Instead, it was a borderland where white settlers of European origin confronted indigenous peoples, besieged their culture, and took away their land. In this long, unhappy saga of Europe's conquest of newly encountered territories — a saga that Turner virtually excluded from his writings — the American story proved fundamentally similar to others.

Similar, too, was the process of white settlement that followed. On many frontiers, traders, missionaries, miners, ranchers, farmers, railroad builders, and land speculators — all with varied agendas — tried to control the pace and character of expansion. In some cases, governments mediated among these competing interests; in others, governments aggressively promoted agricultural and industrial growth. Turner, like many evolutionist thinkers of his day, viewed the frontier's development as an accelerated version of humanity's natural progression from hunter-gatherers to farmers and city dwellers. In the rush to populate North America's frontier and others, six thousand years of social evolution were dramatically telescoped into less than a century. What Turner failed to note, however, was that government plans and absentee owners controlled this process more powerfully than did laws of evolution or the decisions of individual settlers. The frontier became a land of opportunity, but not for all who went there. Less obvious, too, a century ago was the fact that rapid development had terrible consequences for the land. Wherever white settler societies pushed toward the frontier in the nineteenth century, they extracted its resources to satisfy the needs of ambitious central governments and voracious world markets. As a result, environmental plunder replaced the native peoples' practice of living in relative balance with nature. Not until these lands filled up in the twentieth century did expansionist governments begin to curb their wasteful and dangerous ways.

These broad similarities in patterns of conquest and settlement across frontiers form the backdrop for the two comparative essays in this chapter. In the first selection, Roger L. Nichols carefully traces simultaneous attempts on both sides of the American and Canadian border to subdue western Indian tribes and force them to adopt white society's ways. Once native peoples were dispossessed, white migrants and their governments built frontier towns. In the second selection, Kate Brown offers a provocative comparison of two towns across a huge reach of time and space: Billings, Montana, a railroad town founded in the 1880s, and Karaganda, Kazakhstan, a prison settlement erected on the Soviet frontier in the 1930s. These authors choose dramatically different comparative cases and approaches. Nichols's focused narrative points out subtle differences in the fundamentally similar frontier histories of the United States and Canada, while Brown's impressionistic account uncovers broad similarities between the United States and the Soviet Union, societies that are usually seen as opposites. Despite divergent methods, both essays strike a somber note, suggesting that the American experience was one variation of the common frontier theme of tragedy and exploitation.

3

Indian Societies Under Siege in the United States and Canada

ROGER L. NICHOLS

In the decades between the Civil War and the turn of the century, millions of Americans headed west into the vast territory between the Mississippi River and the Pacific Ocean. Across this wide frontier and with astonishing rapidity, they established farms, ranches, mines, and towns. Inevitably, the pioneers' hunger for land and wealth led them to encroach upon Indian villages and hunting grounds, and conflicts between settlers and natives erupted. To reduce the violence, make way for "progress," and help "civilize" the Indians, the federal government decided to confine the Indians to small reservations in remote areas spurned by white settlers. Not surprisingly, many of the western Indians refused to be penned into reservations far from their ancestral lands. Powerful tribes like the Sioux of the northern Great Plains used their skill with horses and guns to defy federal troops sent to hunt them down. Between 1867, when the federal government adopted the reservation policy, and 1890, when the massacre at Wounded Knee closed the era of Indian resistance, armed encounters between the U.S. Army and tribal "hostiles" resulted in thousands of deaths before the government's superior forces overwhelmed the Indians and ended their way of life.

Such frontier bloodletting was not unique. At the same time that the U.S. Cavalry was fighting Indians to secure the West for white settlers, the Canadian national government moved onto Indian lands and suppressed rebellions in Manitoba and Saskatchewan. Both the American and Canadian battles had larger contexts, arising out of long histories of westward expansion and recent successes at consolidating national rule: the Union's victory in the Civil War and the creation of the unified Dominion of Canada in 1867. Seen in an even bigger picture, they were part of what historian James O. Gump calls "a global pattern of intensified conflict in the latter half of the nineteenth century" between European imperial powers and their New World descendants, on the one hand, and less technologically developed native peoples, on the other. By the eve of World War I, this struggle led to Western control over three-quarters of the world's people.

In the following essay, Roger L. Nichols artfully blends the history of Indian-white relations in the United States and Canada from the 1860s to 1890 into a single narrative, highlighting many similarities but also important differences. Although white settlement proceeded at a faster pace in the United States, Nichols finds that on both sides of the border railroads spear-headed the invasion of farmers, miners, and merchants that pressured governments to dispossess Indians. In response, governments negotiated treaties that reduced Indians' lands and curtailed their freedom of movement. On American reservations and Canadian Indian reserves, missionaries and educators attempted to wean natives away from tribal practices. Meanwhile, both governments experimented with allotment programs that offered land to Indian families in exchange for their adopting citizenship and renouncing tribal rights. Finally, Indian peoples in the United States and Canada resisted white incursions by using warfare or more subtle means, such as adapting white people's religion and education to their own ends, but natives inevitably saw their autonomy dwindle in the face of the whites' superior force and numbers.

There were, however, two key differences between these frontier histories. First, the United States experienced a much more violent collision of peoples than its northern neighbor. America's rapid expansion to the Pacific was supported by national policies that were systematically committed to moving Indians aside and enforced by hardened Civil War soldiers. By contrast, Canada's government intervened reluctantly in western affairs, often in response to fears of a possible U.S. takeover rather than Indian uprisings. Canada's vast area, small population, and less aggressive policies resulted in less Indian-white violence. Nichols notes that whereas the U.S. Cavalry was sent to battle Indian tribes, Canada's North West Mounted Police, or "Mounties," were devoted to keeping the peace and establishing civil government. Second, the two nations pursued different ethnic policies. Americans made no special place for mixed-race peoples on the frontier, treating them as Indians, Mexicans, or whites according to whom they lived with. In Canada, on the other hand, the mixed French-Indian Métis were recognized as a distinct people and accorded separate rights. This difference may be related to the rigid black-white dichotomy in American thinking about race, which discouraged mixed-race classifying. It may also stem from Canada's distinctive origin as a hybrid colony that incorporated an existing French minority with a separate language, faith, and territory under British rule.

The special classification of the Métis calls into question the decision that some historians have made to lump together the American and Canadian Wests as "frontiers of exclusion" that sharply separated white expansionists and native peoples, as opposed to Latin American "frontiers of inclusion," where invaders and defenders mixed their races and cultures. In any case, Nichols's account shows that in the late nineteenth century both the U.S. and Canadian governments pursued a contradictory policy that combined exclusion and inclusion, segregation and assimilation. Both nations hoped that Indian reservations would be places of temporary segregation where seminomadic native peoples could be transformed into farmers, converted to Christianity, educated in white ways, and eventually integrated into the market economy. Although some supporters of this forced assimilation policy had good, if misguided, intentions, it violated most Indians' preferences and was exploited by greedy frontier settlers and agents. Thanks to shrunken reservations and foreclosed individual holdings, Indian farmers in the United States lost over 60 percent of their lands in the half-century after Wounded Knee. The results in Canada were somewhat better, in part due to Indians' preference for ranching over farming. Still, because both governments sought to destroy Indians' identities and reduce their lands, they aroused resentment that has embittered Indian-white relations down to the present day.

GLOSSARY

ACCULTURATION AND ASSIMILATION   Terms that describe the process by which one group adopts or absorbs the social and cultural patterns of another; in this case, the Indians' adopting the ways of white society.

CUSTER, GEORGE A. (1839–1876)   A fearless and flamboyant military officer who became the Union army's youngest general during the Civil War. During the postwar campaign against the Sioux, Custer and his entire detachment of about 250 men were killed at Little Bighorn, Montana, in 1876.

ENFRANCHISEMENT ACT (1869)   A law aimed at the rapid assimilation of Indians into mainstream Canadian society. As implemented in 1876, this policy sought to break up Indian land reserves, assign land to individuals, operate schools, and pressure Indians to become citizens. Later, enfranchisement became compulsory, but following protests from many natives, this policy was revoked in 1922.

HAMPTON INSTITUTE   A school for recently freed slaves opened in Virginia in 1868. Its most famous graduate, Booker T. Washington, returned to teach there early in his career as an African American spokesman and educator. Emphasizing basic skills and vocational training, Hampton became a model for educational efforts to assimilate blacks and American Indians into white society.

HUDSON'S BAY COMPANY   A powerful British corporation, organized in 1670, that dominated the fur trade and land development in much of Canada for two hundred years. Its vast holdings, known as Rupert's Land (after the company's first governor, Prince Rupert, a cousin of Charles II), reached from Labrador to the Rocky Mountains. They were sold to the Canadian government in 1870.

MACDONALD, JOHN A. (1815–1891)   The first prime minister of the Dominion of Canada. MacDonald worked to extend the Dominion to the western provinces and to strengthen the powers of the central government. His two terms of office, 1867–1873 and 1878–1891, coincided with two Métis-led rebellions in the Canadian West.

MÉTIS   In Canada, persons of mixed European (usually French) and Indian descent.

MEXICAN WAR (1846–1848)   The war between the United States and Mexico by which the United States gained California and the present-day lands of Arizona, New Mexico, Utah, and parts of Colorado.

NEZ PERCÉ   Indian people of the Pacific Northwest (called "pierced nose" by French traders) whose dispute with white settlers evolved into the Nez Percé War of 1877. Led by Chief Joseph, a band of 250 warriors and their families held off General O. O. Howard's 5,000 men as they trekked from southern Idaho toward refuge in Canada. Captured near the border, they were assigned to Oklahoma, far from their ancestral lands.

QUAKERS   Members of a pacifist Protestant sect who originally settled in colonial Pennsylvania and later were prominent in antislavery and other nineteenth-century reform movements.

RIEL, LOUIS, JR. (1844–1885)   A Montreal-educated Métis who led two rebellions in Canada. Angered by Canada's plans for white settlement of the West, Riel organized the Métis to proclaim their own government in Manitoba in 1869, but fled when the revolt collapsed the following year. Outlawed in 1875, he moved to the United States, where he was recruited in 1884 by Saskatchewan's Métis leaders to help them resist government encroachment. The next year he proclaimed a provisional government, and when the Métis fought alongside western Indians against the Royal Canadian Mounted Police, Riel was captured and executed, ending the rebellion.

ROYAL IRISH CONSTABULARY   An armed peacekeeping force, established by Britain in 1867, whose members enforced civil law in Ireland until it won independence in 1922. It provided the model for the Canadian North West Mounted Police.

SITTING BULL (*circa* 1831–1890)   The Dakota Sioux Indian chief who united the Sioux tribes in resistance against the U.S. Army and America's reservation policy. After his warriors defeated General Custer at Little Bighorn in 1876, Sitting Bull led some followers to Canada, where the government did not aid them and famine forced them to surrender in 1881. Returned to the United States, Sitting Bull toured with Buffalo Bill's Wild West Show for a few years. He was killed by reservation police in 1890 when Sioux warriors tried to prevent his arrest during the Ghost Dance movement.

SUN DANCE   The central annual ceremony of the Sioux religion. In it, male warriors dancing in a circle endured painful tortures to demonstrate their courage and to gain favor for the tribe from the great, unknowable ruling force of the world.

TOOHOOLHOOLZOTE   Nez Percé medicine man and spokesman at the May 1887 council with General O. O. Howard and other U.S. representatives.

WOVOKA   A Paiute medicine man from western Nevada who claimed that he visited heaven during a vision in 1889 and returned as the Indian messiah to rescue Native Americans from invading whites. His teachings supplemented those of his father Tavibo, and formed the basis for the Ghost Dance movement.

Tall and thick-necked, Toohoolhoolzote argued forcefully with the one-armed General Oliver Otis Howard. The soldier, accused of being soft on Indians, strove to disprove that by demanding that the Nez Percé vacate their traditional Wallowa Valley homeland in Oregon. Responding, the older dreamer prophet reminded Howard that this band of Nez Percé had never signed any agreement to move. Rather, he said, the land had come down to them from their fathers and they intended to keep it. Howard interrupted angrily that he had orders from the president and that he wanted to hear no more talk about beliefs, only removal. At that point Toohoolhoolzote answered, "I am telling you I am a chief! Who can tell me what to do in my own country?" Both his tone and words angered the general, who shouted, "I am the man. I stand here for the president. . . . My orders are plain and will be executed." Then he grabbed the Indian by one arm and with an aide walked him across the parade ground to the guardhouse. Following that he issued an ultimatum. The Nez Percé had thirty days to move their property and livestock or the army would drive them to the reservation.

This order set into motion events leading to the tragic 1877 Nez Percé flight toward Canada. It also demonstrated vividly the drastic changes many Indian groups in both nations experienced in their dealings with the rest of society during the last four decades of the nineteenth century. On both sides of the border, railroads stretched across the landscape bringing farmers, miners, and merchants while helping to destroy the plains buffalo herds. Bureaucrats and treaty negotiators followed, greatly reducing tribal land-holdings and bringing freedom of movement to an end for most groups. Increasing numbers of teachers, missionaries, model farmers, and government agents brought renewed demands that tribal people cease practicing some of their cultural and religious ceremonies and adopt the invaders' economy and culture. Such urgings were not new in either country, but after 1860 many of the plains and western tribes encountered them for the first time. That led to bitter interracial conflict and crushing defeats for native peoples in both countries.

During the decades that followed, many western Indians in both countries became administered people. That is, government officials told them what they could do, as well as when, where, and how to do it. By the end of the era their loss of autonomy reached into most aspects of their lives. At the same time, substantial differences marked the tribal experiences on each side of the international border. In the United States the army campaigned repeatedly against tribes and bands declared hostile by government policy. Farther north, on the other hand, the North West Mounted Police usually managed to keep peace. Because of the continuing violence and bloodshed in the American West, churchmen, reformers, and other so-called friends of the Indian launched frequent movements to force the U.S. government to end the fighting, reform the operations of the Indian Office, and give them more say in the way tribal people were being treated. No direct parallel existed in Canada at the time. The issue of how to classify mixed-race peoples and then of what to do with them certainly differentiated actions in the two nations. In Canada the two mixed-race groups, the French-Indian Métis and the English-Scots-lndian country born, came to be recognized as a distinct people with some rights akin to those of the Indians. The United States, in contrast, ignored such people unless they chose to live as Indians with the tribe or band to which they were related.

While the differences appear marked in the two societies, frequent similarities continued as well. In fact, during this era the actions of the two countries became more alike than at any previous time. Both nations used education, particularly boarding schools, to wean the children and young people away from their cultures. Church and missionary activity had a large role in both countries; the churches actually operated many Indian schools in Canada. Both governments sought to isolate tribal people while pressuring them to accept churches, schools, and farms as helpers on the white man's path. While American agents demanded that all Indians become small farmers, their Canadian counterparts at least recognized that some of the Plains groups might succeed as stock raisers and small-time ranchers. Yet neither government would accept communal land use patterns so dear to the hearts of Indians, nor would they protect enough land for the tribal people to have a reasonable possibility of success raising livestock. Officials in both countries assumed that Indians had to become integrated into the society and economic system of their particular country. Regardless, few in either nation expected them to survive as identifiable peoples into the twentieth century.

Some tribal people living in the United States resorted to warfare to protect their lands and customs, while in Canada few violent confrontations occurred. Leaders in both countries responded to the continuing demands for more land cessions with delay, rejection, or compromise, but in almost every case they lost territory to the advancing whites. While a few groups such as a part of the Hunkpapa Sioux followed Sitting Bull into Canada briefly, and some Kickapoos fled from Texas into northern Mexico, this was not a popular option for most Indians. As they had done before, shamans and prophets offered guidance. They upheld past beliefs, offered new insights that combined elements of Christianity and tribal practices, or gradually accepted the missionaries' teachings. On reservations or reserves leaders supported education for the children to help the next generation better deal with the ever-increasing numbers of whites. In all of these choices, however, Indians had ever less chance to take the initiative as the century drew to a close. . . .

MOUNTING CRISES IN THE AMERICAN WEST

. . . Despite nearly a century of experience with tribal people by [the 1860s], American officials found themselves experiencing the most difficult times with the tribal people they could remember. The expansion that followed the Mexican War increasingly brought hordes of pioneers into the new territories of New Mexico, Kansas, and Nebraska. With their creation, the only large territory still reserved for the Indians was the present state of Oklahoma, which soon became established as Indian Territory. There and elsewhere in the West, by 1860 the treaties signed at Fort Laramie with the Plains tribes no longer prevented sporadic violence. The advent of the American Civil War drew most of the regular army forces stationed in the West eastward to help put down the rebellion of the Southern states. This meant that at a time of increasing westward migration and a continuous stream of new mineral discoveries, few regular soldiers stood ready to separate whites and Indians in the West. . . .

With the [army] regulars gone, during the summer of 1862 the eastern Sioux living near Mankato [in Minnesota,] tried to expel the whites from their homeland. Having agreed to land cessions earlier, and feeling closed in by the increasing numbers of pioneers, the Indians struck when their annuities failed to arrive. Actually, the "Great Sioux War," as the settlers called it, began mostly by accident after a minor incident in which several young Sioux men returning from hunting had first been refused water and then offered alcohol. They became drunk and killed a farm family in central Minnesota. Learning of the killings, Chief Little Crow apparently decided that his people had only two choices, flight or battle, so he persuaded his followers to attack. They did so across much of Minnesota, where bitter fighting occurred at the town of New Ulm and several other nearby small communities. Soldiers and militiamen rushed to the scene, tracked the tribe after it fled, and defeated and captured many of the Indians. In December 1862 the army hanged thirty-eight of the captives at Mankato, but some of the warriors had fled, spreading news of their actions among so-called hostile groups on the plains.

By 1864 raiding bands of Sioux, Pawnees, Cheyennes, and Arapahos had cleared many pioneers from the central plains, leading John Evans, the governor of Colorado, to claim that the raiders had virtually isolated Denver and the mining camps in the central Rocky Mountains. That brought retaliation from the Colorado militia, and in November 1864 the Sand Creek Massacre occurred. . . . The militiamen tore into the Indian village, which flew a large American flag to signal peaceful intentions. When the shouting stopped, the pioneers had killed and mutilated two hundred men, women, and children. This carnage prompted investigations by the army and Congress. Meanwhile, the survivors fled, bringing their story of white treachery to other villagers; thus the war continued, shifting northward where the miners pouring into the northern Rockies had to cross Sioux and Cheyenne territory. Even though the Civil War had ended by 1865, Indians and whites fought a bitter contest for much of the next generation in the West. Along the Bozeman Trail leading north from the Platte River Road to the mining camps of Montana, the Sioux bottled up the troops, at times virtually besieging the isolated army outposts. . . .

As citizens called for protection and army leaders proposed crushing the Sioux, humanitarian groups in the East focused public attention on the Indian problem. Looking for a peaceful solution, the Johnson administration agreed to abandon the forts along the Bozeman Trail and established a general peace commission to end the conflict soon. That group, including General William T. Sherman and three other generals as well as three civilians, headed west. In October 1867 they held a treaty council with the tribes of the southern plains at Medicine Lodge Creek in Kansas. Five thousand Indians came together to feast at the commission's expense and to hear what the Great Father's representatives had to say. The negotiators reminded their listeners that the buffalo would disappear soon and that they needed to learn the white man's way if they wanted their children to survive.

At first Indian leaders tried to ignore the commissioners' warnings. Silver Brooch, a Comanche band leader, reminded the negotiators that his people had been ill treated for years and that past promises made to them had gone unmet. Because of white mistreatment many Comanches had died. This time he was openly skeptical about getting any of the benefits promised for signing yet another treaty. "I shall wait until next spring to see if these things shall be given us," he said. If not, he continued, "I and my young men will return with our wild brothers to live on the prairie.". . . Ten Bears, speaking for another Comanche group, stated that his people wanted no part of farming or a sedentary existence. "I wish you would not keep insisting on putting us on reservations," he complained. With considerable feeling, Satanta, the aging Kiowa leader, rejected the commissioners' proposals too. He asked them to tell the president that "when the buffalo leave the country, we will let him know. By that time we will be ready to live in houses."

Despite their reluctance, many Indian leaders on the southern plains realized that each year fewer buffalo appeared and that the number of intruding Americans increased. Clearly the commissioners spoke the truth when they told the tribal people that they had to change their way of life or be destroyed. So, despite their misgivings, on 21 October 1867 leaders of the Kiowas, Kiowa-Apaches, Arapahos, Cheyennes, and Comanches signed the Treaty of Medicine Lodge. They agreed to remain at peace, to surrender vast portions of their hunting territories, to live on assigned reservations, and to accept the white man's instruction in farming. In return for their signatures, the government negotiators promised them annuities for the next thirty years and immediate access to the piles of presents displayed prominently throughout the talks.

Finishing its work in the south, the Peace Commission turned its attention to the tribes of the northern plains. . . . During the summer and autumn of 1868 the bands and tribes of the northern plains signed the Treaty of Fort Laramie. In that agreement the government accepted Sioux demands that Americans stay out of tribal hunting grounds and that no forts or new roads would be built along the Powder River. For their part, the northern plains Indians agreed to stay on fixed reservations in Dakota, Montana, and Wyoming, to remain at peace, and to refrain from harassing railroad survey and construction crews as they moved through Indian country.

No sooner had the ink dried on this latest round of treaty negotiations than violence flared once again. Southern Cheyenne raids in Kansas provided plenty of incidents for headlines in the East. With some of the plains-area people back at war, the peace initiative appeared dead. . . .

Continuing public denunciations of the conduct of Indian relations persuaded incoming president Ulysses S. Grant that he needed competent and honest people in the Indian Office. Even before his inauguration in March 1869 religious leaders asked him to nominate men suggested by the Christian denominations to serve as agents on the new western reservations. Because the first delegation to suggest this plan to Grant happened to be Quakers, his subsequent approach came to be known as the Quaker policy. . . .

As its name indicated, Grant's policy aimed at peaceful relations between the races, but obstacles large and small prevented it from achieving that goal. While the secretary of the Board of Indian Commissioners, Vincent Colyer — dubbed "Vincent the Good" by his detractors — traveled throughout the West negotiating agreements and laying out reservations, neither the Indians nor the local frontier citizens understood or supported his efforts. Worse, agents living among the tribal people had the difficult task of explaining why supplies or annuities promised by previous agents or federal negotiators arrived late or failed to arrive at all. Tribal leaders faced rumblings among their followers, particularly from the young warriors who grew restive while waiting for the Great Father's men to keep their promises. On the plains the large tribes that traditionally followed the buffalo herds found their hunting less successful as each year passed. Correctly blaming the encroaching whites for their troubles, they became restive, and violence often followed. During the years under the peace policy and for another decade into the mid-1880s scattered warfare continued. Sporadic fighting with the Sioux and Cheyennes on the northern plains proved only one part of the story. The Modoc War of 1872–73, the Red River War of 1874–75, the flight of the Nez Percé in 1877, the Ute War of 1879, and the Apache wars of the 1870–80s all punctuated the western story with violence and death.

Most attention, however, fell on the wars with the Sioux on the northern plains. Although technically at peace since the Treaty of Fort Laramie in 1868, the Plains tribes kept up a pattern of minor raids throughout the period. Then, Colonel George A. Custer led a column of soldiers, miners, and reporters into the Black Hills during the summer of 1874, setting the stage for a final showdown in that region. Claiming the Black Hills as a sacred part of their heritage, the Sioux appealed to the agents to remove the illegal miners, but to no avail. When the authorities took no action, the Indians began raiding mining camps and supply trains moving toward the area. Their actions brought a quick response and the most famous military action in American western history. In June 1876 Colonel Custer led a large part of the Seventh Cavalry Regiment to its destruction on the banks of the Little Bighorn — or the Greasy Grass River, as the Indians called it. Mistakenly thinking that Crazy Horse and Sitting Bull led only perhaps 150 lodges of Indians there, Custer charged the camp. Instead of the modest numbers of Sioux he anticipated, the impetuous colonel met the full force of the northern tribes that day. Gall, Hump, and many other war leaders joined with Crazy Horse and Sitting Bull to destroy most of Custer's immediate command. News of the defeat electrified the nation, and soon columns of troops chased the offending Sioux in all directions. The war ended the following summer, but only after Sitting Bull and hundreds of his followers had fled north across the "medicine line" into Canada for refuge.

American violence and warfare with the tribal people resulted from a combination of factors, few of which could have been avoided. The native societies in the West were well led and had strong attachments to their homelands, and some had strong warrior traditions. Moreover, they lived atop land seen as desirable for agriculture or athwart roads and trails over which thousands of pioneers trudged. Some of the tribal lands encompassed valuable mineral bodies or timber stands, and westerners had little patience for the idea that those valuable resources should be monopolized by the Indians. Few accepted the Indians' right to continue living a traditional lifestyle. Although only a small proportion openly called for destroying the tribes, many western Americans wanted the government to push the tribal people out of their way. On that issue they shared values with the Canadians. In both nations the people living nearest the tribes wanted them moved. They gave little thought to where Indians should live, and even those who supported the various acculturation programs failed to accept them as equals or to welcome acculturated Indians as their neighbors with much enthusiasm. By the late nineteenth century this left few options for the western tribes.

Confrontations on the Canadian Plains

While the United States and its tribal people fought bloody wars in the decades after 1860, Canada usually avoided major confrontation and bloodshed. More often than not, this resulted from the vast area and small populations north of the border rather than [from] any superior policy or more careful handling of Indian-related issues by Canadian officials. . . .

During the late 1860s events that shaped the long-term relations between the races took place in London and the provincial capitals in Canada. Moving to grant more local autonomy to parts of their far-flung empire, the British established the Dominion of

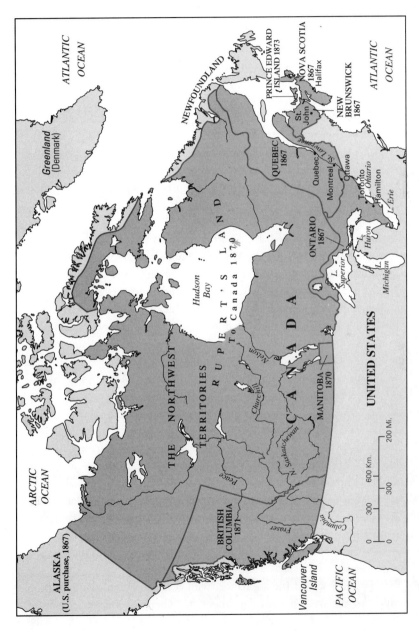

The Dominion of Canada, 1871. Canada's unification as a dominion in 1867 was hastened by the westward expansion of the United States and its purchase of Alaska from Russia that same year. Shortly afterward, new provinces were added (the year that appears near each province's name is the date the province joined the dominion). Still, vast areas of the North and West were too sparsely populated to achieve that status. Manitoba was enlarged in the 1880s and again in 1912, and Alberta and Saskatchewan did not become provinces until 1905.

Canada in 1867 under the provisions of the British North America Act. The new government had authority over Ontario and Quebec (dropping the earlier names of Canada West and Canada East), as well as Nova Scotia and New Brunswick, and within just a few years it would stretch its control west to British Columbia and north and west to encompass all of Rupert's Land, the vast holdings of the Hudson's Bay Company that lay west of Lake Superior and north into the Arctic. As Canadian leaders organized their new government they looked nervously at the United States, fearing American territorial expansion at their expense, and with good reason. In 1867, the same year as Canadian confederation, William Seward, the American secretary of state, purchased Alaska from Russia. The specter of American territorial growth nearly became an obsession for some Canadian leaders. John A. MacDonald, who headed the first government, admitted that "I would be quite willing, personally, to leave that whole country [the West] a wilderness for the next half-century, but I fear if Englishmen do not go there, Yankees will."

For the Indians living beyond Lake Superior this attitude brought mixed results: positive because of governmental determination to keep peace and thus avoid giving the Americans any reason to intervene in the Canadian West; and negative because federal policies encouraged railroad building, settlement, and agricultural development. Despite the growing influx of non-Indians, no army marched west to do combat with the resident tribes. Rather, the North West Mounted Police would serve military, police, and civil governmental functions for the next generation. Their presence in the West showed American authorities that the Canadians could direct western affairs with competence and helped prevent some of the worst difficulties experienced by tribes not too far below the border. At the same time the immense area and the tiny population in western Canada made the Mounties' tasks relatively easy. For example, as late as 1880, when the census of the Dakotas showed 133,147 inhabitants, the 1881 count for the entire Canadian Northwest — excluding Indians, but including Métis and whites — turned up only 6,974 people. . . .

At Confederation the new nation included only four provinces, but in 1869 Rupert's Land, the vast holdings of the Hudson's Bay Company, became part of Canada. The next year, 1870, the government established the new western province of Manitoba, while in 1871 British Columbia joined the country, and two years later Prince Edward Island did the same. In their rush to make Canada a continental power, the Ottawa leaders faced daunting obstacles and at times ignored basic problems. Still, by 1869 they had passed the Enfranchisement Act, which incorporated existing rules about tribal membership and protection for Indian lands. It also created a new system that in theory could sidestep the traditional tribal leaders whenever the bureaucrats decided that was necessary.

Assuming that they had settled Indian matters with that legislation, the leadership turned its attention to the west, present-day Manitoba. There a substantial group of Métis and country-born people had lived for years, mostly south of Lake Winnipeg near the forks of the Red and Assiniboine Rivers, just north of Minnesota. As did the Plains tribes, these people depended heavily on their annual buffalo hunt to provide a large part of their annual food and trade supply. In addition to their hunting, however, they maintained homes and small farms along the Red and Assiniboine Rivers. . . . As long as they lived within the domain of the Hudson's Bay Company, nobody bothered the Métis settlements, and to the villagers it was clear which family owned what land. Once Canada assumed control of the area, however, the peculiar landholdings and the lack of any careful recording of local claims put the westerners and their new and largely unwelcome government on a collision course.

In their fear of possible American intervention and land seizures in the West, Ottawa officials neglected to consult in any way with the Métis people of Manitoba. In 1869, immediately after getting title to the region, the government sent out survey crews to bring landholdings in the West into line with those in Ontario. . . . Fearing that Canadian officials might ignore their customary landholding patterns, angry at having virtually no say in their own government, and deeply suspicious of Canadian motives for moving in on them, the mixed-race peoples of the West organized under the leadership of Louis Riel Jr., a Montreal-educated Métis, to proclaim their own local government, establish courts, and block Canadian penetration of the region until the disputes could be settled. Riel proclaimed a provisional government in December 1869, and the next year Manitoba joined the confederation as a province, if only a small one.

In trying to settle the confusing land claims in the West, the Manitoba Act reserved 1.4 million acres of land for the next generation of Métis. Placing this group with tribal people in the province, the law called for land to be set aside so the government would be able to extinguish the Indian title to lands in the province. As far as Ottawa was concerned, . . . Métis and Indians got the same treatment. Unlike the mixed-race people in the United States, however, in Canada the Métis experienced a different relationship to the government. . . . Although part Indian, they had different rights, and generally the government classed them as a distinct people. By 1870, then, in Canada the classification of native peoples included what would come down to the present as four distinct groups — status Indians, non-status Indians (people who might be Indian by blood or culture but not by legal definition), Métis, and Inuit, the people called Eskimos in the United States. . . .

Despite the differing experiences of mixed-race people in the two countries, Indians on each side of the border faced similar governmental policies toward land acquisition and pioneer settlement. For example, both nations used treaties or other agreements to extinguish tribal land claims. . . . [In Canada,] [e]ach of these agreements varied somewhat because Indian spokesmen insisted on particular provisions such as hunting rights, annuities, schools, tools, farm equipment, and even a medicine chest for each agency. Compared to such accords in the United States, these gave the tribal people smaller land reserves, tiny annuities, and fewer other benefits. Yet the treaties resulted from real and even tense negotiations. Although they came as prepared documents, Indian demands forced Canadian officials to make changes and additions. U.S. officials, in contrast, even after they stopped negotiating treaties, tried to dictate executive agreements in their accustomed unilateral manner.

While the Indians and the Canadian government remained at peace during the nation's first decade in existence, by the mid-1880s this broke down. Without an army, Canada turned to a uniquely British institution for its peacekeeping force. Based on the model of the Royal Irish Constabulary, in 1873 the government created the North

West Mounted Police. Hoping to keep peace, regulate the introduction of alcohol, and discourage American freebooters from crossing the Montana border, the first units marched west a year later. Distinctly Canadian, the NWMP provided an administrative framework that differed substantially from American frontier institutions for government and law enforcement. In place of the divided civil-military authority in the American West, the Mounties combined both functions. An individual Mountie could investigate a crime, pursue, capture, arrest, and incarcerate the accused, gather the evidence, try the defendant, pass sentence, and even escort the criminal to prison. His duties varied widely from serving as a local justice of the police to participating in military actions. In the United States the Indian Office dealt with civil affairs while the army handled military ones. Generally speaking, by combining functions in a single force, the Canadian government avoided some of the worst difficulties that occurred south of the border.

Yet try as they might, the tribes and Canadian officials could not avoid all of the troubles endemic to a large geographical region with few people, inadequate communication facilities, and rapidly diminishing buffalo herds. Although fewer military conflicts occurred than in the United States, the basic issues remained similar. By the mid-1880s most of the vast buffalo herds had disappeared, and some of the Indians began asking for help to change their economy and way of life. While U.S. troops to the south crisscrossed the plains trying to keep the tribes on their assigned reservation land, Canada used no troops because the Indians chose not to flee. With the hunting peoples exhausting their game supply, their economic patterns needed to change rapidly, and neither the government that would have to pay for that change nor the Indians themselves who would have to adapt to a radically different style of life wanted to face the effort needed to do the job.

The Cree and Blackfoot peoples of the plains bore the brunt of the drastic changes sweeping across the west. Because some groups had complained about their benefits under earlier treaties, during the 1875 talks the Cree leader Big Bear voiced suspicions about dealing with the whites. When a government spokesman offered presents to the Indians, Big Bear warned other leaders that by accepting the gifts they might be agreeing to things not spoken there. . . . "We want none of the Queen's presents," he told the government spokesman George McDougall. "Let your Chiefs come like men to talk to us." . . .

Yet neither Big Bear nor other chiefs opposed talking with government officers or considering treaty signing if they saw that as being in the best interests of their people. His contemporary Crowfoot, a Blackfoot leader, admitted that the Canadian Indians could not expect to depend on buffalo hunting for long. In an 1876 meeting with a visiting NWMP inspector, he said that "we shall all see the day is coming when the buffalo will all be killed, and we shall have nothing to live on." He hoped that when that happened, the whites would treat the tribes fairly. He also calmed the inspector's fears that the Canadian tribes would move south and join forces with Sitting Bull and his Sioux followers in their war against the United States.

Three years later Crowfoot confronted Canadian officials again. By then the near-disappearance of the buffalo herds had forced many Plains people to sell their horses in exchange for flour as well as resorting to eating antelope, gophers, and even mice. In

July 1879 Crowfoot told the visiting Edgar Dewdney that "if you will drive away the Sioux and make a hole for the buffalo to come in we won't bother you about grub, but if you don't you must feed us for we are starving." Despite this obvious need, Ottawa officials failed to help. Instead, they ignored or broke several provisions of the 1876 treaty, refused to mark off the lands the Indians wanted, denied some of the bands food vitally necessary for survival, and forced them to move away from the U.S. border to get their treaty payments. . . . [B]y 1884 leaders of a dozen bands met to protest inadequacies of government actions and to negotiate better reserve locations and more assistance from the government. . . .

While violence erupted on the Plains in 1885, growing Indian militancy did not start the rebellion that year. Rather, the fears and dissatisfactions of the Métis people and their recruitment of the erratic Louis Riel from his home in the United States brought matters on the Plains to a head. The administration of John A. MacDonald knew little of western issues and seems to have cared even less. After the 1869 Red River crisis, when some Métis leaders had called for payments to surrender their land, the government had recognized their land claims in Manitoba. Now, however, MacDonald wanted no part of further expenses in the West. . . . [W]hen the federal government refused to consider their complaints, Saskatchewan Métis leaders sent for Riel, hoping that his experiences in negotiating with Ottawa might prove beneficial. Instead, through what might be described as a comedy of errors, the government, the Métis, and the Indians came to blows on the Plains. When the fighting ended the government won, hanged Riel, and sentenced [the Cree leaders] Poundmaker and Big Bear to long prison terms despite the efforts of both men to avoid the fighting. After the massive invasion that the Riel Rebellion called forth, neither the Métis nor the Indians of the Plains raised much public objection to government policies in the West.

EDUCATING FOR ENFRANCHISEMENT

With their military defeats in both countries mainly completed during the 1880s, the tribes awaited further government actions anxiously. Soon they encountered government agents, missionaries, schoolteachers, and demands that they become sedentary farmers. Ironically, bureaucrats decided that the tribal people should live and work in isolation to speed their absorption into the Canadian and American societies. Somehow they thought that Indians would learn personal discipline, the responsibilities of citizenship, and how to function in a capitalist economy in a foreign culture when they had few successful examples on which to model their actions. At the same time, the whites tried to control all decision making within tribal communities. Teachers, government agents, and missionaries told the Indians what to do, when, where, and how they should be doing their tasks, and gave them little to say about how their economy, social life, or even religion was to function. Nevertheless, tribal people continued to choose which parts of the white man's culture they would adopt. . . .

[In Canada, t]he planners decided that education offered the best chance for merging Indians into the general Canadian society. . . . Rather than provide public support for reservation schools, the Indian Department contracted with various church groups to operate the schools. This system reflected attitudes in Quebec and Manitoba, but elsewhere in Canada the church affiliations brought considerable bickering, with the result that many schools had government rather than church support. Getting good teachers continually proved a major obstacle as well. In his annual report one of the inspectors noted that many of the teachers in the Indian schools lacked the qualifications to serve in the ordinary county public schools near the reservations. Often the most experienced teachers avoided tribal schools because they paid only about half as much as the public schools.

Frequently the Indians' actions determined school success. The annual cycle of migration to fish, hunt, or gather took children away for months at a time. Even when seasonal migrations ended, village or band matters directly affected attendance. By the early 1880s some tribal groups ceased cooperating. Some bands refused to pay for schools. Others interpreted their treaties' promises to provide teachers to mean that the government should also provide any buildings or equipment that the teachers might need. One group even suggested that the teachers build their own schools. It is unclear whether this argument reflected Indian understanding of the situation, masked their basic suspicion of the whites and their institutions, or demonstrated efforts to slow acculturation. Clearly, while many traditional leaders wanted education to help their people deal successfully with the encroaching whites, they objected to the curriculum and the methods in use. For example, the Plains tribes objected that they wanted no religion taught to their children. They undermined the missionary efforts so much that the churchmen complained that the "heathen-priests or medicine men do their utmost to prejudice the minds" of the Indian children against what was being taught. . . .

When they realized that the bureaucrats wanted to replace tribal cultures, the Indians resisted openly and covertly. They saw the boarding schools as a means of disrupting their family and village life. If the children remained at those institutions they could not participate in annual hunting or migratory activities. The corporal punishment of the children ran counter to their family practices. Even the job skills each boy or girl got often resulted from forced labor for the schools, which the teachers described as vocational instruction. Because of these objections many of the Plains bands used the sun dance and other annual rituals as a sort of alternative education. At these ceremonies tribal elders, chiefs, shamans, and other adults helped instruct the children in traditional customs and gave a kind of parallel education that included the initiation of young men for marriage, social activities, politics, and band practices and beliefs.

This resistance succeeded so well that in 1884 the government began requiring school attendance for all Indian children between the ages of seven and fifteen. . . .

Regardless of the government efforts many tribal groups continued to ignore the schools. In the mid-1890s one official reported that "only thirteen schools, indifferently patronized, are in operation among the thirty bands occupying this vast district. Two thirds of the Indians are uncompromising heathens, who have for generations successfully resisted all the combined efforts of missionaries to Christianize them." Specific data support this charge, as an 1892 report showed. That year, of the 15,385 school-aged Indian children, only 6,350 even appeared on any school roster, and of those only about half, or 3,630, children showed up in the average daily attendance figures. When asked why they failed to support the schools effectively, one band leader responded that his people did not want to accept many of the whites' customs and ideas at the same time. Rather, they hoped the schools would help the children learn how to earn their living while keeping many of their customs. . . .

To wean the Indian children from their tribal heritage, educators used English to replace their native languages, cut their hair, gave them European-style clothing, and even changed their recreation. Some teachers in the boarding schools hoped that their graduates would move into the general population. As in the United States, however, most Canadians wanted little if anything to do with their Indian neighbors; accordingly, most of the former students returned to the reserves, where they had few chances to use their new skills. . . .

. . . [Over time,] the systems in both nations came to resemble each other. Each agency or reserve had at least one school, but on large reservations where many of the people lived far from the agency headquarters, boarding schools seemed to make good sense. As a result, by 1884 the U.S. government ran seventy-six day schools, eighty-one boarding schools, and six manual-labor or industrial schools. While religious groups operated others on a contract basis, they played a smaller role in Indian education in the United States than they did in the Canadian system.

As in Canada, American authorities saw the schools as a tool that would help erase Indian cultural identity. When they heard suggestions that teaching materials be prepared in the tribal languages, officials objected immediately. Secretary of the Interior Carl Schurz, himself an immigrant from Germany who had to learn English after he arrived in the United States, responded to such suggestions, saying, "If Indian children are to be civilized they must learn the language of civilization. They will become far more accessible to civilized ideas and ways of thinking when they are enabled to receive those ideas and ways of thinking through the most direct channel of expression.". . .

While few officials in either country quarreled with the idea that all Indians needed to learn English, usually they kept the tribes segregated. One of the most outspoken opponents of this approach was Richard A. Pratt, the founder and director of the Carlisle Indian School. An army officer with considerable experience with Indians, in 1878 he persuaded his military superiors to allow him to begin teaching Indian prisoners how to survive in the white man's world. At first he moved the captives into a wing of a building at the Hampton Institute, a school for young blacks in Virginia. Then in November 1879 he opened the Carlisle Indian School, with students from the Dakota and Indian Territories. Pratt insisted that Indian young people had to be integrated into American society right from the start. To accomplish this he placed the students in white homes and businesses for several years, hoping to get them enough education and vocational training that they would not have to or want to return to the reservations. . . . At the time this plan had little chance for success because the white population in both countries refused to accept Indians as neighbors, co-workers, or employees.

Along with the Carlisle Indian School, Hampton Institute in Virginia educated a steady stream of Indian young people. . . . The Sioux, Omahas, and Winnebagos provided most of the students. Both Hampton and Carlisle took the lead in trying to acculturate their pupils, but often they failed to overcome the students' cultural strength. Certainly the returning students lost part of their Indian identity, but they often used their newfound skills to help their communities retain tribal customs and property. The Shawnee leader Thomas Wildcat Alford remembered this clearly. He went to school to learn how "to use the club of white man's wisdom against him in defense of our customs and our Mee-saw-mi [tribal inheritance] as given us by the Great Spirit."

Frequently discussions of the boarding school operations describe how these institutions stripped Indian children of their language, culture, and self-identity, and then sent them home as misfits. Certainly this happened frequently, but that is only part of the story. Many tribal young people returned home determined to remain Indians. The Hampton returnees often used their training well back on the reservation. By 1882 some 122 of these former students toiled as farmers or stock raisers. Thirty-two more taught in reservation schools, while others worked as skilled laborers, merchants, or even professionals. Only 24 held unskilled positions. . . .

MISSIONARIES AND REFORMERS

. . . The presence of large, well-organized, and effective reform groups that watched government actions closely set U.S.-Indian relations apart from the Canadian experience during the late nineteenth century. Although Canadian officials debated policy and how it should be implemented, there seems to have been little of the public outcry that accompanied most federal actions in the United States. . . .

As early as the 1870s the forced removal of the Nebraska Poncas had raised a storm of protest, and throughout the 1880s American reformers who considered themselves "friends of the Indian" publicized federal mishandling of Indian issues by circulating thousands of pamphlets, gathering signatures, presenting petitions, and applying intense political pressure on many government officials. Added to the glare of attention these groups focused on the issue, individuals such as Helen Hunt Jackson helped publicize the government's difficulties with the tribal people. A popular speaker and the author of numerous articles detailing American faults and dishonesty in dealing with the tribes, in 1881 she published her book *A Century of Dishonor.* In it she presented a series of case studies purporting to demonstrate government wrongdoing. Although onesided and only partially correct, her book did raise public and political awareness of the issues after she sent a copy of it to each member of Congress.

A desire to help Indians by bringing them into American society as quickly as possible united almost all of the reformers. The major organizations each represented the currents of late-nineteenth-century Protestantism, and they strove to end tribalism, segregation as represented by the reservations, and limits on full legal and political rights for the Indians. Nearly all of the "friends of the Indian" supported the idea of allotment or dividing reservation land and assigning it to individual families. They based this view on the old idea that if only each Indian had some property, he or she would understand white society more clearly and through self-interest would come to adopt white attitudes about work and property. Having supported allotment, they could not object when the government sold the unassigned land on reservations to individuals or corporations. Once white Americans moved to farm next door, the argument went, the Indians would learn from them as well, and within a generation or two the tribes would disappear as individuals on each reservation, blended into the general society.

Canadian officials had been striving toward the same objective since the 1860s through their unsuccessful enfranchisement program. For years it had remained voluntary; to gain status as an enfranchised person, the individual reserve dweller had to pass muster at a hearing conducted by public officials. In the United States the reformers and the government looked to allotment to do what removal, military defeat, schools, churches, and model farms had failed to accomplish — the acculturation and assimilation of tribal people. The process began in 1887, when Senator Henry L. Dawes of Massachusetts guided the General Allotment Act, or Dawes Severalty Act, through Congress. The new law gave the president authority to allot reservations, giving individual Indians title to the land after twenty-five years and immediate citizenship when they accepted an allotment. During the next generation many Indians became citizens. Once all eligible tribal members got their allotments, the surplus land, or what remained after allotment, could be placed on the market. Once the program began, tribal landholdings shrank drastically. They dropped from 155 million acres in 1881 to just under 78 million in 1900 and continued to decline until 1934, when allotment stopped and the Indians retained only 52 million acres. . . .

. . . [In Canada,] post-Confederacy policy tried to bring about the rapid acculturation and assimilation of tribal people. As in the United States, Canadian officials assumed that individualism, personal property, religion, and education would accomplish that goal quickly. For example, in 1874 Minister of the Interior David Laird wrote that the government should enfranchise eastern Indians, give them an allotment of land taken from the tribal reserves with its title within four or five years, and a few years later divide tribal funds among the members. Laird saw this as doing two important things. First, it would promote individual skills the Indians needed to develop. Second, it would reduce the tribal holdings and weaken Indian attachment to the tribe as an entity.

Laird's proposal got some consideration, but the 1876 Indian Act took a different approach. Rather than assigning land to individual Indians immediately, it demanded that tribal people prove that they had the skills needed to deal with the white society. Before gaining enfranchisement and some land, each Indian had to be able to read and write in either English or French. They had to be free of debt and needed documentation supporting their good moral character. Having passed this first "test," the reserve dweller then got a location ticket for a particular plot of land on the reserve. After a three-year probationary period during which the Indian had to show competence in using and managing the land, he could apply for enfranchisement. This scheme shows the government's basic plan to bring the tribal people into the general society one person at a time. Interestingly enough, these portions of the 1876 law applied only to the eastern tribes. The whites assumed that they might make rapid progress in their acculturation because they had decades or even generations of experience in dealing with Europeans. . . .

In spite of these elaborate efforts to legislate acculturation, the Indians themselves directed the pace of activity. Frequently the white officials proved wildly overoptimistic or simply ill informed when they assessed events in the West. Certainly David Laird did those things. He claimed to see Indians accepting the principle of individual property because they cleared small patches of ground for raising vegetables. What he overlooked, however, was the fact that many Indian groups included some rudimentary agriculture in their economy, and few if any of the people who tilled small fields ever thought about owning that particular piece of the landscape. By 1879, when facing the imminent collapse of the buffalo hunters' livelihood, authorities suggested that the western tribes might prefer cattle raising to farming, a distinct change in thinking and one that would be rejected in the United States for another decade. . . .

Livestock raising on the Great Plains proved a more innovative approach to the need for incorporating Indians into the economy. By 1880 several bands of the Blackfoot Confederacy had begun cattle raising in southern Alberta. The inspector for the western area reported in 1882 that the Piegans' herd seemed to be growing. In June that year the nearby Stoney tribe held a successful cattle roundup. The Indians asked for livestock repeatedly, and by 1888 many bands had herds of cattle, sheep, and swine. Triumphant officials pointed to the care Indians lavished on their livestock, and one reported that at least one tribe had helped to kill their own dogs because the animals attacked their sheep. Certainly not all of them wanted to become herders, but ranching seems to have been more acceptable than farming to most of the Plains groups. In fact, between 1885 and 1895 the tribes in the Northwest Territories increased their cattle herds from 1,230 cattle to 15,378 animals. Clearly these Indians had more success in influencing policy and the direction of their own economic development than had their counterparts south of the border at the same time. . . .

REVITALIZATION AND RELIGIOUS MOVEMENTS

While both governments worked diligently to remake the tribal people, Indians had other ideas. Many villagers turned inward, seeking renewed strength through their religious ideas and cultural practices. . . . Missionaries, educators, and agents denounced the sun dance on both sides of the border as a heathen and barbaric practice, but tribes on the northern plains continued it as well. Other cultural practices such as vision quests, wearing blankets or long hair, and retaining their tribal languages allowed Indian people to assert their cultural pride and retain at least a part of their traditional identity. . . .

In addition to retaining . . . cultural pride in these ways, tribal people turned to new or modified religious beliefs offered by shamans responding to the pressures of drastic change. . . .

By 1881 the Puget Sound region gave rise to [a] prophet, Squsachtun, or John Slocum, who founded the Indian Shaker religion. He . . . experienced a series of visions during which he reported visiting heaven. There he received a divine assignment to teach Indians how to overcome the difficulties of reservation life. Combining tribal religious practices with Christian teachings he learned from the missionaries, his ideas included such Christian elements as heaven, hell, God, and Christ, but the rest of the sacred teachings came from his visions. Limiting the faith to Indians, Slocum taught his followers to meditate and fast, and frequently these produced nervous twitchings, a sign that their bodies were casting off evil thoughts and acts. . . . Squsachtun opposed the acculturation programs being implemented on the reservations, urging his followers to resist them whenever possible. Federal agents arrested him and tried to disrupt the gatherings of his followers, . . . but without success. Groups on both sides of the border accepted his teachings, and adherents of the Indian Shaker religion continue their practices today.

Few Indian groups in the mountains or on the plains ever heard of . . . the Indian Shaker religion, but by the 1880s nearly all of them came to learn about the Ghost Dance religion. Originating in the visions of a Nevada Paiute named Tavibo, this set of beliefs taught that the invading whites were to be destroyed in a massive earthquake. Before gaining many followers Tavibo died, but his son Wovoka, or Jack Wilson, continued the preaching. Adding some of his own ideas to his father's teachings, Wovoka developed the Ghost Dance religion. He taught a return to Indian practices including frequent bathing, living plainly, and avoiding alcohol, and prohibited mourning because all dead Indians were to return once the whites had been destroyed. The worshipers meditated, prayed, and danced for up to five days at a time, and the ceremonies produced a mild group hypnosis.

The teachings spread among the disheartened people on the northern plains reservations, and medicine men among the Sioux turned it from a pacific set of beliefs into a militant antiwhite platform. Worried authorities saw danger in the Ghost Dance's development into a secret society with holy clothes reputed to keep the warriors safe from the soldiers' bullets. In late 1890 agents among the Sioux bands called for soldiers to keep peace, but before the situation calmed, reservation police had killed Sitting Bull. Soon after his death soldiers attacked and destroyed many of Big Foot's followers at Wounded Knee. Thus, while the various religious responses to the unwelcome reservation experience brought some solace to the disheartened Indians, others faced loss of their rations, possible jail terms, and even death at the hands of police or soldiers. After Wounded Knee the Ghost Dance disappeared almost as quickly as it had appeared, but it and the other Indian religious movements of the late nineteenth century show clearly the level of Indian unhappiness and the failure of the acculturative programs to help the tribal people in any substantial way. . . .

QUESTIONS TO CONSIDER

1. What political, economic, and military developments led to conflict between whites and Indians in the late-nineteenth-century American and Canadian Wests? Which of these changes were common to both nations? Which were unique to the United States?

2. Why, according to the author, were Indian-white relations so violent in the American West? Why was Canada able to avoid major frontier warfare? In what ways were the two nations' policies toward natives similar? How were they different? Be sure to

consider treaties, reservations, racial categories, law enforcement, land allotment, and educational programs.

3. Discuss the options that Indian leaders in the United States and Canada could pursue in dealing with white invaders and their government. Despite the Sioux victory at Little Bighorn, why did violent resistance ultimately fail? How did Canadian native peoples negotiate more favorable deals with the government than American Indians did? In what ways did Indians resist white educational and religious indoctrination or turn them to their advantage? Overall, how did Indians have "ever less chance to take the initiative as the [nineteenth] century drew to a close"?

4. C. Vann Woodward argued in Selection 2 that after the Civil War ex-slaves in the South and Indians in the West were treated "in much the same way." Using information from Chapter 1 and the essay by Nichols, compare the U.S. government's policies toward blacks and Indians. Why did the federal government support (for a time) blacks' enfranchisement but deny Indians citizenship and confine them to reservations? What similarities do you see in educational programs aimed at freed slaves and natives? Why did land distribution schemes fail in each case?

5. Many scholars who have studied the overall pattern of European expansion in the New World classify the United States and Canada together as "frontiers of exclusion" that sharply separated white expansionists and native peoples. In contrast, on "frontiers of inclusion" in some Latin American lands natives were used as a labor force and a sizable mixed white-Indian population blended elements of both conqueror and conquered. How "exclusionist" were American and Canadian policies concerning racial categories on the frontier? In what ways did these governments simultaneously pursue contradictory programs of segregation and assimilation? To what extent did both frontiers of exclusion and frontiers of inclusion violate the wishes of native peoples?

Gridded Lives: Why Montana and Kazakhstan Are Nearly the Same Place

KATE BROWN

Once Native Americans were pushed aside, what ways of life replaced them in the West? If popular novels and movies are to be believed, the answer is clear: the western heroes that dominate Americans' consciousness — the cowboy, the mining prospector, the homesteader — celebrate the rugged individualism of the frontier and its promise of opportunity. Lining them up in an orderly sequence, traditional historians of the West chronicle a succession of frontier eras by which fur traders gave way to cattlemen and miners, then to pioneer farmers, and finally to townspeople. But is that really the way it happened? How representative are the western figures of popular legend? Increasingly, younger scholars practicing what has been dubbed "the new Western history" are displacing these colorful figures with a more prosaic but powerful cast of characters: the government planners, corporate bosses, railroad builders, and land speculators who constructed the West, dominated its politics, and controlled its land. When these historians examine the westward movement of millions of Americans, they find not an orderly progression but a mad scramble, a race for wealth in which town promoters jumped the gun — and often reaped the biggest rewards. "The truth is," writes historian John W. Reps, "in every section of the West, towns were in the vanguard of settlement." Their founding preceded most business enterprises, and their dwellers far outnumbered farmers and ranchers. Nearly all western towns were established as planned communities by real estate agents, railroad and mining companies, colonization societies, religious groups, or public officials. Their designs established the framework for future growth, shaping the structure of society rather than simply responding to farmers' or miners' needs for a place to market their goods, buy a drink, or attend church.

From Kansas to California, western towns were surprisingly similar in appearance. Almost all featured a grid plan of square blocks and straight streets oriented to the points of the compass and meeting at right angles. This arrangement was practical and convenient. Used in colonial cities since the Greeks and showcased on America's East Coast by

Philadelphia, it was adopted by western railroad companies and real estate promoters as the quickest and easiest way to lay out a town and sell its lots. The grid plan matched Americans' appetite for "instant cities." Its standardized form made it familiar to newcomers, and its streets could be extended to accommodate the population boom that town boosters breathlessly predicted. At its edges the town grid joined the national grid of farms and roads that had been set up by the first government surveyors of the West. Covering the landscape like graph paper, this grid parceled it into squares for federal auctions, railroad grants, state colleges, and homesteaders, whose famous "quarter section" (160 acres) was deeded to them free of charge after five years of farming or ranching. This grid's checkerboard pattern dominates the view from airplanes crossing the nation today.

The following essay by Kate Brown takes as its starting point this domination of the West by gridded towns and their ties to the national network of farms, railroads, and corporations. But Brown ventures beyond the new western history by proposing a startling transnational comparison. Placing side by side the history of Billings, Montana, a railroad town established in the 1880s, and Karaganda, Kazakhstan, an industrial prison city built on the steppes of Central Asia by the Soviet Union in the 1930s, Brown declares (no doubt with poetic license) that they are "nearly the same place." Despite obvious differences in ideologies and institutions, the United States and Russia became the two great land empires of the nineteenth century and the military superpowers of the twentieth. As they expanded toward their frontiers and industrialized, both imperial powers displaced seminomadic native peoples, imposed instant cities upon the landscape, and used those settlements to feed the national economic machine, leaving behind a trail of scarred landscapes and dashed hopes. The frontier cities of Karaganda and Billings share this history, according to Brown, and both exemplify the "gridded space" that produced settlers' "gridded lives."

In its search for broader parallels, Brown's essay is deliberately provocative, setting aside important distinctions between capitalism and communism, free and totalitarian societies, and homesteaders and deportees. To those who may object that it is misleading to blur the difference between democratic America and Stalinist Russia, Brown responds that "the production of space" speaks its own language and that the land and buildings of her two cities tell a similar tale. Above competing ideologies and social systems were "larger processes" that produced comparably rigid human environments in America and Russia. And to those who might protest that she paints too bleak a picture of opportunity in the American West, Brown suggests that family farmers and company employees endured a much tougher and less rewarding ordeal than nostalgic frontier legends imply.

Whether Brown's evidence supports such sweeping claims is up to you to decide. Whatever your conclusion, as you examine the histories of Billings and Karaganda, consider the lesson that Brown seems to have in mind. What does it mean that industrial nations of such polarized ideologies employed similar strategies to settle their frontier and ended up producing similar spaces? Do national expansion and industrial development follow their own laws regardless of time, place, or belief? Must modern life inevitably produce "gridded spaces" that destroy the natural environment?

GLOSSARY

COLLECTIVIZATION   The Soviet policy that forcibly replaced private farms with huge government-owned collective farms in order to bring agriculture under state control and stimulate industrial growth. Pursued aggressively by Stalin after 1929, collectivization was virtually complete by 1936. Millions of peasants who resisted were deported to prison camps or died in local famines.

CUSTER, GEORGE A. (1839–1876)   A fearless and flamboyant military officer who became the Union army's youngest general during the Civil War. During the postwar campaign against the Sioux, Custer and his entire detachment of about 250 men were killed at Little Bighorn, Montana, in 1876.

ELLIS ISLAND   The main U.S. immigration depot, opened in New York Harbor in 1892, where immigrants were screened for fitness and compliance with immigration laws before being allowed to stay. Over twenty million immigrants passed through Ellis Island before it closed in 1943.

GULAG   The system of forced labor camps and prisons established by the Soviet Union in the 1920s. Expanded enormously by Stalin's purges, agricultural collectivization, and transfer of World War II prisoners, the system held more than five million inmates at a time, 10 percent of whom were killed off annually by harsh conditions, torture, and executions. All told, perhaps fifty million persons were imprisoned in gulags before the system was disbanded in the late 1950s after Stalin's death.

KAZAKHSTAN   A Central Asian land populated for centuries by the Kazaks, a nomadic Muslim people who raised horses, sheep, and camels. As the czar pushed Russian military control and settlement southward and eastward, Kazakhstan was formally incorporated into the Russian empire by 1848. After 1927 the Soviet government pursued an aggressive policy of transforming Kazak nomads into a settled people and colonizing the region with Russians and Ukrainians, and in 1936 Kazakhstan became a republic in the Soviet Union. It achieved independence in 1991 after the breakup of the Soviet Union.

LEBENSRAUM   A German phrase meaning "room to live" that is associated with racial conquest and removal. In the 1930s and during World War II, it was used by Adolf Hitler and his Nazi followers to justify the conquest of eastern European peoples and their replacement with relocated Germans.

PURGE TRIALS   A series of staged trials held in the Soviet Union from 1936 to 1938 that the Stalinist government used to eliminate critics and potential rivals in the Communist Party and the military.

SIBERIA   The vast, sparsely populated region of northern Asia that extends from the Ural Mountains on the west to the Pacific Ocean in the east. Used by Russia in the nineteenth century as a place to exile criminals or political prisoners, Siberia was aggressively industrialized under Stalin and became the location of many Soviet forced-labor camps in the 1930s.

STALIN, JOSEPH (1879–1953)   The ruthless and powerful head of the Soviet Union from 1929 until his death. An early comrade of Bolshevik leader V. I. Lenin, Stalin returned from exile in Siberia during the Russian Revolution and became the first editor of the Communist Party newspaper, *Pravda*. He emerged victorious from the five-year power struggle after Lenin's death in 1924. Once in control, Stalin forcibly collectivized Russia's farms, ordered rapid industrial growth, and imprisoned or executed rivals or dissidents, including millions of ordinary citizens.

STEPPE   The long belt of grassland that extends from eastern Europe through Ukraine and Kazakhstan to Mongolia and Manchuria in eastern Asia. Through much of history, the steppe has been the home of nomadic peoples who raised horses, cattle, sheep, and goats.

UKRAINE   The Soviet republic on the eastern European border from which several hundred thousand people were deported to Kazakhstan and Siberia during Stalin's collectivization and industrialization drives in the 1930s. It became an independent country after the collapse of the Soviet Union in 1991.

✯ ✯ ✯ ✯ ✯ ✯ ✯

From the map of Karaganda, it appears that its city plan was based on the model of the old Roman military camp — set up along a grid, the old Stalin Prospect ran north-south, the former Lenin Prospect bisecting it from east to west. The grid makes sense for a prison city because it creates wide open spaces and straight lines, an architecture designed not to be seen but to see, to survey the city's inhabitants so as to regulate and contain their conduct. Karaganda, located on the arid steppe of northern Kazakhstan, was founded in the early 1930s alongside KarLag, one of the largest labor camps in the Soviet Union. Karaganda constitutes a prison city because it was built largely by convicts, and it was fed on crops grown in the labor camp's farms, while prisoners and deportees worked in the mines and factories of the city's blossoming industries. In 1930, Karaganda was not even a point on the map. By 1939, the city had 100,000 inhabitants, half of them wards (prisoners or deportees) of the Ministry of Interior's Gulag division (NKVD-Gulag).

I had expected Karaganda to have that smoke-belching, wrecked look of industrial cities of Soviet Russia to the north. But I was surprised. After Joseph Stalin died in 1953, the prisoners were gradually given amnesty, the prison barracks were dismantled, the barbed wire was lifted, and, curiously, what remains is a neatly ordered city of broad avenues and shady sidewalks, monumental squares and symmetrically plotted parks, ample and verdant. There is plenty of parking, convenient shopping, and no cramped corners. No sign of the gulag's secrecy or human suffering is written into the urban landscape. Instead, Karaganda is an open-armed embrace that says it has nothing to hide. . . . In fact, Karaganda is so well-ordered, there is no great need to explore it on foot. Rather, it can be read easily from the upholstered comfort of a car at cruising speed.

The car slides by long columns of housing blocks, which replaced the prisoners' barracks in the 1950s. The residential tracts, built with assembly-line efficiency, are the Soviet equivalent of the American suburban development. The same three blueprints echo in row after row, the same efficient economy of occupancy and technology behind

From Kate Brown, "Gridded Lives: Why Kazakhstan and Montana Are Nearly the Same Place," *American Historical Review* 106 (February 2001): 17–48. Reprinted by permission of the *American Historical Review* and the author, Kate Brown. The author would like to thank Richard White, Glennys Young, and Jeff Wasserstror for their generous help with this article.

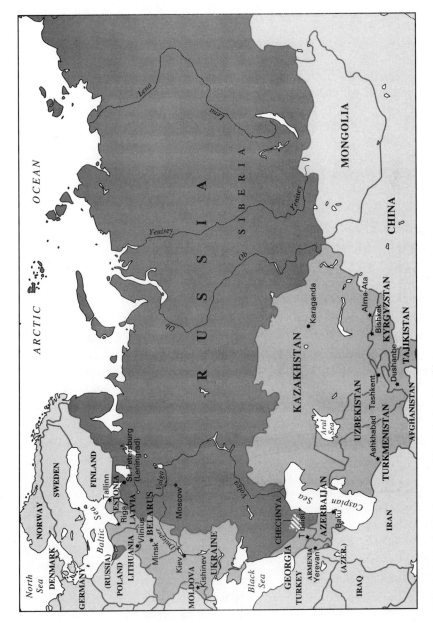

Today's Russia and its former republics, including Kazakhstan.

the lace curtains, the same segregation of space based on the daily repetition of meals, commuting, and recreation around which American homes are also designed. Built rapidly, rapidly looking obsolete, the buildings radiate that temporal quality of much of American architecture, as if designed not for generations of a family but for generations of a professional career, a familiar architecture responding to the unmatched social mobility of the twentieth century.

One evening, I stood on the balcony of the Karaganda hotel room, looking at the neon signs glistening along the rain-soaked streets. . . . In the distance, the comforting lights of thousands of living rooms lit up the expanse, revealing the soothing grid as it marched up and down, partitioning the electrified urban spaces from the black void of the steppe beyond. Here, far from home, in the midst of a former gulag on the Kazakh steppe, I had the uncanny feeling that I had seen this city before. Karaganda, with its gridded composure [and] easy repetition of residential units, . . . seemed oddly familiar, as if I had landed not in Central Asia but in the American middle west, in Wichita, Topeka, Bismarck, or Billings.

Billings, Montana. Like most railroad cities, Billings can be navigated without a map. Broad arteries cut north and south, avenues east and west. The streets are platted out in numbered convenience beginning at one and can multiply to infinity in keeping with the grand aspirations of the founding fathers. The Yellowstone River flows unnoted on the outskirts of town, beyond the grain elevators, the railroad switching yards and oil refineries. Looking at Billings from the height of the cliffs above it, the mind drifts off to high-school geometry, trying to take in the ever-divisible asphalt grid of smaller and smaller blocks that break down to rectangular spaces etched with yellow paint on the parking lots. Fly over Billings, and this chessboard divisibility of space expands to cover the whole land: squared-off fields contained within square-mile sections fit into angular counties in the washboard abdomen of the country, where the states break up into rectangles and trapezoids.

Standing on the bluff overlooking Billings, I was better able to decipher what it was that made it feel like Karaganda: the divisibility and hierarchy of space, the abrupt, fortress-like partition of urban from agricultural territory, the lonely feeling of a city adrift like a ship on a sea of land that is inhospitable and unpredictable. Yet Karaganda is a city erected in the midst of a vast labor camp, a city where children planting trees in the schoolyard still come across human bones. Meanwhile, Billings was founded by railroad entrepreneurs, farmers, miners, and businessmen on the American frontier. One city is the product of an authoritarian state that employed and ruled everyone who toiled there; the other, a conglomerate of competing business interests and individual farmers. Two countries, worlds apart, two different histories, yet cities in the American West share the same modern, expansive, modular feel as Karaganda because Karaganda, like every western American railroad city, is built along a grid.

The fact of the grid may seem like no fact at all. For the grid is no novelty; it has been used as an architectural model for centuries, and it does not necessarily follow that all gridded cities are born of the same motivations. Kazakhstan and the Great Plains fall in the same topographical zone of vast, arid, high plateaus. One could argue that the

BILLINGS, MONTANA
COUNTY-SEAT OF YELLOWSTONE COUNTY.

This lithograph of Billings, Montana, in 1904 highlights its typical grid plan imposed on the High Plains and bisected by the Northern Pacific Railroad (chugging from both directions through the center of town). Commissioned by railroad companies or paid for by subscriptions from local businesses, detailed bird's-eye views of western cities were designed to enhance civic pride and stimulate land sales. (Amon Carter Museum of Western Art, Fort Worth, Texas.)

flat, endless landscapes lend themselves easily to geometric dissection. Yet it seems logical that two such contrasting societies — the communist Soviet Union and democratic United States — would naturally develop cities in distinct patterns expressing the vast differences between the two countries in ideas, politics, and economic structure. For, if one believes that form relates to content — that cities contain their histories, as Italo Calvino writes, "like the lines of a hand, written in the corners of the streets and the gratings of the windows" — then can it be purely coincidental that Karaganda, a prison city, and Billings, a railroad town, look alike?

To attempt any kind of analogy between Karaganda and Billings, however, is to ignore the polarities between the two places. For, at least in terms of imagery, one can conceive of few regions more dissimilar. The American West represents the last, inexhaustible frontier of American individualism, the place where people went to be free. Northern Kazakhstan, conversely, conjures an image similar to that of Siberia; it is a place of unfreedom, exile, and imprisonment, a place where masses of undifferentiated people were sent against their will to serve a monolithic state. Placed in the larger context of the United States and the Soviet Union, the contrasts between the two cities intensify: the free market versus the planned economy, the democracy of the people versus the dictatorship of the proletariat, the pioneer against the exile, the self-made man and free labor versus the machinated relationship of prison guard and convict. To liken Billings to Karaganda is to blur the domains, as we have defined them, of freedom and bondage, of liberty and oppression. People were deported to Karaganda against their will. They were either sentenced to hard labor in camps or exiled to special settlements, and they starved, froze, and worked until they dropped from exhaustion. Of course, it is true that on the Great Plains people also starved, froze, and worked until they dropped from exhaustion, but in the American Plains they did it of their own free will; they bought their own train tickets. . . .

Yet, setting aside for a moment the well-documented differences between the penal Kazakh steppe and free-market American frontier, I wonder if there is a significance to the spatial similarities of the grid in Montana and Kazakhstan — if a comparison would not be fruitful. Comparisons, after all, can be misleading or overtly political. Anything can be compared to anything. It is a trick of historians to place historic eras or regimes in juxtaposition to point out similarities or differences and thus win an argument. For example, since the onset of the Cold War, Stalin's Soviet Union has often been likened to Hitler's Nazi regime. The extremes of left and right are seen to fuse at one common point of total communist/fascist social control, illustrating the apex of state terror. Contrasts, too, can be used for polemical effect. Since the Cold War, historians, journalists, and politicians in the United States have focused on Soviet transgressions such as the purge trials, collectivization, and the suppression of dissidents as a way to spell out what democratic America is not or should never become. In the same way, Soviet historians and journalists for decades fixated on American ghettos, racial strife, social unrest, and rising crime rates as a sign that Soviet socialism was on the right track.

Now, however, with the threat of the Cold War faded, there is more room to question whether knowledge itself has not been gridded into neat polarities, communist and democratic. Histories tend to prioritize texts, written matter, and ideological categorizations. And certainly, in the heated debates of the Cold War, words, rhetoric, and ideologies have been highly evaluated, perhaps over-evaluated, at the cost of ignoring and diminishing the history of the production of spaces and the lives that have been forged by and for those spaces. This is no new idea. Several decades ago, Henri Lefebvre asserted there is no communism, just two myths: "that of anti-communism, on the one hand, and the myth that communism had been carried out somewhere on the other." Lefebvre doubted the existence of communism because it had led to no new architectural innovation, no creation of specifically socialist spaces. In other words, in the history of space, communism and capitalism have produced no qualities that distinguish one from the other.

What would happen, then, if we discarded all that we know about the polarities of communism and capitalism and, just for the sake of argument, explored the spatial affinities? With this approach, it may turn out that historians and politicians in both countries have focused to the point of obfuscation on the differences between Soviet communism and American capitalism and ignored the parallels produced by the industrial-capital expansions of the twentieth century. After all, a mirror image, the Soviet Union and United States, is just the same form reflected backward. We may even recognize how the two countries followed similar paths of development and destruction that differ more in scale than form. . . .

My question, then, is . . . do the gridded spaces of Kazakhstan and Montana constitute the end-point of larger processes that the United States and Soviet Union shared? . . .

. . . [T]here were no cities in northern Kazakhstan or the Great Plains before the steam engine and railroad. Pre-industrial cities in Central Asia and the American plains contained populations that were largely supported by surrounding agricultural communities, and grew only so large as the limits of the land, the reach of the walled fortifications, the scarcities of food, water, and cultivable soil allowed them. Without technology, the short grasslands of the steppe and range, the dry, continental climates, could not support more than small communities of sedentary peoples tilling the soil and were best suited for nomads living off the migratory grazing of range animals adapted to the extreme cold, heat, and aridity of the climate.

Innovations of the industrial age, however, greatly altered the landscape and economies of the Great Plains and Central Asia. Cities in the industrial age did not need to follow the lay of the land or feed populations with foodstuffs produced locally. Montana and Kazakhstan could support urban populations by means of technologies such as railroad networks to move people and goods, steam-powered engines, irrigation systems, the telegraph and telephone, all of which required a concentration of capital investment so large that in both regions it fell to a small group of managers to try to direct from afar the means of production and labor that kept everything going. The managers in both places oversaw these vast networks with the help of time schedules, statistics, and production plans, and with the regimentation and subjection of labor. In both Montana and Karaganda, the rush for land, water, minerals, and cash crops displaced the indigenous peoples who had formerly inhabited the territories, while the European populations who replaced them were sorted according to contrived understandings of race, class, and loyalty.

These patterns of production created corresponding patterns of subjection, which determined that people settled the American high plains and Central Asian steppe in similar ways by carving land into economic units for efficient exploitation. New towns were located for commerce and the quick extraction of resources at railheads and responded not to ecological limits but to the surveyor's rational grid. The grid made space modular and repetitious. The urban grid was a concentration of the expanding rural grid, which linked the hinterland economically and spatially with cities. As a consequence, there were no topographical limits to urban space, and the cities grew and multiplied, supplanting the nomadic cultures that came before. . . .

In both countries, as a result, conquest meant consumption; the newcomers ate — in coal, copper, wheat, sugar beets, ore — the territories they desired. In short, the histories of cities in Montana and Kazakhstan complement one another; taken in tandem, they tell not two stories but one — the history of gridded space.

. . . In 1881, the land on which Billings stands today was considered worthless. It was a barren, waterless alkali flat with only an oasis here and there of sage brush. The settlers and traders who first came to the region settled upstream at Clark's Fork Bottom, where the confluence of two rivers made a good trading post and where the land was fertile and the water supply more plentiful. The residents of Clark's Fork assumed that, when the railroad came through, it would logically create a terminal in their little settlement, as there were a few traders and farmers already waiting for trains to bring in goods and ship their produce off to market. But the railroad executives in St. Paul and New York had a different set of priorities for locating the new town. The federal government had deeded the Northern Pacific line alternating townships of forty miles on either side of the tracks to help offset the cost of building a transcontinental railroad. Frederick Billings, the president of the Northern Pacific, and his engineers studied the U.S. surveyor-general maps and determined that, at a certain point on the map, the odd-numbered townships lay next to each other across the line of the railroad, instead of connecting at the corners as they did elsewhere. Sensibly, Mr. Billings decided to locate the new city at that point where the railroad owned twice as much land as usual.

. . . He and a few associates formed a real estate development company and bought from the railroad 29,394 acres in the newly proposed township for less than $4 an acre. It made no difference to Mr. Billings that the site for the new city planned for 20,000 residents would be established on barren flats, somewhat removed from the swampy edges of the river, without drinking water, two miles north of the closest human habitation. Within the four walls of real estate speculation, the siting of Billings made sense; the fact that the site was barely habitable mattered little to Mr. Billings. After all, Frederick Billings never dreamed of living in Billings.

After the Minnesota and Montana Land and Improvement Company chose the site for Billings, the company designed the city plan, allocated building lots, and proposed future industrial development before any actual building took place, before the "city" was anything but a thicket of squatters' tents. Nonetheless, the founding of the new city was trumpeted for hundreds of miles, and the profits to be made were fabulous. Once it was announced that Billings was going to be the next "Magic City," Frederick Billings's land development company was selling off the alkali flats at $250 for a quarter-acre lot. Whole blocks were sold in New York and Chicago, and a few months later the prices had risen to $1,200. By the summer of 1882, most of the city property was purchased, yet two-thirds of the owners were absentee; people who bought lots never planned to live in the hot, dry, treeless flats but to sell them later at a profit.

The cosmology that ordained the grid in Billings pivoted around economics and administration. Billings's real estate company subdivided land into parcels, uniform and, from the perspective of a map, interchangeable because it made for efficient marketing and sales, especially from remote offices in St. Paul and Chicago. In this way, towns identical to Billings were established throughout the West — Laramie, Reno, Bismarck, Cheyenne. Engineers, land agents, and railroad executives established, planned, and promoted these cities following a uniform gridiron that placed the railroad in the center of the burgeoning city. The pioneering homesteader, the cowboy, and lonesome miner are essential parts of American mythology and self-identity, but historians of the American West have argued that the vanguard of settlement in the West were these corporate-owned towns, run by businessmen who operated on the profits of real estate speculation fueled by federal land grants and the promise of future growth and industrial development.

Karaganda, like Billings, was an unmarked void on the map before its founding as a city in 1930. It consisted of a ramble of shacks, a few abandoned buildings from a czarist-era coal mine, and a small and occasional market where Kazakhs would come to trade in sheep pelts and mutton steaks for salt, flour, and other necessities. In the late 1920s, Soviet geologists rediscovered the Karaganda coal basin, after which the Moscow-based Department of Mines set up the Karaganda Coal Trust and determined that the site would be home to a major new industrial city. Without visiting the region, architects in Moscow drew up plans for a city of 40,000 workers who would dig out a projected twelve new mines. Within the year, several thousand miners, most of them Kazakhs, began working underground in Karaganda. But the Coal Trust found that it could not keep its stores stocked with enough food to feed the miners, and despite the city plan calling for seven square meters of sanitary housing per person, housing conditions stumbled into proletarian disgrace, with most of the miners living in yurts or tents scattered near the mine shafts. In search of food, the Kazakh miners drifted to and from their native *auls* (villages), which made for a sporadic and ill-disciplined labor force, and coal production sagged below prerevolutionary figures.

In February 1931, however, the railroad arrived in Karaganda and with it a whole new form of discipline. The railroad brought supplies, geologists, and experienced miners from the Donbass in Ukraine, and it also brought NKVD officers who quickly realized the limitless possibilities of establishing a labor camp next to the Karaganda mines. Sounding as optimistic as a Billings railroad associate, an NKVD officer wrote that the combination of virgin land, mineral resources, and a rail connection meant that "Kazakhstan offers remarkable potential for the creation of a powerful agricultural base. Only a labor reserve is needed due to the sparsely populated territory." A labor camp, NKVD officials proposed, would funnel a plentiful supply of workers to Karaganda to till the virgin soil and produce food for the miners. In 1931, the Gulag division of the NKVD set up KarLag on 281,000 acres of land around the growing settlement of Karaganda and began to import labor.

The labor camp KarLag helped solve Karaganda's problem of workers and food. City leaders made use of prison labor to grow crops on the outskirts of the city and to work on construction sites in the city to build housing for the miners. To supervise the prisoner-laborers, NKVD guards walled districts into "zones" separated with barbed wire, each about the size of a city block. The guards required avenues straight and broad enough to march prisoners in columns to work sites and needed enough visibility to shoot in case anyone made a run for it. Although it is tempting to postulate that Karaganda's grid grew out of the demands of prison architecture, most modern Soviet cities are platted out in a grid — cities never intended for prisoners. In fact, Soviet planners designed and created many new industrial cities in the 1930s that are nearly interchangeable with Karaganda. . . .

Although private property was outlawed in Soviet socialism, the concepts of ownership and management determined the shape of Karaganda, much as it did Billings. Individuals in the Soviet Union could not own land, but after the Soviet government nationalized all property, it allocated land in vast proportions to state enterprises. The NKVD became a major recipient of huge tracts of land in northern Kazakhstan and one of the major exploiters of natural resources. By 1936, the NKVD controlled 795,600 acres of land appropriated from Kazakh pastureland. By 1941, the NKVD was responsible for 12 percent of all Soviet lumber, 54 percent of all nickel, 75 percent of all molybdenum, and 37 percent of all tungsten production. The total value of all gulag industrial production between 1941 and 1944 reached 3.6 billion rubles. Land that to Kazakh nomads had been a flowing body of winter and summer pastures marked with ancestral burial grounds became to the Europeans who conquered it a series of parcels, surveyed and assigned value in square meters and millions of rubles.

In order to make the transformation from ancestral land to commodified space, European settlers first envisioned indigenous land as empty space, waiting to be populated. Billings and Karaganda were conceived in the minds of people who first saw the territories for the proposed cities as representations on a map. The land for both cities was granted by federal governments to growing bureaucracies charged with settling the territories for the production of raw materials. In both cases, the cities were platted into being by planners from remote locations who drew a series of lines on paper and finalized century-long processes of transferring territory from indigenous to European hands. . . .

In memoir after memoir, what seemed to bother European settlers of the plains and steppe the most was the emptiness: "the stillness with nothing behind it." Soviet deportees refer automatically to the land they first encountered as "the naked steppe"; they found it stripped of all things: water, trees, streams, houses, people — geography itself— empty of everything but space. But what most people failed to mention was that the land was not empty but *emptied*. They came to territory that had recently been cleared of the nomadic pastoralists and hunters who once populated it, people who lived off the arid grasslands by moving through them, following herds that grazed on a carpet of grasses and plants. . . .

. . . Since the Russian Empire first took control of Kazakh territory in the 1820s, Kazakhs had been gradually pushed off good pastureland into the desert interior of Kazakhstan. The final blow . . . came in the early and mid-1930s when Soviet reformers decided to collectivize Kazakh nomads and thus rationalize the production of meat and dairy products on sedentary collective farms.

Not far from Billings, a small marble marker stands in the brown grasses, embossed with a simple Christian cross above the name George A. Custer, Major General. The story of Custer and his defeat by Crazy Horse at the battle of Little Big Horn is well known. So, too, are his infamous trips through the plains shooting bison and leaving behind the stench of rotting flesh that cloud his memorialization as a martyr on the battlefield. Custer was one of a number of Americans who felt that the extermination of the buffalo would inspire Indians to settle down. He understood, as did the Soviet collectivizers later, that to take away the roving sustenance of the indigenous grasslanders would be a sure way to root them. In turn, rooting nomads and transforming the landscape would make it hard to remember "a time," as David Rollison puts it, "when the land was anything other than a commodity to be converted to cash."

But even after the bison were turned into bleached bone, their memory brushed onto canvas, and the remaining Indians settled on the reservation to a form of semi-dependency, the neighboring Crow, who had served as allies of the U.S. Army fighting the Sioux and Cheyenne, came to represent a threat and nuisance to the leaders of Billings. Before all the original lots and homesteads were inhabited by white settlers, city leaders in Billings started itching for more *Lebensraum* and petitioned Congress to move the Crow from their territory south of Billings and open the land for settlement. Frederick Billings and other entrepreneurs of the area wanted the Crow territory in order to build rail lines across it to the coal fields in Red Lodge, and, just as important, they sought to sanitize the valley of the "troublesome Indians" who were held responsible for missing cattle. An editorialist wrote in the *Billings Post* in 1884: "It will be a great boon to this section, when these miserable, idle dogs are moved away, and this valuable section of land thrown open to the use of people who will utilize it."

Perhaps neither Americans nor Soviets anticipated the extent to which forced settlement would exterminate not only the nomadic way of life but nomadic lives as well. Collectivization brought disaster to Kazakh pastoralists. Between 1929 and 1932, the livestock count dropped from 6.5 million heads to 965,000. Of the total population of Kazakhs estimated at 4.4 million in the late 1920s, by the mid-1930s 2 million were missing; they either died from famine or fled across the borders to China, Mongolia, or Afghanistan. In Karaganda, by January 1933, 15 percent of the indigenous Kazakhs remained. In the Great Plains, the bison, which once roamed in immense black clouds totaling around 25 million, had by the 1880s been all but exterminated. Among American Indians, of the estimated pre-colonial population of 5 to 7 million, only 150,000 remained in 1900, 7 percent of the original population. . . .

Once European settlers had marginalized indigenous populations, the emptied spaces needed to be refashioned, and because the land was vacant (or vacated), there was nothing to stop the wholesale appropriation of it as productive, agricultural, and industrial space. After the arrival of the railroad in Billings and Karaganda, European colonizers no longer occupied new territory in a piecemeal fashion — a bend in the river here, a river valley there — but implanted a wholly new figurative and physical architecture in the landscapes. Railroad executives, U.S. Geological Survey officials, and Soviet officials spread out a purposeful map blanketing the landscape, dividing and subdividing territory according to function and use — mining, farming, ranching. And once space was divided according to function, so, too, were the lives that inhabited that space. Indians were to become farmers on land designated for that purpose. Kazakhs were to become collective farm members on land designated for that purpose. And new people were to be imported to fill the recently emptied spaces and implement the destiny described by the maps.

It is logical to think that cities emerge after the accumulation of a critical mass of people, but in Montana and Kazakhstan, this pattern was reversed. Cities came first, then people. Most of the settlers to the Yellowstone Valley arrived a full two decades after the founding of the Magic City. Saddled with a great deal of land bought on speculation, the founders of Billings worked in tandem with the railroad to entice homesteaders to the valley. Booster propaganda lied outright only at times; it usually misled by innuendo and cheerful exaggeration. The *Billings Gazette:*

> Below you lies miles and miles of cultivated farm land, the beautiful Yellowstone Valley, entrancing vistas of woodland and river greets the eye. Delightful attractions of well-laden orchards, with green and brown and yellow fields all dotted with dainty looking farm buildings and pretty red-roofed school houses, form a picture not readily forgotten. And at your feet, the loveliest gem in the beautiful setting, behold the charming city of Billings.

The photo that accompanied this journalistic account contains a waterfall and thick forest, suggesting a shady, refreshing mountain idyll. Imagine the surprise of homesteaders when they arrived in Billings. Mrs. T. W. Wilkinson Polly, a Missouri native, remembered her first night: "It was a tearful set of women and children that evening. There was not a tree, hardly a blade of grass, only sagebrush and dusty streets and untidy surroundings, making it seem as if we had come to the last place on Earth."

Mrs. Wilkinson Polly's tears flowed out of the realization that she and her family had been duped; they had spent their savings and gambled their singular futures on a swindle. The sun-baked flats and tent city could not be recognized as the Eden of the railroad ads and booster press accounts. Yet Mrs. Wilkinson Polly is written into history as a pioneering homesteader because she and her kin made their future themselves. Once they willingly entered the ideological frame of private property and Jeffersonian independence promoted by the railroad and real estate developers, they became the principal force of their own misery.

A few decades after the railroads went into the business of producing homesteaders for Montana, the NKVD took up the task of supplying deportees for agricultural settlement of Kazakhstan. In addition to KarLag, the NKVD deported tens of thousands of people to northern Kazakhstan to till the virgin but often agriculturally marginal land around growing new industrial centers like Karaganda. To colonize and utilize the land most effectively, the Labor Colony department of the NKVD-Gulag gridded the land into 240,000- or 480,000-acre parcels for prospective collective farms, assigning an average of 300 deported families to each farm.

Maria Andzejevskaya was born in a Ukrainian village in the 1920s. One summer day in 1936, NKVD security agents knocked on the door and told Maria's parents they had a week to pack their things and report for resettlement to Kazakhstan. No one in the village knew where Kazakhstan was, but they were told it was to the south, where there was plenty of land for everyone to farm. To many, resettlement, even if by force, sounded like good news; overcrowding and land hunger had plagued the sandy, swampy regions of central Ukraine for decades. Maria and her family joined about half her village in packing up and loading their tools, furniture, and livestock on a train to Kazakhstan. They were part of a mass deportation of over 70,000 Soviet citizens of Polish and German descent, who in 1936 were deemed suspect of collusion with bourgeois Poland and Nazi Germany. Maria's family rode the train for nearly a month, and when they finally disembarked from the cramped cattle cars in mid-September, the landscape had changed drastically. Maria described terrain empty except for a tall pole with a sign on it, labeled "settlement number two": "They told us we were going to Kazakhstan, and they would give us land and homes and we would live well. 'There's no winter, it's the south [they said],' 'everything will be perfect,' and then they dropped us off and there was nothing. The five of us children, mamma and papa, everyone cried, and then it was something horrible, night was coming, what would we do?" Maria's family did what Mrs. Wilkinson Polly did. They built houses out of sod, and in their mud homes they put up with the dampness, snakes, and bugs. They made it through the first winter on their dwindling food stocks, and when those were gone they traded their clothing and dishes to Kazakhs for meat and flour. They learned how to gather up manure and brushwood to burn for heat in the long, sub-zero winters. They figured out the signs of a blizzard and how maybe to survive one if caught outside. In short, they learned to endure.

What is the difference between the homesteader and deportee? At first glance, the two do not belong in the same category. Homesteaders went to Montana voluntarily to break the soil; deportees were rudely coerced from their homes and driven to the virgin Kazakh steppe. Yet, looked at more closely, the categories of free will and coercion begin to fuse. Mrs. Wilkinson Polly's family chose to move based on the hopeful view of Montana advertised by civic boosters and railroad advertisers; an NKVD officer conjured up a rosy picture of Kazakhstan for Maria Andzejevskaya's family. Maria's family was offered no choice in leaving, but there is evidence that many of her neighbors were willing to go, and some even asked to be put on the deportation list so they could also try their fortunes in Central Asia, where there was plenty of untilled land — virgin soil, the same motivation for which Mrs. Wilkinson Polly made the long trek to Montana.

Not to overdraw the comparison, once in Kazakhstan, Maria's family was legally restricted from leaving their village and had to report to a local commandant every month. Mrs. Wilkinson Polly's family could leave if they had someplace else to go and money to get there. In fact, they could be forced to leave if the crops failed and the bank foreclosed on their loans. Many will argue this difference in free will is essential, that to be held in place by decree is entirely different than to be held, or propelled, by debt. And they are quite right, yet these differences themselves point to a set of similarities that cast doubt on assumptions of incompatibility between the Soviet Union and United States. For, in both categories, people became the willing and unwilling tools of larger projects to control huge territories by turning grassland into cash crops. Both families were hoodwinked by visions of a better future. Once they arrived, both homesteaders and deportees expressed a sense of powerlessness, a hazy feeling that their lives were being controlled by outside forces.

Montanans regularly railed against the power of the corporations and the railroads, forces that seemed to seep everywhere, controlling them by setting prices, hiring, firing, overcharging, and underpaying them. In 1912, J. C. Murphy published a book-long diatribe against the corporations in Montana. An excerpt:

> Less than a decade of time had been required to bring the material wealth of the state under combine control . . . to acquire most of the tremendous water power and electric power resources of the state to one ownership . . . to bring the banking interests of the state practically under the domination of a single chain of banks owned by the same interest, to reduce the profits of wage earners and to make their condition in industrial centers little better than bond slaves, to transform the functions of a public press . . . into a perfectly organized machine for the suppression of knowledge . . . all this by lawless corporate combination . . . exercised by absentee bosses.

The corporations remain incorporate, the bosses absentee. Murphy could not visualize the source of his subjection; it came from everywhere and embraced everything at once. In Karaganda, I asked a group of elderly people, former deportees, who was responsible for their imprisonment. The voices rang out immediately: "The System." "The Party." "Stalin." "Moscow." "And what about the guards, the people who are your neighbors now?" Again, a chorus of replies: "It is not their fault. They had no choice. They were good people. They only did what they were ordered to do."

Former deportees in Karaganda saw their lives caught in a "system" so immense it swallowed everyone, even the guards. Settlers in Montana at the turn of the century expressed a similar uneasiness about the corporations that seemed to overtake them at every turn. The "Company," the "Party," two faceless, diffuse entities encircled, or so it seemed, the lives of the people who lived in Kazakhstan and Montana so fully that they never caught sight of the incorporeal, ephemeral forces ruling them.

. . . The biggest obstacles to farming and living on the steppe and plains involved water, or the lack of it. Karaganda and Billings fall into the same precipitation zone, where rainfall deviates from a drought-level eight inches to a cultivable seventeen inches a year. It was decided that farming could only be secured through irrigation, but irrigation seemed a fantasy when even drinking water was in short supply. In Karaganda, people had to cart water for miles by horse or camel. In Billings, residents paid 50 cents a barrel for water hauled from the Yellowstone River. Water was all that was needed to make the land fertile, but large-scale irrigation demanded a concentration of capital and labor well beyond the means of an individual farmer or even of the collective energies of the surrounding urban communities. In Billings, the managers of the land company attracted settlers with the promise of "the Big Ditch" for two decades, but they never succeeded in building it. Only in 1900, when the federal government backed irrigation projects, was there enough capital to build a series of canals and reservoirs. In Karaganda, where the central government dedicated hundreds of thousands of rubles to a 24-kilometer canal, and KarLag had at its disposal a growing labor force swelling into the thousands, digging it still took four years and then only supplied the city and a few hundred acres of farmland. Irrigation presents a metaphor for the large-scale settlement of the continental steppe. It takes the kind of money and concentration of labor and machinery that only government budgets, outside capital, and expertise could provide, which left the farmers of the arid steppe and plains in a state of dependency, waiting on the largess of the state.

In other words, small family farms, the kind Thomas Jefferson envisioned, did not prosper in the Great Plains. To have a predictably profitable crop year after year, farmers needed to irrigate, ideally employing heavy machinery and fortifying the soils with fertilizers. The long arch of agricultural development in Montana points to the replacement of small homesteads with large agri-business farms, an American version of the collective farm, where fields are huge, machinery a must, and a mobile labor force is needed to produce high-yield cash crops to pay for it all. At KarLag, the NKVD specialized in setting up large-scale farm-factories and even ran a model farm that pioneered dry land farming techniques, much as Frederick Billings's son Parmly turned the family ranch into a model "scientific" operation. . . .

. . . On August 28, 1941, a date nearly every adult in Karaganda knows, the Supreme Soviet sent out an executive order to deport people of German heritage east, to Kazakhstan and Siberia. The government feared that Soviet citizens of German descent would serve as a fifth column for the invading German army. As a consequence, more than a million citizens of German descent were uprooted and transferred thousands of miles during the first months of war. The NKVD conscripted the transplanted Soviet-German deportees, among others, into a Labor Army to serve in the Asiatic rear of the country manufacturing, mining, and farming to support the Red Army at the front.

In Billings, of course, there was no NKVD to organize labor. But there were large beet farms and far more beets than any farming family could singly sow, weed, harvest, and ship to the Billings sugar refinery. Meanwhile, in New York at the turn of the century, relatives of the same families of Russian-Germans were arriving on Ellis Island in their homespun clothes, speaking an archaic German dialect. Few knew English, but some saw the Milwaukee Railroad posters of the farmer, biceps bulging, plowing up a field of gold coins over a map of the railroad running straight through Billings. Others were enticed by a railroad recruiter in Russia with a cheap ticket to the Great Plains. The Russian-Germans came most often with no cash or assets, and few could afford to buy land and establish their own farms. Instead, colonies of Russian-Germans became part of the sugar-beet labor force throughout the Great Plains, working the fields in Nebraska, Kansas, Idaho, and Montana. In Russia, they had farmed independently; in North America, they entered the world of agricultural wage labor.

It was a precarious world to inhabit. Work came sporadically, was remunerated half-heartedly, and the winters were long, unproductive, and unpaid. In the summers, parents and their children spent the daylight hours in the fields crawling along the rows of beets, blocking, thinning, and weeding. The back-breaking, punishing hours in the fields paid off for some families, who managed to save enough to buy their own farms. But other families remained on the migrant labor circuit for decades, and their ranks grew in the drought periods when farms were lost to banks. . . .

Germans from Russia weed beet fields just beyond Billings; Germans from Russia weed beet fields near Karaganda. The processes by which the two groups became migrant laborers are quite different, and again the difference hinges on the element of coercion and free will. However, the outcome — membership in a migrant labor force — and the quality of life are quite similar. Russian-Germans in Karaganda and Montana were related not only by family ties but also as subjects of a new kind of expanding agricultural discipline based on cheap and mobile labor. The conditions that encompassed their lives — meager living quarters, long work hours, low pay, few chances for advancement, and continual mobility — bonded them long after time and events broke up their German colonies in Russia. Thanks to migration, legal and illegal, there has never been a sustained shortage of unskilled laborers in the United States. The glut of immigrants and all the disparate, untamed forces of the market produced the same kind of mobile, inexpensive labor force that the NKVD generated with its centrally planned charts, mobilization orders, requisitioned trains, and armed soldiers. The invisible hand of the market and the whimsical breezes of U.S. immigration policy sutured together a migrant labor force on the level of the NKVD, with hardly a flourish of weapons.

There are, of course, other differences between deportees to Kazakhstan and homesteaders of Montana. A major difference is memory. The pioneers are lionized as men and women who with courage and the sweat of their brow and a heap of other slogans remade the West, fought off Indians, broke the virginal soil, and in so doing symbolized the freedom and independence of the American way. The deportees, on the other hand, are memorialized as victims of a heartless, impersonal regime. They stand as an icon of suffering in histories of the Soviet Union. They are driven across the steppe and deposited on a wind-swept plain. They are hungry, are often shown in photographs as children with ribs like knives and pinched women burdened with crying infants. The pioneer, on the other hand, is a man, axe in hand, his jaw projected out, all determination. No one needed to help a pioneer; he did for himself.

Ex-convicts and deportees in Kazakhstan are attached to the memory of themselves as victims of a cruel regime. This is the meta-narrative of their lives, and they feel no remorse for the loss of the nomad, nor do they romanticize life on the agricultural and industrial frontier. The difference in the West lies in the impulse to remember. If you travel through Montana, the stylized ghosts of the past haunt billboards and roadside stands: the dead Indian, the dead pioneer, the long-gone cowboy, the withered family farm, and the displaced miner. Teenagers in American cities, most of whom will never exchange their sweat for wages, walk about in the heavy denim of the farmers' Carhartts; suburbanites negotiate manicured avenues in the rugged jeeps of ranchers. James Bryce's premonition has come true: America's restless, feverish passion for quick results has kicked back up a nostalgia for a past plowed under to make room for an ever-receding future. This grief for what has been paved over is integral to modern life; it is a sign that in the United States, more than in the former Soviet Union, the destruction that accompanies a successfully expanding modernity has been far more complete. . . .

QUESTIONS TO CONSIDER

1. What similarities does the author find in the creation of Billings in the 1880s and Karaganda in the 1930s? What differences? Compare how native peoples were displaced, how land was opened to settlement, how towns were planned, how settlers came and lived, and what impact these urban projects had on the environment. Do the similarities outweigh the differences, or vice versa?

2. The pioneering homesteader, the cowboy, and the lonesome miner dominate popular mythology of the American West. What persons or images does Brown replace them with? Does her essay convince you that hers is a more representative or realistic portrait? Why, according to the author, do Americans romanticize pioneer life on the frontier?

3. In studying the American and Soviet frontiers, Brown attempts to set aside ideologies and focus on "the history of the production of spaces and the lives that have been forged by and for those spaces." In what ways, according to her, were these frontier cities examples of "gridded space"? In what sense did they produce "gridded lives"? Who or what was to blame for this? What does it mean that industrial nations of contrasting ideologies and different time periods used similar strategies to settle their frontiers? Do national expansion and industrial development follow their own laws regardless of time, place, or ideology? Is the author opposed to "modernity" itself?

4. Historians are influenced by current events in their choice of subject, approach, and cases to compare. In what way is Brown's comparison inspired by the end of the Cold War? According to the author, what new insights did the end of Soviet-American polarization make possible?

5. As Brown acknowledges, "Comparisons . . . can be misleading." To what extent, if any, does her essay exemplify this problem? Does Brown's comparison reveal an analogy (a partial resemblance between things otherwise unlike) or a more fundamental similarity ("nearly the same") between Billings and Karaganda? Is it accurate to analyze the history of these cities without highlighting the differences between capitalism and communism, democratic and unfree societies? Would Brown's account look different if basic political and social differences between the United States and the Soviet Union were considered more fully? How so?

III

BUSINESS AND LABOR
IN THE INDUSTRIAL AGE

Scholars conventionally use big words like "industrialization," "immigration," and "urbanization" to describe the developments that transformed American society between the Civil War and World War I. Although ungainly, these terms are fitting. For one thing, they effectively convey the large-scale, impersonal forces that seemed to overwhelm individuals during a time of rapid change. For another, they are meant to give a common label to social processes that have occurred in different times and places yet are fundamentally similar. A glance at western Europe and Japan in the nineteenth century, and much of the rest of the world in the twentieth, makes clear that the United States has not been the only country that has built railroads and factories, taken in migrants from farms or other nations, and spawned huge cities. These are changes that most developed nations have experienced in modern times.

How do we square this fact with the powerful, persisting belief that American society is unique? Did social and economic trends of the late nineteenth century "Europeanize" the United States and rob it of its specialness, as many Americans feared? Or were there political, cultural, or geographic factors that made the urban-industrial transformation of America different from that occurring elsewhere? Are those differences so fundamental that the American experience should be seen as an exception to international patterns rather than a variation of them? The next two chapters address these questions by taking an internationally comparative perspective on the forces that created modern America. Chapter IV will cover immigration and urbanization; this chapter's focus is on industrialization, which its essays explore first from management's and then from labor's point of view. In the first selection, Mansel G. Blackford compares the rise of big business in the late-nineteenth-century United States with parallel developments in Great Britain, where the Industrial Revolution was born, and in Japan, which undertook a crash program of modernization at the end of the century. In the second, Aristide A. Zolberg addresses a long-standing controversy: why were American workers of the industrializing era less willing or able than their counterparts in Europe to challenge capitalism head-on by forming radical labor organizations or joining a socialist political party? Although Blackford's and Zolberg's essays trace the implications of industrialization for different groups, both incorporate multinational comparisons in their analysis. By avoiding the "us-them" dichotomy of most exceptionalist approaches, their essays make it easier to see American social history as a distinctive variant of international trends rather than a unique exception to them.

5

The Rise of Big Business in the United States, Great Britain, and Japan

Mansel G. Blackford

Although the Industrial Revolution came to America later than to Great Britain, it swept through the American economy in little more than a generation. Starting out as a fledgling manufacturing nation before the Civil War, the United States by 1900 was the world's leading industrial power, with a manufacturing output exceeding the combined total of Great Britain, France, and Germany. America's surge to industrial might was aided by its abundant natural resources, investment capital from Europe (which underwrote more than a third of American manufacturing), the cheap labor of immigrants, and a huge domestic market swelled by city dwellers' demands for consumer goods.

Just as startling as the speed of American industrialization was its scale. As business historian Mansel G. Blackford notes in this essay, in the late nineteenth century the American economy was increasingly dominated by huge business corporations. By the end of the century, a few dozen companies controlled their industries nationwide and employed thousands of workers in their sprawling bureaucracies. The largest, J. P. Morgan's U.S. Steel, was capitalized at $1.4 billion, an amount three times bigger than the nation's annual budget. These *giant businesses not only manufactured goods; they also extracted and shipped raw materials and oversaw the distribution and marketing of the finished product to retail outlets under their control — an arrangement called "vertical integration."*

Why nineteenth-century businesses grew to such size is the focus of Blackford's presentation. But since big business was not unique to the United States, Blackford wisely gives his study a comparative cast by including developments in two other industrialized nations: Great Britain and Japan. As his exposition proceeds, it becomes clear that the rise of big business was broadly similar in the three countries. In Britain and Japan as well as the United States, the growing complexity of industrial production and the pressures of domestic and international competition led businesses to centralize management and to assert greater control over distribution of their products. General incorporation laws made it easy to form big firms, and national governments allowed mergers and other business combinations to proceed without much intervention.

Still, Blackford's case studies suggest that within a general framework of similar business practices, important differences in geography and culture made each nation's experience distinctive. The sheer size of the domestic market in the United States, for example, stimulated the creation of big, integrated businesses in a way that tiny England and Japan did not. And unlike American corporations, British and Japanese big businesses were controlled by family ties well into the twentieth century. An important factor that Blackford does not include is the positive role of government in jump-starting economic growth. As latecomers to industrialization compared to Great Britain, American and Japanese businesses relied more on government aid. In Japan during the Meiji period of intense modernization, the national government created a central bank, built the first railroads, and heavily subsidized the shipping industry. In the United States, government assistance to business took the form of protective tariffs, land grants and subsidies to railroads, and virtually free grazing and mining on public lands. Blackford's comparison of national actions and attitudes helps explain why the United States and Japan overtook Great Britain as the world's major industrial powers in the twentieth century. And by placing the rise of big business in an international context, Blackford gives a more nuanced answer to the question of how America's economy is distinctive.

One final word about Blackford's approach: as portrayed in popular histories, the rise of American big business veers between hero worship and muckraking. Some writers praise men such as Andrew Carnegie, John D. Rockefeller, and Cornelius Vanderbilt as successful "captains of industry" who built efficient enterprises and later devoted much of their fortune to philanthropy. Others condemn them as unscrupulous "robber barons" who crushed competitors, exploited workers, and disregarded the law on their way to amassing excess wealth and power. Blackford's story is not without its powerful "great men," but he prefers an approach that stresses underlying, impersonal forces and avoids moral judgments. In his view, the emergence of large-scale corporations was a logical response to changing economic circumstances. To supplement Blackford's interpretation, consider the human dimension in your analysis. How do you view the industrialists' motives and practices? What was the impact, both positive and negative, of the rise of big business upon Americans' lives at the turn of the twentieth century?

GLOSSARY

CARTELS   Organizations of producers who act in concert to fix prices, limit supply, or divide markets. Cartels seek to maximize profits by preventing competition among members, eliminating external competitors, and limiting production in times of over-supply.

CLAYTON ACT (1914)   An American law that strengthened previous antitrust legislation by prohibiting corporate practices such as price discrimination and overlapping membership on boards of directors in the same industry. The act also helped labor unions by excluding from antitrust prosecution such worker protests as strikes, peaceful picketing, and boycotts.

GENERAL INCORPORATION LAWS   Laws enabling businesses to form corporations without a special charter granted by a ruler or legislature. These were enacted by state governments of the United States from the 1830s onward, by the British Parliament in 1862, and by the Japanese government in 1893.

MEIJI RESTORATION   The surrender of power in 1868 by the Japanese shogun, or military ruler, to the young emperor Meiji (1852–1912) after agitation demanding a new government and stronger resistance to foreign economic influence. The restoration brought the downfall of feudalism, the establishment of a centralized administration, and the rise of westernizing leaders determined to make Japan a modern industrial state.

OLIGOPOLY   Control of an industry by a few producers who often act to restrain price competition.

SAMURAI   Members of the aristocratic warrior class of feudal Japan, who followed their own code of honor and pledged loyalty to the nobles. Rising in the twelfth century, the samurai class endured until its privileges were ended shortly after the Meiji Restoration of 1868.

SHERMAN ANTITRUST ACT (1890)   An American law intended to break up monopolies that outlawed combinations or conspiracies in restraint of trade. Vague language and big-business influence impeded its enforcement, and it did not prevent the continued growth of business combinations and monopolies.

THROUGHPUT   The speed of production and the volume of output of a manufacturing business.

TOKUGAWA   The period of Japanese history, between 1603 and 1868, when the Tokugawa dynasty held the shogunate (or military dictatorship) and ruled all of Japan like a feudal overlord.

ZAIBATSU   Large diversified companies in modern Japan. The zaibatsu gather manufacturing concerns, a bank, and an overseas trading company under centralized ownership and management.

Eight million people, 17 percent of America's total population, journeyed to a world's fair held in Philadelphia in 1876 to celebrate one hundred years of progress in the United States. . . . Americans came to the Philadelphia Centennial Exposition to view the inventions of their nation's industries, and the exposition became a song of praise to the economic and industrial prowess of the United States. . . . The center of attraction was the Corliss steam engine, a gigantic piece of machinery housed in the Main Hall, a structure covering 13 acres. When put into motion, the Corliss steam engine powered all of the 8,000 other machines in the hall.

The machinery the fair visitors looked at with such interest was increasingly the product of big business. American industrialists achieved high-volume, low-cost production in the processing of liquids, agricultural goods, and metals after the Civil War. This accomplishment of mass production, encouraged by the existence of a large national market and made possible by technological breakthroughs, led to the rise of big business, fundamentally altering the nature of the business firm in the United States. Despite Great Britain's lead in industrialization, that nation lagged behind the United States in the development of large business firms. America was the first nation to have an economy dominated by big business. Only later did big business come into its own in Great Britain or Japan.

As the nineteenth century progressed, more and more American industrial companies were corporations, as permitted by the general incorporation laws of most states. A shrinking proportion were single-owner proprietorships or partnerships. Manufacturing concerns were capital-intensive and needed to raise vast sums of money to build factories. The corporate form of organization, with its promise of limited liability for investors (investors were not held personally responsible for the debts of the corporations in which they invested), was especially attractive to would-be industrialists. Another advantage of the corporation was that, unlike a partnership, it did not have to be reorganized every time an investor left the business.

As businessmen formed corporations, big businesses arose in America. The size of business firms increased dramatically. In the 1850s, the largest industrial enterprises were cotton textile mills. However, only a handful were capitalized at over $1 million or employed more than 500 workers. In 1901, the newly formed United States Steel Corporation was capitalized at $1.4 billion — to become America's first billion-dollar company — and employed over 100,000 workers. By 1929, the corporation employed 440,000. In 1860, no single American company was valued at as much as $10 million, but by 1904 over three hundred were.

The new big businesses developed internal structures that were different from those of earlier enterprises. These structures evolved in response to the opportunities of the national market and in response to the growing complexity of manufacturing processes. The national market offered pleasing possibilities to American businessmen, a market of continental scope for their products. However, the national market created a problem, that of virulent competition. The railroad and the telegraph fostered competition among businessmen across the nation by destroying local monopolies that had been based on the high cost of inland transportation. Technological breakthroughs in production were also a double-edged sword. The innovations increased production, but this vast increase proved difficult to sell by conventional means.

Vertical integration was *the* common American response to these twin problems. Much more than was or is true even today in either Great Britain or Japan, vertically integrated companies came to dominate the industrial landscape of the United States. In vertical integration a company that initially engages in only one stage of the production and sale of a good may integrate backward to control its sources of raw materials and may integrate forward to control the making and selling of its finished goods. Through vertical integration, big businesses in America combined mass production with mass distribution.

Vertical integration offered several advantages to businessmen who were operating on a large scale in the national market. Through vertical integration businessmen could partially insulate their firms from the buffets of the national market. By controlling his raw materials, a businessman could be assured of adequate supplies during times of peak demand, and by controlling all stages of manufacturing he could keep all the profits within his own firm. There were also advantages in controlling marketing networks, and in key fields big businesses arose when industrialists set up national marketing systems to handle their goods. Marketing systems were established by businessmen who used new types of machinery to turn out high volumes of products such as matches, cigarettes, flour, and canned goods when they found that America's wholesalers were overwhelmed by the increased output. Similarly, producers of perishables such as beer, meat, and citrus fruits set up their own systems when marketers were unable to guarantee the needed speed of delivery to market. Finally, manufacturers of technologically complex goods such as reapers, sewing machines, typewriters, and elevators set up marketing systems because established marketers could not adequately demonstrate such complex products to prospective customers, finance their purchase, or service and repair the products after sale.

Horizontal integration provided a second mechanism by which American industrialists structured their big businesses. In horizontal integration a number of companies joined together to control one step in the production and sale of goods. As in vertical integration, the aim was to decrease competition and control the vicissitudes of the national market. Thus, forty-one companies joined together in 1882 to form the Standard Oil Trust to control much of the refining of petroleum in America. To be successful, horizontal was usually accompanied by vertical integration, as businesses sought to control their raw materials and markets, as well as production. Standard Oil, for example, acquired its own crude oil fields, built its own long distance pipelines, and set up its own sales outlets in the late nineteenth and early twentieth centuries.

Business integration, both vertical and horizontal, took place more through mergers of formerly independent companies than by internally generated growth. Mergers became increasingly common from the 1880s on, culminating in America's first major merger movement. Between 1894 and 1905, over 3,000 individual firms capitalized at over $6 billion merged in the United States.

As industrial firms grew in size and complexity, the personal management so typical of preindustrial times gave way to bureaucratic management. Companies became too large and too complex to be run as one-man shows. With plants spread across the United States, industrial companies became multi-unit enterprises, and four interrelated managerial changes occurred.

Businessmen established strong central (corporate) offices for their companies. Staffed by the top management, these offices were in charge of making strategic decisions for the company, planning for the future, and coordinating the work of the different parts of the company. The central offices soon became functionally departmentalized, with different committees of executives in charge of different functions of the company — production, sales, transportation, and so on. . . . An executive committee of . . . top officers was supposed to oversee and coordinate the work of these committees.

Middle management, which had not existed earlier, developed to oversee the day-to-day operations of the new big businesses and to staff the various production facilities and sales outlets. . . .

To control their growing industrial empires businessmen went beyond the preindustrial merchant's simple accounting methods based on double-entry bookkeeping. Industrialists began using new accounting methods to help plan for the future of their companies as well as to keep track of past and current operations. . . .

Big businesses also began to separate ownership from management. A growing proportion of corporate officers worked on salary for their companies' stockholders. Although not disappearing, family firms became rarer in the realm of big business.

The replacement of personal by bureaucratic management took place first on America's largest railroads, some of which had become big businesses by the 1850s, and then spread to the mammoth industrial enterprises arising in the 1880s and later. Four railroads — the Pennsylvania, the Baltimore & Ohio, the New York Central, and the New York & Erie — controlled trackage from the East Coast to the Midwest by the mid-1850s. As they grew from small local carriers to interregional lines, these railroads faced unprecedented operating difficulties, such as how to schedule large numbers of trains and run them safely on time, and strategic problems, such as how to meet the moves of their competitors and how to raise the enormous amounts of capital needed for their expansion. All responded by establishing bureaucratic management systems. Large industrial firms operating on a national scale encountered the same types of problems and made a similar response — again, the adoption of bureaucratic management — a generation or two later.

The evolution of the American Tobacco Company presents a classic case study in the development of big business in American industry. Its founder, James Buchanan Duke, known by most nineteenth-century Americans as "Buck Duke," transformed the American tobacco industry by introducing mass-production methods and a new product, cigarettes, to the tobacco industry. Moreover, his character was typical, in many important respects, of America's leading big businessmen of that period.

By 1880, Duke had taken over a family pipe tobacco business in North Carolina, and from this base he soon built the largest tobacco-processing company in the world. Realizing that other well-established companies already controlled the plug (chewing) and pipe tobacco fields, Duke looked elsewhere for expansion possibilities. He found his chance in cigarettes, a relatively new field of tobacco processing whose market was rapidly increasing (1.8 million cigarettes were sold in America in 1869, but 500 million in 1880). In those days cigarettes were made by hand, and in 1881 Duke hired a team of ten men to begin producing them. A supervisor and a team of ten could turn out about 20,000 cigarettes a day. In this labor-intensive business there were no economies of scale, and Duke was, at first, simply one of many cigarette makers.

Duke moved ahead of the other cigarette producers with the purchase of rights to the use of automatic cigarette-rolling machines patented by James Bonsack of Virginia. Perfected in 1884, a Bonsack machine could turn out over 100,000 cigarettes a day. The use of Bonsack machines gave Duke a cost advantage over his rivals, and by 1885 he controlled 10 percent of America's cigarette market. He then engaged in horizontal integration, taking over his competitors — Allen and Ginter of Richmond, Kinney Tobacco of New York, Goodwin and Company of Rochester, and others — to form one gigantic company, the American Tobacco Company, in 1890.

Duke next sought to move beyond cigarettes to acquire companies in chewing and pipe tobacco making both in and beyond the United States. By 1910, American Tobacco possessed 86 percent of the cigarette market, 85 percent of the plug market, 79 percent of the pipe tobacco market, and 14 percent of the cigar market in America. Duke went abroad by taking on British cigarette makers in 1901. After a fierce battle, American Tobacco and the leading British company, Imperial Tobacco, agreed to a truce. According to its terms, American Tobacco would get out of the British market, and Imperial Tobacco would leave the American market. Together they would form a new company, two-thirds owned by American Tobacco, to sell cigarettes to the rest of the world.

Some vertical integration followed American Tobacco's horizontal integration, as Duke acquired companies making licorice, cotton bags to hold tobacco, boxes, and tinfoil. American Tobacco also purchased the United Cigar Stores, which had 392 retail outlets.

Eventually, American Tobacco's control over the American market led to its dissolution at the hands of the Justice Department of the federal government. In 1908, the department brought suit against the company under the terms of the Sherman Antitrust Act of 1890, and three years later the United States Supreme Court ordered that the company be split up. From the dissolution of the American Tobacco Company came new firms that long dominated the American tobacco market: the (new) American Tobacco Company, the Liggett and Myers Tobacco Company, the R. J. Reynolds Tobacco Company, and the P. Lorillard Company. Duke left American Tobacco a few months after its breakup, and he died in 1925.

Shortly before his death, Duke told a friend why he thought he had been successful in business. "I resolved from the time I was a mere boy to do a big business," Duke observed. "I loved business better than anything else. I worked from early morning until late at night. I was sorry to have to leave off at night and glad when morning came so I could get at it again." Business was Duke's life. He loved the thrill of the game. He was an empire builder. . . .

American businessmen [like Duke] formed something of an elite in the late 1800s and early 1900s. Most big businessmen were native born (not immigrants), white, from the city (not farms), of middle-class rather than working-class origins, and well educated by the standards of their day. In terms of motivation, most were individualistic and materialistic. They believed in their right to make money, and most viewed the actions of their companies as helping American society as well as themselves. "Have not the great merchants, great manufacturers, great inventors done more for the world than preachers and philanthropists?" Charles Perkins, a railroad president, asked rhetorically in 1888. "Can there be any doubt that cheapening the cost of necessaries and conveniences of life is the most powerful agent of civilization and progress?" he intoned.

Although an elite, America's business elite was a relatively open one. Money was the common denominator that provided access to the upper reaches of American society for the nation's newly rich railroad barons and industrialists. Titles of nobility or the possession of a generations-old family name counted for less in the United States than in Europe. Through what the American economist Thorstein Veblen labeled "conspicuous consumption" — using their wealth to build mansions, acquire art, buy private railroad cars, and host lavish parties (at one the tongues of peacocks were served) — America's big businessmen could buy their way into society.

A major reason for their relative ease of entry into the upper reaches of society was the admiration many Americans had for big businessmen. Americans loved the material abundance, the outpouring of goods, and the rising standard of living that they associated with big business. Yet, there was ambivalence in the attitude of Americans. The rise of big business was so sudden, so new, and so disruptive of traditional ways of doing things that Americans also feared it. The American response to the rise of big business was to try to control it through regulation by the government, especially the federal government.

During the Progressive period, the years 1900 through 1920, the federal government began to regulate big business in a major way. The Interstate Commerce Commission, a federal government agency established by the Interstate Commerce Act of 1887, had its power to regulate railroads greatly enhanced by new legislation in 1906. The Meat Inspection Act and the Pure Foods and Drug Act, both passed by Congress in 1906, gave the federal government responsibility for the regulation of America's food and drug industries, and the Food and Drug Administration was set up in that year. The Federal Reserve Act of 1913 established the Federal Reserve System to regulate banking practices and the money supply in the United States.

Although the main thrust of American public policy was to regulate, not destroy, big business, some antitrust measures were passed by Congress. The Sherman Antitrust Act of 1890, which was used against the American Tobacco Company, and the Clayton Act of 1914 sought to prevent any restriction of trade in America. Congress also established the Federal Trade Commission in 1914 to monitor business practices in the United States in the interests of keeping them competitive. Ironically, some of the very laws designed by Congress to encourage competition, especially the Sherman Antitrust Act, were interpreted by the United States Supreme Court in ways that stimulated combination, not competition. As applied by the Justice Department and as interpreted by the Court in the 1890s, the Sherman Antitrust Act was used to break up only loose combinations among businesses — cartels, for example. Tight combinations, such as single integrated companies like Carnegie Steel, were not attacked as often or as effectively, and as a consequence businessmen continued to form them.

Big business was clearly established in America by the time of World War I. By 1917, the United States possessed 278 companies capitalized at $20 million or more. Of these companies 236 were in manufacturing. Some 171 were in only six fields: food processing, chemicals, oil, metals, machine making, and transportation equipment. Parts of American industry came to be characterized by oligopoly; in these fields a handful of large companies dominated their markets. As early as 1904, just a few major companies controlled at least half of the output of 78 different industries in the United States. . . . Nearly all of the 236 big businesses in manufacturing were vertically integrated, and 85 percent of them were organized around some sort of centralized, functionally departmentalized management structure. . . .

Even though industrialization began earlier in Great Britain than in America, big businesses were slower to develop in Great Britain. As late as 1920, few British companies equaled their American counterparts in absolute size. Nor was British industry as concentrated as American industry. . . .

Particularly noticeable, when compared to business development in the United States, was the lack of vertical integration in British business. . . . Both economic and noneconomic reasons account for the relatively slow development of large, vertically integrated businesses in Great Britain.

British markets differed from American markets. Despite its continuing growth, the domestic British market was smaller and less prosperous than that of the United States. . . . By 1920, the United States had a population and a national income nearly triple that of Great Britain. Moreover, Great Britain's national market was more segmented by regional tastes and preferences than was the American market. . . .

In short, the large unified national market that did so much to stimulate the rise of big, integrated businesses in American manufacturing was not present to the same degree in Great Britain. Great Britain also possessed a much more detailed and better established system of wholesalers and retailers than did the United States. These marketers were able to sell the expanding output of Great Britain's factories, especially because Great Britain was much smaller than America and its markets were more geographically unified in large cities. Thus, British manufacturers did not feel the need to integrate vertically by setting up their own marketing outlets.

Political factors were also significant. As we have seen, in the United States the Sherman Antitrust Act of 1890 outlawed cartels and, thus, ironically encouraged formerly

independent companies to merge and form big businesses. However, no such legal prohibition existed in Great Britain. Small British firms could gain many of the benefits
available to American companies only through merger by simply joining cartels. Cartels
helped preserve small industrial firms in Great Britain.

Finally, social attitudes retarded the development of big business in Great Britain.
More than in the United States, an antibusiness bias lingered, and from the 1850s on was
reinvigorated, in Great Britain. For Great Britain's social elite the ideal came more and
more to be, not an England based on industry and material progress, but an England
grounded in static country values, a "merrie" old England of green pastures and dales.
Like the United States, Great Britain hosted a world's fair in the nineteenth century, the
Great Exhibition, or Crystal Palace Exhibition, of 1851, which featured new industrial
inventions, but this was the last such fair ever sponsored by that nation. . . . By the late
nineteenth century, critics of industrialism and business expansion were railing against
developments in America and warning fellow Englishmen about the dangers of following in America's footsteps. In 1886, Herbert Spencer, a British social thinker, summed
up the attitudes of many English critics of American industrialism when he wrote his
good friend Andrew Carnegie. "Absorbed by his activities, and spurred on by his unrestricted ambitions, the American is," Spencer thought, "a less happy being than the
inhabitant of a country where the possibilities of success are very much smaller."

Industrialization affected management methods and firm structures in Great Britain less
than in the United States. Because British companies were smaller and their operations
less complex, they simply did not have to change as much.

There was less separation of ownership from management in Great Britain than in
the United States. Even after the passage of the Joint Stock Acts of 1856 and 1862,
which limited the liability of investors, few British companies became limited companies, the British equivalent of American corporations. Most remained family-linked
partnerships. As late as 1885, limited companies accounted for only 5 to 10 percent of
the total number of important business organizations in England. Only in shipping, iron
and steel, and cotton textiles was their influence very great. Partnerships could raise the
needed industrial capital from their retained earnings, banks, and personal ties.
Throughout the nineteenth century and into the twentieth, ownership and management remained united in Great Britain.

In Great Britain business remained a personal, not a bureaucratic, affair much longer
than in the United States. Business bureaucracies replete with divisions between top and
middle management, sophisticated accounting systems, and the like were slower to
spread in Great Britain. They were not as urgently needed by the smaller British
firms. . . .

[When big business developed in late nineteenth-century Britain, it retained distinctive
features, as the history of the Imperial Tobacco Company shows.] When it was formed
in 1901, the Imperial Tobacco Company was capitalized at nearly 12 million pounds,
making it the largest company in Great Britain. Imperial Tobacco was a combination of
thirteen formerly independent British firms that joined forces to oppose the entrance of

James B. Duke's American Tobacco Company into the British market. . . . Of the companies coming together to form Imperial Tobacco, the largest was W. D. & H. O. Wills of Bristol, England's leading maker of cigarettes, which was capitalized at almost 7 million pounds. An examination of Wills's rise to dominance of the British tobacco market reveals a lot about the beginnings of big business in Great Britain and provides an instructive contrast to the United States.

Wills began its history in a competitive business environment. The linking of different regions in Great Britain by the railroad began breaking down local monopolies in the 1840s, though regional tastes remained more important than in the United States. In 1846, Wills began giving special brand names to some of its smoking tobaccos as a way of differentiating them from their competitors, and in the 1860s Wills led other tobacco companies in setting up a national selling network. The use of packing machines for loose tobacco and the adoption of airtight tins in the 1880s also moved Wills ahead of the other British companies.

However, it was Wills's movement into cigarette making that gave the company dominance over the British market, in a manner similar to American Tobacco's takeover of the American market. Wills brought out its first handmade cigarette in 1871. In 1884, Wills purchased exclusive British rights to the Bonsack machine for 4,000 pounds and began turning out machine-made cigarettes within the year. Yet, unlike Duke, the managers of Wills hesitated to press home their new competitive advantage against their rivals. For four years, they used the Bonsack machine to produce only existing brands of cigarettes at high prices. The senior partners were cautious and had doubts about the quality of machine-made cigarettes. At least one partner expressed fears that the machines would put men out of work. Beginning in 1888, however, the company began making cheap cigarettes for the mass market with the Bonsack machines. Within two years, Wills had captured 59 percent of the British cigarette market, and, despite the acquisition of the Bonsack machine by other British companies, still held 55 percent of the market in 1901.

As in the United States, the control of technology essential in increasing the throughput of business allowed some British firms to move ahead of their competitors and become big businesses. The Bonsack machine helped Wills, as it had Duke's American Tobacco Company, defeat its rivals in the cigarette industry. Yet, the use of such technologies was more limited in Great Britain than in the United States. There was even some reluctance to use the Bonsack machine to its fullest capacity by Wills's partners. This attitude — a dislike of cutthroat competition as ungentlemanly — may partly explain, as noted previously, the relative lack of big business in Great Britain when compared to the United States. The Imperial Tobacco Company, capitalized in 1901 at 12 million pounds (about $60 million), was large by British standards. But, Imperial Tobacco was a pygmy when compared to America's largest company, United States Steel, which was formed in the same year and capitalized at $1.4 billion. . . .

Not until the years after World War I did big businesses emerge as the dominant force in the British economic system. Firms like Imperial Tobacco were the exception, not the rule, in prewar Great Britain, and even they were considerably smaller than their

American counterparts. Many men of talent went, not into business, which many Britishers held in low repute, but into other occupations such as the civil service. Or, if they did enter business, they went into finance, insurance, and the like — not manufacturing. While building up the "City" of London as a global financial center, this tendency eroded Great Britain's industrial dominance. Great Britain's relative slowness in developing large industrial enterprises placed it at a competitive disadvantage to new industrializing countries such as the United States and Germany, and may well have contributed to its economic malaise in the twentieth century.

In Japan, no less than in the United States or Great Britain, industrialization profoundly affected business firms and business practices. New forms of business arose in Japan, and the status of the businessman underwent a fundamental transformation [during the Meiji period (1868–1912)]. . . . Businessmen in Tokugawa Japan ranked behind other groups in the nation's social order. Samurai, peasants, and artisans all ranked ahead of merchants in Japan's four-class system. This situation changed in Meiji Japan. . . . The creation of industries came to be seen by some Japanese as a service to the state, because new industries would, they thought, make Japan strong. Some Japanese political and economic leaders began to view businessmen as the new samurai of their nation. . . .

Businessmen taking advantage of the new opportunities of the Meiji period to go into shipbuilding, railroads, manufacturing, and banking did so increasingly through the formation of joint-stock companies. Some joint-stock companies existed in an informal way as early as the 1870s and 1880s. Legal recognition through a General Incorporation Act of 1893 and a Commercial Code that went into effect six years later further spurred their development. Several factors accounted for the popularity of joint-stock companies: the ease with which they could mobilize capital, their association with the greatly admired new technology of the West, and the fact that ex-samurai preferred not to work in more traditional family businesses. . . .

Many of the largest businesses in the early and mid-Meiji period were single-industry businesses. Of Japan's fifty largest manufacturing and mining companies in 1896, twenty-eight were cotton textile companies. These firms became even larger as a result of a merger movement, influenced by the model of mergers in the United States. Between 1900 and 1903, the number of companies engaged in cotton spinning decreased from seventy-eight to forty-six.

These and most other Japanese industrial companies were not as highly integrated as American big businesses. The Japanese firms were more like the British ones. Whereas the Japanese cotton textile companies had integrated spinning and weaving by World War I, the firms depended on other companies to buy their raw cotton and sell their finished cloth. Several reasons account for this relative lack of vertical integration, factors similar to those explaining its rareness in Great Britain. Japan had a well-developed marketing system from the Tokugawa period, and so manufacturers did not have to set up their own marketing networks. (To this day, foreign businesses have a difficult time breaking into this marketing network, and this helps explain why they have often had trouble doing business in Japan.) Then, too, Japan's national market was smaller than America's, allowing established marketers to handle adequately the goods bound for that market. For ideological reasons as well, manufacturers did not want to enter marketing, which they viewed as less virtuous than manufacturing. Thus, fully vertically integrated companies were not the norm in Japanese manufacturing. Nor, by the 1910s and 1920s, were single-industry companies such as the independent cotton textile firms the largest businesses in Japan.

Instead, large diversified companies called "zaibatsu" came to dominate industry and some other fields of Japanese business in the opening decades of the twentieth century. The zaibatsu were much more diversified than big businesses in Great Britain or the United States. Zaibatsu were composed of manufacturing ventures (typically in both light industries such as silk reeling and cotton spinning and heavy industries such as shipbuilding, mining, chemicals, and iron- and steelmaking), a bank to finance those concerns, and a trading company to sell the products overseas.

Japan's zaibatsu developed in several ways. A few, such as Mitsui, evolved from Tokugawa merchant houses. More, such as Mitsubishi, grew out of enterprises closely connected with the fortunes of the new Japanese government and, like the government itself, were organizations founded in the Meiji period. Still other zaibatsu, such as Nissan, were so-called "new zaibatsu" formed in the 1920s and 1930s and closely associated with the Japanese government's efforts to build up heavy industry for military purposes. In the years before World War I, eight major zaibatsu emerged — Mitsui, Mitsubishi, Sumitomo, Yasuda, Asano, Okura, Furukawa, and Kawasaki — the first four of which had become known as the "Big Four" by 1920. By the early 1920s, the zaibatsu controlled much of the mining, shipbuilding, banking, foreign trade, and industry of Japan. . . .

. . . The zaibatsu typified the trend toward bureaucratic management. Generally speaking, in the 1890s and early 1900s the zaibatsu operated as fairly loose confederations of companies owned by family groups. Coordination of the activities of the bank, trading company, mining concerns, and manufacturing ventures making up a zaibatsu was not as close as it would later become. In the 1910s and 1920s, a considerable degree of centralization of managerial control over the different enterprises composing a zaibatsu occurred. Most of the zaibatsu came to consist of a center company organized as a family partnership and other companies, sometimes called "core companies" — the bank, trading company, mining ventures, and manufacturing enterprises — that were often joint-stock companies whose shares were owned by the center company. The core companies, in turn, often owned many smaller companies as their subsidiaries. . . . In a typical zaibatsu, officers in the center company, who were usually family members, also held presidencies and directorships in the core companies and helped coordinate the activities of the zaibatsu as a whole. . . .

In many of the zaibatsu professional managers selected from outside of the founding families came to have much of the real power as the managing directors of the various core companies. With the employment of these outsiders as managing directors, owner-ship and management began to become divorced in Japanese business, though not nearly to the degree experienced in the United States or probably even in Great Britain. Fami-lies continued to control the center companies of most zaibatsu until after World War II.

The historical development of Mitsubishi . . . typified common trends in the evolution of big business in Japan. . . .

Yataro Iwasaki founded Mitsubishi. Born the son of a peasant, he purchased samurai status in the Tosa *han* [provincial government] and rose in the *han's* bureaucracy as a pro-curer of arms and ships. After the Meiji Restoration, the *han* was abolished and its ships became the basis for an independent shipping company with Iwasaki as its manager. In 1873, Iwasaki took over this company as his own and renamed it Mitsubishi. He rallied support for his nascent venture by cloaking it in nationalism, saying that the firm would help make Japan strong in shipping. Iwasaki's approach appealed to his employees, many of whom were former samurai of the Tosa *han*. Mitsubishi began business with ten ships. With them the company entered the coastal trade, edging out competitors by cutting rates.

Mitsubishi benefited from government aid, carrying troops and supplies for several military expeditions in the 1870s, and by the late 1870s it controlled 73 percent of Japanese shipping. Mitsubishi's rapid rise attracted the attention of other Japanese businessmen, who formed the Kyodo Unyu Shipping Company to compete with Mitsubishi in the early 1880s. Out of this competition came the formation of a new shipping company in 1885, the Nippon Yusen Company (NYK), with Mitsubishi as the largest single stockholder. However, between 1887 and 1892 Mitsubishi's owners sold most of their holdings in NYK to enter fields that promised larger profits than shipping.

In fact, Mitsubishi's diversification began even before the shipping competition of the 1880s. Yataro Iwasaki led Mitsubishi into warehousing, insurance, coal mining, and ownership of a shipyard in Nagasaki. Under his guidance, Mitsubishi also entered bank-ing in a tentative way with the formation of a foreign exchange and discount bank to serve merchants using its ships. Yataro ran Mitsubishi with force and determination. There was little separation of ownership from management and almost no delegation of authority under his rule.

Yataro Iwasaki died in 1885, and Mitsubishi's management structure changed under the leadership of his successors. After making some preliminary alterations in the late 1880s, Yanosuke Iwasaki, Yataro's younger brother, and Hisaya Iwasaki, Yataro's eldest son, took advantage of Japan's new General Incorporation Law to reorganize Mitsubishi in 1893. Mitsubishi became a limited partnership, consisting of a head office and de-partments in banking, mining, coal sales, and general affairs. The head office continued to run the company with an iron hand. As president, Hisaya Iwasaki delegated few responsibilities to the departments.

Major alterations occurred about a decade later. In 1906, Koyata Iwasaki, Yanosuke's eldest son, who had been attending Cambridge University, returned home and became a vice-president in Mitsubishi. When Yanosuke died in 1908, Koyata assumed his father's share in Mitsubishi and used his power to reorganize radically the company. The mining, shipbuilding, and banking departments became divisions of the company, and by 1913 the company had grown to include six divisions: banking, metal mining, coal mining, trading (a forerunner of Mitsubishi Shoji), shipbuilding, and real estate. Unlike the earlier departments, each division possessed considerable autonomy over its operations. . . . The head office concerned itself with coordinating the work of the divisions and planning for the future of the zaibatsu as a whole. Control was exercised by having thrice-weekly meetings of all the division managers (who were hired from outside the Iwasaki family) presided over by the vice-president of the head office, which continued to be organized as a limited partnership. . . .

Further changes occurred when Koyata Iwasaki took over as president of Mitsubishi in 1916. Over the next three years, he reorganized the six divisions as joint-stock companies. The head office became a holding company owning a controlling share of the stock in each of the joint-stock companies. By selling some of the stock of the new joint-stock companies to the public, Koyata was able to raise funds for Mitsubishi's continuing diversification drive. Finally, in 1919 and 1920 a board of directors was set up as the top authority within Mitsubishi's management. With this reorganization, Mitsubishi moved away from decentralized management, and the joint-stock companies lost some of the power they had possessed over their affairs when they had been divisions.

With new management structures in place, Mitsubishi continued to diversify during the first four decades of the twentieth century. Koyata Iwasaki proved to be an aggressive businessman, much like his uncle Yataro, and his personality dominated Mitsubishi until his death in 1945. Mitsubishi's interests in shipbuilding at its yards in Nagasaki and, from 1905 on, in Kobe led the company in the 1920s and 1930s into a broad range of heavy industries: iron and steel, chemicals, mining, aircraft (including the famous Japanese "Zero" of World War II), and electrical equipment. . . . Mitsubishi eventually established a major bank to finance its concerns and the trading company Mitsubishi Shoji . . . had branches around the world.

Although the Iwasaki family, especially Koyata, continued to run Mitsubishi, non-family, bureaucratic management rose in significance. People from outside the Iwasaki family headed the joint-stock companies that evolved from the divisions, and some standard procedures were developed to coordinate the work of the various components of the Mitsubishi empire. Yet, family ownership and management remained more important than in the United States. The Iwasaki family maintained their overall dominance of Mitsubishi through their control of the head office, which, in turn, owned a controlling share in each of the joint-stock companies until after World War II. . . .

With the development of zaibatsu such as . . . Mitsubishi, big business arrived in Japan. As in the United States, the rise of big business changed Japanese business firms. Large businesses began adopting bureaucratic management systems, although, as the example of Mitsubishi . . . illustrate[s], . . . family control remained strong longer in Japan than in the United States, and in this respect Japanese big businesses resembled their counterparts in Great Britain more than those in America.

QUESTIONS TO CONSIDER

1. What, according to Blackford, were the main reasons that large industrial enterprises developed in the United States in the late nineteenth century? Why, on the other hand, were giant multifunctional corporations slower to develop in Great Britain and Japan? Why was Britain, despite being the first nation to industrialize, the last of these three nations to be dominated by big business? Why did American and Japanese businesses quickly surpass their British counterparts in size and output?

2. How do the histories of the American Tobacco Company, the Imperial Tobacco Company, and Mitsubishi illustrate typical patterns in the development of big business in the United States, Great Britain, and Japan, respectively? What similarities and differences do you find in these three case studies? Be sure to consider the rise of bureaucratic management, attitudes toward competition, and business relations with government.

3. Describe the various routes American corporations took toward bigness: vertical integration, horizontal integration, cartels, and mergers. Were their methods illegal or unfair? To what extent were big businessmen out to make fortunes for themselves, to serve the public good, or to create order out of the chaos of competition? Should we view them as "captains of industry," "robber barons," or something else? Why were the American government's efforts to break up business monopolies ineffective?

4. Try to imagine the impact that centralization of manufacturing and control of distribution by large firms had upon local businesses, workers in manufacturing, and American consumers. Create a "balance sheet" of the positive and negative effects of powerful industrial corporations on late-nineteenth-century America.

5. To what extent do the national patterns Blackford describes help us to understand the conduct of business in each of these countries today? Consider, for example, the greater number of working days (on average) in Japan and the United States than in Britain, or the huge pay gap between chief executives and average employees in the United States (531 to 1) compared to Britain (25 to 1) and Japan (10 to 1). How do Blackford's comparisons help explain the positions of the United States, Great Britain, and Japan in the world economy at the beginning of the twenty-first century?

6

Why Is There No Socialism
in the United States?

ARISTIDE A. ZOLBERG

One special benefit of a comparative approach to American history is its ability to reveal absences that require explanation. Discovering why something did not happen here that happened elsewhere can be just as revealing as explaining what did occur. The question the German sociologist Werner Sombart posed in 1906 — "Why is there no socialism in the United States?" — has stimulated intense debate among historians and social activists. Even before Sombart, commentators on both sides of the Atlantic puzzled over the apparently exceptional course of American political and economic development. The founders of communism, Karl Marx and Friedrich Engels, could not decide whether the United States was ahead of or behind other capitalist societies on the path to socialism. On the other hand, Frederick Jackson Turner's writings suggested that the combination of free land on the frontier and progressive social legislation rendered socialism irrelevant to American workers.

Some participants in this debate have taken a simplistic stance affirming or denying American "exceptionalism," the idea that American history has been exempt from the ills that plague other countries. Others have relied on sweeping and essentially circular generalizations, such as the notion that a pro-capitalist consensus in America excludes the possibility of socialism. In this selection, Aristide Zolberg contributes some chronological precision and a more nuanced touch to the discussion. He begins by narrowing his focus to the period between the 1880s and World War I, the time when the United States experienced its most rapid industrialization. Zolberg reminds us that the American labor movement was more militant and had more of a socialist presence than many people realize. Conversely, European unions and socialist parties were neither as radical nor as powerful as we assume. What needs to be explained, then, is not why there was no socialism here — for there certainly was — but why workers' protests and programs did not take the form of a powerful political party devoted to labor's interests.

Zolberg's answer is framed in three sections, each using different methods and evidence. In the first section, he notes that despite our tradition of worker militancy, the narrow and conservative trade unionism of the American Federation of Labor (AF of L; founded in 1885 by Samuel Gompers) became the dominant thrust of American labor activism. Most *immigrants learned quickly, he says, that "to be an American worker was to be a trade unionist and a Democrat or a Republican, but not a Socialist." To find out why, Zolberg turns in his second section to the distinctive American brand of industrial capitalism. In the late nineteenth century, he says, the American economy produced more material goods for laborers than its European counterparts did. Equally important, it developed two sectors of the work force that proved loyal to the system: a growing sector of "white-collar" office workers, and a "labor aristocracy" of skilled native-born tradespeople who bargained peacefully with employers and who opposed the immigration of cheap unskilled labor. (Note how Zolberg's point about office workers fits well with Mansel Blackford's description in Selection 5 of the rise of business bureaucracies.) Zolberg's third and final section directs our attention to political institutions. In the United States, he says, unlike in western Europe, democratic politics preceded industrialization, so that by the time the workers formulated their demands, the two major political parties were well-entrenched coalitions that vied for the labor vote. This powerful two-party system resisted class-based third parties such as the Populists of the 1890s and the Socialists of the 1910s, and it successfully lured their followers by adopting some of their proposals.*

Zolberg's emphasis on the many subtle ways American economic and political arrangements are distinctive rings truer than simplistic, monocausal explanations for the failure of American socialism. As you analyze his argument and evidence, try to clarify such factors as the role of immigration and the influence of middle-class cultural attitudes among workers. Zolberg also refers to the antilabor hysteria that followed the Haymarket riot of 1886, in which a bomb thrown during a workers' rally killed several policemen. How significant was repression in causing American socialism's weakness? Finally, as you sort out the various obstacles to socialist success here, you might reflect on the implications of the recent collapse of communist regimes in Europe. Does current history discredit the Marxist version of American exceptionalism: the notion that all industrialized nations except the United States are headed inexorably toward socialism? "Only time will tell," historian Eric Foner has written recently, "whether the United States has been behind Europe in the development of socialism, or ahead of it, in socialism's decline."

GLOSSARY

BLUE-COLLAR WORKERS Workers employed in skilled or unskilled manual labor.

BUSINESS UNIONISM A conservative labor union philosophy, typified by the American Federation of Labor, that aimed not to overturn the framework of wage-labor capitalism but to gain higher wages, shorter hours, and better working conditions.

CHARTIST MOVEMENT A workers' political reform movement active in Great Britain between 1838 and 1848. It sought to enact a "people's charter" that called for the secret ballot, annual elections, and universal male suffrage.

CHILD LABOR ACT The Keating-Owen Child Labor Act of 1916, which prohibited the interstate transportation of goods manufactured by children under sixteen.

DEBS, EUGENE V. (1855–1926)   Leader of the Socialist Party of America. Debs gained fame as the forceful and eloquent president of the American Railway Union during the Pullman strike of 1894. He helped to form the Socialist Party in 1900 and was its presidential candidate five times thereafter. A pacifist, Debs was jailed from 1918 to 1921 for his outspoken opposition to American involvement in World War I.

INDUSTRIAL WORKERS OF THE WORLD (IWW)   A revolutionary union organized in 1905. Its members, known as Wobblies, aimed to unite all skilled and unskilled workers into "one big union" to overthrow capitalism in favor of a socialist future. The IWW reached a peak membership of about eighty thousand on the eve of World War I, but wartime strikes led to suppression by the federal government, including the arrest of its entire leadership.

KNIGHTS OF LABOR   Founded in 1869, a union organized by industry rather than by skill level and open to women, blacks, and former wage earners. Among its aims were the promotion of worker-owned shops, the eight-hour day, the abolition of child and convict labor, and currency reform. Victories in railroad and coal strikes in the 1880s boosted the Knights' membership to over seven hundred thousand, but it declined rapidly due to internal divisions and its association in the public mind with the Haymarket bombing.

KNOW-NOTHINGS   Members of a nativist (anti-immigrant) political movement of the 1840s and 1850s. Its organization, the American Party, sought to elect only native-born Americans to office, to slow the naturalization of immigrants, and to prevent them from wielding political and economic power. Originally, its members were sworn to secrecy and told to respond to inquirers that they knew nothing.

MAGNA CARTA   The "great charter," issued by King John of England in 1215, that guaranteed that the king could not encroach upon feudal privileges, proclaimed freedom of the church, and implied the extension of civil rights to royal subjects. It is viewed as the founding document of British constitutional history.

MARXIST   A follower of the economic and political philosophy of Karl Marx (1818–1883), the chief theorist of modern socialism and communism. An economic determinist, Marx interpreted the history of society as the working out of class struggle, which would eventually result in the proletarian (working-class) overthrow of bourgeois society.

POPULISM   A farmer revolt in late-nineteenth-century America that developed into a third political party, the People's Party, organized nationally in 1892. Its platform called for nationalization of railroads, coinage of silver in addition to gold, an eight-hour workday, direct election of senators, and other reforms. Many members left the party when the Democrats, under their presidential nominee William Jennings Bryan, endorsed some of these reforms in 1896.

PROLETARIAT   In Karl Marx's theory, the class of workers who under industrial capitalism are forced to sell their labor in exchange for subsistence. Marx believed that under advanced capitalism this class would become the overwhelming majority and eventually seize power from the bourgeoisie in order to enact a classless communism.

"PURE AND SIMPLE" UNIONISM   The strategy, exemplified by the American Federation of Labor, that confined labor unions to job-related actions and avoided commitments to political parties or causes.

RUSSIAN REVOLUTION   The violent upheavals in Russia ending in the overthrow of the czarist government and the takeover by the Communist Party in 1917.

"SPLIT LABOR"   The theory that workers' solidarity is damaged by a labor force divided between unskilled workers desperate for employment and skilled workers attempting to exclude them from the job market.

TRADE UNIONISM   Reliance upon labor unions organized locally and confined to skilled workers in particular trades.

WHITE-COLLAR SECTOR   The portion of the work force holding salaried or professional jobs generally not involving manual labor. White-collar work ranges from clerical and sales jobs to professional practice to management positions in business and government.

1. The American Working Class in Comparative Perspective

[Werner] Sombart's famous question has somewhat the same effect on historical discussion of working-class formation as the legendary "When did you stop beating your wife?" He does not ask *whether* American workers are socialist, or to what extent, but much more bluntly *why* they are *not*. Moreover, the question takes it for granted that for workers to be socialist is the norm — not only in theory, but in practice as well. There is no doubt that the comportment of American workers, then and now, differed significantly from their fellows in most other capitalist industrial societies: but before we seek to account for this difference, it is important to establish as precisely as possible of what it consisted. This takes us, of necessity, into the realm of comparison. . . . A major source of confusion is that the literature seldom specifies the *time period* to which the explanation is meant to refer: "American workers" as of 1886, when they were renowned throughout Europe for their militancy, or as of 1936, when some of them were involved in a major thrust toward industrial unionism, or yet as of 1956, when the gap between their orientation and that of Europeans perhaps reached its historical maximum? Our focus, here, will be quite specifically on the period that constituted Sombart's "present," i.e., the period immediately preceding World War I.

My starting point is the observation that the historical literature on the German and French cases tends to exaggerate the militancy and revolutionary disposition of the working class in the pre–World War I period because the official doctrine of its leading organizations is taken uncritically as tantamount to the disposition of the workers themselves, and because the effects of World War I and the Russian Revolution as . . .

From "The Roots of American Exceptionalism," by Aristide A. Zolberg, in Jean Heffer and Jeanine Rovet (eds.), *Pourquoi n'y a-t-il pas de socialisme aux Etats-Unis?/Why Is There No Socialism in the United States?* Copyright © 1987. Reprinted by permission of Editions De L'Ecole Des Hautes Etudes en Sciences Sociales.

accounting for post-war radicalism have been underestimated. Mirroring this, there has been a tendency to exaggerate the *conservatism* of the American working class by viewing the policies espoused by the American Federation of Labor (AF of L) in the inter-war era as indicative of the outlook of workers, and by anachronistically projecting into the pre–World War I epoch orientations that owed a great deal to later developments.

. . . [T]he AF of L was committed from the very outset to maximizing the interests of skilled workers by controlling access to crafts, as well as to a narrowly construed "business unionism"; . . . its strategy for achieving political influence entailed avoiding permanent partisan affiliations; and . . . it deliberately rejected socialism. But this does not mean that American "blue-collar" workers, in and out of the AF of L, had no awareness of themselves as a class. On the contrary, there are many indications that they perceived themselves as being engaged in a perennial struggle with their employers; the widespread image of "the bosses," which is still prevalent in the language of the American working class, is hardly a benevolent one. True, the relevant collectivity was narrowly defined — mostly skilled, white, and male — but . . . this was by and large the case among European workers as well. American workers were obviously not revolutionary-minded; but if the criterion of a high degree of class awareness be a revolutionary disposition, then one is led to the absurd conclusion that hardly anywhere in the capitalist world of the early 20th century was a genuinely aware working class to be found.

Lack of interest in revolution did not mean lack of militancy; many observers have noted the high incidence of violence in American industrial relations, a phenomenon which stems largely from the ruthlessness of employers, but to which labor has perennially made contributions of its own. Much as in Europe, union membership was rapidly expanding in the pre-war period. Rising from 447,000 in 1879 to 1.1 million in 1901, the level doubled to 2.2 over the next decade and reached 2.7 million in 1914, approximately one-fourth of the industrial labor force — a level comparable to what was found in Germany, which itself had the highest level in Europe.

Moreover, at the time with which we are concerned, the AF of L was by no means the only working-class organization in America, and a considerable range of outlook was found within its own ranks. The Socialist Party of America, a social democratic organization founded at the turn of the century, rapidly gained ground in the ensuing decade and was on the upswing when Sombart visited the United States in 1904. Its influence within the world of organized labor was by no means negligible. In 1902, the Socialist platform was supported by 46 percent of the votes cast at the AF of L convention, a level which indicated the rapid spread of socialism among component unions. In 1912, a Socialist candidate for the AF of L presidency secured a remarkable one-third of the votes against the incumbent, Samuel Gompers. If these votes were in any way representative of the distribution of opinion among the union rank-and-file, then it can be estimated that nearly 10 percent of the industrial labor force — and perhaps as many as one-fourth of skilled manual workers — were in some sense socialist-minded, a level not out of keeping with what was found in Britain or France around this time.

Concurrently, socialism was also making a breakthrough in the political arena, in a manner very similar to what was going on in Britain. The first Socialist representative was elected to the U.S. Congress in 1910; Eugene V. Debs received 6 percent of the popular vote in the 1912 presidential election; and there were scattered victories at the municipal and state levels. The high point of socialist electoral strength was probably reached in 1914, when in addition to the 1,200 incumbent municipal office-holders, 33 Socialist legislators were elected in 14 states.

The geographical distribution of these votes, as well as circulation patterns of Socialist periodicals, suggests strongly that the largest share of them originated among three specific segments of the working class: skilled operatives of mostly German origin located in the industrial cities of Wisconsin and other mid-western states; miners, often of British origin, in isolated and widely scattered western mining communities, where a native American version of militant producer socialism had recently emerged as the Industrial Workers of the World; and Jewish immigrants from Eastern Europe in the garment trades of the New York metropolitan area.

Conspicuously absent, by all accounts, were the Irish Catholics who . . . made up a very large proportion of America's older urban working class. . . . Moreover, contrary to widespread belief among those who feared socialism, and most ominously for anyone aspiring to a socialist future in the United States, this doctrine appeared to hold little or no appeal for the massive waves of immigrants — with the outstanding exception of the Jews already mentioned — who were at that time contributing to the rapid expansion of the country's industrial labor force.

When considered in the context of a recognition that American workers did share a sense of class founded on their role as *labor,* the fact that only a minority of them acted in class terms within the political arena helps to identify the most distinctive feature of the American outcome, i.e., the orientation of workers qua [as] *citizens* overwhelmingly toward the political mainstream.

. . . [T]he critical turning point in this respect occurred in the wake of the great confrontation of 1886, when the launching of a concerted anti-labor crusade fostered among the leadership of established working-class organizations profound divisions as to how to respond. The Knights of Labor, the leading organization at the time, advocated an escalation of the struggle on the economic front beyond the traditionally narrow objectives of trade unionism "pure and simple," coupled with a more thorough mobilization of the working class by expanding the scope of unions to include the unskilled. Their orientation bears a striking similarity to that of the *bourses du travail* (labor exchange) movement in France, with an emphasis on achievement by the working class of control over its own institutions, while de-emphasizing — if not rejecting outright — action in the established political arena. . . . As it was, within a decade of 1886, the Knights were overtaken by the upstart AF of L, whose strategy was much more narrowly trade unionist. The AF of L set out to consolidate its base in the skilled segment of the working class rather than to mobilize more extensively; to secure acceptance by employers as the sole acceptable antagonist; . . . and to maximize its influence in the political arena by exercising pressure on both the two major political parties to promote policies deemed to be in the interest of labor.

The institutionalization of a practice whereby unions function as intermediating organizations between the working class and the state must be viewed not merely as representing a lower degree of protest than the formation of a working-class party, but rather as a genuine alternative to the latter. . . . Sombart emphasized the originality of the AF of L's political strategy, singling out the "quite special system . . . recently put into operation by those representing the workers' interests," whereby unions demanded that candidates put themselves on record with respect to relevant issues by responding to a questionnaire. Known as the "Winnetka System" after the Illinois city where it originated in the 1880s, the practice was officially taken up by the AF of L in 1901 and generalized in 1904. Sombart also reports that whereas the Winnetka system was denounced by Socialists as a "begging policy," anti-socialist trade union leaders "attach a great deal of hope to this system" as a device for "permanently remov[ing] the threat and danger of an independent Socialist workers' party."

. . . Once elaborated into a doctrine and institutionalized as the official policy of the AF of L, unionism "pure and simple" served as the cultural code which programmed the formation of an outlook among newly arriving waves of industrial workers. Just as they learned to speak English, eat American food, dress in American clothes, and play American games, most immigrants quickly learned that to be an American worker was to be a trade unionist and a Democrat or a Republican, but *not* a Socialist.

Evidence that socialism was gaining ground in the first decade of the century in no way contradicts the proposition that the trend represented by the AF of L was already well under way toward becoming dominant. Looking forward from about 1912, one might have anticipated that socialism, in the sense of an organized formation in the political arena committed to structural change, was sufficiently well entrenched in certain localities and regions to function as a substantial minority force at the national level, possibly taking advantage of cyclical downturns and the like to mobilize a growing share of the American working class. As it was, however, much of the Socialists' thunder was stolen from them by the Democrats in the course of Woodrow Wilson's first term. The establishment of the U.S. Department of Labor in 1913 gave American workers a place of their own in Washington, much as had occurred in France; and the appointment of a former United Mine Workers official as the first Secretary further legitimized organized labor as a component of the American regime. Although U.S. workers had long benefited from more extensive freedom of association than most [workers elsewhere], unions hitherto operated under many legal handicaps. This explains why the Clayton Antitrust Act (1914), which freed unions from the constraints of antitrust regulations, was hailed by Samuel Gompers as labor's "Magna Carta." In addition, the Democrats were credited with ratification of the 16th and 17th amendments, pertaining respectively to the income tax and the direct election of senators, reforms which had long been on the agenda of American Socialists as well as of the AF of L. In 1916, the Wilson administration secured enactment of a long-overdue Child Labor law as well as of an 8-hour day on interstate railroads. J[ames] Weinstein, an historian sympathetic to the American socialist tradition, has belittled these reforms on the ground that they "entailed no substantial change in the lives of most workers"; but he admits that "their cumulative impact was sufficient to halt the steady growth which the Socialist Party had enjoyed during the previous four years." Much of the labor vote that had gone to Debs in 1912 went to Wilson four years later. . . .

2. THE DISTINCTIVENESS OF AMERICAN CAPITALISM AND ITS EFFECTS

With a better understanding of what is to be explained, the contributions of economic and political structures will now be explored. . . . Marx and Engels initially set forth in the [*Communist*] *Manifesto* the general proposition that "the development of class antagonism keeps even pace with the development of industry." However, they subsequently qualified their views on the subject in the light of developments in Britain and in the United States. It was quite evident by the latter decades of the century that if the further development of industrial capitalism in Britain fostered an *enlargement* of the working class and its further *proletarianization,* in the sense that an ever-larger share were working in mechanized factories, the process did not lead to an intensification of the class struggle. . . . [T]his was explained in part by the formation of a "labor aristocracy" in consequence of Britain's paramount position in the world economy; by a general rise in the standard of living; and also by a steady extension of political participation, which had resulted toward the end of Marx's life, and well before the death of Engels, in a substantial democratization of British political life. Engels went even further with respect to the United States, and his remarks on why, despite the spectacular development of industrial capitalism, the American working class showed little inclination toward socialism, provided leads which Sombart subsequently followed.

We are thus led back to the problem of "exceptionalism," albeit in a somewhat different guise: the question has now become, Which form of *capitalism* is the norm, and which the deviant? The answer, of course, must be the same as with respect to the outcome of working-class formation. Capitalism became flesh in a variety of forms, and each of these disparate incarnations functioned as a distinctive experimental matrix for the workers it called into life. Given the multifarious character of industrial capitalism, it stands to reason that the working class emerged . . . as an array of disparate groups subjected to different conditions and hence inclined to respond in different ways. . . .

The peculiarities of capitalism as it developed in the United States can be highlighted by locating the country's economy in relation to [several] variables. With respect to timing proper, Britain preceded all the others by about half a century; then, beginning in 1830, France, the United States, and Germany took off in quick succession within ten years of each other. The literature also suggests that the latter two completed their first major thrust toward industrialization . . . in a somewhat shorter time span than either Britain or France. . . .

With respect to the *pace* of economic development, it would make sense to hypothesize that more rapid growth on a per capita basis would have the effect of delivering greater satisfactions to workers, and hence to reduce the incidence of protest. For the twelve leading western countries as a whole, over the period 1870–1913, the average annual rate of growth of output per capita is 1.6 percent; the highest is Sweden, with 2.3 percent, followed by the United States with 2.2; "lows" include the Netherlands and Italy. Although the status of the overall hypothesis remains moot, it was in fact the case, as Sombart and others observed at the time, that in the decades immediately preceding World War I, American capitalism produced a higher level of material welfare in the form of individual goods than most of its European counterparts.

More directly relevant is the recent literature which emphasizes structural differences as an inherent feature of western economic development. Societies we generally label "industrial" or "advanced" in fact vary considerably with respect to their degree of "industrialness" — an awkward term introduced here to distinguish the size of the industrial sector in relation to the total economy. A useful indicator of this is the proportion of active population employed in the secondary [i.e., manufacturing] sector at each of several points in time.

It is not surprising, given Britain's historical lead, that as of about 1850, the range had become very wide: the appropriate proportion was 48.1 percent for Britain, as against 26.9 percent for France, and 17.6 percent for the United States. Looking forward from that point in time, one might have reasonably predicted that the British proportion would continue to grow, and that others would eventually catch up: this was in fact the assumption made by Marx and Engels. But this projection turned out to be wrong on two quite separate counts, both of which are crucial with respect to working-class formation. First, . . . it turned out that the level achieved by Britain at mid-century was already very close to its historical maximum, 51.6 percent in 1911. Second, and most important here, it turned out that the British level was replicated only in Belgium and Germany. Neither in France nor in the United States did the secondary sector work force ever constitute anywhere as high a proportion of the total labor force. In the United States, the proportion rose from 17.6 percent noted for 1850 to 31.6 percent in 1910. Most strikingly, as of the latter date, the percentage of labor force in the *tertiary* [i.e., sales and services] sector had already reached 35.3 percent. To exaggerate only slightly, at the time Sombart raised his question, the United States was well on the way to becoming a white-collar country. . . .

[T]he high productivity of the American industrial labor force went hand in hand with the rapid growth of the labor force employed in the tertiary sector, which included what came to be called "white collar" [jobs]. Expansion of the latter kept pace with that of the secondary throughout the 19th century, pulling ahead of it in the first decade of the 20th, as indicated. This was, at the time, a quite unique situation, as indicated by the fact that in Britain the size of the tertiary-sector labor force lagged significantly behind the secondary until the 1920s, while in Germany it did so still in 1961, the endpoint of the time series being used. In short, American industrial workers constituted less of a critical mass in the United States than they did in Britain or Germany; and there is little doubt that the precocious development of a large segment of white-collar workers also contributed to the formation of a more diffuse sense of class among Americans more generally.

Other capitalist economies relied on migrant labor as well, and two sorts of hypotheses have been set forth concerning the impact of this pattern of labor procurement on working-class formation. One stream is traceable to Marx himself. Britain received substantial numbers of Irish migrants from the mid-18th century onward; and by the time Marx and Engels observed the British scene, something like one-third of the population of the major industrial cities of England and Scotland was Irish. Marx believed that ethnic hatreds compounded the tensions normally engendered by competition among workers, and asserted that the antagonism between English and Irish proletarians was "the secret of the impotence of the English working-class, despite their organization." But this remains an unverified assertion, and the prominent role which the Irish played in the Chartist movement, for example, suggests that Marx may have underestimated the ability of English and Irish workers to surmount their antagonisms. Nevertheless, there is little doubt that the phenomenon of "split labor" does constitute an obstacle to collective action.

In the United States, there are many indications, going all the way back to colonial times, that native workers tended to regard the incoming flow as a process induced by employers to lower wages, which was indeed very much the case; and such resentment played an important part in the rise of "Know-Nothings" and in the concomitant collapse of the second American party system in the early 1850s. . . . Starting in the 1860s, American labor unions strove to secure the enactment of legislation restricting and later altogether prohibiting the immigration of Orientals, considered as particularly unfair competition because of their willingness to work for lower wages and under worse conditions than whites. In addition, they sponsored the Foran Act of 1885, which prohibited the entry of workers under contract — a practice associated with strike-breaking. . . .

The second line of reasoning pertains to the distinctive outlook of migrants and immigrants. The most comprehensive argument to this effect has been presented by G[erald] Rosenblum, who suggests that in addition to their negative role in muting ongoing mobilization, the newcomers contributed positively to the triumph of business unionism, in that as "target workers" who did not intend to stay — even if in the end many of them did — they were oriented exclusively to the workplace. . . .

The ethnic segmentation of the American working class can also be viewed as a feature of economic rather than of social organization. In this light, it can be seen as an indication of the precocious emergence in the United States of a form of capitalism organized around a segmented labor market. . . . Michael Piore has shown how the consolidation movement "laid the groundwork for a dual economic structure. It divided demand in most major industries into two components: a stable component . . . which the newly formed trusts attempted to reserve for themselves, and which was met through modern, capital-intensive production technologies in relatively large-scale productive units, and a fluctuating component, handled by much smaller enterprises, probably in smaller productive units and using more labor-intensive techniques."

[T]his differentiation fostered a [division] . . . between two categories of labor, skilled natives to man the stable component, and unskilled immigrants to man the fluctuating one. . . .

[T]his analysis provides a structural explanation for the formation of "labor aristocracy" segments within working classes . . . Notwithstanding the understandable resistance of capitalists to unions, accommodation was more likely to be reached with a segment of the working class that was structurally distinctive in the manner indicated, and whose leaders explicitly recognized such distinctiveness at the level of doctrine and organization. . . .

The last feature of the American economy to be noted is the availability of cheap land. Engels, and after him Sombart, placed considerable emphasis on the frontier phenomenon as a factor accounting for the exceptionalism of the American working class; concomitantly, they believed that the waning of the frontier would result in a rapid rise of class consciousness. However, given the low incidence of movement by American urban workers into agriculture, more recent analysts have cast doubt on the importance of this factor with respect to working-class formation.

Yet there is another way in which the availability of land in America may have played a determinative role in shaping the outlook and disposition of the country's working class. Given the vast supply of land, the costs of owning real property of any kind, beginning with a family home, have always been much lower in America than in Europe. . . . [T]he widespread incidence of property ownership among the American populace was already noted in the 1830s by Tocqueville, who believed that this contributed significantly to the tempering of democracy. . . . Even in the absence of appropriate data, there can be very little doubt that the incidence of ownership has continued to be much higher among American than European workers, all the way to the present. This undoubtedly goes a long way toward accounting for [Ira] Katznelson's crucial observation concerning the tendency of American workers to differentiate sharply between their role as labor and their role as residents or as citizens more generally.

3. POLITICAL REGIME AS A CONCEPTUAL VARIABLE

The consequences of variation in the character of political structures on the patterning of working-class formation have been the object of considerable attention ever since this process first aroused the interest of analysts. Marx himself, for example, "went so far as to exclude England and the United States from any postulated necessity of violent overthrow of the state precisely because there was no state [independent of the people] . . . to overthrow." . . . However, there is little agreement in the literature on how to conceptualize these variations so as to render systematic cross-national comparisons more manageable.

Three characteristics of the political system seem to be relevant: (1) the "strength" or "weakness" of the state, . . . (i.e., the extent to which the state has emerged as a highly differentiated and relatively autonomous political actor); . . . (2) the degree of political liberalism; (3) the extensiveness of political participation (i.e., democratization).

In short, where the state is "weak," usually in the absence of absolutist experience — as was the case in Britain and the United States — there tends to emerge a sharp separation . . . between the public and private sectors. Particularly when combined with institutional decentralization and diffused political power, as was the case in the United States prior to its imperial age, this would tend to foster narrowly focused working-class organizations and a tendency to confine their action to the appropriate institutional sector.

Ultimately, however, the single most important determinant of variation in the patterns of working-class politics for the period under consideration seems to be whether, at the time this class was being brought into being by the development of capitalism, it faced an absolutist or a liberal state. In the western world before World War I, the relevant range of variation was defined by the United States at the democratic end of the continuum (at least for the white majority) and Imperial Germany at the other, which may be termed "modernizing absolutism." The effects on working-class formation are evident in both cases. In America, where democracy preceded industrialization, mass political parties arose before a working class was formed; competing middle-class political entrepreneurs had a vital interest in securing support from the populace at large, and through their efforts white workers were thoroughly mobilized into the parties. As a consequence, space in the political arena was pre-empted by trans-class organizations; and established actors, with access to resources by way of the institutional apparatus of the state, held a considerable advantage over subsequent challengers, including class-based parties.

The problems generally faced by third parties have long been noted by students of American politics, and were cited prominently by Sombart in 1905. C. T. Husbands . . . views the matter of political constraints as Sombart's strongest argument for why no social democratic party had yet emerged in the United States. . . . [T]he political alignments established after the mid-19th century crisis remained quite stable until the economic crisis of the 1890s. The latter situation provided an opportunity for a radical movement to attract and maintain support; but populism, which was the prime candidate for this, was a mostly agrarian and Protestant movement, unattractive to urban and often Catholic workers. Consequently, when populism captured the Democratic Party in 1896, many urban workers drifted toward the Republican camp, notwithstanding that party's more conservative stand on social issues. Viewed in this perspective, the Socialist Party's forward surge in 1912 was rendered possible only by a temporary disarray of the electoral system owing to a split in the Republican Party. However, the opportunity of capturing a substantial share of the working-class vote was equally apparent to the Wilsonian Democrats and, as indicated earlier, they quickly took appropriate steps to that effect. Husbands suggests further that it is the difference in the configuration of the British and American two-party systems at this particular time, rather than more profound structural differences between the two societies, which accounts for the failure of the [British] Liberals to pull off what the Wilsonian Progressives did, and hence for the nearly contemporaneous electoral breakthrough of the Labour Party.

In contrast with this, at the time of its industrial development, Germany was not yet even a liberal state, let alone a democratic one. Although the Imperial Reichstag [parliament] was elected on the basis of universal suffrage, this institution had little or no control over the executive; Germans, including workers, were subjects of the Emperor rather than citizens; and Prussian suffrage remained unequal. It is hardly surprising, under such conditions, that the nascent working class was highly responsive to Marxist political doctrine, tailor-made for precisely these conditions.

Viewed in the light of regime, both the United States and Imperial Germany are appropriately seen as exceptional cases. Most countries that experienced industrialization before World War I were neither democracies nor absolutist states; much more typically, they were constitutional monarchies with some governmental accountability to representative institutions, and with limited political participation. The two principal variables considered in this section are interdependent in that the earlier and stronger the thrust of capitalism, the more likely was the emergence of political liberalism. Where an industrial bourgeoisie ruled, the middle classes generally followed; and it is a truism that liberal regimes were more likely than others to seek accommodation with the lower classes.

QUESTIONS TO CONSIDER

1. Describe the goals and strategies of the AF of L as it confronted the conditions of American industrialism. In what sense was it a "conservative" union? Why was it more successful than other unions with American workers and employers? How did the AF of L help to create an American "labor aristocracy"? Why did the AF of L lobby existing political parties rather than start one of its own?

2. How, according to Zolberg, did the massive wave of immigrants coming to the United States between the 1880s and World War I affect the fortunes of American socialism? Which immigrant groups were attracted to socialist doctrines, which were not, and why? How might ethnic and language differences have slowed down working-class organizing?

3. According to Zolberg, what distinctive features of the American economy in the late nineteenth and early twentieth centuries prevented a permanent proletariat from forming? Was the United States more or less industrialized than Great Britain? How did the growth of a large segment of white-collar workers decrease American working-class solidarity? How did the American economy develop a stable and loyal "labor aristocracy"? Compare Zolberg's portrait of American industrialization with that of Mansel Blackford in Selection 5.

4. According to the theory of the "split labor market," skilled workers tend to defend their wages and status by organizing to exclude unskilled cheap labor from the job market. How does this theory apply to American labor history?

5. Zolberg says that the most important factor in American labor politics was that workers thought of themselves as citizens. What impact did access to voting have on the American working class? How did the American two-party system create difficulties for a labor party? How did the Democratic Party under Woodrow Wilson steal much of the Socialists' thunder? What evidence suggests that where capitalism and democracy developed simultaneously, nations experienced less class conflict than others?

IV

IMMIGRANTS
AND CITIES

In the half-century from 1870 to 1920, the United States was transformed from an agrarian society into an urban one. The mechanization of agriculture, the creation of a national transportation system, and the growth of industry laid the foundation for big cities; the arrival of millions of immigrants provided much of their population. Although many immigrants came from small farms and villages, increasingly they settled in the city, where they clustered in ethnic neighborhoods and where factories, construction work, and shopkeeping provided jobs. Anxious native-born Americans worried that urbanization and immigration would "Europeanize" American society. What eventually emerged, however, was a blend of native traditions and foreign influences that gave America's urban landscape and its people their distinctive stamp. No one would mistake American cities for Paris, Rome, or Warsaw. And although other New World peoples took in newcomers from abroad, none absorbed immigrants so thoroughly into its national identity as did the United States.

The selections in this chapter analyze the mixing of Old and New World forces that shaped American urban society during its most explosive era. In the first essay, historian Walter Nugent places immigration to the United States in the context of a vast transatlantic movement of European peoples to destinations throughout the New World. The origins, the process, and the pattern of immigration to Argentina, Brazil, and Canada were quite similar to immigration to the United States, Nugent says, although he does find differences that highlight distinctive features of American culture and history. In the second essay, architect and historian Witold Rybczynski uses the history of Chicago to explore how American cities are different from cities in Europe, and how they got that way. By pursuing subjects such as immigration and urbanization beyond national boundaries, Nugent and Rybczynski (who is Canadian) are able to catch insights not available to scholars who restrict their view to America's shores. Their essays also illuminate other comparative forays in this book. Nugent's tracking of immigrants' motives and moves amplifies Aristide Zolberg's analysis of why there was so little socialism in America (Selection 6), while Rybczynski's tale of urban reform describes an influential attempt to improve what Kate Brown (Selection 4) calls the "gridded lives" of American city dwellers.

7

The Great Transatlantic Migrations

WALTER NUGENT

Between 1870 and 1914, the United States, which had always been a nation of immigrants, took in the largest number of newcomers in its history. Over 23 million foreigners arrived, most steaming past the welcoming torch of the Statue of Liberty before fanning out across the continent in search of jobs and relatives or neighbors who had preceded them. The saga of the immigrant is so tied to American mythology that it is easy to forget that the United States was not the only destination of Europe's wandering peoples. Other New World countries could also justly claim to be nations of immigrants. In the century before 1924, five and a half million foreigners went to Argentina and four and a half million to Canada. Both nations were much smaller in population than the United States, so the newcomers' impact was proportionally greater. By 1914, one out of every three persons in Argentina was foreign-born, compared to one of six in the United States at the peak of foreign influence. Brazil, which took in nearly four million Europeans, boasted more Italian immigrants than the United States, at least until 1900.

These numbers suggest, as Walter Nugent points out in his sweeping overview of the great transatlantic migration of 1870–1914, that the flow of migrants to the United States was one facet of a vast movement of European peoples across the ocean. Transatlantic steamships took Spanish workers to Argentinian construction sites, German peasants to homesteads in the Canadian West, and Italian laborers to Brazilian coffee plantations. If we add the simultaneous transpacific migration of Chinese, Japanese, and Indian workers to places as far away as Hawaii, Peru, and California — a movement outside the scope of Nugent's essay — we can sense how steamship travel, the need for an industrial labor force, and the opening of national borders brought an unprecedented mingling of the world's peoples in the Americas.

Europeans came to the New World for many reasons and they scattered to far-flung places, but Nugent's overview allows us to see patterns in the flux. Most immigrants, he says, were not political or religious refugees but job-seekers, and transatlantic migration was simply the extension of an old practice of traveling within Europe in search of economic opportunity. For European workers, a trip to a nearby city or neighboring nation often proved the first step toward a journey across the Atlantic. Villagers migrated in "chains," following relatives or neighbors who had found work. They settled in ethnic enclaves that replicated familiar ways, as far as possible, in an unfamiliar setting. Unlike the Irish famine exodus or the Jewish refugee migration, the wage-labor immigration was predominantly male, and it flowed in two directions. For every three immigrants coming to the Americas, at least one returned, either unable to find satisfactory work or else bringing earnings home to sustain the family or to invest in land or a business. The high rate of return migration among industrial workers may help account for the weakness of socialism not just in the United States, as Aristide Zolberg noted in Selection 6, but in other New World receiver nations, too.

Immigration to the United States shared these features with the movement to other New World nations. What made the United States different, says Nugent, was the sheer volume of immigration into the country and the diversity of its sources. From the early nineteenth century to World War II, the United States received over three-fifths of all the immigrants Europe sent overseas — more people, in other words, than all other nations combined. (Canada, Argentina, and Brazil received 12 percent, 10 percent, and 7 percent, respectively.) The ability to absorb so many foreigners without major social disruptions testified to the availability of land and to the phenomenal growth of the American economy. While Canada drew its settlers mainly from Great Britain and migrants to South America were overwhelmingly Iberian and Italian in origin, immigrants to the United States came from all over Europe. Here was the origin of the American "melting pot," for without one group dominating the immigrant ranks, immigrants were more likely to mix with other groups and with the native-born population, and to contribute to a common American culture. Ethnic variety, in other words, helped in the long run both to speed the assimilation of immigrants and to create a new idea of what it meant to be American.

At the time, however, not all Americans saw it that way. In the four decades after 1880, the United States developed the most vocal and powerful anti-immigrant (or nativist) movement in the New World. The predominantly Anglo-Protestant host society feared that darker-skinned and non-English-speaking Catholic and Jewish immigrants were so culturally different that their absorption into American life was inadvisable and perhaps impossible. The concentration of newcomers in cities and factories made it easy for natives to blame them for strikes, crime, poverty, and other urban-industrial problems. Even when immigrants returned to their homeland, as Nugent points out, Americans criticized them as "birds of passage" who preyed upon the nation's resources without pledging allegiance to its flag. Anti-immigrant agitation led to a harshly restrictive quota law of 1924, which, along with the Great Depression, slowed the flow of European newcomers to a trickle.

In contrast to the confident welcome of the bronze lady above it, the poem inscribed at the Statue of Liberty's base unintentionally captured Americans' ambivalent attitudes toward immigrants, beckoning "the homeless, tempest-tossed" while labeling them "the wretched refuse" of the Old World. As you analyze Nugent's essay, you might consider its implications for today's controversy over immigration. If migration is primarily a response to international labor market opportunities, is the flow to the United States likely to continue or slow down? Do arguments for restricting immigration echo the ethnic prejudices and unjustified fears of a century ago, or are they realistic and fair social policy?

GLOSSARY

ASSIMILABLE   Possessing qualities enabling absorption into the dominant or mainstream culture.

CHAIN MIGRATION (OR SERIAL MIGRATION)   The pattern by which migrants follow relatives, friends, or neighbors to the same destination, often creating an ethnic enclave in the new country similar to the village or region they left behind.

DOMINION LANDS POLICY   Plans adopted by the Canadian government to promote western settlement. Their most important feature, the Dominion Lands Act of 1872, was similar to the U.S. Homestead Act of a decade earlier. It granted free homesteads of 160 acres to families who would live on and improve them for at least three years.

ELLIS ISLAND   The main U.S. immigration depot, opened in New York's harbor in 1892, where immigrants were screened for fitness and compliance with immigration laws before being allowed to stay. Over twenty million immigrants passed through Ellis Island before it closed in 1943.

EMIGRATION   Migration out of a country, as opposed to immigration, migration into a country.

ENDOGAMOUS   Marrying someone from the same racial or ethnic group.

FAZENDEIROS   Brazilian owners of large estates, or *fazendas,* who forced many small farmers to become agricultural wage laborers. Conditions in such Latin American *latifundia* (the general term for large estates worked by landless laborers) were harsh, but many immigrants got their start with labor contracts there.

GUEST WORKER   Immigrant workers in late twentieth-century Germany and other western European nations who were not eligible for permanent residence or citizenship.

JIM CROW   The practice of legally segregating or discriminating against blacks, especially as it existed in the American South in the late nineteenth and the first half of the twentieth centuries. The term derived from the name of a song in a nineteenth-century minstrel show.

JOHNSON-REED ACT (1924)   Also known as the National Origins Act, a law that culminated the immigration restriction campaigns of the World War I era. The act set restrictive quotas for European immigrants, based on their country of origin, which discriminated harshly against the "new" immigrants from southern and eastern Europe. A separate law passed the same year declared immigrants from Asia inadmissible because they were aliens ineligible for U.S. citizenship.

NATIVIST   Expressing or reflecting hostility to immigrants.

POGROMS   Violent government-condoned attacks in Russia against Jews. They took place between 1881, when Jews were widely blamed for Czar Alexander II's assassination, and the Russian Revolution of 1917. Backed by official anti-Semitism, the pogroms spurred massive Jewish emigration.

SERFDOM   A system of servitude under which peasants called serfs were required to render services to a lord, were commonly attached to the lord's land, and were transferred with it from one owner to another. Common in Europe in the Middle Ages, serfdom lingered into the modern era. Serfs in the Austrian empire were freed in 1781, and Russian serfs were emancipated in 1861.

The forty-five years between 1870 and the outbreak of World War I were the preeminent age of international, especially transatlantic migration. During that period a unique set of factors operated to promote migration: steam-powered transportation, an absence (compared with periods before and since) of legal and political restraints, potential agricultural development on several New World frontiers, and industrialization, hence a demand for non-farm workers both in Europe and in North America — all of which helped extend long-standing European migration patterns to transatlantic distances. Migration had taken place before 1870 within Europe and from Europe to other parts of the world but, thanks to railroads and steamships, the scale of the post-1870 period expanded into something altogether larger. Migration continued after 1914, but it became much reduced because of World War I, the restrictive laws passed by several countries in the 1920s, and the economic depression of the 1930s. Between 1870 and 1914, tens of millions of Europeans and others crossed and recrossed international borders and sailed the North and South Atlantic, often many times. The cumulative picture of movement is one of a swarming or churning of people back and forth across the Atlantic highway, fed by growing railroad networks on either side of it. . . .

PATTERNS OF TRANSATLANTIC MIGRATION

Migration of people encompasses many kinds of geographical relocations. For centuries, and especially in the "swarming" of 1870–1914, Europeans and Americans traveled for various timespans (a harvest season or construction job, a year or two, or a lifetime), over various distances (the neighborhood, the home province, within their country, across national boundaries but within Europe, or across the oceans), and for various reasons (new land, new jobs, new freedoms, and so on). . . . In the histories of all three continents — Europe, North and South America — migration has been a central and crucial constant. For the United States specifically this has certainly been true. Frank Thistlethwaite once wrote that migration can be seen as the "central theme for a history of the American people . . . more lasting, because more profound, than [the frontier theme] of Frederick Jackson Turner; for settlers were emigrants before they

From Walter Nugent, *Crossings: The Great Transatlantic Migrations: 1870–1914* (Indiana University Press). Reprinted by permission of Indiana University Press.

settled and migration has more than the wilderness to do with American character and institutions." Focusing on migration rather than on the frontier would also place the American experience within the broader transatlantic context rather than isolate it as something unique.

Intra-European migration itself is complex, extending from the distant past to the "guest worker" phenomenon of the late twentieth century. In the 1870–1914 period, migration within Europe — whether inside a country (Britons, French, Germans, Italians, and others did a great deal of this) or from one country to another — was in fact greater than transatlantic migration and included one or two million people every year. . . . Moves took place from one rural community to another, or to nearby cities. Kinship relations — a person's place within a family, and how it changed — influenced decisions on when and where to migrate, almost as much as did economics; indeed kinship and economics cannot really be separated. The young and unmarried, both men and women, were especially likely to migrate. So much back-and-forth movement took place, both within Europe and across the Atlantic, that the terms "immigration" and "emigration" are cumbersome; historians find themselves better off with simple "migration." . . .

Transatlantic migration . . . to the Americas in the eighteenth century was . . . somewhere in the hundreds of thousands. But after 1815 the trickle became, to use the inevitable metaphor, a flood, well up in the tens of millions. The time was ripe.

> In the simplest terms, if migration is to take place there must be people who want and are able to leave where they are; countries which they wish and are permitted to enter; and an acceptable means for conveying them. The later nineteenth century not only provided the third of these more amply than any preceding period; it also met the first and second conditions more fully than any preceding period, and the second probably more than any subsequent period.

Serfdom and other institutions hostile to migration had ended, while institutions helpful to migration and to economic development such as free labor, secure private property, and sources of credit had arisen. In that framework, mass migration began and grew.

The total number of migrants will never be known precisely. Three recent, competent estimates put the total migrations of Europeans outside of Europe at 55 million, 1846–1924, of which perhaps 25 percent returned (hence net about 41 million), . . . of whom nearly 60 percent went to the United States. Another estimate restricted to 1871–1915 is 35.4 million. By 1930, perhaps 20 million European-born people were living elsewhere, and of those about 12 million were in the United States, roughly 2 million more in Canada, with 5 million in Argentina, Brazil, and elsewhere in Latin America. About one million lived in Australia, New Zealand, and South Africa, while well under a million lived in other European colonies and in Asia.

The United States received more than the rest of the New World, and probably the entire world, combined (see Table 1). Its absorptive capacity was thus exceptional in sheer numbers. But this was a function of size. In proportion to their populations, several other countries (Argentina, Canada, Australia, and New Zealand) took in more; and Canada, for a time in the late nineteenth century, gave more than it received. . . .

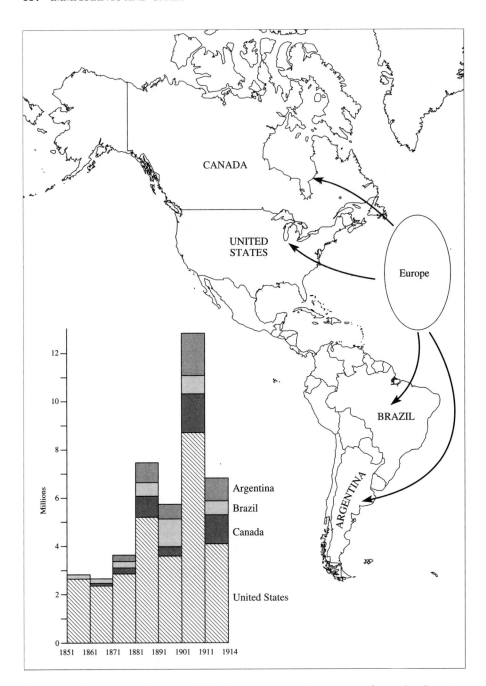

The Atlantic Region and Its Migrations, 1851–1914.   Arrows indicate migration from and to the various donor and receiver countries. The bar graph at bottom left indicates the share of immigrants absorbed by the four major receivers, by decade, 1851–1914. The bar graph at bottom right indicates the share of out-migrants who left the major European countries, 1871–1914.

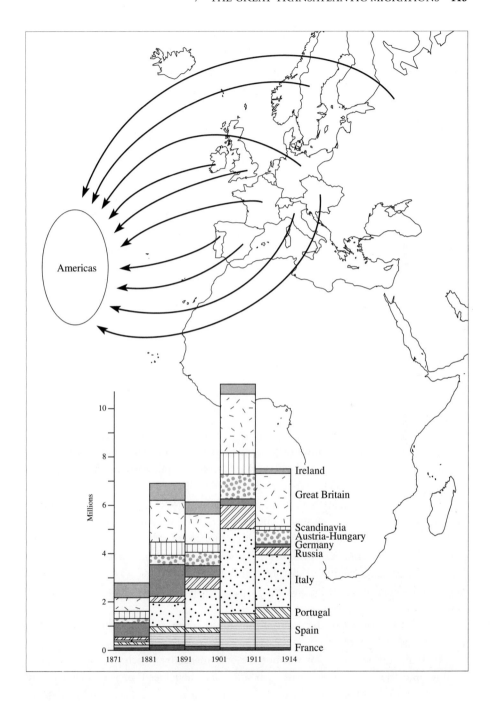

TABLE 1 Major Receivers and Donors of Migrants

Countries Receiving Over 500,000 Immigrants, 1820–1924		
United States	1821–1924	33,188,000
Argentina	1857–1924	5,486,000
Canada	1821–1924	4,520,000
Brazil	1821–1924	3,855,000
British West Indies	1836–1924	1,470,000
Cuba	1901–1924	766,000
Countries Sending Over 1,000,000 Emigrants, 1846–1924		
United Kingdom		16,974,000
Italy		9,474,000
Austria–Hungary		4,878,000
Germany		4,533,000
Spain		4,314,000
Russia		2,253,000
Portugal		1,633,000
Sweden		1,145,000

From Imre Ferenczi, "Migrations, Modern," from *Encyclopaedia of the Social Sciences,* by Edwin R. A. Seligman, Editor in Chief. Vol. X, p. 436. Copyright © 1935 by Macmillan Publishing Company. Reprinted by permission of The Gale Group.

No one doubts that the flow of migrants out of Europe accelerated in the nineteenth century, beginning in the 1840s and 1850s, then leaped forward after 1870 when steamships almost completely replaced sailing ships. Early in the century, the voyage from the British Isles to North America took four to six weeks, plenty of time for contagious diseases to ravage passengers and crew. Up to and including the Irish Famine emigration of the 1840s, deaths from typhus, cholera, or other contagions frequently swept away 10 percent, and occasionally 25 percent, of the passengers during a crossing. In the 1850s mortality fell sharply, thanks to voluntary and government-imposed health and sanitary regulations and faster ships, which began to combine steam power and sails.

. . . [B]y 1863, with half the traffic already under steam, the death rate was a fraction of 1 percent. . . .

The shift from sail to steam was not the only means by which marine technology sped up migration. The size of passenger ships, and their speed, increased almost continuously throughout the period to 1914. The two major German companies, the Hamburg-Amerika line ("HAPAG," out of Hamburg) and the Norddeutsche Lloyd (out of Bremen) began biweekly sailings to New York, often with stops at Southampton, in 1858; the schedule went to weekly sailings about ten years later. During the 1870s and 1880s the German passenger ships as well as those of the British White Star and Cunard lines and the French Fabre and Compagnie Générale Transatlantique were mostly in the 2,500 to 5,000 ton range, roughly 375 feet by 40 feet in size, and normally carried several hundred passengers although as many as 1,500 were occasionally packed into them. Technical improvements in the stroke and bore of propellers and the efficiency of engines brought migrants westward ever faster. . . . By 1873, seventeen companies were operating 173 steamships totaling over 500,000 tons between New York and Europe. . . .

Port cities on both sides of the Atlantic responded to the increase in traffic with sanitary regulations, quarantine facilities, and reception centers. New York's Castle Garden and Ellis Island had counterparts elsewhere. Hamburg's emigrant district of Veddel included boarding houses and hostels to lodge and feed migrants between their arrival by train and their departure by ship. The port also contained indigent aid societies, infirmaries, and a riot of ticket agents, porters, inspectors, innkeepers, expediters, and other service workers (and confidence men). . . .

Emigrants, who increasingly heard from relatives and former neighbors living in the New World of opportunities there, accordingly availed themselves ever more often of the expanding railway networks to reach the seaports. Those from the Austro-Hungarian Empire nearly always departed from Hamburg or Bremen; those from Russia went through Hamburg; and Germans themselves left from either of those ports or from a Dutch or French port. Swedes and Danes appear frequently on the Hamburg passenger lists. People leaving Italy embarked from Naples, Genoa, Trieste, or Marseilles; those from the Balkans, Trieste usually; and many from the Ukraine and the Russian Pale after 1900 used Odessa. By 1900 most emigrants had several options as to ports of embarkation, passenger lines, prices and accommodations, and of course destinations. . . .

Migrants sought better opportunities. As time went on those still in Europe very often learned of opportunities from family members or people from the same village who were already in the Americas. Chain or "serial" migration was common and natural. Changes in legal status sometimes provoked migration; examples are the withdrawal in the early 1870s of German-Russian Mennonites' exemption from czarist military conscription, and the pogroms against Jews in the Russian Pale and Congress Poland after Czar Alexander II was assassinated in 1881. Few members of those groups ever repatriated. Such cases aside, the pervasive motive for migration was economic improvement rather than religion, politics, or persecution.

For some, opportunity lay in farmland, anywhere from northern Argentina to northwestern Canada. In North America, railroad companies whose governments had given them public domain land to help pay for (and provide users for) their lines actively recruited European migrants from the 1870s to the 1920s, bringing Volga Germans to Kansas in the 1870s and Ukrainians to Alberta in the 1920s. From the early 1870s to 1888, when drought and depression struck, homestead and railroad land on the Great Plains was an attractive option for many Germans, Scandinavians, Bohemians, and other Europeans. When agriculture recovered about 1900, North and East Europeans again started new farms on the High Plains, both in the United States (the Dakotas, Montana) and Canada. From about 1887 onward, most migrants to the United States sought non-farming jobs. But Argentina and Brazil drew many Italians, Spaniards, and Portuguese to agriculture from the 1880s onward, and after 1900 Canadian prairie farmland attracted settlers from Britain and from eastern Europe.

For others, opportunity lay in factory, mining, or construction jobs; for a few, it meant employment in skilled trades or services. As a general rule, if farmland was the target, migrants were likely to stay in the New World. But if the target was labor for wages, migrants might well return to Europe or try another country, for their original aim was not settlement in the New World but improvement of life at home. Since the farm frontier in the United States was an unattractive option from about 1888 to 1900, Europeans instead looked toward cities or, in the West, mines (especially gold or copper mines) for opportunities. And their transiency increased. The Atlantic, with steamships making the crossing much less dangerously than sailing vessels, became a two-way street. After 1880 migration to the United States started changing not only according to national origins, as more South and East Europeans arrived, but more importantly it changed according to purpose: from settlement on farmland to wage labor in industry, construction, or mining. . . .

Continuity is a crucial point here: continuity in the practice of migration as a means of self-improvement and as a search for opportunity. The improvement might exist in a New World country, or it might exist at home — in fact it more likely existed at home for most Europeans. This was especially true after farm settlement made truly cheap land unavailable (though the saturation point was not reached until the 1920s in Canada). Much of the transatlantic migration was simply an extension of a long-established pattern of labor migration within Europe, even within countries or districts. Land-seeking migration, implying permanent resettlement, may well have been exceptional in the long history of transatlantic movements, even though it occurred in all four New World receiving societies. . . .

Repatriation — returning home after a season, a year, or a few years — was also a long-established pattern for many Europeans. The size of return flows is unclear because of poor or missing statistics, but it was large. Argentina's official statistics for 1857–1914 indicate that the number leaving was 43.3 percent of the number arriving. For Brazil between 1899 and 1912, the proportion may have been about 66 percent. For the United States (where departure figures were kept only after 1908) from 1908 through 1914, the proportion was 52.5 percent. For Canada, it was undoubtedly much higher. "An educated guess," [J. D.] Gould writes, "would be that for the period 1821–1915 . . . an overall return rate of 30 percent [is probably low], and a rate of 40 percent is quite conceivable. . . . Further, repatriation *rates* on the whole tended to increase through time."

Within Europe, many groups were familiar with seasonal migration. North Italians through much of the nineteenth century migrated to nearby countries in the spring and returned home in the fall, with Piedmontese going to France, Lombards to Switzerland, Venetians to Austria. Indeed, more Italians migrated annually within Europe than to America until very late in the century. Saxons migrated to the lower Rhineland in early and middle century to supplement declining earnings in their cottage textile industry at home. Poles, especially women and children, migrated seasonally to the sugar beet fields of eastern Germany well into the 1880s. And Irish sought work in England, Spaniards in North Africa, Portuguese in France.

. . . [I]ntra-European migration continues today, as anyone can see in European railway stations at certain times of the year, or in Berlin's Little Turkey, or in the service sectors of Germany, France, and Switzerland with their many Yugoslavs, Portuguese, or Catalans. Migration for economic advantage has been a constant feature of European history for millennia, back to Roman or even Celtic times.

. . . The new technology of travel simply extended the possibilities very greatly. The traditional, vast, labor-seeking migration quickly became transatlantic, much larger and much more transient than the transatlantic migrations of the sixteenth through the mid-nineteenth centuries. . . .

IMMIGRATION TO THE U.S.
IN COMPARATIVE PERSPECTIVE

The most immediately striking feature of the migration to the United States is its great size, more than six times the number who went to the second-place receiver, Argentina. But the United States throughout the period was much the largest receiving society to begin with, and the rate of migration into it was lower than Argentina's, even in the peak decade (for rate, not numbers) of the 1880s and the near-peak decade of 1900–1910. [T]he proportion of foreign-born in the Argentine population, at its height (1914), was more than double the American proportion at its height (1910).

Second, migration to the United States came from more places than did migration to Argentina, Brazil, or Canada. Except for the Spanish and Portuguese, very few of whom ventured north of the Caribbean, every group migrating from Europe arrived in some numbers in the United States. Before the creation of the railroad and steamship networks, migrants to the United States came chiefly from the British Isles, Germany, and Scandinavia. Russian-Germans, Czechs, Swiss, and a few other Central Europeans began arriving in the 1870s, most of them in that industrially depressed decade in search of western land. East Europeans, Italians, and various Balkan peoples enriched the mix in the 1880s and 1890s. While Argentina and Brazil took in Mediterraneans for the most part plus small contingents of Germans, Poles, and others, and while Canada (before 1900) took in British and Irish almost exclusively, the United States received everyone. Even Iberia was represented, though in nothing like the numbers farther south; Basques herded sheep in California, Idaho, and Nevada; Cubans of Spanish background, alongside Italians, rolled cigars in Tampa; Portuguese ran fishing boats out of southeastern New England. Eighty-five to 95 percent of the migrant Irish, Germans, and Scandinavians; a smaller majority of Central and East Europeans; a majority of British before 1900 (but not after, when most went to Canada); roughly half the Italians; and a small number of Spanish and Portuguese, came to the United States.

[T]he United States [also] differed from the other New World receivers . . . [in] its possession throughout the period of a large area of cheap, accessible land governed by land laws that encouraged smallholding. Brazil had plenty of land but few ways, legally or logistically, for people to occupy it. The United States had no widespread equivalent of Argentine livestock barons or Paulista *fazendeiros,* who retained title to great acreages and forced small agrarians into various forms of tenancy, as in Argentina, or what amounted to wage labor, as in Brazil.

By 1890, many smallholders in the United States were complaining bitterly about their mortgages, cash shortages, and freight charges. These, however, were problems not of a "traditional" peasantry but of a society with complex market relations. Fewer than half of the gainfully employed Americans were working on farms by 1890, and the economic and demographic future lay, for the most part, in cities and with labor seekers migrating to cities. . . .

Earlier American history had been distinguished by frontier-rural development, which aside from Ontario's had been unique in the transatlantic region. When land was no longer available and the frontier-rural process ceased, so did the United States' chief claim to exceptionalism from a demographic standpoint. Even so, it was not unique. The Canadian West, after 1900 and until 1930, when the Dominion Lands Policy ended, proved to be a frontier of farm settlement much like the already closed American frontier, and for similar reasons: a consistent land survey and policy, railroads, and political order. . . .

Although land seekers outnumbered seekers of wage-earning jobs before 1880 and wage seekers predominated after 1900, the shift was by no means complete or even that dramatic. The United States received both types. By 1914, however, it had become the principal New World receiver of urban-industrial, labor-seeking migrants. Many of the Irish, German, and Scandinavian "older," pre-1890 immigrants came and stayed as non-farm workers, swelling the small and middle-sized cities as well as the metropolises. Germans were always prominent in such cities as Syracuse, Rochester, Cincinnati, and Chicago; Irish were visible and mobile not only in Boston and New York but also on Great Plains farms, mining towns such as Butte, and all over the West.

In 1900, 72 percent of German-stock employed males worked outside agriculture, as did about 84 percent of the Irish-stock. The Irish-Americans by then "had attained relative occupational parity with native white America," their upward mobility aided by the many post-Famine Irish women who were filling a range of white-collar jobs. Jews and Italians contributed to San Francisco's distinct flavor; Scandinavians did the same in Chicago, Minneapolis and St. Paul, Seattle, and Tacoma. The "new" immigrants arriving after 1900 located, it is true, in industrial-urban settings: Hungarians in South Bend, Croatians around the refineries of Whiting, Indiana, Poles in the climatically Polish-like belt from Buffalo to Milwaukee, Italians in distinctly un-Italian-like western Massachusetts and northern New York, and so on. These examples are almost stereotypes. . . .

[As noted above,] . . . serial and chain migration played a huge role in directing specific people to specific places. Although the reasons why the first from somewhere in Europe went to a specific place in the United States are usually obscure, once the migrants were located and employed, the flow of information soon after brought brothers, fiancees, and townsmen. Young men from East Europe arrived at Castle Garden or (after 1892) Ellis Island, followed directions inland, met their relatives or friends at boarding houses, were introduced to shop foremen or others in a position to hire, and went to work. . . . Certain parishes in Pittsburgh, studied by June Alexander, received Slovaks from a band of neighboring villages; and "when firms desperately needed labor, foremen promised jobs to [Slovak] employees' friends or relatives if they would send for them." When these Slovaks became foremen they hired other Slovaks whom they knew or were related to.

Relationships continued outside the workplace. Endogamous in the old country, Slovaks into the second generation in the United States very often married people from the same village or nearby. Jews from Lithuania, the Russian Pale, or Polish Galicia created synagogues whose congregations came from the same areas and founded "a remarkable network of societies called *landsmanshaftn*," expressing "fierce affections for the little places they had lived in, the muddy streets, battered synagogues, remembered fields from which they had fled." Italians were scarcely less renowned for their *campanilismo*, literally their loyalty to the area within the sound of their own church bells, rather than to the recently united abstraction called Italy.

Another point that needs no belaboring is that the economic attractions of the United States were real. Success eluded many, native as well as foreign, but an agricultural ladder did exist, at least in the Midwest and West through World War I. Railroads still had land to sell, and the government had homesteads to give. For the many who lacked the cash and credit to begin as owner-operators, the first rung of the ladder could be tenancy or wage-labor, with the reasonable expectation that, unlike in Europe, one could reach the top of the ladder eventually.

Wages in factories, on railroads, in construction, or in mines surpassed European levels while the cost of living was the same or lower. Wages in Chicago in skilled trades were two to four times higher than in European cities as of 1885; examples could be multiplied. Italians built railroads and other public works all over the Northeast, Midwest, and West. Poles, Slovaks, and other Slavs populated steel mills and coal mines. Jews virtually created the mass-consumption garment industry. Irish men staffed police and fire departments and the post office while Irish women became domestics, then increasingly clerks, office workers, and school teachers. . . .

European migrants, and soon their offspring as well, appeared in every part of the United States where land or labor was available. That meant everywhere except the South, although pockets of immigration existed there too. Within the South as defined by the census, the area stretching from Texas northeastward around the Gulf and Atlantic coasts to Maryland, small groups of Chinese lived in Georgia, Italians in Florida and Louisiana, Irish in New Orleans. In Texas, larger groups of Germans and Poles had been settling farmland since the 1850s, but their migration had more in common with land seeking in the prairies and plains of the Midwest than with typically southern patterns.

A number of southern states tried to attract foreign-born migrants but without much success. The obvious reason was the presence already of a labor force of several million black people who could fill, or were compelled to fill, such industrial and service jobs as there were, and who if on the land were usually relegated to sharecropping or tenancy. Slavery as it existed in Brazil and slavery in the South of the United States have been compared, but comparative histories of the former slaves and their descendants in the two countries *after* emancipation have yet to be done. Such studies might explain why Brazilian ex-slaves disappeared into cities or into the interior, whereas American ex-slaves usually remained on the land, though often not on the plantation where they had been enslaved; and why the Brazilian coffee planters successfully (at least between the late 1880s and 1902) recruited thousands of Italian families to work for them, whereas American cotton planters did not. The lives of black people in the American South in the era of increasingly tight Jim Crowism was most unenviable, but the lives of Brazilian ex-slaves, supplanted by Italian-born *colonos,* was probably worse.

In any event, Europeans kept to the North and the West. They also kept southern black people from migrating north. As Brinley Thomas has pointed out, blacks did not migrate from the rural South to the urban North and Midwest until European mass migration stopped because of World War I, and more definitively by the restriction laws of 1921 and 1924. Only then did the historic "great exodus" of blacks begin. The Northeast, Midwest, and West, in the meantime, attracted European migrants, shutting out the South almost entirely.

Scholars are only beginning to study the history of women migrants. The assumptions have been that in the "older," presumably family-dominated migration before 1880, in which the sex ratio was nearly balanced, women were present as wives and mothers in nuclear families. In the "newer," reputedly individual wage-seeking migration, women were a smaller minority, as the male-skewed sex ratios indicate. . . .

[Donna] Gabaccia, who analyzes women migrants across the whole range of ethnic groups, has shown that sex ratios vary by group and over time. Of all migrants throughout the 1871–1914 period, the majority were male; after 1916 and to the present, the majority have been female. In the 1870s and in 1900 Irish women outnumbered men, and came close at other times. From that level the proportion of males among the migrants and among the foreign-born who persisted in the American population ranged upward to roughly the 55 to 60 percent level among East European Jews, Scandinavians, Germans, and British; to the 65 to 70 percent level among Poles, Magyars, Slovaks, Lithuanians, and other nationalities from the Russian and Austro-Hungarian empires; to above 70 percent among Italians; and finally to almost 90 percent among Greeks, Serbs, and certain other peoples from the Balkans.

Many were indeed wives and mothers. Thousands of them, however, served also as family wage earners — as laundresses, part-time domestics, dressmakers, keepers of boarders or, more elaborately, operators of boarding houses. Outside the home, domestic service occupied migrant women more than any other kind of job throughout the period, as it did native-born women as well. The needle trades collectively employed the next largest group; clerical work, office jobs, retailing, and teaching provided increasing opportunities as those positions gradually expanded within the American occupational structure from the 1880s onward. As the female segment of the gainfully employed rose from 14.7 percent in 1870 to 21.2 percent in 1910, immigrant women shared in and contributed to the rise. . . .

Women returned to Europe less frequently than men did; which . . . allowed immigrant groups in the New World a much more closely balanced sex ratio, thus considerably more marital endogamy than the three-to-one male preponderance among Italian migrants, for example, would suggest. . . .

Return and repeat migration deserves some attention, not only for its intrinsic aspects but also because of the hostile native American reaction to "birds of passage." Attempts to count return and repeat migrants confront a statistical morass even deeper than usual. One can safely say that a strong eastbound flow did take place, perhaps a third to half as large as the westbound flow. The rate varied over time and among national groups. As noted earlier, English, Italians, and several Slavic migrants went back frequently (and many made several visits). Returning and repeating were obviously more attractive after steamships replaced sailing vessels and as steamships became larger, faster, and safer. Also, as labor seekers gradually began outnumbering land seekers after 1880, the return and repeat flows increased. . . .

Impressionistic and anecdotal evidence abounds regarding return migration. French- and Anglo-Canadians, someone noted in the 1880s, "come in the spring, and just as soon as the woodcock takes his flight, they take theirs backward." Umberto Coletti, executive secretary for the Society for Italian Immigrants in New York, dated heavy return migration from 1903. "The Italians started sailing back to their native land in surprising numbers, which increased until the climax of the re-patriation was reached in 1907." Coletti claimed that 38 percent of

> the Italian laborers, after they have worked for a while in this country, return to Italy, where, with their savings, averaging three to four hundred dollars per capita, they look forward to a comfortable future, trading and farming, keeping alive in their mountain villages of Abruzzi, Calabria and Sicily some of the American spirit they acquired in this country. Yet a large majority of the re-patriated sooner or later return to America.

Coletti may have exaggerated, but the return and the repeat migration were common phenomena. Migrants' letters as well as modern scholarship almost universally attest to it.

The "bird of passage" was gravely unsettling to makers of opinion and policy in the United States. Wage-seeking migrant labor had a long history in Europe and, in truth, was hardly unknown in the United States. But the form that it began to take in the 1880s, and very visibly took after 1900 — a Mediterranean or East European young man coming for a season, or for a couple of years, saving or sending money to a home he intended to maintain and improve (and very possibly to a family who needed it) — clashed with certain cherished American notions.

Racist ideas about Anglo-Saxon, Aryan, and Teutonic superiority over Slavic and Mediterranean peoples infected the thinking of many native white Americans, some of whom (business leaders and editorialists) feared that migrants would import anticapitalist ideas and conspiracies. Many, though not all, labor leaders shared doubts about the ability of "new" immigrants to assimilate. Richmond Mayo-Smith, a Columbia University professor who became a leading restrictionist, feared that Hungarians, Bohemians, and probably Italians were "of such a character as to endanger our civilization." Francis Amasa Walker, pioneer statistician and director of the census, pleaded in 1896 for a restriction law, since 40 percent of migrants by then were arriving from East and South Europe. "They are beaten men from beaten races," wrote Walker. "They have none of the ideas and aptitudes which fit men to take up readily and easily the problem of self-care and self-government, such as belong to those who are descended from the tribes that met under the oak trees of old Germany to make laws and choose chieftains." One of the reasons Walker gave for his view was "the complete exhaustion of the free public lands of the United States" — which was an utter misstatement of fact, as were his . . . notions about the origin of democracy in German forests. Yet Mayo-Smith and Walker were highly respected authorities, writing in the most respectable of journals.

Biological and cultural racism appear in the 1907 book of John R. Commons, the progressive labor historian and economist at the University of Wisconsin, who distinguished between the "old" and the "new" immigration in a long series of false dichotomies:

> A line drawn across the continent of Europe from northeast to southwest, separating the Scandinavian Peninsula, the British Isles, Germany, and France from Russia, Austria-Hungary, Italy, and Turkey, separates countries not only of distinct races but also of distinct civilizations. It separates Protestant Europe from Catholic Europe; it separates countries of representative institutions and popular government from absolute monarchies; it separates lands where education is universal from lands where illiteracy predominates; it separates manufacturing countries, progressive agriculture, and skilled labor from primitive hand industries, backward agriculture, and unskilled labor; it separates an educated, thrifty peasantry from a peasantry scarcely a single generation removed from serfdom; it separates Teutonic races from Latin, Slav, Semitic, and Mongolian races.

. . . The birds of passage inflamed opinion in a special way. America was believed to be the haven for Europe's oppressed; immigrants were expected to stay once they arrived. To leave again implied that the migrant came only for money; was too crass to appreciate America as a noble experiment in democracy; and spurned American good will and helping hands. "After 1907," as one historian states, "there was tremendous hostility . . . toward temporary or return migrants. . . . The inference frequently drawn was that [they] considered the United States good enough to plunder but not to adopt. The result was a high degree of antipathy." . . .

The official report of the United States Immigration Commission in 1911 (often called the Dillingham Report after Senator William P. Dillingham of Vermont, who chaired it) stressed that in "the matter of stability or permanence of residence in the United States there is a very wide difference between European immigrants of the old and new classes." The "new" immigrants were to be discouraged from coming, because of their transiency as well as because of their national origins. The commission's position was publicized further in the contemporaneous book by Jeremiah Jenks and Jett Lauck, of the commission's staff, in which transient migrant workers became the number-one target for restriction. The Dillingham Report included a table giving numbers of immigrants admitted in 1907 and numbers who departed in 1908, by nationality, and with some exceptions the old-new distinction did appear (see Table 2).

Among respected academic and social-science authorities on immigration, Peter Roberts was one of the few who argued that the "birds of passage" actually "have not left us poorer, but rather richer." He pointed out that the "Hudson Tunnel is an asset to New York City, [for example]; it is an invaluable agency in the production of wealth; and the Italians who dug it, if all of them had returned to Italy with their savings, would have enriched us by their toil." An economic historian's recent assessment agrees for different reasons. With lowered immigration, the labor force would have been smaller and thus production slower; and land would not have been put to the plow as quickly. Finally, "with fewer savers, capital accumulation would have been less," and overall output would not have been as rapid. . . .

TABLE 2 Return Migrants of 1908 as Percentage of Incoming Migrants of 1907 (Larger Groups Only)

South Italians	61.0
Croatians and Slovenians	59.8
Slovaks	56.1
Hungarians	48.7
North Italians	37.8
Poles	33.9
Finns	23.3
Serbs and Bulgarians	21.9
Germans	15.5
Scandinavians	10.9
English	10.4
Czechs	7.8
Irish	6.3
"Hebrews"	5.1

"Abstracts of Reports of the Immigration Commission," U.S. Senate Document 747, 61st Congress, 3d Session (Washington: Government Printing Office, 1911), I:180, table 14.

More resonant, however, was the "scornful denunciation" of migrants for accumulating American money "for the subsequent consumption of 'porridge, bloaters, maccaroni [*sic*] and sauerkraut' on the other side of the Atlantic." The newer immigrants, therefore, faced hostility on several counts: their habit of return migration, traditional across Europe but regarded as exotically subversive by American authoritative opinion; their search for wage work rather than farm land — indeed the fact that they kept coming despite what was (falsely) believed to be the exhaustion of free land after 1890; their presence as individual young men rather than as families; their suspected anarchism and socialism; and at root, their very nationality, called "race" or "germ plasm," which supposedly made them unassimilable. American opinion regarded the United States as the exception among nations, the antithesis of Europe, yet the worst of Europe seemed to be pouring through the gates. Another nativist bogey was "race suicide," the notion that the native stock would ultimately vanish because of the immigrant's higher fertility. In truth, "the fears of contemporary observers were misplaced," because the fertility of immigrants as well as their children was well below that of the native-born. But "race suicide" added to the nativist chorus. After repeated efforts by restrictionists, a bill excluding migrants who failed a literacy test became law over President Woodrow Wilson's veto in 1917. Following World War I, Congress passed the Johnson Act of 1921 and the Johnson-Reed Act of 1924, which restricted immigration on the more candid and thorough ground of national-origins quotas.

For Europeans, return and repeat migration was normal and traditional. For the increasingly nativist "thinking people" in the United States, fearfully watching their frontier close, it was an added burden, even insult, to the problematic arrival of millions of Europeans. . . . In truth, however, the historical experience of the American frontier was not normal. In the longer European context, it was peculiar and aberrant, an immense but temporary resource to be exploited, even though it took Anglo-America about three hundred years to occupy and conquer that resource. The agrarian frontier was a historical peculiarity, but the American opponents of immigration saw it as normal. Hence they were unprepared to understand the labor-seeking migrants, many of them birds of passage, who arrived in huge numbers during the 1870–1914 period.

In 1914 the World War put a temporary stop to transatlantic migration, and although it resumed for a few years after the Armistice, the 1920s restriction laws and the 1930s Great Depression ended it permanently. In those circumstances, transient labor-seeking migration in and out of the United States — the transatlantic mass migration — did not continue after 1914. Those members of it who managed to stay in the United States did prove as assimilable as their predecessors of the older immigration, though it often took two generations in America — a quicker process, however, than in Brazil. All of these people — Italians coming from Trieste and Naples, Irish and English from Liverpool, and the rest — sought improved life chances. They were assimilable because most of them sought revolutions neither at home nor in the new country, though they did seek to change their own lives. They were, as Alexis de Tocqueville described the people he saw in the Ohio Valley in 1831, a people of "scanty fortunes," loving change but hating revolution, trying to keep the little they had, and hoping to magnify it. The European migrants were, in aspiration if not yet in fact, a lower middle class, whether white collar or blue collar. As such they fit into American society very well, since most of the native-born were similarly situated.

QUESTIONS TO CONSIDER

1. The historian Marcus Hansen said that migration requires people who want to leave, countries willing to accept them, and transportation to take them there. Keeping this in mind, describe some of the factors that promoted increased international migration between 1870 and 1914. In what ways was migration to the Americas an extension of migration within Europe?

2. What features of immigration to the United States were similar to the immigration experienced by other New World receiving nations, such as Canada, Argentina, and

Brazil? Describe common patterns found in immigrants' motives, migration in "chains," sex ratios, and repatriation. On the other hand, what aspects made the U.S. experience different from that of these other countries?

3. What difference does Nugent see in the experiences of farming versus wage-labor immigrants? In which New World countries was frontier farming an attractive option for immigrants? Why and when? As immigrants to the United States after 1880 increasingly sought jobs in industry, construction, and mining, how did the typical immigrant profile change? How do immigrant patterns of job-seeking and repatriation support Aristide Zolberg's claim in Selection 6 that immigrants were unlikely to join radical labor movements?

4. Why did immigrants generally avoid the American South? What contrast does Nugent draw between Brazilian and American plantations after emancipation? How did immigration keep southern blacks from migrating north?

5. What were the arguments against, and in favor of, "birds of passage"? Why was repatriation so unsettling to American leaders? What features of the new immigration did they misinterpret as abnormal? What nationalist, racial, and economic arguments were used to push for immigration restriction? Compare the arguments over the "new immigration" of 1880–1914 with today's debate over immigration.

The City in the Land of the Dollar

WITOLD RYBCZYNSKI

Modern urban life imposes a sameness upon the human environment that has reduced the differences between nations. To the traveler, the railroad station in Florence, the hotel in Vienna, the restaurant in Melbourne, and the museum in Mexico City seem much like the same facilities in cities everywhere. Nevertheless, cities in the United States have a distinctive look, one that is shaped by their history of rapid growth, the predominance of business rather than government, the cultural ideal of the private house, and the relentless rush of the automobile. There is no mistaking Los Angeles for London.

"Why aren't our cities like that?" a friend who had just returned from Paris asked the architect and social historian Witold Rybczynski. Where, she wanted to know, were the elegant tree-lined boulevards, the grand civic spaces, and the stately public buildings? In contrast to the great European capitals, American cities are prosaic grids of long, straight streets with a commercial downtown of tall office buildings set apart from the residential neighborhoods that surround it. And while the center of Paris features buildings of uniform color and scale focused upon public squares and monuments, the centers of American cities, Rybczynski admits, are a "free-for-all" of tall buildings of various shapes and smaller structures interspersed with empty lots and parking garages. The effect, he says, is that of "a Monopoly board in midgame."

Instead of lamenting what American cities are not, Rybczynski set out to explore what they are and how they got that way. For the late nineteenth century there is no better place to begin than Chicago, the fastest-growing city in the United States and the one that best embodied the raw energy, the technological innovations, and the contrasts between wealth and poverty in American urban life. In this excerpt from his book City Life, *Rybczynski introduces Chicago as a city of factories, granaries, and slaughterhouses that grew rapidly thanks to its location at the center of the Great Lakes and the nation's railroad network. Undaunted by the Great Fire of 1871, which destroyed Chicago's business center, confident city leaders rebuilt the downtown with the latest technology. The new Chicago boasted a telephone system, electric streetcars, and steel-framed skyscrapers, and it styled itself the city of the future.*

But whose vision would control that future? Rybczynski constructs his drama around the contrasting agendas of business and art. While businessmen built taller and taller buildings downtown and immigrants crowded into apartments nearby, in a drained marsh on Chicago's South Side an army of planners, architects, and civic patrons erected the magnificent White City of the World's Columbian Exposition in 1893. Its monumental neoclassical buildings, arranged in formal groups of equal height, made a striking contrast to the messy vitality of downtown, with its gritty factories and soaring office buildings. The White City's spacious plazas, watery lagoons, and meandering gardens halted the relentless grid that had shaped Chicago's expansion and, as Kate Brown noted in Selection 4, that of most western cities.

The Chicago Fair inspired the "City Beautiful" movement, a push by planners and other professionals to make over Chicago and other American cities in the image of great European capitals like Paris. In Rybczynski's hands this movement's history becomes a telling parable of the clash between the Old World and the New, the city beautiful and the city profitable. In the end, he says, the civic beautifiers lost because they were unable "to face up to the reality of the American city," a reality better represented by highways, skyscrapers, and gridded streets than grand boulevards and civic buildings. But the early-twentieth-century reformers did leave behind impressive parks, museums, and civic centers for later generations to enjoy. And their idea that planned environments of order and beauty can inspire our common life to rise above the daily rat race, Rybczynski seems to be saying, is one that we should not forget.

GLOSSARY

AXIS   In architecture, an imaginary line along which buildings or parts of buildings are placed, or around which they are arranged symmetrically.

CHAMPS-ELYSÉES   The most famous of the grand boulevards of Paris. The Avenue des Champs-Elysées was laid out in the early 1700s, then enhanced in the nineteenth century by the addition of the Arc de Triomphe and several avenues radiating from the circular Place de l'Etoile.

CORNICE LINE   The horizontal line formed by the projecting ornamental molding along the top of a building.

CRYSTAL PALACE   A huge iron and glass pavilion, housing the London Exhibition of 1851, that was designed by the English architect and gardener Joseph Paxton. Because it demonstrated the possibility of using modern materials and interchangeable parts in large-scale construction, the Crystal Palace is considered a forerunner of the skyscraper.

ECOLE DES BEAUX-ARTS   The French government's school of architecture in Paris, established by Louis XIV, which gave students rigorous training in the principles and forms of classical architecture. Richard Morris Hunt was the first American graduate, and many American architects of the late nineteenth and early twentieth centuries studied there.

FUNCTIONALISM   The aesthetic theory, identified with modern architecture, that buildings should use modern materials, eliminate ornamentation, and have their appearance reflect their structure and function.

L'ENFANT PLAN FOR WASHINGTON   A plan for the new national capital city submitted by French-born engineer and architect Pierre L'Enfant in 1791. It featured broad diagonal avenues intersecting in fifteen squares, special sites for the Capitol and President's House, and a mile-long "mall" or parade ground from the Capitol to the Potomac River. Only partially built because of its cost, L'Enfant's plan was revised in the early twentieth century by the City Beautiful movement and implemented by the federal government.

LOOP   The central business district of Chicago.

PALAZZO   An Italian Renaissance urban palace, usually monumental in scale and often featuring the division of its box-shaped mass into three levels.

"Why aren't our cities like that?" asked my friend Danielle, who . . . had just returned from Paris, obviously impressed by what she'd seen. . . . What did she mean? I asked. Well, she answered, Paris had formal squares, stately parks, and tree-lined boulevards with wonderful vistas. I agreed that it was a beautiful city. Then why didn't we [North Americans] have anything as elegant as the Place des Vosges, she wanted to know, or as stately as the Palais-Royal, as architecturally complete as the arcades along the Rue de Rivoli, as impressive as the *Grands Projets?* Where were the elegant avenues, the great civic spaces, and the impressive public monuments?

. . . No one would describe most North American cities as picture-postcard places, but they . . . are not cities in the accepted sense, or at least not in the traditional sense. Socially fragmented, recklessly entrepreneurial, relying almost completely on the automobile, and often lacking a defined center, they are without many of the conventional trappings of urbanity that have characterized cities in the past. According to their detractors, they are not real cities at all. At least they are not real cities if one assumes that real cities have cathedrals and outdoor plazas, not parking garages and indoor shopping malls; that they have sidewalk cafes, not drive-through Pizza Huts, and movie theaters, not cineplexes; that real cities are beautiful, ordered, and high-minded, not raucous, unfinished, and commercial.

No, our cities are definitely not like Paris. But then what *are* they like? And how did they get that way? . . .

During the last decade of the nineteenth century the fastest-growing city in the United States, probably in the world, was Chicago. The evolution of Chicago bears closer examination, for in many ways twentieth-century American urbanism got its start here. This is where the skyscraper was invented and given its definitive architectural form, this is where the idea of the American commercial downtown took root, and this is also where the issue of urban design, after a hiatus of almost two centuries, emerged as a topic fit for public and political discussion. . . .

Just as Amsterdam was shaped by the Dutch Golden Age or Manchester by the British Industrial Revolution, Chicago was formed by the great commercial and industrial expansion of the late nineteenth century. After the construction of the railroads and a business boom during the Civil War, the city took off like a rocket. Indeed, as far as popular legend is concerned, Chicago was born in a shower of sparks. On October 8, 1871, the preeminent city of the western half of the nation, bursting at the seams with 300,000 people, suffered a calamitous fire that devastated the business center and much of the surrounding area. . . .

The Chicago fire provided a tabula rasa [i.e., blank slate] for land developers, builders, and architects. Not guided by any new planning theories, they kept the same street layout. Nevertheless, the new city emerged dramatically different from the old. This was due to a wide range of new urban technologies. Chicagoans thought of themselves as different, but they were not opposed to adopting urban technologies that had been developed chiefly in eastern cities. In 1878, New Haven introduced the country's first telephone switchboard; Chicago got its own the same year. Thomas Edison invented the electric lamp in 1879; two years later electric lights were installed in a railroad-car factory on Chicago's Far South Side, and the following year in a Prairie Avenue mansion. San Francisco introduced cable cars in 1873; Chicago followed suit in 1881. The first electric streetcar ran in Richmond, Virginia, in 1888; four years later Chicago streetcar companies began switching from horse-drawn and cable cars to electric trolleys.

Electric trolley cars and railroads allowed the city to expand horizontally into the surrounding prairie; at the same time the center of Chicago began to grow in an unexpected direction. Of all the technologies that fashioned the new city, few were more influential than the elevator. . . .

Before the advent of the elevator, the height of buildings had been limited by human endurance in stair-climbing. Urban buildings were four to six stories, with the occasional church steeple or dome protruding above this height — this was no less true in Victorian London than in ancient Rome — but with the introduction of elevators, buildings could be made as tall as construction techniques and engineering would allow. At first, that was not very high. Buildings with solid masonry walls could be built higher only by making the walls thicker and thicker at the base to resist toppling over; the practical height limit was about twelve stories. This limit was pushed to sixteen stories in Chicago's Monadnock Building, whose massive walls were six feet thick at the bottom, but by the time the Monadnock opened in 1891, it was already obsolete. There was now a cheaper and more efficient building material: lightweight structural steel.

Rolled steel had been widely used in Europe and in America for railroad tracks and bridge construction, but not for buildings. Steel-frame construction was pioneered in Chicago, where it was first used in 1884, in the upper floors of an iron-framed building, and where the first complete steel frame was erected in 1890. The steel frame had many advantages: not only was it cheaper and more efficient, it also enabled architects to build higher. In 1892 the steel-framed Masonic Temple Building, designed by Daniel Burnham and John Root, the architects of the Monadnock, rose to 302 feet (twenty-two stories). For a short time it was the world's tallest building, soon exceeded by the office tower of Louis Sullivan's Auditorium Building.

The skyscraper, almost always an office building, changed more than the skyline of Chicago; it greatly increased the value of real estate, which in turn altered the character of the center of the city. When buildings were lower and land was cheaper, the center of all American cities since Williamsburg had been a mixture of commercial, residential, and industrial uses. Inevitably, once the price of land was based on renting sixteen to twenty floors of office space, only sixteen- to twenty-story office buildings could and would be built. The low-rise rooming houses, private residences, workshops, industrial lofts, small manufacturing plants, and factories that had previously stood side by side with commercial offices had to move elsewhere.

Where did people live? The greatly increased price of land in and around the Loop, as well as new fire codes prohibiting inexpensive wood-frame construction, guaranteed that most people would live outside the center of the city. Low-paid factory workers lived in tenements in industrial neighborhoods close to their places of employment, but skilled craftsmen and white-collar workers had another option. They could afford to move to new residential neighborhoods where the new fire codes did not apply; the land was cheap, and so was the cost of traveling by railroad and trolley car. These neighborhoods consisted largely of owner-occupied dwellings, for the most part detached houses with gardens. Although the streets were usually laid out on grids, these new districts did not have a mixture of uses — they were almost exclusively residential.

The character of these outer neighborhoods was initially countrylike, but as the city continued its precipitous growth, they filled up, houses and building lots were subdivided, the density rose, and the hemmed-in streets became less bucolic in appearance. Workingmen's cottages replaced villas, duplexes replaced cottages and, eventually, apartment buildings replaced duplexes. Still, with their broad, tree-lined streets and low buildings, these outlying neighborhoods could not be confused with downtown. No longer rural, but not quite urban either, they presaged the suburban communities that would grow up in the early 1900s on the edges of all large cities.

Thus was the modern American city born. It was different from its European counterpart not just because the buildings were so tall, but also because what people now called "downtown" (the word, too, is of American origin) was a homogeneous, commercial concentration of offices, hotels, and department stores, with a sprinkling of cultural institutions. People worked and shopped and played downtown, but lived elsewhere.

As the fastest-growing city in the world, Chicago was an unprecedented urban phenomenon that would not be duplicated until the explosive growth of Third World cities in the second half of the twentieth century. What attracted people to Chicago was the promise of employment in the stores, offices, factories, warehouses, slaughterhouses, breweries, and railroad yards that filled the city. The image of a place so unrelentingly devoted to work struck foreign visitors as quintessentially American. "Chicago is conscious that there is something in the world, some sense of form, of elegance of refinement, that with all her corn and railways, her hogs and by-products and dollars, she lacks," observed an English writer, G. W. Steevens, who passed through the city in the 1890s. Steevens went on to record his impressions of the United States in the now forgotten but wonderfully titled travel book, *In the Land of the Dollar.*

One could easily slip into condescension when writing about Chicago; it was so new and so raw compared with European cities. No doubt, American cities were unabashedly places for doing business and for making money, and Steevens's opinion is mirrored in Lewis Mumford's description of nineteenth-century American urbanization: "That a city had any other purpose than to attract trade, to increase land values and to grow is something that . . . never exercised any hold upon the minds of the majority of our countrymen. For them, the place where the great city stands *is* the place of stretched wharves, and markets, and ships bringing goods from the ends of the earth; that and nothing else." . . .

[Yet, by the 1890s,] Chicago was trying to put itself on the cultural map, too. . . . Following the example of New York City, whose Central Park was begun in 1858, Chicago, like Brooklyn, Buffalo, Boston, Louisville, Philadelphia, and San Francisco, undertook the construction of large urban parks. Most of the parks were planned by the same man, Frederick Law Olmsted, who exerted a powerful influence on the beautification of cities throughout North America. . . .

Olmsted's original inspiration was European. The English architect and horticulturalist Sir Joseph Paxton, who later designed the Crystal Palace, is credited with creating the first public urban park, the "People's Garden," in Liverpool, in the early 1840s. Similar parks were established in other British cities, as well as in France and Germany. These were not merely fashionable promenades, as had been the case with eighteenth-century fenced urban gardens used exclusively by the upper class; they were specifically intended for the general public. Olmsted visited Liverpool and thought that Paxton's park was a concept ideally suited to American democracy. Moreover, in his opinion, cities like New York and Chicago, bursting at the seams of their tight, practical grids and increasingly disease-ridden, overcrowded, and noisy, needed healthy green open spaces. It is worth recalling that the nineteenth-century city was an *industrial* city, and industry then was extremely dirty. Coal-burning factories and electrical generating plants, polluting stockyards and slaughterhouses, stood side by side with the homes of working people. Hundreds of horse-drawn vehicles, including horsecars, polluted the narrow, crowded streets. To Olmsted and his collaborator on many projects, Calvert Vaux, green spaces were not a mere ornament but a crucial antidote to the nervous, inhospitable city; these parks are not conceived of as urban gardens but rather as large chunks of healthy natural landscape. . . .

At one time, Chicago had intended to build a great linear park — a sort of giant greenbelt, a quarter of a mile wide and fourteen miles long — roughly following the city limits. This would have girdled the city on three sides, leaving the lake to border the fourth. This ambitious plan was ultimately scaled down by Olmsted and Vaux from 2,240 to 1,800 acres, and from a continuous greenbelt to eight individual parks, many named for presidents: Washington, Jefferson, Lincoln, Grant. The parks are large — 200 to 600 acres each — and intended for full-day excursions. They include lakes, canals, sports fields, band shells, conservatories, arbors, zoos, bicycle and pedestrian paths, and broad carriage roads. There were originally no commercial distractions, however — no amusement parks, penny arcades, or beer gardens. This was a conscious effort to provide a civilizing public setting for an urban population with a growing amount of

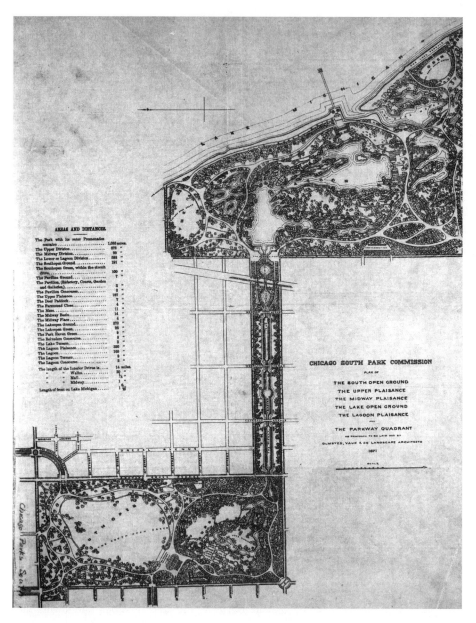

In Frederick Law Olmsted's original plan for the Chicago South Park Commission, 1871, the lower park became Washington Park; the upper one served as part of the Chicago World's Fair site in 1893 and became Jackson Park afterward. Olmsted's curving paths, open recreational space, and romantic lagoons offered relief from the monotonous and cluttered commercial grid. (Chicago Historical Society.)

leisure time. The parks are linked by parkways, a favorite Olmsted device. Parkways were not simply big streets, but were really linear parks that achieved several ends: they brought parklike space closer to more people, they further reduced urban congestion, and they could be a tool in directing urban growth, providing an attractive setting for new residential developments.

The Chicago park and parkway system was successful, but its advocates had seen it chiefly as a counterbalance to the congestion of the city — a green refuge — and so had paid less attention to the character of its urban surroundings. The little grid of the 1830s had multiplied and was now filled with fancy skyscrapers and public parks, but this did not really amount to a beautiful city. The laissez-faire attitude to construction was producing some beautiful buildings, but architecture alone is never enough. What was missing was an urban vision grand enough to encompass Chicago's growing and justifiable sense of importance. . . .

Ultimately, the change in Chicago was accelerated by the World's Columbian Exposition, which took place during the summer of 1893. The master plan of the fair was devised by Olmsted and his associate, Henry Sargent Codman, working with Chicago's most prominent architects, Daniel Burnham and John Root. The fair was located beside Lake Michigan on the site of Jackson Park — originally planned by Olmsted and Vaux, but never built. Olmsted produced a spectacular new plan incorporating his concept of the fusion of town and country. He transformed what had been a 600-acre marsh into an entirely man-made landscape, including a system of canals as well as a great, naturalistic lagoon. Root is generally credited with the idea of the Court of Honor, a formal urban grouping of buildings arranged around a 1,100-foot-long water basin. A 600-foot-wide parkway (part of the original Olmsted and Vaux plan) extended almost a mile inland and contained an amusement park, the Midway Plaisance, and the world's first Ferris wheel, 250 feet in diameter and carrying aloft 1,500 passengers at a time.

Burnham was appointed chief of construction, and after Root's untimely death he assumed the leadership role in planning the exposition. He invited several celebrated architects to design the individual pavilions: Richard Morris Hunt, America's premier society architect, was awarded the choice commission, an imposing 250-foot-high domed building standing at the head of the water basin; Charles Follen McKim of McKim, Mead, and White from New York City designed the Agriculture Building, which he modeled on a Renaissance palazzo; Louis Sullivan built the beautiful Transportation Building; George B. Post was responsible for the largest of the exhibition halls, the Manufacturers Building; Charles B. Atwood designed the train station as well as the Palace of Fine Arts. . . .

The Columbian Exposition was a spectacular combination of naturalistic and formal landscaping combined with grand public buildings. (As many of these buildings were painted white, the exposition became popularly known as the White City.) The architect Robert A.M. Stern has called the Columbian Exposition "the first effectively planned complex of public buildings built in America since the Jeffersonian era," and, indeed, the Court of Honor does recall an enlarged version of Thomas Jefferson's University of Virginia, with Hunt's tall dome at the head of a water basin occupying the place of

This view of the White City of the World's Columbian Exposition, 1893, shows the Court of Honor, with its neoclassical buildings grouped around a central lagoon. A statue of Columbus sits atop its boat-shaped fountain, which faces an arched colonnade and Lake Michigan beyond. (Courtesy of Library of Congress.)

Jefferson's library. The planners conceived of the fair as an explicit exercise in forward-looking urbanism; moreover, they saw it as an opportunity to demonstrate the application of classical design principles to public buildings. Burnham, Hunt, Atwood, and McKim were all confirmed classicists, as was the fair's chief adviser on sculpture, the artist Augustus Saint-Gaudens. The classical approach, as practiced by these American designers, demanded not only the use of the classical architectural vocabulary — fluted columns, capitals, and entablatures — and buildings sited along formal axes, but also restraint. The buildings grouped around the basin, for example, all respected a uniform height for their cornice lines, and all incorporated porticoes, providing an almost continuous colonnade.

As for the public, the experience of the Exposition was an eye opener. Only seven miles from the Loop's undisciplined commercial downtown choked with traffic, they could walk around enjoying water pools, the lake view, landscaping, and public art. It was like going to Europe, which is to say that for most people it was their first experience of the pleasures of ordered urbanism. The implication was there: our cities *could* be like that. . . .

The White City offered Americans a new urban model just when one was needed. By the end of the nineteenth century most cities were in the middle of a period of vigorous growth, and it was apparent that while laissez-faire planning might work in small towns, it had severe drawbacks in large cities. A small grid . . . could be charming, but when it went on for miles, as it did in Chicago, the effect was oppressive. Moreover, the very people who had prospered in the American cities now felt that rough-and-ready planning no longer suited their increasingly genteel way of life. Movers and shakers acquired a taste for the planned avenues and squares of London, Paris, and Rome.

Chicago's Columbian Exposition provided a real and well-publicized demonstration of how the unruly American downtown could be tamed though a partnership of classical architecture, urban landscaping, and heroic public art. Equally important, the planning of the White City brought together an extraordinary group of talented and like-minded creative individuals: . . . Olmsted, . . . Burnham, . . . McKim, . . . Hunt, and . . . Saint-Gaudens.

These men had an ambitious goal. As Werner Hegemann and Elbert Peets, the authors of *The American Vitruvius,* an influential handbook of urban design originally published in 1922, wrote: "Against chaos and anarchy in architecture, emphasis must be placed upon the ideal of civic art and the civilized city." The first chapter of their book was entitled "The Modern Revival of Civic Art," which underlined the common thread that bound together architects like Burnham, McKim, and their followers: a belief in the value of learning from the great urban achievements of the past. Their aim was nothing less than to transplant to the New World the ideals that had underpinned European city building since the sixteenth century — that is, to build classical cities in America. "Classical," in this sense, refers to an architecture derived from the ancient Greeks and Romans, and given its full form by the Renaissance. Classical composition involved a repetition of standardized elements according to predetermined rules, and exemplified, in J. B. Jackson's words, "a devotion to clarity and order." In terms of urban planning, it meant adopting an orderly framework of streets and public spaces within which the work of individual architects could take its place, and introducing such devices as axial views, expansive public squares, and formal groupings of buildings. Although the inspiration was European, the results were distinctive and original. They mirrored the particular conditions of the American city at the turn of the century: available space, rapid urban growth, new urban technologies, and a need for grand civic symbols. . . .

[T]he proponents of classicism achieved some remarkable successes. The most prominent of these was undoubtedly Washington, D.C, where under the leadership of McKim, and with the active involvement of Burnham, Frederick Law Olmsted, Jr., and Saint-Gaudens, the final realization of L'Enfant's 1791 plan was undertaken. . . .

Beginning in 1901, McKim and the members of the Senate Park Commission (also known as the McMillan Commission) visited various European capitals and in less than a year produced a master plan for Washington that included a realigned mall, the placement of the Lincoln and Jefferson memorials, as well as a new railroad terminal with relocated railroad tracks — in a tunnel underground. Some contemporary critics pointed out that the enlarged mall — L'Enfant's "Grand Avenue" was now 1,000-feet wide — had become inhuman, and that replacing the residential scale and atmosphere of Lafayette Square with government offices isolated the White House from the rest of the city.

Others were uncomfortable with what they perceived to be imperial grandeur in a republican capital. On the whole, however, the new plan, widely covered by the press, was well received by the public, and implementation of it began right away.

This time the national capital did become a model for the rest of the country, and it encouraged other cities to undertake similar civic improvements. . . .

Such ambitious projects were possible because the advocates of civic art had an extraordinarily broad base of support, exemplified by the popular movement known as the City Beautiful. According to the architectural historian William H. Wilson, the term "City Beautiful" emerged in 1900 as a slogan for an urban improvement campaign in Harrisburg, Pennsylvania. It became a rallying cry that brought together civic reformers, community volunteers, businessmen, and municipal politicians, with crusading architects and landscape architects. This makes the City Beautiful movement the equivalent of, say, the historic preservation movement today, although it was shorter-lived, lasting only until about 1910. . . .

Thanks to City Beautiful activists, American cities started to look at themselves critically. One way to improve a typical gridded downtown was to introduce a formal civic center. This group of public buildings usually included the city hall, a public library, and an auditorium placed around a square or landscaped mall. In 1902 a commission made up of Burnham, [John] Carrère, and the architect Arnold Brunner prepared a plan for a civic center for Cleveland that was consciously modeled on the concept of the Court of Honor of the White City. . . . There were also civic centers built in Springfield, Massachusetts, Rochester, New York, and other smaller cities. The civic center introduced noncommercial buildings into downtown in a prominent way that was intended to give people a sense of civic pride. . . .

Civic beautification also produced the grand American railroad stations. The urban railroad terminal was a peculiarly characteristic building of the first quarter of the twentieth century when railroads were the preeminent means of transportation. Central terminals served a vital role in the life of cities and were used by both long-distance travelers and commuters. As one historian put it, urban railroad stations were also focal points for the expression of civic values. The symbolic role of the terminal, like the ceremonial gateways of medieval towns, was to signal arrival in the city. Terminal Station at Chicago's World's Columbian Exposition, whose design Peirce Anderson of Burnham's firm adapted in Washington, D.C.'s Union Station, became the architectural model. It was followed by the two New York City terminals: McKim's Pennsylvania Station, modeled on the Baths of Caracalla of ancient Rome, and Grand Central Terminal.

[The urban expert] Jane Jacobs has called the City Beautiful movement an "architectural design cult" rather than a "cult of social reform." This is only partly true. The advocates of civic art did believe in the value of design, both architectural and urban, but they did not think of parks and boulevards as merely civic adornments; these were to be places for leisure and public recreation, and improvements to the very fabric of cities. The focus on railroad stations and on urban transportation likewise reflected a concern for the broad public good. On the other hand, it's true that building grand railroad stations did not address housing issues at precisely the time — the early decades of [the twentieth] century — when the living conditions of most working people were abysmal. But the chief handicap of the practitioners of civic art was not a lack of social concern, nor, even less, their partiality to classicism. It was an inability to face up to the reality of the American city.

This inability is best exemplified by what the urban historian John Reps has described as "one of the great accomplishments of American planning," the Burnham plan for Chicago. In 1906, more than a decade after the Columbian Exposition, Burnham and his associate, Edward H. Bennett, were commissioned by the Merchant's Club, a Chicago businessmen's association, to produce a visionary plan for the city. The project took three years to complete and is estimated to have cost almost $70,000 — a vast sum that did not include Burnham's own time, which he volunteered free of charge. The result was a 164-page report, published in 1,650 copies, with a text by Burnham and many illustrations — photographs, diagrams, plans, and sketches, as well as a beautiful series of colored views of the city-to-be drawn by the New York painter, illustrator, and set designer Jules Guerin.

Burnham and Bennett's extraordinary plan covered an area enclosed by a circle drawn with a sixty-mile radius around the Loop. It was in effect a proposal for the entire metropolitan region of Chicago. It showed how the city should be linked to surrounding suburban towns by highways and railroads, and analyzed the movement of passengers and freight throughout the region. It proposed forest reserves and greenbelts, and within the city, parkways and urban parks, including a long lakefront park built on reclaimed land and forming a series of inland lagoons. Diagonal avenues were cut through the traditional grid, and a thirty-mile circular parkway that recalled Olmsted and Vaux's earlier plan for a linear park provided a "grand circuit" linking half a dozen of the city's major parks. Another dramatic innovation was the creation of a brand-new civic center, not in the Loop but inland, east of the Chicago River. Here, at the exact geometrical center of the entire plan, Burnham and Bennett placed a huge domed municipal administration building facing a great plaza flanked by county and federal offices.

Burnham and Bennett held public hearings and political consultations, and their report included material prepared by numerous committees charged with studying railroads, freight movements, ports, road traffic, and recreation. The comprehensive nature of the plan belies the proposition that the concerns of City Beautiful advocates were solely aesthetic. Burnham's original draft incorporated reforms to public utilities, hospitals, daycare centers, and schools. This was hardly the work of a "design cult." . . .

"We have found that those cities which retain their dominion over the imaginations of mankind achieve that result through the harmony and beauty of their civic works," wrote Burnham, who imagined that the "Metropolis of the Middle West" would be a city along the lines of London, Paris, Vienna, or Berlin. To him, "civic works" meant impressive squares and stately public buildings — features which, in Burnham's view, would provide the chief urban and architectural identity of the city, and which therefore should be given physical preeminence. Guerin's panoramic watercolor views of the new Chicago showed the tall dome of the civic center rising from a city composed entirely of buildings seven to twelve stories high. This low-profile city bore an undeniable resemblance to Paris; not coincidentally, both Guerin, an American, and Bennett, an Englishman, had studied at the Ecole des Beaux-Arts.

Despite its practicality, the Chicago plan had one utopian feature: Burnham and his colleagues, who scrupulously delineated existing streets, public parks, and even railroad rights-of-way, chose to ignore the tall buildings (many built by Burnham's own firm) that were downtown Chicago's most distinctive feature. This rejection of the skyscraper was certainly not an implied criticism of commercial development — the conservative Burnham was not antibusiness — nor was he suggesting that dozens of existing Chicago skyscrapers be demolished. Presumably, Guerin was portraying an ideal future, not merely making pretty pictures. But in that case, how were the heights of buildings to be controlled? The legal section of the report does mention easements that might be applied to lots abutting parks or boulevards, but there is no mention of restricting building height. This is a curious omission, since Washington, D.C., with which Burnham had extensive experience, did have rigorous height limits: 90 feet for residential streets, and 130 feet on wider avenues. . . .

It is possible that Burnham and Bennett simply wanted to avoid the thorny issue of architectural controls altogether, since such prohibitions flew in the face of the American tradition of allowing property owners to build with a minimum of restrictions. It was one thing to have height restrictions in the national capital, quite another to propose them in commercial cities. . . .

It is also possible that the two men could not reconcile their urban theories — which assumed that public buildings would take precedence over commercial and residential structures — with the actual state of affairs in the American downtown. Tall buildings like New York's Municipal Building or Cleveland's Terminal Tower were intended to act as civic symbols, but there was no place in Burnham's vision for downtowns made up of commercial skyscrapers. Yet it was precisely the tall office buildings that impressed the European visitor to Chicago and New York City, and set American cities apart from Europe. In Europe the most impressive urban monuments were public structures like the Eiffel Tower, or religious buildings like the dome of Saint Paul's Cathedral in London, or freestanding campaniles [bell towers]; in Chicago and New York the tallest buildings were privately built and privately owned, and they towered over the cathedral, the city hall, and the public library. . . .

Commercial towers were symbols of the entrepreneurial American city. The tall office building not only made money for its corporate owner but also celebrated and symbolized the making of money. They were also a source of wonderment for the general public, a dramatic index of technological achievement. Having "the tallest building west of the Mississippi" or "the tallest building in the British Empire" marked a city in much the same way as a pennant-winning baseball team does today.

The clash between horizontal ideals and vertical aspirations is dramatically illustrated in the evolution of North Michigan Avenue in Chicago. As early as 1896, Burnham had proposed linking the Loop with the area north of the Chicago River — the so-called Gold Coast — by building a tunnel under the river at Michigan Avenue and broadening the existing street. The 1909 *Plan of Chicago* elaborated this idea, replacing the

tunnel with a bridge and extending Michigan Avenue northward as an elevated boule-
vard in the mold of the Champs-Elysées. Guerin's bird's-eye view shows a broad avenue
lined with trees and flanked by uniform seven-story buildings with distinctly Parisian
mansard roofs. The median strips are marked by heroic sculptures; a sort of traffic island
contains a large fountain. There are crowds of promenaders, including many women
with parasols, both on the sidewalks as well as in the street itself. . . . The chief impression of this charming drawing is a kind of ease and a sense of spaciousness that were in
marked contrast to the busy congested streets of the Loop.

There was a great deal of interest in implementing this proposal, not the least
because of the impact such an important street would have on adjacent property values.
The mayor formed a planning commission to oversee its execution. Four years later the
city council passed an ordinance for the construction of the new bridge and widening
the avenue north of the river. The project incorporated many, though not all, of the
original designers' ideas. . . . The North Central Business District Association, which
had been formed to rule on details of the project, recommended that all buildings on
the avenue maintain a uniform cornice line, just as in Guerin's drawings, and be ten stories (about 120 feet) high, the maximum allowed by the Chicago building code in that
area. . . .

Chicago would finally get its Champs-Elysées. But just as work on the avenue was
beginning, the building code was revised to permit a maximum building height of two
hundred feet, and the first building constructed on North Michigan Avenue rose sixteen stories, or almost exactly two hundred feet. The North Central Business District
Association appears to have been silent on this point — hardly surprising, as the association was composed of property owners who stood to profit by the new height limit.
In 1919 the maximum building height was again revised: now protruding towers were
allowed to soar to four hundred feet. On North Michigan Avenue, the celebrated
Wrigley Building took full advantage of the new code: the top of its central clock
tower is 398 feet above the street.

This is not the end of the story. In 1923 the building code was again rewritten, with
the result that the maximum height of towers was almost unrestricted; so was the height
of buildings that did not cover the entire block but left at least three-quarters of their
site open. The sky was the limit. During the 1920s, North Michigan Avenue became
the site of some of the city's tallest and most spectacular buildings: John Mead Howell
and Raymond Hood's 450-foot-high Tribune Tower (winner of a famous international
competition) and the exuberant 42-story Medinah Club, which was built for the
Shriners and is topped by a minaret and pear-shaped dome. The last tall building erected
in the 1920s was the Union Carbide & Carbon Corporation Building that rose 40 stories straight up from the sidewalk. A poignant footnote: its architects were Burnham
Brothers, Inc., a firm founded by Hubert and Daniel H., Jr., the old man's sons.

"North Michigan's transformation would see the construction of some of Chicago's
most significant individual works of architecture," writes John W. Stamper, . . . "yet at
the same time this would result in a highly inconsistent pattern of urban design." Or
rather, all too consistent. Each building squeezed the economic possibilities of its site to
the utmost and simultaneously celebrated and asserted the individuality and achievement

of its owners and designers. As Stamper notes, the fate of North Michigan Avenue illustrates one of the persistent dilemmas of urban design in American cities: where land values were high, control over development was essentially impossible. And if Burnham's ideals were compromised even in his native Chicago, what chance did they have elsewhere? For a public caught up in the excitement and glamour of seeing taller and taller skyscrapers, a primarily horizontal downtown must have appeared increasingly staid and old-fashioned. In the Land of the Dollar, Burnham's genteel vision of civic harmony was given short shrift; the city profitable replaced the city beautiful. A profitable city was to be as little regulated as possible. It meant a city in which the nononsense street grid was reasserted without any urban frills such as diagonal boulevards or public squares.

Our cities would not be "like that" after all.

QUESTIONS TO CONSIDER

1. What technological innovations made the skyscraper and commuter suburbs possible? How did American "downtowns" develop, and why did tall office buildings come to dominate them? Why did middle-class city dwellers move to the suburbs? What role did the immigrant influx described by Walter Nugent in Selection 7 play in the sorting of American cities into poor center-city and wealthier outlying residential neighborhoods?

2. How were Frederick Law Olmsted's municipal parks meant to improve and "civilize" American city life? In what ways did they provide relief from the "gridded spaces" and "gridded lives" that, according to Kate Brown (Selection 4), characterized American cities?

3. Describe how the World's Columbian Exposition in Chicago embodied classical style and ideals. Was the Chicago Fair a pale imitation of European architecture or an authentically American creation? What influence did the "White City" exert on American city planning?

4. What changes did the City Beautiful movement advocate for American cities? Were the movement's goals too elitist for Americans, or was it a valuable antidote to commercialization and unplanned growth? How did the agenda of civic beautifiers like Daniel Burnham contrast with those of urban businessmen? In what way were they similar? Why were skyscrapers more symbolic of the American city than classically inspired railroad stations and civic centers?

5. After studying Rybczynski's essay, how would you answer the question, "Why aren't American cities like European cities?" Do you think that Rybczynski shares the bleak view of American cities expressed by Kate Brown in Selection 4? Why or why not?

V

IMPERIALISM

The Roman splendor of the Chicago World's Fair of 1893 (described in Selection 8) advertised America's new imperial ambitions. At the end of the nineteenth century, the United States became a world power whose economic and military might vied with industrialized Europe for influence around the globe. Between 1889 and 1904, the United States divided Samoa with the Germans; annexed Hawaii; wrested the Philippines, Guam, and Puerto Rico from Spain; and separated the Panama Canal Zone from Colombia.

Americans are uncomfortable calling their nation imperialist, not just because the term has become a charge that developing countries customarily level against the industrialized West. To label the United States "imperialist" is to place it in the company of the modern British, French, and German empires or even the empires of ancient Greece and Rome. The concept implies an end to America's alleged exemption from the troubles of other nations and suggests its affinity to the bullying "Great Powers" of its era and previous ones. How similar or different was turn-of-the-century America's acquisition of foreign territories from the European imperialism of its day? What political, economic, and racial theories were used to support American expansion? Was American colonial administration unique, and what impact did it have upon subject peoples? Could imperialism be reconciled with America's own colonial past and its republican commitment to the consent of the governed?

The essays in this chapter raise these important questions and use comparative analysis to address them. In the first selection, Robin W. Winks broadly compares American imperialism of the late nineteenth and early twentieth centuries to the European powers' scramble for colonies in Asia and Africa. Winks finds that Americans used many of the same arguments to justify their takeover of foreign lands, but he notes that their way of governing those lands was quite distinctive. In the second selection, Vince Boudreau takes a close look at the workings of American imperialism in a specific setting: the Philippine Islands, which the United States controlled from 1899 to its independence in 1946. Boudreau's analysis can be read as a "case study" testing Winks's generalizations about the American brand of imperialism. To what extent does Philippine history support Winks's claim that democratic values tempered the U.S. commitment to colonial rule? Taken together, these essays are fine examples of breadth and depth in comparative history, and they provide you with ample context and information to assess the nature of America's momentous imperial move in the 1890s.

9

American Imperialism
in Comparative Perspective

ROBIN W. WINKS

After reaching the Pacific and consolidating domestic control by conquering the South and the West, the United States turned outward. Somewhat haltingly but unmistakably, an American empire came into being through the conquest, purchase, or annexation of far-flung territories, from the Virgin Islands in the Caribbean to Hawaii and the Philippines in the Pacific. This flexing of American muscles abroad coincided with the second phase of European imperialism, during which the British took over parts of North and South Africa as well as Southeast Asia, Germany claimed Southwest and East Africa, the French dominated West Africa and Vietnam, and all sought "spheres of influence" in China. When Dutch, Italian, and Belgian claims as well as Russian expansionism are included, European states and their descendants (such as the United States) succeeded in establishing control, directly or indirectly, over almost every part of the world by the eve of World War I.

All this did not happen without fierce resistance from indigenous peoples, or even controversy at home. "I think," declared Mark Twain in 1900, "that England sinned when she got herself into a war in South Africa which she could have avoided, just as we have sinned in getting into a similar war in the Philippines." The debate over imperialism had begun the previous year when the United States decided to annex the Philippines and Britain invaded the Boer republics in South Africa. It has raged ever since. On one side, the search for foreign markets or national glory, the Social Darwinist idea that only the fittest would survive the global "struggle for existence," and the movement (however misguided) to spread

Christianity and "civilization" to "backward" peoples all seemed to justify empire. On the other side, there were charges of hypocrisy in professing democratic values but denying them to others, fears of contact with "nonassimilable" races, and warnings about the evils of a military state. A British critic of imperialism, John Hobson, believed that it stemmed from an excess of capital seeking profitable investment overseas because it could no longer find high dividends at home — an explanation that the Bolshevik leader V. I. Lenin extended into the dictum that imperialism was "the highest stage of capitalism." Whatever its roots and its moral claims, in practice imperialism involved the undeniable exploitation and oppression of colonial peoples, often through brutal violence.

Like Mark Twain, historian Robin Winks adopts the language of sin to describe imperialism. His approach is to admit that we (the United States as well as Europe) are all imperialist "sinners" — not an easy confession for many Americans to share — but then to substitute analysis for confession; in Winks's words, "to see whether and how our sins have differed." Which motives and rationales did American imperialists share with their European contemporaries? How did American imperialism compare in practice to British, French, and Russian colonizing? Roving expertly around the world, Winks finds that, despite Americans' professions to the contrary, their justification for imperialism featured essentially the same ethnocentric and moralistic arguments put forth by European rulers. What made American imperialism different, says Winks, was its commitment to republican institutions, which gave a distinctive flavor to American overseas rule. As a former colony itself, the United States was more reluctant than its mother country or other European nations to take on colonies and to keep them for long. But while they ruled, says Winks, the Americans were, paradoxically, far more intent on imposing their language, customs, and institutions upon the natives than were the British, who governed through an alliance between the imperial bureaucracy and a tiny native elite.

Winks's concise essay offers important distinctions and interpretations to test against the actual historical record. It is a good starting point for the comparative study of imperialism. You will notice, though, that Winks refers to several persons and concepts in the history of imperialism, especially British imperialism, without describing them for you. Be sure to check the Glossary for assistance in identifying these terms. Finally, since the next selection presents a more detailed look at the American venture in the Philippines, it would be a good idea to return to some of the larger questions about American imperialism posed by Winks's essay after you have read Selection 10.

GLOSSARY

BOERS   Descendants of the original Dutch colonists of South Africa. The Boers resisted British imperial rule by trekking northward in the late 1830s to the interior, where they established three republics. One of these (Natal) the British annexed in 1843; the others, the Transvaal and Orange Free State, they conquered in 1902.

BRYAN, WILLIAM JENNINGS (1860–1925)   An American reform politician and spellbinding orator. Bryan won the Democratic presidential nomination in 1896 on a platform that absorbed ideas from the farmer-dominated Populist revolt, but lost the election to Republican William McKinley. Bryan supported the Spanish-American War but opposed the taking of colonies. Nevertheless, he urged Democrats to ratify the treaty annexing the Philippines in order to end the war quickly. He hoped to use the issue of Philippine independence to capture the presidency in 1900, but failed.

CHAMBERLAIN, JOSEPH (1836–1914)   A radical British Whig Party leader of the 1880s who, along with Lord Rosebery, broke with the Whig prime minister William Gladstone and opposed giving Ireland home rule. Rosebery defended British imperialism as a way of "pegging out claims for the future" against competing Great Powers.

COOLIES   Derived from the Tamil and Urdu words for "hireling," a pejorative label for imported contract workers, especially from India or China.

CROMWELL, OLIVER (1599–1658)   A forceful Puritan leader who emerged victorious in the English Civil War of the 1640s. One of the most controversial figures in English history, Cromwell defeated the Royalist forces of Charles I and Charles II and proclaimed England a Republican commonwealth. He led an expedition into Ireland, where he began a policy of dispossessing the Irish. In 1653 he was named Lord Protector, or sole ruler, of England, Scotland, and Ireland, but the monarchy was restored shortly after his death.

DISRAELI, BENJAMIN (1804–1881)   A British author and statesman who rose to leadership of the Tory (now Conservative) Party. His second term as prime minister (1874–1880) was noted for its aggressively imperialist foreign policy. Among other actions, Disraeli annexed the Fiji Islands, waged wars against the Afghans and Zulus, persuaded Turkey to cede Cyprus to Britain, and purchased controlling shares in the Suez Canal. In 1876 he had Queen Victoria crowned empress of India.

GREATER EAST ASIA CO-PROSPERITY SPHERE   The rubric given by Japan to its domination of trade and territory in China and Southeast Asia in the 1930s. Increasingly, this arrangement was a cover for brutal imperialism and exclusionist trade policies.

JESUITICAL   Oversubtle or deceptive.

KIPLING, RUDYARD (1865–1936)   A popular English author who celebrated British imperialism in his poems, novels, and children's stories, such as *The Jungle Books* (1894–1895). Kipling believed in the "white man's burden," the duty to bring European culture and Christianity to the peoples of the "uncivilized" world.

MACKINDER, HALFORD JOHN (1861–1947)   An English geographer who claimed that Eurasia was the geographical pivot and "heartland" of history, a theory that received little attention until it was adopted in Germany to support Nazi imperial ambitions.

MAHAN, ALFRED THAYER (1840–1914)   An American naval officer and historian whose book *The Influence of Sea Power upon History* (1890) argued that foreign trade and overseas bases, and especially a powerful navy to protect them, were the keys to success in international politics. His works had a major influence upon supporters of imperialism in the United States and abroad.

MAORI   The native Polynesian population of New Zealand, subjugated by the British in 1872 after a century of intermittent warfare.

MCKINLEY, WILLIAM (1843–1901)   The Republican president of the United States who followed public opinion into the Spanish-American War after the sinking of the battleship *Maine* in February 1898. Faced with the decision to take colonies as spoils of war, McKinley declared that Puerto Rico, Guam, and the Philippines should be made American territories.

MONROE DOCTRINE   The pronouncement by U.S. president James Monroe in 1823 that from then on the Western Hemisphere was closed to further colonization or intervention by European powers (and that the United States would not interfere in European nations' internal affairs). Initially intended to prevent Europeans from recolonizing the Americas, the doctrine was later used by Theodore Roosevelt and other U.S. presidents to justify American intervention in the Caribbean and Central America for political or economic objectives.

OPEN DOOR NOTES   An American attempt to prevent partitioning of the Chinese empire by imperialist powers and to protect the principle of open trade. In 1899 and 1900, Secretary of State John Hay issued two notes, the first declaring that all foreign powers active in China would respect each other's trading rights, the second calling upon Western powers to preserve China's existing territorial boundaries. Although Hay claimed that European powers accepted his proposal, it was the fear of provoking a general European war that kept imperialists from dismembering China.

PAKEHA   Maori word meaning "white man" and referring to the British colonists who subdued the native peoples of New Zealand.

PAX AMERICANA   "American peace": the maintenance of global peace and stability after World War II through the exercise of American military and economic power.

PAX BRITANNICA   "British peace": the peace imposed by Britain's military and naval supremacy upon its dominions and, by extension, upon the international scene from 1815 to the outbreak of World War I.

POLYGAMY   The practice of having more than one spouse at one time. In the form of polygyny (multiple wives), it was common in many non-Western cultures until recent times.

RAJ   From the Hindu word for "rule" or "dominion," a term referring to British colonial rule in India.

REALPOLITIK   The "realistic" and sometimes amoral understanding of politics reflected especially in the statecraft of Germany's imperial chancellor Otto von Bismarck (1815–1898). Realpolitik involves the recognition that force is the preeminent way to achieve political success and the willingness to brush aside morality and idealism as unrealistic and hence irrelevant.

RHODES, CECIL (1853–1902)   A British imperialist and business magnate who, after making a fortune in the diamond fields of South Africa, became prime minister of the Cape Colony (1890–1896). His British South Africa Company colonized South Africa's northeast frontier, overcame tribal resistance, and claimed the territory (soon called Rhodesia in his honor) for England. Rhodesia is now independent Zimbabwe.

SPENGLER, OSWALD (1880–1936)   A German philosopher whose influential book *The Decline of the West* (1918–1922) declared that all civilizations pass through a life cycle from creativity to decline. Spengler believed that Western civilization had peaked and would soon irreversibly decline.

SUEZ CRISIS   The crisis precipitated in 1956 when Egyptian president Gamal Abdel Nasser took control of the Suez Canal from its imperialist "protector," Great Britain, for economic and military reasons. In the next few months, Israel, Great Britain, and France sent armies against Egypt, but the United States and the Soviet Union, acting through the United Nations, condemned these actions and persuaded all three to withdraw.

SUKARNO (1901–1970)   The leader of the Indonesian independence movement against Dutch rule. Sukarno became Indonesia's first president in 1949, steered its democracy toward one-man rule, and was deposed by a coup d'état in 1966.

SUTTEE   A former Hindu practice in which a widow immolated herself on the funeral pyre of her husband.

TOYNBEE, ARNOLD (1889–1970)   An English historian whose twelve-volume *A Study of History* (1934–1961) analyzed the cyclical development and decline of civilizations as the result of their responses to successive challenges.

TREATY OF VERSAILLES (1919)   The treaty between the Allied Powers and Germany ending World War I. By its terms, Germany's overseas colonies in China, the Pacific, and Africa were taken over by Britain, France, Japan, and others. The British gained Tanganyika (now part of Tanzania).

" "The depositary of power is always unpopular." Benjamin Disraeli knew this, and so did Theodore Roosevelt. Both contributed to their nation's power. Disraeli made Queen Victoria the Empress of India, while Roosevelt took Panama and built a canal there, by his own testimony. Both were imperialists.

But imperialism has proved to be an infinitely elastic term, one to be employed against all men who used power for expansion, consolidation, and conquest. Caesar, Alexander the Great, Genghis Khan, Suleiman the First at the walls of Malta, the Abraham Lincoln who crushed the drive for Southern independence (but not the Lincoln who freed the slaves), Dingaan and Shakar of the Zulu nation, even — according to English historian Christopher Hill — Oliver Cromwell, all were imperialists. As a result of such elasticity, the word is one which now carries almost exclusively a pejorative meaning, and since it has come to cover all those sins for which Western man is thought to be responsible, it is a particularly convenient form of verbal shorthand to demonstrate the gulf that separates the two worlds, the world of those who took and have and the world of those who lack and want. No one wishes to be called an imperialist, no nation wishes to admit to having undergone an imperialist past, and the new and emerging nations like to charge much of their current instability to the imperial tradition.

Many Americans have assumed that there was no period of American imperialism. Others admit to a brief imperialist past but prefer to clothe that past in other words. We were an expansionist nation, some historians argue, but not an imperialist one, a distinction more Jesuitical than useful. Yet other apologists suggest that since American growth was the direct result of a unique American sense of mission, of a Messianic impulse to set the world right which, even if wrongheaded, was sincere, humanitarian, progressive, and in general benevolent, the United States was apart from and above the ventures of the European scramblers for colonies. But most imperialisms have been rooted in a sense of mission, and the American sense differs from that of other nations chiefly in that the United States emphasized different characteristics. The British sense of mission sprang from a conviction of cultural superiority, the Japanese from a racial message thinly veiled in paternal rhetoric, the German from an impulse toward a pre-ordained dialectic, and the Communist sense of mission from what was conceived to be a sure knowledge of the world's ultimate needs and ends. And to say that we all are sinners does not remove the necessity to see whether and how our sins have differed.

Imperialism was not always in ill-repute, of course. In Britain in the 1880's and 1890's, Chamberlain and Rosebery were proud to call themselves imperialists. They were helping unfortunate peoples around the world to come into the light; they were lifting Britain, and not at the expense of nonwhites but at the expense of other, highly competitive European powers. Whatever befell the subjects of imperial control was, on the whole, to their good. . . . [W]hile liberals and conservatives placed different orders of priority upon their respective rationales, they also agreed upon the basic mix: Britain must reform itself at home and make itself fit for an imperial role while expanding abroad in order to extend to the unenlightened the many benefits of a rationalized, or-dered society. Improved sanitation and education, the equal administration of the law and the equal application of justice, the stamping out of slavery, debt bondage, suttee, polygamy, nakedness, and bride price — all seemed legitimate goals when viewed from within the liberal framework of the time. Theodore Roosevelt, too, thought that the vigorous Anglo-Saxon should carry forth the torch of progress; and, not unlike that hoary old radical and voice of the people, Walt Whitman, he wanted a race of splendid mothers.

Liberals, like conservatives, are always capable of highly selective indignation, and if they thought that the abolition of paganism and of slavery were of equal importance, if they thought the disruption of centuries of tribal alliances and of family stability was a small price for Africans to pay in exchange for monogamy, good roads, and a dependable market, they can hardly be blamed for thinking in the nineteenth century in nineteenth-century terms. Consider this statement, written at Brikama, in the Gambia, on the west coast of Africa, by a British traveling commissioner late in that century:

> There are higher purposes in life than merely living. Perhaps I shall die here, but I shall die a better man for having been here. These people are degraded, ignorant, swept by disease; how low, how low, they stand. Yet, they *stand*. I can help move them that inch higher, give them that direction they need, tell them of that truth that, once grasped, lived, proved, may one day make them right-thinking Englishmen, men with souls as white as any other, men I will have been proud to have known. Lift them, lift them. If I pass through the Gate before them, one day they too will pass through it, and I, there before them, will welcome them as men.

Such a sentiment may be found expressed by the *pakeha* among the Maori in the 1840's, by the Dutch in Java in the eighteenth century, by the Australians in New Guinea in the

1960's, and by the Americans in the Philippines in the 1920's. Indeed, one may find the same sentiment scrawled on postcards sent home from foreign parts by members of that most idealistic of all American organizations, the Peace Corps. Can we condemn this sentiment altogether, this amalgam of humanitarianism, of purpose, of drive, of sacrifice; this amalgam of arrogance, of self-righteousness, of superiority; this amalgam of progressivism, of Christianity, of Darwinism, of imperialism?

Imperialism was a practice; colonialism was a state of mind. Whether a powerful nation extended its control, its influence, or merely its advice over another people, those so controlled or so advised not unnaturally resented the controller. Indeed, we have all been colonies mentally at one time or another; no one likes, as they say, to be over a barrel. Much indignity lies in any subservient position, and yet there will always be the powerful and the powerless, and the people with the most power may not escape being the nation that is powerless, as Britain learned at Suez and as the United States is learning today. There is obvious indignity in never being the mover but always the moved, in waiting to see how a foreign capital or a foreign embassy will decide one's fate.

Behind the practice we call imperialism lay many strands of thought which were drawn together near the end of the nineteenth century to provide a rationale for expansive policies. The natural science, like the social organization of the time, emphasized selectivity, categories, hierarchies. There were natural orders of being, as there were natural orders of animal life, and nothing was more natural to political man than to assume that, as Walter Bagehot wrote, there were parallels between physics and politics. The new science taught "objectivity" and in the nineteenth century objectivity meant measurement, not cultural relativism but the opposite, the desire to place races, peoples, and cultures into classifiable categories. Cranial capacity, the length and width of heads, body odor, the color of the skin and the nature of the hair, all were measured, charted, and used to conclude that fundamental differences separated people. The vulgarization of the theories of Charles Darwin was combined with the romanticist's penchant for finding decadence wherever he looked, and the combination justified seeing the world as a jungle in which only the fittest might survive. The opening sentence of Count Arthur de Gobineau's *Essai sur l'Inégalité des Races Humaines,* published in 1853, spoke for the new pessimism that was, in fact, romantic: "The fall of civilization is the most striking and, at the same time, the most obscure of all phenomena of history." This pessimism was to run on through Spengler, through Toynbee, to the present. Arnold Toynbee was to write of the "natural dysgenic effects" that occur in societies; he was to find some groups — the Polynesians and the Jews, for example — suspended on plateaus where insufficient responses to overwhelming challenges had left them. The best men could hope to do was to turn back animality, or animality would take over the world. And to these strands of romance and science were added yet others — the Christian desire to save, to convert, and to enlighten, the commercial impulse to markets, the geopolitical and military notion of strategic values, the desire for adventure, the national thrust to a place in the sun, the national need for *la gloire.*

The very language of imperialism was all-pervasive. Neither the Maori in New Zealand nor the Navajo in America had any name for themselves until Europeans coined the words. Geographical terms of location — Near East, Middle East, Far East — were relative to a European map. Latin America became that portion of the New World where Spanish and Portuguese were spoken, because Americans decided this was so, oblivious of the fact that French Canadians considered themselves Latins too. Indonesia's Sukarno acquired a first name because American journalists refused to believe that a man could have but one. The names of the saints of European churches, like the names of European kings, run across the face of Asia, of Africa, and of the Pacific worlds as dictated by the whims of semiliterate men. The very geography of race itself is European, for it was Leclerc de Buffon who first classified the orders of life so that a later generation would have tools for distinguishing between peoples as well as plants. Long before . . . vine-snared trees fell down in files along the Congo, Europeans had concluded that there, in truth, did lie a heart of darkness in need of both European goods and of European ideas. An imperialism of the mind preceded the imperialism of the gunboat, the adviser, and the investor.

The United States was part of this climate of opinion. American responses to some of the assumptions of European imperialists were bound to be negative, for the United States had grown, after all, out of a former colonial empire. The assumptions that Americans made about imperial responsibility were conditioned by an awareness of distance from the scenes of European conflicts, by a knowledge that the American people were an amalgam of many of the peoples of the world, some themselves representative of the victims of imperial struggles, and from an emotional predisposition to apply the basic tenets of republicanism to the imperial situation.

Perhaps here lies the most significant differences between the American empire and other imperial growths of a comparable time. Most Americans, including their overseas administrators, hoped to make the colonial societies over in the American model so that they could qualify for self-government or for admission into the Union itself. This assumption produced, as Whitney T. Perkins has pointed out, "a safety valve of sorts in an inherent bias toward the extension of self-government." This bias was more far-reaching than the British bias toward establishing representative institutions on the Westminster [parliamentary] model, for it was there from the beginning, and republican principles were maintained for the so-called subject peoples as well as for the dominant nation. The territories acquired from Mexico whether by conquest or by purchase, became states of the Republic. So too did Alaska and Hawaii; and although the time needed to complete the necessary transformation before statehood became a reality was a long one, the assumption always was present that independence or statehood was the goal. The safety valve thus prevented the buildup within the colonies of a long-term ruling elite imposed from outside. It also decreased the intensity of local nationalist movements. While the British moved slowly toward their concept of indirect rule in East Africa, of governing through the already existing tribal structures, the United States applied a form of indirect rule almost immediately, and especially so in the Philippines, in Puerto Rico, and in Samoa. While the British anticipated that the Indians one day would be an independent people, as late as 1930 otherwise farsighted British spokesmen could suggest that such a day would not come for another century. Impatient, as usual, Americans presumed that their imperial role would be a short one, as indeed it was.

Unwilling to admit that dependency was more than a passing phase, American leaders were slow to think through the implications of having an empire. No permanent overseas civil service or military establishment, no educational system meant primarily to provide a continuing imperial tradition, arose to perpetuate imperial dogma. It is not without significance that American romantic novelists of empire, such as Richard Harding Davis, men of the same cloth as . . . Rudyard Kipling, wrote primarily of empires the United States did not hold, seldom using American colonial locales for their adventures. Perhaps the clearest proof that Americans assumed that their empire would be more transient than most may be seen in the fact that there was no Colonial Office, no Ministère des Colonies. The various territories were allocated to the Department of State, of the Interior, the Navy, and War; and when, in 1934, a Division of Territories and Island Possessions was created within the Department of the Interior, Guam and Samoa nonetheless were left to the Navy and the Panama Canal Zone to the Army.

The question is not, therefore, whether the United States or any other nation used power; rather, the questions are, how was this power first mobilized against the less powerful, and how was it ultimately employed? And in the answers to these two questions we may find some areas of contrast between American and, as an example, British imperial experiences.

The facts are clear enough. Most observers would agree in identifying two major periods of American expansion before 1939. The first of these, from perhaps 1803 until 1853, was a period of internal growth, of movement across the land from the eastern seaboard to the west coast, and of two wars — that of 1812–1814 with Britain and the Mexican War of 1846–1848 — which, while not primarily concerned with the acquisition of new territory, nonetheless involved considerable and admitted expansionist interests. When in 1853 the United States purchased an additional corner of land from Mexico for ten million dollars, expansion within contiguous areas was complete.

Was this first period of expansion imperialistic? Perhaps. Certainly the rhetoric that accompanied it was so, and some of the same genuinely held and humanitarian if arrogant views were present in 1812 and in 1846 as sustained the British, for example, during their forward movement in Southeast Asia and Africa after 1870. In 1859 a Congressman from Mississippi envisioned the incorporation of the whole of Mexico, Central America, South America, Cuba, and the West Indies into the Republic, just as Cecil Rhodes later wished to see the entirety of at least the eastern sweep of the African continent painted red on the imperial maps. If the same Congressman also suggested that France and England might be annexed as well, while permitting them to retain their local legislatures for the regulation of local affairs, his hyperbole can be matched by much that [British imperialists] . . . wrote or said about various African kingdoms and reasonably viable Indian states.

Certainly the roots of the later period of American expansion overseas lie in the pre–Civil War past, for it was then that the American idea of a national mission developed. The secularization of the earlier Puritan concepts, the growing sense of the covenant the American people had made with themselves during the Revolution and within their Constitution, and the heightened awareness of and belief in a unique American destiny, led many Americans sincerely to support any of several arguments for expansion. Many believed they were liberating Canadians from British despotism in 1814 and freeing Mexicans from harsh and undemocratic rule in 1847. The doctrine of natural right, the European idea of natural boundaries to which a nation or a people naturally must expand, the desire to extend the "area of freedom" to those less fortunate, the thought that energetic, egalitarian Americans could better use the soil, even that they might regenerate people who too long had lived under effete and declining European institutions, including European churches — all these impulses toward reform lay behind the expansion of the pre–Civil War years.

Because the United States had a continent to conquer, it developed its first empire internally, incorporating territory into the body politic in a way that European nations having to seek overseas outlets for their energies, their people, their goods, their investments, and their doctrines, could neither understand nor attempt. If Britain's third empire lay in Africa, America's first empire lay at hand, merely across the wide Missouri. An imperial democracy might grow within the continent. Thus continentalism, not imperialism, occupied the driving American energies until near the end of the century. As Frederick Jackson Turner was to point out in his essay on the significance of sections in American history, the South and the West at differing times were to think of themselves as colonies of the North and the East. The South was, after all, a conquered territory under military occupation between 1865 and 1877; and the West was, in its eyes and often in the eyes of Wall Street as well, a subject land. Further, Americans did not need coolies or castes in order to create an American *raj*. There always was the Negro to stand at the bottom of the social and economic scale, and there were the Indians to be pressed onto reservations.

The idea of mission was reinforced by the Federal victory in the Civil War. In 1867 the United States purchased Alaska from Russia. Following a period of internal concern for reconstructing Southern state governments, for reshaping the machinery of business, and for general domestic economic and social growth, Americans turned outward. The second major period of American expansion, and the first to propel America overseas, coincided with the world-wide wave of imperial annexations associated with the British, French, and German empires and with the awakening of Japan. If the earlier period were merely expansionist, as some contend, the growth between 1898 and 1920 was genuinely imperialist.

When Cubans renewed their periodic rebellion against the Spanish government early in 1895, *insurrectos* pillaged the land, destroying American and Spanish property indiscriminately, hoping to draw the United States into the conflict. The American Congress passed a concurrent resolution favoring recognition of Cuban belligerency, and anti-American rioting followed in Spain. Rioting in Cuba led the American government to send the battleship *Maine* to Havana Harbor to protect American lives and property; and on February 15, 1898, the *Maine* was sunk with the loss of over 250 lives. A month later a court of inquiry announced that an external submarine mine had caused the explosion, and the American public concluded, probably wrongly, that Spain had been responsible. War followed.

But war might have followed even had there been no incident in Havana Harbor. A generation of Americans that had known no war was seeking adventure. Prosperity had returned to the land following the panic of 1893, and the nation's self-confidence returned with good times. Talk of regenerating Cuba, of driving European powers from the American hemisphere, and of the white man's burden mingled with the pseudo-science of the time. Populist frustrations arising from the defeat of William Jennings Bryan at the polls in 1896 were channeled toward the Cuban adventure, where reforms that had been blocked at home might have at least some compensatory outlet abroad. Free silverites thought that the war might bring remonetization. Businessmen saw the opening up of Eastern markets where, as one noted, if every Chinaman would buy but a single box of matches, the entire match industry would become rich. Unable to resist the many pressures upon him, President McKinley allowed the nation to be swept into war.

From the Spanish-American War flowed a train of events with a logic of its own. The United States won the war with ease; it acquired Cuba, under a pledge to make it free; it became the imperial overlord in Puerto Rico, Guam, and the Philippines. In the

THE WHITE (?) MAN'S BURDEN.—From *Life* (New York).

This anti-imperialist political cartoon was published in the United States one month after the U.S. Senate approved the treaty annexing the Philippines and ending the Spanish-American War. Mocking Rudyard Kipling's poem, which urged Americans to "take up the white man's burden," the cartoon portrays Uncle Sam travelling with John Bull (representing England) and other European imperial lords, carried by their respective colonial subjects. (Life, March 16, 1899/Culver Pictures.)

midst of the war, the United States agreed to a petition from the Hawaiian Islands to annex that kingdom. In 1899, Americans took Wake Island as a link with Guam; and, in 1900, Tutuila in the Samoan group was added. The Open Door Notes of Secretary of State John Hay followed.

Since a direct link with the Pacific was now needed for the Atlantic-locked American navy, Theodore Roosevelt hurried Panama toward independence from Colombia. Without question he connived at the Panamanian revolution, encouraging a puppet state which, in 1904, sold a strip of land across its isthmus so that the new imperial power might build a canal. Caribbean stability thus became important, and Roosevelt added his corollary to the Monroe Doctrine by asserting that America could intervene in any Central American or Caribbean state where financial or political instability threatened European actions. Haiti virtually became an American protectorate in 1915, and the corollary would be used to justify intervention in Nicaragua, Honduras, and the Dominican Republic. In 1917 Denmark sold her Virgin Islands to the United States, a clear example, even though by purchase, of the preventive annexation to which Britain had felt forced to resort in the Pacific and Indian oceans. The Corn Islands were leased from Nicaragua to protect the Caribbean entrance to the new Panama Canal, and tiny coral atolls in the Pacific were claimed for potential communications stations. The Caribbean became an American lake.

To say that these annexations were tempered by the American commitment to re-publicanism is not to say that they were not a form of imperialism. Clearly they were. But to say that the American empire that resulted was identical or even necessarily sim-ilar to other empires is to put one's premise before one's conclusion. At first glance one may find parallels between the cant of an Alfred Thayer Mahan and the pseudo-theories of a Halford John Mackinder, between the pledge made by President Lyndon B. Johnson in Honolulu in 1966 to use American power to defend the freedom of Southeast Asia and the promises made by Japanese leaders in the 1930's to create a Great East-Asia Co-Prosperity Sphere, between the *pax Britannica* and the *pax Americana*. But as pat as these parallels may seem, one cannot deny the presence of some differences between the British and American imperial experiences that are of significance. Mahan, after all, found his chief use not by the American but by the Japanese Imperial Navy, and Mackinder's geopolitical theories were most used not by Britain but by Nazi Germany.

However administered, three differences stand out between the American and other empires. Most British acquisitions between 1870 and 1920 were for the purpose of sta-bilizing already held possessions, arising from turbulent frontiers lying across some un-occupied and intermediate hinterland, turbulence that created vacuums into which the British feared other nations would rush. American annexations, largely consisting of is-lands, shared the strategic and preventive aspects of European imperialism, but in terms of scale alone the American holdings were relatively insignificant, and each acquisition did not to nearly the same extent create an ever-widening circle of new conflicts. Sec-ond, there was no grand design to American expansionism, no overall world strategy, no forward movement as in British Malaya, tied either to a containment policy, as Britain's island acquisitions were in part, or tied to an assumption of semi-permanence.

The American occupations of both Haiti and the Dominican Republic were short-lived, seen from the outset to be temporary, with limited objectives in mind. This makes the occupations no less imperialistic, of course, but it does illustrate the makeshift nature of the American empire.

Most important, perhaps, is the by no means complimentary fact that the American imperialism was more culturally insidious than that of Britain or Germany, although perhaps not more so than that of France. To qualify for self-government among American states, colonial dependencies had to be utterly transformed, and the Americans often showed very little respect for Spanish culture in Puerto Rico, for Samoan life in Tutuila, or for the structure of the old Hawaiian kingdoms. The French, with their *mission civilisatrice,* were equally willing to insist that, to be civilized, the colonized must learn the language and customs of the conqueror. The British, ever more pragmatic, were content to administer through an elite, creating classes of Anglo-Indians and other cultural hyphenates but leaving the fundamental nature of the indigenous culture unchanged. Since they never anticipated the day when India would become part of the United Kingdom, and not until the 1920's did responsible officials give serious thought even to the loose linkage now involved in Commonwealth ties, wholesale Anglicizing was unnecessary. Precisely because the Americans did anticipate rapid progress toward assimilation did they insist upon such brutally fast Americanization.

As a British historian of empire David K. Fieldhouse has pointed out, what set the American empire apart, then, was the attempt to fit colonial possessions into [the mold of] . . . republicanism. No one provided a theoretical base for permanent colonialism, for the new territories were to be ushered into the United States on the basis of the same machinery, already established by the Constitution, that was used for Kentucky and Tennessee in the 1790's, for Colorado in 1876, and for Arizona in 1912. Congress extended full citizenship to the dependencies — to Puerto Ricans in 1917, to the Virgin Islands in 1927, to Guamanians in 1950. Representative government came quickly, responsible government slowly, and Congress exercised over the legislative bodies within the colonies the same kind of ultimate veto that lay in Britain's Colonial Laws Validity Act of 1865.

A difference of considerable importance lay in the fact that the American empire was the only one, other than the Russian, which formed a single economic system. Alaska and Hawaii were brought under the American tariff upon annexation, Puerto Rico in 1900, and the Philippine Islands in 1909. The advantages of such a system accrued almost entirely to the colonies, for all were primary producers who would have found their chief markets in the United States in any event. That the colonies felt more economically benefited than exploited may be seen from the Philippines' rejection of an offer of independence in 1933 because it meant gradual exclusion from the American protective system. Nor did the United States gain economically from the colonies. In 1925, a high point, only 4.9 per cent of American exports went to any of the colonial areas, including those Caribbean states bound to the United States by treaty. Nor did the colonies become important for capital — by World War II, Puerto Rico and the Philippines together held only 2.5 per cent of total overseas American investment, a figure ridiculously tiny compared to the sums placed in independent nations such as Mexico and Canada.

Perhaps here we discover a large area of comparability between American and European imperialisms. France, still primarily concerned with agricultural problems, stands apart from many generalizations, but Britain assuredly also realized little direct economic gain from her colonies. The British also preferred to place investment capital in areas that need not be annexed. The British informal empire, an empire of trade, investment, and influence, extended into the Middle East, to Argentina, and to the Baltic states, just as an American informal empire existed in Latin America, in Canada, and in parts of China. But such nations also gained from such contacts, as any study of the growth of Canadian industry or of Argentine rails would show. Informal empires were a mixed blessing, but mixed they were, doctrinaire ideologies notwithstanding.

The American empire may be contrasted to those of the European powers in another way, however. The United States had grown out of an earlier empire, and having fought a revolutionary war to gain its independence of Britain, it continued to hold to certain principles which, as we have seen, injected republican assumptions into colonial relationships. Further, all of the colonial possessions acquired by the United States, with the exception of Hawaii, had belonged to another nation before. They were not formerly independent states, they had not experienced a recent period of local autonomy, as Natal did under the Boers, as the Indian princely states had done before the British East India Company arrived upon the scene, or as the Malay States did under their sultans. Cuba, Puerto Rico, the Philippines, and Guam had been under Spanish control, the Virgin Islands under Danish, Alaska under Russian, Samoa under German and British, and the Canal Zone under Colombian. Former concepts of independence were not silenced and, in some cases, were introduced for the first time. The American imperial acquisitions might thus be best compared to those areas added to the British Empire at the Treaty of Versailles, as the spoils of war, not the spoils of trade. In effect, the American empire was not unlike the new colonial holdings of Australia and New Zealand — a ricochet empire, picked up as the by-product of other events, and ironically acquired by nations which themselves had grown out of former dependency status.

No European power gave any colony independence before the end of World War II. But the United States released Cuba from its administrative embrace in 1934 and promised in the same year to give the Philippines independence after a decade's transition period, a promise kept immediately following World War II. Puerto Rico was offered independence or statehood and chose neither, so that today it is a unique commonwealth, within the American nation, self-governing, and in part untaxed.

The United States rejected empire in 1945. Victorious, wealthy, clearly the most powerful nation on earth, the United States could have insisted upon retaining much, had nineteenth-century doctrines of power been operative. Perhaps it did not, as some of its critics say, because it recognized that through military occupation in Germany and Japan, through advantageous treaties with war-torn nations, and through the pervasive presence of American capital, there no longer was any need to build an empire in the old ways. Perhaps so; but if so, this was another kind of imperialism than was usually meant. It may be that American commitments overseas which arose in connection with Cold War diplomacy constituted another form of imperialism. But . . . whatever imperial content the diplomatic and military events of the 1960's may hold, that content is not comparable with the events of the classic period of world imperialisms that fell between 1870 and 1920. . . .

What, then, have we said of American imperialism? That, like all imperialisms, it was contradictory and that it could make an entire people appear to be hypocritical. When Woodrow Wilson set out to make the world safe for democracy, he spoke for *Realpolitik* as well as for humanitarianism, for the kind of democracy for which he wished to make the world safe was American democracy. But if he thought that he must teach South Americans to elect good men, he also remembered himself sufficiently not to do so. "We can afford," he thought, "to exercise the self-restraint of a really great nation which realizes its own strength and scorns to misuse it."

We have also said that similarities in motivation do not prove similarities in execution. The imperial experience, whether viewed from the gunboats of the expanding powers or from the beaches of the colonized peoples, must involve more than the first part of the story. Because the United States had no established church, no class of permanent civil servants, no entrenched system of private and privileged education, and no well-established military tradition, the American imperial movement was reinforced by fewer institutions. While G. A. Henry rode *Through the Khyber Pass* and Henri Fauconnier sought out *The Soul of Malaya,* American novelists did not write of Samoa, Guam, or Puerto Rico. Racism, romanticism, pseudo-science, and Christianity worked in roughly similar ways in British and American societies but they were projected into the colonies somewhat differently.

There are, perhaps, four questions which one might pose of any imperial relationship. What was the nature of the white settlers sent into the new country? What was the nature of the indigenous people? What was the degree of commitment on the part of the metropolitan power to retention of the territory and for what purposes? Within what geographical compass would the drama be played out? Since the United States sent few settlers into its empire, and since the areas, with the exception of the Philippines and Alaska, were quite small, the American answer to the first and last of these questions usually differed from the British, French, or Russian response. There rise the differences. In the answers to the second and third of the questions rise the similarities. One does not wish to reduce a complex problem to futile simplicities, but nonetheless one suspects that the American imperial experience is comparable to that of other nations only briefly, somewhat incidentally, and then but half the time.

QUESTIONS TO CONSIDER

1. Imperialism, the author says, is "an infinitely elastic term." How does Winks define imperialism in this essay? Is it the same as or different from territorial expansion? conquest in war? economic domination? What is Winks's attitude toward imperialism?

2. What nineteenth-century ideas about religion, race, nationalism, and progress provided justifications for imperialist ventures? What practical considerations fueled the quest for empire? Which of these motives and rationales did the United States share

with other late-nineteenth-century imperial powers? Which, if any, were uniquely American? Is there evidence to support the theory of Hobson in the American case?

3. Using specific examples and episodes, describe the two phases of American imperialism prior to 1920. What elements did they have in common? How did they differ?

4. In what ways did American imperialistic practices differ from those in European empires of the period from 1870 to 1920? How did the U.S. commitment to republicanism and the nation's history as a former colony shape its decisions about its own colonies? In what sense was the American empire small, "makeshift," and temporary? What evidence is there that the Americans, more than the British, imposed their customs and language upon their colonies?

5. Why have many Americans denied that there was such a thing as American imperialism? What features of imperialism, and what aspects of American national ideals, make it hard for Americans to admit that theirs was — and may still be — an imperialist nation?

America's Colonial Rule in the Philippines

VINCE BOUDREAU

To see American imperialism at work in a specific setting, we turn from the overview by Robin Winks in the preceding selection to a detailed analysis of the workings of American rule in the Philippines. Few Americans are aware that the nation fought not one but two wars to acquire these tropical Pacific islands. The first, the Spanish-American War of 1898 described by Winks, stemmed from American support for Cuba's anticolonial rebels and public anger over the sinking of the battleship Maine *in Havana harbor, which the "yellow press" mistakenly blamed on Spanish subterfuge. Although the main target of this "splendid little war" (as American pro-imperialist John Hay called it) was the Spanish empire in the Caribbean, halfway across the globe an American naval squadron moved quickly into Manila Bay and destroyed its Spanish fleet, and the squadron was followed by an army expeditionary force that captured Manila itself. American president William McKinley, who had forsworn annexing Cuba, had different ideas about keeping up with European imperial powers in the Pacific. After wrestling with the question of annexing the Philippine Islands, he decided that "there was nothing left for us to do but to take them all and to educate the Filipinos, and uplift, and civilize, and Christianize them." McKinley apparently did not realize that the Spanish had converted many Philippine natives to Catholicism. He also underestimated how many Americans would oppose his decision. American public opinion was sharply divided between imperialists and anti-imperialists, and the Treaty of Paris (1899), by which Spain ceded the Philippines, Guam, and Puerto Rico to the United States for $20 million, barely survived its struggle for ratification in the U.S. Senate.*

A different kind of resistance was put up by the Filipinos themselves, who had not been consulted and had no desire to exchange Spanish overseers for American ones. A popular independence movement led by Emilio Aguinaldo had been fighting the Spanish years before the Americans arrived. When the Spanish surrendered, these rebels declared the islands independent and expected American support. Rebuffed, they waged war on U.S. occupying forces. America's second, less-remembered Philippine war was a much longer and bloodier conflict than the first. Aguinaldo's rebels adopted guerrilla tactics, hiding in jungle and mountain retreats from which they conducted hit-and-run attacks. The Americans responded by herding native villagers into "concentration camps" in order to isolate the guerrillas. By the time the main body of rebels was subdued in 1902, more than seven thousand Americans had been killed or wounded and two hundred thousand Filipinos had died through battle, disease, and famine.

Ironically, after such a bloody beginning, American rule in the Philippines took a very different turn. Mindful of popular misgivings back home and smoldering Filipino resentment, a series of pragmatic American governers-general, including future U.S. president William Howard Taft, worked hard to win the support of the islands' people. Under an orderly "Filipinization" process begun in 1901, the Americans granted the colony increasing measures of self-rule. An elected legislative assembly was created in 1907, then a bicameral legislature in 1916 by the Jones Act, which also promised the Philippines eventual independence. Commonwealth status, proclaimed in 1935, replaced the American governor with an elected president, who presided until the Philippines became fully independent after Japan's defeat a decade later. This systematic transfer of power was a rare case in which an imperial government voluntarily relinquished colonial rule. Furthermore, as Vince Boudreau notes in the following essay, the Philippines' growing political autonomy was supplemented by other American policies, including restrictions on American ownership of plantations and the establishment of an American-style public school system that spanned the islands and reached from kindergarten to the university level.

Boudreau, a political scientist who studies protest movements, is concerned with "methods of [colonial] domination" and "modes of resistance." His inquiry is explicitly comparative. Starting with the question of why popular protests against American rule in the Philippines were less radical and powerful than anticolonial movements elsewhere in Southeast Asia, Boudreau looks for answers not only in Filipino society but also in the distinctive nature of American colonial rule. He places both American policies and Filipino responses in a wider context through comparisons with colonial arrangements in Dutch Indonesia, British Burma, and French Vietnam. You may have some difficulty getting used to his social science jargon (with its "political elites," "bureaucratic corps," and "nationalist mobilization"), and you should use the Glossary to help with references to people and events in Philippine history. But Boudreau's wide-ranging discussion will reward your close reading with new information and insights about American colonial policy, a topic too often left out of U.S. history courses. And his overall emphasis should be clear: a combination of fortunate timing, divisions in Philippine society, and comparatively enlightened U.S. colonial policies created "successful" American rule that enabled the Philippines to make a relatively peaceful transition to independence.

Of course, in what sense American colonialism in the Philippines was "successful" and for whom are complex questions that you should address once you have read Boudreau's essay. Ask yourself, too, whether the evidence presented by Boudreau supports the claim made by Robin Winks in Selection 9 that American imperial rule was tempered by its commitment to republican values and institutions. Finally, lest you emerge from your reading with the impression that American imperialism was an unmixed blessing, you should balance Boudreau's findings with important considerations his essay alludes to but does not highlight. First, recall that American control over the Philippines came only after victory in a prolonged, brutal war against national independence forces. Second, note that, although

American rule brought the apparatus of popular government to the Philippines, it did little to rectify the islands' economic problems, strengthening the power of large landholders, widening the gap between rich and poor, and creating an economy heavily dependent upon exports to the United States. Third, consider the larger issue posed by domestic opponents of American colonial rule: is it appropriate for the United States, a republic born from a colonial revolt and proclaiming the right of all peoples to self-government, to take on the mantle of empire?

GLOSSARY

AGUINALDO, EMILIO (1869–1964)   The nationalist leader who fought Spain and then the United States for Philippine independence. Exiled by the Spanish to Hong Kong, he returned to assist in the U.S. war of 1898 against Spain. During the war, the Filipinos declared their independence and named Aguinaldo president, but after Spain ceded the islands to the United States, hostilities broke out between Philippine and American troops. The "Philippine Insurrection" turned into a brutal guerrilla war. Aguinaldo was captured in 1901, pledged allegiance to the United States, and returned to private life, but organized resistance continued for several years on southern Philippine islands.

ARCHIPELAGO   A group of islands; in this case, the roughly seven thousand islands that make up the Philippines.

BOLSHEVIK REVOLUTION   The second phase of the Russian Revolution of 1917, in which the Bolsheviks under V. I. Lenin seized control of the provisional government that had been established when the czar was overthrown in February. This inaugurated communist rule of the Soviet Union.

CREOLE QUESTIONS   Disputes between European (or Europeanized) colonists and the imperial mother country.

FILIPINIZATION   The process, begun in 1901, by which American colonial authorities granted expanding spheres of legislative, law enforcement, and administrative action to Filipino elites while maintaining ultimate control.

HUK REBELLION (1946–1954)   A communist-led peasant uprising in central Luzon. Begun as guerrilla warfare against Japanese occupation during World War II, it escalated into an attack on large landowners. Banned from the Philippine Congress in 1946, the Huks opened a rebellion against the newly independent government that was suppressed by a combination of U.S. military aid and the promise of land reforms.

ILUSTRADOS   Filipino educated elites, based in Manila, who led a disjointed drive for national independence between 1872 and 1898 but accommodated to American rule thereafter.

KATIPUNAN NG BAYAN   The Filipino nationalist society, founded in 1892 and led by Aguinaldo, that opposed Spanish rule.

MARCOS, FERDINAND (1917–1989)   President of the Philippine Republic, elected on the Nacionalista Party ticket in 1965. The U.S.-supported Marcos pursued a moderate agenda in his first term. After reelection in 1969, he became increasingly authoritarian and corrupt, declaring martial law, jailing political opponents, and taking over the army. In 1986 he fled the country after charges that he had assassinated a potential rival and rigged his recent reelection.

MCKINLEY, WILLIAM (1843–1901)   The Republican president of the United States who followed public opinion into the Spanish-American War after the sinking of the battleship *Maine* in February 1898. Faced with the decision to take colonies as spoils of war, McKinley declared that Puerto Rico, Guam, and the Philippines should be made American territories.

METROPOLE   The parent or ruling nation of a colony: in the case of the Philippines, the United States.

MYOTHUGYIS   The local hereditary authorities in Burma who were displaced by British colonial rule.

NACIONALISTA PARTY   The Philippine political party, advocating a peaceful path to independence, that dominated colonial politics after its formation in 1907. A shifting coalition of groups, it was shaped by personal rivalry between its founder, Sergio Osmena, and Manuel Luis Quezon y Molina.

PHILIPPINE SOCIALIST PARTY   The leftist party founded in 1929 by the wealthy lawyer Pedro Abad Santos. The Socialists formed a disciplined coalition of tenant farmers and urban workers in the wake of the failed Sakdal uprising. This party made substantial electoral gains in the years before the Japanese takeover of 1942.

QUEZON Y MOLINA, MANUEL LUIS (1878–1944)   President of the commonwealth government of the Philippines from 1935 to 1942. A member of Aguinaldo's independence movement, Quezon entered colonial politics under U.S. rule and in 1909 was appointed nonvoting representative to the U.S. Congress. There he helped to pass the Jones Act (1916), which gave the Philippines an elected bicameral legislature and promised future independence. Returned to Manila, Quezon gained control of the Nacionalista Party and was elected president of the new commonwealth government. As president, Quezon established central control over the military, developed the southern island of Mindinao, and fought government graft and corruption. He formed a government in exile in the United States when Japan occupied the Philippines in 1942 but died shortly before independence was established following World War II.

SAKDAL UPRISING (1935)   An agrarian revolt against large landowners and control of the Philippines by the Nacionalista Party and the United States. Named for the opposition newspaper *Sakdal,* this uprising tried to prevent a plebiscite (popular vote) that would ratify the islands' commonwealth status and delay independence for ten years. It was easily suppressed.

SAYA SAN REBELLION (1930–1932)   A peasant uprising against British rule in Burma. Precipitated by heavy taxes and falling rice prices, it was led by Saya San, who sought to restore the Burmese monarchy. Captured by the British, San was hanged in 1931 and more than ten thousand of his followers were killed.

★ ★ ★ ★ ★ ★

R elative to activity in colonial regimes across Southeast Asia, Philippine protest during the American period was distinct. Although many Filipinos were dissatisfied with the pace or terms of promised independence over the course of the American period, the promise itself sufficed to draw emerging national elites away from mass-mobilizing contention. The absence of national elites in protest movements left a distinct imprint on protest and mobilization during this period; it also shaped broader political alliances that would emerge under U.S. rule and beyond.

Hence, whereas nationalist student activists spearheaded resistance movements in Burma and Indonesia and provided an important push to Vietnamese nationalism, they remained marginal to Philippine nationalist protest from 1898 until the regime of Ferdinand Marcos (1965–1986). Coalitions between peasants and local intellectuals helped focus vast agrarian resistance movements such as the Burmese Saya San rebellion and Vietnam's 1908 tax rebellion; early-twentieth-century Philippine agrarian revolts, including the comparatively large Sakdal uprising in 1935, were mainly local affairs with weak national alliances and relatively parochial orientations. Whereas the Burmese civil service applied sustained pressure for independence, Philippine bureaucrats seldom produced sharp or radical political demands, except when members of that service lost their positions. Although Philippine labor organizations did mount several important strike and protest waves under U.S. rule, their most important national connections were to electoral parties, and Philippine labor never acquired the large-scale revolutionary stature that Burmese oil workers or the northern Vietnamese proletariat gained in their struggles. [On the other hand,] Philippine protest under U.S. colonialism . . . developed modes of activity, such as suffragist movements and heated electoral contests between recognized political parties, that were unique in the region.

Distinct elements of U.S. colonial rule significantly shaped Philippine protest and resistance. Most particularly, without a coherent national elite leadership, Philippine protest tended toward limited and localized mass expressions or more civil demonstrations to demand broader voice or resources *within* existing or proposed arrangements. . . .

To make this argument, I take a comparative perspective that considers contrasts and comparisons between the Philippines and [European] colonies in Burma, Indonesia, and Vietnam. According to one classic typology, colonists govern either directly, by bringing or creating their own administration, or indirectly through existing local authorities. As will be shown, however, this distinction says comparatively little about how colonialism created and transformed administrative elites, about how such elites positioned themselves in relation to colonialism itself, or about the forces that pushed some toward anticolonial struggles and some toward collaborative interactions. . . .

From Vince Boudreau, "Methods of Domination and Modes of Resistance: The U.S. Colonial State and Philippine Mobilization in Comparative Perspective," in *The American Colonial State in the Philippines: Global Perspectives,* ed. Julian Go and Annie L. Foster. Copyright © 2003 by Duke University Press.

Three aspects of U.S. colonial practice worked unique influences on Philippine society in comparison with other Southeast Asian cases. First, the United States acquired a Philippine colony that had developed some coherence under Spanish rule — and in resisting that rule. More important, Americans could imagine the territory as a single package, defined as that which Spain had governed and the United States acquired by treaty. . . . [Thus,] the U.S. administration regarded the puzzles attendant in acquiring a territory with a resident population differently from earlier colonial regimes. The initial model for the U.S. colonial project could be neither jungle exploration nor [the] rolling conquest of nineteenth-century pre-national colonialism. Rather, it was the pacification of territory already acquired and the subsequent extension of governance over whatever territory the administration decided to retain. Hence, whereas colonial powers in Indonesia, Vietnam, and Burma incrementally established dominion over colonial territory, constructed colonial states and social institutions piecemeal, and confronted questions of governance and representation only when compelled to by pressures against their rule, the United States dealt with these questions up front and arrived more quickly at the construction of integrated political institutions, including local security forces, representative assemblies, and a far-reaching civil service. Municipal governments were rapidly organized in the first years of U.S. rule in the Philippines, and a major consideration before the U.S. Congress in 1901 was the drafting of an "organic law or constitution" for the colonial government.

This orientation, in turn, contributed to distinct ideas about representation, education, and the bureaucracy. Governing the Philippines raised questions about political responsibilities toward the islands' residents, not least because the question of colonial rule required justification at home beyond the economic exhortations of expansionist Republicans. The United States, as many have noted, approached the construction of governing institutions at least partly as a way to create a tractable political elite positioned and inclined to deflect and temper grievances generated by Philippine society under U.S. rule. These governing policies, discussed in more detail later, prevented potentially explosive nationalist alliances between political elites and the bureaucratic corps; encouraged political elites to recruit, socialize, and tame young college graduates; and placed many contentious decisions about bureaucratic hiring and promotion under Filipino, rather than American, authority.

The contrasts with other Southeast Asian cases are impressive. Dutch reforms in Indonesian educational and administrative policy increasingly placed aristocratic and upwardly mobile students together inside colonial schools and offices and outside them as unemployed, resentful graduates. When French schools in Vietnam began to produce their own Western-trained functionaries, local scholarly elites detached themselves from the larger educational system and provided important political and moral leadership to a nationalist movement of students and a growing class of "new intelligentsia." The destruction of the old Burmese court (the Hutladaw) in 1888 and of local authorities (*Myothugyis*) gave young Burmese graduates of British colonial schools a nationalist mistrust of British intentions (bolstered by the importation of Indian and Tamil bureaucrats) and a relatively free hand to assume leadership of the nationalist campaign. Quite obviously, . . . these policies, and the apparent persistence of colonial rule, provided nationalism with a more robust political vehicle. But it also produced models of protest and contention that outlasted the nationalist phase and shaped models of collective resistance into the independence period.

A third, ideological peculiarity underpins the distinctive arrangement of U.S. colonial institutions. America's colonial epoch began after its own Civil War helped dispatch the aristocratic ideology on which the U.S. South's plantation economy had rested. In its place, an orientation favoring individual rights and equality before the law linked to Northern industrialization and Western expansion captured Americans' imagination. This orientation produced support for universal education, broad suffrage, and upward mobility, which did not sit well with Philippine agrarian elites who formed the political backbone of the Philippine Assembly: Most of the Philippine members of this new representative institution had far less liberal orientations and relied on more explicitly unequal social and political conventions designed to insure a docile labor force. Not surprisingly, therefore, indigenous elites often labored to preserve their prerogatives against the grain of U.S. policy and inclination. Hence, from the outset, U.S. domination of the Philippines was somewhat at odds with local class domination, and local elites drew more fire and ire than Americans from upward-striving nationalists, particularly during moments of electoral competition and bureaucratic reorganization.

THE PHILIPPINES AT THE DAWN OF U.S. COLONIAL RULE

Although distinctive aspects of the U.S. administration set the Philippine regime apart, the entire arrangement also sat atop a society that in many ways was already distinct from the rest of Southeast Asia. In one respect, this distinctiveness consists in the recent Philippine revolutionary climax and the original connection that existed, however briefly, between arriving U.S. forces and elite Philippine nationalists. By 1898, the struggle against Spain had passed from its political to its military phase, and many of the nation's brightest leaders had given their lives in pushing the independence struggle to that point. In addition, by 1898 the logic of the revolution's military phase had placed particular burdens on Philippine society. In moving to open military struggle against a weakened Spain, Filipino revolutionaries shed important tactical and political advantages associated with secret societies, unions, and local mass organizations. For example, although the Katipunan ng Bayan had begun as a decentralized collection of social and secret forces based in Filipino neighborhoods, the war took soldiers out of these neighborhoods, forged them into an army (the revolution's first organization with national scope), and strained the more organic connection between local society and the resistance. After 1898, anticolonial forces faced a vigorous American adversary instead of the worn-out Spanish administration, and the Americans developed new tactics, such as concentration camps in Cavite, Batangas, and Laguna, that isolated revolutionaries from their social base. Differences also began to emerge between the military under Emilio Aguinaldo's Cavite-based leadership and the Ilustrado movement's (a nationalist movement of the elite) Manila intellectuals — triggered largely when Americans offered incentives to the latter at a time that the revolutionary organization was still mainly unconsolidated. Hence, in important ways the revolution paid for its early victory over Spain through substantial sacrifices in political capacities necessary to defeat the United States.

Moreover, the 1898 revolution took place about twenty years before anticolonialism had developed a substantial global political and organizational infrastructure, and this bit of timing had significant consequences. The decrepitude of the Spanish colonial regime, at war with the United States and already bereft of prime acquisitions in Latin America, accounted in substantial measure for Filipinos' early successes at the nineteenth century's close. But the Philippines' comparatively early revolutionary upsurge also segregated the Philippine struggle from some of the more important events in that global history, such as the impact (especially in Asia) of the Japanese victory over Russia in 1905 and of the Bolshevik Revolution in 1917. These events pushed anticolonialists' resolve toward more resolute demands for self-rule rather than for expanded representation. Filipino nationalists in 1898 were therefore somewhat different from nationalists who soon emerged elsewhere in Southeast Asia. . . . Anticolonial questions in the late nineteenth century were still primarily creole questions, potentially resolved by imperialism's concessions to local elites' aspirations for greater standing within the colonial regime. . . . But the more global anti-imperialism of [the twentieth century] and the supporting institutions of transnational movement and party organizations, had not yet clearly emerged. Hence, elite Filipino nationalists had little in the way of a global movement with which to counterbalance absorption into the U.S. system. If anything, the early conclusion of the revolutionary war against Spain, and clear strategies to supplant Spanish culture with Americanism, left the society plastic and defenseless in the face of U.S. efforts to develop a base in the archipelago.

PHILIPPINE COLLECTIVE ACTION UNDER U.S. RULE

It is possible to divide Philippine protest and collective action under U.S. colonialism roughly into three periods. The first period . . . divides into two American wars: one against Muslims (Moros) in Mindanao, and the other against Christians in Luzon and the Visayas. Both began in 1899. The Moro wars lasted until 1912, and the Christian wars lasted until 1907. Filipinos at first engaged Americans in artillery battles along the railway corridor from Manila to Pangasinan, but heavy casualties soon forced them to switch to guerrilla tactics. After the switch, the Americans shifted their attention to severing the connection between the guerrilla fighters and their mass base. In Luzon, the United States built concentration camps that held entire provinces hostage to their soldiers' surrender. In the south, the army preferred to pound Muslim population centers into submission with artillery rather than imprison their residents. After brutal tactics in both theaters had killed an estimated 13 percent of the archipelago's population, the United States forced surrender on the resistance.

Even before this killing ended, some Filipinos began new forms of struggle and collective action, designed to secure positions within and under the U.S. regime rather than to displace that rule. As the Philippine-American War moved out of Manila and into the countryside, rapid capitalist expansion produced new activity among workers in Manila and would shortly do so in important secondary cities such as Iloilo and Cebu. At first, working communities fell back on autonomous forms of self-help organized among a *balangay* (community) of those practicing a similar trade. . . . Before long, mutual-aid societies gave way to more outward-directed strategies of strikes and union politics. The U.S. regime, transporting ideas of rule and governance to its new colony, began a policy of limited toleration for mutual-aid associations . . . and in 1908 established an institution that would have been unheard of under the Spanish or, indeed, in other colonial regimes across the region: the Bureau of Labor. This bureau, alongside Nacionalista Party efforts to win worker support in 1907 elections, legitimized labor politics and unions within limited economic and electoral parameters. Over the next several decades, workers' strikes largely reflected economic pressures on poor consumers, such as the ebb and flow of rice prices. More broadly, the advent of electoral politics opened the question of suffrage in various ways; encouraged by contact with American women, Filipinos began organizing the suffragist movement to lobby for the women's vote. In both instances, unfolding representative opportunities encouraged urban populations to launch civic demonstrations designed to secure access to and standing in the new regime.

A much different, and more militant, struggle emerged frequently after 1923. A wave of small-scale peasant and worker-based rebellions began in the countryside, initially in reaction to central-state interference in local religious practices . . . and subsequently as capitalist expansion changed agrarian social relations and impoverished farmers in the countryside. In the cities, labor protest radicalized in the mid-1920s and 1930s and benefited from new educated and middle-class allies with axes to grind against Manuel Quezon's efforts to centralize and purge the state. In both agrarian and rural rebellions, new themes entered the struggle. Mobilized and disaffected groups accused elites of betraying Philippine nationalist aspirations — something that suggests a diversification of nationalist perspectives beyond those of the national leadership. But it also suggests something that became increasingly prominent as independence drew near: The primary cleavages inflamed by nationalist debate did not separate American and Filipino adversaries; rather, they divided Filipinos. Tactically, the movements left behind the more civil modes of struggle within "pacified" territory during the century's first decades in favor of armed clashes with the constabulary that led predictably to one-sided defeats for activists. Rebellions from 1923 to 1935 were partly the fallout of political centralization that forged an increasingly closed and exclusive national elite. Agrarian rebellions were usually led by fairly parochial elites and tended to attract localized and limited support for violent outbursts rather than sustained struggles. Labor movements, and other, more urban modes of contention, often pulled together under former or aspiring members of the government bureaucracy who had been removed from or denied positions in the government. Urban protests . . . often were more center-directed and sustained, but they still levied their sharpest and most radical criticism against collaborating Filipino elites.

If Philippine collective action under U.S. rule is in many ways distinct from that in other Southeast Asian colonies, the utter absence of a truly integrative and national elite leadership for Philippine collective action is central to this difference. The question is not so much why Filipino elites did not join a more radical nationalist movement against U.S. rule, for their more passive and patient activity makes perfect sense in light of the United States' promise of impending self-rule and the economic advantages elites enjoyed during the U.S. regime. Rather, how did the absence of broad and cross-class nationalist alliances set the tone for other forms of collective action and political contention? Without strong and national elite allies, demonstrations that began in the early 1900s, and continued through their more militant phase in the 1920s and 1930s, remained the limited affairs of small sections of society. Activists in these movements championed the explicitly segmented interests of people organized in bounded groups of women or workers rather than the more integrated demands framed as emanating from a Filipino nation.... A reason may be that, beyond U.S. promises of Philippine self-rule, administrative and class divisions wrought on Philippine society by the structure of the American colonial state also greatly influenced mobilization and dissident patterns in the archipelago.

THE DISTINCTIVENESS OF U.S. COLONIAL RULE IN THE PHILIPPINES

In terms of world time, it makes sense to begin a consideration of the U.S. colonial state by setting it alongside Japan's burgeoning imperial efforts. Both countries walked onto the colonial stage as colonialism itself began to creak under the weight of its gathering obsolescence. . . . What distinguished the two regimes from each other, however, were their varying orientations and motivations for colonial acquisition. In late developing Japan, the state's competitive haste to enhance industrial production and accelerate national capacities required both vast external reserves of raw materials and a patriotic mission of expansion to deflect increased pressure on local populations. Pushed by these stimuli, Japanese imperialism developed into a strong state-led effort at domination and extraction that in most ways was utterly unconflicted and focused on overcoming competition from established colonial powers expanding through its Asian hinterland.

U.S. contrasts with the Japanese pattern lie rooted in America's comparatively earlier and more self-contained industrialization process. The United States approached its colonial period without a serious shortfall of natural resources to spur a state-led mercantilist expansion and without the need to relieve social pressure from an overworked domestic society. Instead, U.S. business desired a base from which to explore and exploit market opportunities in China, but this position was strongly supported by only a small circle of expansionist Republicans. Thus, the United States' colonial enterprise required domestic justification elaborated in terms of other-directed missions, including a mission to govern justly, rather than as the mere acquisition of resources and markets. Acquisitive races with other large states to obtain a market share of China did not, therefore, strongly attract social support in the United States. America's political competition with rivals, primarily European rivals, was in fact more popularly expressed in the ironically *anti*colonial Spanish-American War. Hence, while President McKinley's operatic confusion over the Philippine question never quite rang true, Americans (even powerful and politically involved Americans) did not agree about the purpose the colony would serve. In the pitched debates over retention, therefore, the justification for the Philippine colony was largely made in terms of the character of U.S. rule, and expansionist Republicans had a ready model for Philippine exploitation in the recently completed conquest of the American frontier.

Lacking Japan's imperial drive and armed with its own individualist ideology, U.S. colonialism did not attempt to place economic activities under state auspices. The greatest U.S. colonial presence occurred during the Philippine-American War and fell off sharply immediately thereafter. Having attained military ascendency over the Filipino anticolonial resistance, the United States soon reduced its troops, and by 1903 the number of American soldiers in the country had fallen to 17,748 from a 1901 high of 71,528. The maintenance of civil law and order passed from the U.S. War Department to a newly created Philippine Constabulary, with more localized staffing, command, and control. By 1904, only 345 American officers led 7,000 Filipino constables. As the American fighting force underwent this transformation, the broader logic of U.S. control in the Philippines emerged. The state would separate colonial administration from accumulation and insure American society's untrammeled access to Philippine markets and productive resources. In setting up this system, the United States strove to establish laws and treaties regulating commerce and trade that insured American ascendency; to that end, Americans dominated any governing body responsible for drafting these regulations. In contrast, authorities charged with implementing and maintaining the rules were judged to have less discretionary power, and such posts could pass to Filipinos (suitably trained in the new U.S. educational system) through the much publicized Filipinization policy.

The educational system that prepared Filipino bureaucrats for their new responsibilities constitutes one of the most important elements of the American system. Soon after it gained control over the Philippines, the U.S. colonial government began an astoundingly broad effort at non-vernacular [non-native language] education, unprecedented in its number of both students and Americans deployed as teachers. . . . This, and the colonial state's decision to replace predominantly Spanish administrators with Filipinos, rendered educational attainment one of the great engines for upward mobility for middle- and lower-class Filipinos at that time. But perhaps of equal importance to the system's development was that educational institutions stood on a national, rather than international, framework. While young Indonesians, Vietnamese, and Burmese could acquire a passable administrative education in their own countries, those who aspired to advanced university education typically traveled to Europe. In the Philippines, several old Spanish colleges already existed to provide such education, and the Americans soon built others, such as the University of the Philippines (1908) on American University models — that is, not as mere training academies for administrators but as vehicles for providing higher, professional education. Some students still traveled abroad to study, but from the early 1900s, it became possible for local people to obtain advanced,

The Philippines and other colonies and protectorates in Southeast Asia in 1900. *As this map indicates, in this region the United States competed with France, Britain, Holland, Portugal, Germany, and Japan for trade and territory. Japan moved southward to annex Taiwan in 1895. Among the colonies mentioned in Selection 10, British Burma lay to the west of Siam (Thailand); Vietnam was the later name for Annam, the coastal region of French Indochina from the Chinese border to Saigon; and Indonesia was the name taken by the Dutch East Indies after independence. Note the Philippines' strategic location near China, whose ports the United States had sought to access since the 1880s.*

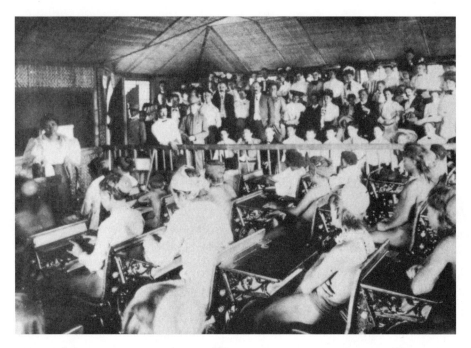

Americans established a tax-supported public school system in the Philippines that featured English-language instruction, dramatically improved popular literacy, and promised upward mobility to ordinary Filipinos. This class of Filipino students was put on display at the St. Louis World's Fair of 1904 to show American spectators (in the background) the benefits of their nation's imperial rule. (Missouri Historical Society.)

professional degrees in the archipelago. Hence unlike their counterparts across Southeast Asia, many of the Philippines' twentieth-century leaders had not studied abroad for any length of time. Rather, they rose within domestic networks that continued to connect them to campus life even as they moved into government.

From 1901 onward, as the coercive American presence declined, the shock troops of U.S. colonialism arrived in robust numbers: Newspapermen, entrepreneurs, bankers, and lawyers flooded Manila and streamed into the provinces. They took charge of a massive effort to meet greatly expanded Western demand for tropical products such as sugar, copra [coconut], and abaca [hemp]. They established the great sugar centrals, mapped out strategies for broader fruit production for export markets, and accelerated timber and mining operations. In these efforts, they worked hand in hand with the landed provincial elite who had been gathering power and productive resources during the last years of Spanish rule — an alliance rendered indispensable by legal restrictions on U.S. participation in the Philippine plantation economy, and . . . by some American ambivalence in the metropole about Philippine economic opportunities. For these local elites, it was a time of great opportunity: Credit was readily available; new production strategies energized all types of industry; and formerly tight Spanish export controls were replaced with preferential access to the larger U.S. market and a more open orientation toward global trade in general. Under the new American regime, local businessmen made a killing both by taking over industrial niches previously dominated by the Spanish and by rapidly acclimating themselves to the more freewheeling and liberal American system of trade and production.

Soon, two important alliances emerged between U.S. colonialism and Philippine society. First, the U.S. colonial state nurtured the new Filipino bureaucrat corps. This upwardly mobile civil service benefited from the comparatively egalitarian and democratic impulse of the United States' colonial administration. Second, the rush of American business planted entrepreneurial seeds among landed provincial elites who were awakening to the new possibilities of a global economy. . . . Such Filipino elites were often as wary of the administrative opportunities afforded their lower-class countrymen as they were eager themselves to participate in more aggressive capitalist accumulation. . . . Hence, a tension existed in the regime's social base between mass-educated and upwardly mobile colonial bureaucrats from a new middle class and a revitalized and aristocratic principalia [landed provincial elite]. These new political elites could take advantage of capitalist opportunities but were neither willing nor compelled (by the need to recruit mass support) to share power with the middle and lower classes.

The Philippine Assembly's institutional arrangement combined with the class tension at colonialism's social base to influence protest and mobilization under the U.S. regime. In part, the idea behind the Philippine Assembly replicated the United States' own bicameral pattern of regional representation: Its Filipino members came from across the archipelago and both protected regional interests and integrated regional elites nationally. But the evolution of the electoral system also insured the hegemony of landed interests over the newer working and administrative classes. Severe literacy and property requirements initially restricted the franchise to roughly 2 percent of the population. Elections began in 1902 with municipal-level contests that the local elite easily dominated, then used to establish patronage machines for larger contests. The Philippine Assembly's lower house was first elected in 1907, and broader bicameral contests followed in 1916. . . .

The Philippine Assembly's distinct aspect was its position between society and the colonial state in importantly ambiguous relations to both power and national aspiration. Its members accommodated themselves to colonial rule, but its Nacionalista Party grounded recruitment on the demand for immediate independence. The assembly's independence debates, although tamed by their perch inside the U.S. colonial state, nevertheless drew attention from student activists and others who might otherwise have looked elsewhere for political leadership. Moreover, the pageantry of periodic electoral competition gave these debates, demonstrations, and rallies a hothouse radicalism that both channeled dissent in directions that U.S. rule could accommodate and squarely fixed rival Filipino politicians, rather than American colonists, in the rhetorical crosshairs. Because assembly members held elected office, moreover, they constructed specific sorts of relationships with voting segments of Philippine society, and these relationships influenced dissent. In the first two decades of U.S. rule, for instance, workers pursuing mutual aid and socioeconomic unionism expended great efforts to link themselves to electoral machines. Labor militancy outside electoral arenas could neither attract enough attention from assembly members to influence legislative debates nor distract national elites from these formal representative institutions. . . .

The relationship between the Philippine Assembly and the broader society, then, explains some peculiar aspects of political mobilization under U.S. rule. First, the absence of any significant national anticolonial movement or organization outside the political parties reflects the influence of the Americans' promise of self-rule, and the consequent efforts of Filipinos to concentrate on representative institutions that would secure position in that new dispensation. Those who may have been expected to construct a national political movement — such as labor-union members and the students who, by the late 1920s, periodically protested on university campuses — instead drew near party politics and often demonstrated in the service of party campaigns. Agrarian protest had virtually no cosmopolitan leadership: The electoral dynamic was overwhelmingly patronage-based, which quarantined mass communities from national politics and alleviated the need for national figures to work out a political posture that agrarian society would support. Even movements that would eventually develop into more national challenges, such as the Huk rebellion, began as local and mainly parochial collectives and achieved national stature only in the struggle against the Japanese occupation. . . .

COMPARATIVE PERSPECTIVES ON THE COLONIAL STATE AND SOCIAL RESISTANCE

. . . Although each [colonial] case [in Southeast Asia] stands apart from the others in important respects, there is considerable reason particularly to distinguish the engagement between Philippine society and U.S. colonialism. The combination in the Philippines of promised independence, economic and political concessions to new elites, and the creation of separate political and administrative classes early on scattered nationalist energies. The space for maneuver gained in those first years, at least partly (for the Americans) a lucky consequence of the revolutionary climax against Spanish rule, allowed the United States to establish a more responsive approach to governance — or, at least, an approach that was responsive enough to overcome skeptics in the United States and some dissidents in Philippine society. At the same time, this particular brand of U.S. colonial rule . . . made it more possible for U.S. colonists to co-opt Filipino nationalists. Having attracted important elements of the anti-Spanish movement to the American side, U.S. colonists needed to outflank not a nationalism running at flood tide but one that had ebbed considerably.

In contrast, representative institutions in Indonesia, Burma, and Vietnam were a step behind, and they struggled to overtake, mobilized anticolonialism — and an anticolonialism with new and more powerful global support and precedence that managed to hold national elites and mass followers firmly together. Dutch, British, and French struggles with colonial societies therefore encountered adversaries who stood atop socially broader and more powerfully adversarial coalitions. Liberal reforms in each of these settings never successfully undercut nationalism. Rather, they inspired vibrant and broadly based counteroffensives. Although it may be true that U.S. colonialism pursued some exceptional policies in the Philippines, . . . profound differences between Philippine experiences and those of Indonesia, Burma, and Vietnam probably had more to do with the timing and global context of colonial rule, because these conditions influenced the political consequences of colonial practice. It is in this particular global context that the practices of U.S. imperialism exercised their special effect in the Philippines.

Flashpoints of local resistance against Dutch, British, and French rule all resulted from increases in the rate or directness of colonial economic exploitation that were triggered by growing demands for tropical products or the rising cost of empire. Peasant resistance on Dutch plantations after the cultivation system ended, Burmese resistance to increased rice exports to India, and the Vietnamese tax revolts in 1908 all occurred when a statist economic system attempted to raise revenues. In contrast, U.S. colonialism progressed under the cloak of social mission that was necessary in a recently, and still partly anti-imperialist, United States, and this mission motivated explicit restrictions on U.S. business activity in the archipelago. In any event, the most avid imperialists on the American side regarded the Philippines as a base for expansion elsewhere and so were willing to tolerate such restrictions to secure support for retaining the colony. In the Philippines, Americans largely worked to reorganize production, extend greater amounts of credit, and link Philippine agriculture to the world economy — activities that enabled Philippine elites to make a great deal of money. When economically statist colonial regimes created new elites (as in Burma) or worked through existing elites (as in Indonesia), they restricted the elites' economic opportunities. Such elites had comparatively less interest in buffering economic discontent that increased state extraction produced. Indeed, anti-imperialist political elites lent significant support to agrarian rebellions in each case. With rare and individual exceptions — notably, Pedro Abad-Santos's leadership of the Philippine Socialist Party — the Philippine political elite never championed grassroots complaints about colonial extraction.

Much has been said about the broad scope of educational opportunity in the Philippines under U.S. rule. Yet educational-policy changes also opened substantial opportunities for study in Indonesia and Vietnam. The distinctive impact of the U.S. educational system seems to lie in its content and more complete local elaboration. In Indonesia and Vietnam, most colonial schools imparted rather narrow administrative and bureaucratic skills. Those who wished for something more needed to cross over to European schools and, in many cases, travel out of the colony to the metropole. . . . In the Vietnamese case, foreign travel contributed both intellectual and organizational resources to the demand for national self-determination, particularly in the wake of post–World War I negotiations at Versailles. Even for Indonesians (who on the whole traveled abroad in smaller numbers and for shorter durations), the glimpse of a larger world introduced a new language of organizational and revolutionary modernity that invigorated politics. By that time, however, Filipinos were directing themselves more toward new educational opportunities *in* the Philippines that provided educational opportunities that were less narrowly administrative and more professional. Filipinos were able to attain an approximation of an American education on home soil, and elite political opportunity focused on climbing locally elaborated political networks. Thus, Filipinos were less exposed to anticolonial Marxist discourse than elites elsewhere in

Southeast Asia. Hence, the United States' educational reforms not only kept many Filipinos apart from global nationalist movements, it also encouraged stronger integrative links between students and established representative institutions, which had broad political consequences down the line.

American economic and educational policies helped establish conditions under which the United States administrative design could work its characteristic effect. First, the United States planned from the outset to set up governing institutions in the Philippines or in those portions of the archipelago that it wanted to control and soon after placed the issues of self-government and representative institutions on the table. Because self-government and prosperity seemed within the grasp of elites early on, national electoral institutions were not saddled with the burden of diffusing an active nationalist movement. Instead, they could provide the framework for a new political and economic elite to emerge and grow strong. In contrast, all three of the other colonial regimes undertook representative reforms only when nationalism was cresting. It helped the Americans that the Philippine revolution divided in 1900 into two groups: wealthy elites willing to participate in American plantation capitalism, and soldiers for whom independence was less negotiable. Yet the initial U.S. framework that colonial control was a problem of governance helped insure that the self-interested collaborating elite would evolve into a political buffer against less satisfied members of colonial society. The recruitment of wealthy Ilustrados to the American side; the creation more generally of broad social opportunities for less powerful people; and the tendency (largely rooted within the Philippine elite) to keep political and administrative classes separate from one another all undercut the scope of subsequent nationalist struggle by converting the strongest potential nationalists into supporters of incremental transitions to independence. When voices rose to demand more comprehensive nationalist advance, they did so without strong national leadership and in patterns of mobilization that favored localized and limited, if often violent, modes of struggle.

Yet U.S. colonial policies did not succeed merely by empowering an elite allied with American interests — for indeed, the French had built a similar group with less political success in Vietnam. Rather, the United States created differentiated bases of support for its colonial regime in Philippine society. In important ways, the class and functional divisions between the civil service and the political elite prevented alliances between the two against U.S. interests. Indeed, by working through a political elite, the Americans were assured that many of the most volatile labor and agrarian movements in the 1920s and 1930s would be directed against Filipino politicians rather than U.S. colonialists. In contrast, Indonesia after educational reform and Burma after the monarchy's destruction suggest that too great a concentration of power in a state-constructed indigenous elite tends to sharpen the contrast between European and indigenous prerogatives, spurring nationalist mobilization. In Vietnam, by contrast, too large a segment of an autonomous elite existed outside the circle of colonial sponsorship. By creating an internally differentiated elite in the Philippines divided into administrators and politicians, who themselves needed to build constituency support (and, not incidentally, who attacked one another during elections), the United States prevented sharp oppositions between U.S. and Filipino power.

The consequences of interactions among these factors — of the United States' economic, educational, and administrative programs in the Philippines — should remind us of how vastly world time influenced colonial politics in these cases. By the time the Indonesian, Burmese, and Vietnamese anticolonial movements were gathering steam in earnest, it was virtually impossible to conceive of these struggles without Marxist referents. Ideas of a global, scientific workers' revolution were as inseparable from these later movements as they were alien to the 1898 Philippine revolution. Battles between French and Vietnamese forces raged across Asia, and both Burmese and Indonesians thought about great-power politics and the possibility of Japanese support for their anti-imperialist struggles. By the time these same global and Marxist currents entered Philippine political discussions, U.S. colonialism had already established (and segregated) political and bureaucratic institutions that pushed the likely audience for revolutionary politics a considerable way down the social scale. In most of Southeast Asia, the entrance of an explicitly Marxist framework of struggle attracted significant bourgeois attention and targeted local collaborators and (primarily) foreign occupying forces. By the time Marxism established a foothold in the Philippines, the new elite had gained such control over Philippine society that revolutionary politics concentrated far more on struggles among different Filipino classes.

The consequence of the absence of a Marxist component to nationalist struggles for contentious politics in the Philippines, beyond even its influence on nationalism itself, has been profound. Most strikingly, patterns of rule that emerged under the Americans prevented any serious Marxist discourse from occurring among Filipino political elites and sparked a concomitant failure of leftist politics in general to find sponsorship among mainstream Philippine forces or institutions. . . .

QUESTIONS TO CONSIDER

1. Why, according to Boudreau, were popular protest movements against American rule in the Philippines less radical and powerful than anticolonial movements elsewhere in Southeast Asia? How did the two wars against Spain and the United States weaken the Philippine nationalist movement? Why was it difficult for Philippine protesters to form durable national or cross-class alliances? How did U.S. policies and governing arrangements encourage Philippine dissenters to work *within* the colonial system rather than overthrow it? In what sense was American colonialism "successful," and for whom?

2. Describe American colonial policies in the Philippines in the areas of political representation, government bureaucracy, law enforcement, economic development, and education. Try to gauge their impact on Philippine society. How did America's commitment to republican ideals and institutions influence its treatment of the Philippines? What effect did "Filipinization" of the army and bureaucracy have? Did the Philippine Assembly successfully demonstrate democratic principles? How did its operation channel opposition to American domination into conflict between Filipinos? To what extent did educational reforms and government bureaucracy

create a rising professional class? Did American policies support or weaken the landed elites who opposed greater economic equality in the Philippines?

3. How does the author contrast American and Japanese imperialist ventures in Asia? How did their economic motives and policies differ? How did Americans' domestic debate over imperialism influence their nation's colonial policies?

4. What differences does Boudreau find between America's imperial rule in the Philippines and European colonialism in Indonesia, Burma, and Vietnam? Be sure to consider the timing and context of colonization, methods of economic exploitation, educational arrangements, and the formation of political elites. What impact did these differences have upon Philippine society?

5. To what extent does Boudreau's evidence support the generalizations about American imperialism that are presented by Robin Winks in Selection 9? Did Americans expect colonialism in the Philippines to be a "passing phase"? Did their promise of independence "decrease the intensity of local nationalist movements"? Did the United States rapidly impose its customs and language upon Filipinos? Were Filipinos "more economically benefited than exploited" by American policies? What implications, if any, does Boudreau's analysis have for later American attempts to build democratic institutions in foreign countries?

PROGRESSIVE REFORM
AT HOME AND ABROAD

A wave of reform that historians call Progressivism swept through both American political parties in the early twentieth century, leaving behind important laws that expanded the role of government. Although usually studied in isolation, Progressivism was paralleled by similar movements in other Western countries and was even connected to them by direct influence. Throughout the Euro-American world, the expansion of cities and industries was accompanied by distressing problems such as urban slums, violent conflicts between capital and labor, and the tightening grip of big business on political and economic power. Wherever ordinary citizens were allowed to vote, they addressed these problems by advocating electoral reforms, more government planning, and labor and welfare legislation. In Europe, Latin America, and Australia as well as the United States, reform and socialist parties of various kinds took up demands for efficient government and social justice that were voiced by women, organized labor, and middle-class professionals. Whether they were British Liberals or Labour Party members, Argentine Radicals, French socialists, or American Progressives, their struggles played a crucial part in creating the modern "welfare state," a national government that takes responsibility for the well-being of the country's workers and citizens.

Progressivism was an international movement in another sense. As the United States became a world power, Progressives debated how the nation could best play the role of moral leader on the global stage. On the movement's conservative wing were vocal champions of American imperialism who identified the extension of American rule and Anglo-Saxon civilization with progress and enlightenment. Progressive presidents Theodore Roosevelt and Woodrow Wilson did not hesitate to intervene militarily, especially in nearby Latin America, to promote American interests. In a more idealistic mood, Wilson and other reform-minded Progressive internationalists wanted to replace the old European balance-of-power system among nations with a new regime of cooperation in pursuit of world peace. American radicals who pursued direct contacts between labor and women's groups across national borders were intent upon adding social justice to this internationalist agenda. Since all these factions believed in America's God-given mission to redeem the world, Progressivism featured a confident but sometimes contradictory blend of reform and empire, exceptionalism and missionary nationalism. This enhanced its appeal among Americans but undermined its credibility abroad and its proponents' ability to work with other peoples and nations as equals.

The selections in this chapter set out to place the domestic and international agendas of American Progressivism in a global context. In the first essay, Kathryn Kish Sklar focuses on the long-term expansion of government's role to include legislation related to health, safety, labor, and social welfare. The United States, she acknowledges, evolved a welfare state more slowly than most European countries. But, she asks, why in the United States did so much of the pressure for the government to address human needs come from women? Her response shows that Progressivism was the logical outcome of a long history of reform agitation by American women that began with the abolitionist movement before the Civil War and crested, ironically, just before the Nineteenth Amendment allowed women to vote in federal elections.

In the second essay, Alan Dawley recounts the dramatic story of Woodrow Wilson's crusade to make the Treaty of Versailles that ended World War I embody the ideals of "Progressive internationalism." By promoting his Fourteen Points as the basis for peace, Wilson galvanized the hopes of Progressives that extending American traditions of democratic government, social justice, and peaceful cooperation worldwide would eliminate war forever. At Versailles, however, Progressive idealism ran up against the harsh reality of national self-interest as well as its own contradictions, and suffered a shattering defeat. By the 1920s, the domestic and international plans of Progressives were in retreat. But history sometimes vindicates idealists if they have patience. A decade later, the Great Depression revived calls for an American welfare state, and two decades later, after another devastating world war, Americans acknowledged the wisdom of Wilson's vision of a "concert of nations" by helping to establish the United Nations.

Women and the Creation
of the American Welfare State

Kathryn Kish Sklar

The emergence of modern industrial society produced strongly analogous political movements in several Western countries. Middle- and working-class voters injected a reform agenda into existing political parties or created new ones to press their demands for universal suffrage, greater government planning, and labor and welfare legislation. In the United States, the label "progressive" became attached to the mainstream of this reform current, signifying those who sought a middle course between conservative defenders of the status quo and socialists who sought to overturn the system. Elsewhere, "liberal," "radical," or "social democratic" were the names that legislative crusaders for social justice gave themselves. In many of these countries, as in the United States, the reform surge peaked before World War I and then became a casualty of the general rightward retreat in the war's aftermath.

Unlike narrow studies that chart the rise and fall of Progressive political parties, Kathryn Kish Sklar examines over the long haul the Progressives' expansion of government's role. Between 1870 and 1940, every industrial nation developed its own version of the "welfare state," a national government that takes responsibility for the economic and physical well-being of its citizens. The American welfare state, Sklar notes, was slower to evolve than that of most Western countries because of a national tradition of private enterprise and limited government. Yet as it moved from state and local organizing to the halls of Congress and the White House under Theodore Roosevelt and Woodrow Wilson, the Progressive movement began Americans' adjustment to the concept of federal regulation and social-welfare legislation. Popular acceptance would come only later when the crisis of the Great Depression made Franklin Roosevelt's New Deal programs crucial to the nation's survival. Even then, the victory of the welfare state was far from complete. The United States remained, for example, the only Western industrialized country without a national health care system. And as the "Reagan Revolution" of the 1980s and later Republican electoral victories demonstrated, American voters felt lingering discomfort with the welfare state and cheered politicians who promised to dismantle "big government."

Besides its long chronological sweep, a second original aspect of Sklar's essay is her focus on gender. Working through such organizations as the National Consumers' League and the General Federation of Women's Clubs, Progressive-era women mobilized grass-roots support for mothers' pensions, child labor laws, and shorter workday legislation. Why was it, Sklar asks, that in the United States, unlike western Europe, so much of the push for government to address basic human needs came from middle-class women? She answers by deftly weaving together the story of American women's and men's separate political cultures from the mid-nineteenth century onward. Along the way, she pauses to cast sideways glances at countries such as Germany and England, where class seemed more powerful than gender as an organizing principle for reformers and radicals. As early as the 1830s, white middle-class women in America formed voluntary associations addressing such social problems as slavery, prostitution, and alcohol abuse. In the late nineteenth century, the process was accelerated by women's gains in education and social work. Thus women were poised to take the initiative when labor unions and male professionals failed to break the hold of laissez-faire doctrines on politicians. The combination of men's votes and women's agitation "meant that cooperation between [female and male reformers] . . . could produce spectacular rewards." An unprecedented burst of Progressive legislation in the 1910s regulated big business, outlawed child labor, limited the working hours of women, and recognized unions' right to exist.

Sklar's account takes several interpretive directions that you will want to follow and then evaluate. It modifies the traditional view of Progressivism as a reform movement of male politicians and intellectuals by showing its roots in women's organizations. It supports the theory of some social-welfare historians that women's activism flourished better in "weak states" like the United States without a tradition of big government than in paternalistic "strong states" like Germany, where male-dominated government agencies simply imposed social-welfare measures on the public. It argues that female reformers were not just "maternalists" interested in mothers and children, but champions of all workers' interests. And it shows how American women were able to influence public policy even before they had the vote. (Sklar barely mentions the campaign for woman suffrage, but politicians' interest in wooing potential female voters no doubt played a part in their passing some reform measures.) Beyond these specific points — and even more important — Sklar's essay demonstrates how rich the story of American history becomes when it is framed comparatively and when men's and women's histories are skillfully integrated.

GLOSSARY

ADDAMS, JANE (1860–1935)   An influential American social reformer. Addams founded Hull House in Chicago in 1889. This was a social settlement, based on the English model of Toynbee House, where humanitarians and social workers lived among immigrants and sought to improve economic conditions and civic life in the slums. Addams became a crusader for Progressive legislation and for international peace and was awarded the Nobel Peace Prize in 1931.

CHARTIST MOVEMENT   A workers' political reform movement active in Great Britain between 1838 and 1848. It sought to enact a "people's charter" that called for the secret ballot, annual elections, and universal male suffrage.

CIVIL SERVICE REFORM   Reform that aimed to have officials (i.e., nonelected civilian government administrators) selected on merit and not subject to political appointment or dismissal. It was spurred by the assassination of President Garfield in 1881 by a disappointed office-seeker and by opposition to political bosses generally. The Civil Service Reform Act of 1883 set up examinations for all positions classified as civil service, but most federal jobs were not classified until the twentieth century.

FABIAN SOCIALISM   The ideology of the Fabian Society, a British organization founded in 1884 to promote nonviolent, evolutionary socialism, which, it argued, could be achieved through the ballot. Leading exponents of this form of socialism included George Bernard Shaw, Beatrice Potter Webb, and Sidney Webb. The Fabians helped to create the British Labour Party in 1906.

KELLEY, FLORENCE (1859–1932)   A leading Progressive-era reform crusader. Kelley joined Jane Addams at Chicago's Hull House, the nation's preeminent social settlement, in 1891. She was chief factory inspector of Illinois from 1893 to 1896, then headed the National Consumers' League, which promoted social-welfare legislation in legislatures and the courts, from 1899 until her death.

MULLER V. OREGON (1908)   A U.S. Supreme Court decision upholding an Oregon law limiting the maximum working hours of women. The case was notable not only for its validating of the government's regulatory power over "freedom of contract," but also for the massive use of statistical and social science data, rather than legal arguments, by attorneys for the state.

PATRONAGE   The distribution of offices, jobs, or favors by political elites to reward their supporters.

PULLMAN STRIKE   A strike called in 1894 by the American Railway Union to protest wage cuts at the Pullman Company, which made railroad cars. When violence broke out, President Cleveland sent federal troops to restore order and a federal court issued an injunction forbidding interference with operation of the mails or interstate commerce. Union president Eugene V. Debs was jailed for contempt, and the strike was smashed.

SHAFTESBURY, ANTHONY ASHLEY COOPER (1801–1885)   An aristocratic English social reformer who advocated laws to limit child labor and the workday, provisions for care of the insane, the building of model tenements, and other measures to alleviate injustices of the Industrial Revolution.

SOCIAL GOSPEL MOVEMENT   A liberal movement within late-nineteenth- and early-twentieth-century American Protestantism that attempted to apply biblical teachings to problems associated with urbanization and industrialization. Optimistic about human nature and the prospect of a kingdom of heaven on earth, Social Gospellers often supported Progressive legislation.

SOCIAL SECURITY ACT (1935)   A social-welfare law passed as part of President Franklin Delano Roosevelt's New Deal program. This act set up a federal-state program of unemployment compensation, a federal program of old-age pensions for retirees (including wives not in the labor force), and federal grants to state programs for child welfare, citizens with disabilities, and public health.

This essay examines . . . features of American life that help us explain the power that middle-class women exercised in the white polity between 1890 and 1920 as they channeled the resources of the state in new directions. . . .

. . . To an extent unequaled elsewhere, middle-class American women were crucial and central to the responses state and federal governments made to social pressures created by massive immigration and rapid industrialization and urbanization. Nowhere else did protective labor legislation focus so extensively on women workers, and nowhere else were women so extensively involved in its enactment. Nowhere else did women reformers design and administer a major government bureau responsible for the health and welfare of the nation's infants and children. Every national polity developed its own version of what became known in the 1940s as "the welfare state." Why in the United States was so much of the path to the welfare state blazed by middle-class women?

This essay offers a[n] . . . answer to that question. For complex historical reasons that derived partly from the political culture of middle-class women, partly from American political culture generally, women were able to provide systematic and sustained grass-roots support for social-welfare programs at a time when the working-class beneficiaries of those programs could lend only sporadic support. Of course not all middle-class women participated in this effort. Middle-class women were an extremely diverse group. Some were uninterested in legislation benefiting working people, some were eventually persuaded to support such statutes, and some led the way in campaigns for "industrial democracy." This essay focuses on that vanguard and the women who provided it with grass-roots sustenance.

In their analyses of the prominence of American women in social-welfare provisions, historians have emphasized the gendered qualities of their efforts, characterizing their achievements and their methods as "maternalist." In many ways that term rings true, but it does not go far enough. It fails to capture the class struggle that shaped the creation of the American welfare state, and the role middle-class women played in that struggle. Using gender as a substitute for class strategies, women championed more than motherhood. True, their agenda advanced middle-class notions of gender and family relations, focusing as it did on bettering the lives of women and children. True, their leaders tended to benefit personally from the reform upsurge of 1890–1920, moving as they did into new jobs and positions of power that they themselves created. Yet their story embraces more than motherhood and self-interest. Responding to horrific conditions spawned by industrialization — conditions that threatened to poison middle-class as well as working-class life — large numbers of middle-class women sought to improve the welfare of working people generally. . . .

THE ORIGINS OF MIDDLE-CLASS
WOMEN'S POLITICAL CULTURE

. . . The two most remarkable features of the political activism of white Protestant middle-class women after 1900 — its massive grass-roots scale and its institutional autonomy — emerged during the transforming social changes of the antebellum [pre–Civil War] era. . . .

Between 1830 and 1860 white middle-class American women constructed vital and autonomous political institutions on the basis of their ability to speak for the needs of women of other races and classes. . . .

To explain the vitality of middle-class women's social activism in this era, we need to consider how it was fueled by fundamental aspects of male political culture. Most important was a widespread commitment to limited government. After 1776 this commitment dismantled the traditional merger of church and state. Religious "disestablishment" steadily withdrew tax support from churches, thereby greatly enhancing the power of the laity, upon whom ministers now had to rely for financial backing. Since a majority of the laity were women, and since most Protestant churches were self-governing congregations, in contrast to the hierarchically governed Church of England in Great Britain, this change substantially augmented women's social authority, especially their ability to forge autonomous pan-Protestant organizations independent of ministerial direction.

Women's organizations profited from the extension of universal white-male suffrage, albeit indirectly. By the 1830s and 1840s the few remaining limitations on white-male suffrage were abolished, and "the age of the common man" eroded class-based patterns of political deference. While this process was far from complete, it did preclude trends that in England channeled women's energies toward the male-dominated objective of the expansion of male suffrage. There many politically active women joined the Chartist movement, where they devoted their energies to the advancement of universal male suffrage. Although some Chartist leaders paid homage to the rights of women, women's issues never became a major focus of the movement. British restrictions on the political participation of . . . non-Anglican men meant that insofar as the female relatives of these men were politically active, they championed the rights of male dissenters rather than the female-specific agendas more common in the United States. In 1853 a British abolitionist explained to her American friend:

> I find very few people who are aware that with you all *white men* are on a legal equality & that consequently our class restrictions, religious disabilities, landed propertied monopolies etc. etc. all the host of oppressions under which we groan resolve themselves with you into distinctions of *sex* or of color. If the English public had this key to the enigma they would be a little more merciful to the transatlantic Amazons as they suppose all the advocates of woman's rights to be.

Due to the early introduction of universal white-male suffrage in the United States, distinctions of sex and race became relatively more salient within the polity than distinctions of class. Women's rights "Amazons" were merely the most visible expression of the formation of a vibrant, autonomous women's political culture in the United States. Far from a fluke created by a few visionary women, that culture was deeply rooted in American social and political realities.

THE POLITICAL CULTURE OF URBAN MEN, 1870–1900

Opportunities for the expression of women's political activism multiplied after 1870, when traditions of limited government in the United States curbed forces that in England and Europe aided in the creation of welfare legislation. Traditions of limited government had three consequences. They undercut the development of problem-solving governmental agencies and bureaucracies; they promoted the power of professional politicians within the two major political parties; and they invested an uncommon degree of authority in the judiciary branch of government.

Although a few governmental bureaus, such as the U.S. Department of Labor, brought together experts and collected data capable of guiding public policy in attacking social problems created by rapid industrialization, explosive urban growth, and massive immigration, for the most part such expertise remained sequestered in universities, private foundations, and voluntary organizations. Whereas British and German governments were prominent employers of men trained in the new social-science methods of collecting and analyzing data about social problems, this was not the case in the United States, where most social scientists ended up in academic jobs that kept them on the political sidelines.

The failure of civil-service reform in the U.S. illuminates the process by which male middle-class experts were shut out of policy-making positions. Civil-service reform was the top priority of the elite "Mugwump" movement of the 1880s, which succeeded in obtaining the passage of the Civil Service Reform Act in 1883. Yet the effects of the act were negligible. In England civil-service management of public policy was successfully instituted as a way for university-trained elites to retain their control of government despite the growing enfranchisement of working-class men. In the United States this maneuver was not possible because universal white-male suffrage had already recast political life in ways that gave to professional politicians — the men who maintained the heart and soul of the American polity, the two-party system — the power to block civil-service reform. . . . In the United States the popular will was constrained not by a civil-service elite, but by men who shaped the agendas of the Democratic and Republican parties. . . .

Increasingly in the last quarter of the nineteenth century, especially in American cities, Democratic politicians were oriented toward working-class, immigrant constituencies, and Republicans toward powerful economic interests, neither of which embodied the desires of middle-class men and women for government more responsive to their interests. Josephine Shaw Lowell, the most politically powerful woman in New York City, wrote to a friend in 1886 that she wished all "decent people would come out of your disreputable party, as we have come out of our disreputable party, and let us all join to make a decent one of our own!" Such criticism of "politics as usual" grew steadily between 1890 and 1920, giving rise to municipal-reform regimes that waxed and waned in many American cities, some of which arose from within the major parties, some of which formed "fusion" movements with party discontents, some of which expressed the growing strength of municipal socialism. A few states, particularly Wisconsin and Minnesota, and to some degree New York, implemented statewide reform programs, including the passage of labor and other social-welfare legislation, but only in 1912 with the Progressive party's unsuccessful presidential campaign in support of Theodore Roosevelt did this reform impulse achieve national scope. . . .

Notably lacking in this milieu was a strong national political movement representing the class-specific interests of urban working people. . . . The Socialist Party of America, founded in 1901 and headed by Eugene V. Debs, did provide a serious national forum for policies benefiting working people when it reached its peak in 1912, the year it won one-third of the vote within the American Federation of Labor to replace Samuel Gompers as president, and the year it attracted six percent of the vote in the presidential election. Yet the socialist upsurge did not prevent the wider political process from undercutting class-specific strategies among working-class men. Because universal white-male suffrage preceded industrialization, political class consciousness did not evolve, as it had in England, in response to the exclusion of the industrial working class from political rights. On the contrary, individualistic ideologies appealed to all segments of the political spectrum. . . .

In addition to blocking the establishment of problem-solving bureaucracies and to fostering the entrenched power of the two major parties, traditions of limited government also enhanced the power of the nation's courts, and, through them, the power of unregulated capital. The empowerment of courts, especially their ability to limit the authority of popularly elected bodies by overruling legislative actions, was a key element in the design of limited government in the United States. In the 1880s and 1890s that power began to be applied systematically to repress organized labor and overturn legislative strategies designed to benefit working people. Following a pattern of repression begun with the use of state militias and the national guard to combat strikes in the 1870s and 1880s, courts began during the 1894 Pullman strike to issue antistrike injunctions. Injunctions rendered strikes illegal and justified the use of armed force to suppress them.

Moreover, by the mid-1880s courts had begun to overrule prolabor statutes passed by state legislatures. . . . The effects of that process on organized labor were profound. When the New York Supreme Court ruled 1881 legislation banning the production of cigars in tenements unconstitutional, Samuel Gompers, head of the fledgling American Federation of Labor, decided that "the power of the courts to pass upon the constitutionality of the law so complicates reform by legislation as to seriously restrict the effectiveness of that method." The power of the courts to block prolabor legislation steered Gompers and other labor leaders into strategies that avoided political solutions for labor problems. . . . [American] labor's chief initiatives lay in "pure and simple unionism," which meant keeping clear of entangling political alliances and concentrating on direct

negotiations with employers. . . . [Thus b]efore 1920 the embattled position of organized labor within the American polity undercut labor's ability to shape the emerging
welfare state. . . .

Industrialists themselves constituted another group who elsewhere stimulated the
creation of state welfare policies but in the United States did not. In Germany, for example, industrialists often supported public initiatives for working-class health and
welfare because they were threatened by a highly politicized labor force and, in a context of falling birth rates, had to be concerned about the survival of a population large
enough to sustain industrial growth. Yet . . . in the United States even such elementary
social indices as high rates of infant and maternal mortality or extraordinarily high
rates of occupational deaths and injuries prompted less anxiety among industrialists
because the labor force was not politically mobilized and the colossal scale of European
immigration guaranteed an abundant labor supply. In this context American industrialists often took the lead in instituting welfare legislation that benefited business (such
as workmen's compensation plans that ended costly court settlements arising from
occupational injuries), but energetically fought legislation that primarily aided workers, such as shorter hours, minimum wages, unemployment plans, and social security
pensions.

County-based gentry were another group that in England made significant contributions to the development of state strategies for remedying social problems arising
from industrialization, but in the United States did not do so. Lord Shaftesbury in the
mid-nineteenth and Winston Churchill in the early twentieth century both criticized
the noxious effects of industrialization from radical perspectives engendered in part by
their aristocratic place in the social order. In the United States Theodore Roosevelt
embodied the equivalent of this tradition but also demonstrated its relative weakness.
Although born into a wealthy rural Dutch-American family and educated at Harvard
and Columbia, Roosevelt could acquire no electoral sinecure. His choice of a political
career obliged him to enter the rough-and-tumble world of machine politics; compro-
mises with the Republican-party bosses were essential to his electoral success. Around
1900 when he became an important ally of men and women social reformers, Roosevelt
drew his ideas from them rather than from an aristocratic critique of American industrial society.

Historians once believed that political bosses met the social-welfare needs of urban
immigrant constituencies, but recent scholarship challenges that assumption. While
municipal governments did dispense most nonfederal state spending before 1940, and
hundreds of patronage-based jobs were distributed on the basis of party loyalty, taxes remained low and social services rudimentary. Partly due to a lack of imagination among
party bosses, partly due to the restraining influence of the tax-conscious middle class,
urban political machines did not meet their constituencies' needs for positive government. They distributed food at Christmas, and mediated between members of their
constituencies and social-service agencies. Sometimes they championed pure-milk
campaigns, supported woman suffrage, and welcomed the construction of new schools,
but most machine politicians were fiscal conservatives who, except in the business of
getting votes, shunned policy innovations. . . .

Thus policies to help the working poor survive the negative effects of industrialization went against the grain of American political structures, and crucial groups that advanced those policies elsewhere were hobbled in their attempts to do so in the United States. These circumstances created unprecedented opportunities for women reformers. When they moved into the political arena in large numbers in the 1890s, women became crucial catalysts, forming effective coalitions with men and with them constituting a new majority of politically active middle-class people in support of systematic changes in the political status quo. Men in every social group capable of advancing social legislation — lawyers, labor leaders, social scientists, industrialists, party politicians, middle-class male reformers, and even socialists — worked closely with middle-class women and their class-bridging organizations to achieve what men had not been able to accomplish separately.

THE FLOWERING OF MIDDLE-CLASS WOMEN'S POLITICAL CULTURE, 1860–1900

The same forces that limited men's power to solve social problems actually promoted the power of women's political culture. . . .

In the 1870s middle-class northern women propelled autonomous, mass-based women's organizations into the nation's political mainstream. This was the development stage of women's political culture. By far the most important organization, the Woman's Christian Temperance Union (WCTU), formed in 1874, carried women's pan-Protestant voluntarism into a new scale of political activism and a new depth of cultural meaning for its participants. Organizing their locals geographically to coincide with congressional districts, the WCTU endorsed woman suffrage as early as 1879. Through its "do everything" policy the Union became an umbrella organization with thirty-nine departments in 1896, twenty-five of which dealt wholly or mostly with nontemperance issues. In Chicago in 1889 the Union built a twelve-story "Woman's Temple" to serve as a national headquarters, hotel, and office building. Moving into openings created by American traditions of limited government, WCTU members generated a wide range of needed social services. In Chicago alone they maintained

> two day nurseries, two Sunday schools, an industrial school, a mission that sheltered four thousand homeless or destitute women in a twelve-month period, a free medical dispensary that treated over sixteen hundred patients a year, a lodging house for men that [before 1890 had] provided temporary housing for over fifty thousand men, and a low cost restaurant. . . .

We gain insight into the reciprocal relationship between the WCTU and its social and political environment by noting that the British Women's Temperance Union remained a smaller, more scientific group of relatively elite women that did not swell into an umbrella organization, did not massively mobilize British women, and did not fill public-policy needs disregarded by men. The British group lacked the militancy and the . . . power that flowed from the "Christian" identity of the WCTU. . . . Much more than was the case in the United States, class structures dominated British political life and tended to channel women's activism into male-dominated struggles. Between 1830 and 1900 British women participated in a wide range of male-dominated movements from Chartism to Fabian socialism, and they built their own institutions, such as the Women's Cooperative Guild and the Women's Trade Union League, but the scale of autonomous organization expressed by the "White Ribbon Army" of the WCTU had no British equivalent.

At the same time, other changes in American life democratized access to higher education and opened institutions of higher learning to women on an unprecedented scale. By 1880 more than forty thousand women were pursuing higher education, and one out of every three undergraduates was female. . . .

. . . By 1890 the number of female undergraduates had risen to about 56,000, or 36 percent of the total. The founding of elite women's colleges, including Vassar (1865), Smith (1875), and Wellesley (1875), lent greater visibility to this trend. As Vida Scudder wrote in 1890,

> It is impossible to deny, in the presence of the amazement with which our great women's colleges are still viewed by visitors from distant lands, that we do embody a type, in some respects hitherto unknown. We stand here as a new Fact — new, to all intents and purposes, within the last quarter of a century. Our lives are in our hands.

When the American welfare state began to emerge in the 1890s, a sizable second generation of college graduates was mobilized for action.

Tens of thousands of urban middle-class women put their education to use in the women's club movement. In 1890 the General Federation of Women's Clubs (GFWC) drew together a vast network of local women's organizations, which since 1869 had emerged as the secular equivalent of the WCTU. Generating an effective intermediate level of organization through state federations, and channeling women's energies into concerted political action, the GFWC became the chief voice of "organized womanhood" after 1900. By 1910 it represented 800,000 women, some of whom could vote in local elections, and most of whom had at least some influence on the male voters in their families. . . .

. . . In 1898 the Federation resolved:

> That each club in this Federation shall appoint a standing committee whose special duty it shall be to inquire into the labor conditions of women and children in that particular locality. That each state federation shall appoint a similar committee to investigate its state labor laws and those relating to sanitation and protection for women and children.

Each committee was expected "to influence and secure enforcement of labor ordinances and state laws." A national committee collected local reports and presented them at national conventions.

Opposed to the employment of mothers of young children, the Federation energetically campaigned for the passage of state mothers' pensions laws. Its rhetoric critiqued industrialization from the perspective of exploited women and children. The Federation's official history in 1912 expressed the moral outrage that regularly aroused hundreds of thousands of women to social action. "Probably the most piteous cry which has reached the ears of the mothers of the nation is that which goes up from the little children whose lives are sacrificed to the greed of manufacture," it noted in a chapter on "Federation Ideals." Although the "advent of machinery" had been a great blessing to some, it also increased "the labor of women and little children." . . .

Just as important as education . . . in drawing middle-class women into public activism was the growth of their consciousness as consumers. This consciousness reflected the unprecedented market in consumer goods and the emergence of a consumer culture that linked producers, sellers, and buyers. Waves of immigrants who entered industrial and manufacturing jobs between 1880 and 1900 lifted most northern native-born working-class Americans into white-collar work, creating a large and relatively new group of middle-class consumers. New forms of marketing emerged, visible in the size and number of advertisements in popular magazines and the scale and diversity of department stores. Consumer culture had two striking effects on women within the older, well-established middle class. It made them more conscious of their relatively elite position within emerging middle-class consumer culture; and it highlighted the contrast between their relatively privileged lives and the lives of women who toiled to produce consumer goods. The National Consumers' League and its scores of local branches embodied the new consciousness of middle-class consumers.

Amplifying the trends that deepened and intensified the potential for political activism among middle-class women, a vanguard of talented leaders emerged within the social-settlement movement. Choosing to live in working-class, immigrant neighborhoods, this vanguard acquired potent leadership skills for cross-class cooperation with working-class women, and the ability to speak for the welfare of their entire society, not merely for the needs of women and children, or for the interests of their own class. . . .

A product of the Social Gospel movement, settlements drew on the religious roots of women's justifications of their public power. . . . Nevertheless, the primary tone of women's settlements was secular and professional. For hundreds of young women between 1890 and 1920, the question, "After college, what?" was answered with a few years of settlement work before marriage. Moreover, for dozens of talented college graduates like Jane Addams, Florence Kelley, Julia Lathrop, Alice Hamilton, Grace Abbott, and Mary Simkhovitch, settlement life sustained lifelong careers in reform activism. In many ways settlements served as the equivalent of graduate schools where women gained professional training in a supportive and innovative milieu, and of academic apprenticeships where women learned to practice their specializations — Addams and Simkhovitch in settlement work itself, Kelley in labor legislation, Lathrop in social-welfare administration, Hamilton in occupational medicine, and Abbott in immigrant welfare and child welfare. Settlements situated women to make the most of their new methods of social-science analysis. They could collect social data and use it to design remedies for social problems just as well as any university professor.

Although women's settlements received money from wealthy male benefactors and some settlements were sustained by church funds, the leading women's settlements were emphatically autonomous institutions whose destinies were shaped by their founders and the resident communities they nurtured. Hull House, by far the most important women's settlement, was supported primarily by women donors. Others were sustained by women's colleges. . . . These independent institutions permitted women reformers to draw upon male assistance without succumbing to their control.

. . . Women's very prominence within the American social-settlement movement . . . served as a substitute for the political, professional, academic, and religious careers from which they were excluded by reason of their gender. In England settlements were attractive to women for the same reason, but men were most visible because settlements became training centers for public office and the civil service. In the United States, where political parties remained the chief route to public office, men who were attracted to settlement life tended to be ministers trying to combine a religious calling with social action — a smaller and less dynamic group than the throng of reform-minded American settlement women.

The years between 1900 and 1920 marked the maturation of the political culture of middle-class women. Able to vote in only a few states before 1910, excluded by law from public office in most states, and perceived as outsiders by lawmakers in Congress, and in state and municipal governments, women had to find ways to overcome these gender-specific "disabilities" if they were to affect public policy. They did so by drawing on the most fundamental and enduring features of women's political culture — the strength of its grass-roots organizations, and the power of its moral vision.

Structured representationally, women's organizations, even those with strong national leaders like the National Consumers' League, gave great weight to the views of state and local affiliates. This sparked grass-roots initiative. It also fostered belief in democratic processes and the capacity of large social organizations — like state and federal governments — to respond positively to social needs. Whereas the predominant moral vision of men's political culture tended to regard the state as a potential enemy of human liberty, the moral vision of women's political culture viewed the state as a potential guarantor of social rights.

The grass-roots strength and moral vision of women's political culture resided in groups like the General Federation of Women's Clubs, the multitude of local and state organizations affiliated with the Federation, the National American Woman Suffrage Association, the Woman's Christian Temperance Union, the National Council of Catholic Women, the National Council of Jewish Women, the National Consumers' League, the National Women's Trade Union League, the Young Women's Christian Association, the Congress of Mothers, the League of Women Voters (after 1920), and (before 1925) even the Daughters of the American Revolution and the National Federation of Business and Professional Women's Clubs.

To a remarkable degree the creation of the American welfare state before 1930 was due to the endorsement these predominantly middle-class women's associations gave to the expansion of governmental responsibility for the welfare of able-bodied wage earners and their families. They lobbied for legislative interventions in the relations between capital and labor to protect those they viewed as the weakest and most exploited by the forces of industrial capitalism. Shorter hours, higher wages, safer work sites would, they thought, create sounder citizens and a better society. Many of these organizations were explicitly class-bridging, such as the Women's Trade Union League, the National Consumers' League, and the YWCA. All invited the influence of the vanguard of reform leadership concentrated in the social-settlement movement. All cooperated closely with a variety of men's groups.

WHITE MIDDLE-CLASS WOMEN AND MEN CREATE THE WELFARE STATE

. . . Gender differences meant that since women could accomplish some things that men could not, and men could achieve some of what women could not, together they might produce what neither could realize separately. Common goals made it possible for groups of women and men to work together, but differences in their institutional settings, their constituencies, and their beneficiaries meant that cooperation between them could produce spectacular rewards.

Above all, women needed access to the institutional power and positions of public authority that men held, and men needed the grass-roots support that women could mobilize. Thus the National Congress of Mothers drew on the help of juvenile-court judges to launch a successful campaign for state mothers' pensions laws between 1910 and 1915. The National Consumers' League relied on prominent male attorneys to argue their cases before the U.S. Supreme Court. The General Federation of Women's Clubs worked with state superintendents of education and other state and municipal officials in designing and implementing their legislative agendas. And during the early stages of the effort to found the United States Children's Bureau, Lillian Wald and Florence Kelley reached Theodore Roosevelt only through the intervention of Edward T. Devine, professor of sociology at Columbia University, director of the New York School of Philanthropy, and head of the Charity Organization Society in New York.

Other instances of male-female cooperation, though less prominent, alert us to the significance of this dominant pattern of women's grass-roots organizations and official male expertise. Sometimes, for example, women's grass-roots strength combined with that of men. This was the case with child-labor reforms, which were passed exclusively at the state level before 1938, and were generally endorsed by organized labor as well as by women's organizations. This dual support for child labor statutes may explain why they were implemented and enforced more extensively than any other form of early social-welfare legislation. . . .

What happened when measures gained the support of neither male nor female grass-roots organizations? Good examples were unemployment insurance and old-age-pension proposals, which languished in legislative committees until the economic disaster of the Great Depression demonstrated their necessity. When I. M. Rubinow, head of the American Association for Social Security, sketched the history of unemployment insurance, he noted that although "the Scientific Societies" . . . promoted plans similar to the one implemented in England in 1911, and successfully inaugurated one in Wisconsin in 1921, popular support for a national measure developed only as a result of "the obvious overwhelming force of the depression." Until 1932 representatives of organized labor opposed unemployment benefits, exclaiming "a job not a dole!"

The questions then become: "What was it about the combination of women's grassroots activism and small groups of male experts and leaders that accounted for their success at passing welfare legislation before 1930?" "What did this partnership accomplish and what does it tell us about the forces that created the American welfare state?" The success of these forces was limited. For example, their effort to outlaw child labor through a constitutional amendment failed, as did their attempts to create unemployment insurance nationally — two reforms that became possible only after the devastating depression of the early 1930s — and they failed to establish state-sponsored health care for workers, an issue that continues to bedevil the American polity in the 1990s. But their efforts built a foundation on which it was possible to construct the "New Deal" of the 1930s.

On their own the enormous numbers of women who supported protective labor legislation for women and children, who demanded schools large enough to accommodate the burgeoning population of immigrant working-class children, and lobbied state governments for mothers' pensions for poor widows constituted a vital political force. Linked in various capacities with the full range of male-dominated political groups who advocated some sort of social-welfare legislation after 1900 — from municipal socialists to the National Civic Federation — they tipped the balance of the political process heavily in favor of such legislation. Middle-class women remained central to the debate about the welfare of working people — job-related health perils, the length of the working day, the need for a "living wage" — that absorbed the nation's courts, its legislative bodies, and public-opinion forums at the height of American industrialization between 1900 and 1920.

Middle-class white northern women were merely the largest, most prominent (because most elite), and most vocal group of women to address the needs of poorer, working-class people. Similar class-bridging motivations inspired the activism of black club women in the North and South who, through the National Association of Colored Women and its multitude of affiliated organizations, ministered to the needs of black migrants who had left their rural homes. In the same way, German-American Jewish women, through the National Council of Jewish Women, the Henry Street Settlement, the Hebrew Immigrant Aid Society, and other organizations, aided recent Eastern European Jewish immigrants. White women differed from African-American women in their ability to use the state to remedy social problems, but otherwise the dynamic was similar: women took the lead in remedying social problems. Self-interest motivated all three groups, since they each wanted to avoid the threat to their middle-class security posed by the poverty, disease, illiteracy, and degradation of their poorer counterparts. But they were also committed to visions of social justice that transcended their own class interests. . . .

. . . [I]n this context Jane Addams became the preeminent woman and probably the preeminent citizen of her era through her ability to articulate the new values she called "social democracy." In the United States, in contrast to Europe, this term expressed ethical reformism rather than revolutionary political insurgency, but those carrying its banner, women as often as men, marched at the forefront of social change. Occupying a place on the executive boards of almost every reform organization in the Progressive

Era, including men's groups like the American Association for Labor Legislation as well as women's groups like the National Consumers' League, and mixed groups like the National Child Labor Committee, Addams embodied the aroused conscience of middle-class women and their readiness to take collective action, not only in the name of womankind, but in the name of democracy and social justice.

Perhaps the most fundamental characteristic of the emerging welfare state was the effort to provide minimum standards for living and working conditions. Early labor legislation for women was central to that effort, as were the strategies . . . by which gender did the work of class. In *Lochner v. New York* (1905), the U.S. Supreme Court reaffirmed its commitment to abstract notions of workers' contract rights, making health the only avenue for arguments designed to limit the exploitation of workers through long hours. Therefore in *Muller v. Oregon* (1908) Louis D. Brandeis, a prominent Boston attorney, and Josephine Goldmark, NCL research director, justified state intervention by emphasizing women's physiological weakness. Less often noted by historians, but no less important, were similar efforts by Brandeis, Goldmark, and the NCL in 1916 in *Bunting v. Oregon,* which successfully defended the limitation of men's working hours by emphasizing men's physiological weakness. Florence Kelley, for example, rallied public opinion to support Oregon's law "to the end that the present wholesale using up and wearing out of fathers of families in the manufacturing industries may be checked." As Kelley later wrote, the Bunting decision "took a long step forward" in American judicial history by upholding the constitutionality of the regulation of the workplace of "men in private industry in a non-injurious employment." This precedent smoothed the way for . . . the [federal] protection of unions in 1935 as well as the regulation of hours and wages in the Fair Labor Standards Act [of 1938]. . . .

Women's collective action in the Progressive era certainly expressed a maternalist ideology, as historians have frequently pointed out. But it was also sparked by a moral vision of a more equitable distribution of the benefits of industrialization, and the vitality of its relatively decentralized form of organization. Within the political culture of middle-class women, gender consciousness combined with an awareness of class-based injustice, and talented leaders combined with grass-roots activism to produce an impressive force for social, political, and economic change. Issues regarding women and children wage earners captured the imagination of tens of thousands of middle-class women between 1890 and 1920, so much so that gender — women's organizations and female-specific legislation — achieved much that in other industrialized nations was done through, and in the name of, class. Women did what Florence Kelley called "the nation's work" by reaching beyond the betterment of their own class to shape a new social compact for the society as a whole.

THE END OF AN ERA

The commitment of women's organizations to "welfare legislation" waned considerably in the 1920s. In that decade of . . . change for middle-class women, nineteenth-century notions that valued gender differences gave way to twentieth-century presumptions about the similarity of the sexes. Along with this undermining of "maternalist" motivations, the political climate underwent a sea change: social reform in general and efforts to achieve more equitable distribution of social resources in particular met determined resistance. Florence Kelley and Jane Addams were slanderously attacked as members of a communist conspiracy. American religious life, which between 1890 and 1920 had nurtured social-justice convictions and fostered a "Social Gospel" discourse shared by middle-class and working-class churchgoers, also underwent a sea change. New forms of fundamentalism among poor Protestants and a business-promoting positivism among middle-class Protestants both discouraged commitments to social justice.

Women's organizations persisted, but many lost their interest in social legislation, and their belief that women brought unique capacities to public life diminished. The membership of the General Federation of Women's Clubs no longer provided grass-roots support for social legislation. Though still at the forefront of social-justice campaigns for working people, the National Consumers' League evolved into a much smaller organization. Without the grass-roots support that had sustained their class-bridging campaigns before 1920, the power of the U.S. Children's Bureau steadily ebbed. . . . These changes within women's political culture coincided with the end of Progressive reform in men's political culture and marked a sharp swing to the right in the nation's political climate. Thus concluded thirty years of nation building by women, and three decades of productive interaction between women's and men's political cultures.

The Progressive Era formed a watershed in the history of state recognition of its responsibility for human welfare. Before 1880 that responsibility was extremely limited, but by 1920 the foundations had been laid for the construction of a modest welfare state. Women were central to that striking transition. In many ways their organizations filled gaps left by American traditions of limited government and other features of male-dominated polity. Taking advantage of those structural opportunities, they used gender-specific legislation and gender-based moral imperatives as surrogates for class-specific laws and visions. As a result, the interaction between women's and men's political cultures combined to produce changes that neither group could have achieved alone. In countries with stronger traditions of state authority, women did not encounter equivalent opportunities and men did not rely so heavily on their talents.

What conclusions can we draw about the centrality of women in the construction of the American welfare state? The strength of social-justice and class-bridging efforts within middle-class women's organizations illuminates the vitality of American civic culture between 1890 and 1920, and the ability of that culture to envision a better society and to take effective action to implement that vision. The crucial significance of women within American grass-roots democracy was never better demonstrated.

Women's organizational heyday between 1890 and 1930 brought a new and vital constituency into American political life at a time when women's political perspectives and resources were urgently needed. When the crushing effects of the nation's worst economic crisis prompted a "New Deal" in American public policy, many of their achievements were incorporated into national law. Women ceased to engage in autonomous political action on behalf of expanded state responsibility, but they worked effectively within the Democratic party to overcome, however temporarily, some of the deleterious effects of American traditions of limited government.

QUESTIONS TO CONSIDER

1. What differences between the United States and countries such as England and Germany encouraged American women's independent organizing? How did universal male suffrage and especially the American tradition of limited government open up opportunities for women's activism? Why did labor unions, industrialists, and wealthy landowners not play important roles in shaping the American welfare state, as they did in some European countries? What forces drew American middle-class women into public activism?

2. Describe some of the organizations through which American women became politically active between the 1880s and the 1910s. What were their goals, successes, and failures? How did male and female Progressive reformers complement each other's work? In what ways were they at odds? To what extent did women have a different view of government's role from men? Why?

3. In what sense did American women's activism serve, according to Sklar, as a surrogate for working-class agitation? To what extent did female reformers reach beyond a "maternalist" program aimed at helping mothers and children? What evidence does the author provide that they transcended their own middle-class interests?

4. Why is it that women's "organizational heyday" coincided with the national campaign for woman suffrage? Was it a coincidence that the surge of Progressivism reform ended just when women began voting in federal elections in 1920? What changes in the 1920s helped to sideline Progressive reform and its commitment to social justice?

5. Sklar has written elsewhere that the Progressive era recast "the American social contract" so that "state and federal governments assumed greater responsibility for human welfare." Do you think that today's government cutbacks are rewriting that social contract, or have Americans basically accepted the welfare state?

Woodrow Wilson and the Failure of Progressivism at Versailles

ALAN DAWLEY

"Sometimes people call me an idealist," President Woodrow Wilson told a South Dakota crowd in 1919 as he stumped the country to build support for the Treaty of Versailles that ended World War I. "Well, that is the way I know I am American. America is the only idealistic nation in the world." Although Wilson had vowed to keep the United States out of the fighting in Europe, by April 1917 this minister's son and Progressive reformer reversed himself; now he believed that America's entry into the war was essential to its mission to redeem the world. Rallying around the flag, Wilson predicted, would unite Americans who were torn by conflicting allegiances to their ancestral homelands. Wartime mobilization would further the Progressives' domestic agenda by demonstrating the efficiency of government regulation and federal agencies. Most of all, with America's moral guidance this bloody brawl between nations could be transformed into the war to end all wars, a struggle to "make the world safe for democracy." In January 1918, long before the war's outcome was clear, Wilson announced his visionary formula for peace: the Fourteen Points. The first five were based upon the principles of free-market democracy: open international agreements, freedom of the seas, free trade, arms reduction, and self-determination of peoples. The next eight points demanded specific territorial adjustments to recognize nationalist groups in eastern Europe. The fourteenth point, which Wilson considered the heart of his proposal, called for a "concert of nations," a new international organization that would adjudicate conflicts between nations through arbitration and persuasion, in effect relegating war to the dustbin of history.

As historian Alan Dawley makes clear in the sweeping narrative that follows, the response to Wilson's vision of "peace without victory" was overwhelming. The Fourteen Points, writes Dawley, acted as a "magic mirror" in which many groups saw their postwar dreams projected. American reformers, radicals, and conservatives; socialists and pacifists in Europe; exhausted publics in all the warring nations; colonial peoples chafing under imperialist rule — all placed their desperate hopes on Wilson during the anxious months when the fighting wound down and the Paris Peace Conference got under way. As the world looked to Wilson for leadership, America experienced its first critical moment on the world stage.

Dawley's account is notable for the way it meshes the domestic and international agendas of Progressive reformers, who saw Wilson's proposed League of Nations as American democracy writ large. It also models a "multiple-perspective" version of international history. While placing Wilson's diplomacy in its widest global context, Dawley incorporates the varied perspectives of Wilson's contemporaries, from conservative proponents of American empire to socialist advocates of a "people's peace," into his story. This comparative technique, essential for seeing the range of options available at a given historical moment, helps us to differentiate competing versions of "Progressive internationalism," the attempt to replace the old balance-of-power system of national alliances with new, American-inspired arrangements. Among Progressives intent upon engaging the world outside America, it made all the difference that Wilson, who shared the idealistic hopes of radical agitators for a people's peace, was far less critical of imperial prerogatives — including America's — and more concerned with preserving social order than ensuring social justice.

Partly because of what Dawley calls the "limitations, evasions, and hypocrisies" of Wilson's vision, his holy crusade ended in colossal disappointment. During the negotiations at Versailles, Wilson's idealism ran up against the harsh reality of reactionary fear and national self-interest. Determined to punish Germany, expand their borders, and retain their colonies, Wilson's Allied counterparts, David Lloyd George of Britain and Georges Clemenceau of France, conspired to undermine his agenda. Meanwhile, the "Big Three" — Wilson included — redrew the map of eastern Europe to contain the "Bolshevik menace" and sent troops to Russia to help defeat it. Only minor territorial provisions of the Fourteen Points found their way into the Treaty of Versailles. The first five points were scrapped altogether. Worst of all, the treaty contained punitive clauses that blamed Germany for starting the war and required impossibly high "reparations" payments as revenge. Ever the optimist, Wilson convinced himself that the treaty's "Covenant" for a league of nations would make up for its fatal flaws. Yet in an ultimate irony — which occurred beyond the time frame of the excerpt reprinted here — the U.S. Senate, piqued by Wilson's snubbing of Republicans and fearing international checks on American intervention abroad, rejected the Versailles Treaty and U.S. membership in the League of Nations. Wilson had sold the war as a Progressive crusade to remake the world in America's image, but in the end a disillusioned Congress would have none of it.

Dawley recounts this tale of naïve idealism and crushed hopes with clarity and drama, but leaves his conclusion open-ended. Rather than proposing a single explanation or "lesson" of the fiasco at Versailles, he consigns the task of interpretation largely to the reader. As you analyze his essay, ask yourself who or what was to blame for the failure of Wilson's version of Progressive internationalism at its critical moment. Was it Wilson's contradictory blend of democracy and imperialism? the delusion of bringing peace through war? the enduring problem of nation-states and national self-interest? or the Allies' obsessive fear of the Bolshevik menace? Although Dawley is careful to stick to the record of the 1910s, the conclusions you draw from his account may well be relevant to the present, when the United States dominates the world stage and when many of the world's peoples again look to its leadership in addressing pressing questions of peace and justice.

GLOSSARY

AMERICAN FEDERATION OF LABOR (AF of L)   A coalition of craft unions formed in 1886. Concentrating upon skilled workers and seeking to improve working conditions through collective bargaining rather than labor politics, the AF of L became the longest-lived American labor organization. It resisted socialist influence in the early 1900s and sought accommodation with corporate capitalism. At President Wilson's urging, the AF of L's president, Samuel Gompers, joined with Europeans to create the International Labor Organization (ILO) in 1919 in order to counter communist influence in Western labor movements, but Gompers soon renounced the ILO over concern for the AF of L's autonomy.

BALFOUR DECLARATION (1917)   Issued by British foreign secretary Arthur Balfour, a statement pledging British support for a Jewish homeland in Palestine, with the proviso that the rights of existing non-Jewish communities would be respected. It was endorsed by France and the United States. In the postwar treaty negotiations, Britain was given a mandate over Palestine, in part to implement the Balfour Declaration.

BOLSHEVIKS   A highly disciplined Marxist faction of the Russian Social Democratic Party that, led by V. I. Lenin, seized control in October 1917 of the Provisional Government set up by the Russian Revolution of February that year. In 1918 the Bolsheviks changed their name to the Russian Communist Party and began suppressing rival political organizations and establishing a communist government in Russia.

CAPORETTO, BATTLE OF   A disastrous Italian defeat in October 1917 in which Italian troops failed to halt an Austro-German offensive northwest of Trieste and the Italian army experienced almost total collapse.

CLEMENCEAU, GEORGES (1841–1929)   A veteran journalist and French political leader. Clemenceau became prime minister in 1917 and reinvigorated the French war effort. At the Paris Peace Conference, he frequently opposed Wilson's proposals because he sought to protect France's borders and interests.

CLEVELAND, GROVER (1837–1908)   The Democratic president of the United States in 1885–1889 and 1893–1897. Cleveland championed a lowered tariff on imports and the gold standard for currency. His Protestant moralism and free-trade liberalism made him an American counterpart to Britain's William Gladstone.

CONGRESS OF VIENNA (1815)   The international congress that restored the monarchies of France and Spain and redrew the map of Europe to assure conservative predominance and a balance of power among nations in the wake of Napoleon's defeat.

DEBS, EUGENE V. (1855–1926)   Leader of the Socialist Party of America. Debs gained fame as the forceful and eloquent president of the American Railway Union during the Pullman strike of 1894. He helped to form the Socialist Party in 1900 and was its presidential candidate five times thereafter. A pacifist, Debs was jailed from 1918 to 1921 for his outspoken opposition to American involvement in World War I.

EASTMAN, CRYSTAL (1881–1928)   A prominent American feminist and peace activist who opposed U.S. involvement in World War I. Active in the short-lived Women's Peace Party, she helped found the American Civil Liberties Union in 1917 to protect free speech and formed the American Union for a Democratic Peace to influence the postwar treaty negotiations.

GLADSTONE, WILLIAM (1809–1898)   The leader of Britain's Liberal Party from 1868 to 1894 and prime minister four times during that interval. Gladstone was a tireless promoter of Protestant morality, free trade, and open markets.

HABSBURGS   The Catholic dynasty that ruled the Austrian empire from 1282 to 1918. In 1867 the Habsburg empire was reorganized into the Austro-Hungarian monarchy, which was dissolved by the Allied victors after World War I.

AL-HUSEIN, FAISAL (1885–1933)   The son of Husein ibn Ali, sherif (governor) of Mecca, and leader of an Arab revolt against the Turkish empire during World War I with the assistance of British agent T. E. Lawrence. Proclaimed king when Arab forces took over Syria in 1918, al-Husein was deposed by the French, but the British, who held a postwar mandate in Mesopotamia, sponsored him as king of the territory (and later nation) of Iraq, and he was confirmed monarch by a plebiscite in 1921.

KOLCHAK, ALEXANDR (1874–1920)   The leader of the anti-Bolshevik forces in western Siberia during the Russian civil war of 1918–1920. Admiral Kolchak assumed dictatorship over Siberia and was supported by U.S. and Allied troops before being defeated and executed by the Bolsheviks.

LEAGUE OF NATIONS   The "concert of nations" formed after World War I to promote international peace and security. Advocated by President Wilson at the Paris Peace Conference, its "Covenant," or constitution, was inserted in the Treaty of Versailles that formally ended the war in 1919. Initially excluded from the League, Germany joined in 1926 but withdrew under Adolf Hitler's leadership in 1933. Since the U.S. Senate failed to ratify the Versailles Treaty, the United States never became a member of the League, which collapsed after the outbreak of World War II.

LENIN, VLADIMIR ILICH (1870–1924)   The head of the Bolshevik faction of the Russian Social Democratic Party. Lenin denounced World War I as a conflict of competing imperialist powers. When the Russian Revolution of February 1917 removed the czar and established a provisional government, Lenin returned from exile to agitate for communism and take Russia out of the war. In October 1917 the Bolsheviks seized power and declared the world's first communist government. The following March, Lenin's government signed the Brest-Litovsk peace agreement with Germany, ending Russia's involvement in World War I.

LIBERTY BONDS   Securities issued by the U.S. government and sold to the public to fund America's military effort in World War I.

LLOYD GEORGE, DAVID (1863–1945)   A leading British Liberal Party statesman who was elected to Parliament in 1890 and served until 1945. The reform legislation he advocated before World War I became a model for Woodrow Wilson and American Progressives. Chosen prime minister in 1916, Lloyd George guided Britain through World War I and played a major role in shaping the Treaty of Versailles.

MASARYK, THOMAS (1850–1937)   The Czech philosopher and nationalist leader who before World War I advocated parliamentary democracy and Czech autonomy within the Austro-Hungarian Empire. Fleeing Czechoslovakia during the war, he organized a Czech army abroad and a government in exile. At the war's end, Masaryk became the first president of the Czechoslovak Republic.

MONROE DOCTRINE   The pronouncement by U.S. president James Monroe in 1823 that from then on the Western Hemisphere was closed to further colonization or intervention by European powers (and that the United States would not interfere in European nations' internal affairs). Initially intended to prevent Europeans from recolonizing the Americas, the doctrine was later used by Theodore Roosevelt and other U.S. presidents to justify American intervention in the Caribbean and Central America for political or economic objectives.

SECOND INTERNATIONAL (1889–1915)   A loose federation of socialist parties and trade unions that influenced labor politics in Europe and the United States. It collapsed during World War I when most socialist parties ignored its antiwar doctrine and supported the efforts of their respective countries.

SINN FEIN   An Irish nationalist movement opposed to British rule. Revitalized after the failed Easter Uprising of 1916, it set up an Irish parliament in Dublin that declared independence and resisted the British army. When negotiations with Britain produced the Irish Free State in 1922, the militant wing of Sinn Fein opposed the exclusion of northern Ireland and eventually turned to terrorism.

STOCKHOLM CONFERENCE   A "people's peace" conference that socialists and peace advocates in Britain, France, Germany, Russia, and the United States planned to hold on neutral ground in Sweden in the summer of 1917. These activists hoped to negotiate an end to World War I on the basis of peace without annexations, indemnities, or suppression of nationalities. Their efforts were blocked by the belligerent governments, and the conference never took place.

TREATY OF BREST-LITOVSK (1918)   The peace agreement signed by Germany and the new communist government of Russia during World War I. Under its terms, the communists were forced to concede the Russian territories of Poland, the Caucasus, and Ukraine in return for ending the war with Germany. The treaty's signing sparked a brutal civil war in Russia between the Bolshevik Red Army and the White Army of czarist loyalists and various anticommunist factions. The fighting ended in 1921 with the Bolsheviks' victory.

ZIONISTS   Advocates of reconstituting a Jewish national state in Palestine, Zionists formed an international congress in 1897 and pressured Turkey and Great Britain, the most prominent regional powers, for territorial concessions. After World War I, Britain received a mandate over Palestine but limited Jewish immigration in order to mitigate Arab hostility. Following World War II, most Zionists accepted the U.N. plan to partition Palestine into the nations of Israel and Jordan.

The period from the proclamation of Wilson's Fourteen Points in January 1918 to the start of the Peace Conference a year later marked an American moment in world affairs. For the first time in history, an American army, backed by the most powerful economic engine in the world, was shaping the outcome of a war in Europe, and an American president was being hailed as the prophet of a new world order. Other times may have been more significant in the internal history of the United

Entitled "Let her be heard," this illustration from the New York Evening
Post, *circa 1917–1919, conveys a message of messianic Americanism. An
upright President Wilson clutches a scroll — perhaps the Fourteen Points —
and defends Humanity, a ravished female victim of war. At the outset of the
Versailles conference, many people at home and abroad saw the progressive
American president as humanity's best hope. (Library of Congress, Prints and
Photos Division.)*

States — the Revolution, the Civil War — but this was by far America's most important moment in world history.

The emergence of American leadership marked a portentous shift in world power.
As the European powers tore themselves apart, the baton of Western leadership — or
hegemony — passed temporarily to the United States, just as it would pass for a much
longer lap after the Second World War. It was as if, in the midst of the great conjunc-
ture that was remaking world history, the curtains parted to reveal its deepest inner
workings.

If this was an American moment, it was not because of messianic Americanism, but because of the universal message of liberty and peace enfolded in progressive internationalism. To be sure, American influence was not the result of ideas alone. Wartime changes in political economy elevated the United States to the top rank among the world's creditors, underwrote the power of U.S. banks and industrial corporations, and ushered in an administrative state that promoted efficient production and consumption. But the more Woodrow Wilson advanced the idea of a just peace enforced by a concert of nations, the more he became the first American to be recognized as a true world figure. Indeed, as he surged past Lenin in the race for world opinion and past Allied heads of state, as well, it is not too much to say that he became the first world leader of the twentieth century.

THE FOURTEEN POINTS

The single most important force in winning moral authority was Wilson's formulation of Allied war aims in the famous Fourteen Points. They appeared at the beginning of 1918 against a background shrouded in gloom, because things were going badly on the battlefield. The Italian war effort had collapsed in a heap at the battle of Caporetto in October, and, far worse, the Eastern Front simply disappeared. Negotiations between the Bolsheviks and the Germans produced a Christmas truce that confirmed what generals on both sides already knew: Russian armies were no longer willing to fight. With the Eastern Front closed down, the main obstacle to German victory was gone. The fact that American troops were not yet available in large numbers only made the situation more dire.

Things were not going well on the morale front, either. . . . Civilian morale, already low, was dealt another blow by the Bolsheviks' publication of the Allies' secret treaties, which revealed Allied war aims to be an all-around imperialist landgrab. Against the sordid deals of the old diplomacy, the Bolshevik call for peace based on the formula of no annexations or indemnities was looking better and better.

Given this unfavorable turn of events, pressure mounted on the Allies to redefine their war aims. In Britain, radical democrats in the Union for Democratic Control called for a renunciation of territorial and punitive aims, while the Labour party embraced terms similar to Wilson's "peace without victory." Although the Stockholm idea for a "people's peace" was held in check, the fact that Germany's independent socialists were pressing their government for a negotiated settlement rekindled a spark of the old socialist internationalism.

The French government, however, would have none of it. Largely because of Clemenceau's adamant opposition to a negotiated settlement, an inter-Allied conference in late November adjourned without any formal statement of war aims. The British were only slightly less opposed to negotiations, and when Wilson sent Colonel Edward House on another diplomatic mission to the Allies, they failed to craft a joint statement. Lloyd George's tepid support for some kind of international organization to reduce armaments did not go far enough. All in all, Allied diplomacy seemed as paralyzed as the armies on the Western Front. . . .

When the Allies continued to temporize, Wilson took things into his own hands. On January 8, 1918, he issued the Fourteen Points. As one of the most important state papers of the twentieth century, Wilson's stunning manifesto of the new diplomacy deserves close attention. To understand why it generated so much excitement at the time, it is necessary to set it in the context of ongoing revolutionary upheavals. Far from condemning revolt in eastern Europe or rejecting Bolshevik peace proposals out of hand, the Fourteen Points expressed sympathy for the popular aspirations they represented. Calling for the evacuation of Russian territory by foreign forces, point 6 warmly welcomed Russia into the family of nations with a promise to respect "the independent determination of her own political development." In the face of conflicting reports from Americans on the scene, this promise of self-determination seemed to keep the door open for acceptance of a radical regime in Moscow. . . . By showing sympathy with the cause of Russian freedom, the president was trying to bolster moderate political forces, such as they were, and, at the same time, reinvigorate Russian resolve to fight.

It was an extraordinary gesture, one that resonated with the best in American history. Wilson's support for revolution in Europe harked back, consciously or not, to the founding generation of American revolutionaries. Playing the role of Jefferson to the hereditary princes of Europe, he echoed the Declaration of Independence with its appeal to the "opinions of mankind" in his universal call to liberty. In seeking to rally world opinion to the cause of human freedom, Wilson was, in truth, the last of the Founding Fathers.

The same message of liberation was embodied in the call for a new diplomacy. Point 1 stated the cardinal principle of "open covenants of peace, openly arrived at." The message contained implicit criticism of the Allies' no-longer-secret war aims. Since the United States had not been a party to the secret treaties, Wilson had clean hands in making this pious proposal, a fact which helped offset the damage of their publication. Freedom was also embodied in the promise of "political and economic independence" for the nations and would-be nations of Europe — occupied nations such as Belgium, suppressed nations such as Poland, and the thwarted nationalities of the Balkans.

In the end, what convinced people that Wilson really was out to create a new world order was the last of the Fourteen Points. The overarching proposal for a "concert of nations" aimed to create a kind of world parliament where conflicts could be worked out in a peaceable manner. In one of the most influential progressive ideas of the century, Wilson proposed to substitute "mutual guarantees of political independence and territorial integrity" — what later came to be called collective security — for the destructive alliances of the old balance-of-power system.

For something that seemed so incendiary at the moment, it is striking how much the Fourteen Points owed to the past. Reverting to the liberal internationalism of the pre-war years, Wilson appeared in the frock coat of the Victorian gentleman to trade in the common commodities of nineteenth-century liberals. Points 2, 3, and 4 restated the basic tenets of free-trade liberalism: freedom of the seas, open markets, and reduction of armaments. There was nothing here to disturb the slumber of William Gladstone or Grover Cleveland, no battle cry of social reform, no hint of bringing big business to heel, no forecast of the social liberalism to come later in the century. There was not even a promise to make the world safe for democracy, for fear of disturbing conservative regimes.

Given all the damage being done by the warring nations, it is also striking that Wilson chose to found his new world order on the rock of the nation-state. In points 6 through 13, he went Lenin one better in spelling out terms for territorial settlements of national questions. Some of these points have all the moral eloquence of a deed to property, which, in a basic sense, is exactly what they were — promises of "territorial integrity" to both the nations and would-be nations of Europe.

Unfortunately, it was not at all clear how guarantees of nationhood to the fractious peoples of the Balkans would prevent them from replaying the bloody battles that had set the stage for the Great War itself. Nor was it clear how creating a Polish state would prevent it from preying on Jews and other enemies. Nationalism was like the proverbial wolf — anyone who got a hold of it could neither safely hold it, nor safely let it go. In embracing nationalism, Wilson blindly ignored the danger.

If nationalism was right for Europe, Wilson believed it was wrong for Europe's overseas empires. Conspicuously absent was any reference to self-determination for colonial peoples. In rather elliptical language, point 5 proposed an "impartial adjustment of all colonial claims," not between colonizer and colonized, but among colonial powers themselves. Despite a nod to the "interests of the populations concerned," the intention was clearly to sort things out within an imperial framework. References in the text to "the Imperialists" were meant to apply only to the empires of the enemies, not of the Allies. Wilson's manifesto of the new diplomacy was no charter of independence for the subject peoples of Asia, Africa, or Latin America.

Reading between the lines, it was also apparent that Wilson's new diplomacy was perfectly consistent with American self-interest. The world's biggest economy was likely to prosper in an open-door world where American business could go wherever it pleased. In the war of words against German autocracy on one side and Russian bolshevism on the other, Wilson's salvos of liberal capitalism contained a good deal of economic benefit for the United States.

Despite these limitations, evasions, and hypocrisies, Wilson's progressive internationalism captured the imagination of the world. What was historic about the proposals was not their old-fashioned liberal principles, nor the prosaic attempt to settle territorial claims. Rather, it was the vision of humanity acting for the first time in concert.

Immediately, the Fourteen Points became a kind of magic mirror in which different segments of humanity saw their best face reflected. To the European left, Wilson's message was the call for a just peace they had long been waiting for. British progressives in the Union of Democratic Control abandoned the Bolsheviks and went over to Wilson, while their French counterparts were also drawn to Wilson's transatlantic republicanism. Delegates from both countries arrived at the second Inter-Allied Labor and Socialist Conference in late February 1918 ready to support the Fourteen Points as the best chance for a people's peace, despite the fact that the Wilson administration was nervous about unauthorized peacemaking and had refused to issue a passport to a would-be American delegate.

Wilson's star rose even higher after Russian humiliation in the Treaty of Brest-Litovsk signed at the end of March. . . . The treaty transferred a huge chunk of Russian

territory — upwards of one-third — to German hands, while freeing Germany's eastern divisions for service on the Western Front. Within two months Germany began the
last great offensive of the war.

With Russia out of the fighting, the American contribution loomed much larger.
The Fourteen Points had a vital impact on Allied morale. The *Times* of London saw
nothing less than "the reign of righteousness" in Wilson's message, and Lloyd George
extended his appreciation. Across the Channel, the French press and public were also
very enthusiastic. Clemenceau, however, was predictably frosty. "Wilson has his Fourteen Points," he sneered, "God needed only Ten Commandments. We shall see." But
elsewhere in conquered Belgium and disheartened Italy, Wilsonism became a popular
phenomenon.

Even in Germany, Wilson's message was well received. In another speech in
September, Wilson appealed directly to the German people over the head of their government, extending the promise of self-determination to them, provided they overthrew the kaiser. Needing little prodding, they replaced the centuries-old Hohenzollern
dynasty with a new republican regime. And when German authorities finally decided
to sue for peace in November, it was not the Allies they contacted, but Woodrow
Wilson. . . .

When American conservatives looked into the magic mirror of the Fourteen Points,
they, too, saw much to their liking in the prospect of great power status for the United
States. Far from accepting American isolation, some conservatives had taken the lead in
promoting overseas expansion ever since the Spanish-American War. . . . Standing next
to Wilson on a high peak overlooking the future, they envisioned a role for the United
States as Britain's successor as world hegemon. . . .

Conservatives also pushed their own agendas. Arch-nationalists, such as Henry
Cabot Lodge, collaborated with the champions of 100 percent Americanism in the National Security League and other patriotic societies to preserve maximum freedom of
action for U.S. diplomacy. Although Lodge was a thoroughgoing Anglophile, he opposed any wartime "entangling alliance" and, instead, insisted on fighting not as an
"ally" but as an "associated power." The fact that Lodge was a militant nationalist did
not mean he was an isolationist. Far from supporting a stay-at-home foreign policy,
Lodge rubbed his hands with glee over the projection of U.S. power overseas, so long
as it came on U.S. terms. He was, instead, a unilateralist who wanted nothing to do with
collective security. Unilateralists would soon join forces with isolationists to oppose [the]
collective security provision of the Versailles Treaty. But for the time being, Wilson's
enemies had to bide their time.

Reformers of all stripes were predictably enthusiastic. Christian idealists were taken
by the illusion that the foreign policy of the United States could be made the instrument of a higher power. Many Christians who had opposed U.S. intervention now
clambered up the hill to stand with Wilson on the moral high ground, including the
prewar secretary of the pacifist Church Peace Union, who endorsed Wilson's program
as the embodiment of Christian idealism.

Secular progressives, for their part, saw in Wilson's magic mirror a vision of democratic internationalism. In the new world to come, the main actors on the world stage

would be nations and peoples, not nation-states and diplomats. Their idea of a league of nations was a democratic legislature writ large, comprised of *peoples'* representatives from around the world, not a league of nations, strictly speaking. The democratic message effectively silenced Wilson's progressive critics in Congress. . . .

Even radicals saw what they wanted. Wilson's call for a concert of nations seemed to be just what radicals had been demanding since the previous April. . . . Persuading herself that a "democratic peace" and an "American peace" might be the same thing, the ever-resilient Crystal Eastman helped fashion the American Union for a Democratic Peace out of the wreckage of earlier peace and justice organizations. Echoing Wilson almost word for word, she took a leaf from the book of messianic Americanism to proclaim that democracy and America were synonymous in the sense in which "America has stood for the hope and freedom of all peoples."

What a predicament for the radicals to be in! World history was heading their way, the president was talking their language, and all they could do was cheer from the sidelines. What was worse, the leader they were cheering was throwing a lot of them in jail. Shortly before being arrested under the Sedition Act, Eugene Debs was heard to give "unqualified approval" to the Fourteen Points. Max Eastman wrote in private, "I was still regretting we had entered the war, but I felt that Wilson might find a fruitful way out of it." Unfortunately, he could not write this in his own magazine, because *The Masses* had been shut down by Wilson's government. . . .

Despite these blows, a parade of leftists repented their former antiwar views. The *Appeal to Reason,* the largest circulation socialist paper in the country, urged its readers to support the League of Nations idea. Mother Jones, "the Miner's angel" with impeccable radical credentials, endorsed Liberty Bonds. By the spring of 1918, conservatives, progressives, and radicals alike had been co-opted by Wilsonian internationalism.

By raising impossible hopes, Wilson's efforts to win over reluctant crusaders succeeded too well. In retrospect, it is easy to spot the illusion. Nation-states tend to be the pursuers of self-interest conservatives said they were. They rarely put high moral principle first, the way progressive internationalists hoped. Progressives might have done a better job guarding against the illusion that the United States was an exceptional nation, the only nation that could transcend self-interest to be a beacon of redemption for a warring world.

Yet posterity should not judge them too harshly. All those who ever set out to change the world have tried to make their country behave ethically. Who can blame progressives for trying to turn national traditions in internationalist directions? Reconciling national and international impulses was exactly what Walter Weyl, a leading progressive writer, was trying to do. In a book on "the end of the war," the Philadelphia-born son of German-Jewish immigrants called upon his fellow citizens to turn U.S. intervention into a new American mission: "We leave behind our old Americanism to find abroad a new and broader Americanism; an Internationalism." Just as Americans ought to adopt a new spirit of internationalism, so American influence might make the new international order more democratic. . . .

Weyl's credibility on the point of democratic internationalism was enhanced by his willingness to criticize imperialist impulses in his own country. Knowing that Debs had landed in jail for just such a statement, Weyl nonetheless warned that in the pursuit of post-war spoils the United States "is as likely to become imperialistic as are the other nations." Noting that the United States had acquired a string of colonies and protectorates in the Western Hemisphere, he predicted that "small economic groups possessing vast influence" would seek to expand American power, just as the emergence of America as the world's biggest creditor pointed toward full-scale "financial imperialism."

The specter of American capital haunting the world's less developed peoples became manifest in American participation in the Allied intervention in Russia. Refusing to accept the Bolshevik separate peace at Brest-Litovsk, the Allies sent troops into Russia in the spring of 1918 with the ostensible purpose of reopening the Eastern Front. Although reluctant at first, Wilson actually supplied more troops than the Allies in a futile effort fatally flawed by association with tsarist counterrevolutionaries. The Russian imbroglio drew fire from some progressives, including Senator Hiram Johnson, who growled, "the real thing behind the scenes in this Russian situation is the international banker." Somehow Wilson escaped the blame for the Russian intervention. It was put down to the French, or international bankers, or monarchists.

In fact, nothing seemed to diminish the luster of his ideas. For a fleeting moment all of humanity looked into Wilson's magic mirror and saw themselves not as they were, but as they hoped to be. In Europe, the vision of a just peace lifted demoralized spirits. In the United States, it illuminated a shining moment of common purpose. In colonial regions, it carried the promise of self-determination, despite itself. After the collapse of the socialist Second International and before the Communist International gained purchase, the lines between reform and revolution blurred, and progressive internationalism seemed capable of becoming the vehicle of popular hopes for radical change everywhere.

Was that enthusiasm misplaced? In some ways, yes, since it rested on a good deal of smoke and mirrors. Yet, at a time when the old balance-of-power politics stood disgraced; when rebels had overthrown autocrats in Mexico, China, and Russia; when aged dynasties — the German *Kaiserreich,* the mighty Habsburgs, the Ottoman Turks — were about to tumble; under these circumstances, enthusiasm was understandable. As the weight of centuries lifted, it seemed possible that the "war to end all wars" might just bring about a better world. . . .

PEOPLE'S PEACE

Released from the confinements of war, social movements immediately rushed toward Paris to get in on the peace conference which began in January 1919. "Paris was the capital of the world that spring of the Peace Conference," wrote young John Dos Passos, who was there basking in the excitement. Actually, there were two very different gatherings: the official meeting of diplomats at the old Bourbon Palace of Versailles, to be discussed shortly, and the unofficial gatherings of people's representatives, most of whom were not welcome in Paris and had to find someplace else to meet.

The idea of a "people's peace" — even Wilson used the phrase — rose like a phoenix from the ashes of war. Social movements from the Western countries sought entry to the gates of Paris to press their demands for labor legislation, women's rights, and the Stockholm idea for a people's peace conference. Brandishing Wilson's Fourteen Points, American progressives came to support a "league of free peoples." Even Walter Lippmann and other members of The Inquiry, the official team of policy experts brought along to advise the American peace commissioners, were warm to the notion of a people's peace.

Also drawn into the vortex of Paris were colonial peoples, most of whom came knocking on President Wilson's door. According to George Seldes, an American correspondent on the scene, "All the oppressed nations sent kings, princes, premiers and delegations to Mr. Wilson and called him the sole arbiter of the New World." Among the supplicants was a young Vietnamese student named Ho Chi Minh, who, like all the other colonials from Asia or Africa, went away disappointed. . . .

In the flux of the moment, the line between a people's peace and a peace among nations grew indistinct. In pressing their claims for self-determination against imperial rulers, nationalist leaders in the cause of Irish, Polish, or Arab freedom were seen to be on the side of democracy, and in many respects, they were. In some cases — Masaryk of Czechoslovakia, Sinn Fein in Ireland — they were aligned with social reform or even social revolution. Moreover, the very fact that Asians and Africans were claiming the right of self-government, never mind the character of the government they would set up, ran contrary to European colonialism. . . .

Like the supplicants from the colonies, social activists from Western countries discovered that Versailles was not very hospitable. Socialists trying to reconstitute the Second International were thwarted when Allied governments denied citizens of the Central powers access to Paris, just as the Stockholm conference had been thwarted during the war. That forced the socialists to move to Bern, Switzerland, where delegates from the battered socialist parties of the former warring countries tried with little success to overcome the nationalist hatreds that had divided them since 1914. Mary Heaton Vorse, an American radical on the scene in Bern, found the timidity and bickering pathetic. Clearly, socialism had not recovered its prewar momentum, and it never would.

Other eyes were on communism. Although red Russia was excluded from official Paris, the influence of communist internationalism was felt everywhere. Partly because so many radicals in the West were hitching their wagons to the Soviet star, the manifestos coming from Petrograd fluttered like red flags over Western capitals. Built on the iron will of Lenin and his followers, the communist Third International, founded in March of 1919, managed to achieve the organizational discipline its rivals lacked. From that day forth, all efforts to rebuild internationalism from below had to reckon with this new force.

Recognizing the challenge from the left, Wilson picked up the pace in what he saw as a race between reform and revolution. On his way to the Peace Conference, he told his advisors that "liberalism must be more liberal than ever before, it must even be radical, if civilization is to escape the typhoon." Badly needing something to counter the bolshevik menace, Allied statesmen authorized the creation of an international labor commission to promote stable relations between labor and capital. The idea was to co-opt the international labor movement into any future league of nations in the same way that trade unions had been incorporated so effectively into the state machinery of the warring nations. . . .

. . . Together with their European counterparts, American women dared to believe they might serve in some kind of advisory role in the peace conference. But it was not to be. Disappointed to find all doors closed in Paris[,] . . . they sailed off to Washington. Refusing to allow exclusion from official circles to keep them out of the public square, the National Women's Trade Union League, led by Margaret Drier Robins (wife of Wilson's unofficial emissary to Russia, Raymond Robins), offered to host the first International Congress of Working Women in October 1919.

. . . Over the next four years, the Congress (later Federation) of Working Women agitated for industrial and social legislation of special interest to women around the world. But like many international efforts, it, too, foundered on national differences, with European women choosing to affiliate with the International Federation of Trade Unions, while their American sisters acceded to the wishes of the AFL [American Federation of Labor] and bowed out.

The spirit of 1919 lived longest in the quest for peace and justice. Women reformers reforged international links that had been broken during the war. . . . When German and Austrian sister delegates were barred from Paris, the intrepid organizers chose a neutral Swiss city, Zurich, as the location for the founding in May 1919 of the Women's International League for Peace and Freedom. Believing that the root causes of war lay in structures of inequality — social, economic, and political — they issued Cassandra-like warnings that the seeds of future war were being sown in the unequal terms of the Versailles Treaty. Great power domination of the proposed League of Nations, they believed, would reinforce imperialism, underwrite poverty, and deny oppressed peoples access to power.

The Women's International League brought moral realism into the swelling pacifist movement. Picking up the thread where it had been dropped upon U.S. entrance into the war, Jane Addams, Emily Green Balch, and other leaders worked to temper power politics with the universal ethics of peace and justice. As such, they represented the best in the new postwar progressivism, sadder and wiser, but with ideals intact. . . .

The chief focus of idealism was Wilson himself. In the winter of 1918–19, the author of the Fourteen Points became a vessel into which all the hopes and dreams of the moment were poured. When he made his procession from the Brittany seacoast to the French capital on his way to the peace conference, Catholic villagers along the rail route were said to have stood in the December cold and prayed for his success. Upon arrival in Paris, he was welcomed with a tumultuous celebration that even exceeded the reception given arriving American soldiers two years earlier. When he made a triumphal procession to Rome, he was received as "the King of Humanity." His call for self-determination made him the champion of oppressed peoples from eastern Europe to East Asia. . . .

The legend of Wilsonian idealism was born out of this moment. Harboring no territorial ambitions or imperial claims of his own, so the story went, the president of the New World republic was the only one to arrive in Paris with clean hands. Compared to the sordid self-seeking of Old World diplomats, Wilson seemed to stand for the universal principles of peace without victors, freedom of the seas, and self-determination. "Wilson the Just," as Clemenceau mockingly called him, carried the hopes of the dispossessed from the streets of Paris into the very den of the possessing classes at Versailles. . . .

VERSAILLES

Amid great expectations, the official gathering got underway in January 1919 in the baroque palace of the Bourbon kings at Versailles just outside Paris. Meeting in the Hall of Mirrors surrounded by the gilded trappings of the *ancien régime* [the old monarchical order], the victorious statesmen hammered out peace terms to be presented to the vanquished Germans and Austrians. The irony of meeting in a prime symbol of the old regime while attempting to forge a new world order was not lost on contemporaries. The Versailles conference was often compared to the 1815 Congress of Vienna, which had attempted to reestablish the old order in the aftermath of the French Revolution and the Napoleonic Wars.

The comparison, however, was misleading. The Allied statesmen were not hidebound reactionaries. They had not come to Versailles to restore plumed aristocrats and hereditary princes to the throne. Except for a few diehards, everyone acknowledged that the old aristocratic order was gone forever. Rather, they came to recast the modern bourgeois order. Flickering newsreel images showed the diplomats in their formal morning coats and top hats looking like Victorian gentlemen on their way to redraw the map of the world in a way that would foster prosperity and political stability. . . .

Republican men of affairs would no doubt have given their right arms to be in Paris. . . . However, in a fateful decision that would have dire consequences in the fight over ratification, not a single Republican of stature had been invited. Bypassing the grand old men of the Grand Old party — ex-President Taft, former presidential candidate Charles Evans Hughes, and senior statesman Elihu Root — Wilson chose only one low-profile member of the opposition. The mistake was in not joining forces with those outward-looking Republicans who relished America's new great power status and eagerly anticipated a leading role for the United States in the proposed League of Nations. Instead, they were left behind to choke on their anger.

The reason has to do with Wilson's desire to take all the glory for himself. Convinced of his own unsurpassed virtue, Wilson succumbed to his own megalomania. He took along only the most trusted advisors, above all, Colonel Edward House. The suave Texas Democrat was a promoter of Mexican investment schemes, a thoroughgoing Anglophile, and the first American to become an influential member of the elite club of world-class diplomats. Another member of the team was Robert Lansing, Wilson's son-in-law. Lansing had come to the War Department from Wall Street, and he was an arch-Presbyterian obsessed with the Bolshevik threat. . . .

Americans rubbed elbows with leaders of the Atlantic nations. The key figures were Lloyd George, the wily Welshman who was Liberal prime minister, and Georges Clemenceau, the tenacious French premier known as "the Tiger." Together with Wilson, they were seen to personify the new regime of commoners and self-made men. Certainly, in comparison to the deposed Kaiser Wilhelm II and the Habsburg emperor, they were elected leaders of constitutional regimes (unwritten, in Britain's case) and, in some sense, heirs of the great republican revolutions of the eighteenth century.

Yet they were by no means revolutionaries themselves. Despite Wilson's rhetoric about the need for radical change, the more they got down to the business of constructing a new world order, the more the emphasis shifted from "new world" to "order." Against what Wilson had called the "typhoon" of revolutionary threats to family and property, they set out to reconstruct an order where contracts were sacrosanct, debts repaid, marriages revered, and authority respected. Wartime promises had to be set aside. The revolt against the old civilization had gone far enough.

The first to go was the new diplomacy. Never mind what the Fourteen Points had said about open covenants openly arrived at. The peacemakers were not about to conduct their solemn business under the pressure of a mob. At first, the representatives of popular movements were allowed to stand outside the Hall of Mirrors with their noses pressed against the glass, so to speak, looking in on the official proceedings. Early on, however, plenary sessions became unwieldy, and what had begun as open discussions were increasingly closed to the press and public. Key decisions were referred to the Supreme Council of Ten, then the Council of Four, and when the Italian premier Orlando went home in a huff over the disputed city of Fiume, it was reduced to the Big Three.

The most fateful decision was made even before the conference opened. Without even a hint of protest from the one-time spokesman for "peace without victory," Germany and Austria were excluded from the deliberations. In a decision fraught with danger for the future, the victors undertook to make peace without any representation from the most powerful single country on the continent. The absence of Germany permitted the victors to write the soon-to-be-infamous "war guilt" clause, saddling Germany with full blame for the war, and with responsibility for paying damages in the form of reparations. Whether or not reparations were justified, they fostered resentment that would soon come back to haunt the world.

An equally weighty matter was international political economy. Some of the wiser heads at Versailles urged reestablishment of the more or less open borders that had characterized the prewar world, but four years of intense nationalism ruled that out. Instead, both at Versailles and after, each nation pursued its own narrow economic interests without regard to the stability of the international system as a whole. In addition to millions in reparations demanded of the Germans, Americans also demanded repayment of wartime loans extended to the British, instead of regarding them as a sound investment in Allied victory. With each nation jealously looking out for its own industries, there were no agreements on reducing tariffs. To the contrary, import duties rose sky high.

In the face of Bolshevik repudiation of tsarist debts, a prime goal in recasting the bourgeois world was ensuring that everyone pay their debts. What was new in the international equation was that the biggest share of world debt was now owned in the United States. Thanks to its wartime credits to British and other European borrowers, the United States had emerged as the world's biggest creditor, with some $10 billion in private and public debt outstanding. With Wall Street making ready to challenge the City of London as the headquarters of world lending, Americans such as Thomas Lamont, associated with the House of Morgan, became key players in international finance.

The Big Three also confronted a shambles in international relations. Seeking to consolidate a new system, they chose to rebuild international relations around a much-expanded system of nation-states, large and small. Thus a whole new tier of nation-states came into being in eastern Europe all the way from the Baltic republics on the north through Poland, Austria, Hungary, and Czechoslovakia down to the Balkan states on the south. Some of the new states were top-down creations of the great powers, but they also embodied widespread popular demands for national self-determination.

Even so, the complete ascendancy of nationalism is something of a puzzle. Nationalism had much to do with conflict between the great powers and everything to do with the wars in the Balkans which had been the tinderbox of the Great War itself. If national rivalries had helped start the war and nationalist hatreds had kept it going, why add fuel to this fire?

In explanation, the first thing that stands out is the place of nation-states in the prevailing ideology of the day. As representatives of their respective nation-states, the statesmen simply could not conceive of an alternative. Since the bourgeois societies of the West took the form of national markets, most everything else took national form, as well — currencies, armed forces, flags, ruling interests, and ruling ideas. It was not just rulers who thought in terms of national interest, but ordinary people, too, who imagined themselves to be nations. Once the system of national states was in place, no nation could afford to be left out, with the result that nations without states, like the Poles, demanded that a state be created for them.

Efforts to create viable nation-states were immensely complicated by eastern Europe's complex cultural diversity. In the arc stretching from the Baltic Sea in the north to the Balkan peninsula in the south, the architects of the new world order confronted a bewildering array of languages, religions, and ethnic identities. . . .

No matter how many times they retraced the maps of the region, members of The Inquiry, the special team of American academic advisors, were unable to carve uniform nations out of this jungle. As everyone recognized at the time, the new states confounded the link between state and cultural nation. Poland had Jewish and German minorities; Czechoslovakia was made up of two different nationalities; and Yugoslavia topped them all, a wholly artificial conglomeration of cultural minorities — Serbs, Croats, Montenegrans, Albanians — sure to be restive under any central government.

The best hope was that, once in place, the new states would somehow generate the kind of civic nationalism of the sort pioneered by the American and French republics. In his eloquent public addresses, Wilson, the last of the Founding Fathers, never failed to link peacemaking to the civic ideals of liberty and self-determination, hoping these would bring a measure of cohesion to a potentially chaotic situation.

The nation-state found its apotheosis in the League of Nations. Heedless of national rivalries, such as that between Germany and France over Alsace-Lorraine, that had done so much to bring on the Great War, the commissioners proposed an international forum for working out national disputes, and if that failed, a "concert of nations" under which member states would join together against an aggressor nation, of which Germany was taken as the arch-example. No matter how much Wilson declaimed about a "league of peoples," it was neither that, nor even a true league of nations, but, in fact, a league of nation-states.

In the view from the top at Versailles, nation-states were a safe answer to people's movements, unless they happened to be colonial peoples. For anyone living under Western rule, Versailles was the graveyard of national liberation. None of the Big Three, not even Wilson, had any intention of extending the principle of self-determination outside Europe. The colonial world would have to remain a giant chessboard in the game of imperial power.

So it was in the Middle East. Anticipating the defeat of the Ottoman Empire, British and French diplomats began making promises during the war for the future of the region. Palestine, in particular, was promised to the Jews (Balfour Declaration), to the Arabs (to induce the Saudis to join the Allies), and to the British (in the Sykes-Picot agreement, one of the infamous secret treaties). In a quip that made the rounds at Versailles, Palestine became a "much-promised land."

There was little in the way of democracy or progressive politics among any of the would-be nations. Certainly Emir Faisal of the Arabian peninsula could present no liberal credentials whatsoever. Accompanied by General Nouri Pasha and Colonel T. E. Lawrence ("Lawrence of Arabia"), Faisal and his fellow potentates may have been "the most resplendent figures that had ever entered the Quai d'Orsay," but no one could have mistaken the elegant robes of the patriarchal, monarchical, theocratic son of the Sherif of Mecca for the trappings of democracy. Meanwhile, Zionists conveniently forgot that Palestine was no more unoccupied territory than was New England before the arrival of the Puritans.

In the end, neither Arabs nor Jews were able to play the Big Three against one another; instead, European imperial control was preserved behind the fig leaf of League of Nations "mandates." Japan got into the mandate game by taking control of Shandong, the former German territory in China. The Japanese proposal to insert a "racial equality" clause into the treaty threatened to upset the imperial applecart, but in return for backing away from the incendiary proposal, the Big Three accepted the Japanese landgrab in China. For his part, Wilson pretended ignorance of the secret treaties and refused to have anything to do with the mandate system (Armenia had been suggested for U.S. oversight), but he made sure to protect American protectorates, colonies, and spheres of influence in Latin America by winning explicit recognition for the Monroe Doctrine in the treaty.

What added special urgency to the deliberations were the fires of social revolution burning on the horizon. Every day, the Big Three could look outside the windows of the Hall of Mirrors and imagine these fires getting closer. Having already consumed Russia, they were flaring up in central and eastern Europe, feeding on the highly combustible fuel of starvation and economic dislocation. For this reason, no one wanted to allow Lenin's Russia a place at the table. In western Europe, too, hunger and hardship were a threat, and even in America, so rich and secure, elites were gripped by a fear of disorder. With events between Moscow and Paris spinning out of control, a bewildering set of social changes — women's suffrage, ethnic revolt, race riots, industrial discord — looked more threatening to otherwise secure rulers than they actually were.

That was why bolshevism seemed such a menace. To Western elites, bolshevism began and ended in chaos. It was a product of economic dislocation and moral decay, and once in power, it set about creating chaos through tyrannical methods of proletarian dictatorship that destroyed the good order of civilization. . . . It was not so much the seizure of state power that aroused opposition in the West, as the seizure of banks, mines, and Orthodox churches under an ideology of collectivism that seemed to strike at the propertied family, the very foundation of the social order.

Every major decision at Versailles was made with one eye on the revolutionary fires. To deal with the Bolsheviks themselves, the Big Three sent troops into Russia. The ill-fated Allied intervention had begun a year earlier with the purpose of reopening the Eastern Front. Troops were sent to Arkhangel'sk and Murmansk in northern Russia and to Vladivostok in Siberia, where they remained without a clear mission when the war ended. The Big Three considered a proposal brought back by a special mission under William Bullitt for a peace conference to be held at the island of Prinkipo in the Black Sea. When that idea was vetoed by Clemenceau, the most ardent anticommunist of the three, Lloyd George and Wilson swallowed their disappointment and agreed to change the mission of the intervention and come to the aid of Russian counterrevolutionaries in an effort to overthrow or at least cripple the Bolshevik regime. In their last formal act at Versailles in June 1919, they agreed to support Admiral Kolchak in his increasingly desperate campaign to restore the old ruling classes to power. . . .

Erecting a firewall against the westward spread of bolshevism was a main reason the Big Three had set up the tier of new nation-states in eastern Europe in the first place. Called a *"cordon sanitaire"* [quarantine line], it was intended to get new states up and running as quickly as possible to fill the vacuum of authority left by the collapse of the defeated empires, just as the mandate system was supposed to seal off colonial regions from Bolshevik ideas.

There is no doubt that the situation in eastern and central Europe was fraught with peril. Journalists and diplomats on the scene from the Baltic to the Balkans regaled their respective contacts at Versailles with terrifying tales of bloated bellies swelling the ranks of street demonstrators. Tracing communist insurrections in Germany to hunger and privation, Lloyd George called for an immediate lifting of the blockade so that food could be sent in. "As long as order was maintained in Germany, a breakwater would exist between the countries of the Allies and the waters of Revolution beyond." The Americans were even more convinced that food was the answer to revolution. Putting it crudely, Lansing said, "Empty stomachs mean bolsheviks. Full stomachs mean no bolsheviks."

What made leaders doubly nervous was the unsettled situation in their own back-yards. France, with its ruined villages and broken economy, and Britain, suffering economic dislocation and high inflation, were home to restive workers demanding the redemption of wartime pledges of "a land fit for heroes." In a typical rhetorical flourish, Lloyd George warned that unless the peacemakers acted quickly to stabilize Germany, "he could not speak for France but trembled for his own country." He was worried because a "state of revolution among the working classes of all countries would ensue with which it would be impossible to cope."

Did the fires of revolt threaten the United States? Opinion was divided. With a whiff of smoke in their nostrils, some Americans at Versailles worried that somehow the flames might leap across the Atlantic. Lansing, for example, believed the peril to America was "very great" because of the high level of disorders in American streets. . . .

Others agreed with [Herbert] Hoover that the United States was immune to revolution. Believing the Atlantic Ocean was a deep firebreak between two vastly different ways of life, he was sure "the irreconcilable conflicts between Old and New World concepts of government and of social and economic life" would keep America safe. The essential difference, in his view, had to do with class. The Old World was imperiled because "the gulf between the middle classes and the lower classes is large, and where the lower classes have been kept in ignorance and distress, this propaganda will be fatal and do violence to normal democratic development." Fortunately, the New World had been spared deep class division and was, therefore, immune to bolshevism. "For these reasons," he said, "I have no fear of it in the United States."

Seeking to recast the bourgeois order, the peacemakers did their best to bury the remains of aristocratic and autocratic Europe and replace it with an order based on modern property, the middle-class family, and self-governing nation-states under the "covenant" of the League of Nations. Although Germany was excluded from the League, adding punishment to defeat, everyone assumed that after a period of probation it, too, would join the community of nations. Meanwhile, acceptance of the United States as a great power was a sign of European willingness to augment European global hegemony of the past with a broader reign of the West.

With Germany excluded and Russia sidelined, most of the political battles had taken place among the Big Three themselves. Given all the wrangling, they came to be seen in many quarters not as peacemakers but as deal makers. John Dos Passos spoke for a disillusioned generation in portraying them as three old cynics playing a diplomat's game of cards, dealing out decisions on one issue after another — the Rhineland, the Polish corridor, Fiume, Shandong. In this high-stakes poker game, Dos Passos added with some cynicism of his own, "Oil was trumps."

Ever the optimist, Wilson hailed the Versailles Treaty as the fulfillment of the Fourteen Points. His supporters went along, portraying it as a triumph of Wilsonian idealism. In reality, it was anything but. Instead of making a place for common people at the table of wealth and power, the Big Three rejected social reform, spurned power-sharing in the colonies, and gave only weak support to international labor standards. Far from embracing radicalism, as Wilson had once proposed, they sent an army to Russia to crush it. By the end, Wilson's magic mirror lay shattered. When many progressives looked into the treaty, they beheld not their hopes for a better world, but the ghastly face of reaction. Characterizing it as the work of "reactionaries," The Nation declaimed, "In the whole history of diplomacy there is no treaty more properly to be regarded as an international crime than the amazing document which the German representatives are now asked to sign."

By the time the peace conference concluded in June, the Big Three had forfeited their hold on the imagination of the world. Feeling betrayed by world leaders, the forces of change lost their enthusiasm for "Wilson the Just" and his new world order.

The millennial moment had been brief. What Dos Passos had called "the first year" [of a new era in history] ended a few short months after it began. . . .

QUESTIONS TO CONSIDER

1. In what ways was America's involvement in World War I "America's most important moment in world history"? How did the emergence of Wilson's leadership reflect a deeper shift in world power?

2. Many historians have pointed out the paradox that Americans believe simultaneously in their nation's exceptional history and in its mission to convert the world to its ways. To what extent did Woodrow Wilson exemplify this paradox? How was he "the last of the Founding Fathers"? What version of "Progressive internationalism" did he advocate? In what ways did Progressive reformers turn American national traditions in internationalist directions? How did they believe that America could save the world? How did Republican Progressive Herbert Hoover's claim that the United States was "immune to revolution" reflect exceptionalist thinking?

3. According to the author, Wilson's Fourteen Points acted as a "magic mirror" in which different people "saw their best face reflected." Describe the ways that American conservatives, reformers, and radicals interpreted Wilson's vision for the postwar peace. Were their views complementary or contradictory? How did people in Britain, France, and Germany react to Wilson's plan? How were colonial peoples given hope by it? What "limitations, evasions, and hypocrisies" were obscured by the initial attractiveness of the Fourteen Points?

4. In what ways did the settlement at Versailles demonstrate the persistence of European and American imperialism? How did secret treaties, the mandate system, and recognition of the Monroe Doctrine put a "fig leaf" on imperialist takeovers? Why did Wilson, who had advocated the "self-determination of peoples," not call for colonial independence? Why did he challenge only German imperialism?

5. What do you think is the overall point or "lesson" of Dawley's tale of crushed hopes? Who or what does the author blame for the failure of Wilson's version of Progressive internationalism? its internal contradictions and hypocrisies? the "impossible dream" of international cooperation? the illusion that the United States could redeem the world? the delusion that nation-states could represent ordinary people? the relentless pursuit of national self-interest? the Allies' obsessive fear of the Bolshevik menace? What implications, if any, does your response have for America's role in the world today?

VII

CULTURAL CHANGE
IN THE 1920s

As Americans recovered from the trauma and disappointment of World War I, their political mood turned conservative. Longing for "normalcy" at home and less intervention abroad, they elected old-fashioned Republican presidents who gave them both. In other ways, however, the 1920s ushered in a new, more modern America. Prosperity and economic innovation created conditions that eroded the Protestant work ethic and outmoded the old values of thrift and self-denial. Automobiles and other mass-produced consumer goods fed a new emphasis on consumption and leisure, and advertising became big business. Jazz, short skirts, and cigarette smoking suggested that a new, looser morality was replacing Victorian ways. These changes did not come without conflict. Many Americans were disturbed by the new secular lifestyle of the 1920s and feared that white Protestant dominance of the nation's values was slipping away. Tension over change broke out into cultural and political conflict over such issues as immigration, race relations, and Prohibition.

As Robert Sklar notes in his essay, the movies played a key role in this cultural drama of tradition versus change. Silent-film movie palaces provided an arena of fantasy where Americans' ambivalence about the new hedonistic lifestyle was played out. As they thrilled to passion-filled melodramas or laughed at silent-film comedies, filmgoers could challenge traditional Protestant morality vicariously, then return to their conventional real lives. Glamorous European movie stars helped Americans to push the boundaries of Victorian morality while retaining their "respectable" self-image.

Something similar was happening in France at the same time, as Jeffrey H. Jackson shows in his essay. The French "Crazy Years" matched the American "Roaring Twenties" in their live-for-the-moment spirit and looser attitudes toward sexuality and consumption. A popular mania for American jazz music that swept through Paris in the 1920s suggested that the French, like Americans, found "foreignness" alluring but also somewhat troubling. Analyzing French commentary on the new music, Jackson contends that discussing jazz provided a way for Europeans to register their conflicting views on the momentous changes of the postwar world, from the "Americanization" of European life and the decline of French cultural authority to the giddy discarding of old manners and morals.

Taken together, these two essays act as mirror images reflecting the cultural transformations of the 1920s from both sides of the Atlantic. After you have read them, think about the similarities and differences they reveal. What common patterns do you see in the American craze for European movie stars and the French interest in American jazz? What national differences do these borrowings disclose? What role did foreignnness play in the loosening of manners and morals after World War I, and why? The transatlantic exchange that these essays document offers rich material for a comparative look at cultural change in the 1920s. It should also prompt you to reflect upon today's debates over the impact of American culture abroad. Is American popular culture homogenizing the world, or do national issues and traditions continue to govern people's views?

13

Americans, Europeans, and the Movies

Robert Sklar

A "revolution in manners and morals" swept through middle-class America in the 1920s, fueled by postwar prosperity, new attitudes toward sexuality, Prohibition (which seemed to make drinking more attractive), and the automobile. It surfaced in many ways, ranging from the appearance of "flappers" and "speakeasies" to the growing popularity of Sunday drives (instead of churchgoing) and divorce. But the "Roaring Twenties" were not one big party. They were more like a cultural battleground where the painful transition from Victorian norms to modern habits of consumption and leisure was being contested. Ranged against the new hedonism were Protestant traditionalists such as Henry Ford and William Jennings Bryan (defender of biblical creation in the famous Scopes "Monkey trial" of 1925), who clung to the work ethic and a literal interpretation of the Bible. Fears that America was departing from a white Protestant cultural consensus spurred the crusade to restrict immigration, the revival of the Ku Klux Klan in northern cities, and calls to censor perhaps the most visible transgressor of the Victorian moral code — the movies.

Fans and detractors alike agreed that the movies played a central role in freeing middle-class manners and morals from their Victorian confines. Millions of young men and women flocked to their local theaters to see films whose advertisements promised "brilliant men, beautiful jazz babies, champagne baths, midnight revels, petting parties in the purple dawn, all ending in one terrific smashing climax that makes you gasp." "It seems," pronounced sociologist Herbert Blumer ponderously, "that emotional possession induced by passionate love pictures represents an attack on the mores of our contemporary life." The motion picture autobiographies Blumer collected from high school and college students at the decade's end appeared to bear him out. Over and over again, young people described how they put into practice the smoking, drinking, flirting, dressing, and undressing they had thrilled to on the screen. "Our children," complained one editor, "are rapidly becoming what they see in the movies."

It is easy to overstate the extent of this rebellion against convention, which was generally limited to the urban white middle class and was opposed by traditionalists of many ages. Even those who tested the warm water of passion often kept one foot on the solid ground of Victorian morality. As Robert Sklar shrewdly notes in this selection from his book Movie-Made America *(1975), American film audiences were basically ambivalent about the new morality. They were eager to see lurid and sinful behavior on the screen, but they wanted to preserve their respectability in the process. The result was the dominance of formula pictures, with easily identifiable male heroes and villains, virginal girlfriends and dangerously alluring "other women." While steamy seduction scenes and nude baths magnetized viewers, the films' endings usually featured the reconciliation of the "good" couple and an appropriately gruesome punishment for the "heavies." As Sklar demonstrates, in order to violate conventions safely, Hollywood imported foreign actors and directors and revived old stereotypes of Europeans as more sensual, emotional, and sinful than innocent Americans. Through European stars such as Rudolph Valentino and Greta Garbo, American filmgoers could vicariously escape their puritanical roots and smooth their transition to an acceptance of modern sexuality.*

According to Sklar, it was not the passion-filled melodramas of the 1920s but the silent-film comedies of Harold Lloyd and Buster Keaton that really exploded middle-class pieties. Sometimes this happened literally, as in Keaton's One Week *(1920), in which a passing train smashes a newlywed couple's house to pieces; more often it occurred metaphorically, as in Lloyd's harrowing "climb to success" in* Safety Last *(1923), which Sklar describes vividly. Sklar's analysis takes a comparative turn when he notes that European filmgoers seemed to understand and enjoy these comic artists more than American audiences did. While Americans went to the movies to feel European "passion," European moviegoers marveled at the open spaces and freewheeling action of American comedies and cowboy films.*

Sklar's thoughtful tour through the silent-film era has important implications for students of American history. It shows that American movies are products of a particular time and place and (like popular culture generally) often contain "cultural messages" that address prevailing social and moral codes. It suggests some of Americans' shared cultural traits as well as their stereotypes of other peoples. And to those who fear that mass culture is making everyone everywhere the same, it offers some reassurance. No doubt the movies, in becoming an international entertainment medium, spread modern consumption habits and sexual behavior wherever they were seen. Yet audiences in different nations brought their own cultural baggage into the theater, and because of this they took home different memories and messages. Silent films may have used the universal language of pictures, but that language was interpreted quite differently by Americans and Europeans.

GLOSSARY

CHAPLIN, CHARLIE (1889–1977)   A British-born pantomimist who came to the United States in 1910 and three years later adopted the Little Tramp costume and character that made him famous. Chaplin's sentimental silent-film comedies were enjoyed around the world in the 1920s.

FLAPPERS   Young women of the 1920s who defied Victorian conventions by wearing short skirts, smoking and drinking, and dancing the Charleston. Combining frank female sexuality and boyish athleticism, the flapper challenged traditional prudishness but not male domination.

GATSBY, JAY   The wealthy protagonist of F. Scott Fitzgerald's famous Jazz Age novel, *The Great Gatsby* (1925).

JAMES, HENRY (1843–1916)   A preeminent American novelist noted for his complex style and subtle psychological characterizations. His early novels, such as *The American* (1877) and *Daisy Miller* (1879), compared the sophisticated culture of Europeans with the naïve quality of Americans.

KU KLUX KLAN   An ex-Confederate secret society that terrorized blacks and their supporters in the South during Reconstruction. Revived in 1915, the Klan was wider in scope and mainly northern in membership. Anti-Catholic, anti-Semitic, and anti-immigrant as well as racist, the Klan was fueled by the conformist Americanism of the World War I years and the Red Scare that followed.

MUCKRAKER   The name applied to Progressive-era journalists, novelists, and critics who exposed the abuses of business and corruption in politics. They included Upton Sinclair and Lincoln Steffens as well as David Graham Phillips. The label was given to them by President Theodore Roosevelt in a 1906 speech criticizing their methods.

PROHIBITION   The outlawing of the production and sale of alcoholic beverages by the Eighteenth Amendment to the Constitution in 1919. Prohibition opened new opportunities for organized crime, spurred increased consumption of alcohol, and proved unenforceable. The Twenty-first Amendment repealed it in 1933.

SENNETT, MACK (1880–1960)   A film director and producer whose Keystone studios (1912–1935) made thousands of short and full-length slapstick comedies. Charlie Chaplin, Buster Keaton, and other film comedians began their film careers at Keystone.

SLAPSTICK   A broad style of comedy featuring nonstop action and cartoonlike violence such as clubbing and pie-throwing. Slapstick dominated silent-film comedy.

SPEAKEASIES   Barrooms or similar places where alcoholic beverages were illegally sold during Prohibition.

UFA (UNIVERSUM-FILM-AKTIENGESELLSCHAFT)   The major German film producing company in the 1920s and early 1930s. UFA was formed when subsidies from the German government encouraged a merger of leading film studios in 1917. Many of its directors, stars, and cameramen were lured by Hollywood studios in the 1920s.

VAUDEVILLE   Variety-show entertainment consisting of unconnected songs, dances, acrobatic and magic acts, and comic skits. Called "music hall" in England, vaudeville was the most popular theatrical attraction for British and American working-class audiences at the turn of the twentieth century. Many film comedians began their careers in vaudeville.

T he silent feature film as a medium of art and mass commercial entertainment was born, flourished and died within a span of less than twenty years. Of more than ten thousand silent features produced in the United States between 1912 and 1929, only a handful remain in circulation for screening on television, at museums or by university film societies — the tip of an uncharted iceberg of surviving prints in archives, studio vaults and private collections. Though they date back little more than half a century, well within memory for many, they are, no less than Etruscan vases, artifacts of a departed culture, an irrecoverable past.

Who can re-create the experience of going to the pictures in the radiant dawn of popular mass culture? By the late 1920s every large city and most medium-sized towns boasted at least one brand-new sumptuous picture palace. Outside on the sidewalk stood a doorman, attired in frock coat with white gloves, waiting to open your car door and direct you to the ticket booth. If it was raining, he held an umbrella over your head; if snowing, an usher in the lobby rushed forward to brush off your coat.

You passed from usher to usher as you moved through ornate lobby corridors, hushed by the atmosphere of an Egyptian temple or a baroque palace that had provided the inspiration for architectural imitation. (A *New Yorker* cartoon of the period shows a child in a picture-palace lobby, asking, "Mama — does God live here?") Eventually you came to the auditorium itself, or one of its serried balconies, where additional ushers stood, poised beside automatic seating boards that indicated which seats, if any, were empty. One, holding a flashlight to direct your steps, personally escorted you to your seat. There, after live stage performances, musical interludes played by an orchestra numbering up to thirty pieces, a newsreel and a travelogue, you saw what you had come for — a feature film, accompanied by its own especially arranged musical score.

Of the feature films exhibited in such picture palaces, and at every other movie theater large or small throughout the country, no more than a tiny number were produced without the expectation or at least the strong hope of reaping a profit. . . . The almost undiluted commercialism of motion-picture production was a constant source of exasperation to critics and reviewers in the silent era, who looked, most often vainly, for redeeming aesthetic value in the stream of feature films pouring out of Hollywood at the rate of nearly two a day.

Posterity, however, has found it easier to recognize enduring artistry in American silent films. In a world-wide poll of critics published in 1972 by the British Film Institute in its quarterly, *Sight and Sound,* some twenty American silent features were named at least once on the various critics' lists of the top ten motion pictures in the history of world cinema. . . .

. . . It would be as false, however, to tell the story of moviemaking in the silent era on the basis of a few artistic achievements as it would be to leave art out of it. For producers, movie workers, audiences and observers alike, the meaning of American movies lay in the multiple and cumulative messages of the more than ten thousand good, bad and indifferent films that played selectively across the vision and consciousness of their viewers. . . .

. . . All the evidence suggests that the vast majority of silent films fell into well-defined categories of subject and treatment: the crime story, the Western story, the historical costume story, the domestic melodrama, the romance. Overwhelmingly, films of contemporary life, crime movies, melodramas and love stories centered on men and women from the upper-middle and wealthy classes: people who lived in large spacious houses, kept servants, owned cars and earned their money from business, finance or the professions.

This was as true before World War I as after. But the dramatic changes in American cultural styles and values in the war years and after have sometimes confused historians of motion pictures, who, like other historians of the arts, sometimes oversimplify about the larger culture in which their medium was shaped. . . .

. . . [I]n this period American society and culture were changing faster and more fundamentally than the movies themselves. . . . Members of the urban leisure and professional classes . . . led the way in discarding the social code symbolized by that Victorian drawing-room scene. The traditional middle-class moral order had, even before the war, been losing ground in its effort to maintain small-town values in an increasingly urban, industrial and ethnically heterogeneous society. Its drive to recover dominance during the war through excessive patriotism, moralism and repression, though leading to impressive victories with the enactment of Prohibition and immigration restriction, also drove segments of the culturally influential urban elites away from adherence to traditional beliefs and behavior.

The targets of the campaign for conformity — the recently arrived immigrants and their children, the "hyphenated Americans" — related in a more confused and ambiguous way to the dominant social order. They sought success, comfort, status on the same terms as other Americans; many newcomers were quite willing to adhere to American standards because they marked the path to the American rewards they had come for. Yet they were told in painfully explicit ways, from discrimination and restrictive legislation to Klan violence, that their character and traits, their religions, languages, dress styles, complexions, features, cuisines, mores and habits were barriers to full admission into American life. . . .

To the spokesmen and spokeswomen of the dominant order, the movies stood in direct opposition to respectable American values and institutions: power over movies rested largely in the hands of foreign-born producers; even native-born movie workers came from marginal and disreputable subsocieties of vaudeville and stock company theater; and the movies were full of incitements to crime and salacious behavior.

Movies thus came to play a central role in the cultural conflicts that followed World War I. On both sides of the struggle, movies came to be seen as offering values distinctly different from those of the older middle-class culture, and providing greater opportunities for ethnic minorities than other economic sectors. Immigrants and their children were attracted to movie culture not merely because movies were cheap, ubiquitous and appealing as fantasy or entertainment; their preference became a conscious, one might almost say a political, choice.

In American society, movies became a major factor in the reorientation of traditional values — [the German critic] Walter Benjamin's word "liquidation" in the American context would be too strong. For no matter how despised they were by defenders of traditional middle-class culture, movies were, after all, made by men deeply committed to the capitalist values, attitudes and ambitions that were part of the dominant social order. Any new options they offered would clearly avoid breaking away from the fundamental economic and social mold. . . .

Faced with an audience more divided, more defensive, and yet increasingly avid for visions of alternative styles and behavior, moviemakers not unnaturally sought the subjects and treatments that pleased the most and alienated the fewest. The noisy and well-organized opposition and their own settled beliefs and filmmaking practices kept them from straying too far beyond the remaining stereotypes and formulas of the middle-class order. What they became adept at was reformulating older conventions; only when the need was obvious and overwhelming did they dare generate a new formula.

The results were not so different from traditional culture as reformers and censors sometimes made it appear. The overall effect of the movie version of reality was as always to place audiences at a distance from direct contact with their social environment. To choose between movies and traditional culture was essentially to choose one highly elaborated social code over another — a fact of which movie patrons were never totally unaware.

The tactics of moviemakers in transforming social codes were nowhere more successful than in the films of Cecil B. DeMille. He became notorious early in 1918 when he unveiled the first in a series of spicy morality tales of extramarital temptation, *Old Wives for New*. His audacity has since become a centerpiece of the Hollywood legend, but like many such stories, the facts are much more interesting.

The DeMille legend focuses especially on the most controversial of his early postwar films, *Male and Female* (1919). Moralists grew outraged as soon as they learned of DeMille's suggestive change of title from its source, James M. Barrie's play *The Admirable Crichton,* and the picture disappointed no one's expectations. In its famous bathroom scene Gloria Swanson, as Lady Mary, steps into a sunken bath the size of a small swimming pool, revealing a momentary glimpse of her breasts. Later DeMille introduced a lavish Babylonian fantasy sequence not to be found in the original, taking his inspiration from a poem by William Ernest Henley, whose lines the butler Crichton quotes in the play: "I was a king in Babylon/And you were a Christian slave."

By all accounts, *Male and Female* could never have been made before World War I. It was "a highly moral picture," Adolph Zukor, whose Famous Players-Lasky company produced the film, recalled in his autobiography, "yet its emotional theme — the noble lady falling in love with the butler — would probably not have been acceptable to pre-war audiences." In Lewis Jacobs' classic study, *Male and Female* is called "more daring in its subject matter than any other picture Hollywood had produced."

Is it merely the narrow moral climate in which movies have been judged that has led such commentators to ignore the relation of DeMille's films to their sources? Barrie's satire on the British aristocracy and its servants had been a stage favorite for nearly twenty years before *Male and Female* was produced (its original performances took place in London in 1902 and on Broadway in 1903). Similarly, David Graham Phillips' novel *Old Wives for New,* the source of DeMille's film of the same title, had been published back in 1908 and had aroused considerable controversy over its portraits of plutocratic American women. Perhaps the point is that before the war, playwrights and novelists, with smaller and higher status audiences, had been permitted more freedom of expression than filmmakers.

The more we learn of early motion-picture history, however, the more difficult it is to validate such judgments. Glimpses of nudity did not originate with *Male and Female;* not only were women with bare breasts shown in the Babylonian sequence of *Intolerance,* but Annette Kellerman, the champion swimmer, appeared nude in *A Daughter of the Gods* (1916). Nor was infidelity a novel topic — indeed, the attraction and danger of dalliance was the constant theme of Theda Bara's many "vampire" films, beginning in 1914 with *A Fool There Was.* (Long before *Dracula,* the term "vampire" described a predatory woman whose sexual desires, if fulfilled, were sure to drain a man's life blood; after World War I, as American society became more relaxed about sex, it was shortened to "vamp" and described a woman whose sexual forwardness was, though ambiguous, a great deal less harmful.) Nor was the subject of romance across the master-servant barrier so daring in DeMille. As far back as 1903, Biograph had made a comic film on that theme, *With a Kodak.* Filmmakers before the war explored nearly all the aspects of the subjects and the images that were to occupy their successors for half a century more; only in our own era have innovations gone further, with the display of male and female genitals and the performance of sex acts in commercial movies.

DeMille's daring lay not in subject matter, theme or revelation of the human form; what he did was give familiar topics a treatment that precisely suited audience desires in the immediate aftermath of the war. He was able to free the subject of marriage from the overstuffed parlors of Victorian melodrama, to infuse it with wit, style, vicarious pleasures, and above all, practical hints on contemporary ways to behave. . . . [Yet he was] far from being a realist, muckraker or impassioned critic of the upper bourgeoise. DeMille's triumph was one of manner, not matter. Though his films suggested new attitudes, none challenged moral order. In Phillips' novel [*Old Wives for New,*] "modern" marriage ends in adultery and divorce; in DeMille's movie, in temptation and reconciliation. DeMille's films angered moralists largely because they were popular with respectable middle-class audiences; and they would not have been so popular had they not been so conservative.

DeMille, was, above all, a consummate sentimentalist. He had the knack of titillating audiences while at the same time reinforcing their conventional standards — of letting them eat their cake and have it too. A few years later he discovered the most congenial form for his particular skills, the religious epic, which proved the perfect vehicle for his deft combination of moral didacticism and orgiastic fantasy. His "modern stories" in the early postwar period were preliminary expressions of this long-enduring formula. They told moviegoers of the necessity for, and the boundaries of, social change that would not disturb the inherited moral order; and in dream sequences of opulent sensuality, set in ancient times, they provided a voyeuristic glimpse of forbidden pleasures and desires.

There was one serious difficulty about eating one's cake and having it too: as a steady diet it quickly led to undernourishment. DeMille's modern dramas of temptation could gratify middle-class ideological expectations only when they insisted that adult men and women would not let lures and desires override their fundamental morality. Yet the films also frustrated a basic emotional expectation American audiences had traditionally brought to their popular arts — the wish to experience vicariously the sweet succumbing to temptation, and the guilt and retribution of those who step beyond the boundaries of the social code. Ultimately DeMille's formula narrowed the range of behavior too much. Of its kind it was superior, but alone it was not a strong enough base for Hollywood popularity and profits. In a period of cultural change, moviemakers could never feel certain that their conventions and stereotypes would last beyond a season. The longings of postwar audiences set them on a perpetual quest for more commercially and emotionally satisfying entertainment formulas.

The extent of alternative human behavior was, of course, never limitless. The vast majority of the world's nonwhite peoples were not considered subjects for the movies, any more than they were treated as other than stereotypes in the fiction, travel books, social sciences and political rhetoric of the time. An artist could rise above the barriers of his own culture and carry an audience with him, as Robert Flaherty proved with his classic silent documentaries *Nanook of the North* (1922), about Eskimo people in Canada's Hudson Bay, and *Moana* (1926), about the people of the western Samoan island Safune. But the audience for Samoans was smaller and did not go to movies so frequently as those who preferred to see Gloria Swanson on a tropical island, and Flaherty had few followers in the documentary field.

There were, however, Caucasian people known to behave very differently from Americans. These exotics inhabited such countries as France, Italy, Germany, Russia,

Sweden, even Great Britain. Natives of these countries, though much on American minds during the European war of 1914–1918, did not often appear on the screens of American movie theaters, since the war had diverted European film industries from making fiction feature films. American moviemakers were thus given a free hand to perpetuate their own versions of the character of European nationalities, which generally did not rise above the gross stereotypes of blacks or American Indians, though normally they were more favorable.

Europeans were more sensual, decadent, emotional, sinful than Americans, and also more calculating, rational and willful. They dared what the innocent American flirts in a DeMille movie would never dare — to be direct and clear in their intentions, to express themselves emotionally, to seek fulfillment of their desires. They were charming, fascinating, beguiling, dangerous and possibly evil.

They could do so many things forbidden to Americans! In one of the most interesting sexual dramas of the 1920s, Herbert Brenon's *Dancing Mothers* (1926), a married woman begins her flirtation with a single man (for the highly moral purpose, in the beginning at least, of distracting him from her frivolous flapper daughter) by posing as a Frenchwoman and speaking to him in French. One of the memorable scenes of romantic pathos in silent films is in the long tracking sequence in King Vidor's war epic *The Big Parade* (1925), when Renée Adorée, as the French peasant girl, runs frantically along the dusty line of marching American soldiers to carry his boots to her departing doughboy lover. The silent movies would not have risked depicting an American woman acting in the same open, vulnerable, loving way.

As a ground for sexual expressiveness, the stereotyped European had already become a familiar figure in American movies by the time of World War I. The war, however, infused even the most mundane European caricatures in the popular arts with a new intensity. It was the most emotional of America's overseas conflicts; the fate of civilization itself seemed to rest on combating the despicable Hun and supporting the brave French and British. The waves of popular sentiment engulfing the country gave new life to the settled forms of the movies.

Erich von Stroheim was among the first to experience the changed audience response to stock European figures. The war gave him a chance, after several years of hand-to-mouth work as a bit player and production assistant, to use his Austrian military background and play a series of villainous German officers. His personal appearance in public could set off angry murmurs and threats of violence. He had superseded the old stereotypes and become himself an archetype, the cruel, overbearing Prussian aristocrat, "the man you love to hate." When the war ended he was able to capitalize on this infamous characterization to launch a new career as a director, with himself as star of his own films.

In Von Stroheim's early postwar films his warrior is transformed into a seducer, and the struggle between America and the Central Powers becomes a battle of the sexes. He is Von Struben in *Blind Husbands* (1919), vacationing at the same Alpine resort as a young American couple; in *Foolish Wives* (1921) he is Count Sergius Karamazin, an adventurer in Monte Carlo who seeks to take advantage of an American diplomat and his wife. Both films follow a basically similar format: the suave and graceful European beguiles the idle American wife; he very nearly seduces her, but in each case her own feeble will and timely outside intervention save her from violation; in the end the European is unmasked as evil and meets a just death at the hands of someone he has wronged. American husband and wife are strengthened in their loyalty.

Though such a brief summary hardly does justice to Von Stroheim's qualities as a director, . . . it does suggest how little his formula varied from the sentimental conventions developed by DeMille. No marriage vows are breached; the American man learns a trim little lesson about not neglecting his wife, the woman learns to beware of continental lovers; and the European reveals how weak and miserable he is before meeting an ignominious death. Compared to DeMille, Von Stroheim adhered far more strictly to traditional American morals. He did allow audiences more of a chance to flex some larger emotions, but these were mainly negative: revenge, retribution and relief that the moral order was not seriously breached. Where were the warm, outgoing cathartic emotions to come from, love and sympathy, admiration and awe, pity and sorrow?

They were not to be found in the leading postwar films about contemporary American men and women, nor in Von Stroheim's films about Americans encountering Europeans. Only one possible alternative form of human interaction remained, and moviemakers were not required to think of it themselves, because the American reading public gave them the idea: for more than a year after the Armistice, book buyers and readers had clamored to get Vicente Blasco Ibáñez's *The Four Horsemen of the Apocalypse,* a romantic novel about an Argentine playboy in Europe who at first disdains the struggle, then converts to the cause of civilization, enlists in the French army and dies a hero's death in battle. The answer had been on the tip of every Hollywood tongue all along: if you were used to putting Europeans in your movies to hike up the emotion, think of the emotion you could generate by making *all* your characters European.

Metro got the chance to pioneer this new conception by buying the rights to the Ibáñez novel. For the part of Julio, the playboy, they assigned a young Italian, a former tango dancer who had been biding his time in movies playing bit parts as a south-of-the-border villain. His name was Rudolph Valentino. The rest, one is tempted to say, is history. In the brief span of years before Valentino's sudden death in 1926 at the age of thirty-one, Metro as well as Valentino's subsequent employers and the women and men of America got considerably more emotion than they had bargained for.

Valentino was a presence the silver screen had never seen before. He had passion; he loved, openly and fully; his love was strong but could be tragic weakness, too, as in *Blood and Sand* (1922), based on another Ibáñez novel, where he plays a famous matador whose desire for a "vamp" leads to self-destruction and death in the bull ring. Valentino's remarkable screen persona was not mere happy accident; he was also a skillful actor. . . .

It is instructive to compare Valentino with the most popular American male star of the period, Douglas Fairbanks. Valentino's character in Clarence Brown's *The Eagle* (1925) was clearly patterned after the carefree adventurer Fairbanks had so successfully portrayed in such films as *The Mark of Zorro* (1920), *Robin Hood* (1922) and *The Thief of Baghdad* (1925). Valentino demonstrated skill in horsemanship, sufficient athletic prowess — though nothing equal to Fairbanks' gymnastic feats — and a surprising

Rudolph Valentino, the European film lover at his most ardent, plays a British aristocrat disguised as an Arab, and overcomes Agnes Ayres in The Sheik *(1921). (Corbis-Bettmann.)*

capacity for wit and self-irony in his semicomic role as a Russian Robin Hood. The telling difference between the two men was that Valentino always projected himself in a way that Fairbanks, the smiling, clean-cut, genteel American hero, rarely did, if ever — as a sexual being.

In the as yet unwritten history of the revolution in modern American sexual attitudes and behavior, Valentino must play a considerable part. It was not only that he seemed to fulfill the fantasies of millions of American women — a collective dream that received its quintessential embodiment in his performance in *The Sheik* (1921), the film version of E. M. Hull's sensational novel, where, as an Arab chieftain, he ravishes an Englishwoman, then reveals himself an Anglo-Saxon aristocrat — there was also the tangled resentment and emulation he aroused in American men.

His grace, his ease with his body, his skill as a dancer, all clearly attractive to women, seemed to cause some men considerable unease. For a man to make himself appealing to women they considered a certain sign of his effeminacy. Valentino's masculinity was questioned because, among other things, he wore a bracelet, given him by his second wife. His deviance from the "cave man" ethic of male sexual behavior was particularly galling to the Chicago *Tribune,* which several times attacked him editorially; one such diatribe, published only a few weeks before Valentino's fatal illness, was blamed by Valentino's business manager for hastening the actor's death.

The equation Europe = passion was not, however, a discovery Americans made wholly through the screen image of Rudolph Valentino. It was a time-honored theme of American fiction, in the works of, among others, Henry James; and Europeans, using the logical calculating side of their natures, had long before figured out the value of passion as a means of achieving rational ends. The Germans, for example, deliberately turned to the theme of passion as a way of reviving their film industry after the war.

Burdened with their nation's defeat and the accumulated odium of Allied anti-German propaganda, the UFA studios and director Ernst Lubitsch planned to regain their international audience by a tour de force, making intimate sexual dramas about great figures in the histories of their conquerors. Curiosity and outrage would persuade British and French exhibitors to book their films, and their quality would win over hostile audiences — so it was plotted, and so, by and large, it occurred. The first of these films, *Madame Dubarry,* appeared in 1919, with Pola Negri in the title role and Emil Jannings as Louis XV, and was hailed as a classic. It was taken up by American distributors and opened a year later in New York, the first postwar German film to be shown in the United States . . . , although its origins were described vaguely as Central European. *Madame Dubarry* also was given a new name for its American run — *Passion*.

The alternative to traditional American behavior that movie audiences most clearly demanded was passionate behavior. And as the food industry turned to Latin America for its bananas, the movie industry looked to Europe for its supplies of passion. Passionate actresses, actors, directors and writers answered the call, and passionate philosophers as well. Foremost among the latter was the British novelist Elinor Glyn, who propagated the philosophy of "It," a form of personal magnetism not to be confused with sexual attraction — though everyone managed to, anyway.

The list of Europeans who came to Hollywood reads like the guest list of Gatsby's parties. Lubitsch, Negri and Jannings all came, the first two to stay, and the director continued his brilliant career, bringing an altogether new kind of sophistication and wit to Hollywood comedy. From Germany also came Conrad Veidt, the leading actor of *Dr. Caligari,* and directors Paul Leni, E. A. Dupont and F. W. Murnau. Murnau's first American film, *Sunrise* (1927), was ranked in the *Sight and Sound* poll mentioned earlier as one of the half-dozen greatest silent films of world cinema.

Hungary gave the American movies director Paul Fejos and actress Vilma Banky, whose blond beauty made an attractive contrast to Valentino's dark good looks when she played opposite him in *The Eagle* and *Son of the Sheik*. France contributed director Jacques Feyder, and the Swedish film industry lost its two leading directors, Mauritz Stiller and Victor Sjöström (known as Seastrom in Hollywood). Sjöström (who was an outstanding actor and matinée idol in Sweden) directed Lillian Gish in *The Scarlet Letter* (1926) and an extraordinary work of cinema naturalism, *The Wind* (1928). With Stiller to Hollywood came his protégé, Greta Garbo, a young actress who became the new embodiment of European passion in the same year Valentino died.

There is an uncanny lesson to be learned from Garbo's Hollywood debut: American moviemakers, then and for decades after, held fast to their formulas as faithfully as a newborn duckling adheres to the first moving thing it sees. Garbo was cast in her first two American films, *The Torrent* and *The Temptress* (both 1926), as a female Valentino, a sultry Spanish siren drawn from novels by none other than Vicente Blasco Ibáñez. If these were tests of her skill as an actress, she passed with flying colors, for as the *Variety* reviewer wrote of her first American performance, when a Scandinavian "can put over a Latin characterization with sufficient power to make it most convincing, need there be any more said regarding her ability?"

As it turned out, much more needed to be said, and was — no one doubted Garbo's appeal, but everyone seemed puzzled as to its nature. Though she was obviously a fine actress, her studio, MGM, gave her little chance to show it. Her ten American silent films were not exactly alike in their plots, but to all intents and purposes they were the same; following the first two came *Flesh and the Devil, Love, The Divine Woman, The Mysterious Lady, A Woman of Affairs, Wild Orchids, The Single Standard* and *The Kiss.* Garbo's principal challenge was to show how a passionate Russian woman differed from a passionate Austrian, French or English woman (and because everyone knew she was European, she was even allowed to portray passionate American women).

On the screen Garbo shone with an inner intensity few other performers in motion pictures came even close to. Director Fred Niblo demonstrated Garbo's power with a clever opening sequence in *The Mysterious Lady* (1928). The film begins at a party. The camera moves among the guests. Then a woman appears at the top of a staircase. You see parts of her, her legs, her arms, you see her from the back, she moves downstairs among the others, and still you have not seen her face. It does not matter. She has created an excitement in the audience, an emotional quickening, that makes the other players appear mere mannequins. This was Garbo; if her career had any major flaw, it was that she made Hollywood's most romantic male stars look callow and inadequate beside her.

It is pertinent to ask how European audiences reacted to all the passion committed in their name. Overseas exhibition accounted for more than a third of the American movie industry's total income during the 1920s and provided the vital margin for the high profits, high salaries and extravagant life style of the moguls and stars. Clearly, then, they did not mind it. But it would be fair to say that Europeans did not go to American movies to see themselves, nor did they consider Gloria Swanson or John Gilbert "Europeans" no matter what nationality they were presumably portraying. They wanted to see Americans, the wild raw new people of the Western world, doing what Americans do, in characteristically American ways.

To Europeans, what epitomized American life was movement. Compared to themselves — encrusted with traditions, weighted down by forms, customs, habits, procedures; measured, lugubrious, drained of life — American motion, and therefore American motion pictures, possessed an enchanting, irresistible allure. "There were long sequences of action — without a single dull passage — portraying sensational abductions," Philippe Soupault wrote of the early postwar American movies in France; "there were the pictures of Douglas Fairbanks, of Rio Jim, and of Tom Mix; there were complicated stories ending in the robbing of banks, in violent deaths, in discoveries of gold mines. . . . Doors open and close; bronzed men, strong men, terribly refined or terribly frivolous women come and go with happiness or unhappiness in their hands." Americans had physical genius; they held the secret of action, and Europeans went to American movies to learn the secret.

There was a time after the war when the arrival of the latest American Western was an exciting cultural event in European cities. With its tough, lean men, spectacular riding and blazing guns, the Western seemed to represent American action at its purest. But the novelty of Western stereotypes quickly paled. American producers began sending over films that combined a more refined, supple, versatile kind of physical genius. After a time Westerns came to seem unintentionally comic; these new films were comic by design. European audiences were among the first to recognize that the silent comedians were artists as well as funny men, and that in their antics the heritage of cultural values was more thoroughly explored and exploded than anywhere else in American movies.

. . . [After World War I,] the field was open for performers who could create a comic style specifically tailored to American middle-class values; and so a new group of bourgeois comedians emerged in the 1920s, with Harold Lloyd and Harry Langdon among its stars, and Buster Keaton its consummate artist.

At the core of the difference between prewar slapstick and postwar bourgeois comedy lies their respective treatments of that most sensitive area of middle-class behavior and belief — sex. In Keystone comedies, sex was all buffoonery and conflict: villains kidnapped young maidens; lovers thwarted censorious parents; wives and husbands schemed against each other and flirted with every available member of the opposite sex. Sexual attraction in [Charlie] Chaplin's films, whether the Tramp loved and won or loved and lost, was imbued with romance and sentiment, with tender glances and spontaneous emotion.

In contrast, bourgeois comedy steered a middle way between [Mack] Sennett's chaotic sexual struggles and Chaplin's sweet, unrestrained expression of love. Sex in the middle-class comedies was rigidly structured, and linked with preservation of the social order. Sexual attraction occurred only between unmarried youth, and marriage was its goal. It was a goal, however, to be attained not through the intimate attention of the prospective lovers, but rather through separation and action in the world — through challenge by the young woman, and in response, achievement by the young man in the face of obstacles placed in his way.

This was a familiar theme in American novels and stories of earlier days, but what marked the movie comedians as special was their firm roots in the comic tradition of extravagance and grotesque exaggeration. Their physical skills, and the vividness of their visual medium, pushed the young man's imagination to new heights of foolhardiness, danger and absurd complications. In the films of Lloyd and Keaton the traditional social order was never breached (that, it turned out, was one of their strengths), but within the bourgeois framework, comic formulas were carried to such extremes that they became parodies of themselves and struck at the roots of the cultural heritage no less powerfully than the films of Chaplin and Sennett.

Harold Lloyd's *Safety Last* (1923), directed by Fred Newmeyer and Sam Taylor, is a classic example of what happens to the aspiring young man in silent-movie comedy. Harold is a small-town boy going off to the city to start his career and earn wealth and status sufficient to enable him to marry his small-town girl. He takes a job in a department

In this famous shot from a classic silent comedy Safety Last *(1923), Harold Lloyd hangs on by the minute hand in his precarious climb to success and the girl. (The Museum of Modern Art/Film Stills Archive.)*

store and writes glowing but false letters home telling of rapid advancement. When the girl comes to visit he must go through elaborate comic byplay to demonstrate his exalted position without being caught.

Meanwhile, in an effort to promote himself, he arranges a publicity stunt for the store, a climb up its outside walls by a "human fly." An earlier joke played on a policeman backfires, however, and the cop chases the human fly, so that as the crowd gathers Harold has lost his performer. To save his idea Harold goes up the wall himself, in one of the superb comic stunts in the history of motion pictures. His climb is impeded successively by pigeons, a tennis net, a painter's board, a clock, a mouse and a weather gauge. Each new encounter throws him into graver danger. After one harrowing comic escape after another, he finally reaches the roof and falls into his girl friend's arms. One could hardly ask for more graphic satire on the theme of "upward mobility."

Keaton, the greatest of the comedians to emerge in the 1920s, derived his comic persona from the same stereotype, but he created an entirely different figure out of it. Lloyd was the quintessential middle-class climber, brash and knowing, caught up in a comedy of excess and panic; Keaton was stoic and naïve, an impassive inventor of solutions to life's bizarre challenges. . . . Where Lloyd accepted middle-class order and made comedy from the foolish antics of the man on the make, Keaton's existence within the same social setting was predicated on a recognition of not his but *its* absurdities. His comedy always had as its goal the restoration of order in the face of society's errors and false judgments.

After a career in vaudeville that began virtually in his infancy, Keaton began making movies in 1917 with Fatty Arbuckle. In 1920 he went into production for himself, making five to seven two-reelers a year over a three-year period. Beginning in 1923 he made features, ten in five years, of which no fewer than six received at least one vote in the *Sight and Sound* poll — recognition of one of the most concentrated periods of high creativity of any motion-picture artist. Of these, four are considered the classic examples of Keaton's comic art: *The General* (1926), *Sherlock Jr.* and *The Navigator* (both 1924), and the earlier two-reeler, *Cops* (1922).

In each of these four films Keaton is cast in the familiar role of a young man courting a young woman of more respectable position than his own. Each film opens with a rebuff — "I won't marry you until you become a big businessman," says the girl bluntly in *Cops,* in straightforward parody of the middle-class formula; while in *Sherlock Jr.* and *The General* the spurning is motivated by accusations of theft or cowardice. The stage is thus set for Buster, a perfect blend of ineptitude and ingenuity, to stand up to the challenge, perform feats of daring and imagination, right wrongs, clear his name and win back the woman. *Cops* is the only one of these films where the rebuff is repeated at the end; this utterly destroys his reason for being and he voluntarily submits himself to the police he has been eluding.

More than any other silent comedian, Keaton developed mechanical ingenuity and contrivance as basics of his comic style; they served, among other things, as counterpoints to his astounding acrobatic skill, an ability that always made his triumphs over machinery the result of neither brains nor blind luck but of his full comic persona. He locked himself in struggle and alliance with a wide range of the nineteenth-century's machinery of motion: a locomotive in *The General,* a steamship in *The Navigator,* a motorcycle and a motion-picture projector in *Sherlock Jr.*

Keaton's dream encounter with the movies in *Sherlock Jr.* is one of the greatest parodies of the medium ever made. Keaton plays a projectionist who falls asleep. In his dream, a double arises from his sleeping form, sees his girl friend threatened on the screen and rushes forward to rescue her. He steps into the screen, is pushed away, re-enters, and then the scenes begin to change. Over and over again in mid-movement Keaton is shifted from one setting to another, each more fraught with danger: from a doorstep he finds himself in a garden; sitting down, he is suddenly in the midst of traffic; beginning to walk, he finds himself on the edge of a cliff; and so on, through a lion's den, a desert, a hill, an island, a snowbank and back to the garden again. Ironically, the motion-picture projector is the only machine over which he cannot assert control. In the end he becomes its pupil: reunited with his girl in the projection booth, he courts her by following each move of the celluloid lovers, until a shot shows the screen couple with three babies.

If Chaplin's comic fantasy rested on an underlying realism of class distinctions, Keaton's was firmly anchored in the outer world of American mechanical civilization in its encounter with nature. In a Chaplin film the locus of movement was always the Tramp; movement was a principle of the entire Keaton motion-picture universe, emanating from machinery, from the natural setting and from the camera, as well as from Buster himself. Keaton was a master of outdoor action, in part because he refused to stint the money, time or detail necessary to achieve authentic action shots: in *The General* a real bridge is blown up, and a real locomotive, not a miniature, plunges into the water; in *Steamboat Bill Jr.,* a real frame wall falls on Keaton, who is spared because he is standing in a space corresponding to an open window frame, and neither a double nor trick shots were used. The physical genius that Europeans regarded as the hallmark of American silent movies found its embodiment in one man, Buster Keaton, and in his struggle to wrest order from the recalcitrant machinery, natural environment and moral values of the American landscape.

QUESTIONS TO CONSIDER

1. Analyze the tensions between traditional Victorian values and the looser moral and social codes of the 1920s. How did the urban leisure and professional classes lead the way in transforming traditional behavior? What part did Prohibition, the revival of the Klan, and immigration restriction play in the "culture wars" of the 1920s? Where did immigrants stand in the struggle between the old middle-class culture and the revolution in manners and morals?

2. Sklar contends that movies of the 1920s were superficially daring but basically supportive of traditional middle-class ways. How do the films of Cecil B. DeMille demonstrate this? Why were the moviemakers of the 1920s fearful of alienating audiences? Did the comedies of Harold Lloyd and Buster Keaton mock or reaffirm traditional ideas about the family and success?

3. How did European screen stars such as Rudolph Valentino and Greta Garbo differ from American film actors? What function did stereotyped European characters play for American film audiences? Why did moviegoers of the 1920s flock to see "passionate behavior" on the screen?

4. Why, according to the author, were European audiences drawn to American westerns and silent comedies after World War I? What do the Americans' attraction to passion and the Europeans' interest in action suggest about their respective cultures?

5. Do the patterns Sklar found in films of the 1920s still shape the movies today? Draw upon evidence from recent movies to discuss the use of stereotypes of non-Americans, or the relationship between mass culture and changing sexual norms.

The Meanings of American Jazz
in France

Jeffrey H. Jackson

*"There are only three things America will be known for two thousand years from now,"
historian Gerald Early recently declared: "the Constitution, jazz music, and baseball." Jazz
developed in the late nineteenth century out of a long tradition of African American musical
expression that included work songs, marches, dance music, and spirituals. Spontaneous,
emotional, and improvisational, jazz blended African harmonic and rhythmic elements with
American themes. Born in New Orleans, jazz music spread north, east, and west to American
cities where blacks migrated in huge numbers seeking jobs during and after World War I.
Outside black neighborhoods, however, jazz gained acceptance slowly because of its racial
origin and its suggestion of loose morals or low living. Only when white orchestras adapted
or imitated it in the late 1930s did jazz become popular with America's mass public.*

*European audiences were far more receptive. Introduced by American soldiers and spread
by black entertainers such as James Reese Europe, Louis Mitchell, and Josephine Baker,
jazz took Europe by storm in the 1920s. Especially in Paris, where crowds flocked to
cabarets and clubs in the bohemian districts of Montmartre and Montparnasse to drink,
dance, and revel in the wild and exotic sounds, jazz took over the music scene. Adored by
French fans and feeling more welcome than in their segregated homeland, Baker, Henry
Crowder, and many African American jazz musicians became permanent expatriates.*

*The jazz craze of Paris in the 1920s and the cultural exchange it represented formed
one episode of a larger transatlantic cultural shift. In a way analogous to the Americans described by Robert Sklar in Selection 13, Europeans experienced a "revolution in manners
and morals" in the 1920s. The American "Roaring Twenties" were paralleled by the "Crazy
Years" in France, and the two were described in strikingly similar language. If American
movie posters promised "beautiful jazz babies, champagne baths, [and] midnight revels,"
French clubgoers described "women with men's coats and cigarettes, . . . crazy virgins . . .
and the feverishness in everyday pleasure." The French had less prudishness to overcome
than American descendants of Puritanism, and being more deeply disillusioned by the recent
European bloodbath, they were more eager to throw off conventional ways. But France's
variant of cultural revolution arose from causes broadly similar to those of the American*

movement: a surge of postwar prosperity, new attitudes toward sexuality, the influence of records and movies, and the contribution of immigrant minorities. And both nations looked elsewhere for their models: like Americans who flocked to see "passionate" Europeans in the movies, the French imported the culture of transatlantic "others" — in this case, American blacks — to inspire their revolution.

How American jazz migrated to Paris is the subject Jeffrey Jackson addresses in his lively essay. Jackson offers a revealing comparison between black musicians' experience in the United States and in France. His primary focus, though, is not the transmission of jazz but its reception, not the migration of Americans abroad, but the impact of their music upon a foreign culture. Probing the many meanings of American jazz expressed by the audiences, writers, and music critics of Paris, Jackson discovers that talking about jazz was a way for the French to understand and debate momentous cultural changes that were overtaking their nation and the Western world in the wake of World War I.

Because jazz was American, it symbolized the "Americanization" of France that took off in the 1920s thanks to the influx of American tourists, the invasion of the French market by American products, and the cultural inroads of American movies. As they linked jazz to the spread of American "modernity," French commentators were both fascinated and frightened. While some thrilled to the energy and newness of American culture, others deplored its materialism and mass-produced sameness, and they worried that importations like jazz might blur or even eliminate French national identity.

Jazz was also black. Slighting the music's origins in the American South, French critics traced it instead to the jungles of Africa. Jackson's analysis becomes especially subtle when he compares American and French racial ideas, indicating their different reference points but detecting a similar tone of ambivalence. While Americans identified jazz with the urban ghetto, the French believed that its rhythm and sensuality expressed timeless racial qualities of blacks that recalled their African homeland. Yet French commentators were not uniformly enthusiastic. If, on the one hand, jazz offered a healthy dose of primal emotion to a stilted culture, on the other it raised the specter of cultural regression or "racial degeneration." In the 1920s France experienced a surge in immigration from its African colonies that caused anxieties similar to those that spurred apprehensive Americans to close their nation's doors in 1924 (see Selection 7).

On the surface, these jazz-induced images of American modernity and black primitivism seem contradictory, but Jackson claims that they offered complementary alternatives to the tired conventions of French civilization that had been discredited by the catastrophe of World War I. The prospect of discarding tradition and starting life over by combining modern conveniences and primitive pleasures made jazz alluring to some French observers and horrifying to others.

By reflecting the cultural transformations of the 1920s from the other side of the Atlantic, Jackson's essay presents a mirror image of Robert Sklar's in Selection 13. After you have read both, analyze the similarities and differences between these cases of cultural borrowing. What common patterns do you see in the Americans' craze for European movie stars and the French adoption of American jazz? What do these borrowings reveal about the distinctive concerns of each culture? What larger contexts and explanations do they suggest for the transatlantic cultural changes of the 1920s? Finally, explore what implications the reception of jazz in 1920s France might have for today's raging debates over the Americanization of popular culture around the world. What meanings and messages do foreigners find in American music, movies, and TV? Why is American popular culture still loved and feared in other countries? The rich transatlantic dialogue sampled in Sklar's and Jackson's essays demonstrates that the impact of American culture abroad is a fitting and especially revealing subject for a globalized American history.

GLOSSARY

ARMSTRONG, LOUIS (1900–1971)   An African American jazz trumpeter and singer who became perhaps the most influential jazz performer ever. Starting his career in New Orleans, he later played with bands in Chicago and New York. Already known in France by his recordings, Armstrong made the first of his many European tours in 1933 and became a worldwide ambassador for jazz.

AVANT-GARDE   An advanced group of artists, writers, or intellectuals exploring unorthodox or experimental methods.

BAKER, JOSEPHINE (1906–1975)   An African American dancer and singer who took Paris by storm in the 1920s. Appearing scantily clad in an all-black revue in Paris in 1925, she introduced the *danse sauvage* that launched her European music hall career. Her uninhibited dancing to sultry jazz songs symbolized what Europeans saw as the exotic primitivism of Africa. Less popular in the United States and an outspoken critic of segregation, Baker became a French citizen in 1937.

CAKEWALK   Initially, a strutting dance performed by slaves to mock their owners (with a cake as the prize for the best dancer). The cakewalk was later performed by black variety shows and vaudeville revues and became a popular dance craze in the 1890s. Many historians see it as a precursor of the dancing that accompanied jazz.

CARTESIAN HERITAGE   The legacy of René Descartes, a seventeenth-century French philosopher and mathematician who emphasized the power of logic and analytical precision.

DU BOIS, W. E. B. (1868–1963)   A prolific African American scholar and activist. Du Bois was an early advocate of full equality for blacks and a cofounder of the National Association for the Advancement of Colored People (NAACP) in 1910. Over his long career Du Bois increasingly championed nationalist movements in black Africa and the liberation of colonized blacks elsewhere.

ENLIGHTENMENT   The name given to the rationalist, humanitarian, and scientific trend of eighteenth-century Western thought during what is often called the Age of Reason. French thinkers such as Montesquieu, Diderot, and Voltaire were among its leaders.

EUGENICS   The pseudoscience of selective reproduction to improve the qualities of future generations. Whether "positive" (encouraging propagation among the healthy and intelligent) or "negative" (discouraging or preventing propagation by the "unfit"), eugenics was advocated in many Western nations in the early twentieth century by white elites intent on preventing "racial degeneration" through unregulated intermarriage or immigration.

FORDISM   A term that became popular in Europe to describe the new industrial regime of assembly-line production and cheap, standardized products, so called because it was pioneered by the American auto manufacturer Henry Ford.

HARLEM   The major black neighborhood in New York City in the early twentieth century. Harlem grew rapidly from an influx of southern black migrants during and after World War I. It became a focal point for a "renaissance" of black artists and writers and internationally renowned for its entertainment spots and jazz clubs.

JIM CROW LAWS   Laws that legally segregated or discrimated against blacks, especially in the American South in the late nineteenth and the first half of the twentieth centuries. The term derived from the name of a song in a nineteenth-century minstrel show.

MCKAY, CLAUDE (1890–1948)   An African American poet and novelist who was involved in radical political activities and became a major figure in the "Harlem Renaissance" of the 1920s.

MONROE DOCTRINE   The pronouncement by U.S. president James Monroe in 1823 that from then on the Western Hemisphere was closed to further colonization or intervention by European powers (and that the United States would not interfere in European nations' internal affairs). Initially intended to prevent Europeans from recolonizing the Americas, the doctrine was later used by Theodore Roosevelt and other U.S. presidents to justify American intervention in the Caribbean and Central America for political and economic objectives.

RAGTIME   The earliest form of jazz to gain wide appeal. Ragtime was a piano style emphasizing syncopation and multiple rhythms. Popularized through sheet music and player-piano rolls, it was sometimes used to accompany the cakewalk.

SORBONNE   The first college of the University of Paris, which opened in 1253. The Sorbonne became the core of this world-renowned university and is often used as a shorthand name for it.

TAYLOR, FREDERICK WINSLOW (1856–1915)   An American engineer whose theory of "scientific management" subdivided workers' tasks into small mechanical movements in order to maximize efficiency. Adopted by many industries in the United States and abroad, Taylorism was criticized as inhumane and often resisted by workers.

TIMBUKTU   A city on the southern edge of the Sahara Desert in present-day Mali. Founded in the eleventh century, Timbuktu gained fame as a commercial center for the trans-Sahara trade in gold, salt, and slaves with North Africa and the Arab world.

World War I represented a watershed in the relationship between France and the United States. The influx of some two million U.S. soldiers into the European theater of battle meant that thousands of French and Americans experienced an unprecedented level of contact with one another — now as individuals, not merely as abstractions. And this interaction occurred not only in Paris but in towns and villages in the countryside. Unlike the earlier generations of Americans in France, the soldiers were generally neither wealthy nor highly educated. Instead, they offered the French people a much more representative cross-section of U.S. society, including its racial diversity. Black Americans had traveled to France before, but never in such large numbers (around two hundred thousand). Although most French villagers had never seen a black person, either from the United States or one of France's African colonies, many had the chance to do so by the war's end.

These new wartime contacts begin to explain how French listeners first came to hear jazz music. The Americans brought jazz to the troops and Parisians for entertainment and morale boosting. At first, the French were not quite clear how to evaluate this new music or what impact it would have. In fact, they sometimes had difficulty defining it. During the 1920s, musicians, critics, and audiences alike worked to make sense of the new sound, trying to decide whether it portended good or ill for the future of French entertainment. But common to their assessments was the belief that jazz represented something transformative — above all, something modern. Jazz was a sign of the times because it challenged previous musical norms. It seemed "noisy" and "mechanical." To those who heard bombs and explosions in jazz, the music soon extended the wartime chaos into the post-war age. Furthermore, it represented culture in motion. Jazz was an American music, but it quickly gained widespread popularity in France, Britain, Germany, Italy, and elsewhere. Jazz posed a crucial challenge to many in France by suggesting the arrival of an era when old national boundaries and artistic categories were far more porous than before. . . .

If World War I opened up many questions about Americans and their culture for the French, one of the clear conclusions that many in France drew during the war was that not all Americans were the same. In particular, the war introduced African Americans to a greater number of French people than ever before, often to the delight of black soldiers, who felt more warmly accepted in France than in their own country. French civilians were, to be sure, happy to meet anyone willing to fight on their behalf, but their reactions to African Americans were especially positive. Many French officers disdained the U.S. regulations that kept whites and blacks in separate units, criticizing the hypocrisy of an army that was supposedly "making the world safe for democracy," in the words of President Woodrow Wilson. French generals who failed to understand such segregation sometimes destroyed American literature that advocated racial discrimination.

These kinds of French actions added to the long-standing belief among African Americans that France was a color-blind country truly practicing the equality that the United States only preached. Previous generations of black American writers, intellectuals, and entertainers who had visited France brought back stories of a nation that was open and racially tolerant compared to the United States. Many black Americans, urged by leaders who continued to describe France in these terms, joined the U.S. army in order to fight for France as the true land of liberty. And contact between African Americans and French civilians reinforced many of these notions. In one oft-quoted story, the mayor of a French village complained when white troops arrived, saying, "Take back these soldiers and send us some real Americans, black Americans." In fact, though, the French army did not treat its own sub-Saharan African troops and laborers or colonial subjects in Africa with the same kind of generosity, and the contradiction between French words and actions on this issue was beginning to make some African American intellectuals, like W. E. B. Du Bois and Claude McKay, doubt the truth of France's claims to racial tolerance. Furthermore, not everyone in France welcomed black American visitors to Paris, as the debates over jazz would soon reveal. But in spite of an evolving understanding of French attitudes toward race in the early twentieth century, the generally positive wartime experience of African American soldiers set the stage for many others, including jazz musicians, to thrive in Paris afterward.

Even if such a large number of black Americans was new to many Parisians, their music was not entirely unknown. By the time jazz players arrived, black American musicians and white musicians playing black music had already been entertaining French audiences with minstrel songs, ragtime, and cakewalks, the latter having been wildly popular as a dance craze around 1900. But the war did provide an opportunity for Parisians to hear black musicians in greater numbers than ever before. One of the central figures in bringing jazz to France during the war was James Reese Europe and the military orchestra that he conducted. By the time he went to France, Europe was already a well-established popularizer of black American music. As a famous New York bandleader in the 1910s, Europe had helped to organize his fellow black musicians to ensure that they could find performing jobs. Touring around the United States with the popular white dancers Vernon and Irene Castle, Europe introduced many white audiences to the rapidly developing sounds of ragtime and early jazz. World War I provided yet another occasion for Europe to employ his talents as a disseminator of black American music, but this time he did so across the Atlantic as an army lieutenant. In 1917, Europe's commanding officer asked him to recruit "the best damn band in the United States Army." Advertisements in black newspapers and personal persuasion enabled Europe to create an orchestra that included the composer Noble Sissle along with the dancer Bill "Bojangles" Robinson as the ensemble's drum major. The band was known as the Hellfighters and originally traveled with the 369th United States Army Infantry Regiment, whose nickname they took. They were later attached to a French army unit. Europe's band toured throughout wartime France to boost the morale of the troops and civilians.

The uniqueness of James Reese Europe's music frequently took the French by surprise. Since his orchestra played many tunes already familiar to audiences, the novelty was not what Europe performed but how he and his band played. Europe noted the distinction between his performance and that of the French when a Parisian bandleader asked him for a copy of his musical score. The French band could not replicate the sound, with its "jazz effects," Europe reported. Some of the French musicians "felt sure that my band had used special instruments." On one occasion, Europe's band performed a rendition of the French national anthem, "La Marseillaise," that confused many French listeners since the sound of its rhythm and the arrangement were so unusual. But the effects of "filling France full of jazz," as one wartime reporter described Europe's accomplishments, were astounding. Along with several other bands, Europe's orchestra performed at a concert at the Tuileries garden near the end of the war. Europe quickly overshadowed the others, and the crowd turned its full attention to his musicians. "We played for 50,000 people, at least," he marveled, "and, had we wished it, we might be playing yet." Noble Sissle recalled that, at another concert, "the audience could stand it

Lieutenant James Reese Europe conducts the U.S. Army's 369th Infantry Band, nicknamed the Hellfighters, at the Hotel Tunis in Paris, 1919. (Photographs and Prints Division, Schomburg Center for Research in Black Culture, The New York Public Library.)

no longer; the 'Jazz germ' hit them and it seemed to find the vital spot, loosening all muscles and causing what is known in America as an 'Eagle Rocking Fit.'"

Europe was not the only African American to bring his music to France during these years. While his orchestra was entertaining on behalf of the war effort, the drummer Louis Mitchell and his band played at the music hall Le Casino de Paris and also made a few records. . . . In 1917, Mitchell was drumming at Le Casino de Paris when the management sent him back to New York to recruit a jazz band, suggesting that they believed the venture to be a potentially profitable one. [Robert] Goffin remembered their 1917 group called Mitchell's Jazz Kings as the first black jazz band he ever heard, seconding the description of one U.S. observer of Mitchell at the time: "The big attraction at the Casino Theater here and the big attraction for every Parisian theater that can bid enough for his services, is Louis A. Mitchell, who just drummed his way to Paris and into the hearts of Parisians." Goffin also noted the financial rewards for such affection by Parisian audiences. "Paris, at the end of the war was a wide-open and exciting place," he proclaimed. "Louis Mitchell earned money hand over fist. He received seven thousand francs for a week's engagement, or just about ten times the salary of a Cabinet member." . . .

As Paris settled back into civilian life after the war, jazz musicians struck up their rhythms in venues all over the city. Audiences heard it in cabarets, nightclubs, dance halls, restaurants, and theaters. Many music halls first presented jazz during the regular show's intermission, but they soon moved it to the main program. In cafés, owners often decided to take advantage of the music's growing popularity and hired jazz bands to lure customers into their establishments. These kinds of commercial concerns were crucial motivations in introducing jazz to Paris. As the story . . . of Louis Mitchell being sent back to the United States to recruit a band suggests, many theater owners were already sensitive to the money-making potential of jazz. And during the 1920s, the spread of jazz increased as that potential became reality. Jazz musicians, as a result, soon seemed to many to be everywhere. . . .

Just as jazz musicians were fanning out across Paris, important changes in the city's entertainment culture were also underway to accommodate the new tastes of audiences. The evolution was particularly striking in one of the favorite gathering places of the 1920s, the dance hall. The "dance craze" of the postwar years provided a business incentive to revamp old venues into flashy and fashionable hot spots so that they could provide space to do the latest steps. Many critics believed that not only was the music different in these places because of the introduction of jazz, they were also beginning to lose their traditional character. Some came to see the growing presence of jazz throughout the city along with the ways in which it altered where and how Parisians enjoyed themselves as an indication of the changing nature of modern life more generally. And talking about jazz was one way of debating what those changes meant.

Another modern development, the new media that were created or improved in the early twentieth century, allowed the sounds of jazz to be carried across great distances. Indeed, perceptions about jazz music cannot be separated from the technology — especially phonographs and radios — from which it roared. Being connected with such devices further equated jazz with the cutting edge of cultural developments. Easily linking jazz to other innovations of the day, one French observer captured the range of overlapping associations between the music and spirit of the age when he wrote: "I like modern dances because I live in 1924, because I have seen the theater, music, the arts, dance evolve, because we live in the century of radio, of the jazz-band, of electricity, of thermal rays, and of negromania . . . because I live in my century." . . .

[As jazz grew in popularity, it] provoked controversy all around Europe. It drew the ire of the British monarchy and the pope, among many others. Italy banned jazz dancing in

1926, and German musicians protested the presence of U.S. musicians. In Paris, the archbishop banned what he believed to be provocative dances. According to the *New York Times,* the rector of the Sorbonne removed three black saxophone players and drummers when they appeared in a dance class not knowing that only the classical Greek style would be taught. Even outside the French capital, police sometimes tried to keep a lid on the music. In 1923, law enforcement officials stopped the performance of a jazz band at a funeral in the town of Udine. The deceased had requested that one of his close friends conduct a jazz band for his funeral procession, but the police, "scandalized at the sight," as the *New York Times* reported, "descended on the band and ordered it to stop playing." After the bandleader pleaded with the officers, they allowed him to continue, but only if he would play at a slower cadence.

If many listeners had difficulty coping with the shock of jazz, the task of the commentators who tried to interpret the music was even more challenging. For them, jazz was problematic because it symbolized much more than just a fad for crazy dancing or a loud, new sound. It also signaled a broader cultural shift. "Knee-length skirts, neck-length hair, women with men's coats and cigarettes," wrote journalist Lucien Farnoux-Reynaud, for example, in his 1926 article "The Epoch of the Jazz-Band,"

> multicolored pullovers and the silk underwear of their companions . . . , crazy virgins . . . race cars . . . , and confusion of the sexes; the anguish of living and the feverishness in everyday pleasure; all of this starts again, blends itself, with a suspicious cosmopolitan shiver, in the cadences born at the conjunction of a shady bar in Jackson City and an ancestral memory of Tombouctou [Timbuktu].

Such a statement vividly captured the sense of upheaval that inspired the French to dub the 1920s "the crazy years." It also demonstrated just how easily jazz could be connected to other changes of the post–World War I era.

Farnoux-Reynaud's observations were particularly remarkable because they brought together some of the paradoxical ways in which French commentators described jazz as they tried to make sense of it. Most notably, as Farnoux-Reynaud suggested, jazz had come to represent the "modern" world of the twentieth century and, at the same time, the "primitive" culture of the music's purportedly African origins. Jazz was a fitting sound for an increasingly technological era ("race cars"), even while it recalled the presumed simplicity of the lives of "noble savages" in a nearly forgotten other time (the "ancestral memory of Tombouctou").

These connotations were not random, however, because they stemmed from two important and immediately clear facts: jazz was an American music and simultaneously, as the French called it, *une musique nègre* [Negro music]. In many ways, jazz was one of the best representatives of the often debated américanisation of France that began in the 1920s and then exploded after World War II. By the first decades of the twentieth century, more Americans now traveled and invested throughout the continent than ever before, and Europeans were beginning to buy new mass-produced consumer goods from the United States in larger quantities. With its seemingly endless mechanical rhythms and broad commercial success, jazz reflected the qualities of modern life in the United States that occupied the minds of many French writers and critics in the interwar years.

Like other kinds of American consumer culture, especially films, jazz seemed to be pushing aside older types of French entertainment. As a result, it frequently served as a harbinger of life in the new century and signaled to many the loss of a more traditional French culture to the rising Americanism.

At the same time, jazz was une musique nègre whose immediate origins were African American, but whose ultimate roots French writers generally traced to the jungles of Africa. The African sensibilities, French critics stressed, had been preserved in jazz because of the common racial connection between its performers and their ancestors on the so-called Dark Continent. Even when white musicians played jazz, they were believed to be performing a black musical style. At the height of its popularity, jazz music could suggest an "Africanization" of France — an ironic reversal of the colonial project simultaneously underway in sub-Saharan Africa in the 1920s and 1930s. Jazz rested at the intersection of these two powerful and controversial trends, thereby making it all the more meaningful and controversial.

AMERICAN MODERNITY

. . . In light of [the success of earlier American bands,] the presence of another American music like jazz was not necessarily remarkable to audiences. But jazz's roots assumed a much larger significance against the backdrop of changes in the U.S.-French relationship during the war and in the interwar years, including an influx of Americans and their ways into Paris. For example, although they were still usually outnumbered by British visitors, U.S. tourists were among the most prominent foreigners in 1920s Paris, in large part because of the dollar's strength during these years. . . .

The tourist-fueled entertainment industry in the 1920s was a visible sign of the increasing economic strength of the United States in Paris. Americans found the continent a hospitable economic environment as well as a pleasant place to visit, and they began to exert a wider range of economic and cultural influences. The Great War had ravaged the European economy, so U.S. companies had a more-than-competitive edge in postwar business. Although the more famous segment of the American presence in Paris consisted of the literary and intellectual figures who inhabited the Left Bank, the Right Bank financial, industrial, and commercial concerns were far more central to the larger U.S. community. . . . Branches of American banks such as the influential Morgan Bank and various corporations worked with the U.S. Chamber of Commerce in Paris, which had been founded in 1894 to promote business interests, or the Office of the American Commercial Attaché, an arm of the U.S. Department of Commerce. In these years, the United States went from being a debtor to a creditor nation and poured millions of dollars into Europe.

Investments and loans were not the extent of U.S. economic interests. American companies saw the Old World as a vast new marketplace for manufactured goods that were now more abundant because of mass-production technology. The United States had been sending agricultural products and raw materials to Europe, typically cotton, wheat, copper, tobacco, and lumber. In the years before the war, finished manufactures represented only about 16 percent of U.S. exports to Europe, but by 1927 that figure had risen to just over 26 percent and included new products like steam shovels, washing machines, razor blades, cars, and adding machines. . . .

Many French business leaders had begun to study U.S. industrial practices and adapted them to their own factories. The dynamic French car manufacturer André Citroën, for example, heartily embraced the new innovations in production being developed in the United States. Citroën prided his country on being "a good second" to the United States in the number of cars on the road. He introduced an assembly line into his factory — "chain work," as he called it — and emblazoned his name on the Eiffel Tower as a flashy, American-style advertisement for his cars. The Michelin tire company also adapted U.S. techniques and propagated the ideas of the scientific management theorist Frederick Winslow Taylor in its company publication, *Prosperité*. . . . The secretary of the French Federation of Labor spent a year working and studying in the United States in hopes of learning more about how factories there worked. . . .

Many French critics, however, were not as excited about these kinds of changes as were Citroën or U.S. trade officials. They frequently objected to such transformations in production techniques as being harmful for French workers and consumers. Moreover, they saw developments in the United States as a warning for what France might become if it continued down such a path of intensive economic and technical evolution. The United States had entrapped itself in a "myth of production," alleged conservative cultural critics and opponents of américanisation Robert Aron and Arnaud Dandieu in *Décadence de la nation française* (1931). Once a bastion of democratic ideals, the United States was developing a more intense form of industrialization that replaced freedom with Fordism — a new slavery to the machine and the assembly line. Taylorization, the reorganization of work according to scientific principles designed to improve efficiency, promised a more rational production method, but as many inquired, at what cost to the workers' moral and spiritual being? People in this kind of society, critics feared, would lose their individuality to the uniformity required and produced by the machine. . . .

. . . French reactions to Americans and their ways were [similarly] ambivalent in the 1920s. Americans remained the source of amusement for many Parisians who dressed in their fashions, including sometimes as cowboys. Parisians were famous for hailing the U.S. pilot Charles Lindbergh for his daring crossing of the Atlantic. And the love of jazz was an important part of the French fascination with things American. Yet at the same time, the presence of Americans and their culture could be worrisome. As jazz grew in popularity, it came to represent for some a particularly troubling example of everything that was wrong with the New World. It also threatened to bring those problems to France. In his visit to the United States, [Georges] Duhamel did not see mechanization and industrial standardization only in workplaces. He also heard these forces in the sounds of jazz because the music could be easily associated with other noises from the era. Duhamel linked the new "modern" music with the age from which it came in a fascinating passage in his diatribe against the decay of American culture:

> The music suddenly burst forth from a corner. It was the falsest, the shrillest, the most explosive of jazz — that breathless uproar which for many years now has staggered to the same syncopation, that shrieks through its nose, weeps, grinds its teeth, and caterwauls throughout the world.

For Duhamel, the "shrieks" and "grinds" of the music were part of the mechanistic world that he deplored. . . .

Writer and diplomat Paul Claudel echoed Duhamel's sentiments in one of his essays on the United States when he wrote of "the rhythmic pulsation and nervous uniformity of the pistons of a steam engine interrupting the cyclical roaring of the dynamo that one feels across all of American life and of which jazz is the supreme expression." Jazz, maintained one music critic, "is the music of . . . mass-produced men."

Other French listeners rejected jazz because it reflected the encroachment of a more general American way of life that went far beyond the machine culture. "Jazz is not made for us," insisted journalist Jacques Janin. "Everything in us rejects it: spirit and tradition." This U.S. export was not welcome, he concluded sarcastically: "Let us not put up the Monroe Doctrine for discussion. America for the Americans." Others were even more outraged in their responses to an imported music. Stressing its foreignness in an article called "The Infernal Rhythm of Jazz," one essayist ended by calling for the prefect of police to take action. "Will you let the strangers who come to France," he demanded, "import this abominable vision from their countries?" . . .

Movies and jazz along with the changes they represented were often attacked by critics, but they had their defenders and celebrators as well. For many intellectuals, the modern spirit that these innovations brought to France were precisely their value. The Surrealist writer Philippe Soupault, for example, looked to new kinds of entertainment like films and jazz precisely because they were American. . . . Soupault had fought in the war and became disgusted with the culture for which he was supposed to have been fighting: "Those who in early youth were witnesses of nothing but death and destruction . . . , turned with a kind of fever toward life." He found that life impulse in modern entertainment. Soupault demonstrated his appreciation for the pace and style of U.S. culture . . . in his brief book *The American Influence in France* (1930). . . .

. . . For Soupault, jazz was . . . a crucial part of American culture and a way to get at the more authentic essence of the United States. Jazz "has helped us finally to discover and to understand the United States," he wrote. But for Soupault, to understand the United States and its art was part of his larger intellectual quest of blending art and life. European music had been long divided into "popular music (songs, marches, operettas)" and "highbrow music, that is to say, concert music," Soupault claimed. Yet American music had no such distinctions within it. Instead, he argued, "One of the most definite qualities of the American influence resides in the close relationship between art and life." Like film, jazz expressed something about life that Soupault found irresistible in the wake of the war's destruction — the energy, the breaking down of barriers.

Writer Paul Morand also saw and felt the energy and drive of the United States as the herald of a new age. In his book *New York* (1930), Morand took readers on a tour of Manhattan from one end to the other, commenting on the scenery, people, and customs that he observed. Not everything was praiseworthy for Morand, such as the predilection in the United States for eating quickly and poorly. But his account was filled with wonder and respect for the new power and influence of the United States. . . . Indeed, this newness and sense of motion was one of the things that drew his attention: "To have America, you need only to put the adjective 'New' in front of Rochelle,

Jersey, London, Utrecht or Brighton, repaint these old European signs, and add twenty floors." Inventions like the car liberated Americans for the modern age since the "American car spreads out over the world, an instrument of escape, the tool of speed, which after freeing the United States, is shattering Puritanism, volatilizing savings, demolishing the family, reversing the law, leading the world toward catastrophe and the glory of adventure." For Morand, jazz was also part of the landscape of New York, particularly in Harlem. There, he heard a blending of sounds since "jazz is the Negro melody of the South arriving at Pennsylvania Station and suddenly maddened by adorable Manhattan, where everything is noise and light." Jazz reflected the modern mixture of black and white America, of both rural and urban settings. Jazz was "the Mississippi's dream become a nightmare, cut across by motor-horns and sirens." . . .

As the sound of the United States, jazz was also the sound of a broader set of cultural changes in the way that people lived, worked, and played in Paris. It could be the sound of the machine or stockyard — frightening and foreign images that suggested the impending brutalization of a French tradition. But the United States was a land of promise and renewal, as people like Soupault and Morand noted, and new kinds of art, like film and jazz, were at the forefront of that hopeful image that was attractive precisely because it was foreign.

AFRICAN PRIMITIVISM

Like music from the United States more generally, African American entertainment was not new to Paris in the 1920s. Black performers had been traveling to France for many decades, and Parisians had become familiar with black choirs, minstrel shows, and especially with the cakewalk and ragtime — respectively, a dance and a music created by African Americans in the nineteenth century that music historians often describe as the immediate precursors to jazz and jazz dancing in the United States. . . .

The French were not just receptive to black Americans as performers, however, but to African Americans as people. A long-standing belief that France was a color-blind nation led many black Americans to perceive an atmosphere of openness in Paris that they could not find at home. That assumption gained credence during World War I, when many black soldiers felt more at liberty among the French. In the 1920s, that sense of freedom continued since overt racial discrimination was not part of the regular Parisian way of life. "Paris affords to black men," remarked the U.S. writer Robert Forrest Wilson, "an equality of treatment unknown in the United States even in the North. . . . We see black men walking with white girls and white mothers leading mulatto children." This seemingly more generous French attitude played a critical role in encouraging many jazz musicians and other entertainers to relocate across the Atlantic. Josephine Baker described the relative freedom, saying, "Why did I leave America? Because one day I realized that I lived in a country where I was afraid to be black. In Paris, I feel liberated." Henry Crowder, a trumpet player who became the lover of the white, British heiress Nancy Cunard, echoed Baker's sentiment when he wrote of his departure from the United States, "France! No color bar there. No discriminations! Freedom! A chance to live as every other man lived regardless of his color. No taboos. Not a single sigh escaped my being because I was leaving. Only unbounded joy existed." Baker and Crowder were not alone, nor were they unique as performers. Whether opening successful businesses — including Montmartre nightclubs — working as laborers, attending school, or engaged in the arts, blacks from the United States created an exile community in interwar Paris that existed in relative harmony with its French neighbors. . . .

Still, simply because the French did not discriminate against black Americans in traditional U.S. terms, such as Jim Crow–type laws, did not mean that the French were truly color-blind in the 1920s. Rather, they operated with a range of assumptions about what blacks, including those from the United States, were like. The French understanding of race, especially as it related to jazz, was different from definitions of racial characteristics in the United States. "Blackness," in other words, meant something different on each side of the Atlantic. The French perception of les nègres had been shaped under quite different circumstances than attitudes about blacks in the United States, and that understanding, along with France's own set of racial stereotypes about people of color, influenced views about jazz.

In the United States, jazz emerged from a large domestic black population. But because of the nation's racialized history, many Americans viewed "black culture" as something distinct from "white culture," even though the two had been intertwined since colonial days. Black and white entertainment in the United States had frequently intersected in significant ways throughout the nineteenth century. The cakewalk . . . emerged as a kind of resistance by blacks against white, southern plantation owners. Moreover, blackface minstrelsy was an important genre of performance that brought black entertainment to white audiences in a more acceptable form — one that historian Eric Lott has described as tinged both with "racial insult and racial envy" — and thus reflected a historically ambiguous relationship between whites and blacks in the United States. . . . In other words, as these and other scholars argue, black performance in the United States cannot be separated from domestic cultural politics that includes questions of slavery, racism, and definitions of national identity.

French audiences were certainly familiar with U.S. stereotypes of African Americans, and those views were perpetuated by many of the jazz-accompanied shows of the interwar years. Images of black America, particularly of antebellum plantation life, were not uncommon in interwar Paris, and they served to reinforce a view of African Americans as only partially civilized and working in a "primitive" agricultural setting. For example, *La Revue Nègre*, in which Josephine Baker starred, featured scenes of southern U.S. plantations, and this show was not unique. A 1927 exhibition at the Jardin d'Acclimatation called *Charleston City* even claimed to re-create an authentic southern plantation for display. It "is the exact reconstruction of a black village in the southern United States," proclaimed one newspaper. "We have before our eyes, like words come to life, the life of blacks, we know their customs, their work, their hobbies, and notably their dances. . . ."

Many French critics translated common stereotypes of African Americans into musical terms, taking note of what they described as a pronounced emotionalism within jazz along with a kind of sadness and melancholy in the music due to the history of black Americans. Critic René Dumesnil, for instance, portrayed . . . black "plantation songs," and jazz as . . . illustrating a characteristically black way of singing or playing music in which the innate emotional qualities of les nègres combined with the tortuous past of African Americans. Born out of oppression, as Dumesnil put it, black American songs "are examples to vanquish the oppressor or reasons to hope for liberation." Playing jazz, observers like Dumesnil argued, offered a form of emotional freedom from the lives that blacks had led in the United States.

Unlike in the United States, however, there was never a very large black (African or American) population in France, even in the 1920s. And French observers were never particularly clear on the distinction between Africans and African Americans, who they often believed had more in common than not. Because many listeners assumed that jazz expressed certain essential racial qualities that transcended specific historical circumstances or experiences, jazz easily turned the minds of French critics from antebellum America to sub-Saharan Africa and the colonial project at its height in the interwar years. For the French, jazz was "jungle music" more often than "plantation music."

As many scholars have pointed out, the French response to Africans was contradictory at best. . . . As colonial interests expanded at the end of the nineteenth century along with an increasing attention to economic exploitation, scientific research, and political experimentation on the African continent, knowledge of its people became more widespread, even if that understanding was not always more accurate. Those within France who hoped to exploit Africa for its resources frequently presented Africans as "noble savages" and the Dark Continent as an unspoiled territory waiting to be explored. But this attitude changed in the wake of African resistance to French colonial advances in the late 1800s. Africa soon began to seem like a territory with a vicious race of people that needed to be conquered and controlled.

During World War I, relations between the French and Africans from the colonies became increasingly complicated. France welcomed colonial soldiers to its soil because they were seen as valuable members of a Greater France and were fighting on behalf of the nation and its values. At the same time, though, many French workers feared that laborers from the colonies could threaten their jobs, and the resulting resentment sparked race riots, which themselves helped to bring about more highly politicized perceptions of race in the 1920s. Unrest within the colonies from educated Africans demanding French citizenship after the war added to the French desire to keep a reasonable distance between themselves and their colonial subjects by employing a policy of "association." Also in the wake of World War I, eugenics, social hygiene movements, and . . . concerns about declining birthrates all stressed a more clearly biological conception of racial categories, including those in the colonies, and emphasized the need to protect the French "race" by preventing racial decline or dilution. Therefore, by the time of jazz's arrival, foreigners in general, and Africans in particular, could seem at least as dangerous as they were exotic.

The most basic fact about jazz to most French listeners was that even though many white musicians played it, the music was still la musique nègre. Writing in *La Revue musicale,* musicologist Blaise Pesquinne, for example, argued that "in spite of its popularity in Europe and in all the countries of the white race, one must not forget that jazz is, for us, an essentially exotic product. . . . Jazz is by no means an internal phenomenon from within Western music, it is the artistic manifestation of a race that is different from our own." Underlying this common idea of a distinct musique nègre was the notion that it was an expression of a universal category of blackness — an essential set of qualities common to all people of color — that transcended the individual experience of each musician. . . . La musique nègre, as many French saw it, contained certain special qualities peculiar to all black people because of its beginnings on the Dark Continent. . . .

One supposed proof of this link with Africa that many French critics offered was the sense of nostalgia that they perceived in jazz, the musical expression of a longing for a world that had been lost. . . . Modern technology and the movement of populations from the countryside to cities took people away from home and familiar surroundings and "civilized" them, but it stripped something of their old self in the process. . . . [F]or cultures or individuals believed to be caught in the middle of the process, longing for another time and place was seen as common. Nostalgia linked life in the present with a memory of the past.

. . . Having been uprooted from Africa by slavery, American blacks expressed through their music a sadness and longing for an idyllic past before their forced emigration to the United States, in the view of French commentators. . . . From this point of view, jazz was the music of exiles whose real home was Africa, and depicting jazz as nostalgic emphasized the essential racial nature of the music. Demonstrating the partially civilized state of black Americans, one author stated of jazz: "From this duality, the tam-tam and the fever of the combustion engine, a fantastic humor, sometimes a little monkeylike, alternates with a tragic nostalgia of exiled slaves curiously corresponding to that of an extreme civilization bullied by the machine culture.". . .

The most important argument for the deep racial origins of jazz music came in the 1926 book *Jazz* by André Cœuroy, an editor of the journal *La Revue musicale,* and ethnomusicologist André Schaeffner. . . . Their book was a landmark not only because it was the first French text that purported to be about jazz as a musical form but also because it drew together some of the other critical writing on jazz up to that time from articles in France and the United States, and it linked jazz with other musicological discussions. . . .

In *Jazz,* Cœuroy and Schaeffner maintained that . . . [t]he music of Africans and African Americans should be seen as part of a single black musical continuum of which jazz was simply the latest form. . . . "The violent music of Africa to the planting songs of the Antilles or Louisiana, to *spirituals,* finally to *jazz,*" were all members of the same musical family. In this scheme, there was no significant difference between black Africans and black Americans, who remained united above all by ancient and ultimately immutable characteristics. Blacks were united in particular by a love of music and dance with a special affinity for rhythm, they suggested. Much of their book traced the development of la musique nègre as a background to jazz, and it cited the observations of seventeenth- and eighteenth-century travelers as evidence of the longevity of a specifically black style of performance. They also followed the history of various instruments, such as the drum and banjo, along with the traditions of song and dance that they believed defined black music. . . .

Many listeners were attracted to jazz precisely because of its perceived blackness, including Belgian poet Robert Goffin, who became an important figure in early jazz criticism in France. . . . His new book in 1932, *Aux frontières du jazz* (At the borders of jazz) reflected a decade of listening to and thinking about the music. In it, he did not seek to analyze the origins of the music, as Cœuroy and Schaeffner had done, but rather the music as he heard it in the 1920s.

Goffin's earliest experiences with syncopated music came, like those of many other listeners, during the Great War. While serving as an interpreter for a Canadian battalion, "among the soldiers," he remembered, "were some Americans who taught me their songs." Later, as a student, he listened to Belgian, French, and English orchestras perform music that they called jazz, but his real introduction to the music came when he encountered Louis Mitchell in Paris. Inspired by what he heard, Goffin wrote his early articles and poems "possessed immediately by a sort of frenzied lyricism." Goffin took a few lessons from the black trumpeter Arthur Briggs in 1922 while playing in a "humble orchestra which some friends and I formed." Experiences with Mitchell and Briggs confirmed for Goffin that jazz was a black music set apart by its players' unique expression. "How I prefer *les nègres,* the beautiful *nègres* who laugh with all their teeth," he proclaimed in *Le Disque vert* in 1922. By contrast, for Goffin, the music of whites was cold and overly rational. Jazz was about feeling rather than reason, and for him black American musicians were in touch with the more emotional side of human experience.

Unlike Cœuroy and Schaeffner's book, which ended where jazz began, *Aux frontières du jazz* was the first book-length work in French to treat jazz as it actually existed in the 1920s. . . . [Goffin] was among the first to praise Louis Armstrong at a time when white bands were experiencing their greatest popularity in Paris, and in doing so, he reemphasized the crucial contribution of black American musicians to jazz. The stress on musicians and the techniques of their performances also distinguished Goffin from other critics. Most French writers referred to jazz as a single musical entity with little distinction between bands or styles. . . . Goffin, however, discussed an entire range of performers, commenting on their performances not as a general music critic but rather as a jazz critic using a specialized set of criteria to judge and elaborate on the music. . . . "Open your dictionaries because here are the beautiful new words that France accepts as they are instead of translating them," he announced. "Jazz, drummer, lyrics, hot, break, chorus," were some of the new American terms that those who wrote and spoke of the music must use, declared Goffin. . . .

Jazz also fascinated anthropologist and author Michel Leiris, who, as a young man in Paris in the 1920s, was also cultivating an interest in African art and cultures. As part of the intellectual and literary avant-garde drawn to exploring exotic peoples, Leiris sought to investigate realms outside of traditional Western experience, whether in Africa or within himself. Indeed, the two became closely intertwined in his ethnographic writing in which he cast aside the objectivity of scientific inquiry in favor of an intensively psychological engagement, both with himself and his subjects. Leiris's depictions of jazz blended the richness of an ethnographic study with the confessional self-revelation and "personal ethnography" for which his writing is known, as if the music had penetrated to that deep level as well.

Leiris remembered his first encounter with jazz in 1918 during the intermission of a music hall program at Le Théâtre Caumartin, where one of Louis Mitchell's bands, the Seven Spades, performed. In the following years, as jazz grew in popularity and moved

This publicity photo of Josephine Baker, the African American jazz dancer who rose to stardom in Paris, combines sexual allure and a fashionable 1920s hairstyle with an exotic costume and allusions to Africa, such as the elephant figurine she holds. (Hulton/Archive by Getty Images.)

from a music hall intermission to a headlining act, Leiris became an enthusiastic fan. He visited various nightclubs around the city and participated in surprise parties that brought jazz into people's homes. Josephine Baker's performance in *La Revue Nègre* fascinated him, as it did so many French intellectuals, because of its provocative blending of "primitive" images with modern music and themes. Leiris was drawn to jazz as part of his search for something new, disgusted as he was with what Europe had become by the early twentieth century. "What is certain," he recalled in an interview later in life, "is that I enjoyed jazz as something exotic and non-European, as an affront to European music and art." Like many intellectuals and artists in the interwar years, Leiris thought that cultures outside Europe offered the hope of regenerating a seemingly dead Western imagination that had been exhausted in the war. . . .

   Although many in France were attracted to the blackness of jazz, for others this quality, drawing on the dangerous aspects of the stereotype about Africans, was precisely the music's problem. *La musique nègre* was frequently seen as part of a more general l'art nègre that, for some, threatened to turn black everyone around it. "If the *'folie noire'* [black craze] is not stopped soon," declared one critic in an article that rejected everything black including jazz, "in a few months, I won't see any whites!" In a 1930 article titled "Progress toward the Simian," another author argued that because of jazz, "the reign of the Negro is nearly finished. The reign of the monkey is starting again."

Criticisms of the blackness of jazz begin to make sense against the larger backdrop of other concerns in the interwar period, especially fears of racial degeneration. Particularly important during the 1920s were eugenicists' concerns about how the presence of foreigners would affect the "quality" of the French people. Already troubled that an invasion of immigrants in the postwar period might weaken France physically, many French critics also saw jazz as the symptom and a further cause of such degeneration. They cast the music in terms that emphasized its potential for producing nothing but the basest physical responses in listeners. Writing in *La Revue musicale,* critic André Suarès called jazz "an orchestra of brutes with nonopposable thumbs," saying that it "is all excess.". . . Playing jazz as the black musicians did, some critics suggested, constituted a step backward and away from civilization toward the jungles, and echoed the fear of "going native" that some observers voiced about the French in their African colonies. "Is one still in Paris?" asked one critic in desperation on hearing the sounds of jazz. "Is one still in a civilized country?"

The case of jazz in Paris helps to clarify and emphasize some French views of blackness in the 1920s and 1930s. Whether or not the French were racist in the interwar years, it is clear that they, along with most Westerners, thought in increasingly racialized terms. And as the history of interaction with colonial subjects indicates, French racial attitudes evolved through a series of often competing responses depending on historical circumstances, perceptions, and the needs of the moment. Jazz could evoke many such racialized reactions depending on whether one heard it as friendly or frightening, especially when linked with colonial Africa. Observers of jazz perceived blackness as a biological category that produced cultural manifestations. Musical qualities like rhythm emanated from supposedly inborn traits, even though the unique history of African Americans had played a role in shaping how jazz developed and sounded. Most important, whether one liked jazz or despised it, the music's blackness — like its Americanness, although for different reasons — made it alien to French traditions.

FRENCH CIVILIZATION

In spite of the apparent differences between these two ways of characterizing jazz — American music linked with economic and cultural influence and la musique nègre based on a racial category — both pointed to still larger challenges. One question centered around the influence that foreigners and foreign cultures were, for better or worse, exercising in postwar France. As a music that blended the symbolism of both the United States and Africa, jazz was doubly foreign and therefore a touchstone of debate about how France interacted with those from beyond its borders. This debate itself was double-sided. Many in France celebrated the seemingly new and refreshing influence of foreigners. Others, however, decried the erosion of what they deemed to be a more traditional French culture by immigrants, feeding the xenophobic [antiforeign] nationalism for which the interwar era is already well-known. Those on both sides of the debate about jazz employed the terms *American* and *black* to their own ends.

The issue of jazz's foreignness can be set against the backdrop of a wave of immigration into France that had begun during the Great War and changed Paris dramatically in the 1920s. Most of the foreign laborers and colonial troops that had come to France to assist in the war effort were repatriated, but some Allied soldiers did remain afterward. In the early years of postwar reconstruction, . . . the government and businesses brought in new workers, largely from other European countries, to fill gaps in the labor force and as a way to increase the French population at a time when France feared a further decline in its numbers. . . . Official immigrants to France numbered between 150,000 and 200,000 each year of the 1920s with only three years of the decade falling below these figures. The number of foreigners residing in France more than doubled between 1911 and 1931. Although foreigners were never a large percentage of the population — between approximately 4 and 7 percent from 1921 to 1931, after which the number dropped off somewhat — their increasing presence in the 1920s aroused a wide range of responses, from interest and sympathy to suspicion and fear, and each reaction became intensified as their numbers grew. . . . Neither Americans generally nor African Americans more specifically were the most numerous foreigners in postwar Paris, and their numbers were not large compared to the overall population of the city. But because of their economic impact and visibility in the arts, these particular individuals from outside France signaled to many a significant change in the postwar era. . . .

Another issue underlay the discussions about foreigners and jazz, however. In particular, the perceived modernity of the United States and the so-called primitivism of la musique nègre both threatened to erase a more traditional notion of French *civilisation,* one important element of how many people in France conceived of their nation. By virtue of their language, their Cartesian heritage, their Enlightenment and revolutionary roots, and their purported clarity of ideas, the French claimed a cultural leadership within Europe. And they had been exporting those values, along with the accompanying idea of "mastery" of self and others coupled with a belief in the moral power of improvement, as part of their "civilizing mission" in the colonies. World War I had been, for many combatants, a struggle on behalf of these traditional conceptions of what civilization meant, but the brutality and shock of the war had also called into question whether those values could continue to survive. Perhaps poet Paul Valéry best captured the postwar sense of despair when he remarked, "We modern civilizations have learned to recognize that we are mortal." And in the 1920s, the perceived modernity and primitivism of jazz music forced many French listeners to ask whether their unique and privileged civilization was again being challenged, this time by foreign influences.

Bringing these ideas together in the 1939 *L'Age d'homme* (Manhood), an exploration of his youth and psyche, Leiris wrote that

> jazz was a sign of allegiance, an orgiastic tribute to the colors of the moment. It functioned magically, and its means of influence can be compared to a kind of possession. It was the element that gave these celebrations their true meaning: a *religious* meaning, with communion by dance, latent or manifest eroticism, and drinks, the most effective means of bridging the gap

that separates individuals from each other at any kind of gathering. Swept along by violent bursts of topical energy, jazz still had enough of a "dying civilization" about it, of humanity blindly submitting to The Machine, to express quite completely the state of mind of at least some of that generation: a more or less conscious demoralization born of the war, a naive fascination with the comfort and the latest inventions of progress, a predilection for a contemporary setting whose inanity we nonetheless vaguely anticipated, an abandonment to the animal joy of experiencing the influence of a modern rhythm, an underlying aspiration to a new life in which more room would be made for the impassioned frankness we inarticulately longed for.

This complicated and beautiful passage connects many of the themes in the debate surrounding jazz in the interwar years. Ultimately, it suggests that there was very little difference between the modern, machine-age qualities of jazz and the primitive, Dionysian [uninhibited] responses that this music was thought to bring out in people. As he described jazz, "modern rhythm" effortlessly met "animal joy." Leiris also coupled the search for new artistic inspiration in the postwar years with the belief that jazz drew from a timeless and transcendent culture of black people.

Like Leiris, some listeners appreciated the vitality of jazz because of its ability to cut through layers of old art and culture, thereby finding a new inspiration at the beginning of a new century. . . . That it also appeared to have non–Western origins was all the better for many as the West seemed to have proved itself bankrupt in the war. In this pairing of the modernity of the twentieth century and primitivism of black Africa, fans of jazz invoked a liberationist fantasy implying that the nineteenth century could be shed by embracing the newest developments where "all that is solid melts into air" and, at the same time, returning to a golden past and the beauty of the noble savage. Writer and artist Sem . . . put the second half of this formulation plainly when he maintained, "We have been civilized for too long, and this primitive music communicating to us its naïveté gives us once again for a moment the simple souls of children." Both the modern and primitive in jazz promised its fans the ability to rebuild France and start life over in a new, modern world that was also a rediscovered state of nature like the imagined primitive society.

In this, both America and nègre represented modernity and primitivism at the same time. The United States could be both the height of technological advancement and the land where everything was starting anew. Likewise, blackness could represent both the primitive, savage world of Africa and the modern world that promoted change and novelty, that reveled in exoticism. The modern and primitive values that jazz emulated were simultaneous welcome attacks on the venerable institutions of French civilization — the mores, values, and principles on which many aspects of French culture had been built for so long, but that many now found oppressive and antiquated.

But to its enemies, both the modernity and primitivism of jazz were its worst qualities for the very same threat they posed to French civilization. "The last war has abolished the aesthetics as well as the ethics of the past," lamented conservative critic Henry Malherbe in language similar to that of jazz fans. "We have been obliged to return to the beginning of art and civilization," he claimed, and "with its elementary melody" and other qualities, jazz was part of that process. As much as anything, the criticisms of the Americanness of jazz were attacks on the modern, post–World War I world and the kinds of economic as well as cultural changes that France was undergoing. In that respect, jazz was a sign of the times. Jazz "continues its crazy song!" wrote one critic, "Crazy like the age in which we live." Yet the noise of the modern world and its psychological effects were, in the end, not far from what many called primitive; indeed, they were two sides of the same coin. The modern world — in its very desire for progress and renewal in the wake of the war, and as the result of technological change that eroded old ways of seeing the world — had become primitive again, stripping away all the previous morals, values, tastes, and rules to return to a new, and for many frightening, state of nature. And for many critics, jazz was the sound track of this era. . . .

QUESTIONS TO CONSIDER

1. How was the experience of African American soldiers and musicians more positive in France than in the United States during World War I and the 1920s? Why? Were the French truly "color blind," or did they have different racial stereotypes and prejudices than Americans? How did the French racial atmosphere encourage the migration of black workers and performers?

2. In what ways did French commentators interpret jazz as a symbol of the ongoing "Americanization" of their country? Was their response to this trend positive, negative, or both? What essential racial qualities did French observers see in jazz? How did the French response to jazz reflect ambivalent attitudes about Africans? How did it relate to French colonialism? to immigration in the 1920s?

3. According to the author, French views of jazz as a symbol of "American modernity" and "black primitivism" were two sides of the same coin. In what ways did jazz music suggest an appealing alternative to the traditional values and norms of European (or French) civilization? How was that civilization discredited by World War I?

4. Compare the essays by Jackson and Robert Sklar (Selection 13) as mirror images reflecting the cultural transformations of the 1920s from different sides of the Atlantic. What similarities do you see between Americans' use of European movie stars and the French adoption of American jazz? What differences? Is there a common thread in Europeans' enjoyment of American silent-film comedies and jazz? What role did "foreignness" play in the loosening of manners and morals in the 1920s?

5. What implications does the reception of jazz in 1920s France suggest for today's debates over the Americanization of popular culture around the world? Are American music and film imposed upon foreign audiences or welcomed by them? What meanings do Europeans or others abroad attach to American TV, movies, and music? Are these interpretations the same as Americans'? In what sense is today's American culture loved and hated, admired and feared?

VIII

THE GREAT
DEPRESSION

The prolonged slump that descended on the American economy at the end of
the 1920s was part of a worldwide crisis. Since the United States had been more
prosperous than most countries in the 1920s, its fall was more dramatic, but not
exceptional. The pattern of plunging production, prices, and employment was
similar almost everywhere. It provided somber proof that by the early twentieth
century a complex, intermeshed world economy had come into existence. Most
national economies hit bottom in 1933, but the slump lasted, despite some
spotty improvement and a few national exceptions, until the outbreak of World
War II in 1939. By that time, the world's political landscape had been profoundly altered. Western democracies, including the United States, responded to
the crisis by delegating to national governments the responsibility for providing
jobs and relief to their beleaguered populations. Thus, the modern welfare state
came into its own. There was also a more ominous response. In Germany, Italy,
and Japan, authoritarian governments took control amid the turmoil of the Depression. These repressive and militaristic regimes ended unemployment, but
they also destroyed democracy and eventually brought the world itself to the
brink of destruction.

Despite the global spread of "hard times" and its momentous international
impact, most histories of the Great Depression are resolutely national in focus.
The selections in this chapter are exceptions. The first essay, taken from a
multivolume world history by the British historian Eric Hobsbawm, analyzes
the causes and sketches some of the consequences of the "Great Slump of
1929–1933." Hobsbawm writes within a thoroughly international framework
that allows him to situate the United States in the world economy and to consider its particular economic and political pattern as a variant of global trends.
The second essay, by the American historian John A. Garraty, features a

provocative binational comparison between the United States and Germany. Comparing Nazism and the New Deal, Garraty uncovers surprising similarities in the leadership skills and economic programs of Franklin Roosevelt and Adolf Hitler as they wrestled with the Depression. Hobsbawm's transnational survey and Garraty's focused comparison not only offer contrasting assessments of Depression-era events and movements; they also demonstrate two quite different ways to internationalize the study of American history. As you read them, try to assess the strengths and weaknesses of their different approaches as well as the soundness of their insights.

15

Into the Economic Abyss

Eric Hobsbawm

In hindsight, it is easy to tell when the Great Depression began. On "Black Tuesday," October 29, 1929, the New York stock market began a tumble that lowered stock prices by almost half within three weeks. The Wall Street crash demoralized American banks, investors, and consumers, whose curtailed activities deepened the economic crisis. It sent shock waves around the world, triggering declines in securities markets, decreasing lending, and deflating prices in other industrialized countries. Yet the roots of the worldwide Depression go farther back in time than the Great Crash and extend over a much wider area than the United States. As Eric Hobsbawm notes in his analysis of the world's descent "into the economic abyss" of the 1930s, historians and economists still argue over the causes of the Great Depression. Many explanations are basically enlarged descriptions of the capitalist business cycle, the recurring up-and-down syndrome by which good times inevitably lead to speculation and overproduction, which are then "corrected" by deflation and unemployment, until inventories are spent and investors and consumers resume the expansion. But, says Hobsbawm, other factors combined to deepen the crisis and to prolong it beyond any other international slump in modern times. Western Europe's crushing debt from World War I (to be paid, supposedly, by Germany's impossibly high reparations), agricultural overproduction in the 1920s, the reluctance of the United States to take over Britain's role as the world's banker, and the wrong-headed nationalistic economic policies that many countries pursued — all these meant that what looked like a typical economic downturn was really a world catastrophe in the making.

Whatever the Great Depression's causes, there is no disputing its devastating impact. Between 1929 and 1933, over eleven thousand American banks failed; national production was cut in half; and thirteen million people (representing one-fourth of the labor force) were put out of work. Some European economies were hit even harder because they had not yet fully recovered from World War I. Throughout the industrialized world, unemployment ranged between 15 and 30 percent of the work force in the early 1930s. Ironically, agricultural countries tended to fare better. Plummeting crop prices hurt Brazil and India, for example, but peasants could grow their own food, and local businessmen recovered quickly by developing textile manufacturing and other industries.

Hobsbawm acknowledges the immediate devastation caused by the "Great Slump of 1929–1933," but he steps back in order to note the Depression's long-term effects. First, he says, the collapse of Western economies fatally discredited the orthodox economic theory that free trade abroad and government noninterference at home were the best guarantees of prosperity. Even if the European and American economies rebounded by themselves after hitting bottom, massive unemployment made doing nothing politically unacceptable to angry voters. One by one, Western governments attacked joblessness with planned production, public works programs, and other deficit-spending measures. They were egged on not only by the new economic theories of John Maynard Keynes, but also by the apparent success of the Soviet Union's planned economy in avoiding the decade's economic woes. The modern welfare state had come, and with it came the second effect of the Depression: a move toward stronger central governments. Throughout the West, frightened and desperate citizens anxious to restore order and confidence ceded authority to powerful governments run by charismatic leaders. The new regimes were sometimes left-leaning, as in the case of President Franklin Roosevelt's New Deal in the United States or Lázaro Cárdenas's land-reform administration in Mexico. More often, however, they proved to be far-from-benevolent dictatorships of the Right. Economic depression prepared the ground for dangerous fascist regimes in Germany and Italy as well as a civil war that gave victory to the fascists in Spain.

Hobsbawm's international approach is a fine corrective to textbooks that discuss the American Great Depression in isolation. And his insight that fascism and the New Deal were in a sense analogous responses to the Depression is a good preparation for the reading by John Garraty that follows it. As you move to the next essay, you should compare Hobsbawm's generalizations about the Depression's political effects with the detailed comparison of Roosevelt's and Hitler's economic policies undertaken by Garraty.

GLOSSARY

COMMUNIST INTERNATIONAL (COMINTERN)   An organization formed in 1919 by V. I. Lenin to assert communist leadership over the international socialist movement and to promote communism around the world. It was disbanded in 1943 as a gesture of support for the Allied coalition during World War II.

DEFLATION   A time of falling prices, slower business activity, and high unemployment, the opposite of inflation.

ECONOMIC LIBERALISM   The doctrines of classical economics as applied to governments and economies in the nineteenth century. In general, economic liberalism prescribed free trade internationally and a laissez-faire (noninterventionist) policy for the domestic economy.

ELASTIC AND INELASTIC DEMAND   Concepts that express how consumers respond to changes in the price of goods or services. Elastic demand is a situation in which a change in price produces a distinct change of the opposite direction in the quantity purchased; that is, if the price goes up, demand goes down. With inelastic demand, price changes do not affect the amount purchased.

FASCISM   A political philosophy that glorifies the nation over the individual and encourages "benevolent" dictatorship. Its elements often include opposition to democratic and socialist movements, racist ideologies, aggressive military policy, and faith in an authoritarian leader who is said to embody the nation's ideals. The term was first used by the party of Benito Mussolini in Italy, and it also applied to right-wing movements such as National Socialism (Nazism) in Germany and the regime of Generalissimo Francisco Franco in Spain (1939–1975).

FORD, HENRY (1863–1947)   A pioneer American automobile manufacturer. Ford used assembly-line techniques to produce the Model T, an inexpensive, standardized car that made Ford's company the largest auto producer in the world.

GOLD STANDARD   The practice of making gold the basis of a monetary system by giving a unit of currency, such as a dollar bill, the value of a particular weight of gold, for which, under certain conditions, it could be exchanged.

HOOVER, HERBERT (1874–1964)   The Republican president elected in 1928 but soon overwhelmed by the Great Depression. Hoover's response to the economic crisis reflected the limitations of Progressives' expansion of government: he insisted that only state and local agencies and private charities deal with unemployment relief. By 1932 Hoover was seen by many Americans as an aloof and uncaring leader, and shantytowns set up by the unemployed were called Hoovervilles.

INFLATION   A persistent and large rise in the general price level of goods and services. Inflation often results from an increase in the amount of circulating currency due to shortages of goods or to heavy borrowing by individuals or government.

KEYNES, JOHN MAYNARD (1883–1946)   An English economist whose theories departed from classical laissez-faire doctrines by advocating government intervention in the market. Keynes argued that during depressions, government spending and easier monetary policies would raise the employment level and stimulate business recovery. His theories influenced Western governments during the Great Depression and especially after World War II.

STALIN, JOSEPH (1879–1953)   The ruthless and powerful head of the Soviet Union from 1929 until his death. An early comrade of Bolshevik leader V. I. Lenin, Stalin returned from exile in Siberia during the Russian Revolution and became the first editor of the Communist Party newspaper, *Pravda*. He emerged victorious from the five-year power struggle after Lenin's death in 1924. Once in control, Stalin forcibly collectivized Russia's farms, ordered rapid industrial growth, and imprisoned or executed rivals or dissidents, including millions of ordinary citizens.

I

The First World War was followed by one kind of breakdown that was genuinely worldwide, at least wherever men and women were enmeshed in, or operated by, impersonal market transactions. Indeed, the proud U.S.A. itself, so far from being a safe haven from the convulsions of less fortunate continents, became the epicenter of this, the largest global earthquake ever to be measured in the economic historians' Richter Scale — the Great Inter-war Depression. In a sentence: between the wars the capitalist world economy appeared to collapse. Nobody quite knew how it might recover.

The operations of a capitalist economy are never smooth, and fluctuations of various length, often very severe, are integral parts of this way of running the affairs of the world. The so-called "trade cycle" of boom and slump was familiar to all businessmen from the nineteenth century. It was expected to repeat itself, with variations, every seven to eleven years. A rather more lengthy periodicity had first begun to attract attention at the end of the nineteenth century, as observers looked back on the unexpected peripeties [sudden changes] of the previous decades. A spectacular, record-breaking global boom from about 1850 to the early 1870s had been followed by the twenty-odd years of economic uncertainties . . . and then another evidently secular forward surge of the world economy. In the early 1920s a Russian economist, N. D. Kondratiev . . . discerned a pattern of economic development since the late eighteenth century through a series of "long waves" of from fifty to sixty years, though neither he nor anyone else could give a satisfactory explanation of these movements, and indeed skeptical statisticians have even denied their existence. . . .

In the past, waves and cycles, long, medium and short, had been accepted by businessmen and economists rather as farmers accept the weather, which also has its ups and downs. There was nothing to be done about them: they created opportunities or problems, they could lead to bonanzas or bankruptcy for individuals or industries, but only socialists who, with Karl Marx, believed that cycles were part of a process by which capitalism generated what would in the end prove insuperable internal contradictions, thought they put the existence of the economic system as such at risk. The world economy was expected to go on growing and advancing, as it had patently done, except for the sudden and short-lived catastrophes of cyclical slumps, for over a century. What was novel about the new situation was that, probably for the first, and so far the only, time in the history of capitalism, its fluctuations seemed to be genuinely system-endangering. . . .

The history of the world economy since the Industrial Revolution had been one of accelerating technological progress, of continuous but uneven economic growth, and of increasing "globalization," that is to say of an increasingly elaborate and intricate worldwide division of labor; an increasingly dense network of flows and exchanges that bound every part of the world economy to the global system. Technical progress continued and even accelerated in the Age of Catastrophe [1914–1948] . . . [and] economic growth during these decades did not cease. It merely slowed down. . . .

Yet . . . [t]he globalization of the economy, it seemed, had stopped advancing in the inter-war years. Any way we measure it, the integration of the world economy stagnated or regressed. The pre-war years had been the greatest period of mass migration in recorded history, but now these streams died out, or rather, were dammed by the disruptions of wars and political restriction. In the last fifteen years before 1914 almost fifteen millions had landed in the U.S.A. In the next fifteen years the flow shrunk to five-and-a-half millions; in the 1930s and the war years it came to an almost complete stop; less than three quarters of a million entered the U.S.A. Iberian migration, overwhelmingly to Latin America, fell from one-and-three-quarter millions in the decade 1911–20 to less than a quarter of a million in the 1930s. World trade recovered from the disruptions of war and post-war crisis to climb a little above 1913 in the late twenties, then fell during the slump, but at the end of the Age of Catastrophe (1948) it was not significantly higher in volume than before the First World War. . . .

Why this stagnation? Various reasons have been suggested, for instance that the largest of the world's national economies, the U.S.A., was getting virtually self-sufficient, except in the supply of a few raw materials; it had never been particularly dependent on foreign trade. However, even countries which had been heavy traders, like Britain and the Scandinavian states, showed the same trend. Contemporaries focused on a more obvious cause for alarm, and they were almost certainly right. Each state now did its best to protect its economy against threats from outside, that is to say against a world economy that was visibly in major trouble. . . .

The Anglo-Saxon world, the wartime neutrals and Japan did what they could to deflate, i.e. to get their economies back to the old and firm principles of stable currencies guaranteed by sound finance and the gold standard, which had been unable to resist the strains of war. Indeed, they more or less succeeded in doing so between 1922 and 1926. However, the great zone of defeat and convulsion from Germany in the West to Soviet Russia in the East saw a spectacular collapse of the monetary system, comparable only to that in part of the post-communist world after 1989. In the extreme case — Germany in 1923 — the currency unit was reduced to one million millionth of its 1913 value, that is to say in practice the value of money was reduced to zero. Even in less extreme cases, the consequences were drastic. The writer's grandfather, whose insurance policy matured during the Austrian inflation, liked to tell the story of drawing this large sum in devalued currency, and finding it was just enough to buy himself a drink in his favorite café.

In short, private savings disappeared totally, thus creating an almost complete vacuum of working capital for business, which does much to explain the massive reliance of the German economy on foreign loans in the following years. This made it unusually vulnerable when the slump came. . . . When the great inflation was ended in 1922–23, essentially by the decision of governments to stop printing paper money in unlimited quantities and to change the currency, people in Germany who had relied on fixed incomes and savings were wiped out, although at least a tiny fraction of the value of money had been saved in Poland, Hungary and Austria. . . .

By 1924 these post-war hurricanes had calmed down, and it seemed possible to look forward to a return to what an American president [Warren Harding] christened "normalcy." There was indeed something like a return to global growth, even though some of the producers of raw materials and foodstuffs, including notably North American farmers, were troubled because prices of primary products turned down again after a brief recovery. The roaring 1920s were not a golden age on the farms of the U.S.A. Moreover, unemployment in most of Western Europe remained astonishingly, and by pre-1914 standards, pathologically, high. It is hard to remember that even in the boom years of the 1920s (1924–29) it averaged between 10 and 12 percent in Britain, Germany and Sweden, and no less than 17–18 percent in Denmark and Norway. Only the U.S.A., with average unemployment of about 4 percent, was an economy really under full steam. Both facts pointed to serious weaknesses in the economy. The sagging of primary prices (which were prevented from falling further by building up increasingly large stockpiles) simply demonstrated that the demand for them could not keep pace with the capacity to produce. Nor should we overlook the fact that the boom, such as it was, was largely fueled by the enormous flows of international capital which swept across the industrial worlds in those years, and notably to Germany. That country alone, which took about half of all the world's capital exports in 1928, borrowed between 20,000 and 30,000 billion Marks, half of it probably on short term. Once again this made the German economy highly vulnerable, as was proved when the American money was withdrawn after 1929.

It therefore came as no great surprise to anyone except the boosters of smalltown America, whose image became familiar to the Western world at this time through the American novelist Sinclair Lewis' *Babbitt* (1922), that the world economy was in trouble again a few years later. The Communist International had indeed predicted another economic crisis at the height of the boom, expecting it — or so its spokesmen believed or pretended to believe — to lead to a new round of revolutions. . . . However, what nobody expected, probably not even the revolutionaries in their most sanguine moments, was the extraordinary universality and depth of the crisis which began, as even non-historians know, with the New York Stock Exchange crash of 29 October 1929. It amounted to something very close to the collapse of the capitalist world economy, which now seemed gripped in a vicious circle where every downward movement of the economic indices (other than unemployment, which moved to ever more astronomic heights) reinforced the decline in all the others.

As the admirable experts of the League of Nations observed, . . . a dramatic recession of the North American industrial economy soon spread to the other industrial heartland, Germany. U.S. industrial production fell by about a third from 1929 to 1931, German production by about the same, but these are smoothing averages. Thus in the U.S.A., Westinghouse, the great electrical firm, lost two-thirds of its sales between 1929 and 1933, while its net income fell by 76 percent in two years. There was a crisis in primary production, both of foodstuffs and raw materials, as their prices, no longer kept up by building stocks as before, went into free fall. The price of tea and wheat fell by two thirds, the price of raw silk by three quarters. This prostrated — to name but the countries listed by the League of Nations in 1931 — Argentina, Australia, the Balkan countries, Bolivia, Brazil, (British) Malaya, Canada, Chile, Colombia, Cuba, Egypt, Ecuador, Finland, Hungary, India, Mexico, the Netherlands Indies (the present Indonesia), New Zealand, Paraguay, Peru, Uruguay and Venezuela, whose international trade depended heavily on a few primary commodities. In short, it made the Depression global in the literal sense.

The economies of Austria, Czechoslovakia, Greece, Japan, Poland and Great Britain, extremely sensitive to the seismic shocks coming from the West (or East), were equally shaken. The Japanese silk industry had tripled its output in fifteen years to supply the vast and growing U.S. market for silk stockings, which now disappeared temporarily — and so did the market for the 90 percent of Japan's silk that then went to America. Meanwhile the price of the other great staple of Japanese agricultural production, rice, also plummeted, as it did in all the great rice-producing zones of South and East Asia. Since, as it happened, the wheat price collapsed even more completely than that of rice, and wheat was therefore cheaper, many Orientals are said to have switched from the one to the other. . . . Farmers tried to compensate for falling prices by growing and selling more crops, and this made prices sink even further.

For farmers dependent on the market, especially the export market, this meant ruin, unless they could retreat to the traditional ultimate redoubt of the peasant, subsistence production. This was indeed still possible in much of the dependent world, and insofar as most Africans, South and East Asians and Latin Americans were still peasants, it undoubtedly cushioned them. Brazil became a byword for the waste of capitalism and the depth of the Depression, as its coffee growers desperately tried to prevent the price-collapse by burning coffee instead of coal on their steam railroad engines. (Between two thirds and three quarters of the coffee sold on the world market came from that country.) Nevertheless the Great Slump was far more tolerable for the still overwhelmingly rural Brazilians than the economic cataclysms of the 1980s; especially since poor people's expectations of what they could get of an economy were still extremely modest. . . .

For those who, by definition, had no control over or access to the means of production (unless they could go home to a peasant family in some village), namely the men and women hired for wages, the primary consequence of the Slump was unemployment on an unimagined and unprecedented scale, and for longer than anyone had ever expected. At the worst period of the Slump (1932–33) 22–23 percent of the British and Belgian labor force, 24 percent of the Swedish, 27 percent of the U.S., 29 percent of the Austrian, 31 percent of the Norwegian, 32 percent of the Danish and no less than 44 percent of the German workers were out of jobs. What is equally to the point, even the recovery after 1933 did not reduce the average unemployment of the 1930s below 16–17 percent in Britain and Sweden or below 20 percent in the rest of Scandinavia, Austria and the U.S.A. The only Western state which succeeded in eliminating unemployment was Nazi Germany between 1933 and 1938. There had been nothing like this economic catastrophe in the lives of working people as long as anyone could remember.

What made it even more dramatic was that public provision for social security, including unemployment relief, was either non-existent, as in the U.S.A., or, by late twentieth-century standards, extremely meager, especially for the long-term unemployed. That is why security had always been such a vital concern of working people: protection against the terrible uncertainties of employment (i.e. wages), sickness or accident and the terrible certainties of an old age without earnings. That is why working people dreamed of seeing their children in modestly paid, but secure and pensionable jobs. Even in the country most fully covered by Unemployment Insurance schemes before the Slump (Great Britain) less than 60 percent of the labor force were covered by it — and that only because Britain since 1920 had already been forced to adjust to mass unemployment. Elsewhere in Europe (except for Germany, where it was above 40 percent) the proportion of working people with claims for unemployment relief ranged from zero to about one quarter. People who had been used to fluctuating employment or to passing spells of cyclical unemployment were desperate when no job turned up anywhere, after their small savings had gone and their credit at the local grocer's shop had been exhausted.

Hence the central, the traumatic, impact of mass unemployment on the politics of the industrialized countries, for that is what first and foremost, the Great Slump meant, to the bulk of their inhabitants. What did it matter to them that economic historians (and indeed logic) can demonstrate that the majority of the nation's labor force, which was in employment even at the worst moments, was actually getting significantly better off, since prices were falling throughout the inter-war years, and the price of foodstuffs fell more rapidly than any other in the worst depression years. The image which dominated at the time was that of soup kitchens, of unemployed "Hunger Marchers" from smokeless settlements where no steel or ships were made converging on capital cities to denounce those they held responsible. Nor did politicians fail to observe that up to 85 percent of the membership of the German Communist Party, growing almost as fast as the Nazi Party in the slump years, and, in the last months before Hitler's accession to power, faster, were unemployed. . . .

Curiously enough, the sense of catastrophe and disorientation caused by the Great Slump was perhaps greater among businessmen, economists and politicians than among the masses. . . . It was precisely the absence of any solutions within the framework of the old liberal economy that made the predicament of the economic decision-makers so dramatic. To meet immediate, short-term crises, they had, as they saw it, to undermine the long-term basis of a flourishing world economy. At a time when world trade fell by 60 percent in four years (1929–32), states found themselves building increasingly high barriers to protect their national markets and currencies against the world economic hurricanes, knowing quite well that this meant the dismantling of the world system of multilateral trade on which, they believed, world prosperity must rest. The keystone of such a system, the so-called "most favored nation status" disappeared from almost 60 percent of 510 commercial agreements signed between 1931 and 1939 and, where it remained, it was usually in a limited form. Where would it end? Was there an exit from the vicious circle?

We shall consider the immediate political consequences of this, the most traumatic episode in the history of capitalism, below. However, its most significant long-term implication must be mentioned immediately. In a single sentence: the Great Slump destroyed economic liberalism for half a century. In 1931–32 Britain, Canada, all of Scandinavia and the U.S.A. abandoned the gold standard, always regarded as the foundation of stable international exchanges and by 1936 they had been joined even by those impassioned believers in bullion, the Belgians and Dutch, and finally the very French. Almost symbolically, Great Britain in 1931 abandoned Free Trade, which had been as central to the British economic identity since the 1840s as the American Constitution is to U.S. political identity. Britain's retreat from the principles of free transactions in a single world economy dramatizes the general rush into national self-protection at the time. More specifically, the Great Slump forced Western governments to give social considerations priority over economic ones in their state policies. The dangers of failing to do so — radicalization of the Left and, as Germany and other countries now proved, of the Right — were too menacing.

So governments no longer protected agriculture simply by tariffs against foreign competition, though, where they had done so before, they raised tariff barriers even higher. During the Depression they took to subsidizing it by guaranteeing farm prices, buying up surpluses or paying farmers not to produce, as in the U.S.A. after 1933. . . .

As for the workers, after the war "full employment," i.e. the elimination of mass unemployment, became the keystone of economic policy in the countries of a reformed democratic capitalism, whose most celebrated prophet and pioneer, though not the only one, was the British economist John Maynard Keynes (1883–1946). The Keynesian argument for the benefits of eliminating permanent mass unemployment was economic as well as political. Keynesians held, correctly, that the demand which the incomes of fully employed workers must generate, would have the most stimulating effect on depressed economies. Nevertheless, the reason why this means of increasing demand was given such urgent priority — the British government committed itself to it even before the end of the Second World War — was that mass unemployment was believed to be politically and socially explosive, as indeed it had proved to be in the Slump. . . .

[A]nother prophylactic measure taken during, after and as a consequence of the Great Slump [was] the installation of modern welfare systems. Who can be surprised that the U.S. passed its Social Security Act in 1935? We have become so used to the universal prevalence of ambitious welfare systems in developed states of industrial capitalism — with some exceptions, such as Japan, Switzerland and the U.S.A. — that we forget how few "welfare states" in the modern sense there were before the Second World War. Even the Scandinavian countries were only just beginning to develop them. Indeed, the very term welfare state did not come into use before the 1940s.

The trauma of the Great Slump was underlined by the fact that the one country that had clamorously broken with capitalism appeared to be immune to it: the Soviet Union. While the rest of the world, or at least liberal Western capitalism, stagnated, the U.S.S.R. was engaged in massive ultra-rapid industrialization under its new Five-Year Plans. From 1929 to 1940 Soviet industrial production tripled, at the very least. It rose from 5 percent of the world's manufactured products in 1929 to 18 percent in 1938, while during the same period the joint share of the U.S.A., Britain and France, fell from 59 percent to 52 percent of the world's total. What was more, there was no unemployment. These achievements impressed foreign observers of all ideologies, including a small but influential flow of socio-economic tourists to Moscow in 1930–35, more than the visible primitiveness and inefficiency of the Soviet economy, or the ruthlessness and brutality of Stalin's collectivization and mass repression. For what they were trying to come to terms with was not the actual phenomenon of the U.S.S.R. but the breakdown of their own economic system, the depth of the failure of Western capitalism. What was the secret of the Soviet system? Could anything be learned from it? Echoing Russia's Five-Year Plans, "Plan" and "Planning" became buzz-words in politics. Social Democratic parties adopted "plans," as in Belgium and Norway. Sir Arthur Salter, a British civil servant of the utmost distinction and respectability, and a pillar of the Establishment, wrote a book, *Recovery,* to demonstrate that a planned society was essential, if the country and the world were to escape from the vicious cycle of the Great Slump. Other British middle-of-the-road civil servants and functionaries set up a non-partisan think-tank called PEP (Political and Economic Planning). . . . Even the very Nazis plagiarized the idea, as Hitler introduced a "Four-Year Plan" in 1933.

II

Why did the capitalist economy between the wars fail to work? The situation of the U.S.A. is a central part of any answer to this question. For if the disruptions of war and post-war Europe, or at least the belligerent countries of Europe, could be made at least partly responsible for the economic troubles there, the U.S.A. had been far away from the war, though briefly, if decisively, involved in it. So far from disrupting its economy, the First World War, like the Second World War, benefited it spectacularly. By 1913 the U.S.A. had already become the largest economy in the world, producing over one third of its industrial output — just under the combined total for Germany, Great Britain and France. In 1929 it produced over 42 percent of the total world output, as against just under 28 percent for the three European industrial powers. This is a truly astonishing figure. Concretely, while U.S. steel production rose by about one quarter between 1913 and 1920, steel production in the rest of the world fell by about one third. In short, after the end of the first World War the U.S.A. was in many ways as internationally dominant an economy as it once again became after the Second World War. It was the Great Slump which temporarily interrupted this ascendancy.

Moreover, the war had not only reinforced its position as the world's greatest industrial producer, but turned it into the world's greatest creditor. The British had lost about a quarter of their global investments during the war, mainly those in the U.S.A., which they had to sell to buy war supplies; the French lost about half of theirs, mainly through revolution and breakdown in Europe. Meanwhile the Americans, who had begun the war as a debtor country, ended it as the main international lender. Since the U.S.A. concentrated its operations in Europe and the western hemisphere (the British were still by far the biggest investors in Asia and Africa) their impact on Europe was decisive.

In short, there is no explanation of the world economic crisis without the U.S.A. It was, after all, both the premier exporting nation of the world in the 1920s and, after Great Britain, the premier importing nation. As for raw materials and foodstuffs, it imported almost 40 percent of all the imports of the fifteen most commercial nations, a fact which goes a long way to explaining the disastrous impact of the slump on the producers of commodities like wheat, cotton, sugar, rubber, silk, copper, tin and coffee. By the same token, it was to become the principal victim of the Slump. If its imports fell by 70 percent between 1929 and 1932, its exports fell at the same rate. World trade dipped by less than a third from 1929 to 1939, but U.S. exports crashed by almost half.

This is not to underestimate the strictly European roots of trouble, which were largely political in origin. At the Versailles peace conference (1919) vast but undefined payments had been imposed on Germany as "reparations" for the cost of the war and the damage done to the victorious powers. To justify these a clause had also been inserted into the peace treaty making Germany *solely* responsible for the war (the so-called "war-guilt" clause) which was both historically doubtful and proved to be a gift to German nationalism. The amount Germany was to pay remained vague, as a compromise between the position of the U.S.A., which proposed fixing Germany's payments according to the country's capacity to pay, and the other Allies — chiefly the French — who insisted on recovering the entire costs of the war. Their, or at least France's, real object was to keep Germany weak and to have a means of putting pressure on it. In 1921 the sum was fixed at 132 billion Gold Marks, i.e. $33 billion at the time, which everyone knew to be a fantasy.

"Reparations" led to endless debates, periodic crises and settlements under American auspices, since the U.S.A., to its former Allies' displeasure, wished to link the question of Germany's debts to them, to that of their own wartime debts to Washington. These were almost as crazy as the sums demanded of the Germans, which amounted to one and a half times the entire national income of the country in 1929; the British debts to the U.S. amounted to half the British national income; the French debts to two-thirds. A "Dawes Plan" in 1924 actually fixed a real sum for Germany to pay annually; a "Young Plan" in 1929 modified the repayment scheme and, incidentally, set up the Bank of International Settlements in Basel (Switzerland), the first of the international financial institutions which were to multiply after the Second World War. . . .

There was the question of how reparations were to be paid. Those who wanted to keep Germany weak wanted cash rather than (as was rational) goods out of current production, or at least out of the income from German exports, since this would have strengthened the German economy against its competitors. In effect they forced Germany into heavy borrowing, so that such reparations as were paid came out of the massive (American) loans of the mid-1920s. For Germany's rivals this seemed to have the additional advantage that Germany ran into deep debt rather than expanding its exports to achieve an external balance. . . . However, the whole arrangement, as we have already seen, made both Germany and Europe highly sensitive to the decline in American lending which began even before the crisis and the shutting of the American loan-tap, which followed the Wall Street Crisis of 1929. The entire house of cards of reparations collapsed during the Slump. . . .

However, wartime and post-war disruptions and political complications in Europe can only partly explain the severity of the inter-war economic breakdown. Speaking economically, we can look at it in two ways.

The first will see chiefly a striking and growing imbalance in the international economy, due to the asymmetry in development between the U.S.A. and the rest of the world. The world system, it can be argued, did not work, because, unlike Great Britain, which had been its center before 1914, the U.S.A. did not much need the rest of the world, and therefore, again unlike Great Britain, which knew that the world payments system rested on the Pound Sterling [the British unit of currency] and saw to it that it remained stable, the U.S.A. did not bother to act as a global stabilizer. The U.S.A. did not need the world much, because after the First World War it needed to import less capital, labor and (relatively speaking) fewer commodities than ever — except for some raw materials. Its exports, though internationally important — Hollywood virtually monopolized the international movie market — made a far smaller contribution to the national income than in any other industrial country. How significant this . . . withdrawal of the U.S.A. from the world economy was, may be debated. However, it is quite clear that this explanation of the Slump was one which influenced U.S. economists and politicians in the 1940s, and helped to convince Washington in the war years to take over responsibility for the stability of the world economy after 1945.

The second perspective on the Depression fixes on the failure of the world economy to generate enough demand for a lasting expansion. The foundations of the prosperity of the 1920s, as we have seen, were weak, even in the U.S.A., where farming was virtually already in depression, and money wages, contrary to the myth of the great jazz age, were not rising dramatically, and actually [were] stagnant in the last mad years of the boom. What was happening, as often happens in free market booms, was that, with wages lagging, profits rose disproportionately and the prosperous got a larger slice of the national cake. But as mass demand could not keep pace with the rapidly increasing productivity of the industrial system in the heyday of Henry Ford, the result was overproduction and speculation. This, in turn, triggered off the collapse. . . .

When the collapse came, it was of course all the more drastic in the U.S.A. because in fact a lagging expansion of demand had been beefed up by means of an enormous expansion of consumer credit. . . . Banks, already hurt by the speculative real-estate boom which, with the usual help of self-deluding optimists and mushrooming financial crookery, had reached its peak some years before the Big Crash, loaded with bad debts, refused new housing loans or to refinance existing ones. This did not stop them from failing by the thousands, while (in 1933) nearly half of all U.S. home mortgages were in default and a thousand properties a day were being foreclosed. Automobile purchases alone owed $1,400 million out of a total personal indebtedness of $6,500 million in short- and medium-term loans. What made the economy so much more vulnerable to this credit boom was that customers did not use their loans to buy the traditional mass consumption goods which kept body and soul together, and were therefore pretty inelastic: food, clothing and the like. However poor one is, one can't reduce one's demand for groceries below a certain point; and that demand will not double if one's income doubles. Instead they bought the durable consumer goods of the modern consumer society which the U.S.A. was even then pioneering. But the purchase of cars and houses could be readily postponed, and, in any case, they had and have a very high income elasticity of demand.

So, unless a slump was expected to be brief, or was short, and confidence in the future was not determined, the effect of such a crisis could be dramatic. Thus automobile production in the U.S.A. *halved* between 1929 and 1931 or, at a much lower level, the production of poor people's gramophone records ("race" records and jazz records addressed to a black public) virtually ceased for a while. In short, [according to W. W. Rostow] "unlike railroads or more efficient ships or the introduction of steel and machine tools — which cut costs — the new products and way of life required high and expanding levels of income and a high degree of confidence about the future, to be rapidly diffused." But that is exactly what was collapsing.

The worst cyclical slump sooner or later comes to an end, and after 1932 there were increasingly clear signs that the worst was over. Indeed, some economies roared ahead. Japan and, on a more modest scale, Sweden, reached almost twice the pre-slump level of production by the end of the 1930s, and by 1938 the German (though not the Italian) economy was 25 percent above 1929. Even sluggish economies like the British showed plenty of signs of dynamism. Yet somehow the expected upsurge did not return. The world remained in depression. This was most visible in the greatest of all the economies, the U.S.A., for the various experiments in stimulating the economy undertaken under President F. D. Roosevelt's "New Deal" — sometimes inconsistently — did not really live up to their economic promise. A strong upsurge was followed, in 1937–38, by another economic crash, though on a rather more modest scale than after 1929. The leading sector of American industry, automobile production, never regained its 1929 peak. In 1938 it was little more than it had been in 1920. Looking back from the 1990s we are struck by the pessimism of intelligent commentators. Able and brilliant economists saw the future of capitalism, left to itself, as one of stagnation. . . .

III

The Great Slump confirmed intellectuals, activists and ordinary citizens in the belief that something was fundamentally wrong with the world they lived in. Who knew what could be done about it? Certainly few of those in authority over their countries, and certainly not those who tried to steer a course by the traditional navigational instruments of secular liberalism or traditional faith, and by the charts of the nineteenth century seas which were plainly no longer to be trusted. How much confidence did economists deserve, however brilliant, who demonstrated, with great lucidity, that the Slump in which even they lived, could not happen in a properly conducted free-market society, since (according to an economic law named after an early nineteenth century Frenchman [Jean-Baptiste Say]) no overproduction was possible which did not very soon correct itself? . . . Economists who simply advised leaving the economy alone, governments whose first instincts, apart from protecting the gold standard by deflationary policies, was to stick to financial orthodoxy, balance budgets and cut costs, were visibly not making the situation better. Indeed, as the depression continued, it was argued with considerable force not least by J. M. Keynes who consequently became the most influential economist of the next forty years — that they were making the depression worse. . . .

It is therefore not surprising that the effects of the Great Slump on both politics and public thinking were dramatic and immediate. Unlucky the government which happened to be in office during the cataclysm, whether it was on the right, like Herbert Hoover's presidency in the U.S.A. (1928–33), or on the left, like Britain's and Australia's labor governments. The change was not always as immediate as in Latin America, where twelve countries changed government or regime in 1930–31, ten of them by military coup. Nevertheless, by the middle 1930s there were few states whose politics had not changed very substantially from what they had been before the Crash. . . .

Probably nothing demonstrates both the globality of the Great Slump and the profundity of its impact more than . . . the virtually universal political upheavals it produced within a period measured in months or single years, from Japan to Ireland, from Sweden to New Zealand, from Argentina to Egypt. Yet the depth of its impact is not to be judged only, or even mainly, by its short-term political effects, dramatic though these often were. It was a catastrophe which destroyed all hope of restoring the economy, and the society, of the long nineteenth century. The period 1929–33 was a canyon which henceforth made a return to 1913 not merely impossible, but unthinkable. Old-fashioned liberalism was dead or seemed doomed. Three options now competed for intellectual-political hegemony. Marxist communism was one. After all, Marx's own predictions seemed to be coming true[,] . . . and, even more impressively, the U.S.S.R. appeared to be immune to the catastrophe. A capitalism shorn of its belief in the optimality of free markets and reformed by a sort of unofficial marriage or permanent liaison with the moderate social-democracy of non-communist labor movements was the second, and, after the Second World War, proved to be the most effective. However, in the short run it was not so much a conscious program or policy alternative as a sense that once the Slump was over, such a thing must never be allowed to happen again and, in the best of cases, a readiness to experiment stimulated by the evident failure of classical free-market liberalism. . . . An alternative theory to the bankrupt free market economics was only in the process of elaboration. J. M. Keynes' *General Theory of Employment, Interest and Money,* the most influential contribution to it, was not published until 1936. An alternative government practice, the macro-economic steering and management of the economy based on national income accounting did not develop until the Second World War and after, though, perhaps with an eye on the U.S.S.R., governments and other public entities in the 1930s increasingly took to seeing the national economy as a whole and estimating the size of its total product or income.

The third option was fascism, which the Slump transformed into a world movement, and, more to the point, a world danger. Fascism in its German version (National Socialism) benefited both from the German intellectual tradition which . . . had been hostile to the neoclassical theories of economic liberalism that had become the international orthodoxy since the 1880s, and from a ruthless government determined to get rid of unemployment at all costs. It dealt with the Great Slump, it must be said, rapidly and

more successfully than any other (the record of Italian fascism was less impressive). . . .
But as the tide of fascism rose with the Great Slump, it became increasingly clear that in
the Age of Catastrophe not only peace, social stability and the economy, but also the
political institutions and intellectual values of nineteenth century liberal bourgeois society,
were in retreat or collapse. . . .

QUESTIONS TO CONSIDER

1. Analyze the international causes of the Great Depression. How did the peace settlement following World War I contribute to Europe's economic woes? What was
   wrong with agricultural production and prices after the war? What trends damaged
   the world economy in the 1920s? How did nationalistic economic policies, such as
   high tariffs and currency deflation, contribute to the problem?
2. According to Hobsbawm, what role did the United States play in causing, or at least
   not preventing, the Great Depression? How did American "hard times" affect other
   countries? Why was the United States, the world's wealthiest nation, among those
   hardest hit by the Depression?
3. Hobsbawm says that the Great Depression "destroyed economic liberalism for half a
   century." In what sense did the Depression cause a crisis for the conventional wisdom of classical (liberal) economics? Which national economic policies helped the
   public to weather the crisis, and which failed? Why? How did the experience of the
   Depression change governments' economic role after World War II?
4. Discuss the impact that the "Great Slump" had on different peoples. Why were some
   nations less affected by it than others? Which occupational groups suffered the most?
   Which groups prospered? Which remained the same?
5. Analyze today's debates in the United States over the government's role and its economic policies. In what ways have attitudes toward unemployment and government's
   responsibility for the economy changed since the 1930s? How have they remained
   the same? If another severe depression were to occur today, would its economic and
   psychological impact be as devastating as in the 1930s? Do you think that American
   politics would shift to the left or the right? Why?

Roosevelt and Hitler: New Deal and Nazi Reactions to the Depression

John A. Garraty

It is not surprising that people adrift in poverty, resentment, and despair would turn to confident and charismatic political leaders during the Great Depression. Two such men were Franklin Roosevelt and Adolf Hitler, whose personalities and programs are compared by John Garraty in this selection. Both leaders came to power at almost precisely the same time, following inept and unpopular predecessors. Neither had a consistent economic program to end the crisis, Garraty shows. Their improvised policymaking reflected their ignorance about economics as well as their political pragmatism when faced with pressures from various interest groups. But both Roosevelt and Hitler symbolized "energy and commitment," and they were willing to experiment with government initiatives on an unprecedented scale in order to bring economic recovery.

Putting aside obvious differences between the American political system and Hitler's Third Reich, Garraty finds that New Deal and Nazi economic policies were remarkably similar. From government work programs and youth camps to farm subsidies and rural resettlement, both combined deficit spending on modern improvements with an old-fashioned idealization of rural life. Both leaders began by advocating a form of "corporatism," or government-supervised cooperation between business and labor. By the mid-1930s this relationship had broken down and was replaced by anti-business rhetoric and new programs promising economic and social security for the nation's workers. In the end, Garraty says, neither Roosevelt nor Hitler solved the riddle of the Great Depression, although Hitler was more successful at restoring full employment. Yet the sense of action, confidence, and purpose both men brought to their roles — highlighted by their skillful propaganda — kept the masses on their side and helped to carry the common people through the crisis.

Comparing the most revered American president of the twentieth century with its most evil dictator should raise some eyebrows; emphasizing similarities between them may well cause outrage. Garraty intends his comparison to be provocative, and he certainly succeeds. Do his parallels cynically equate democracy and dictatorship by suggesting that their results were essentially the same? Was Roosevelt's desire to preserve the American way of life the equivalent of Hitler's dreams of world conquest, or do policymakers' motives not matter?

*Is Garraty suggesting that the New Deal was a form of fascism or that Nazism had a pos-
itive side? Can Hitler's economic policies be separated from his destruction of democratic institutions or his extermination of German Jews? (Between 1933 and 1938, the Nazis
boycotted Jewish businesses, established anti-Jewish quotas in professions and schools,
forbade intermarriage between Jews and Gentiles, and built the first concentration camps,
although Hitler's order to exterminate the Jews was not given until 1941.)*

*However you answer these questions, it is hard to deny that Garraty's comparison un-
covers striking similarities between the two nations' anti-Depression policies. What does it
mean that industrial nations of various ideological stripes, from democracies to dictatorships,
adopted similar strategies during the Depression? Do economic laws limit modern policymakers to only a few options, or is a failure of imagination responsible? Do depressions
always lead to more authoritarian governments? Can economic prosperity be maintained
without military buildups and war? Garraty's essay is rooted in the context of the 1930s,
but it poses by implication questions that are crucial for the future as well as the past.*

GLOSSARY

AGRICULTURAL ADJUSTMENT ACT (AAA; 1933)   Part of President Roosevelt's
New Deal program, a law seeking to eliminate surplus farm production and maintain
crop prices. Farmers were paid to reduce crops or acreage voluntarily, the money coming from a tax on food processors. Key features of the AAA were declared unconstitutional by the Supreme Court in 1936.

BRÜNING, HEINRICH (1885–1970)   The leader of Germany's Catholic Center
Party who was appointed chancellor in 1930 and governed for two years without a parliamentary majority. Brüning's deflationary economic policies did not mitigate the
Depression and made him unpopular. When President Hindenburg was reelected in
1932, he replaced Brüning with the ineffective Franz von Papen, who helped to negotiate Hitler's appointment in 1933.

CARTELS   Organizations of producers who act in concert to fix prices, limit supply,
or divide markets. Cartels seek to maximize profits by preventing competition among
members, eliminating external competitors, and limiting production in times of over-
supply.

CORPORATISM   An economic philosophy stipulating that government-supervised
associations of employers and employees administer various sectors of the national
economy. Corporatism was adopted in modified form by fascist regimes in Europe during the Great Depression.

DEUTSCHE ARBEITSFRONT (GERMAN LABOR FRONT)   A Nazi organiza-
tion uniting employers and employees and claiming to represent all working Germans.
Formed in 1933 after the government abolished trade unions, the front was primarily a
propaganda instrument to integrate the German working class into the Nazi regime.

ERBHOF   A German landed estate of a specified size that could not be sold or mort-
gaged, but had to be bequeathed to particular heirs.

FAIR LABOR STANDARDS ACT (1938)   A New Deal law that established a minimum wage of twenty-five cents an hour and a maximum work week of forty-four
hours and forbade labor by children under sixteen. These provisions applied only to

workers engaged directly or indirectly in interstate commerce, and they exempted farm laborers and domestic servants. This was the first federal wages and hours law applying to nongovernment workers.

FARM SECURITY ADMINISTRATION (FSA)   A New Deal agency, established in 1937, that offered loans to farm tenants and laborers, regulated the wages and hours of migrant workers, and built model migrant camps and health clinics. Its Historical Section hired photographers such as Dorothea Lange and Walker Evans to document and publicize the plight of small farmers.

FASCISM   A political philosophy that glorifies the nation over the individual and encourages "benevolent" dictatorship. Its elements often include opposition to democratic and socialist movements, racist ideologies, aggressive military policy, and faith in an authoritarian leader who is said to embody the nation's ideals. The term was first used by the party of Benito Mussolini in Italy, and it also applied to right-wing movements such as National Socialism (Nazism) in Germany and the regime of Generalissimo Francisco Franco in Spain (1939–1975).

HITLER, ADOLF (1889–1945)   The leader of the National Socialist movement who became dictator of Germany. Born in Austria, Hitler won the Iron Cross for service in the Bavarian army during World War I. He was enraged by the Treaty of Versailles and blamed Germany's defeat on Jews and communists. In 1920 Hitler helped to found the National Socialist Party, and he was arrested after the "beer hall putsch," the Nazis' failed attempt to seize the Bavarian government in 1923. In prison Hitler wrote *Mein Kampf* (My Struggle), which publicized his ideas of racial purity, his amoral worship of power, and his vision of German domination of the world. The Great Depression brought Hitler mass support. President Hindenburg named him chancellor in 1933, and the Reichstag (the German parliament) gave him dictatorial powers. After 1933 Hitler as "Führer" (leader) consolidated his political control, persecuted German Jews and others, and began building the economic and military machine that in 1939 would invade Poland to begin World War II.

KEYNES, JOHN MAYNARD (1883–1946)   An English economist whose theories departed from classical laissez-faire doctrines by advocating government intervention in the market. Keynes argued that during depressions, government spending and easier monetary policies would raise the employment level and stimulate business recovery. His theories influenced Western governments during the Great Depression and especially after World War II.

KRAFT DURCH FREUDE (STRENGTH THROUGH JOY, KDF)   Founded in 1933 as the recreational organization of the German Labor Front. The KdF helped finance workers' vacations and provided other cultural benefits.

MUSSOLINI, BENITO (1883–1945)   The leader of the Fascist movement who became dictator of Italy. Mussolini broke with the Socialist Party during World War I and became an aggressive nationalist. In the troubled postwar period, his Fascist Party preached forcible restoration of order and opposition to leftists. Once named premier in 1923, Mussolini transformed the government into a dictatorship. During the 1930s, he invaded Ethiopia and Albania and formed an alliance with Hitler, which eventually took Italy into World War II.

ROOSEVELT, FRANKLIN DELANO (1882–1945)   President of the United States during most of the Depression and World War II. Born into a wealthy New York family, Roosevelt became a Progressive Democrat who campaigned for Wilson, served as assistant secretary of the Navy, and ran as vice president when the Democrats lost to

Warren Harding in 1920. The next year he was stricken with polio and regained only partial use of his legs, but his energy was undiminished. In 1928 he was elected governor of New York, where he signed into law old age pensions, public works projects, and unemployment insurance. In 1932, in the depths of the Great Depression, American voters chose him over President Herbert Hoover. Within months, Roosevelt rushed through Congress a series of reform measures and new programs aimed at reviving the economy, which eventually became known as the New Deal.

TENNESSEE VALLEY AUTHORITY (TVA)   A government-owned corporation established by New Deal legislation in 1933 that built dams and power plants along the Tennessee River and provided electricity to nearby farms and villages. A celebrated example of government planning, the TVA coordinated regional development and undertook improvements in health and education as well as land use.

WAGNER LABOR RELATIONS ACT (1935)   A New Deal law that created a federal agency to supervise workers' elections and certify the winning union as a collective bargaining agent. Important sections of the law upheld employees' right to join a labor organization and to bargain collectively, and defined unfair labor practices that the courts could order stopped. This was the most important law putting the federal government's support behind labor unions.

WORKS PROGRESS ADMINISTRATION (WPA)   A New Deal program that funded extensive building and improvement projects to provide work for the unemployed. The WPA (1935–1943) constructed over one hundred thousand buildings, seventy-eight thousand bridges, and six hundred and fifty thousand miles of roads, and also provided work for actors, writers, and artists.

I n early 1933, the Great Depression was at its low point, and the worst-hit countries were Germany and the United States. In both nations, industrial production had plumbed the depths. Unemployment was in the area of 25 percent of the work force, somewhere between 13 and 16 million in America, 6 million or more in Germany. Both countries had experienced periods of poor or at best, uninspired, leadership. Herbert Hoover lacked both political skill and popular appeal. One biographer mentions his "inability to master the political techniques of leadership," and the *New York Times* columnist Arthur Krock, who admired Hoover and shared his political philosophy, spoke of his "awkwardness of manner and speech and lack of mass magnetism."

Like Hoover, the German chancellors in 1932 proved incapable of dealing with the deepening depression. Heinrich Brüning was too rigid to be a good politician and too reserved to win the affection of the public. . . .

Brüning's successor, Franz von Papen, was a political lightweight. When a friend said to General Kurt von Schleicher, who had recommended Papen to President Hindenburg,

Excerpts from "Roosevelt and Hitler: New Deal and Nazi Reactions to the Depression" in *The Great Depression,* copyright © by John Garraty, reprinted by permission of Harcourt, Inc.

that "Papen did not have much of a head," Schleicher replied with a smile, "He need not have, but he'll make a fine hat!" . . . As for Schleicher, who replaced Papen in December 1932, he was primarily a behind-the-scenes manipulator. He soon resigned.

On January 30, 1933, Adolf Hitler became chancellor, and on March 4, 1933, in the midst of a financial panic that had caused thousands of banks to close their doors, Franklin D. Roosevelt took the oath as president of the United States. Thus, barely a month apart, the two most powerful and effective depression leaders of the western world took office. Although it is possible to argue that the long-sought economic upturn had already begun, their rise marked, if it did not cause, the beginning of the end of the Great Depression. Their methods and their personalities had enormous effects, both on their own nations and on the rest of the world.

Although two more different people than Roosevelt and Hitler would be hard to imagine, at the time neither seemed particularly well suited for his position. Roosevelt had been born to wealth and social prominence. He had attended elite private schools (Groton, Harvard, Columbia Law). His political career, culminating in two terms as governor of New York, had been successful but not particularly brilliant. He was widely regarded as an intellectual lightweight; the political commentator Walter Lippmann, in a now-famous phrase, described Roosevelt in 1932 as "a pleasant man who, without any important qualifications for the office, would very much like to be President."

Roosevelt had only the sketchiest understanding of economics, and that outdated, as witness his referring to John Maynard Keynes as "a political economist," a term rarely used since the nineteenth century. That such a person could be elected president at a time when entrenched wealth was in disrepute and when everyone believed that solving complex economic problems was the nation's top priority is best explained by Hoover's inadequacies and the widespread public feeling that no matter what, it was time for a change in the White House and in Congress.

Hitler was the son of an Austrian customs official of modest means. He had been a poor student and lazy. He dropped out of school at the age of 14. Later he lounged around Vienna for five years, pretending to be studying art but mostly absorbing his ultranationalist, anti-Semitic ideas. He spoke a most uncultivated form of German, and of course with an Austrian accent — not the kind of speech that one would expect to appeal to German voters. After serving in the army in the Great War, Hitler became involved in reactionary political movements. His National Socialist Party was scorned by most decent Germans in the 1920s, both for its ideology and because of the rowdy, violent behavior of its members.

Yet despite all these apparent disadvantages, Hitler became the leader of a country whose citizens were supposed to have an exaggerated respect for hard work, education, high culture, and family lineage, and who had a reputation for orderliness and rigid obedience to the law.

For some reason, Roosevelt and Hitler were especially appealing to their social and economic opposites: Roosevelt to industrial workers, farmers, the unemployed, Hitler to hard-working shopkeepers and peasants and then (after he achieved power) to industrialists, large landowners, and the military.

These strange contradictions may not be significant. Probably any Democrat would have defeated Hoover in 1932, and what Hitler did after he became chancellor was accomplished without the formal consent (though not necessarily without the approval) of a majority of the German people. Yet the personal impact of Roosevelt and Hitler on the two societies in the depths of the depression was very large. Their policies aside, both exerted enormous psychological influence on the people.

Roosevelt's patrician concern for mass suffering, his charm, his calm confidence, his gaiety, even his rather cavalier approach to the problems of the day had an immediate effect on most Americans. Hitler's resentment of the rich and well born, while probably psychotic in origin, appealed powerfully to millions of Germans. His ruthless, terrifying determination, always teetering on the brink of hysteria, combined with the aura of encapsulated remoteness that he projected to paralyze his opponents and turn his supporters into toadies. He inspired awe among millions of ordinary Germans. Both the euphoria of the early days of Roosevelt's New Deal and the nationalistic fervor that swept over Germany in early 1933 made millions almost incapable of organized thought, let alone of judgment. . . .

The sweeping approval that Roosevelt and Hitler won on first taking office was due to a spontaneous public reaction based mostly on the hope that things would get better. But not entirely. Both Roosevelt and Hitler employed the latest technologies to dramatize themselves and to influence public opinion. When the Democratic convention nominated him in 1932, Roosevelt flew to Chicago in order to make his acceptance speech on the floor of the convention. Both the flying and the personal appearance before the delegates were unprecedented acts for a presidential nominee. Hitler pioneered in making whirlwind speaking tours. By using airplanes, he spoke at 21 different cities in a seven day period, 50 in two weeks on another occasion. Here is how the German historian Joachim Fest has described the effect: "Hitler descended like a saviour to the seething crowds of despairing people; on one day alone he would address several hundred thousands, sweeping them into a 'forward-thrusting hysteria,' as he called it himself. The collective feelings, the fascination of the vast mass, of which each individual could feel himself a part, gave people a sense of power which they had long lacked and which found fulfillment in Hitler's rhetoric in this atmosphere of rapturous emotion: extreme self-elevation was brought about by extreme self-surrender."

Roosevelt and Hitler were masters at speaking on radio, a skill that was still quite undeveloped by politicians in the early 1930s. Roosevelt specialized in low-key "fireside chats," Hitler in shrill harangues delivered before huge audiences. . . .

The depression-oriented policies of New Deal America and Nazi Germany also displayed many remarkable similarities. Both gave providing aid to the unemployed a top priority. Building on a program begun by Papen, the Nazis offered subsidies and tax rebates to private companies that hired new workers. They granted marriage loans to persuade women to leave the work force and to encourage consumer spending, and they launched a huge public works program that included numerous railroad and navigation projects, the building and repair of private homes, the construction of public buildings, and the *Motorisierung* [motorization] program that involved the design and construction of the autobahn [superhighway] network. Soon wits in Germany were saying that Hitler was going to put the unemployed to work painting the Black Forest white and laying linoleum on the Polish Corridor.

American work creation programs were relatively smaller — at no time were more than one-third of the unemployed enrolled. The programs were nonetheless impressive. Besides swiftly appropriating federal funds for direct relief for the jobless, in 1933 Congress set up a $3.3 billion program under which more than 4 million people were put to work. Somewhat later came the Works Progress Administration (WPA) and the Public Works Administration (PWA), which employed more millions building roads, schools, bridges, and similar public structures. . . .

. . . It is fashionable, and also accurate, to note the military aspect of Nazi public works policies, although in fact, the Nazis spent relatively little on arms before 1935. It is less fashionable, but equally correct, to point out that in the United States, PWA money — more than $824 million of it — went into armaments. The aircraft carriers *Yorktown* and *Enterprise,* four cruisers, many lesser warships, as well as more than a hundred army airplanes and about 50 military airports were built with these funds.

Another way that both regimes dealt with the jobless was by opening work camps; one of Roosevelt's first actions in March 1933 was to propose the creation of the Civilian Conservation Corps [CCC]. Unlike the German and American public works projects, these camps did not employ many idle industrial workers. They were not expected to have much stimulating effect on private business. Both used enrollees for forestry and similar projects to improve the countryside, and both were intended primarily to keep young men out of the overcrowded labor market. Roosevelt described work camps as a means of getting youth "off the city street corners." Hitler said they would keep young men from "rotting helplessly in the streets." In both countries, much was made of the beneficial social results of mixing thousands of young people from different walks of life in the camps, and of the generally enthusiastic response of youth to the camp experience.

Furthermore, both were organized on semimilitary lines, with the subsidiary purposes of improving the physical fitness of potential soldiers and stimulating public commitment to national service in the emergency. . . .

Army authorities soon concluded that six months in the CCC was worth a year's conventional military training, and the secretary of war, George Dern, said that running the camps had given the army the best practical experience in handling men that it had ever had. . . .

New Deal and Nazi attempts to stimulate industrial recovery also resembled each other. Despite the "Socialist" in National Socialist and the charge of American mossbacks [ultraconservatives] that Roosevelt was a "traitor to his class," neither administration sought to destroy the capitalist system. In both cases, there was at the start much jockeying for positions of influence between small producers and large, between manufacturers and merchants, between inflationists and deflationists, between planners, free enterprisers, and advocates of regulated competition.

In Germany the great financiers and the heads of cartels, most of them determinedly antidemocratic, demanded an authoritarian solution that would eliminate the influence of organized labor and increase their own control over the economy. Small operators, shopkeepers, and craftsmen wanted to reduce the power of bankers and to destroy not only the unions but the industrial monopolies and the chain stores. The tycoons sought to manipulate the Nazis, the others comprised the Nazis' most enthusiastic supporters, but Hitler and the party responded to pressure from both camps.

In the United States, most big-business interests had no open quarrel with the existing order. But because of the depression, by 1933 many were calling for suspension of the antitrust laws in order to end competitive price cutting. Other interests wanted to strengthen the antitrust laws. Still others favored some attempt at national economic planning. All clamored for the attention of the new administration.

The goals of these groups were contradictory, and neither Roosevelt nor Hitler tried very hard to resolve the differences. Roosevelt's method was to suggest that the contestants lock themselves in a room until they could work out a compromise. But Hitler, who freely admitted to being an economic naïf, was no more forceful. "I had to let the Party experiment," he later recalled in discussing the evolution of his industrial recovery program. "I had to give the people something to do. They all wanted to help. . . . Well, let them have a crack at it."

Out of the resulting confusion came two kinds of that conservative, essentially archaic concept of social and economic organization called corporatism. . . .

In Germany the concept of government-sponsored cartels that regulated output and prices had a long tradition. Before 1933, however, the existence of powerful trade unions precluded the possibility of an effective corporatist organization. Hitler's success changed that swiftly. The Nazis created a complex system of 13 "estates" governing all branches of industry. These estates were, in effect, compulsory cartels. Each was subdivided into regional organizations, and at least in theory, the whole system was controlled by the Nazi minister of economics.

In America the process did not go nearly so far. But the system of self-governing industrial codes established under the National Recovery Administration (NRA) was in the same pattern. No less an authority on corporatism than Benito Mussolini saw the relationship. "Your new plan for coordination of industry follows precisely the lines of our cooperation," he told an American reporter in June 1933, though elsewhere he pointed out that Roosevelt had refused to go to the root of the problem by setting up labor-management associations and labor courts and by outlawing strikes. . . .

Under the law, the code system was voluntary. Each industry was supposed to draft its own code, tailored to its particular needs. But when the codification progress bogged down, a generalized "blanket" code called "the President's Re-employment Agreement" was drafted. The blanket code exempted arrangements made by previously competing companies from the antitrust laws so that they could fix prices and limit output. It also provided for minimum wages and maximum hours of labor, and it supposedly guaranteed workers the right to form unions and bargain collectively.

Production controls to prevent gluts, limitation of entry of new companies to lessen competition, and price and wage manipulation were characteristics of industrial policy in both countries. So were the two governments' justifications of drastic and possibly illegal or unconstitutional changes in the way the economy functioned on the ground that a "national emergency" existed, and so were the enormous propaganda campaigns they mounted to win public support.

During the early stages, big-business interests dominated the new organizations and succeeded in imposing their views on government. In Germany the radical Nazi artisan socialists who wanted to smash the cartels and nationalize the banks, led by Gregor Strasser and Gottfried Feder, lost out to the bankers and industrialists, represented by the financier Hjalmar Schacht. In the United States, victory went to the large corporations in each industry, which dominated the NRA code authorities. . . .

But bewildering crosscurrents of interest and persistent factional rivalries hampered the functioning of corporatist organizations. In theory the system promised harmony and efficiency within industries. In practice it seldom provided either. It did not even pretend to solve interindustry problems, yet these were often more disturbing to government authorities. Under corporatism workers were supposed to share fairly in decision making and in profits resulting from the elimination of competition. In both countries, industrialists resisted allowing them to do so, with the consequence that the governments found themselves under pressure to enforce compliance. In America workers were a potent political force and vital to the New Deal coalition. German workers did not count as voters after 1933, but their cooperation and support remained essential to Nazi ambitions. Small businessmen also maintained a drumfire of complaint, and New Dealers and Nazis were sensitive to their pressure too. . . .

To the Nazis, corporatism seemed at first compatible with the political process called *Gleichschaltung,* or coordination. This was a process by which nearly every aspect of life was brought under the control of Hitler and the party. It quickly became apparent, however, that the autonomous character of any corporatist organization made precise control from above difficult. America, fortunately, was never *gleichgeschaltet.* But in any case, by 1935 and 1936, the Roosevelt and Hitler governments were abandoning corporatism and taking a more anti-big-business stance.

In America, after the Supreme Court declared NRA unconstitutional [in 1935], this meant the passage of the Wagner Labor Relations Act, a far more effective guarantee of the right of workers to unionize and bargain with their employees in good faith. A government board was created to supervise elections and empowered to issue cease-and-desist orders when employers engaged in unfair labor practices. The Public Utility Holding Company Act made the pyramiding of control of gas and electric corporations illegal and gave the government power to regulate utility rates. In addition, the Social Security Act of 1935, which provided for both old age and unemployment insurance, was financed in part by a tax paid by employers, and other taxes paid by corporations were raised.

In Germany, although the cartel structure was retained, the Nazis limited the size of corporate dividends. The government constructed and operated steel, automobile, and certain other facilities in competition with private enterprise and imposed higher taxes on private incomes and corporate profits. As in the United States, but to a much greater degree, freedom of managerial decision making was curtailed.

After 1935 the increasing emphasis of the Nazis on preparing for war had much to do with the new restrictions on private business interests. They placed strict controls on imports in order to conserve the foreign exchange needed to buy raw materials used in the manufacture of munitions and other military necessities. These controls put nearly all industries at the mercy of the regime, whether they were making military or civilian goods. Under the Four-Year Plan of 1936, Hitler made Air Marshall Hermann Göring a kind of economic czar. The government undertook the manufacture of synthetic oil and rubber as well as steel and motor vehicles. Some businessmen earned profits from this activity, but their influence shrank, and their freedom of action disappeared. . . .

This kind of ruthless subordination of economic interests did not occur in the United States. Nevertheless, when military considerations began to dominate American policy after 1939, Roosevelt was also prepared to substitute guns for butter. One need only mention his famous announcement that he was replacing "Dr. New Deal" with "Dr. Win the War" as his prime consultant. . . .

New Deal and Nazi labor policies were also shaped by the Great Depression in related ways. On the surface, this statement may seem not merely wrong but perverse, but only if one identifies labor with unions. Hitler destroyed the German unions and forced all workers into the *Deutsche Arbeitsfront* (German Labor Front) controlled by the Reich Trustee (another euphemism) for Labor. It is also true that Roosevelt, in part unwittingly, and with some reluctance, enabled American unions to increase their membership and influence enormously.

However, New Deal and Nazi policies toward unions had little to do directly with the depression, and they do not throw much light on national policies toward workers. Hitler would no doubt have destroyed the German unions as autonomous organizations in any case — he destroyed all autonomous institutions in Germany. But it was because they were anti-Nazi that he smashed the unions so quickly. Roosevelt was at first indifferent to the fate of organized labor. He encouraged the American unions in order to gain labor's support, not because he thought doing so would speed economic recovery. In each instance the decision was essentially political.

The important New Deal labor legislation, especially the Social Security Act of 1935 and the Fair Labor Standards Act of 1940, benefited *workers,* not merely those who happened to belong to unions. Although the immediate effects of these laws were not dramatic, in the long run, they had an enormous impact. It is also possible to demonstrate Nazi concern for industrial workers. The "battle against unemployment" had first priority in Germany in 1933, and it was won remarkably swiftly. By 1936 something approaching full employment existed. Soon thereafter an acute shortage of labor developed. Of course the military draft siphoned thousands of men out of the German labor market. But this was also true in the United States after 1940. Full employment was never approached in America until the economy was shifted to all-out war production. . . .

. . . Nazi ideology (and Hitler's prejudices) inclined the regime to favor the ordinary German over any elite group. Workers — as distinct from "Marxist" members of unions — had an honored place in the system. . . . The Nazis created what were called Courts of Social Honor. These courts may be compared with the New Deal National Labor Relations Board. They did not alter power relationships between capital and labor the way the National Labor Relations Board did in the United States; they represented the interests of the Nazi party rather than those of labor. But they did adjudicate disputes between workers and bosses, and there is considerable evidence that the Courts of Social Honor tended more often than not to favor workers in these disputes. Furthermore, the very existence of the courts put considerable psychological pressure on employers to treat labor well. . . .

It is beyond argument that the Nazis encouraged working-class social and economic mobility. They eased entry into the skilled trades by reducing the educational requirements for many jobs and by expanding vocational training. They offered large rewards and further advancement to efficient workers. In the *Kraft durch Freude* (KdF) Strength Through Joy movement, they provided extensive fringe benefits, such as subsidized housing, low-cost excursions, sports programs, and more pleasant factory facilities. It was under Hitler that the famous Volkswagen ("the Bug") was developed as part of the *Motorisierung* policy. The name of course means "people's automobile." . . . In a speech at the Berlin Motor Show in 1934, Hitler promised that besides "giving bread and work to thousands of men," *Motorisierung* would "offer ever greater masses of our people the opportunity to acquire this most modern means of transport."

Eventually the Nazi stress on preparation for war meant harder work, a decline in both the quantity and quality of consumer goods, and the loss of freedom of movement for German workers. But because of the need to win and hold the loyalty of labor, the hierarchy imposed these restrictions and hardships only belatedly and with great reluctance. If the question is: "Did the Nazi system give workers more power?" the answer is that it did not. But that question, albeit important, has little to do with the economic position of workers or with the effectiveness of the Nazi system in ending the depression.

New Deal and Nazi methods of dealing with the agricultural depression also had much in common. Both sought to organize commercial agriculture in order to increase farm income. The New Deal Agricultural Adjustment Act set up supposedly democratic county committees to control production. In Germany the centralized Estate for Agriculture (*Reichnäherstand*) did the job. The purpose was to raise agricultural prices and thus farm income through a system of subsidies, paid for in each instance by processing taxes that fell ultimately on consumers. Both governments also made agricultural credit cheaper and more readily available, and they protected farmers against the loss of their land through foreclosures.

These similarities are not remarkable. . . . Under the impact of the depression, farmers everywhere, large and small alike, were expressing the same resentments and demands and . . . these affected governments in related ways. What *is* remarkable, given the profound differences between American and German agriculture, is the attitude of the two governments toward the place of farmers in society.

Both Roosevelt and Hitler tended to idealize rural life and the virtues of an agricultural existence. Each hoped to check the trend of population to the cities and to disperse urban-centered industries. Roosevelt spoke feelingly of the virtues of close contact with nature and of the "restful privilege of getting away from pavements and from noise." Only in the country, he claimed, did a family have a decent chance "to establish a real home in the traditional American sense." Roosevelt did not deny the attractions of city life. He reasoned that electricity, the automobile, and other modern conveniences made it possible for rural people to enjoy these attractions without abandoning their farms. . . .

Because they were property owners, had large families, and were, in general, good Nazis, Hitler called the German peasants "the foundation and life source" of the state, "the counterbalance to communist madness," and "the source of national fertility." The superiority of rural over urban life was a Nazi dogma — especially the life of the self-sufficient small farmer, free from the dependency and corruption of a market economy. "The fact that a people is in a position to nourish itself from its own land and through that to lead its own life independent of foreign nations has always in history been significant," a Nazi agricultural expert wrote in 1935. To make sure that the peasants remained as they were, a law of 1933 (the *Erbhofgesetz*) forbade the sale or mortgaging of farms of a size "necessary to support a family . . . independent of the market and the general economic situation." About a third of the farms in Germany were thus entailed. As the historian J. E. Farquharson notes, this law, along with Nazi agricultural price supports, made the possessor of an *Erbhof* a member of "a privileged class, sheltered from all the worst effects of free market forces."

Nazi leaders described Berlin as a den of iniquity and deplored the influx of Germans from the east into the capital. Nazi housing policy sought to stimulate suburban development in order to bring industrial workers closer to the land and to reduce urban crowding. They placed all construction under government control and made funds available for low-interest, state-guaranteed mortgage loans.

The New Deal Tennessee Valley Authority and the rural electrification program made important progress toward improving farm life, but efforts to reverse the population trend in the United States yielded limited results. Despite Roosevelt's dreams of decentralizing industry and relocating millions of city dwellers on farms, during the whole of the New Deal, his Resettlement Administration placed fewer than 11,000 families on the land. The Resettlement Administration had a Greenbelt Town program for planned suburban development. It produced minuscule results. . . . [O]nly three of the 60 originally planned greenbelt towns were built.

Nazi rural resettlement efforts proved equally disappointing. Between 1933 and 1938, the Nazis resettled about 20,000 families, but this was barely more than half the number that the Weimar government had managed to relocate between 1927 and 1932. In both the German and American cases, efforts to check the movement of the people to the cities foundered on the opposition of real estate and construction interests. The unwillingness of the politicians to allocate sufficient funds to enable much progress to be made was another reason for the failure of rural resettlement. . . .

There were significant differences between the objectives of American and National Socialist agricultural policies: the former, plagued by surpluses, sought to limit output; the latter, seeking to become self-sufficient, sought to increase it. All in all, the New Deal was the more successful in solving farm problems; far less was accomplished in Germany toward modernizing and mechanizing agriculture during the thirties. On the other hand, Nazi efforts on behalf of farm laborers were more effective than those of the New Deal. As is well known, the AAA programs actually hurt many American agricultural laborers and also tenants and sharecroppers. In both nations, agricultural relief brought far more benefits to large land owners than to small. . . .

There is still another way in which New Deal and Nazi practices were similar, and different in degree from those of other industrial nations. This was in the way the two governments tried to influence public opinion. The Nazi use of parades, banners, rallies, and of every instrument of propaganda are well known. During the New Deal, the American government never went so far, but it did make efforts to sell its policies to the public that were unprecedented in peacetime. The NRA slogan "We Do Our Part" served the same function as the Nazis' incessantly repeated *Gemeinnutz geht vor Eigennutz* (the public interest before the individual's interest). With Roosevelt's approval, General Hugh Johnson, head of NRA and designer of its Blue Eagle symbol, organized a massive campaign to muster support for the NRA. Like the Nazi swastika in the Reich, the Blue Eagle was plastered everywhere — on billboards, in shop windows, even on cans of beans and applesauce. Johnson's office blanketed the land with posters, lapel buttons, and stickers. . . .

This was the positive side of the NRA campaign. There was also a negative side. "Those who are not with us are against us," Johnson orated. "The way to show that you are part of this great army of the New Deal is to insist on this symbol of solidarity." He denounced opponents of NRA as "chiselers" and "slackers," thereby suggesting that disagreement was equivalent to criminality and cowardice. President Roosevelt himself, in a fireside chat, compared the Blue Eagle to a "bright badge" worn by soldiers in night attacks to help separate friend from foe.

Placed beside the overpowering Nazi displays at Nuremburg, even the ten-hour, 250,000-person NRA parade up Fifth Avenue in September 1933 would not appear especially impressive. But it and other NRA hoopla were designed to serve the same functions: rousing patriotic feelings and creating in the public mind the impression of support for government policies so extensive as to make disagreement appear unpatriotic. As Johnson himself explained, the purpose was to "put the enforcement of this law into the hands of the *whole* people."

Another example of New Deal propaganda is provided by the efforts of the Resettlement Administration and the Farm Security Administration. Pare Lorenz's documentary films, *The Plow That Broke the Plains* (1936) and *The River* (1938), and the still photographs of sharecroppers taken by Dorothea Lange, Walker Evans, Margaret Bourke-White, Gordon Parks, and others were aesthetic achievements of the highest order. They were also a form of official advertising designed to explain and defend the New Deal approach to rural social and economic problems. They differed from Leni Riefenstahl's *Triumph of the Will* (also a cinematic masterpiece) and the annual volumes of photographs celebrating National Socialism chiefly in style — "soft" rather than "hard" sell — and point of view.

New Deal efforts at mass persuasion reflect the attitude of Roosevelt's government — an attitude shared by Hitler's government — that the economic crisis justified the casting aside of precedent, the nationalistic mobilization of society, and the removal of traditional restraints on the functions of the state, as in war. The two regimes also agreed that the crisis called for personal leadership more forceful than that needed in normal times. That all these attitudes were typical of Hitler goes without saying, but Roosevelt held them too. When we think of Roosevelt's first inaugural nowadays, we tend to re-member his fatherly reassurance, "the only thing we have to fear is fear itself." But he also said:

> Our true destiny is not to be ministered unto but to minister to ourselves. . . . I assume un-hesitatingly the leadership of this great army of our people. . . . In the event that the Congress shall fail . . . I shall ask the Congress for the one remaining instrument to meet the crisis — broad Executive power to wage a war against the emergency, as great as the power that would be given to me if we were in fact invaded by a foreign foe.

This last sentence evoked the loudest cheering that Roosevelt's speech produced. Eleanor Roosevelt found the response "a little terrifying." Commenting on it later, she said, "You felt that they would do *anything* — if only someone would tell them *what* to do."

Roosevelt was neither a totalitarian nor a dictator, real or potential, but his tactics and his rhetoric made it possible for anti–New Dealers and outright fascists to claim that he was both. Many of the accusations of both conservatives and communists in the United States were politically motivated, as were, of course, Nazi comments on the president. But during the first years of the New Deal German newspapers praised him and the New Deal to the skies. Before Hitler came to power, he was contemptuous of the United States, which he considered an overly materialistic nation dominated by Jews, "millionaires, beauty queens, stupid [phonograph] records, and Hollywood."

Nevertheless, Hitler and the Nazi party hierarchy were impressed by Roosevelt's suc-cess during the Hundred Days in dominating Congress and pushing through the New Deal depression policies so swiftly. "Mr. Roosevelt . . . marches straight toward his ob-jective over Congress, over lobbies, over stubborn bureaucracies," Hitler told Anne O'Hare McCormick of the *New York Times* in July 1933. The *Völkischer Beobachter* [*People's Observer*, the official Nazi newspaper] announced smugly that Roosevelt's lead-ership proved that representative government, which the paper described as "govern-ment without a head," had "outlived its usefulness generally, not only in Germany." By July 1934, that newspaper was describing Roosevelt as "absolute lord and master" of the nation, his position "not entirely dissimilar" to a dictator's. Roosevelt's collected speeches, *Looking Forward* (1933) and *On Our Way* (1934) were translated into German and enthusiastically reviewed, the critics being quick to draw attention to parallels in New Deal and National Socialist experiences. . . .

At the end of Roosevelt's first year in office, Hitler sent him a private message through diplomatic channels offering sincere congratulations for "his heroic efforts in the interests of the American people. The President's successful battle against economic distress is being followed by the entire German people with interest and admiration," Hitler claimed. . . .

This friendly attitude ended in 1936, although even after Roosevelt made his famous speech denouncing the dictators and calling for a "quarantine" of Germany and Italy, the Nazi propaganda machine refrained for tactical reasons from attacking him person-ally. It is clear, however, that New Deal depression policies seemed to the Nazis essen-tially like their own and the role of Roosevelt not very different from the Führer's.

So far as the Great Depression is concerned, Roosevelt and Hitler, the one essentially benign, the other malevolent, justified far-reaching constitutional changes as being necessary for the improvement of economic conditions in a grave emergency. But they used change also as a device for mobilizing the psychic energies of the people. Both their administrations were plagued by infighting and confusion, partly because of genuine conflicts of interest and philosophy within the two diverse societies and partly because of ignorance. No one really knew how to end the depression or even how best to serve the different interests that the governments presumed to represent. Time after time, major American and German policies produced results neither anticipated nor desired. Some of them were directly contrary to the leaders' intentions — the effect of New Deal farm policy on sharecroppers and of its public housing policy on racial segregation, and that of Nazi rearmament on urban concentration, for example.

Hitler papered over confusion, doubts, and rivalries with the *Führerprinzip*, command from above, unquestioning obedience to one's leader, who was presumed to know what was best. Roosevelt, on the other hand, made a virtue of flexibility and experimentation. Both, however, masterfully disguised the inadequacies and internal disagreements in their entourages and to a remarkable extent succeeded in convincing ordinary citizens of their own personal wisdom and dedication.

The differences in the degree and intensity with which psychological pressures were applied by Nazis and New Dealers were so great as to become differences in kind. Nevertheless, the two movements reacted to the depression in similar ways, distinct from those of other industrial nations. Of the two, the Nazis were the more successful in curing the economic ills of the 1930s. They reduced unemployment and stimulated industrial production faster than the Americans did. Considering their resources, they handled their monetary and trade problems more successfully, certainly more imaginatively. By 1936 the depression was substantially over in Germany but far from finished in the United States.

This was partly because the Nazis employed deficit financing on a larger scale. Between 1933 and 1939 the German national debt nearly quadrupled, the American rose by less than 50 percent. It was also partly because the Nazi totalitarian system better lent itself to the mobilization of society, both by force and by persuasion. There was no German parallel to the combination of timorousness and stubborn resistance to change characteristic of American business interests. Unlike the New Dealers, the economist H. W. Arndt wrote while Hitler was still in power,

> the Nazi Government . . . was not hampered in its expansionist policy by "low business confidence." . . . German business which, rightly or wrongly, had thought itself threatened by imminent social revolution, breathed again under a government which . . . appeared as the saviour and benefactor of private property. . . . During the later years of the Nazi régime when profit expectations of a good many business men must have been low, State control of investment insured that private investment absorbed what factors of production and savings were not required by the demands of the State.

Yet neither regime solved the problem of maintaining prosperity without war. The German leaders wanted war and used the economy to make war possible. One result was "prosperity": full employment, increased output, hectic economic expansion. The Americans lacked this motivation. But when war was forced upon them, they took the same approach and achieved the same result.

QUESTIONS TO CONSIDER

1. What similarities does Garraty find between Roosevelt's and Hitler's economic strategies against the Depression? Describe each leader's public works programs, "corporatist" pacts with industry, and farm policies. How did Hitler and Roosevelt deal with workers and labor unions? Are there important differences in their programs that Garraty minimizes or neglects?

2. How did Roosevelt's and Hitler's personal qualities contribute to their success? Why were both able to exert tremendous psychological influence on the masses? What similarities and differences do you see in their personalities, propaganda skill and techniques, and constituencies?

3. Kate Brown, author of Selection 4, warns that "comparisons . . . can be misleading." Is it misleading to compare Roosevelt and Hitler? Is Garraty suggesting that the New Deal was a form of fascism? Does Garraty contend that Nazism had positive effects in Germany? Why do you think he omits Hitler's persecution of the Jews? Can Hitler's economic policies be separated from his destruction of democracy or his attacks on Jews? What view would Eric Hobsbawm (Selection 15) take of Garraty's parallels between Roosevelt and Hitler?

4. In what ways, if any, does Garraty's account of Roosevelt and his New Deal help to explain why the United States had no change of government or drastic social upheaval during the 1930s? Does the evidence support the claim often made that Roosevelt "saved American capitalism"?

5. On the basis of Garraty's comparison of Roosevelt and Hitler as well as Eric Hobsbawm's international survey in Selection 15, what generalizations can you make about the impact of depressions on a nation's political climate? Why do depressions tend to produce authoritarian leaders and expanded national government? How are war and economic depression related to each other?

WORLD WAR II

The war that began in Europe in 1939 and reached America at the end of 1941 proved a decisive turning point for the United States and indeed for the whole world. Mobilization for war ended the Great Depression here and abroad. Allied success on the battlefield, with its ghastly toll of casualties, saved the West (but not six million Jews) from Nazi dreams of racial purity and world conquest. There were other, less welcome changes for Americans. The global scale of the conflict banished perhaps for good the dream of American isolationism. As historian Otto Friedrich has written, World War II "changed Americans from a nation of provincial innocents . . . ignorant of the great world . . . into a nation that would often have to bear the burdens of rescuing that world." The aftermath of war brought the collapse of all overseas Western empires, a cold war between communist and noncommunist nations, and, finally, the arrival of Japan at the world's economic and political center.

The essays in this chapter relate to two of these changes: the end of American isolationism and the emergence of American rivalry with Japan. They use comparative perspectives to tell the two-sided story of America's relations with its chief ally and with a major enemy. In the first selection, David Dimbleby and David Reynolds show how America's Franklin Roosevelt and Britain's Winston Churchill put aside Anglo-American disputes and prejudices to forge an alliance that committed the United States not only to join the war effort, but also to take up Britain's role as world policeman after the war. In the second essay, John W. Dower analyzes the imagery of mutual hatred that pervaded American and Japanese propaganda during the war. The sharp contrast between Anglo-American cooperation and Japanese-American enmity displays the range of (in Winston Churchill's words) unsordid and sordid acts that war calls forth from its participants. Fortunately, Japan's postwar surge would involve a generally friendly political partnership and an intense but peaceful economic rivalry with the United States.

17

An Ocean Apart:
The Anglo-American Relationship
on the Eve of War

DAVID DIMBLEBY AND DAVID REYNOLDS

During the 1930s, Adolf Hitler repudiated the Treaty of Versailles and boldly reasserted Germany's military power. The Nazi leader took Germany out of the League of Nations; formed an alliance with Italy's fascist dictator, Benito Mussolini; and began a series of territorial seizures that culminated with the invasion of Poland in 1939, which plunged Europe into war. Throughout these events the United States stood on the sidelines, and President Roosevelt declared the nation neutral at the outset of World War II. But after France fell to the German onslaught in June 1940, Roosevelt resolved to save England at all costs. Isolationists in Congress had passed Neutrality Acts in the mid-1930s that restricted American trade with belligerents. Now Roosevelt convinced Congress to permit the sale of arms to England on a "cash-and-carry" basis. He arranged to transfer fifty destroyers to Great Britain in exchange for long-term leases on several British bases in the Americas. And after overcoming strong isolationist resistance, Congress passed Roosevelt's Lend-Lease bill in 1941, which gave billions of dollars of military aid to Britain and the Soviet Union, which Hitler invaded in June 1941. That summer, American destroyers began escorting British convoys most of the way across the Atlantic, and navy ships approached Ireland to track German submarines for the British. It was only a matter of time before a showdown in the Atlantic would bring the United States into war with Germany. When the Japanese launched a surprise attack on Pearl Harbor in December, the United States was drawn abruptly into a war it was already entering step by step on the other side of the globe.

In this excerpt from An Ocean Apart *(1988), their book derived from the BBC television series of the same name, David Dimbleby and David Reynolds narrate the story of America's gradual entry into the European theater of World War II. Their special contribution is to analyze events from the viewpoints of both American and British policymakers. It is a truism that all stories have at least two sides. This seems especially true for international affairs, where major events can be understood best by examining the aims and actions of all the nations involved, not just the United States. Using their dual-perspective approach as a narrative device as well as a comparative tool, Dimbleby and Reynolds alternate between the United States, where President Roosevelt trod a difficult path between isolation and intervention, and Great Britain, whose Prime Minister Winston Churchill tried desperately to bring Roosevelt into a military alliance against Hitler.*

Dimbleby and Reynolds's narrative is enlivened by colorful anecdotes and stories from television interviews. Especially impressive is their sympathetic attempt to understand the world views of both the isolationists and the interventionists. But they never lose sight of their central question: how did the leaders of two Western democracies put aside their prejudices, surmount their domestic political obstacles, and negotiate their conflicting national interests in order to fight together against Hitler's Germany? Instead of indulging in hindsight to reprimand British and American policymakers for allowing the dictators of the 1930s to bully Europe for so long, their account looks through the eyes of the participants. It shows the Western leaders' hopes that Hitler could be stopped short of war, the constraints that made their cooperation difficult, and how Roosevelt and Churchill managed in the end to overcome them.

GLOSSARY

ARYANS Prehistoric peoples of Iran and northern India from whom the Indo-European languages are descended. Nazi doctrine asserted the superiority of the "Aryan race" over all others and regarded the Nordic, or Germanic, peoples as the purest Aryans. This spurious anthropology was used to justify the German government's policy of exterminating Jews, Gypsies, and other "non-Aryans."

ATLANTIC CHARTER A statement of common principles issued in August 1941 by President Roosevelt and Prime Minister Churchill. It became the unofficial list of American and British aims in World War II and the ensuing peace. It named eight goals, including renunciation of territorial aggression, no territorial changes without the consent of the people involved, the restoration of self-government to conquered peoples, freedom of the seas, and world economic cooperation.

BULL, JOHN The personification of England, a portly character often portrayed in cartoons but introduced in satirical political pamphlets written by John Arbuthnot in 1712.

CHAMBERLAIN, NEVILLE (1869–1940) The Conservative chancellor of the exchequer who became Britain's prime minister in 1937. Hoping to avoid a military showdown and believing that Hitler was a rational statesman, Chamberlain pursued a policy of "appeasement" that culminated in the Munich Pact of 1938, which ceded part of Czechoslovakia to Germany. He remained in office after World War II broke out, but resigned in 1940 following the British retreat from Norway.

CHURCHILL, WINSTON (1874–1965) A prominent British statesman and wartime leader. Churchill fought in British imperialist campaigns in India, Sudan, and South Africa before being elected to Parliament in 1900. He served in several cabinet positions in the Liberal government of Lloyd George and supported domestic reforms. Switching to the Conservative Party after 1924, Churchill served as a cabinet member in the late 1920s but was out of office from 1929 to 1939 and a vocal critic of his party's appeasement policy. In May 1940 he replaced Neville Chamberlain as prime minister and rallied the British military and public to eventual victory over Germany.

EDEN, ANTHONY (1895–1977)   A Conservative Party leader and veteran of foreign affairs. Eden served as Britain's foreign minister three times, including from 1935 to 1938, when he resigned to protest Prime Minister Neville Chamberlain's appeasement of Nazi expansionism, and 1940 to 1945, when he was a leading member of Churchill's war cabinet.

FOURTEEN POINTS   President Woodrow Wilson's formula for postwar peace, announced in January 1918 following U.S. entry into World War I. They included open international agreements, freedom of the seas, free trade, arms reduction, and self-determination of peoples. The fourteenth point, the heart of the plan, called for an international organization, the League of Nations, to keep the peace through arbitration and sanctions. Several points were compromised or omitted in the Treaty of Versailles (1919), but the signers agreed to Wilson's League.

FRANCO, FRANCISCO (1892–1975)   The Spanish general and head of the fascist Falange Party who led a Nationalist rebellion against the republic in 1936. With help from Hitler and Mussolini, he won the Spanish Civil War in 1939, ruthlessly punished his Republican opponents, and set up a dictatorship. Franco kept Spain neutral in World War II and retained power until his death.

LINDBERGH, CHARLES A. (1902–1974)   An American aviator who in 1927 made the first solo, nonstop transatlantic flight and became a national hero. In 1938–1939 he was a prominent spokesman for America First, which advocated strict American neutrality in the European war. Branded as a Nazi sympathizer, he resigned from the service, but later he flew combat missions in the Pacific against Japan.

MUNICH PACT   An 1938 agreement signed by Germany, Great Britain, France, and Italy that surrendered the Sudetenland (nearly half of Czechoslovakia) to Germany in return for Hitler's pledge to demand no more territories. The pact culminated British prime minister Neville Chamberlain's policy of appeasement. Although it won public approval in Britain and the United States at the time, the pact soon was regarded as a fatal concession that only encouraged Hitler's appetite for world conquest.

MUSSOLINI, BENITO (1883–1945)   Leader of the Fascist movement in Italy. Mussolini broke with the Socialist Party during World War I and became an aggressive nationalist. In the troubled postwar period, his Fascist Party preached forcible restoration of order and opposition to leftists. Once named premier in 1923, Mussolini transformed the government into a dictatorship. During the 1930s, he invaded Ethiopia and Albania and formed an alliance with Hitler, which eventually took Italy into World War II.

NEUTRALITY ACT OF 1935   An American law designed to keep the United States out of a possible European war by banning shipment of war materiel to belligerents and forbidding American citizens to travel on belligerent vessels, except at their own risk.

TORY   A member of the Conservative (formerly the Tory) Party in Britain, which dominated British politics in the 1920s and 1930s under the ministries of Stanley Baldwin and Neville Chamberlain. Conservatives generally defended social and ecclesiastical privileges, sought to preserve the British Empire, and (until 1939) pursued a policy of appeasement toward Hitler.

★ ★ ★ ★ ★ ★

It is a commonplace that if Britain and America had stood up to the dictators in the 1930s the Second World War would never have happened. Winston Churchill dubbed it "the unnecessary war," and the first volume of his war memoirs took as its theme "how the English-speaking peoples, through their unwisdom, carelessness and good nature, allowed the wicked to rearm." With hindsight it is easy to castigate the leaders of both countries for their blindness to the dangers that threatened them and for a complacency that at times seems almost supine. It is harder to step back, to see the threats as they saw them at the time, and to understand the constraints that made effective Anglo-American cooperation so difficult.

By the early 1930s the world economy had collapsed into depression, and threats to peace were already apparent. In 1931 an expansionist Japan had taken Manchuria on the Asian mainland from China, with only ineffectual protest from the League of Nations. After Hitler came to power in January 1933, he rapidly rearmed Germany and planned a vast Aryan empire in Europe and beyond. The Italian dictator Mussolini, emboldened by Hitler's success, invaded Ethiopia virtually unchallenged in 1935, and from 1936 both dictators intervened on the side of Franco and the fascists in the Spanish Civil War.

Britain and America watched these events from the sidelines. Both countries were preoccupied with recovery from the depression. Both were inhibited by a popular backlash against the slaughter of the Great War [World War I]. They both shared a suspicion of the motives of the armaments industry and a reluctance to become entangled again in the continent of Europe. Rearmament was therefore slow, diplomacy hesitant and indecisive.

President Franklin D. Roosevelt, who succeeded Herbert Hoover in 1933, wanted to break the isolationist mold. Although he had lost faith in the League of Nations, which he had originally supported when a junior member of the Wilson administration, Roosevelt still believed that the United States should use its influence in the cause of world peace. That was not only a moral duty, he believed, but also a matter of self-interest. In 1937 he compared war to an infectious disease whose spread could be prevented only by putting the aggressors in "quarantine" through diplomatic isolation or economic sanctions.

Practical politics, however, made it difficult to implement any such remedies. The Congress was isolationist by conviction, not wanting to involve America in another war or even to take action entailing the risk of war. The Neutrality Act of 1935 was designed to prevent the economic entanglements of trade and loans that had helped drag America into the Great War. Roosevelt himself shared these anxieties. "I have seen war. . . . I hate war," he insisted in 1936. He was also acutely sensitive to political realities, having watched the disintegration of Wilson's policies in the confrontation with the Senate in 1919. For Roosevelt, diplomacy had to be tailored to the public mood. His political posture was cruelly caricatured by Congresswoman Clare Boothe Luce as an index finger wetted and held up in the air.

In the 1930s it was understandable for Americans to display little interest in world affairs. Three thousand miles of Atlantic Ocean seemed ample protection against Hitler's Germany, and the expansion of Italy or Japan was of limited concern to a country with few overseas possessions and little dependence on foreign trade. Britain, however, could not afford to take such a detached view. The English Channel, her moat in the past, was no barrier to the growing German air force, and British power and wealth depended on the survival of the empire and the protection of vulnerable trade routes. The First Sea Lord Admiral Chatfield summed up British thinking in 1934: "We are in the remarkable position of not wanting to quarrel with anybody because we have got most of the world already, or the best parts of it, and we only want to keep what we have got and prevent others from taking it away from us."

Britain therefore had to maintain a delicate balance. Her interests lay in preventing not just renewed war but also the further erosion of her power. She wanted peace, but not at any price. The problem was that she lacked the means for a firm policy that would deter worldwide aggression. Rearmament was not popular with the British electorate, nor with the Treasury, which feared that it would damage economic recovery and so undermine foreign confidence in sterling [British currency]. In particular Britain's Navy, the main instrument for protecting her trade and empire, was inadequate for her responsibilities, after the reductions of the 1920s and successive arms control agreements. . . .

Since a policy of deterrence seemed impossible, British leaders adopted a policy of appeasement. The attempt to buy off potential foes, often denigrated as shortsighted and even cowardly, was really a calculated gamble by Britain to negotiate her way out of danger. The aim was to reduce the number of enemies by satisfying their grievances in return for guarantees of peace and disarmament. Appeasement was the policy of the Tory-dominated National Government throughout the 1930s, but it was adopted with particular enthusiasm by Neville Chamberlain, who became prime minister in May 1937.

Chamberlain effectively seized control of foreign policy, trying to reach personal agreements with Hitler and Mussolini. He and most of his colleagues underestimated Hitler's long-term ambitions and exaggerated Germany's immediate military strength. Fearful of being plunged into a war on three fronts simultaneously, they were unwilling to risk calling Germany's bluff, or Italy's or Japan's. Chamberlain was also pessimistic about the chances of significant help. The British Dominions were isolationist, France was in turmoil, and Russia was engulfed in Stalin's bloody purges. Like most of his colleagues, Chamberlain was particularly skeptical about the United States after the bitter experiences of the 1920s and early 1930s. "It is always best and safest," he once observed, "to count on *nothing* from the Americans except words."

As the crisis worsened Roosevelt wanted to reinforce Britain's efforts to reduce international tension, but his plans were often frustrated by rifts between the two governments.

Trade was a major issue. America was becoming increasingly irritated by British discrimination against U.S. products. In 1937, 16 percent of all the goods America exported went to Britain, making her America's most valuable trading partner, but their importance to Britain, who was expanding her trade with the empire, was declining. By 1937 only 11 percent of British imports came from America, whereas 39 percent came from the empire. Roosevelt's secretary of state, Cordell Hull, was alarmed at the effects of this trend on American farmers and manufacturers. He put the blame on Britain's policy of Imperial Preference, which imposed lower tariffs on imports from the empire than on those from other nations. Hull felt the discrimination was unfair and was convinced that trade barriers and economic nationalism were the root causes of war. The British took a different view. Building up the empire's trade seemed the best way out of the depression, and they were not willing to reduce Imperial Preferences until America offered drastic cuts in its own tariffs. Negotiations on lowering trade barriers between the two dragged on from 1934 to 1938.

The political damage of this stalemate was considerable. It became a State Department axiom that there could be no cooperation on other matters with Britain until a trade agreement had been reached. "At present," a senior U.S. diplomat complained in 1936, "she [Britain] thinks she can count on our help politically and yet hit us below the belt commercially all over the world."

The lack of cooperation was particularly apparent in East Asia. In 1937 Japan, encouraged by the lack of any effective reaction to her invasion of Manchuria, once again attacked China in violation of the 1922 treaty. Instead of coordinating their actions against Japan, Britain and America acted independently and ineffectually. . . .

Early in 1938 Roosevelt turned his attention to the ominous situation in Europe. He put forward a proposal suggested by his under secretary of state, Sumner Welles, for a peace conference to be held under the auspices of the United States. He hoped it would establish basic principles for the conduct of international relations, reduce the level of armaments and open up world trade. Roosevelt secretly asked for Chamberlain's support, urging him to reply within a week, but the prime minister was not impressed. "The plan appeared to me fantastic," he wrote in his diary, "and likely to excite the derision of Germany and Italy. They might even use it to postpone conversations with us."

Without consulting his foreign secretary, Anthony Eden, who was on a brief holiday in France, Chamberlain sent Roosevelt a cool reply, outlining his own plans for talks with Mussolini and Hitler and asking the President to hold off for the moment. . . .

For the rest of 1938 and 1939, until the outbreak of war with Germany, Chamberlain conducted increasingly fruitless negotiations with Hitler and Mussolini. Such sympathy as there had been in Britain for Germany's expansion had now abated. . . . [D]uring 1938 Hitler invaded Austria and then threatened Czechoslovakia. By September war seemed inevitable. In London air raid sirens were tested, trenches were dug in the parks, and millions of anti-gas masks were made ready for distribution. In a last effort to maintain the peace Chamberlain flew to Munich and made an agreement that gave Hitler half of Czechoslovakia in exchange for pledges that he would make no further territorial demands and that Britain and Germany would never fight each other again.

Roosevelt, who had been watching from the sidelines since the failure of his peace initiative, was relieved that war had been averted and hopeful of a lasting peace. After

Munich he cabled Chamberlain: "I fully share your hope and belief that there exists today the greatest opportunity in years for a new order based on justice and law." Privately, however, he became increasingly doubtful during the winter that any agreement with Hitler would stick, and began pressing for American rearmament. Yet he still believed it was the responsibility of the democracies in Western Europe to mount their own defense. America would back them up but not take the lead. . . .

Relations between the two governments improved during 1939. The British were encouraged by Roosevelt's plans for rearmament and his condemnation of totalitarianism. The Americans applauded Britain's decision to end appeasement after Hitler took the remainder of Czechoslovakia in March 1939. . . .

On the night of August 31, 1939, Hitler invaded Poland, ignoring Britain's ultimatum, and three days later Britain and France declared war. Unlike Wilson in 1914, Roosevelt at once made clear that American sympathies lay with the Allies. In a "fireside chat" radio broadcast he said, "I cannot ask that every American remain neutral in thought. Even a neutral cannot be asked to close his mind or conscience."

But neutrality was still America's official policy. The Neutrality Act had been amended in 1937 to permit Americans to trade with belligerent nations, except in armaments. To avoid the country being dragged into war by attacks on its ships and by foreign loans, as had happened in World War I, all these goods had to be collected by the buyer and paid for at the time of purchase, a system called Cash and Carry. Within two months of the outbreak of war Roosevelt persuaded Congress to modify the Act further. Britain needed supplies of armaments, which she had been ordering in increasing quantities from America as war loomed, but at the outbreak of hostilities, in keeping with the Neutrality Act, these supplies had been halted. American munitions factories fell idle. By early November, arguing that it was in America's own economic interest to supply Britain, Roosevelt secured the repeal of the arms embargo. Britain could now buy whatever she wanted, as long as she paid cash and arranged delivery.

For the British the revised Neutrality Act was a welcome improvement. As in the Great War, they could now draw on the vast industrial resources of the United States. But the ban on loans was worrying, and the inconvenient "carry" clauses drove the two countries to subterfuge. Airplanes, for instance, could not be flown directly from factories in America to Canada and then on to Britain. Some were dismantled and shipped in crates by sea. Lockheed in California, a small company that was expanding with orders from Britain, found an original solution that kept strictly within the terms of the Neutrality Act. The company bought a stretch of flat land in the far north of North Dakota on the Canadian border. Lockheed pilots flew the planes to the grass airstrip. The engines were turned off and the pilots disembarked. A local farmer hitched a team of horses to the front undercarriage and drew the machines a few yards across the border into Canada, thus ensuring that the planes had not left the United States under their own power. British or Canadian pilots then went aboard, restarted the engines and took off for Britain.

For seven months after war was declared there was little fighting. Poland was swiftly dismembered by Germany and Russia, with whom Hitler had signed a nonaggression pact. There then followed the period of inactivity known as the phony war. During it a last attempt was made by Roosevelt to explore the chances of peace. Sumner Welles was sent to Europe on a special mission. Chamberlain wrote scathingly of the intervention: "Heaven knows I don't want the Americans to fight for us — we should have to pay too dearly for that if they had a right to be in on the peace terms — but if they are so sympathetic they might at least refrain from hampering our efforts and comforting our foes."

In April 1940 the phony war came to an abrupt end. Germany invaded Scandinavia. A British expeditionary force arrived in Norway too late and was soon forced to withdraw. On May 10 the German army invaded the Netherlands, Belgium, Luxembourg and northern France. The Allied forces were soon in headlong retreat. At six o'clock that night the British prime minister resigned, having lost a vote of confidence over Norway in the House of Commons. His successor was Winston Churchill.

Although a diehard Tory, Churchill had been out of office for most of the 1930s, when he had been an outspoken advocate of rearmament and a frequent critic of appeasement. Ed Murrow, head of CBS operations in Europe, reported to American radio listeners that evening that Churchill "enters office with the tremendous advantage of being the man who was right. . . . Mr. Churchill can inspire confidence. And he can preach a doctrine of hate that is acceptable to the majority of this country." Unlike Chamberlain, Churchill was also an ardent champion of cooperation among what he liked to call "the English-speaking peoples." He had an American mother, knew the United States well and, on his appointment as First Lord of the Admiralty in September 1939, had responded eagerly to Roosevelt's secret request for regular information on naval matters. After his appointment as prime minister their correspondence was to develop into the most important channel of communications between the two governments. Between May 1940 and April 1945 Churchill sent Roosevelt a message, on average, once every thirty-six hours. "No lover," he said after the war, "ever studied the whims of his mistress as I did those of President Roosevelt."

But all this was in the future in May 1940. When Churchill assumed office there were many in Washington who were wary. His belligerent stance on naval disarmament in the 1920s had not been forgotten. He was also suspected of erratic judgment and an excessive fondness for alcohol. When news of his appointment reached Washington, Roosevelt commented dryly that he "supposed Churchill was the best man that England had, even if he was drunk half of his time."

It was the disastrous course of the war itself as much as the change of leaders that transformed Anglo-American relations. Within two weeks of Churchill's assumption of office the German Army had reached the Channel coast. Three hundred and thirty thousand British and French troops, miraculously evacuated from Dunkirk, reached Britain bedraggled and without most of their weapons and equipment. By the middle of June France had surrendered. Britain stood alone with an army wholly inadequate for the task of defending her shores from the attack that seemed imminent. In the House of Commons Churchill rallied his countrymen. "We shall never surrender; and even if, which I do not for a moment believe, this Island or a large part of it were subjugated and starving, then our Empire beyond the seas, armed and guarded by the British Fleet, would carry on the struggle until, in God's good time, the New World, with all its power and might, steps forth to the rescue and the liberation of the Old."

As Churchill's rhetoric acknowledged, Britain now had nowhere to turn but to America. Doubts about American reliability still lingered. Chamberlain and others had not forgotten World War I and the price extracted then for American military help. But under Churchill's guidance the British government came to accept that without the United States Britain was lost. Disregarding the dangerously low level of her gold and dollar reserves, which could not, as in World War I, be covered by U.S. loans, Britain placed huge orders for munitions. When the money ran out, the government hoped that supplies would continue to flow. But new orders could not meet the current crisis. Ships and planes would take months to build, and by then Britain might have been overrun. Churchill begged Roosevelt for immediate practical help. On the East Coast of the United States were fifty Great War destroyers, "mothballed" in their dockyards. If these could be recommissioned and lent to Britain, they could be used to help repel a German invasion and to protect the sea-lanes, with their vital supplies of food, from German submarines.

"Not a day should be lost," Churchill cabled Roosevelt, emphasizing the urgency of his request. Roosevelt's reply, one that Churchill would become used to receiving, was that he wanted to help but that Congress was unlikely to allow it. Again Churchill cabled: "We must ask . . . as a matter of life or death to be reinforced with these destroyers." Roosevelt did not reply, and for two months after the fall of France sent no messages at all. Finally, in desperation, Churchill cabled on July 31: "Mr. President, with great respect I must tell you that in the long history of the world, this is a thing to do now."

Roosevelt's reluctance to meet Churchill's appeal was partly political. Cautious as ever, he was unwilling to abandon formal neutrality before Congress was ready. But there was also the fear fostered, among others, by the American ambassador in London, Joseph Kennedy, that Britain was on the verge of collapse. "If we had to fight to protect our own lives," Kennedy advised, "we would do better fighting in our own backyard." Roosevelt himself assessed Britain's chances of survival in early July 1940 as no better than one in three. Offering destroyers, which America itself would need if Britain fell, could be a futile, even suicidal, gesture.

The President's military advisers were particularly reluctant to see too much given away. Although America was an industrial giant, its military strength was puny. In April 1940 the United States ranked twentieth among the world's military powers. The Dutch were nineteenth. A country with an army of 250,000 men with outdated equipment and a navy only adequate to defend either the Pacific or the Atlantic, not both, simply did not have resources to spare. After Dunkirk five hundred thousand U.S. rifles were sold cheaply to the British Army, but this was still a commercial arrangement, paid for from Britain's dwindling foreign exchange. Lending fifty destroyers was a very different matter.

By the middle of August, however, Roosevelt felt able to act. Intelligence reports reaching Washington suggested that Britain might, after all, survive into 1941. Equally important was legal advice to the President that he need not go to Congress for special legislation but could act independently, under his authority as commander in chief. At last Roosevelt put a proposal to Churchill. Britain could have the destroyers, but she would have to offer something in return. The President wanted ninety-nine-year leases on eight British possessions in the Americas, stretching from Newfoundland to the Caribbean, on which the United States could build air and naval bases to strengthen its own defenses. Roosevelt also requested a pledge from Churchill that if Britain fell the Royal Navy would not be surrendered but would carry on the fight from ports in the British Empire. The bases and the promises, Roosevelt explained[,] were "molasses" to sweeten the pill in America.

When the British Cabinet received the proposal, its first reaction was to refuse. The secret War Cabinet minutes read: "The view of the War Cabinet was that a formal bargain on the lines proposed was out of the question." Even Churchill was against giving what he called "a blank cheque on the whole of our transatlantic possessions." But Britain no longer called the tune: she had little choice but to accept aid on whatever terms America proposed. Eventually a compromise was reached: two of the leases were designated a "gift" from the British government; the rest were made part of the formal deal that Roosevelt needed in order to persuade Americans that they were not, once again, being taken as suckers by the wily British. Even at a moment of world crisis, old suspicions died hard.

On September 2, 1940, the "destroyers for bases" deal was signed. It was of symbolic as well as practical importance. The United States was formally neutral, and yet, with this unneutral act, it had effectively pledged support for Britain as America's own front line of defense. . . .

Roosevelt's caution during this early part of the war, though unwelcome to Britain, was understandable. The presidential election was due in November 1940. Roosevelt had decided to run for a third term of office, an unprecedented and controversial decision. He had secured the endorsement of the Democratic party in July but did not want to do anything during the campaign that would give credence to Republican charges that he was a "war-monger."

The President was, however, encouraged by the growing public support for Britain in the United States. In May 1940 a Committee to Defend America by Aiding the Allies had been formed by a Kansas newspaper editor, William Allen White. The White committee soon established chapters across the country that agitated for every help to be given to Britain, short of declaring war. One of its leading members was the film star Douglas Fairbanks, Jr., who joined to warn America of the dangers of isolationism. He recalls Roosevelt telling him that as president he "had to be like the captain in front of his troops. If he got too far ahead in expressing his own sympathies and opinion, then he would lose the people behind. He could only be a little ahead . . . and it was *our* job to push public opinion."

At times it took some pushing. Only two days after the "destroyers for bases" agreement there was a sharp backlash. A new committee was formed to keep America out of the war. America First was a direct rival of the White committee, and drew its strongest support from the Midwest, particularly around Chicago. This area had particularly large German populations, although opposition to entering the war did not come from just them or from the Italians, or from Britain's traditional opponents[,] the Irish. Among supporters of America First were many pacifists, those who did not believe the war was

America's concern, and mothers who simply wanted to prevent their sons being sent as cannon fodder to Europe. By December 1941 the organization had 850,000 members. Its basic policy was to build up America's own defenses and not to get entangled in Britain's war.

The figurehead of America First, who was always in demand at their rallies, was the aviator Charles Lindbergh, whom some suspected of fascist sympathies. Having toured German aircraft factories, he reported back to America the scale of German superiority to Britain in the air and warned about the folly of believing that Britain could win. Another supporter was the young Kingman Brewster, in later years to be president of Yale University and American ambassador to Britain. He believes the movement reflected a broadly based sentiment in the country. There were many who feared that total war could mean the destruction of American institutions, perhaps even of democracy itself. In particular, America Firsters disputed the claim that Britain was the United States' front line. "There was a feeling that Hitler could not invade us and we could not invade him. The Atlantic was just too big. . . . " Looking back now, Brewster concedes that for America to have followed the isolationists' cause "would have been a disaster. . . . But it wasn't because we thought Europe ought to go hang. It was because we didn't think America should hang in order to prevent that."

Roosevelt and those who believed America must do everything possible to help Britain had powerful allies among the American war correspondents stationed in London. During August and September the Battle of Britain was being fought out in the skies over southern England. Day after day the Luftwaffe [German air force] came to attack Britain's airfields and bomb her cities, to meet with a daring and effective defense from Britain's fighter squadrons. It was a dramatic battle for survival, watched and reported back each evening to America by radio. . . .

By the autumn of 1940, with the presidential election only weeks away, the argument over America's response to the war was becoming bitter and sometimes violent. Fairbanks remembers abuse from the isolationist press, his films being banned or boycotted, his wife and children threatened with violence and kidnapping. He went to speak to a huge rally in Chicago. "We were scared to death. My knees were cracking together like biscuits on the platform, but I got through it all right."

Roosevelt's opponent for the presidency was the Republican Wendell Willkie, a New York attorney and businessman with Midwestern roots. Willkie sympathized with Britain and personally supported Roosevelt's policy of aid short of war, but as the campaign developed he began to slip behind in the polls and succumbed to pressure to attack Roosevelt on the war issue. He implied that the President had made secret commitments to the Allies and warned "if you re-elect him you may expect war in April 1941." With two weeks of the campaign to go, Willkie was recovering and Roosevelt was forced to fight back. In Boston he gave a pledge for which he was later much criticized: "Your boys are not going to be sent into any foreign wars." Willkie fumed, "That hypocritical son of a bitch! This is going to beat me!" On November 5, 1940, Roosevelt was reelected for a third term with 449 electoral votes to Willkie's 82, a massive vote of confidence that gave the President more freedom of maneuver to conduct foreign policy.

The election over, Roosevelt went for a rest in the Caribbean. There, early in December 1940, he received a message from Churchill that was timed to catch him in a relaxed, responsive mood. Churchill later called this letter "one of the most important I ever wrote." He followed the advice of the British ambassador in Washington, Lord Lothian, by explaining Britain's predicament in detail. It was an alarming analysis. Britain urgently needed deliveries of munitions and aircraft. The worsening Battle of the Atlantic was threatening to strangle her lifelines and starve her into surrender. Every ton of merchant shipping surplus to American requirements, Churchill argued, should be put at Britain's disposal, as should American naval escorts to accompany cargoes across the Atlantic. He also reminded the President that "the moment approaches when we shall no longer be able to pay cash for shipping and other supplies." The letter ended with a moving request that Roosevelt "regard this letter not as an appeal for aid, but as a statement of the minimum action necessary to the achievement of our common purpose."

Roosevelt's reaction, unlike his response to the request for fifty destroyers earlier in the year, was swift and imaginative. On his return from his Caribbean holiday he gave a press conference in which he warned of Britain's imminent dollar crisis. "The best immediate defense of the United States is the success of Great Britain in defending itself," he insisted, and put forward a proposal not, as in World War I, for financial loans to be repaid after the war but for America to lend Britain the goods she needed, leaving repayment or the return of the goods to be arranged later. . . .

On January 10, 1941, the Lend-Lease bill was introduced into Congress and ran the gauntlet of committee hearings by both houses, at which members of the administration and other witnesses were cross-examined in open session and with maximum publicity. The hearings provided a new forum for the debate about America's proper relationship with Britain.

Opponents of the scheme, the anti-interventionists like Congressman Hamilton Fish and Charles Lindbergh, concentrated their attack on two points: that the bill would give the President far too much power, making him a virtual dictator, and that it would suck America into war. The counterargument, put by Senator Claude Pepper and others, was that the proponents of Lend-Lease were the true America Firsters, since helping Britain was the only realistic way of defending America. The bill itself was shrewdly entitled "An Act to Promote the Defense of the United States."

The debate was acrimonious. Pepper had long supported more help for the Allies, and had spoken on the subject all over the country. For his pains he was hanged in effigy outside the Senate by a group of women protesting that he was trying to murder their sons. "I was trying to explain to everyone that this was the only way we could stay out of the war. We could not afford to let Hitler become the master of Europe and then maybe a master of a large part of the world. We would have to fight him all over the world by ourselves."

The debate was not simply about the best means of defending America. It also reflected the deep-rooted American suspicions about Britain. The bill's opponents claimed that America was once more being taken for a ride by Britain, that cunning John Bull was inveigling a generous Uncle Sam into paying for a war that was not yet beyond his means. Many Americans found it hard to believe that Britain was short of cash when, as they saw it, she still owned a vast empire.

Roosevelt expected Churchill to make some gestures to help him with these political problems. These included releasing gold held in South Africa and selling one of Britain's major companies in the United States, American Viscose, a highly successful subsidiary of the textile giant Courtaulds. An American destroyer was sent to Cape Town to collect $50 million of gold, and American Viscose was compulsorily sold, only to be resold immediately at a much higher price by the consortium of American bankers who bought it — a profit that did not come back to Britain.

"Certain things were done," Churchill wrote after the war, "which seemed harsh and painful to us." At the time he drafted a message of complaint to Roosevelt. "It is not fitting that any nation should put itself wholly in the hands of another, least of all a nation which is fighting under increasingly severe conditions for what is proclaimed to be a cause of general concern." But Churchill controlled his anger and the message was never sent. As with the destroyers deal, Britain was in no position to dictate the terms of American help.

It took Roosevelt two months to push Lend-Lease through Congress. On March 11, 1941, after votes that split on party lines — Democrats mainly for, Republicans mainly against — the bill was signed into law. The businessman Averell Harriman was dispatched across the Atlantic to run the London end of Lend-Lease. His instructions from Roosevelt were blunt: "Recommend everything that we can do, short of war, to keep the British Isles afloat."

Churchill later described Lend-Lease as "the most unsordid act in the history of any nation." It came as essential relief to a hard-pressed government and, compared with the arrangements for lending funds in World War I, it was a generous and farsighted gesture. Roosevelt was determined to avoid another disastrous row over war debts. Lend-Lease was not, however, pure altruism. Supporting Britain was seen as a way of defending America by keeping it out of the war. Claude Pepper admits that he saw Britain as "a sort of mercenary" doing America's fighting for her. Nor was Lend-Lease a gift. The terms had not been agreed upon, but repayment in some form was expected.

Churchill's overriding aim was still to persuade America to join forces with Britain. In 1917 President Wilson had finally declared war against Germany because of attacks on American shipping in the North Atlantic. In 1941 it seemed possible that this would happen again. German sinkings of merchant ships had reached new heights: 530,000 tons in March, 668,000 tons in April. At this rate, even allowing for new construction, Britain would have lost a quarter of her merchant fleet in a single year. Roosevelt issued secret orders that the American Navy should be ready to escort Allied convoys across the North Atlantic beginning in April, but at the last moment drew back in response to a renewed America First campaign against "convoying." Instead, to Churchill's dismay, he moved cautiously, extending U.S. patrols to the mid-Atlantic at the end of April, and in July taking over the garrisoning of Iceland from Britain.

The weary Prime Minister needed more than this. His government was demoralized by setbacks in Greece and North Africa. There were fears that once Hitler had achieved total dominance in the eastern Mediterranean he would turn once again to the invasion of Britain. For the first time since the desperate days of June 1940 Churchill now pleaded with Roosevelt to enter the war. On May 4 he cabled: "Mr. President, I am sure that you will not misunderstand me if I speak to you exactly what is in my mind. The one decisive counterweight I can see . . . would be if the United States were immediately to range herself with us as a belligerent power. . . . ". . . In Washington many of Roosevelt's advisers agreed with Churchill's analysis, but the President balked at leading his people into war, convinced that this would only be possible when Hitler affronted American interests or honor in such a way that national unity would be guaranteed.

The two leaders had now been corresponding as heads of government for over a year, but they had not yet met, except briefly in 1918. In the summer of 1941, however, the moment was opportune. Hitler's surprise attack on Russia in June 1941 and Russia's stout defense meant that the main thrust of the war was for the moment being pursued on the Eastern European front, giving Churchill a breathing space. He took advantage of it by accepting Roosevelt's invitation to a full-scale conference to be held in Placentia Bay, Newfoundland, in August. Churchill arrived aboard the battleship HMS *Prince of Wales.* He had rested on the voyage, taking exercise, striding the decks, and watching films in the wardroom at night. He was in high spirits, hopeful, like many in London, that Roosevelt now meant to call for a declaration of war. "I do not think," he had told the Queen before his departure, "that our friend would have asked me to go so far for what must be a meeting of world-wide importance, unless he had in mind some further forward step.". . .

The four-day meeting confirmed the friendship between the two leaders and created new links among their advisers.

. . . [Still,] Roosevelt resisted Churchill's call for a declaration of war. Instead he proposed a statement of joint war aims, which, while they confirmed America's determination to see Hitler defeated, exacted a price from Britain in the form of pledges that could imperil the continuance of her empire after the war.

It was not just opponents of Lend-Lease who suspected Britain's long-term motives. Elliott Roosevelt, the President's son, who was present at the conference, remembers his father also having doubts about Churchill. "He felt that in the period following the war . . . Churchill believed that Great Britain would have a bigger empire and greater influence, that he would take advantage of the help given by America, and that we would still be in a secondary role."

It was the same fear that Woodrow Wilson had expressed on America's entry into World War I. Wilson had put forward his Fourteen Points to establish that America's aims were not the same as the Allies'. Roosevelt used the Atlantic Charter, the agreement signed at the end of the Placentia Bay conference, to try to bind Britain and America in common war aims that would satisfy the American people and embody America's distinctive vision of the postwar world.

Clause Three of the charter stated that both countries "respect the right of all peoples to choose the form of government under which they will live; and they wish to see sovereign rights and self-government restored to those who have been forcibly deprived of them." Although these words were mainly aimed at the subject peoples of Hitler's

Europe, they were soon seized on by politicians in Britain's empire and by American anticolonialists to justify demands for independence. Clause Four of the charter was also significant. It pledged both governments "to further the enjoyment of all States, great or small, victor or vanquished, of access, on equal terms, to the trade and to the raw materials of the world." This latest American attempt to break down Britain's Imperial Preference system was weakened by the saving condition, inserted at British insistence, of "due respect for their existing obligations." Nevertheless the Atlantic Charter served as a warning that the United States would use its leverage to try to force Britain to adopt policies in keeping with its own plans for the postwar world.

What mattered to Churchill, though, in the heat of war, was not the future import of Clauses Three or Four, but how to identify America firmly with Britain's cause. From that perspective the joint statement of war aims was invaluable. And although he failed to secure the American declaration of war he hoped for, Churchill did obtain further promises of American naval help in the North Atlantic. The President had promised, he told the Cabinet on his return, to "become more and more provocative" in the Atlantic. "Everything was to be done to force an 'incident'. . . which would justify him in opening hostilities."

On September 4 such an incident occurred. A U-boat attacked the U.S. destroyer *Greer,* and Roosevelt used the opportunity to announce a state of virtual, though still undeclared, naval war. American warships now began escorting British and Canadian convoys, laden with vital military supplies and food, through "American defensive waters," which ran up to longitude 10 degrees west, or roughly three-quarters of the way across the Atlantic. The relief for Britain was immense. German vessels were warned that they would enter the area at their peril. In November these "Shoot on sight" orders were strengthened by the repeal of further sections of the Neutrality Act. Roosevelt could now arm American merchant ships and send them direct to Britain. He could also use the U.S. Navy to escort convoys all the way to British ports. But he did not rush to do so, aware of the strength of antiwar feeling in the country and in Congress. According to a Gallup poll on October 22, for instance, only 17 percent of the American people favored a declaration of war on Germany.

The incident Roosevelt was waiting for, the affront that would unite the people behind him, was finally delivered not by Germany but by Japan. Germany's surprise attack on Russia removed Japanese fears that Stalin would be able to resist Japan's expansion in Asia. Britain was unable to spare large forces for Singapore and Malaya or capital ships to patrol the China Sea. Only the Americans with their main fleet at Pearl Harbor, Hawaii, offered any deterrent.

In July 1941 Japan overran the remainder of Indochina. The Americans reacted by imposing an oil embargo and strengthening their forces in the Philippines. By December it was expected that Japan would mount an attack on British and Dutch possessions in Southeast Asia. The attack on Pearl Harbor took everyone by surprise. On the morning of Sunday December 7 Japanese planes bombed the American base, sinking or immobilizing eight American battleships and leaving 2,400 dead. It was the most humiliating military disaster in American history. . . .

At first some members of America First thought the news was a hoax, or some clever trick of Roosevelt's. But when the appalling truth dawned, they abandoned their campaign and joined forces behind the President. On the eve of Pearl Harbor the chairman of the New York chapter of America First had sent a long critical letter to Roosevelt. The Monday following the attack he wrote again: "Please consider the contents of our letter, dated December 6, 1941, null and void."

America declared war on Japan, and Hitler, in turn, declared war on America. Roosevelt cabled Churchill, "Today all of us are in the same boat with you and the people of the Empire, and it is a ship which will not and can not be sunk." The Prime Minister was jubilant. After nineteen months of lonely leadership Britain was now assured of survival and victory. On the night of Pearl Harbor, he recalled later, "I went to bed and slept the sleep of the saved and thankful."

QUESTIONS TO CONSIDER

1. Compare the positions of British and American policymakers toward German expansionism in the late 1930s. Why did the British adopt the policy of appeasement? What events led Britain to take a tougher stand in 1939? What was Roosevelt's attitude toward Hitler? toward the Munich Pact? toward Great Britain? In what way did conflicting positions on international trade and the British Empire affect Anglo-American cooperation?

2. How did the experience of World War I affect American foreign policy during the international crises of the 1930s?

3. Once World War II broke out, why did Roosevelt support the British war effort gradually and cautiously? How did domestic politics affect Roosevelt's decisions? Was Roosevelt waiting for an event to draw the United States into war? Was he hoping to avoid war by supporting Britain? Or was he attempting to create an incident that would bring America into the conflict?

4. Analyze the debate between isolationists and interventionists in the United States prior to the attack on Pearl Harbor. Were isolationists Nazi sympathizers, anti-British, or afraid of an American defeat? Did those who advocated aid to Britain aim to go to war or to avoid entering it? What factors led to victory for the policy of intervention?

5. How does the authors' focus on the Anglo-American relationship make their analysis different from one that concentrates on American policymakers alone? What new impressions or interpretations of American actions emerge through this dual-perspective approach?

Race War:
American and Japanese
Perceptions of the Enemy

JOHN W. DOWER

For people all over the globe, World War II was a catastrophe, the costliest and deadliest war in human history. Yet Americans suffered much less than others. Because there was no invasion of the mainland, Americans were spared the terrors of an occupying army, the destruction of their cities, the mass killing of civilians, and the ordeal of homelessness — commonplace horrors for over four years in Europe, Asia, and the Soviet Union. Of the more than nineteen million soldiers killed in the fighting, three hundred thousand were Americans — less than 2 percent of the total.

On the home front, the contrast was especially dramatic. While factories in Europe and Japan were being bombed, wartime production finally lifted the United States out of the Great Depression. Unemployment disappeared, wages were high, and white women and African Americans were recruited to work in war industries. The American public rallied behind the war with far more conviction and unity than during World War I. Few questioned the justice of fighting Hitler's hated Nazis or retaliating against Japan, which had drawn the United States into war with its surprise attack on Pearl Harbor. No wonder that during the war's fiftieth anniversary in 1995, Americans still in the shadow of divisive conflicts in Korea and Vietnam remembered World War II as "the good war."

There was, however, a darker side to America's war, part of which John Dower reveals in the following essay. After Pearl Harbor, dehumanizing, racist stereotypes of the Japanese pervaded the American media and stirred up popular hatred. While anti-German propaganda concentrated on the evil figure of Adolf Hitler, in the Pacific war American venom was directed at the Japanese in general. Denigrated as monkeys, children, "little men," or simply "Yellow bastards," the Japanese people, rather than their leaders, were held responsible for the war, were disparaged as an inferior race, and were targeted for revenge by American soldiers and civilians.

American racism was not unique. Dower's analysis takes a revealing comparative turn by presenting Japanese opinion-makers' perceptions of their nation's enemies during the war. Reviewing the ugly catalog of slurs and stereotypes on both sides, he notes that Anglo-American racism "denigrated the other," while Japanese racism "elevated the self." Such images of superiority and inferiority can be traced to the contrasting histories of the two nations, one the victor and the other often the victim of imperialistic expansion. But Dower also finds deep roots of dangerous hierarchical thinking in long-standing Western and Asian cultural ideas about family, gender, and class. In both cultures, ideas about the inferiority of women, children, and the poor could easily be transferred onto national enemies.

Dower's sensitive presentation suggests how understanding American and Japanese racial thinking can illuminate such wartime incidents as the American response to Pearl Harbor, the forced relocation of one hundred ten thousand West Coast Japanese Americans to internment camps, and the brutal Japanese treatment of American POWs. More generally, his study raises troubling questions that should lead you to ponder the persistence of prejudice and the ugly effects of war upon societies that wage it. Must societies at war always dehumanize their enemies? Where do racist stereotypes come from? Why do they show such remarkable durability?

GLOSSARY

BATAAN DEATH MARCH   A Japanese atrocity during World War II in which American and Filipino troops captured on the Philippine peninsula of Bataan in April 1942 were forced to march to a distant prison camp. Due to harsh treatment and starvation, nearly ten thousand died.

CONFUCIUS (551–479 B.C.)   A Chinese sage who founded a system of practical ethical and social precepts called Confucianism. Its important doctrines include benevolence (the enlightened self-interest expressed by the Golden Rule) and ritual propriety (correct behavior according to one's station in society or time of life). His teachings are the source of much of traditional Chinese (and, by extension, East Asian) ethics and culture.

EMPIRICISM   The practice of research or experiment.

GENOCIDE   The deliberate and systematic extermination of a national or racial group.

GREATER EAST ASIA CO-PROSPERITY SPHERE   The rubric given by Japan to its domination of trade and territory in China and Southeast Asia in the 1930s. Increasingly, this arrangement was a cover for brutal imperialism and exclusionist trade policies.

HOLOCAUST   The persecution and extermination of European Jews by Nazi Germany between the late 1930s and the end of World War II. By the end of the war, six million Jews had been murdered and their communal life destroyed.

IWO JIMA   A Pacific island seven hundred miles south of Japan. The site of a Japanese airbase, it was captured in March 1945 by U.S. Marines after fierce fighting.

KOREMATSU V. UNITED STATES (1944)   A U.S. Supreme Court decision that upheld the wartime removal of Japanese Americans from the West Coast and their forced relocation to inland internment camps due to fears of sabotage or espionage. Partial restitution for their financial losses did not come until 1988, when Congress voted to issue a public apology and $20,000 to each of the surviving sixty thousand internees.

MANDALA   In Asian art, a symbolic diagram of the universe in concentric geometric shapes, each containing an image or attribute of a deity.

MANDARINS   Intellectuals or experts who serve those in power (named after the public officials of imperial China).

MANICHEAN   Divided starkly into light and dark, good and evil (named after the dualistic religious system of the third-century Persian prophet Manes, which saw the world as an arena of conflict between light and spirit, which represented God, and darkness and matter, which represented Satan).

MANTRA   In Hinduism or Buddhism, a mystic word or phrase to be recited or sung in ritual and meditation. Chanting it establishes a link with the deities or spiritual forces it represents.

NOBLESSE OBLIGE   The moral obligation of the rich or highborn to practice charity toward those less fortunate.

If one asks Americans today in what ways World War II was atrocious and racist, they will point overwhelmingly to the Nazi genocide of the Jews. When the war was being fought, however, the enemy Americans perceived as most atrocious was not the Germans but the Japanese; and the racial issues that provoked their greatest emotion were associated with the war in Asia.

With few exceptions, Americans were obsessed with the uniquely evil nature of the Japanese. Allan Nevins, who twice won the Pulitzer Prize in history, observed immediately after the war that "probably in all our history, no foe has been so detested as were the Japanese." Ernie Pyle, the most admired of American war correspondents, conveyed the same sentiment unapologetically. In February 1945, a few weeks after being posted to the Pacific following years of covering the war in Europe, Pyle told his millions of readers that "in Europe we felt that our enemies, horrible and deadly as they were, were still people. But out here I soon gathered that the Japanese were looked upon as something subhuman and repulsive, the way some people feel about cockroaches or mice." Pyle went on to describe his response on seeing Japanese prisoners for the first time. "They were wrestling and laughing and talking just like normal human beings," he wrote. "And yet they gave me the creeps, and I wanted a mental bath after looking at them." Sober magazines like *Science Digest* ran articles titled "Why Americans Hate Japs More Than Nazis." By incarcerating Japanese Americans, but not German Americans or Italian Americans, the United States government — eventually with Supreme Court backing [in *Korematsu* v. *United States*] — gave its official imprimatur to the designation of the Japanese as a racial enemy. It did so, of course, in the most formal and judicious language.

Japan in War and Peace: Selected Essays by John W. Dower. Copyright © 1995. Reprinted by permission of The New Press. (800) 233-4830.

It is not really surprising that the Japanese, rather than the Germans and their decimation of the Jews, dominated American racial thinking. In the United States, as well
as Britain and most of Europe, anti-Semitism was strong and . . . the Holocaust was
wittingly neglected or a matter of indifference. Japan's aggression, on the other hand,
stirred the deepest recesses of white supremacism and provoked a response bordering on
the apocalyptic. As the Hearst papers took care to editorialize, the war in Europe, however terrible, was still a "family fight" that did not threaten the very essence of occidental civilization. One Hearst paper bluntly identified the war in the Pacific as "the
War of Oriental Races against Occidental Races for the Domination of the World."

There was almost visceral agreement on this. Thus Hollywood formulaically introduced good Germans as well as Nazis but almost never showed a "good Japanese." In
depicting the Axis triumvirate, political cartoonists routinely gave the German enemy
Hitler's face and the Italian enemy Mussolini's, but they rendered the Japanese as plain,
homogeneous "Japanese" caricatures: short, round-faced, bucktoothed, slant-eyed, frequently myopic behind horn-rimmed glasses. In a similar way, phrasemakers fell unre-
flectively into the idiom seen in the *Science Digest* headline: Nazis and Japs. Indeed,
whereas the German enemy was conflated to bad Germans (Nazis), the Japanese enemy
was inflated to a supra-Japanese foe — not just the Japanese militarists, not just all the
Japanese people, not just ethnic Japanese everywhere, but the Japanese as Orientals. Tin
Pan Alley [that is, the popular music industry] . . . immediately placed its finger on the
American pulse. One of the many popular songs inspired by Pearl Harbor was titled
"There'll Be No Adolph Hitler nor Yellow Japs to Fear." Pearl Harbor and the stunning
Japanese victories over the colonial powers that followed so quickly in Southeast Asia
seemed to confirm the worst Yellow Peril nightmares.

World War II in Asia was, of course, not simply or even primarily a race war. Alliances cut across race on both the Allied and Axis sides, and fundamental issues of
power and ideology were at stake. Where the Japanese and the Anglo-American antagonists were concerned, however, an almost Manichaean racial cast overlay these other
issues of contention. This was true on both sides. The Japanese were racist too —
toward the white enemy, and in conspicuously different ways toward the other Asians
who fell within their "Co-Prosperity Sphere." Thus the war in Asia offers an unusually
vivid case study through which to examine the tangled skein of race, language, and violence from a comparative perspective — not only with the luxury of retrospect, moreover, but also at a time when United States–Japan relations are very different and yet still
riven with racial tension. . . .

That racist perceptions shape behavior may seem obvious, but the war experience
calls attention to how subtly this occurs, and at how many different levels. Myths, in this
case race myths, almost always override conclusions drawn from sober, rational, empirical observation — until cataclysmic events occur to dispel or discredit them. It took
Pearl Harbor and Singapore to destroy the myth cherished by Caucasians that the
Japanese were poor navigators and inept pilots and unimaginative strategists, for example, and it required a long, murderous struggle to rid the Japanese of their conceit that
the Anglo-Americans were too degenerate and individualistic to gird for a long battle
against a faraway foe. We have become so mesmerized by the contemporary cult of

military intelligence gathering that we often fail to recognize how extensively unadulterated prejudice colors intelligence estimates, causing both overestimation and underestimation of the other side. Beyond this, in its most extreme form racism sanctions extermination — the genocide of the Jews, of course, but also the plain but patterned rhetoric of exterminating beasts, vermin, or demons that unquestionably helped raise tolerance for slaughter in Asia.

Five categories subsume the racist perceptions of the Japanese that dominated Anglo-American thinking during World War II. The Japanese were subhuman. They were little men, inferior to white Westerners in every physical, moral, and intellectual way. They were collectively primitive, childish, and mad — overlapping concepts that could be crudely expressed but also received "empirical" endorsement from social scientists and old Japan hands. At the same time, the Japanese also were portrayed as supermen. This was particularly true in the aftermath of their stunning early victories, and it is characteristic of this thinking that the despised enemy could be little men and supermen simultaneously. Finally, the Japanese in World War II became the nightmare come true of the Yellow Peril. This apocalyptic image embraced all others and made unmistakably clear that race hates, and not merely war hates or responses to Japanese behavior alone, were at issue.

Dehumanization of the enemy is desirable among men in combat. It eliminates scruples and hesitation from killing, the reasoning goes, and this contributes to self-preservation; the enemy, after all, is simultaneously dehumanizing and trying to kill you. Among Allied fighting men in the Pacific, this attitude emerged naturally in the . . . metaphor of the hunt. Fighting Japanese in the jungle was like going after "small game in the woods back home" or tracking down a predatory animal. . . .

The kill did not remain confined to the combat zones, however. . . . In the United States, signs appeared in store windows declaring "Open Season on Japs," and "Jap hunting licenses" were distributed amid the hysteria that accompanied the incarceration of Japanese Americans. The psychology of the hunt became indistinguishable from a broader psychology of extermination that came to mean not merely taking no prisoners on the battlefield, but also having no qualms about extending the kill to the civilian population in Japan. Here the more precise language and imagery of the race war became apparent. The Japanese were vermin. More pervasive yet, they were apes, monkeys, "jaundiced baboons." The war in Asia popularized these dehumanizing epithets to a degree that still can be shocking in retrospect, but the war did not spawn them. These were classic tropes of racist denigration, deeply embedded in European and American consciousness. War simply pried them loose.

Vermin was the archetypal metaphor Nazis attached to the Jews, and the appalling consequences of that dehumanization have obscured the currency of this imagery in the war in Asia. On Iwo Jima, the press found amusement in noting that some marines went into battle with "Rodent Exterminator" stenciled on their helmets. Incinerating Japanese in caves with flamethrowers was referred to as "clearing out a rats' nest." Soon after Pearl Harbor, the prospect of exterminating the Japanese vermin in their nest at home was widely applauded. The most popular float in a day-long victory parade in

New York in mid-1942 was titled "Tokyo: We Are Coming," and depicted bombs falling on a frantic pack of yellow rats. . . .

. . . Among Western political cartoonists, the simian [ape] figure was surely the most popular caricature for the Japanese. David Low, the brilliant antifascist cartoonist working out of London, was fond of this. The *New York Times* routinely reproduced such graphics in its Sunday edition, at one point adding its own commentary that it might be more accurate to identify the Japanese as the "missing link." On the eve of the British debacle at Singapore, the British humor magazine *Punch* depicted Japanese soldiers in full-page splendor as chimpanzees with helmets and guns swinging from tree to tree. *Time* used the same image on its cover for 26 January 1942, contrasting the monkey invaders with the dignified Dutch military in Indonesia. . . . The *Washington Post* compared Japanese atrocities in the Philippines and German atrocities in Czechoslovakia in a 1942 cartoon pairing a gorilla labeled "Japs" and a Hitler figure labeled simply "Hitler." In well-received Hollywood combat films such as *Bataan* and *Guadalcanal Diary*, GIs routinely referred to the Japanese as monkeys.

The ubiquitous simian idiom of dehumanization came out of a rich tradition of bigoted Western iconography and graphically revealed the ease with which demeaning racist stereotypes could be floated from one target of prejudice to another. Only a short while before they put the Japanese in trees, for example, *Punch's* artists had been rendering the Irish as apes. Generations of white cartoonists also had previously refined the simian caricature in their depictions of Negroes and various Central American and Caribbean peoples. The popular illustrators, in turn, were merely replicating a basic tenet in the pseudoscience of white supremacism — the argument that the "Mongoloid" and "Negroid" races (and for Englishmen, the Irish) represented a lower stage of evolution. Nineteenth-century Western scientists and social scientists had offered almost unanimous support to this thesis, and such ideas persisted into the mid-twentieth century. President Franklin D. Roosevelt, for example, was informed by a physical anthropologist at the Smithsonian Institution that Japanese skulls were "some 2,000 years less developed than ours."

In the world outside the monkey house, the Japanese commonly were referred to as "the little men." Their relatively short stature contributed to this, but again the phrase was essentially metaphorical. The Japanese, it was argued, were small in accomplishments compared with Westerners. No great "universal" achievements were to be found in their traditional civilizations; they were latecomers to the modern challenges of science and technology, imitators rather than innovators, ritualists rather than rationalists. Again, the cartoonist provided a good gauge of this conceit. More often than not, in any ensemble of nationalities the Japanese figures were dwarfish.

Such contempt led, among other things, to a pervasive underestimation of Japanese intentions and capabilities by British and American observers at even the highest levels. Before Pearl Harbor, it was common wisdom among Westerners that the Japanese could not shoot, sail, or fly very well. Nor could they think imaginatively; as a British intelligence report carefully explained, this was because the enormous energy required to memorize the ideographic writing system dulled their brains and killed the spark of creativity. There can be few better examples of the power of myth and stereotype over the weight of objective analysis than the unpreparedness of the Westerners when Japan attacked. Almost everything was a shock: the audacity of the Pearl Harbor attack and the ability of the Japanese to bring it off, the effectiveness of the Zero aircraft (which had been in operation in China for over a year), the superb skills of the Japanese pilots, the esprit and discipline of the Japanese ground forces, the lightning multipronged assault against the European and American colonial enclaves. . . .

At the same time, the little-men thesis also was elaborated on in ways that shed harsh light on racist bias in the academic disciplines by revealing how Western social sciences could be used to support popular prejudices. The war years witnessed the emergence of anthropologists, sociologists, psychologists, and psychiatrists as the new mandarins of theories of "natural character," and on the whole they performed a valuable service in repudiating the old theories of biological determinism. What the social scientists did not dispel, however, were the racial stereotypes that had been associated with biological determinism. On the contrary, they essentially reaffirmed these stereotypes by offering new cultural or sociopsychological explanations for them. . . .

In the final analysis, the "national character" studies amounted to a new way of explaining what the presumedly discredited biological determinists had concluded long ago: that the Japanese as a people displayed arrested development. Although this was not inherent in their genes, it was the inevitable consequence of their peculiar history and culture. . . .

When all was said and done, however, these designations of Japanese peculiarity possessed a universal quality. They were formulaic and rested in considerable part on code words that transcended Japan and even transcended racial and cultural discourse in general. In suggestive ways, these code words also overlapped with vocabularies associated with discrimination based on gender and class. The central image of arrested growth, or "childishness," for example, was and remains one of the most basic constructs used by white Euro-Americans to characterize nonwhite peoples. This could be buttressed with pseudoscientific explanations (nonwhites being lower on the evolutionary scale, and thus biologically equivalent to children or adolescents vis-à-vis the "mature" Caucasian races) or meretricious social scientific equations (the "less developed" peoples of "less developed" nations, for example, or peoples alleged to be collectively blocked at a primitive or immature state psychologically by indigenous cultural practices or mores). In the milieu of war, the image of Japanese as children conveyed utter contempt, . . . but in less harsh circumstances it also was capable of evoking a condescending paternalism (as reflected in the depiction of Japanese after the surrender as "MacArthur's children" or as the beneficiaries of a student-teacher relationship with Americans). This same metaphor also is integral to the rationale of male domination and rule by elites. Thus, to describe women as childish or childlike is one of the most familiar ways men traditionally have signified both the inherent inferiority of women and their own obligation to protect or at least humor them. Similarly, dominant social and political classes commonly affirm their privileged status and inherent right to rule by dismissing the masses as irrational, irresponsible, and immature. In its softer guise, the elite sense of noblesse oblige masks class inequalities with a paradigm of parent-to-child obligations. . . .

Because nothing in the "rational" mind-set of Western leaders prepared them for either the audacity and skill of Japan's attack or the debacle of British, Dutch, and American capitulations to numerically inferior Japanese forces that followed in Southeast Asia, it was natural to look to nonrational explanations. Scapegoating helped obfuscate the situation — the United States commanders at Pearl Harbor were cashiered, and the West Coast Japanese Americans were locked up — but this was not enough. It also became useful to think of the Japanese as supermen. Graphic artists now drew the Japanese as giants on the horizon. Rhetorically, the new image usually emerged in a more serpentine or backhanded fashion. Thus the United States print media from 1941 to the end of the war featured a veritable "between the lines" subgenre debunking the new myth of the supermen. Battle A proved they could be beaten at sea, battle B that they could be beaten in the jungle, battle C that they were not unbeatable at night fighting, battle D that the myth of the "invincibility of the Zero" was finally being destroyed. The *New York Times Magazine* took it upon itself to address the issue head-on with a feature article titled "Japanese Superman: That Too Is a Fallacy." Admiral William Halsey, the most blatantly racist officer in the United States high command, later claimed that he deliberately belittled the Japanese as "monkeymen" and the like in order to discredit "the new myth of Japanese invincibility" and boost the morale of his men.

The myth of the superman was never completely dispelled. To the end of the war — even after most of the Japanese navy and merchant marine had been sunk; after Japanese soldiers in the field, cut off from support, had begun starving to death and were being killed by the tens and hundreds of thousands; after the urban centers of the home islands had come under regular bombardment — Allied planners continued to overestimate the will and capacity of the Japanese to keep fighting. There are surely many explanations for this, but prominent among them is a plainly racial consideration: the superman image was especially compelling because it meshed with the greatest of all the racist bogeys of the white men — the specter of the Yellow Peril.

Hatred toward the Japanese derived not simply from the reports of Japanese atrocities, but also from the deeper wellsprings of antiorientalism. *Time* magazine's coverage of the American response to Pearl Harbor, for example, opened on this very note. What did Americans say when they heard of the attack, *Time* asked rhetorically. And the answer it quoted approvingly as representative was, "Why, the yellow bastards!" *Time's* cover portrait for 22 December 1941, depicting Admiral Yamamoto Isoroku, who planned the Pearl Harbor attack, was colored a single shade: bright yellow. At one time or another almost every mainstream newspaper and magazine fell into the color idiom, and yellow was by far the dominant color in anti-Japanese propaganda art. Among the music makers, we already have encountered Tin Pan Alley's revealing counterpoint of Hitler and the "Yellow Japs." Other song titles included, "We're Gonna Find a Fellow Who Is Yellow and Beat Him Red, White, and Blue." . . . In some American pronouncements, the Japanese were simply dismissed as "LYBs," a well-comprehended acronym for the double entendre "little yellow bellies."

Spokesmen for Asian Allies such as China were aghast at such insensitivity, and the war years as a whole became an agonizing revelation of the breadth and depth of anti-Asian prejudice in the United States. In the very midst of the war these revelations prompted a year-long congressional hearing to consider revision of the notorious "Oriental Exclusion Laws" — the capstone of formal discrimination against all people of Asian origin. What the Japanese attack brought to the surface, however, was something more elusive and interesting than the formal structures of discrimination: the concrete fears that underlay the perception of a menacing Orient.

Since the late nineteenth century, when the Yellow Peril idea was first expressed in the West, white people had been unnerved by a triple apprehension — recognition that the "hordes" of Asia outnumbered the population of the West, fear that these alien masses might gain possession of the science and technology that made Western domination possible, and the belief that Orientals possessed occult powers unfathomable to Western rationalists. By trumpeting the cause of Pan-Asianism and proclaiming the creation of a Greater East Asia Co-Prosperity Sphere, Japan raised the prospect that the Asian hordes might at last become united. With their Zero planes and big battleships and carriers, the Japanese gave notice that the technological and scientific gap had narrowed dramatically. And with the aura of invincibility that blossomed in the heat of the early victories, the Japanese "supermen" evoked the old fantasies of occult oriental powers. All this would be smashed in August 1945, when Japan capitulated. And it would all resurface three decades later when Japan burst on the scene as an economic superpower and other Asian countries began to emulate this "miracle."

Racism also shaped the Japanese perception of self and other — again in patterned ways, but patterns different from those of the West. History accounts for much of this difference. Over centuries, Japan had borrowed extensively from India, China, and more recently the West and had been greatly enriched thereby; and it acknowledged these debts. And over the course of the preceding century, the Japanese had felt the sting of Western condescension. Even when applauded by the Europeans and Americans for their accomplishments in industrializing and "Westernizing," the Japanese were painfully aware that they were still regarded as immature and unimaginative and unstable — good in the small things, as the saying went among the old Japan hands, and small in the great things.

Thus Japanese racial thinking was riven by an ambivalence that had no clear counterpart in white supremacist thinking. Like the white Westerners, they assumed a hierarchical world; but unlike the Westerners, they lacked the unambiguous power that would enable them to place themselves unequivocally at the top of the racial hierarchy. Toward Europeans and Americans, and the science and civilizations they exemplified, the national response was one of admiration as well as fear, mistrust, and hatred. Toward all others — that is, toward nonwhites including Asians other than themselves, their attitude was less complicated. By the twentieth century Japan's success in resisting Western colonialism or neocolonialism and emerging as one of the so-called Great Powers had instilled among the Japanese an attitude toward weaker peoples and nations that was as arrogant and contemptuous as the racism of the Westerners. The Koreans and Chinese began to learn this in the 1890s and early 1900s; the peoples of Southeast Asia learned it quickly after 7 December 1941.

For Japan, the crisis of identity came to a head in the 1930s and early 1940s, taking several dramatic forms. Behind the joy and fury of the initial attacks in 1941–42, and

indeed behind many of the atrocities against white men and women in Asia, was an un-
mistakable sense of racial revenge. At the same time, the Japanese began to emphasize
their own destiny as a "leading race" (*shido minzoku*). If one were to venture a single
broad observation concerning the difference between the preoccupation of white supremacism and Japanese racism, it might be this: that whereas white racism devoted in-
ordinate energy to the denigration of the other, Japanese racial thinking concentrated
on elevating the self. In Japanese war films produced between 1937 and 1945, for example, the enemy was rarely depicted. Frequently it was not even made clear who the
antagonist was. The films concentrated almost exclusively on the admirable "Japanese"
qualities of the protagonists. The focus of the broader gamut of propaganda for domestic consumption was similar. In its language and imagery, Japanese prejudice thus appeared to be more benign than its white counterpart — by comparison, a soft racism —
but this was misleading. The insularity of such introversion tended to depersonalize
and, in its own peculiar way, dehumanize all non-Japanese "outsiders." In practice, such
intense fixation on the self contributed to a wartime record of extremely callous and
brutal behavior toward non-Japanese.

The central concept in this racial thinking was that most tantalizing of cultural fixations: the notion of purity. In Japan as elsewhere, this has a deep history not merely in
religious ritual, but also in social practice and the delineation of insider and outsider
(pure and impure) groups. By turning purity into a racial ideology for modern times,
the Japanese were in effect nationalizing a concept traditionally associated with differentiation within their society. Purity was Japanized and made the signifier of homogeneity, of "one hundred million hearts beating as one," of a unique "Yamato soul"
(*Yamato damashii,* from the ancient capital of the legendary first emperor). Non-Japanese
became by definition impure. Whether powerful or relatively powerless, all were beyond
the pale.

. . . At a superficial level, this fixation on the special purity or "sincerity" of the
Japanese resembles the mystique of American "innocence." Whereas the latter is a sub-
theme in the American myth, however, the former was cultivated as the very essence of
a powerful racial ideology. Like esoteric mantras, a variety of evocative (and often archaic) words and phrases were introduced to convey the special racial and moral qualities
of the Japanese; and like esoteric mandalas, certain visual images (sun, sword, cherry
blossom, snowcapped Mount Fuji, an abstract "brightness") and auspicious colors (white
and red) were elevated as particularistic symbols of the purity of the Japanese spirit.

Where Westerners had turned eventually to pseudoscience and dubious social science
to bolster theories of the inherent inferiority of nonwhite and non-Western peoples,
the Japanese turned to mythohistory, where they found the origins of their superiority
in the divine descent of their sovereign and the racial and cultural homogeneity of the
sovereign's loyal subjects. Deity, monarch, and populace were made one, and no words
captured this more effectively than the transcendent old phrase resurrected to supersede
plain reference to "the Japanese": *Yamato minzoku,* the "Yamato race." "Yamato" — the
name of the place where Jimmu, grandson of the grandson of the sun goddess, was alleged
to have founded the imperial line in 660 B.C. — was redolent with the archaic mystique of celestial genetics that made Japan the divine land and the Japanese the chosen

THE CODE OF THE SAMURAI

Wartime imagery dehumanized the Japanese and belittled their culture. This cartoon from the Chicago Tribune *typifies the stereotype of the Japanese as monkeys and the American sense of waging a just war of retribution. American soldiers, it implied, were the real samurai, enforcing a code of honor the Japanese had abandoned. (Copyrighted Chicago Tribune Company. All rights reserved. Used with permission.)*

people. In *Yamato minzoku*, the association became explicitly racial and exclusionary. The race had no identity apart from the throne and the traditions that had grown up around it, and no outsider could hope to penetrate this community. This was blood nationalism of an exceptionally potent sort.

Many of these themes were elaborated in the ideological writings of the 1930s and early 1940s, and the cause of blood nationalism was elevated when 1940 became the occasion for massive ceremony and festivity in celebration of the 2,600 year anniversary

Annihilating demons was the Japanese counterpart to the Anglo-American imagery of killing beasts or vermin. In this Japanese poster of 1942, Japanese bayonets skewer Anglo-American demons designed to look like Franklin D. Roosevelt and Winston Churchill. The caption reads, "The death of these wretches will be the birthday of world peace." (Osaka Puck, February and December 1942.)

of the "national foundation day." At the same time, the racial ideologues took care to emphasize that purity was not merely an original state, but also an ongoing process for each Japanese. . . . Purity lay in transcendence of ego and identification with a greater truth or cause; and in the crisis years of the 1930s and early 1940s this greater truth was equated with the militarized imperial state. War itself, with all the sacrifice it demanded, became an act of purification. And death in war, the ultimate expression of selflessness, became the supreme attainment of this innate Japanese purity. We know now that most Japanese fighting men who died slowly did not pass away with the emperor's name on their lips, as propaganda claimed they did. Most often they called (as GIs did also) for their mothers. Still, they fought and died with fervor and bravery, enveloped in the propaganda of being the divine soldiers of the divine land, and this contributed to the aura of a people possessed of special powers.

Both the Western myth of the superman and the bogey of the Yellow Peril had their analogue in this emphasis the Japanese themselves placed on their unique suprarational spiritual qualities. In Western eyes, however, this same spectacle of fanatical mass behavior also reinforced the image of the little men, of the Japanese as a homogeneous, undifferentiated mass. There is no small irony in this, for what we see here is the coalescence of Japanese indoctrination with the grossest anti-Japanese stereotypes of the Westerners. In the crudest of Anglo-American colloquialisms, it was argued that "a Jap is a Jap" (the famous quotation of General John DeWitt, who directed the incarceration of the Japanese Americans). In the 1945 propaganda film *Know Your Enemy — Japan,* produced by Frank Capra for the United States Army, the Japanese were similarly described as "photographic prints off the same negative" — a line now frequently cited as the classic expression of racist American contempt for the Japanese. Yet in essence this "seen one seen them all" attitude was not greatly different from the "one hundred million hearts beating as one" indoctrination that the Japanese leaders themselves promoted. Homogeneity and separateness *were* essential parts of what the Japanese ideologues said about themselves. In their idiom, this was integral to the superiority of the Yamato race. To non-Japanese, it was further cause for derision.

. . . In proclaiming their own purity, the Japanese cast others as inferior because they did not, and could not, share in the grace of the divine land. Non-Japanese were, by the very logic of the ideology, impure, foul, polluted. Such sentiments usually flowed like an underground stream beneath the ornate paeans to the "pure and cloudless heart" of the Japanese, but occasionally they burst to the surface with extraordinary vehemence. Thus, in a book of war reportage titled *Bataan,* Hino Ashihei, one of the best-known Japanese wartime writers, described American POWs as "people whose arrogant nation once tried to unlawfully treat our motherland with contempt." "As I watch large numbers of the surrendered soldiers," he continued, "I feel like I am watching filthy water running from the sewage of a nation which derives from impure origins and has lost its pride of race. Japanese soldiers look particularly beautiful, and I feel exceedingly proud of being Japanese." These were the American prisoners, of course, whom Japanese soldiers brutalized in the Bataan death march. Hino's contempt for the "impure" American prisoners provides an almost perfect counterpoint to Ernie Pyle's revulsion on seeing his first "subhuman" Japanese POWs.

As a rule, however, the Japanese turned to one particular negative image when referring directly to the Anglo-American enemy: the demon or devil. "Devilish Anglo-Americans" (*kichiku Ei-Bei*) was the most familiar epithet for the white foe. In the graphic arts the most common depiction of Americans or British was a horned Roosevelt or Churchill, drawn exactly like the demons (*oni, akuma*) found in Japanese folklore and folk religion. As a metaphor of dehumanization, the demonic white man was the counterpart of the Japanese monkeyman in Western thinking, but the parallel was by no means exact. The demon was a more impressive and ambiguous figure than the ape, and certainly of a different category entirely from vermin. In Japanese folk renderings, the demon was immensely powerful; it was often intelligent, or at least exceedingly crafty; and it possessed talents and powers beyond those of ordinary Japanese. Not all demons had to be killed; some could be won over and turned from menaces into guardians. Indeed, Japanese soldiers killed in battle often were spoken of as having become "demons protecting the country" (*gokoku no oni*) — easy to imagine when one recalls the statues of ferocious deities that often guard Buddhist temples. Here again, like the flexible Western metaphor of the child, was an intriguingly malleable stereotype — one that would be turned about dramatically after the war, when the Americans became the military "protectors" of Japan.

During the war years, however, this more benign potential of the demonic other was buried. For the Japanese at war, the demon worked as a metaphor for the enemy in ways that plain subhuman or bestial images could not. It conveyed a sense of the adversary's great power and special abilities, and in this respect it captured some of the ambivalence that had always marked Japan's modern relationship with the West. At the same time, the demonic other played to deep feelings of insecurity by evoking the image of an ever-present outside threat. Unlike apes or vermin, the demon did not signify a random presence. In Japanese folklore, these figures always lurked just beyond the boundaries of the community or the borders of the country — in forests and mountains outside the village, on islands off the coast. In origin, they exemplified not a racial fear, but a far more basic fear of outsiders in general.

Contrary to the myth of being homogeneous, Japanese society was honeycombed with groups suspicious of one another, and the blue-eyed barbarians from across the seas became absorbed into patterns of thinking that had emerged centuries earlier as a response to these tense and threatening insider/outsider relationships. The Westerners who suddenly appeared on Japan's horizon in the mid-nineteenth century were the most formidable of all outsiders, and the response to them mobilized nationalist and racist sentiments in unprecedented ways. Symbolically the demonic other was already present to be racialized. . . .

Where images and actions come together most decisively, however, demon, ape, and vermin functioned similarly. All made killing easier by dehumanizing the enemy. The rhetoric of "kill the American demons" and "kill the British demons" became commonplace not only in combat, but also on the home front. A popular magazine published in late 1944 conveyed the fury of this rhetoric. Under the title "Devilish Americans and English," the magazine ran a two-page drawing of Roosevelt and Churchill as debauched ogres carousing with fellow demons in sight of Mount Fuji and urged all Japanese, "Beat and kill these animals that have lost their human nature! That is the great mission that Heaven has given to the Yamato race, for the eternal peace of the world!" . . .

Demonization was by no means an essential precondition for killing, however. The most numerous victims of Japanese aggression and atrocity were other Asians, who were rarely depicted this way. Toward them the Japanese attitude was a mixture of "Pan-Asian" propaganda for public consumption, elaborate theories of racial hierarchy and Japanese hegemony [domination] at official and academic levels, and condescension and contempt in practice. Apart from a small number of idealistic military officers and civilian officials, few Japanese appear to have taken seriously the egalitarian rhetoric of Pan-Asian solidarity and genuine liberation of colonized Asian peoples. Never for a moment did the Japanese consider liberating their own Korean and Formosan colonies, and policy toward Southeast Asia — even when "independence" was granted — was always framed in terms that made Japan's preeminence as the "leading race" absolutely clear. The purity so integral to Japanese thinking was peculiar to the Japanese as a race and culture — not to "oriental" peoples in general — and consequently there emerged no real notion of "Asian supremacism" that could be regarded as a close counterpart to the white supremacism of the Anglo-Americans.

Before the 1930s, the Japanese did not have a clearly articulated position toward other Asians. The rush of events thereafter, including the invasion of China and the decision to push south into Southeast Asia, forced military planners and their academic supporters to codify and clarify existing opinions on these matters. The result was a small outpouring of studies, reports, and pronouncements — many of a confidential nature — that explicitly addressed the characteristics of the various peoples of Asia and the appropriate policy toward them. That these were not casual undertakings was made amply clear in 1981, when a hitherto unknown secret study dating from 1943 was discovered in Tokyo. Prepared by a team of some forty researchers associated with the Population and Race Section of the Research Bureau of the Ministry of Health and Welfare, this work devoted over three thousand pages to analysis of race theory in general and the different races of Asia in particular. The title of the report gives an inkling of its contents: *An Investigation of Global Policy with the Yamato Race as Nucleus.* . . .

The focus of this massive report was on Asian rather than Western peoples, and its dry language provides insight into how racial inequality in Asia was rationalized. The central metaphor was the family. The critical phrase was "proper place" — a term that had roots in Confucian prescriptions for domestic relationships but was carefully extended to cover international relations beginning in the late 1930s. The family idiom is another example of the malleable social construct, for it suggests harmony and reciprocity on the one hand, but clear-cut hierarchy and division of authority and responsibility on the other; and it was the latter that really mattered to the Japanese. . . . The Japanese writers made clear that Japan was not merely the head of the family in Asia, but also destined to maintain that position "eternally." Whether the Yamato race also was destined to become the head of the global family of races and nations was left unanswered, although passing comments suggested that this was the ultimate goal. The opening pages of the study flatly declared that the war would continue "until Anglo-American imperialistic democracy has been completely vanquished and a new world order erected in its place." And as the *Investigation* made amply clear, the Japanese-led imperium in Asia would assume a leading role in this new world order.

Despite their Confucian overtones, the family metaphor and proper-place philosophy bore close resemblance to Western thinking on issues of race and power. The Japanese took as much pleasure as any white Westerner in categorizing the weaker peoples of Asia as "children." In their private reports and directives, they made clear that "proper place" meant a division of labor in Asia in which the Yamato race would control the economic, financial, and strategic reins of power . . . and thereby "hold the key to the very existence of all the races of East Asia." . . . For other Asians the real meaning of Japan's racial rhetoric was obvious. "Leading race" meant master race, "proper place" meant inferior place, "family" meant patriarchal oppression.

Given the virulence of the race hate that permeated the Pacific war, at first it seems astonishing that Americans and Japanese were able to move so quickly toward cordial relations after Japan's surrender. Intimate face-to-face contact for purposes other than mutual slaughter enabled each side to rehumanize the other in the highly structured milieu of the Allied Occupation of Japan, which lasted from 1945 to 1952. Although the United States–dominated Occupation was ethnocentric and overbearing in many respects, it also was infused with goodwill and — in its early stages — a commitment to "demilitarization and democratization" that struck a responsive chord among most of the defeated Japanese. Contrary to the wartime stereotypes of propagandists in both the Allied and Japanese camps, most Japanese were sick of regimentation, indoctrination, and militarism. At the same time, the cold war facilitated a quick diversion of enmity, and anticommunism became a new crusade uniting the two former antagonists at the state level. Enemies changed, enmity did not.

On both sides, the abrupt metamorphosis from war to peace was cushioned by the malleability of racial, cultural, and ideological stereotypes. With only a small twist, patterns of perception that had abetted mass slaughter now proved conducive to paternalistic patronage on the American side — and to acquiescence to such paternalism by many Japanese. Racism did not disappear from the United States–Japan relationship, but it was softened and transmogrified. For the Americans, the vermin disappeared but the monkeymen lingered for a while as charming pets. The September 1945 cover of *Leatherneck,* for example — the first issue of the marine monthly to appear after Japan's capitulation — featured a cheery cartoon of a GI holding a vexed but thoroughly domesticated monkey wearing the cap, shirt, and leggings of the Imperial Army. . . .

Other racist stereotypes traveled from war to peace in comparable ways. Although defeat temporarily extinguished the superman mystique, it reinforced the perception of the Japanese as little men or lesser men. Stated conversely, victory over Japan reinforced the conceit of inherent white and Western superiority. . . . The American overseers of Occupied Japan thought in terms of a civilizing mission that would eliminate what was primitive, tribal, and ritualistic — an old but idealistic colonial attitude indeed. They would guide an immature people with backward institutions toward maturity. The Japanese "children" now became pupils in General MacArthur's school of democracy, learners and borrowers of advanced United States technology, followers of United States cold war policies. . . .

Neither democratization and demilitarization nor — later — economic reconstruction and remilitarization were ethnocentric American goals forced on unwilling Japanese. The overall relationship, however, was inherently unequal and patronizing on the part of the Americans, and it is here that racist attitudes survived. United States policymakers at the highest level also were not above cynically manipulating Japanese racism to serve their own purposes. In 1951, when Japan's allegiance in the cold war was still not entirely certain, for example, [the American diplomat] John Foster Dulles recommended that the Americans and British take advantage of Japanese feelings of "superiority as against the Asiatic mainland masses" and play up the "social prestige" of being associated with the Western alliance. . . .

On the Japanese side, defeat was bitter but peace was sweet, and certain attitudes associated with wartime racial thinking also proved adaptable to the postsurrender milieu. Proper-place thinking facilitated acceptance of a subordinate status vis-à-vis the victorious Allies, at least for the time being. In this regard it is helpful to recall that the "leading race" rhetoric of the war years was a relatively new ideology in Japan, and that for most of their modern history the Japanese had played a subordinate role in the world order. The militarism of the 1930s and early 1940s arose out of a desire to alter that insecure status, and it ended in disaster. To seek a new place in new ways after 1945 was in fact the continuation of a familiar quest.

In fascinating ways, the wartime fixation on purity and purification proved adaptable to this commitment to a new path of development. Individuals who had been exhorted to purge self and society of decadent Western influences before the surrender now found themselves exhorted to purge the society of militarism and feudalistic legacies. This sense of "cleansing" Japan of foul and reactionary influences was truly phenomenal in the early postwar years, and while this tapped popular aspirations for liberation, it also politicized the militarists' ideology of the pure self in undreamed-of ways. Universal "democratic" values now became the touchstone of purity. And the guardians at the gates, to cap these astounding transmogrifications, were the erstwhile American demons. The United States assumption of a military role as protector of postwar Japan was a hard-nosed, rational policy, but from the Japanese perspective it had a subtle, almost subconscious logic. The fearsome demons of Japanese folklore, after all, were often won over and put to use by the ostensibly weaker folk.

The transitional adaptations of proper place, purity, and the demon more or less deracialized the wartime fixations. They did not, however, eliminate racial tensions latent in the structure of institutionalized inequality that characterized postwar United States–Japan relations until recently. So long as Japan remained conspicuously inferior to the United States in power and influence, the structure and psychology of what is known in Japan as "subordinate independence" could be maintained. When relations of power and influence changed, neither side could be expected to rethink these fundamental relationships without trauma. The great change came in the 1970s, when it became apparent — abruptly and shockingly for almost everyone concerned — that Japan had become an economic superpower while America was in relative decline. In this situation, war talk became fashionable again: talk of trade wars; ruminations on who really won the Pacific war; doomsday warnings of a new yen bloc, a seriously rearmed Japan, a "financial Pearl Harbor." In American rhetoric, the simian subhumans were resurrected as "predatory economic animals," the old wartime supermen returned as menacing "miraclemen," garbed in Western business suits but practicing sumo capitalism. Japanese, in turn, often in high government positions, decried America's demonic "Japan bashing" and at the same time attributed their country's accomplishments to a "Yamato race" homogeneity and purity that "mongrelized" America could never hope to emulate.

As times change, the malleable idioms of race and culture, power and status, change with them. They never completely disappear.

QUESTIONS TO CONSIDER

1. Analyze Anglo-American racist perceptions of the Japanese. In what way did the image of Japanese as monkeys connect with biological and cultural theories about human development? Why did Westerners consider the Japanese childlike or "little men"? How similar were anti-Japanese stereotypes to traditional negative images of women or colonial peoples? Why? How does Dower reconcile the coexistence of "little men" and "supermen" images of the Japanese?

2. Compare the Anglo-American ideology of white supremacy with Japanese racist ideology during World War II. Why did white racism "denigrate the other," while Japanese racism "elevated the self"? Did the ideology of Japanese racial superiority embrace all Asian peoples, or was it nationally specific? How did Japanese images of the American enemy contrast with American images of the Japanese? What similarities do you see between American and Japanese racist propaganda?

3. How does Dower's presentation of American and Japanese racial thinking illuminate such wartime incidents as the American reaction to Pearl Harbor, the incarceration of Japanese Americans in the United States, Japan's treatment of American POWs, and Japanese reluctance to apologize for the nation's subjugation of East Asia? Do you think it is relevant to America's dropping of the atomic bomb on Hiroshima (which Dower does not discuss)?

4. How, according to Dower, did racist stereotypes "travel from war to peace"? In what ways were racial ideas adjusted to accommodate the conditions of America's postwar occupation of Japan and the new relationship between the two countries? What role did the Cold War play in this adjustment?

5. Do hostile racial images or cultural caricatures still play a role in U.S. military or economic confrontations around the world? Consider the images that appeared in media coverage or government pronouncements during the U.S.-Iraq wars of 1990 and 2003, or the emnity between Islamic and Christian "civilizations" being invoked by people on both sides during the current U.S. war against terrorism. If it is true that Americans have avoided official campaigns of hatred based on ethnic caricatures in recent wars (unlike World War II), why is this the case? Why are such images still invoked on talk radio or other mass media?

THE COLD WAR IN
EUROPE AND ASIA

Instead of peace, the end of World War II brought a different kind of war, one that erupted into military conflict only sporadically but loomed over the earth's people for nearly fifty years, threatening their very survival. The Cold War between the Soviet Union and the United States began during World War II, continued in their postwar rivalry for control of Eastern Europe, then became a worldwide struggle as communism in various forms spread to China and elsewhere in Asia. At home, the Cold War had a chilling effect on American politics and culture, triggering a Red Scare that intimidated those who disagreed with government policies or criticized the American way of life. Abroad, American efforts to "contain" communism and to promote democracy and capitalism led to tense showdowns with the Soviets over Eastern Europe and Cuba, and to controversial and costly wars in Korea (1950–1953) and then in Vietnam (1965–1975).

The essays in this chapter span three decades of American Cold War policy, from its origins in postwar European events to its apex in the Vietnam War. In the first selection, John Lewis Gaddis adopts a dual-perspective approach to contrast Soviet and American policymakers' motives and strategies toward Europe in the years immediately following World War II. Gaddis sees a basic clash between the Soviet "empire by imposition" — Russian leader Joseph Stalin's aggressive expansion into Eastern Europe — and the American presidents' "empire by invitation" — their defensive alliance with the anticommunist nations of Western Europe. The second selection, by T. Christopher Jespersen, suggests that in Vietnam the United States attempted its own "empire by imposition." Pursuing an analogy between the Vietnamese Revolution of 1945–1975 and the American Revolution of 1776, Jespersen finds striking parallels in the actions of the imperial powers that tried to suppress these independence movements.

Despite its own birth in a colonial war for independence, the United States, he shows, responded to the Vietnamese struggle in ways that echoed Britain's fight against its North American colonies, and met with a similar defeat.

It is noteworthy that both Gaddis and Jespersen use the word "empire" to describe the international involvements of Cold War America. By implication, this invites you to compare America's Cold War policies with the earlier, more formal kind of American imperialism discussed in Chapter V. In other ways, however, the two essays are very different. The first offers a close comparison of contemporary rivals; the second makes an imaginative leap across time and space to pursue a telling analogy. The first emphasizes Soviet and American differences and declares the American brand of empire benign; the second finds the British and American imperial responses to revolution eerily similar and equally mistaken. As you assess the strengths and weaknesses of these essays, consider how well they demonstrate the value of different comparative approaches as well as what they tell us about the nature of America's Cold War commitments.

19

The American and Soviet Cold War Empires

John Lewis Gaddis

For decades, American historians wrote about the Cold War as if they were fighting it. On one side, scholars who were dubbed "Cold Warriors" by their critics described the American policy of containing communism as a moral response to Soviet aggression in Eastern Europe and against the "Free World." On the other side, "revisionist" historians portrayed the United States as the aggressor. Americans, they claimed, exaggerated the Soviet threat and used their superior economic and military power to dominate the postwar world.

The destruction of the Berlin Wall in 1989 and the dissolution of the Soviet Union two years later turned down the heat of this scholarly debate and promised to increase its light. The end of the Cold War after nearly a half-century of excruciating tension eased Americans' fear of perishing in a superpower showdown. It also influenced historians' views of the past. For one thing, the opening of the Kremlin archives began to reveal the secret motives and actions of Soviet policymakers, while declassification of American records provided new information about matters ranging from nuclear policy to the machinations of the Central Intelligence Agency. For another, the end to hostilities opened the way for interpretations of the Cold War that are less intent on assigning blame than on analyzing processes, and more evenhanded in the attention they give to both sides of the superpower rivalry, or even to third parties. Longer time spans and larger contexts provide an excellent environment for comparative history to flourish.

This by no means eliminates moral judgments from history. As Kate Brown's pairing of the American and Soviet frontiers in Selection 4 showed, comparative analysis can pack its own moral punch. The same is true for the following excerpt from John Lewis Gaddis's We Now Know (1997), a post-Soviet assessment of the origins of the Cold War in Europe. Gaddis distances himself from Cold War polemics by using memoirs and other new evidence in his account. He acknowledges the revisionist insight that American foreign policy was rooted domestically in the expansionist ambitions of corporate capitalism. Above all, he proposes that the concept of empire provides the best way of understanding the Cold War international system. This includes the striking admission, unthinkable to many Americans during the Cold War, that their nation was acting as an imperial power.

Nevertheless, as Gaddis charts the escalating tensions between Americans and Soviets over the fate of Eastern Europe after 1945, he makes clear which of the "Cold War Empires" he favors. Beginning with the Soviet Union, he shows how dictator Joseph Stalin updated old-fashioned Russian imperialism by fusing it with Marxist ideology, so that the expansion of Russian territory and power was provided the cover of righteous anticolonialism. Since Stalin would take as much land as the West would allow, Gaddis writes, it was essential that Americans abandon their isolationist tendencies and join with Europe to "contain" the Soviet menace through military alliances as well as economic initiatives such as the Marshall Plan. The American empire was thus a defensive response to Soviet expansionism. At first, American leaders preferred a "multilateral" approach to international affairs in which the United Nations, the World Bank, and similar institutions would ensure world peace and prosperity. Only when Stalin prevented the Soviet Union and its satellites from participating did Americans turn to containment, which revived the traditional "balance-of-power" methods of European empires. Critics labeled containment a "balance of terror" that threatened to blow up the planet, but Gaddis calls it a success and wonders whether Americans and Europeans should have adopted it sooner.

By juxtaposing the American and Soviet "empires" and carefully considering counterarguments to his conclusions, Gaddis attempts a measured Cold War postmortem based on what "we now know." Whether his essay succeeds as a fair and balanced comparison is up to you to decide. How persuasive is Gaddis's contrast between the American "empire by invitation" and the Russian "empire by imposition"? In blaming Stalin's expansionist blend of imperialism and communism for the impasse, does Gaddis ignore a corresponding American mixture of imperialism and democratic capitalism that dates back to Woodrow Wilson (as Alan Dawley suggested in Selection 12)? Does Gaddis take self-interested motives sufficiently into account when discussing American Cold War policy? Would his contrast look as favorable to the United States if policy toward Asian nations such as China, Korea, and Vietnam were his focus? (This is a question you might return to after reading Selection 20.)

Comparisons of momentous historical events will always be influenced by the shifting concerns and creeds of later eras, and they should not avoid moral judgments or conclusions. At the same time, comparative history, like all good history, must remain faithful to the evidence. For all their differences, Gaddis and his critics would surely agree that the goal of an accurate comparative history of the Cold War is worth pursuing if we are to learn lessons from its frightening history rather than repeat it.

GLOSSARY

BERLIN BLOCKADE (1948–1949)   A land and water blockade of the West German capital begun by the Soviets to force the United States and its allies to abandon their postwar occupation of West Berlin. The Allies responded with a massive airlift of food and fuel until the Russians lifted the blockade.

BOLSHEVIKS   A highly disciplined Marxist faction of the Russian Social Democratic Party that, led by V. I. Lenin, seized control in October 1917 of the Provisional Government set up by the Russian Revolution of February that year. In 1918 the Bolsheviks changed their name to the Russian Communist Party and began suppressing rival political organizations and establishing a communist government in Russia.

CHURCHILL, WINSTON (1874–1965)   A prominent British statesman and wartime leader. Churchill fought in British imperialist campaigns in India, Sudan, and South Africa before being elected to Parliament in 1900. He served in several cabinet positions in the Liberal government of Lloyd George and supported domestic reforms. Switching to the Conservative Party after 1924, Churchill served as a cabinet member in the late 1920s but was out of office from 1929 to 1939 and a vocal critic of his party's appeasement policy. In May 1940 he replaced Neville Chamberlain as prime minister and rallied the British military and public to eventual victory over Germany. Forced to step down when the Conservatives lost an election in July 1945, Churchill warned Westerners of the Soviets' expansionist aims and coined the term "Iron Curtain" to describe the barrier raised by Soviet control over Eastern Europe. Churchill was reappointed prime minister in 1951 and directed Britain's Cold War policies until he resigned in 1955.

CONTAINMENT POLICY   The American policy of halting the spread of Soviet communism, which was pursued by Presidents Truman and Eisenhower as the basis of Cold War strategy.

GREAT RUSSIAN NATIONALISM   The belief, subcribed to by most of the czars, that Russia should extend its control over neighboring non-Russian peoples and incorporate them into an empire dominated by ethnic Russians.

KENNAN, GEORGE F. (1904–)   An American diplomat who planned policy in the State Department in the late 1940s and served in 1952 as U.S. ambassador to the Soviet Union. Kennan was the primary author of the American Cold War strategy of "containment."

KHRUSHCHEV, NIKITA (1894–1971)   Premier of the USSR during part of the Cold War. A Ukrainian peasant who climbed through the Soviet ranks in the 1930s, Khrushchev managed to escape Stalin's purges by directing technical agricultural and construction projects. When Stalin died in 1953, Khrushchev vied for power with several prominent communists and emerged triumphant in 1956. That year he denounced Stalin's crimes, but as Soviet premier (1956–1964) Khrushchev continued the Cold

War, including the arms race, support for client states such as Cuba, and an attempt to outproduce Western economies.

KOREAN WAR (1950–1953)   A conflict between communist North Korea and noncommunist South Korea that was joined by U.S. and U.N. forces, which assisted the South under the policy of "containment," and Chinese (but not Soviet) troops, which aided the North. After intense fighting that cost fifty-four thousand American lives and many more Koreans and Chinese, an armistice agreement restored the original boundary dividing North and South Korea.

KREMLIN   The walled center of Moscow, enclosing the czar's residence, three cathedrals, and the Soviet parliament. After 1918 the Kremlin was the seat of government of the Soviet Union.

LENIN, VLADIMIR ILICH (1870–1924)   The head of the Bolshevik faction of the Russian Social Democratic Party. Lenin denounced World War I as a conflict of competing imperialist powers. When the Russian Revolution of February 1917 removed the czar and established a provisional government, Lenin returned from exile to agitate for communism and take Russia out of the war. In October 1917 the Bolsheviks seized power and declared the world's first communist government. The following March, Lenin's government signed the Brest-Litovsk peace agreement with Germany, ending Russia's involvement in World War I.

MARSHALL PLAN   Officially called the European Recovery Program, a program, proposed by American secretary of state George C. Marshall and established in 1948, that provided over $13 billion in American aid to promote economic rebuilding and political stability in Western Europe after the war. The USSR and Eastern European countries were invited to participate, but declined.

MOLOTOV, VYACHESLAV MIKHAILOVICH (1890–1986)   Stalin's faithful lieutenant. Molotov was chairman of the Council of People's Commisars (the equivalent of prime minister) from 1930 to 1941 and served as the Soviet Union's foreign minister from 1939 to 1949 and again from 1953 to 1956.

NAZI-SOVIET PACT (1939)   A treaty between Stalinist Russia and Nazi Germany that shocked the world, reversing years of antifascist propaganda by the Soviets. It featured a nonaggression and trade agreement as well as secret protocols that provided for the German and Soviet partition of Poland and Soviet occupation of the Baltic States. Hitler used the pact to clear the way for the Nazi invasion of Poland; Stalin used it to grab territory and to delay, if not prevent, a German attack. It remained in force until Hitler invaded the USSR in June 1941.

RUSSO-JAPANESE WAR (1904–1905)   A conflict over the rival claims of Russia and Japan on Manchuria and Korea during which Japan's land and naval victories announced its arrival as a world power. Russia's concession of Korea to Japan and its return of Manchuria to China helped to spark the Revolution of 1905, which forced the czar to make modest constitutional reforms.

SOMOZA GARCÍA, ANASTASIO (1896–1956)   The Nicaraguan army leader who overthrew the elected president in 1936 and became virtual dictator until his assassination. The Somoza family controlled the Nicaraguan presidency until 1979.

STALIN, JOSEPH (1879–1953)   The ruthless and powerful head of the Soviet Union from 1929 until his death. An early comrade of the Bolshevik leader V. I. Lenin, Stalin returned from exile in Siberia during the Russian Revolution and became the first editor of the Communist Party newspaper, *Pravda*. He emerged victorious from the five-year power struggle after Lenin's death in 1924. Once in control, Stalin forcibly collectivized Russia's farms, ordered rapid industrial growth, and imprisoned or executed rivals and dissidents, including millions of ordinary citizens.

TOCQUEVILLE, ALEXIS DE (1805–1859)   The French statesman and political philosopher whose book *Democracy in America* (1835) became a classic analysis of political democracy and American society. Tocqueville famously predicted that the United States and Russia would become the dominant "great powers" of the twentieth century.

TREATY OF VERSAILLES (1919)   The treaty between the Allied powers and Germany ending World War I. Its terms, which rejected U.S. President Woodrow Wilson's plans for peace, punished Germany by imposing reparations payments, reducing its territory, and distributing its colonies to rival powers. Only the treaty's blueprint for a peacekeeping League of Nations reflected Wilson's influence.

TRUJILLO MOLINA, RAFAEL LEÓNIDAS (1891–1961)   The dictator of the Dominican Republic from 1930 until his assassination in 1961.

YALTA CONFERENCE   An important planning meeting among Churchill, Stalin, and Roosevelt in the Russian Crimea in February 1945. There they agreed on a four-power occupation of Germany (including French troops), a founding conference for the United Nations to be held later in 1945, entry by the Soviets into the war against Japan ninety days after Germany surrendered (the USSR to receive in return some island territories of Japan, trade privileges in China, and occupation areas in Korea), and a guarantee of representative government and free elections in Poland.

B y 1947, it was clear that cooperation to build a new order among the nations that had vanquished the old one was not going to be possible. There followed the most remarkable *polarization* of politics in modern history. It was as if a gigantic magnet had somehow come into existence, compelling most states, often even movements and individuals within states, to align themselves along fields of force thrown out from either Washington or Moscow. Remaining uncommitted, in a postwar international system that seemed so compulsively to require commitment, would be no easy matter. The United States and the Soviet Union were now as close as any great powers have ever been to controlling — as Tocqueville had foreseen Americans and Russians someday would — "the destinies of half the world."

Theorists of international relations have insisted that in seeking to understand such a system we need pay little attention to the "units" that make it up. Because states exist within an anarchic environment, survival has to be their common objective; power is the means by which all of them — regardless of their internal makeup — seek to ensure it. Nations

The Big Three at Yalta, February 1945.   As their armies converged upon Berlin, Roosevelt, Churchill, and Stalin met at a resort on the Black Sea. Their multilateral agreements on the occupation of Germany, the fate of Poland, Russia's entry into the war against Japan, and plans for the United Nations disguised fundamental differences between Soviet and American visions of the postwar world. (National Archives.)

therefore behave like featureless billiard balls: their collisions are significant, but their character is not. Tocqueville's distinction between authoritarian and democratic traditions in the Russian-American relationship, from this perspective, would be quite irrelevant.

The historian must point out, though, that however "great" the United States and the Soviet Union were during the Cold War, the "power" they obtained and wielded was rarely comparable. If these were billiard balls, they were not of the same size or weight or mass. Nor did the spheres of influence Washington and Moscow dominated resemble one another, whether from a military, economic, ideological, or moral perspective — a fact that has become obvious now that one of them no longer exists. Apples and oranges might be the better metaphor: at least it would allow for asymmetry, irregularity, and the possibility of internal rot.

But even this model has its deficiencies, because it leaves little room for the role of third parties — to say nothing of fourth, fifth, and nth parties — in shaping the Soviet-American relationship. It makes a big difference if great powers have to extend their authority against, rather than in concert with, the wishes of those subjected to it. The choice is between resistance and collaboration, and it falls to those incorporated within spheres of influence, not to those who impose them, ultimately to make it. If we are to grasp the nature of the post–World War II international system, then we will need an analytical framework capable of accounting for the rise and fall of great powers; but also one that incorporates variations in the nature of power and the influence it produces, as well as the limitations on power that permit peripheries to make a difference, even when things are being run from very powerful centers.

Such a framework exists, I think, in a more ancient method of governance than either democracy or authoritarianism: it is *empire*. I mean, by this term, a situation in which a single state shapes the behavior of others, whether directly or indirectly, partially or completely, by means that can range from the outright use of force through intimidation, dependency, inducements, and even inspiration. Leaders of both the United States and the Soviet Union would have bristled at having the appellation "imperial" affixed to what they were doing after 1945. But one need not send out ships, seize territories, and hoist flags to construct an empire: "informal" empires are considerably older than, and continued to exist alongside, the more "formal" ones Europeans imposed on so much of the rest of the world from the fifteenth through the nineteenth centuries. During the Cold War years Washington and Moscow took on much of the character, if never quite the charm, of old imperial capitals like London, Paris, and Vienna. And surely American and Soviet influence, throughout most of the second half of the twentieth century, was at least as ubiquitous as that of any earlier empire the world had ever seen.

Ubiquity never ensured unchallenged authority, though, and that fact provides yet another reason for applying an imperial analogy to Cold War history. For contrary to popular impressions, empires have always involved a two-way flow of influence. Imperializers have never simply acted upon the imperialized; the imperialized have also had a surprising amount of influence over the imperializers. The Cold War was no exception to this pattern, and an awareness of it too will help us to see how that rivalry emerged, evolved, and eventually ended in the way that it did.

I

Let us begin with the structure of the Soviet empire, for the simple reason that it was, much more than the American, deliberately designed. It has long been clear that, in addition to having had an authoritarian vision, Stalin also had an imperial one, which he proceeded to implement in at least as single-minded a way. No comparably influential builder of empire came close to wielding power for so long, or with such striking results, on the Western side.

It was, of course, a matter of some awkwardness that Stalin came out of a revolutionary movement that had vowed to smash, not just tsarist imperialism, but all forms of imperialism throughout the world. The Soviet leader constructed his own logic, though, and throughout his career he devoted a surprising amount of attention to showing how a revolution and an empire might coexist. Bolsheviks could never be imperialists, Stalin acknowledged in one of his earliest public pronouncements on this subject, made in April 1917. But surely in a *revolutionary* Russia nine-tenths of the non-Russian nationalities would not *want* their independence. Few among those minorities found Stalin's reasoning persuasive after the Bolsheviks did seize power later that year, however, and one of the first problems Lenin's new government faced was a disintegration of the old Russian empire not unlike what happened to the Soviet Union after communist authority finally collapsed in 1991.

Whether because of Lenin's own opposition to imperialism or, just as plausibly, because of Soviet Russia's weakness at the time, Finns, Estonians, Latvians, Lithuanians, Poles, and Moldavians were allowed to depart. Others who tried to do so — Ukrainians, Belorussians, Caucasians, Central Asians — were not so fortunate, and in 1922 Stalin proposed incorporating these remaining (and reacquired) nationalities into the Russian republic, only to have Lenin as one of his last acts override this recommendation and establish the multi-ethnic Union of Soviet Socialist Republics. After Lenin died and Stalin took his place it quickly became clear, though, that whatever its founding principles the USSR was to be no federation of equals. Rather, it would function as an updated form of empire even more tightly centralized than that of the Russian tsars.

Lenin and Stalin differed most significantly, not over authoritarianism or even terror, but on the legitimacy of Great Russian nationalism. The founder of Bolshevism had warned with characteristic pungency of "that truly Russian man, the Great-Russian chauvinist," and of the dangers of sinking into a "sea of chauvinistic Great-Russian filth, like flies in milk." Such temptations, he insisted, might ruin the prospects of revolution spreading elsewhere in the world. But Stalin — the implied target of Lenin's invective — was himself a Great Russian nationalist, with all the intensity transplanted nationals can sometimes attain. "The leaders of the revolutionary workers of all countries are avidly studying the most instructive history of the working class of Russia, its past, the past of Russia," he would write in a revealing private letter in 1930, shortly after consolidating his position as Lenin's successor. "All this instills (cannot but instill!) in the hearts of the Russian workers a feeling of revolutionary national pride, capable of moving mountains and working miracles."

The "Stalin constitution" of 1936, which formally specified the right of non-Russian nationalities to secede from the Soviet Union, coincided with the great purges and an officially sanctioned upsurge in Russian nationalism that would persist as a prominent feature of Stalin's regime until his death. It was as if the great authoritarian had set out to validate his own flawed prediction of 1917 by creating a set of circumstances in which non-Russian nationalities would not even *think* of seceding, even though the hypothetical authority to do so remained. The pattern resembled that of the purge trials themselves: one maintained a framework of legality — even, within the non-Russian republics, a toleration of local languages and cultures considerably greater than under the tsars. But Stalin then went to extraordinary lengths to deter anyone from exercising these rights or promoting those cultures in such a way as to challenge his own rule. He appears to have concluded, from his own study of the Russian past, that it was not "reactionary" to seek territorial expansion. His principal ideological innovation may well have been to impose the ambitions of the old princes of Muscovy, especially their determination to "gather in" and dominate all of the lands that surrounded them, upon the anti-imperial spirit of proletarian internationalism that had emanated from, if not actually inspired, the Bolshevik Revolution.

Stalin's fusion of Marxist internationalism with tsarist imperialism could only reinforce his tendency, in place well before World War II, to equate the advance of world revolution with the expanding influence of the Soviet state. He applied that linkage quite impartially: a major benefit of the 1939 pact with Hitler had been that it regained territories lost as a result of the Bolshevik Revolution and the World War I settlement. But Stalin's conflation of imperialism with ideology also explains the importance he attached, following the German attack in 1941, to having his new Anglo-American allies confirm these arrangements. He had similar goals in East Asia when he insisted on bringing the Soviet Union back to the position Russia had occupied in Manchuria prior to the Russo-Japanese War: this he finally achieved at the 1945 Yalta Conference in return for promising to enter the war against Japan. "My task as minister of foreign affairs was to expand the borders of our Fatherland," Molotov recalled proudly many years later. "And it seems that Stalin and I coped with this task quite well."

II

From the West's standpoint, the critical question was how far Moscow's influence would extend *beyond* whatever Soviet frontiers turned out to be at the end of the war. Stalin had suggested . . . that the Soviet Union would impose its own social system as far as its armies could reach, but he was also very cautious. Keenly aware of the military power the United States and its allies had accumulated, Stalin was determined to do nothing that might involve the USSR in another devastating war until it had recovered sufficiently to be certain of winning it. "I do not wish to begin the Third World War over the Trieste question," he explained to disappointed Yugoslavs, whom he ordered to evacuate that territory in June 1945. Five years later, he would justify his decision not to intervene in the Korean War on the grounds that "the Second World War ended not long ago, and we are not ready for the Third World War." Just how far the expansion of Soviet influence would proceed depended, therefore, upon a careful balancing of opportunities against risks. "[W]e were on the offensive," Molotov acknowledged:

> They [presumably the West] certainly hardened their line against us, but we had to consolidate our conquests. We made our own socialist Germany out of our part of Germany, and restored order in Czechoslovakia, Poland, Hungary, and Yugoslavia, where the situations were fluid. To squeeze out capitalist order. This was the cold war.

But, "of course," Molotov added, "you had to know when to stop. I believe in this respect Stalin kept well within the limits."

Who or what was it, though, that set the limits? Did Stalin have a fixed list of countries he thought it necessary to dominate? Was he prepared to stop in the face of resistance within those countries to "squeezing out the capitalist order"? Or would expansion cease only when confronted with opposition from the remaining capitalist states, so that further advances risked war at a time when the Soviet Union was ill-prepared for it?

Stalin had been very precise about where he wanted Soviet boundaries changed; he was much less so on how far Moscow's sphere of influence was to extend. He insisted on having "friendly" countries around the periphery of the USSR, but he failed to specify how many would have to meet this standard. He called during the war for dismembering Germany, but by the end of it was denying that he had ever done so: that country would be temporarily divided, he told leading German communists in June 1945, and they themselves would eventually bring about its reunification. He never gave up on the idea of an eventual world revolution, but he expected this to result — as his comments to the Germans suggested — from an expansion of influence emanating from the Soviet Union itself. "[F]or the Kremlin," a well-placed spymaster recalled, "the mission of communism was primarily to consolidate the might of the Soviet state. Only military strength and domination of the countries on our borders could ensure us a superpower role."

But Stalin provided no indication — surely because he himself did not know — of how rapidly, or under what circumstances, this process would take place. He was certainly prepared to stop in the face of resistance from the West: at no point was he willing to challenge the Americans or even the British where they made their interests clear. Churchill acknowledged his scrupulous adherence to the famous 1944 "percentages" agreement confirming British authority in Greece, and Yugoslav sources have revealed Stalin's warnings that the United States and Great Britain would never allow their lines of communication in the Mediterranean to be broken. He quickly backed down when confronted with Anglo-American objections to his ambitions in Iran in the spring of 1946, as he did later that year after demanding Soviet bases in the Turkish Straits. This pattern of advance followed by retreat . . . would reappear with the Berlin Blockade and the Korean War, both situations in which the Soviet Union would show great caution after provoking an unexpectedly strong American response.

What all of this suggests, though, is not that Stalin had limited ambitions, only that he had no timetable for achieving them. Molotov retrospectively confirmed this: "Our ideology stands for offensive operations when possible, and if not, we wait." Given this combination of appetite with aversion to risk, one cannot help but wonder what would have happened had the West tried containment earlier. To the extent that it bears partial responsibility for the coming of the Cold War, the historian Vojtech Mastny has argued, that responsibility lies in its failure to do just that.

Where Western resistance was unlikely, as in Eastern Europe, Stalin would in time attempt to replicate the regime he had already established inside the Soviet Union. Authority extended out from Moscow by way of government and party structures whose officials had been selected for their obedience, then down within each of these countries through the management of the economy, social and political institutions, intellectuals, even family relationships. The differentiation of public and private spheres that exists in most societies disappeared as all aspects of life were fused with, and then subordinated to, the interests of the Soviet Union as Stalin himself had determined them. Those who could not or would not go along encountered the same sequence of intimidation, terror, and ultimately even purges, show trials, and executions that his real and imagined domestic opponents had gone through during the 1930s. "Stalin's understanding of friendship with other countries was that the Soviet Union would lead and they would follow," Khrushchev recalled. "[He] waged the struggle against the enemies of the people there in the same way that he did in the Soviet Union. He had one demand: absolute subordination."

Stalin's policy, then, was one of imperial expansion and consolidation differing from that of earlier empires only in the determination with which he pursued it, in the instruments of coercion with which he maintained it, and in the ostensibly anti–imperial justifications he put forward in support of it. It is a testimony to his skill, if not to his morality, that he was able to achieve so many of his imperial ambitions at a time when the tides of history were running against the idea of imperial domination — as colonial offices in London, Paris, Lisbon, and The Hague were finding out — and when his own country was recovering from one of the most brutal invasions in recorded history. The fact that Stalin was able to *expand* his empire when others were contracting and while the Soviet Union was as weak as it was requires explanation. Why did opposition to this process, within and outside Europe, take so long to develop?

One reason was that the colossal sacrifices the Soviet Union had made during the war against the Axis had, in effect, "purified" its reputation: the USSR and its leader had "earned" the right to throw their weight around, or so it seemed. Western governments found it difficult to switch quickly from viewing the Soviet Union as a glorious wartime ally to portraying it as a new and dangerous adversary. President Harry S. Truman and his future Secretary of State Dean Acheson — neither of them sympathetic in the slightest to communism — nonetheless tended to give the Soviet Union the benefit of the doubt well into the early postwar era. A similar pattern developed within the United States occupation zone in Germany, where General Lucius D. Clay worked out a cooperative relationship with his Soviet counterparts and resisted demands to "get tough" with the Russians, even after they had become commonplace in Washington.

Resistance to Stalin's imperialism also developed slowly because Marxism-Leninism at the time had such widespread appeal. It is difficult now to recapture the admiration revolutionaries outside the Soviet Union felt for that country before they came to know it well. "[Communism] was the most rational and most intoxicating, all-embracing ideology for me and for those in my disunited and desperate land who so desired to skip over centuries of slavery and backwardness and to bypass reality itself," [Yugoslavian ex-communist Milovan] Djilas recalled, in a comment that could have been echoed throughout much of what came to be called the "third world." Because the Bolsheviks themselves had overcome one empire and had made a career of condemning others, it would take decades for people who were struggling to overthrow British, French, Dutch, or Portuguese colonialism to see that there could also be such a thing as Soviet imperialism. European communists — notably the Yugoslavs — saw this much earlier, but even to most of them it had not been apparent at the end of the war.

Still another explanation for the initial lack of resistance to Soviet expansionism was the fact that its repressive character did not become immediately apparent to all who were subjected to it. With regimes on the left taking power in Eastern and Central Europe, groups long denied advancement could now expect it. For many who remembered the 1930s, autarchy [economic self-sufficiency] within a Soviet bloc could seem preferable to exposure once again to international capitalism, with its periodic cycles of boom and bust. Nor did Moscow impose harsh controls everywhere at the same time. Simple administrative incompetence may partially account for this: one Russian historian has pointed out that "[d]isorganization, mismanagement and rivalry among many branches of the gigantic Stalinist state in Eastern Europe were enormous." But it is also possible, at least in some areas, that Stalin did not expect to *need* tight controls; that he anticipated no serious challenge and perhaps even spontaneous support. Why did he promise free elections after the war? Maybe he thought the communists would win them.

One has the impression that Stalin and the Eastern Europeans got to know one another only gradually. The Kremlin leader was slow to recognize that Soviet authority would not be welcomed everywhere beyond Soviet borders; but as he did come to see this he became all the more determined to impose it everywhere. The Eastern Europeans were slow to recognize how confining incorporation within a Soviet sphere was going to be; but as they did come to see this they became all the more determined to resist it, even if only by withholding, in a passive but sullen manner, the consent any regime needs to establish itself by means other than coercion. Stalin's efforts to consolidate his empire therefore made it at once more repressive and less secure. Meanwhile, an alternative vision of postwar Europe was emerging from the other great empire that established itself in the wake of World War II, that of the United States, and this too gave Stalin grounds for concern.

III

The first point worth noting, when comparing the American empire to its Soviet counterpart, is a striking reversal in the sequence of events. Stalin's determination to create his empire preceded by some years the conditions that made it possible: he had first to consolidate power at home and then defeat Nazi Germany, while at the same time seeing to it that his allies in that enterprise did not thwart his long-term objectives. With the United States, it was the other way around: the conditions for establishing an empire were in place long before there was any clear intention on the part of its leaders to do so. Even then, they required the support of a skeptical electorate, something that could never quite be taken for granted.

The United States had been poised for global hegemony [domination] at the end of World War I. Its military forces played a decisive role in bringing that conflict to an end. Its economic predominance was such that it could control both the manner and the rate of European recovery. Its ideology commanded enormous respect, as Woodrow Wilson found when he arrived on the Continent late in 1918 to a series of rapturous public receptions. The Versailles Treaty fell well short of Wilson's principles, to be sure, but the League of Nations followed closely his own design, providing an explicit legal basis for an international order that was to have drawn, as much as anything else, upon the example of the American constitution itself. If there was ever a point at which the world seemed receptive to an expansion of United States influence, this was it.

Americans themselves, however, were not receptive. The Senate's rejection of membership in the League reflected the public's distinct lack of enthusiasm for international peace-keeping responsibilities. Despite the interests certain business, labor, and agricultural groups had in seeking overseas markets and investment opportunities, most Americans saw few benefits to be derived from integrating their economy with that of the rest of the world. Efforts to rehabilitate Europe during the 1920s, therefore, could only take the form of private initiatives, quietly coordinated with the government. Protective tariffs hung on well into the 1930s — having actually increased with the onset of the Great Depression — and exports as a percentage of gross national product remained low in comparison to other nations, averaging only 4.2 per cent between 1921 and 1940. Investments abroad had doubled between 1914 and 1919 while foreign investment in the United States had been cut in half; but this shift was hardly sufficient to overcome old instincts within the majority of the public who held no investments at all that it was better to stand apart from, rather than to attempt to dominate, international politics outside of the Western hemisphere.

This isolationist consensus broke down only as Americans began to realize that a potentially hostile power was once again threatening Europe: even their own hemisphere, it appeared, might not escape the consequences this time around. After September 1939, the Roosevelt administration moved as quickly as public and Congressional opinion would allow to aid Great Britain and France by means short of war; it also chose to challenge the Japanese over their occupation of China and later French Indochina, thereby setting in motion a sequence of events that would lead to the attack on Pearl Harbor. Historians ever since have puzzled over this: why, after two decades of relative inactivity on the world scene, did the United States suddenly become hyperactive? Might the administration have realized that it would never generate public support for the empire American elites had long desired without a clear and present danger to national security, and did it not then proceed to generate one? Can one not understand the origins and evolution of the Cold War in similar terms?

There are several problems with such interpretations, one of which is that they confuse contingency with conspiracy. Even if Roosevelt had hoped to maneuver the Japanese into "firing the first shot," he could not have known that Hitler would seize this opportunity to declare war and thereby make possible American military intervention in Europe. The Pacific, where the United States would have deployed most of its strength in the absence of Hitler's declaration, would hardly have been the platform from which to mount a bid for global hegemony. These explanations also allow little room for the autonomy of others: they assume that Hitler and the Japanese militarists acted *only* in response to what the United States did, and that other possible motives for their behavior — personal, bureaucratic, cultural, ideological, geopolitical — were insignificant. Finally, these arguments fail to meet the test of proximate versus distant causation. The historian Marc Bloch once pointed out that one could, in principle, account for a climber's fall from a precipice by invoking physics and geology: had it not been for the law of gravity and the existence of the mountain, the accident surely could not have occurred. But would it follow that all who ascend mountains must plummet from them? Just because Roosevelt *wanted* the United States to enter the war and to become a world power afterwards does not mean that his actions alone made these things happen.

A better explanation for the collapse of isolationism is a simpler one: it had to do with a resurgence of authoritarianism. Americans had begun to suspect, late in the nineteenth century, that the internal behavior of states determined their external behavior; certainly it is easy to see how the actions of Germany, Italy, and Japan during the 1930s could have caused this view to surface once again, much as it had in relations with tsarist

Russia and imperial Germany during World War I. Once that happened, the Americans, not given to making subtle distinctions, began to oppose authoritarianism everywhere, and that could account for their sudden willingness to take on several authoritarians at once in 1941. But that interpretation, too, is not entirely adequate. It fails to explain how the United States could have coexisted as comfortably as it did with authoritarianism in the past — especially in Latin America — and as it would continue to do for some time to come. It certainly does not account for the American willingness during the war to embrace, as an ally, the greatest authoritarian of this century, Stalin himself.

The best explanation for the decline of isolationism and the rise of the American empire, I suspect, has to do with a distinction Americans tended to make — perhaps they were more subtle than one might think — between what we might call benign and malignant authoritarianism. Regimes like those of Somoza in Nicaragua or Trujillo in the Dominican Republic might be unsavory, but they fell into the benign category because they posed no serious threat to United States interests and in some cases even promoted them. Regimes like those of Nazi Germany and imperial Japan, because of their military capabilities, were quite another matter. Stalin's authoritarianism had appeared malignant when linked to that of Hitler, as it was between 1939 and 1941; but when directed against Hitler, it could come to appear quite benign. What it would look like once Germany had been defeated remained to be seen.

With all this, the possibility that even malignant authoritarianism might harm the United States remained hypothetical until 7 December 1941, when it suddenly became very real. . . . Pearl Harbor was, then, the defining event for the American empire, because it was only at this point that the most plausible potential justification for the United States becoming and remaining a global power as far as the American people were concerned — an endangered national security — became an actual one. Isolationism had thrived right up to this moment; but once it became apparent that isolationism could leave the nation open to military attack, it suffered a blow from which it never recovered. The critical date was not 1945, or 1947, but 1941.

It did not automatically follow, though, that the Soviet Union would inherit the title of "first enemy" once Germany and Japan had been defeated. A sense of vulnerability preceded the identification of a source of threat in the thinking of American strategists: innovations in military technology — long-range bombers, the prospect of even longer-range missiles — created visions of future Pearl Harbors before it had become clear from where such an attack might come. Neither in the military nor the political-economic planning that went on in Washington during the war was there consistent concern with the USSR as a potential future adversary. The threat, rather, appeared to arise from war itself, whoever might cause it, and the most likely candidates were thought to be resurgent enemies from World War II.

The preferred solution was to maintain preponderant power for the United States, which meant a substantial peacetime military establishment and a string of bases around the world from which to resist aggression if it should ever occur. But equally important, a revived international community would seek to remove the fundamental causes of war through the United Nations, a less ambitious version of Wilson's League, and through new economic institutions like the International Monetary Fund and the

World Bank, whose task it would be to prevent another global depression and thereby ensure prosperity. The Americans and the British assumed that the Soviet Union would want to participate in these multilateral efforts to achieve military and economic security. The Cold War developed when it became clear that Stalin either could not or would not accept this framework.

Did the Americans attempt to impose their vision of the postwar world upon the USSR? No doubt it looked that way from Moscow: both the Roosevelt and Truman administrations stressed political self-determination and economic integration with sufficient persistence to arouse Stalin's suspicions — easily aroused, in any event — as to their ultimate intentions. But what the Soviet leader saw as a challenge to his hegemony the Americans meant as an effort to salvage multilateralism. At no point prior to 1947 did the United States and its Western European allies abandon the hope that the Russians might eventually come around; and indeed negotiations aimed at bringing them around would continue at the foreign ministers' level, without much hope of success, through the end of that year. The American attitude was less that of expecting to impose a system than one of puzzlement as to why its merits were not universally self-evident. It differed significantly, therefore, from Stalin's point of view, which allowed for the possibility that socialists in other countries might come to see the advantages of Marxism-Leninism as practiced in the Soviet Union, but never capitalists. They were there, in the end, to be overthrown, not convinced.

IV

The emergence of an opposing great power bloc posed serious difficulties for the principle of multilateralism, based as it had been on the expectation of cooperation with Moscow. But with a good deal of ingenuity the Americans managed to *merge* their original vision of a single international order built around common security with a second and more hastily improvised concept that sought to counter the expanding power and influence of the Soviet Union. That concept was, of course, containment, and its chief instrument was the Marshall Plan.

The idea of containment proceeded from the proposition that if there was not to be one world, then there must not be another world war either. It would be necessary to keep the peace while preserving the balance of power: the gap that had developed during the 1930s between the perceived requirements of peace and power was not to happen again. If geopolitical stability could be restored in Europe, time would work against the Soviet Union and in favor of the Western democracies. Authoritarianism need not be the "wave of the future"; sooner or later even Kremlin authoritarians would realize this fact and change their policies. "[T]he Soviet leaders are prepared to recognize *situations,* if not arguments," George F. Kennan wrote in 1948. "If, therefore, situations can be created in which it is clearly not to the advantage of their power to emphasize the elements of conflict in their relations with the outside world, then their actions, and even the tenor of their propaganda to their own people, *can* be modified."

342 THE COLD WAR IN EUROPE AND ASIA

This idea of time being on the side of the West came — at least as far as Kennan was concerned — from studying the history of empires. Edward Gibbon had written in *The Decline and Fall of the Roman Empire* that "there is nothing more contrary to nature than the attempt to hold in obedience distant provinces," and few things Kennan ever read made a greater or more lasting impression on him. He had concluded during the early days of World War II that Hitler's empire could not last, and in the months after the war, he applied similar logic to the empire Stalin was setting out to construct in Eastern Europe. The territorial acquisitions and spheres of influence the Soviet Union had obtained would ultimately become a source of *insecurity* for it, both because of the resistance to Moscow's control that was sure to grow within those regions and because of the outrage the nature of that control was certain to provoke in the rest of the world. "Soviet power, like the capitalist world of its own conception, bears within it the seeds of its own decay," Kennan insisted in the most famous of all Cold War texts, his anonymously published 1947 article on "The Sources of Soviet Conduct." He added, "the sprouting of those seeds is well advanced."

All of this would do the Europeans little good, though, if the new and immediate Soviet presence in their midst should so intimidate them that their own morale collapsed. The danger here came not from the prospect that the Red Army would invade and occupy the rest of the continent, as Hitler had tried to do; rather, its demoralized and exhausted inhabitants might simply vote in communist parties who would then do Moscow's bidding. The initial steps in the strategy of containment — stopgap military and economic aid to Greece and Turkey, the more carefully designed and ambitious Marshall Plan — took place within this context: the idea was to produce instant intangible reassurance as well as eventual tangible reinforcement. Two things had to happen in order for intimidation to occur, Kennan liked to argue: the intimidator had to make the effort, but, equally important, the target of those efforts had to agree to be intimidated. The initiatives of 1947 sought to generate sufficient self-confidence to prevent such acquiescence in intimidation from taking place.

Some historians have asserted that these fears of collapse were exaggerated: that economic recovery on the continent was already underway, and that the Europeans themselves were never as psychologically demoralized as the Americans made them out to be. Others have added that the real crisis at the time was within an American economy that could hardly expect to function hegemonically if Europeans lacked the dollars to purchase its products. Still others have suggested that the Marshall Plan was the means by which American officials sought to project overseas the mutually-beneficial relationship between business, labor, and government they had worked out at home: the point was not to make Wilsonian values a model for the rest of the world, but rather the politics of productivity that had grown out of American corporate capitalism. All of these arguments have merit: at a minimum they have forced historians to place the Marshall Plan in a wider economic, social, and historical context; more broadly they suggest that the American empire had its own distinctive internal roots, and was not solely and simply a response to the Soviet external challenge.

At the same time, though, it is difficult to see how a strategy of containment could have developed — with the Marshall Plan as its centerpiece — had there been nothing to contain. One need only recall the early 1920s, when similar conditions of European demoralization, Anglo-French exhaustion, and American economic predominance had existed; yet no American empire arose as after World War II. The critical difference, of course, was national security: Pearl Harbor created an atmosphere of vulnerability Americans had not known since the earliest days of the republic, and the Soviet Union by 1947 had become the most plausible source of threat. The American empire arose *primarily,* therefore, not from internal causes, as had the Soviet empire, but from a perceived external danger powerful enough to overcome American isolationism.

Washington's wartime vision of a postwar international order had been premised on the concepts of political self-determination and economic integration. It was intended to work by assuming a set of *common* interests that would cause other countries to *want* to be affiliated with it rather than to resist it. The Marshall Plan, to a considerable extent, met those criteria: although it operated on a regional rather than a global scale, it did seek to promote democracy through an economic recovery that would proceed along international and not nationalist lines. Its purpose was to create an American sphere of influence, to be sure, but one that would allow those within it considerable freedom. The principles of democracy and open markets required nothing less, but there were two additional and more practical reasons for encouraging such autonomy. First, the United States itself lacked the capability to administer a large empire: the difficulties of running occupied Germany and Japan were proving daunting enough. Second, the idea of autonomy was implicit in the task of restoring European self-confidence; for who, if not Europeans themselves, was to say when the self-confidence of Europeans had been restored?

Finally, it is worth noting that even though Kennan and the other early architects of containment made use of imperial analogies, they did not see themselves as creating an empire, but rather a restored balance of power. Painfully — perhaps excessively — aware of limited American resources, fearful that the domestic political consensus in favor of internationalism might not hold, they set out to reconstitute *independent* centers of power in Europe and Asia. These would be integrated into the world capitalist system, and as a result they would certainly fall under the influence of its new hegemonic manager, the United States. But there was no intention here of creating satellites in anything like the sense that Stalin understood that term; rather, the idea was that "third forces" would resist Soviet expansionism while preserving as much as possible of the multilateralist agenda American officials had framed during World War II. What the United States really wanted, State Department official John D. Hickerson commented in 1948, was "not merely an extension of US influence but a real European organization strong enough to say 'no' both to the Soviet Union and to the United States, if our actions should seem so to require."

The American empire, therefore, reflected little imperial consciousness or design. An anti-imperial tradition dating back to the American Revolution partially accounted for this: departures from that tradition, as in the Spanish-American War of 1898 and the Philippine insurrection that followed, had only reinforced its relevance — outside the Western hemisphere. So too did a constitutional structure that forced even imperially minded leaders like Wilson and the two Roosevelts to accommodate domestic attitudes that discouraged imperial behavior long after national capabilities had made it possible.

And even as those internal constraints diminished dramatically in World War II — they never entirely dropped away — Americans still found it difficult to think of themselves as an imperial power. The idea of remaking the international system in such a way as to transcend empires altogether still lingered, but so too did doubts as to whether the United States was up to the task. In the end it was again external circumstances — the manner in which Stalin managed his own empire and the way in which this pushed Europeans into preferring its American alternative — that brought the self-confidence necessary to administer imperial responsibilities into line with Washington's awareness of their existence. . . .

It would become fashionable to argue, in the wake of American military intervention in Vietnam, the Soviet invasions of Czechoslovakia and Afghanistan, and growing fears of nuclear confrontation that developed during the early 1980s, that there were no significant differences in the spheres of influence Washington and Moscow had constructed in Europe after World War II: these had been, it was claimed, "morally equivalent," denying autonomy quite impartially to all who lived under them. Students of history must make their own judgments about morality, but even a cursory examination of the historical record will show that these imperial structures could hardly have been more different in their origins, their composition, their tolerance of diversity, and as it turned out their durability. It is important to specify just what these differences were.

First, and most important, the Soviet empire reflected the priorities and the practices of a single individual — a latter-day tsar, in every sense of the word. Just as it would have been impossible to separate the Soviet Union's internal structure from the influence of the man who ran it, so too the Soviet sphere of influence in Eastern Europe took on the characteristics of Stalin himself. The process was not immediate: Stalin did allow a certain amount of spontaneity in the political, economic, and intellectual life of that region for a time after the war, just as he had done inside the Soviet Union itself after he had consolidated his position as Lenin's successor in 1929. But when confronted with even the prospect of dissent, to say nothing of challenges to his authority, Stalin's instinct was to smother spontaneity with a thoroughness unprecedented in the modern age. This is what the purges had accomplished inside the USSR during the mid-1930s, and Eastern Europe underwent a similar process after 1947. There was thus a direct linkage from Stalin's earliest thinking on the nationalities question prior to the Bolshevik Revolution through to his management of empire after World War II: the right of self-determination was fine as long as no one sought to practice it.

The American empire was very different: one would have expected this from a country with no tradition of authoritarian leadership whose constitutional structure had long ago enshrined the practices of negotiation, compromise, and the balancing of interests. What is striking about the sphere of influence the United States established in Europe is that its existence and fundamental design reflected as frequently pressures that came *from those incorporated within it* as from the Americans themselves. Washington officials were not at all convinced, at the end of World War II, that their interests would require protecting half the European continent: instead they looked toward a revival of a balance among the Europeans themselves to provide postwar geopolitical stability.

Even the Marshall Plan, an unprecedented extension of American assistance, had been conceived with this "third force" principle in mind. It was the Europeans themselves who demanded more: who insisted that their security required a military shield as well as an economic jump-start.

One empire arose, therefore, by invitation, the other by imposition. *Europeans* made this distinction, very much as they had done during the war when they welcomed armies liberating them from the west but feared those that came from the east. They did so because they saw clearly at the time — even if a subsequent generation would not always see — how different American and Soviet empires were likely to be. It is true that the *extent* of the American empire quickly exceeded that of its Soviet counterpart, but this was because *resistance* to expanding American influence was never as great. The American empire may well have become larger, paradoxically, because the American *appetite* for empire was less [than] that of the USSR. The United States had shown, throughout most of its history, that it could survive and even prosper without extending its domination as far as the eye could see. The logic of Lenin's ideological internationalism, as modified by Stalin's Great Russian nationalism and personal paranoia, was that the Soviet Union could not.

The early Cold War in Europe, therefore, cannot be understood by looking at the policies of either the United States or the Soviet Union in isolation. What evolved on the continent was an interactive system in which the actions of each side affected not only the other but also the Europeans; their responses, in turn, shaped further decisions in Washington and Moscow. It quickly became clear — largely because of differences in the domestic institutions of each superpower — that an American empire would accommodate far greater diversity than would one run by the Soviet Union: as a consequence most Europeans accepted and even invited American hegemony, fearing deeply what that of the Russians might entail.

Two paths diverged at the end of World War II. And that, to paraphrase an American poet, really did make all the difference.

QUESTIONS TO CONSIDER

1. How, according to the author, is the concept of "empire" a better way to understand the Cold War international system than the notion of rivalry of two "great powers"? In what sense were the American and Soviet empires "informal"? Describe Gaddis's contrast between them. How does he compare the motives and methods of the two imperial powers? What does he mean when he says that American imperialism was "defensive" and proceeded without desire or design? How does this contrast with Russian imperialism? In what sense was American hegemony an "empire by invitation" and Soviet hegemony an "empire by imposition"?

2. Describe Joseph Stalin's imperialist vision as Gaddis interprets it. How did Stalin's views contrast with Lenin's? In what way did Stalin fuse "Marxist internationalism" with "tsarist imperialism"? Was Stalin interested in territorial acquisitions or "spheres of influence"? What spatial or temporal limits did Stalin set on Soviet

expansion? Why did opposition to Stalin's ambitions by Americans and Europeans take so long to develop?

3. Discuss America's "imperial" Cold War policy. In what sense were the necessary pre-conditions in place for empire in the United States rather than in the Soviet Union? Why was the American "isolationist consensus" slow to break down, and what changed it? What framework of international relations did the United States project for the post–World War II world? Was the policy of "containment" an example of "multilateralism" or a return to "balance-of-power" diplomacy? Where did the Marshall Plan fit in American designs for Europe?

4. How convincing is Gaddis's stark contrast between the American and Soviet empires? Try to critique his selection and presentation of the evidence before you render a final judgment. Does Gaddis assume the worst about Soviet leaders' motives and the best about Americans'? Was American military and economic power always "invited" and Soviet power always "imposed"? Does Gaddis take into account America's own expansionist blend of imperialism and capitalism? How would Gaddis respond to the claim by Kate Brown (in Selection 4) that Cold War polarities obscured basic similarities between the United States and the Soviet Union?

5. Gaddis writes that the Japanese surprise attack on Pearl Harbor was "the defining event for the American empire" because it destroyed isolationism. The terrorist attacks of September 11, 2001, on the Pentagon and New York's World Trade Center have frequently been compared with Pearl Harbor. What similarities or differences do you see between these events and between the American responses to them? Were the attacks of 9/11 the actions of an enemy nation? Why were Americans so unprepared for them? In what sense has the threat of terrorism revived or revised notions of American empire?

Imperial Responses to Revolution in Colonial America and Vietnam

T. CHRISTOPHER JESPERSEN

The long and divisive war in Vietnam was a traumatic experience for the United States. In Vietnam, America's leadership of the "Free World" seemed to falter. Because of policies shaped by the Cold War, what began as a Vietnamese war for national independence became an American counterrevolutionary struggle, and the United States became identified around the world as an imperialist bully. The frightful cost of the war in money and lives, and the difficulty of setting up a viable anticommunist government in South Vietnam, led many Americans to question their country's involvement. As the conflict dragged on, the American people divided into pro-war and antiwar factions whose bitter dispute colored the nation's political and social scene for more than a decade.

The origins of the American war in Vietnam go back to the end of World War II, when the nationalist forces of Ho Chi Minh fought the French to liberate their homeland from colonial rule. During the World War, Franklin Roosevelt had committed the United States to anticolonialism in Southeast Asia. But because American policymakers disapproved of Ho's communist connections and because they wanted to soften French opposition to the rebuilding of Germany, the United States ultimately supported France's reoccupation of Indochina. By 1954 the Eisenhower administration was paying 80 percent of the French war bill. The following year, after suffering a humiliating defeat at Dien Bien Phu, the French withdrew from Vietnam, and an international agreement signed at Geneva divided Vietnam into two regions to be reunited by free elections in 1956. To prevent Ho Chi Minh's almost-certain victory at the polls, Eisenhower urged the indefinite postponement of elections and helped install in South Vietnam a pro-Western government headed by President Ngo Dinh Diem. American support for Diem was backed by the belief that the international communist movement would spread through Asia like falling dominoes if not checked in Vietnam.

After Eisenhower, Cold War considerations dictated an increasing flow of American men and money to Vietnam. As an insurrection by the communist-led Viet Cong gained ground in South Vietnam, three presidents escalated the war into a major test of America's stand against communism. President Kennedy proved he was "tough on communism" by expanding foreign aid and sending more than fifteen thousand U.S. troops to advise the South

Vietnamese on counterinsurgency operations. His successor, Lyndon Johnson, took decisive steps to Americanize the war after several American military advisers were killed and American intelligence-gathering ships may have been fired upon. By late 1965, more than one hundred fifty thousand American soldiers were fighting the Viet Cong and their North Vietnamese allies (who received support from China and the Soviet Union) without a declaration of war from Congress or even a substantial debate at home. By the time Richard Nixon took office in 1969, more than half a million American troops had ravaged the Vietnamese countryside and killed nearly one million Vietnamese in a fruitless effort to achieve victory for unpopular South Vietnamese military regimes. The majority of Americans now opposed the war, but Nixon, worried about American prestige and "credibility," prolonged the agony with brutal bombing attacks of the North and an invasion of Cambodia to destroy communist hideouts. Gradually, however, Nixon withdrew American ground troops, and in 1975 the South Vietnamese army was overrun by North Vietnamese and Viet Cong forces, which then set up a united Vietnam under Hanoi's communist government.

As America's longest and least successful war, the debacle of Vietnam remains controversial. Historians have interpreted it in widely divergent ways: as an assertion of American economic ambitions in Asia, a mistaken application of the Cold War "containment" policy, a good cause ruined by military blunders, or a winnable war lost by political decisions at home. In the essay that follows, T. Christopher Jespersen views America's intervention in Vietnam as an imperial war against a movement for independence. Drawing an analogy between the post–World War II revolution in Vietnam and colonial Americans' own struggle for independence two centuries earlier, Jespersen discovers close parallels in the behavior of the imperial powers that tried to suppress these revolts. Both Great Britain in 1776 and the United States in the 1960s trumpeted a version of the "domino theory" warning that the revolutionary outbreak would spread to neighboring regions if not quelled immediately. Both suffered key military setbacks because they underestimated their enemy's resources and will. And both mistakenly believed that "loyalists" in the colonies would rally sufficient support to put down the rebellion. Led by Cold War ideology and imperial ambitions, the United States, Jespersen says, reacted to the Vietnamese struggle in ways that echoed Britain's campaign to subdue its upstart American colonies, and met with a similar defeat. Years ago, historian Richard Ketchum labeled the American Revolution "England's Vietnam." Jespersen reverses the focus, declaring in effect that the war in Vietnam was "America's Yorktown."

Why did the United States, which was born in a colonial war for independence, oppose a similar struggle in Vietnam? How did Americans "end . . . up becoming an imperial power very much like Great Britain"? Jespersen does not offer a sweeping response but instead lets readers reflect upon the overall import of his analogy. This leaves several avenues for you to explore. As you ponder the parallels Jespersen uncovers, ask what they suggest about the dynamics of revolutions, changes in America's world position, the Cold War, the nature of imperialism, or even the idea that history repeats itself. Since Jespersen's account of America's involvement in Vietnam contrasts with John Lewis Gaddis's claim in Selection 19 that the American empire expanded by "invitation," not "imposition," you should compare America's Cold War initiatives in Europe and Asia. Finally, because Jespersen treats Vietnam as an example of colonialism in Southeast Asia, his essay should prompt you to review Vince

Boudreau's analysis of America's colonial rule in the Philippines (Selection 10). Why did the United States succeed in installing a viable colonial government in the Philippines but fail in South Vietnam?

GLOSSARY

ARVN   The Army of the Republic of Viet Nam. President Diem's South Vietnamese military force was modeled after the U.S. Army, advised by Americans, and trained mainly in conventional warfare.

CATHERINE II (1729–1796)   Also known as Catherine the Great; the empress of Russia who was crowned in 1762 after deposing her husband, the unpopular Peter III. During her reign, she extended Russian control over Poland and the Crimea and she integrated Russia into the political and cultural life of Europe, continuing the work begun by Peter the Great.

COSSACKS   Fiercely independent farmers and horsemen from southern Russia who fought to maintain their autonomy within the Russian empire. By the nineteenth century, however, they were subdued by the czar, who used them as a ruthless cavalry policing Russia's borders and suppressing domestic dissent.

DIEM, NGO DINH (1901–1963)   An ardent anticommunist and prominent Roman Catholic who became president of the Republic of Vietnam. Diem served briefly in the French colonial government in the 1930s. At the end of the French Indochina War he was named premier of Vietnam, and after the Geneva Agreement of 1954 divided the country in two, Diem ruled South Vietnam with American support. In 1956 he proclaimed South Vietnam a republic and became president. His authoritarian rule and hostility toward Buddhists led to popular discontent, and Diem was assassinated during a military coup apparently backed by the United States.

GIA LONG (1762–1820)   The founder of the Nguyen dynasty of Vietnam, who became emperor in 1802 after defeating his rivals with the help of French troops. Gia Long permitted French missionaries to preach Christianity in Vietnam but otherwise resisted France's claim to special privileges.

HO CHI MINH (1890–1969)   The first president of the Democratic Republic of Vietnam (North Vietnam). Ho left Vietnam as a young man and lived in England, the United States, and France. He agitated for Vietnamese civil rights at the Paris Peace Conference in 1919 and the following year became a founding member of the French Communist Party. He established the Indochinese Communist Party in 1930 and lived in the USSR and China during that decade. Returning to Vietnam, Ho organized the communist-controlled Viet Minh resistance to Japanese rule in 1941, and at the end of World War II he proclaimed the independence of Vietnam and became its president. For the next two decades, he led the Viet Minh in warfare against the French and then the U.S.-backed South Vietnamese government. He died six years before Vietnam was reunified under northern rule.

SARATOGA, BATTLES OF (1777)   Two battles in upstate New York in September and October 1777 in which the Continental Army defeated British troops led by General John Burgoyne and forced their surrender. The American victory at Saratoga marked a turning point in the Revolutionary War. It shifted British war efforts to the southern colonies, where the British hoped to rely upon Loyalist support. It also helped convince France to recognize U.S. independence and to join the war on the American side.

TET OFFENSIVE (1968)   A coordinated attack on major South Vietnamese cities, including Saigon and Hue, by North Vietnamese and Viet Cong troops during Tet (the lunar New Year) in January and February 1968. Although it was repulsed, this offensive convinced many Americans that their nation was not winning the war in Vietnam and led the U.S. government to shift its strategy toward slowly withdrawing from the war.

THIEU, NGUYEN VAN (1923–2001)   The president of South Vietnam from 1967 until it was overrun by North Vietnamese forces in 1975. An anticommunist who fought with the French against the Viet Minh and rose in the ranks of the South Vietnamese army, Thieu was one of the leaders of the coup against President Diem. He staunchly opposed a political settlement with North Vietnam and fled the country when his government fell.

USAID   The U.S. Agency for International Development. Established in 1961 by President Kennedy, it provides economic, humanitarian, and development assistance to foreign countries in furtherance of U.S. foreign policy goals. Kennedy believed that promoting growth and stability in developing nations would prevent the advance of communism.

VIET CONG   The insurgent guerrilla movement that fought the South Vietnamese government and its ally, the United States. The Viet Cong was dominated by South Vietnamese communists but included several noncommunist groups. In 1960 these groups united into a political coalition called the National Liberation Front (NLF), modeled on the earlier Viet Minh, and began a full-scale insurrection. The movement depended increasingly upon North Vietnamese aid and troops. The NLF formed a provisional revolutionary government in 1969, which took part in the Paris peace ne-gotiations and later in the government of a unified Vietnam.

VIET MINH   The communist-dominated League for the Independence of Vietnam, which was formed in 1941 by Ho Chi Minh. The Viet Minh led the resistance to Japanese occupation during World War II, then battled the French for independence. It was dis-solved after the French were defeated in 1954 and the government of North Vietnam was established.

VIETNAMIZATION   President Richard Nixon's policy after 1968 of turning over the ground war in Vietnam to South Vietnamese troops in order to minimize American casualties and quell dissent at home.

YORKTOWN (1781)   The climactic battle of the American Revolution, in which General Lord Cornwallis's British troops were entrapped on a peninsula at Yorktown, Virginia, by a combined French–American force on land and French ships by sea. Cornwallis's surrender to General George Washington ended the fighting and assured the colonists' independence from England.

I

The case for comparing the American and Vietnamese revolutions is not an obvious one. The United States fought for its independence against the nation and government whose policies had created the loose association of colonies in the first place. The familial and fraternal bonds across the Atlantic Ocean were strong. Both colonists and British spoke the same language. Economic ties were vigorous, and many well-to-do families in North America sent their children to England for schooling.

The relationship between Vietnam and the United States had none of the same qualities. In fact, Vietnam was not a significant part of American history, culture, politics, or diplomacy prior to 1950. Vietnam did not rebel against American control; rather, the United States tried to interpose itself in the course of a determined Vietnamese independence movement, one that had its origins in opposition to French colonial rule in the nineteenth century. When the United States officially supplanted France in 1954 out of concern over how Vietnam fit into the global competition with the Soviet Union, it sought to contain the independence movement by setting up an indigenous government capable of competing for power. In most respects, therefore, Vietnam's fight was not akin to the American colonial effort to wrest control of North America from the British.

Despite the significant differences that separate the two revolutions in time, origin, and temperament, the responses to them deserve comparison because of how many things are so strikingly similar. In the 1770s, Great Britain possessed an empire that stretched from a budding presence in South Asia to a more fully established outpost in North America. Its size and extent were impressive, although it was to grow even larger in the coming decades. By the 1960s, the United States had troops stationed in countries from West Germany to Japan, and it had military and economic agreements with even more nations. The scope of American hegemony was daunting, even if it was on the decline. Both revolutions became enmeshed in larger conflicts between competing imperial powers. Both were fought with the goal of securing independence from foreign control. Both were civil wars and forced the dislocation of tens of thousands of people. And both were met with determined resistance during their struggle for victory and afterward.

It is through a comparison of the British reaction to the American Revolution in the late eighteenth century with the U.S. response to the Vietnamese revolution of the latter twentieth century that certain aspects of empire can be discerned. In the process of juxtaposing them, some things become clearer in terms of the general conclusions that can be drawn and the undeniable distinctions that must be made. Finally, in comparing these two responses to revolution, it is important to note that the common thread remains the United States. It is thus possible to examine the nature of American society over a two-hundred-year period and, from there, to draw conclusions about the nature of its politics, culture, and diplomacy.

II

The battle between the North American colonists and the Crown grew out of the British victory over the French in 1763. That conflict, alternately labeled the French and Indian War, the Seven Years' War, and the War for Greater Empire, pitted British forces against French troops in places as far away from each other (and from England) as India and the western frontier of the North American colonies. The burden of victory was heavy: Britain's national debt rose from £74.6 million to £132.6 million. In addition, maintaining and protecting the North American holdings necessitated stationing troops there, which, in turn, led to a series of efforts to tax the colonies in order to offset the costs. American colonists rebelled at the idea, challenging parliament's authority through various means for a decade before the onset of war. King George III, who "foresaw ruin ahead if the home country conceded American independence," was determined to put down the rebellion, and he had the backing of "significant sections of public opinion — probably by the majority of the political nation." Bolstered by highly optimistic reports from the colonial governors about the ease with which the rebellion would be broken, reports that were further encouraged by the secretary of state for the colonies, Lord George Germain, the king committed Great Britain to putting down the revolution with force. He was unabashed about involving himself in the details of the matter. "The King was not one to sit back and allow his politicians and generals to conduct the war on their own — or at least not without liberally proffered advice."

From April 1775 until the battle at Saratoga in October 1777, British military leaders focused their energies on New England and the mid-Atlantic states of New York and New Jersey. The demands of empire, however, meant that fewer British soldiers could be spared for the war in North America than were needed, putting a premium on foreign forces and necessitating alliances with Indian tribes in North America. The push for assistance began with an effort to recruit 20,000 Russian soldiers, the view being that "the mutinous Bostonians" were the "American version of the Cossacks." Russian troops, moreover, were "expected to have fewer scruples than British troops, who could be restrained by a belief they were fighting fellow subjects." When Catherine II rejected the idea, Britain looked to the Dutch, who also refused. Ultimately, it was the Hessian states of Central Europe that supplied 18,000 troops at one time and 30,000 total for the duration of the war.

General John Burgoyne's defeat [at Saratoga] in upstate New York markedly altered the military situation. The quick victory anticipated at the beginning of hostilities gave way to the realization that the fighting was going to require a greater cooperative effort with those subjects in North America still loyal to the king. After Saratoga, British strategy focused on securing the South, where it was believed a strong Loyalist base would assist in yielding decisive results. "It was at last admitted that, ultimately, restored British authority would have to depend on Americans themselves, and that even the strongest army and navy could do no more than create favorable conditions for the Americanization of the war." Indeed, as John Shy has written, "during 1778, Loyalists moved from the periphery toward the center of the war."

The British defeat at Saratoga bolstered Patriot spirits at a time when they were sagging badly. In writing to General George Washington, John Page extolled Saratoga as a vindication for the American side. "I have all along looked upon our Cause, as favored by Heaven; & I think I have seen many Instances of a divine Interposition in our Favour." He contrasted this with the arrogance of the other side: "Britain grown great & powerful & put into a Condition, by Heaven, to do infinite good to Mankind wickedly abused that Power — intoxicated with its success it ungratefully & impiously attributed them to its own Strength — For such abuse of power it seems consistent with the infinite Goodness & Justice to deprive them of it & for such Ingratitude & Pride they deserved to be humbled." . . .

Despite the change in regional strategy, the British effort limped on, failing to gather anything but limited popular support in the southern states. However sympathetic to the Crown many individuals in the region may have been, "Readiness to die for King George was harder to enlist." After partially subduing the Carolinas, General Lord Cornwallis headed north into Virginia, whereon American troops recaptured most of the areas he had occupied. Still, many in England were not ready to concede defeat. In 1780, John Adams reported on arguments being publicized in England in favor of continuing the war. According to the ardent Loyalist Joseph Galloway, should America achieve its independence, it would have profound consequences for all aspects of British economic life, which would jeopardize the nation's strategic position, even its sovereignty, vis-à-vis the other nations of Europe. He concluded, "It does not require the spirit of *divinatio* [prophecy] to perceive that Great Britain, robbed of her foreign dominions and commerce, her nurseries of seamen lost, her navy weakened, and the power of her ambitious neighbors thus strengthened and increased, will not be able to maintain her independence among nations."

Continuation of the war, however, was becoming increasingly absurd. . . . Cornwallis's surrender at Yorktown seemed to indicate that the game was up; certainly the king was forced to rethink his position. He conceded that independence for the colonies was unavoidable, a conclusion he reached with considerable remorse and anguish. Commenting on the state of Anglo-American relations and quoting British sources on the matter, Henry Laurens, the South Carolinian diplomat who had been imprisoned in London for part of the war after the British captured his vessel, wrote the president of Congress in 1784, "His Majesty was dragged into the late war as reluctantly as ever a bull was dragged to a baiting." The king confessed to Laurens his regret "at the shedding of so much blood." What, however, could he have done to prevent it? "They drew me in little by little," he said of his advisers; "I have been deceived."

Preliminary articles for peace were not signed until a little over a year after Yorktown, on November 30, 1782; the actual signing ceremony took place in Paris on September 3,

1783; and the king's signature came the following year. There were three provisions that quickly became critical for subsequent relations. The first, and from the American standpoint the most important, was the British retention of forts along the western frontier. Coupled with the Crown's support for Indian tribes in lower Canada as well as the Ohio and Mississippi river valleys, the occupation of the forts was seen as part of a larger effort to restrain the new nation's territorial growth. Second was the American treatment of Loyalists. The treaty called for the states to recognize legitimate claims made by Loyalists to confiscated property. It also recommended that the states be advised to cease further confiscations and treat the Loyalists fairly and without recrimination. The third issue centered around the payment of American debts contracted to British merchants prior to the outbreak of war in 1775.

With respect to the confiscation of Loyalists' property, many Americans had other ideas. Certain states, upon getting wind of the final stipulations of the peace treaty, passed resolutions outlawing any compensation to Loyalists and denying any legal claims they might make on confiscated property. Some Virginians reasoned that, at the time of independence, individuals were forced to make a choice, and those who elected to remain loyal to the Crown lost their standing because they had opted not to become members of the new social compact. They could not subsequently appeal for legal protection under the laws of the new nation. . . .

This ran counter to the treaty, of course, but with no strong national government to ensure compliance, other states, along with Virginia, passed resolutions precluding Loyalist claims to lost property. The *Pennsylvania Packet* had expressed the idea during the war that Tory property "would become securities for the repairs" the states would have to make after the fighting ended. And that, in many instances, is just what some of the states did after 1781.

The Loyalists were aware of what was coming, and the defeat of the British at Yorktown sealed their fates. William Franklin, former governor of New Jersey and son of the famous inventor, political operative, and diplomat, Benjamin Franklin, wrote Lord George Germain that had the British army only managed to extricate itself from Yorktown, and thus not suffer such a humiliating defeat at the hands of the combined French and Patriot forces, many in North America, "as well rebels as loyalists," were prepared to take up arms to compel Congress to end the resistance not so much because all were ready to join the British cause but because of their collective weariness over the continuation of hostilities. Yorktown dealt a fatal blow to their hopes. . . .

The Yorktown debacle did not force the complete or immediate evacuation of the United States. Instead, British forces remained in New York, Charleston, and other sections of the South for the next two years, pending final negotiations between the two parties.

During this period, the battle for control over the United States continued as Loyalists held out hope that they would be rewarded. . . . [But a]s terms of the impending peace treaty became known, many Loyalists expressed their dismay. "Deserted as we are by our King, banished by our country, what resource is left us in the combination of calamities? I had hitherto during many distressing events supported a uniform cheerfulness (being determined never to despair) and hoped for the best but alas! there is now not left the least glimmering of hope." Cataloging the exact manner in which he felt abandoned, the writer continued, "It's no small comfort, though, 'that it's not our crimes but our virtues that have distressed us.'" Specifically objecting to one of the articles of the peace agreement, he asserted, "but we who have borne arms, exposed our lives and sacrificed our properties, encountering innumerable hardships in the service of Britain, are particularly thrown out in a most severe and pointed manner instead of being the first provided for." He concluded, with no small amount of sarcasm, "I shall ever, though, remember with satisfaction that it was not I deserted my King but my King that deserted me."

The number of Loyalists who left the United States during and immediately after the American Revolution is estimated at between sixty thousand and one hundred thousand. Considered as a percentage of the population, which in 1780 was a little under 2.8 million, the figure is higher than the number of emigres who left France during the French revolution. Of those who fled, some relocated to the British islands in the Caribbean; others tried to establish lives in England, largely to discover how much higher the cost of living was there; some even tried returning to the United States with decidedly mixed results. But the vast majority settled in present-day Canada, specifically Nova Scotia and western Quebec, creating a British colonial diaspora that had a major impact on the demographics of the Western Hemisphere and the national evolution of Canada. According to Peter Marshall, "defeat in 1783 generated an influx of settlers on a scale that had long been unavailingly sought, even if the newcomers now came as refugees." The Crown paid greater attention to Canada and played a more aggressive role in developing the remaining colonies in the hemisphere. . . .

The signing of the Paris Peace Treaty in 1783 did not end the friction between the United States and Great Britain. As the principal architect of the peace, the Earl of Shelburne preferred a cooperative course with the Americans, one that included strong economic ties and possibly even a coordinated defense strategy. The economic fit certainly seemed clear enough: America could retain its status as a principal supplier of raw materials to Britain and, in return, the United States would serve as a customer for British goods. In this sense, Shelburne's plan was devious and ingenious. He proposed generosity toward the United States in return for resurrecting the colonial relationship in new guise.

Shelburne's plan did not prevail, however. First, "He greatly underestimated the enmity caused by seven years of fighting and civil war. It was impossible — on either side of the Atlantic — to wipe away the bitterness and bloodshed by one apparently magnanimous gesture." Second, his plan withered under the fierce attack led by the diplomat William Eden (later Lord Auckland) and his friend Lord Sheffield, the two of whom, with the Order in Council of July 2, 1783, managed to restrict American trade with the British West Indies for the next decade. They played upon popular fears of economic decline as well as the frustration and anger focused at Americans for their ingratitude, insolence, and revolutionary success. Permitting the Americans to conduct trade freely, Sheffield demonstrated, "would be to invite the loss of the carrying trade and, inevitably, maritime decadence. The roar of approval which greeted his performance was the voice of the nation."

The reaction was not surprising. The failed effort to put down the American Revolution cost Great Britain £115 million and nearly doubled the national debt. To Emperor Joseph II of Austria, the British position appeared to have declined so much that he declared in 1783, "England had fallen to the status of a second class power." Or as it was put another way by one Loyalist, "O Englishmen, where is now your national honour? Nothing but bribery, corruption and treason prevails in your senate who promised protection and then basely betrayed."

As it turned out, predictions of Great Britain's imperial demise were greatly exaggerated. There was a period of governmental uncertainty, but it was followed by a resurgence that lasted more than a century and catapulted the nation to historic international preeminence.

III

The Vietnamese revolution differed from the American Revolution in almost every respect. Instead of involving one group of people in rebellion against the government that had greatly assisted in their historical development, the Vietnamese situation revolved around three major developments: two international, the other domestic. First was French colonialism. During the nineteenth century, it began with missionary assistance to Emperor Gia Long shortly after 1802 and culminated with French troops subduing Vietnamese forces in the early 1860s.

The second (domestic) issue was the development of a coherent nationalist ideology. Over the three-quarters of a century after France imposed its rule on Vietnam, indigenous nationalism evolved haphazardly, but it continued to grow just the same, eventually becoming a potent and cohesive force. Ultimately, it was the Vietnamese Communists under the leadership of Ho Chi Minh who came to the fore of the opposition against foreign domination. When Ho declared the creation of the Democratic Republic of Vietnam shortly after Japan's surrender in 1945, the Viet Minh's history of resistance, Ho's statements as well as his international travel and learning, and his actions during the war comprised a mélange of nationalism, communism, antiforeignism, and opportunism, all of which resonated with the majority of the Vietnamese people.

When France decided to oppose Vietnam's bid for independence, the United States sided with its European ally out of concern for what might happen to the French position in Europe should it not be able to re-establish its colonial empire. In making this choice, American foreign policy makers denied the nationalist character of Vietnam's push for independence and emphasized, exclusive of all other factors, its communist ideology. Thus, the Cold War competition between the Soviet Union and the United States constitutes the third element.

U.S. support for France began in a small and indirect fashion, but between 1950 and 1954 it became substantial — to the tune of $2 billion — and afterward, it became direct. French forces were unable to stem the tide; they surrendered ignominiously in May 1954. It was the subsequent determination — when the United States decided to back Ngo Dinh Diem as an alternative to Ho's claim on authority — that led to the decades-long involvement in Vietnam. Diem was propped up through a series of mech-anisms, including military assistance in the training and supply of his South Vietnamese army (Army of the Republic of Viet Nam, or ARVN). It also included massive eco-nomic assistance. In the process, the United States fostered a coterie of sorts, or more accurately, it expanded the existing group of Vietnamese whose livelihood had been de-pendent upon the French. This began with an effort to provide Diem with a base of support. Given that he was Catholic, American advisers enticed, cajoled, and even scared nearly 800,000 Vietnamese co-worshipers to relocate from the north to the south in the aftermath of the French withdrawal. From there, fidelity to Diem provided ac-cess to a system of economic rewards through a number of different avenues, including government or military service. The result of all this activity was that the United States created its own group of loyalists.

American hopes that these faithful would stabilize the situation in Southeast Asia proved to be misguided. Aid begot more aid, and the South Vietnamese government became entirely dependent on the United States for its survival. Diem, not popular to start with, became increasingly isolated during his reign and finally fell victim to his own generals, who killed him in a coup in 1963. Subsequent South Vietnamese leaders were even more dependent on the United States. Meanwhile, as the Viet Minh organ-ized North Vietnamese society and pressed for elections to unify their country, a process opposed by the United States, an indigenous resistance movement developed in South Vietnam. When the National Liberation Front (NLF) began its armed struggle to top-ple Diem's rule in 1960, it was a small but rapidly growing force. Its success led policy makers and military personnel in the Kennedy and Johnson administrations to conclude that the only way to retain suzerainty [political control] was for American forces to as-sume a greater share of actual combat.

But why Vietnam? Unlike the North American colonies, which had been populated by so many British settlers with the assistance of the Crown over a century and a half and thus clearly represented a major investment and interest to England, Vietnam had received no such attention from the United States prior to 1950. In the end, the length or extent of the previous commitment mattered less than the perception of where North America and Vietnam fit into the larger imperial scheme of things and as pieces in the competition with archrivals France and the Soviet Union. A little over a decade before the American Revolution, for example, Britain had fought to deny France the opportunity to expand its holdings in North America. Having expended so much money, material, and men on ousting the French, the British were not about to allow the colonists their freedom in 1775. The Crown believed it could not permit the United States to act independently.

Similarly, the United States decided to make its stand in South Vietnam because of its importance for the larger empire in Asia. Japan was pivotal to American designs but it needed trading partners, and Southeast Asia, specifically a noncommunist South Vietnam, was critical. As Thomas McCormick has argued, "Empires were of a piece, and the loss of one member affected the organic health of the whole." More commonly known as the domino theory, this idea posited that if Vietnam fell to communism, other nations would succumb, ultimately leaving the United States without a stake in the region. Equally unacceptable was the idea that a neutral South Vietnam could develop. When Diem made overtures to the NLF in 1963 with the intent of exploring just such an idea, his fate was sealed. According to the Kennedy administration, Diem had to be removed. A neutral South Vietnam was almost as bad as a communist-controlled one.

It was necessary for the United States to organize the periphery and keep it from the clutches of its chief international competitor, just as it had been essential for Great Britain to prevent France from expanding in North America. As Don Higginbotham has summed up the comparison, "The Johnson government and to some extent the king and the North administration persisted in the face of dissent as long as they did because they believed in the domino theory — for Britain this meant the loss of the colonies would lead to secessionist movements in Ireland, the West Indies, and elsewhere; for the Johnson team, 'the best and the brightest,' it meant the fall to communism, one by one, of most Southeast Asian states." But in opposing Vietnamese unification and independence, American foreign policy makers pushed Vietnam into closer cooperation with the Soviet Union and China.

Within five years, the Kennedy and Johnson administrations led the nation into a greater military commitment in South Vietnam. By the end of 1965, American ground troops totaled 180,000; a year later there were another 200,000, and the number came to just over 530,000 in 1968. Given its vast military commitments around the globe in the mid-1960s and considering the need for at least the appearance of an allied effort in Southeast Asia, the Johnson administration had to find its own Hessians to fight alongside American troops. In this respect, the American endeavor, which took shape in the form of the Many Flags Program, paralleled two aspects of the British struggle against the Americans. One was the recruitment of foreign mercenaries, be they Hessians or South Koreans, Thais, or Filipinos. The Many Flags Program had two principal attractions, according to George Kahin: "It had the potential of significantly reducing the U.S. military burden, and it also had the political advantage . . . of providing visible proof that the increased military intervention was sanctioned by, and enjoyed the tangible support of, some of Washington's allies."

The other resemblance came in the economic benefits that accrued to areas in proximity of the fighting. During the American Revolution it was Canada and the British West Indies, especially the former, that received supplies, increased trade, and enjoyed the economic benefits from having troops and administrators stationed there. After Saratoga, for example, "British North America became an essential line of supply rather than a battleground. This brought about an increase of Imperial expenditures in Nova Scotia of 250 percent over the average for the previous decade." Farther west, "The necessary deployment of troops in Quebec and the use of Halifax as the reception point of ships and supplies ensured that local economies received a powerful, if not a transforming, stimulus."

During the Vietnamese revolution, it was Japan, followed by South Korea, Thailand, and the Philippines, that benefited the most from American military largesse. As Michael Schaller pointed out, between 1965 and 1972 "Japan earned at least $7 billion in 'extra' sales of goods and services related to Vietnam." From 1967 through 1969, South Korean soldiers in Vietnam sent home over $500 million, and the country earned about $1 billion from 1966 to 1970. Proportionate to the number of troops they committed, Thailand and the Philippines did about as well.

By the end of 1967, the United States had just under five hundred thousand troops stationed in Vietnam. The war continued without signs of abating and despite the insistence of the American military leaders that the "cross-over point" had been reached — that is, the point at which North Vietnamese casualties exceeded their ability to replace them. Then again, American military personnel, like their British counterparts from the eighteenth century, had insisted from the start that the enemy would not be able to withstand a concerted military effort. In the eighteenth century, British assessments of the average American soldier ran from "a very effeminate thing, very unfit for and very impatient of war" to characterizations of the citizenry as "a worthless lot, a rabble, without discipline and without courage, running away from battle, deserting to the British ranks, leaving Mr. Washington with no army at all."

In the summer of 1965, while discussing the consequences of escalating the conflict through the introduction of large numbers of American troops, the chairman of the Joint Chiefs of Staff, Earle Wheeler, spoke confidently of how the North Vietnamese would be placed in a bind. When Johnson asked about their matching the buildup, Wheeler asserted, "This means greater bodies of men from North Vietnam, which will allow us to cream them." And when Johnson followed up with an assessment of the likelihood of a greater North Vietnamese commitment, Wheeler stated, "The North would be foolhardy to put one-quarter of their forces in S[outh]V[iet]N[am]. It would expose them too greatly in the North." But North Vietnamese regulars and Viet Cong guerrillas proved those predictions wrong and tenaciously battled American troops throughout South Vietnam. Nevertheless, according to many American military and civilian advisers in late 1967, the war was about to be brought to a conclusion.

Although not a surprise, the Tet Offensive that came in January 1968 was a significant shock to the United States, and its impact was very similar to the effect Saratoga had had on Great Britain. Tet came a little less than three years after the onset of major hostilities. The period from Saratoga to the final peace treaty was five-and-a-half years; Tet to the Paris peace agreement was almost exactly five years. But far more important, and very much like Saratoga, Tet forced a fundamental reconsideration of strategy: The United States looked to rely more heavily on the indigenous forces, in this case ARVN, to shoulder a greater share of the fighting. According to George Herring, by March 1968, after the brunt of the Tet Offensive had been borne, the Johnson administration decided "the United States was willing to send limited reinforcements and substantial quantities of equipment but that continued American assistance would depend upon South Vietnam's ability to put its own affairs in order and assume a greater burden of the fighting."

Tet signaled the beginning of the painful end of the American effort to control Southeast Asia. Upon his election in 1968, Richard Nixon embarked upon a twofold strategy to extricate the nation from the war: first was the withdrawal of American forces while maintaining military credibility by escalating the conflict through aerial bombardment, which included Cambodia; second was the buildup of South Vietnam through massive military and economic assistance. What John Shy has written about the impact of Saratoga holds true for Tet: "The new approach which emerged during 1778 emphasized the role of loyal Americans. It was at last admitted that, ultimately, restored British authority would have to depend on Americans themselves, and that even the strongest army and navy could do no more than create favorable conditions for the Americanization of the war."

When the Paris Peace Accords were signed in January 1973, Nixon and his chief foreign policy adviser, Henry Kissinger, claimed that they had achieved an honorable peace and that South Vietnam was prepared to move forward as a viable political entity.

In truth, the situation looked a good deal different. South Vietnam was about as viable as the Loyalist governments set up in Georgia and South Carolina during the American Revolution. Once the supporting troops from abroad departed, the claims of the South Vietnamese government to legitimacy dissolved, less quickly than in the case of the Loyalists, but they vanished just the same. And with the disintegration of their state, South Vietnamese leaders lashed out at their American supporters who had deserted them. In writing to President Gerald R. Ford in March 1975, General Nguyen Van Thieu sounded like William Franklin and so many other Loyalists two hundred years earlier. He asked for immediate and substantial American military support to stem the communist advance. He called "to the credibility of American foreign policy, and especially to the conscience of America." When his solicitation proved futile, Thieu resigned and expressed his deep frustration at the lack of support from the United States. "The United States is proud of being an invincible defender of the just cause and the ideal of freedom in this world," he lamented. "I ask them: Are U.S. statements worthy? Are U.S. commitments still valid?"

At the very bitter end it was the chief executives who remained defiant, impervious to the truth. For some time King George III had rejected "the arguments of his ministers that colonial independence was inevitable and refuse[d] to accept that the rebellion had succeeded." In 1975, Ford and members of the Executive Branch seemed to be the only ones who failed to realize that the game was up, that the North Vietnamese had won. Beginning in January and continuing until just a few days before the actual collapse of the South Vietnamese government in late April, Ford tried repeatedly to secure congressional consent on a variety of military and economic assistance packages totaling anywhere from $300 million to $2 billion. In a cabinet meeting at the end of January, the president outlined a plan for supplemental assistance for South Vietnam and Cambodia and asked for support from everyone. He spoke of a "guilt complex" that afflicted the nation by withdrawing from Southeast Asia. Kissinger went further. Although the United States had "brought 550,000 troops home with honor," he worried about the impact that leaving South Vietnam to the communists would have on the nation's "international negotiating power" and "international negotiating ability," in addition to general credibility around the world. Two years after the signing of the Paris Peace Accord, South Vietnam faced imminent destruction, Ford said, "and we apparently stand helpless, our fidelity in question, our word at stake." The American pledge to South Vietnam stood as a test for other commitments around the world. And Ford wondered whether America's allies would not suddenly doubt the advisability of working closely with the United States: "In this world of ours, it is not without hazard to be a friend of the U.S." Failure to provide additional assistance to South Vietnam in its time of need would have serious and far-reaching complications. From negotiations in the Middle East to allies making "other accommodations to protect themselves," Ford foresaw a potentially catastrophic series of consequences emanating from the failure to provide supplemental assistance to South Vietnam and Cambodia. "The results would be an alien world in which the costs for our survival would dwarf anything we have ever known." With the president and his advisers denying the reality of the situation while jockeying for political position, worried as they were about their positions in history, Congress made the hard decision and cut off the moribund Thieu regime from additional assistance.

In the war's aftermath, the United States placed severe restrictions on the Vietnamese economy through a number of punitive measures. The Ford administration froze $150 million in Vietnamese assets, expanded the embargo on North Vietnam — in place since the early 1960s — to include all of Vietnam and Cambodia, and denied Vietnam's entry into the United Nations. The embargo effectively undercut discussions between American oil companies and Vietnam about developing offshore reserves.

The Nixon-Ford administrations, like the government of Lord North, failed to live long beyond the end of the fighting. And in their place came the American version of Lord Shelburne: Jimmy Carter. He wanted to heal the wounds of the war; he wanted to end the rancor. He wanted to put the war firmly into the past, and he tried to accomplish this by extending a diplomatic hand to Vietnam in 1977 through the normalization of relations without preconditions. But like Lord Shelburne, who had discovered that the "enmity caused by seven years of fighting and civil war" was impossible to expunge so quickly, Carter ran into strong emotions on both sides. Vietnamese negotiators were determined to get something for their long suffering. An equally resolute Congress was intent on providing nothing. In the end, the United States refused to give any consideration to the $4.75 billion in reconstruction assistance promised by Nixon in separate codicils to the 1973 peace agreement. Moreover, Congress passed legislation in the spring preventing the payment of reparations and disallowing key international lending agencies from providing funds to Vietnam. For their part, the Vietnamese continued to press for something, almost anything, but the Americans remained firm and negotiations dragged into 1978, when they came up against the American desire to normalize diplomatic relations with the People's Republic of China.

The Vietnamese, who were initially as eager and expectant with regard to establishing diplomatic and economic relations with the United States as Americans had been with respect to Great Britain in the early 1780s, became frustrated at the impasse created by the American refusal to acknowledge its debt. Vietnam turned to the Soviet Union, signing a Treaty of Friendship and Cooperation in 1978 that, along with the Vietnamese invasion of Cambodia in December 1978, precluded a rapprochement with the United States for another decade and a half.

The cost of the war to the United States was staggering. Between 1962 and 1975 South Vietnam was the largest recipient of USAID funds, a fact that bespeaks the distorting impact the war had on the nation's priorities. One estimate places the total cost of the war at $168 billion. Approximately 150,000 Vietnamese escaped with the hastily departing Americans in 1975. Nearly one-and-a-half million left afterward, particularly during 1979 when Vietnamese "boat people" drifted in regional waters, searching for a place to land. Since 1975, approximately three-quarters of a million Vietnamese have settled in the United States. Others relocated to countries in Southeast Asia, creating a Vietnamese diaspora of growing economic importance.

Of those Vietnamese who left, Hamilton's earlier warning held true: Many of the most productive citizens fled, along with their education, training, and skills. They departed just like the Loyalists did — out of fear of the reprisals against themselves and their families. The bloodbath predicted by American right-wing commentators never materialized, but the re-education camps were harsh and brutal environments. Release meant a greater degree of freedom, but jobs were scarce for everyone, especially former loyalists to the American cause.

From a comparative perspective, if two million Vietnamese left after 1975, the figure represents less than 4 percent of the total population, which surpassed fifty million upon unification. If only sixty thousand Loyalists fled the United States during and after the revolution, the number comes to a little over 2 percent of the total population of roughly 2.8 million in 1780; if the higher figure of one hundred thousand is taken, it exceeds 3 percent. Some Loyalists who remained or tried to return after the end of the war found themselves imprisoned. The luckier ones were simply run out of town; the less fortunate ones were killed by mobs.

IV

What, then, are the major conclusions to be drawn from a comparison of the two revolutions and the principal responses they elicited from the powers that worked to thwart them? First, Great Britain and the United States sought a military solution once it became clear that the indigenous forces favorable to the imperial position were inadequate to stem the tide of revolution. By 1775, the British colonial authorities in North America had clearly lost control of the situation. With the Patriot attacks on British troops at Lexington and Concord in April, the Crown decided it was time to take stern action, to teach the colonists certain lessons. And from then until General Burgoyne's defeat in October 1777, those lessons would come from a contingent of British and foreign troops.

In Vietnam, it was the South Vietnamese government that was clearly losing the initiative by 1965, so much so that members of the Johnson administration concluded that the only way to bolster morale and instruct the North Vietnamese in the manner of American resolve was through a bombing campaign. That led to the introduction of regular ground troops to protect the airbases. When that strategy proved inadequate to the task, a major commitment of ground troops was deemed necessary, including foreign troops.

Second, both British and American military efforts failed in spectacular fashion to achieve their goals. Saratoga and Tet have come to represent turning points in both wars in similar ways. The former was clearly a British defeat, militarily speaking, and as such the plan to cleave New England from the other colonies gave way to the southern strategy and a greater reliance on Loyalists. Tet was not so much a military defeat for U.S. forces on a tactical level as it was a complete repudiation of the strategic assertions that the war was being won and that the Vietnamese were depleting their material and human resources to such levels that they no longer would be able to fight. The Vietnamese had to wait until 1972 to conduct another major military offensive, but comparatively speaking, colonial troops under General Washington never conducted a major offensive. Taking the offensive mattered less than outlasting the imperial power, something that both American and Vietnamese forces managed to do in the end and something that their opponents failed to comprehend at the time.

Third, faced with a longer and more costly conflict than they had anticipated, the British Crown and the U.S. government tried to rely on indigenous elements to assume a greater share of the fighting. In the case of the former it was the Loyalists; in the latter it was the ARVN troops in a process labeled Vietnamization, but in neither instance were these forces capable of stemming the tide of the revolutions they faced. With their defeat, the individuals who had fought for the empire looked for protection and assistance, sometimes during the hasty and mass exodus on the heels of the departing imperial troops, other times in the form of governmental aid for relocating somewhere else in the region.

Fourth, both Great Britain and the United States sought to curb the ambitions and activities of the victorious revolutionary nations immediately after they won independence. For Great Britain, this came through restricting Americans' access to the Caribbean trade they had previously enjoyed. It also meant maintaining and sometimes furthering alliances and relations with Indians along the western frontier of the new nation. And it included diverting resources to strengthen Canada. For the United States, this took shape in continuing a punitive economic embargo, freezing assets, and normalizing relations with Vietnam's principal nemesis in the region, China.

Fifth, the efforts to thwart the revolutions were costly both economically and politically. The British government saw a brief period of instability — from the North to the Shelburne administrations — before William Pitt the Younger became prime minister. In the United States, Nixon became the first president to resign from office. He was caught covering up an illegal break-in run by a group initially established to find and stop leaks concerning the administration's Vietnam policies. His hand-picked successor lasted a little over two years, and he was followed by the only Democratic president (other than John F. Kennedy, who was assassinated in his first term) not to be re-elected in the twentieth century. By the end of the Carter administration, commentators were writing about how the presidency had become an impossible job. Ronald Reagan changed all that.

Finally, despite assertions to the contrary, at the time of their defeat neither Great Britain nor the United States went into a dramatic decline as a result of having lost the fight. Instead, it was their global rivals who collapsed, leaving the international arena far less threatening for the immediate future. What is remarkable, then, is how many similarities exist between the American and Vietnamese revolutions and how strikingly alike are the responses they evoked from the principal imperial powers that sought to thwart them.

Ho Chi Minh appreciated enough of American history, both its eighteenth-century fight for independence and its more recent declarations about self-determination and anticolonialism during World War II, that he quoted portions of Thomas Jefferson's most famous work in proclaiming Vietnamese independence on September 2, 1945. And it is here that the comparison between the two revolutions and the decisions made in response to them becomes most poignant: The United States had the opportunity to act differently, especially given its own history, from the European powers that had colonized so much of the globe. Instead, Americans chose the path more heavily traveled and ended up becoming an imperial power very much like Great Britain, a fate the leaders of the revolution had anxiously sought to avoid.

QUESTIONS TO CONSIDER

1. How, according to the author, were the American and Vietnamese revolutions similar in their character and impact? On the other hand, what major differences does he see in their global context, their colonial situation, and their ideologies? Why did the United States intervene if Vietnam was not its colony?

2. What parallels does Jespersen point out between Britain's reaction to the American Revolution and America's response to the Vietnamese Revolution? How did the "domino theory" apply in both cases? How were nearby nations or colonies benefited by the conflict? How were the British defeat at Saratoga and the American setback during the Tet Offensive analogous? In what ways were America's South Vietnamese allies in a position similar to Loyalists in the British colonies? How did British and American leaders react to defeat?

3. What overall conclusions does Jespersen draw from his pairing of these counterrevolutionary wars? What lessons do *you* find in his comparison? Be sure to consider questions about military strategy, the dynamics of revolutions, changes in America's world position, the Cold War, the nature of imperialism, and the way "history repeats itself." Why did the United States, which was born in a colonial war for independence, oppose analogous struggles in Vietnam and elsewhere in the twentieth century?

4. Compare America's Cold War stance toward Vietnam with its strategy against communist expansion in Europe, as described by John Lewis Gaddis in Selection 19. Was America's approach toward Vietnam consistent with "empire by invitation," or was it more like the Soviets' "empire by imposition"? Why?

5. Review the essay by Vince Boudreau on America's colonial rule in the Philippines (Selection 10). What similarities and differences do you see between America's war in Vietnam and its war against Philippine independence in 1899–1902? Why were the Vietnamese communists able to triumph, while the Philippine rebels were defeated? How did the timing of the Vietnamese Revolution change the way Americans viewed it? Why did the United States succeed in installing a viable colonial government in the Philippines but fail in South Vietnam? In what way, if any, does the war in Vietnam alter the portrait of American imperialism that emerged from Boudreau's analysis?

XI

RIGHTS
REVOLUTIONS

Nationally as well as internationally, the early 1960s brought a breath of fresh, warming air into Cold War culture. The Cuban missile crisis of 1962, which took the United States and the Soviet Union to the brink of nuclear war, left in its wake an easing of Cold War tensions. When the Soviet Union and China broke their communist alliance and a bloc of nations emerged that were committed to neither the Americans nor the Soviets, the threat of a climactic nuclear confrontation lessened. As the Cold War began to thaw, the chilling atmosphere of political conformity that had pervaded the McCarthy era began to dissipate, opening up room for liberals and radicals to express their views candidly on domestic issues. During the Cold War, opponents of segregation had argued that America's racial divide undermined its position as a model for the "Free World." With John F. Kennedy's election as president in 1960, there was a clear mandate for reform. The young president took the reins of government away from an older generation of wartime leaders like Dwight Eisenhower. Kennedy's idealistic rhetoric and his ambitious plans for legislation to end discrimination and provide federal aid to education seemed to prefigure a new activist spirit in domestic politics.

The idealism and the unprecedented prosperity of the years flanking 1960 bred "revolutions of rising expectations" among groups previously left on the margins of American society. The two most important social movements of the post–World War II era, the civil rights and women's rights crusades, began as equal-rights movements but evolved into more multifaceted causes. Both were built upon a history of discrimination and protest in the United States. Yet as the essays in this chapter show, neither operated in an isolated national context. The first essay, by George M. Fredrickson, compares the American Civil Rights movement's struggle against segregation with South African blacks' simultaneous campaign against the repressive white apartheid regime. Both movements, he notes, were inspired by the surge of anticolonial protests among people of color following World War II, especially by the philosophy of nonviolent resistance that Mahatma Gandhi had used to lead India to independence from British control. In the second essay, Olive Banks finds many parallels between the American and British feminist movements, ranging from their common roots in women's greater participation in the paid work force to their similar evolution toward radical feminism. Both authors also point out key ways in which the American "rights revolutions" were different from the others. Fredrickson finds the American Civil Rights movement initially more successful than its South African counterpart, for instance, and Banks notes how American feminists were in the vanguard of women's liberation. But the fact that both American movements stalled in the 1970s as the world economy dipped into recession and voters took a conservative turn suggests that progress toward equality in the United States was far from inevitable.

21

Resistance to White Supremacy in the United States and South Africa

GEORGE M. FREDRICKSON

In the 1950s and the early 1960s, nonviolent protesters tried to end the rule of racial segregation in South Africa and the American South. These were, according to the comparative historian George Fredrickson, "the only two places where such blatant manifestations of white supremacy could then be found." The American Civil Rights movement rallied around an eloquent young Baptist preacher, Martin Luther King Jr., who energized audiences by blending Christian scriptures and American political ideals with the philosophy of nonviolence he had learned from the saintly father of Indian nationhood, Mahatma Gandhi. Overcoming every obstruction that southern whites placed in the way, King's interracial coalition boycotted, walked, sat-in, litigated, and marched its way to victories over segregationist practices. The movement's idealism and perseverance impressed the nation and eventually led Congress to pass landmark civil rights legislation in 1964 and 1965.

In South Africa, the result was quite different. There the Defiance Campaign of 1952–1960 led by the African National Congress (ANC) used many of the same nonviolent tactics to oppose laws requiring blacks to live in segregated townships and carry passes wherever they went. But the South African government responded with force, brutally massacring dozens of protesters at Sharpeville in 1960, banning the ANC, and outlawing public demonstrations. Some members of the ANC, forced underground, resorted to acts of sabotage and violence. The ANC's Nelson Mandela was imprisoned by the government in 1964 and remained in custody for a quarter century.

In retrospect, it is not surprising that the American movement succeeded and the South African one failed. For after World War II, the two nations were clearly heading in opposite directions. The wartime surge of black migration to the North and West brought considerable economic gains that raised the expectations of young African Americans. Railway union leader A. Philip Randolph threatened a massive march on Washington unless President Roosevelt ordered an end to discrimination in defense jobs. Membership in the National Association for the Advancement of Colored People (NAACP) increased tenfold, and the Congress of Racial Equality was founded in 1942 as a nonviolent protest alternative to the NAACP. The Cold War's ideological struggle against totalitarianism made many Americans anxious to prove that democracy was color blind. President Truman desegregated the army in 1948 and introduced civil rights legislation in Congress. The NAACP pressed the legal battle against segregation through court cases, winning some minor victories in the late 1940s. Then in 1954, in Brown vs. Board of Education of Topeka, the NAACP scored a spectacular triumph when the U.S. Supreme Court declared public school segregation unconstitutional. Reversing the doctrine of "separate but equal" that had prevailed since the Plessy vs. Ferguson decision of 1896, the Court pulled away the legal props that had supported the Jim Crow system of racial separation for more than half a century. The following year, a black boycott of segregated city buses in Montgomery, Alabama, became the first mass protest by African Americans since the war, and it brought Reverend King to prominence.

By contrast, after World War II the ruling white minority in South Africa, worried about the spread of communism and black nationalism in the region, asserted white supremacy with increased ferocity. The National Party, representing the most conservative Afrikaners (whites descended from the Dutch colonists of the seventeenth century) triumphed in the elections of 1948 on a platform of "apartheid," or "separate development," for whites and blacks. Immediately, its leaders extended the nation's already harsh segregationist practices. They designated tiny territorial "homelands" where African natives were to be confined, leaving urban blacks — the majority — to be treated as "guest workers" with few rights. In 1953, the year before the U.S. Supreme Court's desegregation decision, the South African legislature declared separate and unequal facilities its official policy. Voting rights were taken away from the Coloreds (the mixed-race offspring of Asians, whites, and blacks), who now joined black Africans as outcasts. All residents were required to carry racial identification cards.

As Fredrickson shows, the American and South African protest movements had much in common. Both were influenced by Gandhi, whose writings King encountered in divinity school and who had personally directed the Indian struggle for equal rights in South Africa early in the century. Also, both campaigns were led by a black elite that mobilized the masses *for boycotts and marches. Fredrickson, however, finds important differences between them, especially the greater grass-roots support for black activism in the American South and the Civil Rights movement's fervently religious character. Perhaps the biggest difference was in their environments: whereas African blacks faced a white minority determined to preserve its power at all costs and unhampered by legal obstacles, American blacks could build alliances with northern white liberals and use the Constitution and the courts to their advantage.*

On the surface, it is hard to deny that the American movement was a success and the South African one a failure. Yet it is important to note that Fredrickson puts strict thematic and chronological limits on his study. Without them, his conclusion would be more mixed. On the American side, several factors make the civil rights story less triumphant. For one thing, there was the stiff resistance of southern whites to desegregation, which delayed implementation of the Brown vs. Board of Education ruling and cost several protesters' lives. For another, the Civil Rights movement's climax of 1964–1965 was followed by a division in black leadership between King's integrationist, nonviolent message and that of Malcolm X and other Black Power spokesmen, who advocated militant racial separatism. Angry blacks in northern cities lashed out in dozens of riots between 1965 and 1970, protesting continuing discrimination and unemployment. The climate of violence took a frightful toll as Malcolm X was assassinated by rival Black Muslims in 1965, and King, who was planning a "Poor People's Campaign" for jobs and peace, was killed by a white racist in 1968. Despite the civil rights victories of the 1960s, the public's receptiveness to black protests cooled in the recession-dominated 1970s, and the goal of economic equality for African Americans remains elusive.

On the African side, black protests, buoyed by international support, eventually defeated apartheid. In 1976 a series of riots in black townships re-ignited the protest movement, and in ensuing years international sanctions isolated the South African government and increasingly hurt its economy. During the 1980s, the beleaguered Nationalist Party combined concessions to blacks with stepped-up violence against protesters, a policy that only alienated die-hard white supremacists and increased black activism. Under the United Democratic Front, South African blacks organized antirent strikes, consumer boycotts, and work stoppages. Over seventeen thousand South African blacks died when nonviolent protests were met with force and black political and tribal factions engaged in internecine warfare. Finally bowing to foreign pressure and the threat of internal chaos, South African president F. W. de Klerk in 1990 declared an end to segregated facilities, lifted the ban on the ANC, and released Nelson Mandela from jail. The following year, complex negotiations were begun to determine the shape of a new government. After a preliminary constitution was drafted, the first free elections in South African history were held in April 1994. Mandela was elected president, vindicating years of black protest and inaugurating a new era in South African history. The road to peace and racial harmony will surely be difficult, but South Africa has come a long way from the days of the Defiance Campaign.

GLOSSARY

AFRICAN NATIONAL CONGRESS (ANC)   The foremost South African black political pressure group. The ANC was formed in 1912 by middle-class black professionals and chiefs as an organization promoting interracial dialogue and peaceful protest. In 1955 the ANC collaborated with organizations representing South Africa's Coloreds, Asians, and white liberals to issue a freedom charter calling for nonracial democracy. Banned in 1961 by the government, the ANC went underground, advocating sabotage and guerrilla operations and establishing bases in neighboring countries. After Nelson Mandela was released in 1990 and the ban against it was lifted, the ANC suspended its armed struggle against white rule. In the 1994 elections, it became the majority party in the South African parliament.

CIVIL RIGHTS ACTS OF 1964 AND 1965   American laws passed at the height of the Civil Rights movement. The first, the Civil Rights Act of 1964, prohibited discrimination in public accommodations, schools, and employment on the basis of color, race, religion, sex, or national origins. The second, the Voting Rights Act of 1965, authorized the federal government to register black voters and suspended literacy tests in states with low voter turnout.

CONGRESS OF RACIAL EQUALITY (CORE)   A civil rights organization founded in 1942 in Chicago by James Farmer. It sought to end discrimination through nonviolent direct action. CORE first gained national attention through the 1961 Freedom Rides, in which interracial groups traveled south by bus to protest segregated busing facilities. By the mid-1960s, CORE turned toward a philosophy of Black Power and racial separatism.

GANDHI, MOHANDAS K. "MAHATMA" (1869–1948)   The Indian political and spiritual leader who became the father of independent India. After practicing law in South Africa, where he fought for Indian civil rights, Gandhi returned to India in 1915 to work for independence. He renounced Western ways to lead a life of abstinence and spirituality, and became an advocate of *satyagraha* (love-force or passive resistance) against British rule. Jailed several times by the British, he was released in 1944 and helped guide the negotiations that led to independence in 1947. He was assassinated the following year by a Hindu fanatic who objected to his tolerance for Muslims.

JIM CROW   The practice of legally segregating or discriminating against blacks, especially in the American South in the late nineteenth and the first half of the twentieth centuries. The term derived from the name of a song in a nineteenth-century minstrel show.

LUTULI, ALBERT (1898–1967)   A Zulu chief and protester against the apartheid regime. A fervent Christian, Lutuli advocated nonviolent resistance to apartheid and the formation of a multiracial democratic society. He was elected president of the ANC in 1952 and was repeatedly arrested by the South African government for allegedly promoting racial "hostilities." Lutuli was awarded the Nobel Peace Prize in 1960.

MANDELA, NELSON (1918–)   A leader of the South African movement to end apartheid. Trained as an attorney, Mandela helped form the Youth League of the ANC in 1944 and participated in the Defiance Campaign. In 1961 when the ANC was outlawed, he abandoned peaceful protest and became commander of the ANC's military wing. He was sentenced to life imprisonment in 1964 for conspiracy to overthrow the government and became a symbol of resistance to apartheid. Mandela was released in 1990 and a year later was chosen head of the ANC. He and President de Klerk were named co-recipients of the Nobel Peace Prize in 1993, during negotiations to end the Nationalist regime. Elected president of South Africa in 1994, Mandela served until 1999.

NATIONAL ASSOCIATION FOR THE ADVANCEMENT OF COLORED PEOPLE (NAACP) An organization founded in 1910 by a coalition of white liberals and black activists and dedicated to ending racial inequality and segregation in the United States. The organization works mainly through lobbying and litigation, and it has sometimes been accused of passivity by more militant groups.

PETTY BOURGEOISIE The middle-class element composed of white-collar workers, shopkeepers, and tradespeople, as opposed to the high bourgeoisie of bankers and corporate owners.

SOUTHERN CHRISTIAN LEADERSHIP CONFERENCE (SCLC) A civil rights organization founded by Martin Luther King Jr. and other black ministers in 1957. It worked through local churches to push for desegregation and social change.

STUDENT NONVIOLENT COORDINATING COMMITTEE (SNCC) Established in 1960 by southern black students with King's help to organize sit-ins against discriminatory businesses and segregated facilities as well as voter registration drives. In 1966 young militants took over SNCC, rejecting white members or assistance and advocating black separatism and even violent resistance.

TUTU, DESMOND (1931–) A black bishop who became the head of the entire Anglican Church in South Africa. Tutu helped to form the United Democratic Front committed to nonviolent protest against apartheid. He was awarded the Nobel Peace Prize in 1984 and in 1995 was appointed head of the Truth and Reconciliation Committee, which investigated human rights abuses that had occurred during the apartheid era.

During the 1950s and early 1960s non-violent protesters challenged legalized racial segregation and discrimination in the only two places where such blatant manifestations of white supremacy could then be found — the southern United States and the Union of South Africa. Comparing these roughly contemporaneous movements and looking for connections between them may give historians a better perspective on the recent history of black liberation struggles in the two societies. . . .

The ANC's [African National Congress's] "Campaign of Defiance against Unjust Laws" in 1952 resulted in the arrest of approximately eight thousand blacks (including Indians and Coloreds as well as Africans) and a handful of whites for planned acts of civil disobedience against recently enacted apartheid legislation. The campaign did not make the government alter its course, and it was called off early in 1953 after riots broke out in the wake of non-violent actions in the Eastern Cape. Repressive legislation, making deliberate transgression of the law for political purposes a serious crime in its own right, made the ANC wary of again attempting a nation-wide campaign of civil disobedience,

"Resistance to White Supremacy in the United States and South Africa," by George M. Fredrickson. From Brian Ward and Tony Badger (eds.), *The Making of Martin Luther King and the Civil Rights Movement.* Copyright © 1996. Reprinted by permission of New York University Press, and Macmillan Press Ltd.

but it could not prevent the Congress and other black or interracial organizations from protesting non-violently in other ways and refusing generally to cooperate with the regime in its efforts to erect barriers between blacks and whites in all aspects of life. School boycotts, bus boycotts, non-cooperation with the program of removing blacks to new townships, and mass marches to protest efforts to force African women to carry passes were among the actions of the mid-to-late fifties which the ANC led or supported. In 1960, the Pan-Africanist Congress — a militant faction that had recently seceded from the ANC because of its objections to the parent organization's policy of cooperating with the congresses established by other racial groups as well as to its relatively cautious approach to mass action — launched a campaign of civil disobedience against the pass laws that ended with the massacre of 69 unarmed protesters at Sharpeville. Chief Albert Lutuli, president-general of the ANC, showed his sympathy for the Sharpeville victims by publicly burning his own pass, and the one-day stay-at-home which the Congress called to register its solidarity with the PAC was well supported. But the government quickly suppressed all public protest, and both the ANC and the PAC were banned and driven underground. After Sharpeville, non-violent direct action no longer seemed a viable option for the liberation movement, and in 1961 some ANC leaders, in cooperation with the South African Communist Party, inaugurated the era of armed struggle by establishing a separate organization to carry on acts of sabotage against hard targets.

The non-violent phase of the American Civil Rights Movement began with the Montgomery bus boycott of 1955–6 and culminated in the great Birmingham, Mississippi, and Selma campaigns of 1963–5. Viewed narrowly as an attack on legalized segregation and disfranchisement in the southern states, the movement was remarkably successful. It led to the Civil Rights Acts of 1964 and 1965, which effectively outlawed Jim Crow and assured southern blacks access to the ballot box. It becomes immediately apparent therefore that an obvious and fundamental difference between the two movements is that one can be regarded as successful in achieving its immediate objectives while the other was a conspicuous failure.

Fully explaining success or failure obviously requires an assessment of the context — what each movement was up against and what outside help it could expect in its struggle. But before looking at such limiting or favoring circumstances, the movements themselves have to be described and analyzed in an effort to compare the resources and capabilities that each brought to the confrontation with white power. Furthermore, it would be mechanistic and ahistorical to ignore the possibility that movements emerging at about the same time and involving people who in both instances defined themselves as black victims of white oppression may have influenced each other in some direct and important way. We need to know what they shared or had in common and how they differed — in ideology, organization, and leadership. What do similarities and differences in political thought and behavior as well as in social and cultural characteristics tell us about the situation of black people in these two racist societies during the 1950s and 60s? What role, if any, did internal differences play in determining the success or failure of non-violence?

Somewhat surprisingly, little evidence has come to light that the two non-violent movements influenced each other in a significant way. Before World War II, African-American influence on black South African ideologies and movements had been substantial, but the use of black America as inspiration and example appears to have tapered off during the post-war years. Before the triumph of the Nationalists in 1948, black American interest in South Africa had been limited and intermittent; the African Methodist Episcopal Church had provided the most important and durable connection when it had established itself in South Africa at the turn of the century. For most African-Americans Africa meant West Africa, but awareness of the white-dominated nation at the tip of the continent increased rapidly after the rise of apartheid showed that South Africa was out of step with a world that seemed at last to be moving towards an acceptance of the principle of racial equality.

Nevertheless, the Defiance Campaign does not seem to have made a great impression on African-Americans. The Council on African Affairs, a group of black radicals who sought to influence American opinion on behalf of decolonization, circulated a petition supporting the Campaign that garnered 3800 signatures — many of which came from white radicals — and $835 in donations; but this appears to be the most significant expression of African-American concern. . . .

Black Americans might have been more aroused by the Defiance Campaign if it had not occurred at a time when interest in direct action as a possible form of protest in the United States was at a low ebb. Non-violence had been placed on the agenda of civil rights activity during and immediately after World War II with A. Philip Randolph's March on Washington Movement of 1941–5 and the founding and first sit-ins of CORE; but by 1952 McCarthyism and the generally conservative mood in the country had made established black leaders reluctant to endorse actions that opponents of civil rights could describe as radical or subversive; they feared a backlash that would weaken popular support for a legalistic and gradualist reform strategy that was beginning to bear fruit, especially in court decisions affirming the basic constitutional rights of African-Americans. When interest in non-violence revived after the onset of the Montgomery bus boycott in 1955–6, scarcely anyone seems to have thought of invoking the South African precedent.

Montgomery, in turn, does not appear to have inspired in any significant way the dramatic bus boycott that took place in the Johannesburg township of Alexandria in 1957. . . . The Alexandria boycott was a desperate act of resistance to a fare increase, not a protest against segregation or denial of civil rights, and replicated a similar action in the same township during World War II. At the time when Martin Luther King and the American non-violent movement was first attracting the attention of the world, the faith of black South Africans in passive resistance was in fact wearing thin. When direct action on a broad front commenced in the United States in 1960 and 1961, the ANC was in the process of rejecting non-violence in favor of armed struggle.

The movements were connected historically in one sense, however. Both were inspired to some extent by the same prototype — Mahatma Gandhi's use of militant non-violence in the struggle for Indian independence. King of course made much of the Gandhian example and tried to apply the spirit and discipline of *Satyagraha* [passive resistance] to non-violent protests in the American South. The official statements of purpose or philosophy issued by SCLC [Southern Christian Leadership Conference] and SNCC [Student Nonviolent Coordinating Committee] in the early 1960s were permeated with Gandhian rhetoric and philosophy. Gandhi was less often invoked explicitly by the Defiance Campaigners, but their methods, especially their public announcements of where, when, and by whom laws would be disobeyed and their refusal to make bail in an effort to "fill the jails," could have been learned from a Gandhian textbook.

If both movements drew inspiration from the great Indian apostle of non-violence, they received the message by different routes. Gandhism came to King and the American movement by way of a radical pacifism that derived mostly from the left wing of the Protestant social gospel tradition. King's non-violent antecedents and mentors were from the Christian pacifist FOR [Fellowship of Reconciliation] and its anti-segregationist offshoot, CORE [Congress of Racial Equality]. Mainly the creation of white Christian radicals like the Rev. A. J. Muste, this intellectual and spiritual tradition lacked deep roots in the black community, although it did have some notable black adherents like Bayard Rustin and James Farmer. Nevertheless, as a recent study has shown, there was a long history of African-American admiration for Gandhi as a brown man who was fighting for the freedom of his people from white or European oppression. Black newspapers sometimes expressed the hope that a Negro Gandhi might someday appear to lead a non-violent movement against racial oppression in the United States.

Gandhi cast an even longer shadow in South Africa, because he had first experimented with *Satyagraha* as the leader of the South African Indian community's struggle for rights as British subjects in the period between 1906 and 1914. The South African Native National Congress had been so impressed with Gandhi's mobilization of Indians for non-violent resistance that they included "passive action" as one of the methods they proposed to use in their struggle for African citizenship rights. In 1919, the Congress actually engaged in "passive action" on the Witwatersrand in an unsuccessful attempt to render the pass laws unenforceable through a mass refusal to obey them, but for the next 30 years this potential weapon lay rusting in the ANC's arsenal as the politics of passing resolutions and petitioning the government prevailed. A politically aroused segment of the Indian minority revived the Gandhian mode of protest in 1946 and 1947 when, with the encouragement of Gandhi and the newly independent Indian government, it engaged in "passive resistance" against new legislation restricting Indian residential and trading rights. With the triumph of the Nationalists in 1948 and the coming of apartheid, the Indian passive resisters gave up their separate struggle and allied themselves with the ANC. The Defiance Campaign itself was in fact jointly sponsored by the ANC and the South African Indian Congress, and several veterans of earlier Indian passive resistance struggles played conspicuous roles teaching and demonstrating Gandhian non-violent techniques, as well as helping to plan the campaign and participating in its actions.

In neither case, however, does a tracing of the Gandhian legacy provide a full picture of the ideological origins of mass non-violent action. Mass pressure tactics do not require a specifically Gandhian rationale; they may derive simply from a sense that less militant and confrontational tactics have proved fruitless and that it is now time to challenge the oppressor in a more direct and disruptive way. The decision of a group to engage in non-violent direct action usually constitutes a major escalation of resistance, a shift from legally authorized protest by an elite to initiatives that are more threatening and potentially violence-provoking because they involve bringing masses of aggrieved people into the streets. A philosophical or religious commitment to non-violence is not necessary to a choice of boycotts and civil disobedience as vehicles of resistance. In fact groups committed ultimately to a revolutionary overthrow of the existing order often embrace non-violent action as a means of raising consciousness and encouraging the kind of polarization that will make a revolutionary upheaval more likely. In the United States, the Communist Party and its allies had engaged in a variety of non-violent protests against racial discrimination during the 1930s, including the first mass march on Washington.

Communists were excluded from A. Philip Randolph's March on Washington Movement of 1941, but Randolph was clearly influenced by their example in his effort to create an all-black movement for equal rights that would go beyond the customary legalistic methods of the NAACP and use mass action to pressure the government. As a trade unionist, he was also aware of the sit-down strike and other examples of labor militancy that owed nothing to Christianity or pacifism. Neither religious nor a pacifist, he found Gandhi's campaigns attractive because they showed what could be achieved by "non-violent goodwill direct action." He represented a way of thinking that could endorse everything Martin Luther King Jr. was doing without accepting his non-violent theology. For Randolph and those in the movement who shared his views, it was sufficient that non-violent direct action was a practical means for African Americans to improve their position in society — while violent resistance, however defensible it might be in the abstract, was not in their view a viable option for a racial minority. . . .

In South Africa, non-Gandhian pressures for non-violent mass action came during the 1940s from the young rebels in the ANC Youth League who had grown impatient with the older generation's willingness to work within the system of black "representation" established by the pre-apartheid white supremacist governments of Prime Ministers J. B. M. Hertzog and Jan Smuts. The Youth Leaguers, among whom were Nelson Mandela, Walter Sisulu and Oliver Tambo, favored a boycott of segregated political institutions and experimentation with more militant and confrontational methods of protest than the organization had hitherto employed. In 1949, the Youth Leaguers won control of the ANC, and the Program of Action that was subsequently enacted called for "immediate and active boycott, strike, civil disobedience, non-cooperation. . . ." The spirit of the Youth League and of the Defiance Campaign that was the fruit of its action program was not based to any significant degree on a belief in the power of love to convert enemies into friends or in the higher morality of non-violence. Indeed the very use of the term "defiance" suggests that anger more than agape was the emotion being called forth. The campaign, as its chief planner Walter Sisulu and its tactical leader, volunteer-in-chief Nelson Mandela, conceived it, was designed to enable an unarmed and impoverished majority to carry on its struggle against the tyrannical rule of an armed and wealthy minority in a more forceful and effective manner. If non-violent methods failed, there was no firm ideological barrier to prevent the young turks of the ANC from embracing other means of struggle.

But there were still influential older figures in the Congress who were non-violent in principle and not purely out of expediency. Among them was Chief Albert Lutuli whose fervent Methodist Christianity strongly predisposed him against taking up arms and sustained his hopes that oppressors could be redeemed by the sufferings of the oppressed. "The road to freedom is via the cross" was the memorable last line of the statement he made after the government had dismissed him from his chieftainship because he would not resign from the ANC. The fact that the idealistic Lutuli was elected President-General of the ANC in 1952 showed that the ANC of the 1950s, like the southern civil rights movement of the 1960s, brought together those who regarded non-violence simply as a tactic and those who viewed it as an ethic. . . .

In addition to such similarities of ideology and ethos, the leadership of the two movements came from a similarly situated social group — what might be described as the educated elite of a subordinate color caste. Studies of the social composition of the ANC through the 1950s have shown conclusively that the organization was dominated by members of "an African Bourgeoisie" or "petty bourgeoisie" that was characterized mainly by educational and professional achievements. Examinations of the origins of the southern civil rights movement have found the spur for militant action in the rise in southern cities and towns of what one historian calls "a relatively independent black professional class."

It was a special product of legalized racial segregation that such elites were not . . . subject to detachment and alienation from their communities by a system of rewards and opportunities that allows a favored few to move into the lower ranks of the governing institutions established by the dominant group. It might be taken as axiomatic that where race *per se* is the main line of division in a society, as it obviously was in South Africa and the American South, that resistance will take the form of a cross-class movement led by members of the educated middle class. This does not mean, however, that less-educated and working-class blacks made little contribution to whatever success these movements achieved. It was of course the plain folk who sustained the boycotts, often at great personal sacrifice. The point is that these freedom struggles were, and had to be, movements of peoples or communities rather than of social classes.

These similarities in the ideological and social character of the two movements did not preclude significant structural and cultural differences, to say nothing as yet of the obvious contrast of situations. The most significant structural difference between the Defiance Campaign and the non-violent civil rights movement was that the latter grew out of a number of local struggles and was sustained by strong organizations and institutions at the community level, whereas the former was for the most part a centrally planned, from-the-top-down operation. The one area where the Defiance Campaign achieved something like mass involvement was in the cities of the eastern Cape, where, as historian Tom Lodge has shown, it was able to build on the firm base provided by a recent history of local mobilization and protest activity. But nothing like the network of "movement centers" that was the source of the American movement existed to buttress non-violent campaigns in South Africa. Where such centers existed in South Africa they were usually tied to labor organizations and trade unions; in the United States it was the black churches and black colleges that did most to sustain local activism. Since every southern city had relatively prosperous black churches and many had some kind of higher educational facility for blacks, such an institutional matrix for community protest was widely available, whereas black unions were well-established in only a few places in the South Africa of the 1950s. Furthermore, South African black townships of the 1950s were quite different from southern black urban communities. Their populations, which included a large number of transients and illegal residents, were less socially stable and significantly poorer; there were fewer well-established cultural or religious institutions; there was a proportionately much smaller middle class and relatively little black entrepreneurship or business activity. . . .

Even if the forces opposing each movement had been identical in strength and determination — which of course they were not — there seems little doubt that a centralized movement like the South African one would have been easier to repress than the more decentralized and diffuse American movement. Even before the ANC was outlawed, the government was able to hobble it severely simply by banning or arresting its top leaders. In the American South in the 1950s, the NAACP was rendered ineffectual by state legal harassment that in some states amounted to an outright ban. It was partly to fill the vacuum created by persecution of the NAACP that independent local movements developed. These grass-roots movements were more difficult to suppress by state action, and they flourished in places where the NAACP could no longer show itself. If such strong local communities and institutions had existed in South Africa, the government might have faced a variety of local actions that would have been much more difficult to counter than the centrally directed campaign of the ANC in 1952. (This in fact is what happened in the 1980s with the rise of the United Democratic Front, which was a federation of the community organizations that had sprung up in the 1970s and early 1980s.) . . .

Besides differing structurally, the two campaigns also diverged in the less tangible realm of movement culture and ethos. As the special prominence of ministers and churches in the American movement strongly suggests, religious belief and emotion directly inspired and animated the Afro-American protesters to an extent that could not be paralleled in South Africa. The charisma of King as prophet/saint of the movement was instrumental in making it a moral and religious crusade rather than merely the self-interested action of a social group. . . . The South African struggle, unlike the American, did not produce a Gandhi-like figure who could inspire the masses by persuading them that non-violent protest was God's will. There was a reservoir of religious belief and practice that might have been tapped — it surfaced at times in local actions that featured prayer and hymn-singing. But the ANC leadership was composed of highly educated men who had gone to mission schools and whose religious beliefs had little connection with those of the masses of Africans, especially those who were members of the independent "zionist" churches that served a large proportion of urbanized Africans. . . . What King did that no South African leader was able to do was to weave together the black folk Christianity that was his own cultural heritage with the Gandhian conception of non-violent resistance to empower a cause that both inspired its followers and disarmed the opposition of many whites. Hence the non-violence of the American movement had a soul-stirring quality, both for its practitioners and for many white observers, that the more obviously conditional and pragmatic civil disobedience characterizing the Defiance Campaign normally failed to project. Of course this resonance was in part the

Martin Luther King Jr. led the voting rights drive in Selma, Alabama, in 1965. Note that King is speaking in a church. Black civil rights activists in the United States used Protestant Christianity and American national ideals to bolster their cause. (UPI/Corbis-Bettmann.)

result of the extensive and usually sympathetic way that the national press covered the American movement and, by the sixties, of its exposure on national television. The Defiance Campaign by contrast received relatively little attention from the white South African press and was not widely noticed abroad (which is one reason why it did not serve as a model for African-American passive resisters).

The possibly decisive effects of contrasting press or media treatment suggests that the differences in the nature of the movements may tell us less about why they ultimately succeeded or failed than we are likely to learn from examining their external circumstances — what they were up against. The American protesters faced a divided, fragmented and uncertain governmental opposition. The most important division among whites that the movement was able to exploit was between northerners who lacked a regional commitment to legalized segregation and southerners who believed that Jim Crow was central to their way of life. The success of the movement stemmed ultimately from its ability to get the federal government on its side and to utilize the US constitution against the outmoded states' rights philosophy of the southern segregationists. When King proclaimed that "civil disobedience to local laws is civil obedience to national laws," he exploited a tactical advantage the South African resisters did not possess; for they had no alternative to a direct confrontation with centralized state power. South African black protest leaders had long tried to drive a wedge between British imperial and South African settler regimes, but the withdrawal of British power and influence beginning as early as 1906 and virtually complete by the 1930s had rendered such hopes illusory. For all practical purposes, South African whites in the 1950s were monolithic in their defense of perpetual white domination. In the United States it was of course federal intervention to overrule state practices of segregation and disfranchisement in the southern states that brought an end to Jim Crow. In South Africa there was no such power to which protesters could appeal against apartheid.

The geopolitical context of the Cold War and decolonization of Africa and Asia also cut in opposite ways, ultimately helping the American movement and hindering the South African. In the United States, the competition with the Soviet Union for the "hearts and minds" of Africans and Asians, especially by the early sixties when several African nations achieved independence, made legalized segregation a serious international liability for the Eisenhower, Kennedy and Johnson administrations. As reasons of state were added to other factors working against Jim Crow, the federal government became more susceptible to pressures from the civil rights movement. In South Africa, on the other hand, fears of Communist subversion within the country and of Soviet influence in the newly independent African states of southern and central Africa panicked the white political leadership into pressing ahead with more radical schemes for the "separate development" and political repression of the black majority. Underlying these contrary assessments of the dangers of black insurgency was the basic difference between a white majority facing a demand for the inclusion of a minority and a white minority conscious that the extension of democratic rights would empower a black majority.

It would be cynical, however, to see nothing in the positive responses of many white Americans to the civil rights movement except self-interested calculations. White America has not been of one mind historically on the place of blacks in the republic. In the North, at least, there was an alternative or oppositional tradition in white racial thought, originating in the antislavery movement, that advocated the public equality of the races and offered a standing challenge — although one that was only intermittently influential — to the deeply rooted white supremacist tradition that was a legacy of African-American slavery. At times, as during Reconstruction and in the mid-1960s, racial liberals became ideologically dominant and were in a position to respond to black demands for civil and political equality with major reforms. . . . In South Africa, by contrast, there was no white liberal tradition that went beyond a benevolent paternalism and no deep reservoir of theoretically color-blind attitudes toward democratic reform that could be appealed to. Nelson Mandela caught this difference when asked by an American journalist in one of his rare prison interviews during the 1980s why he had not followed the example of Martin Luther King and remained non-violent:

> Mr. Mandela said that conditions in South Africa are "totally different" from conditions in the United States in the 1960s. In the United States, he said, democracy was deeply entrenched, and people struggling then had access to institutions that protected human rights. The white community in the United States was more liberal than whites in South Africa, and public authorities were restrained by law.

Was it therefore inevitable that a non-violent movement for basic civil rights would succeed in the United States and fail in South Africa? As probable as these outcomes might seem to be, one can imagine things turning out differently. It is arguable that without the astute and inspirational leadership provided by King and others the struggle for black civil and political equality would have taken much longer. Any claim that the Civil Rights Acts of 1964 and 1965 were inevitable obscures the creative achievements of the liberation movement. For South Africa the argument has been made that the 1961 decision of the ANC to sanction some forms of violence was a mistake; the full potential of non-violent resistance had not been exhausted, and the sabotage campaign . . . that became the center of resistance activity in the 1960s posed little threat to white domination and turned out very badly for the ANC because it exposed its top leadership to arrest and imprisonment. If non-violence had its inherent limitations as a resistance strategy under the kind of conditions that prevailed in South Africa, it would be hard to establish from its record of achievement in the 1960s and 1970s that the resort to violence, however justifiable in the abstract, represented a more effective method of struggle. Of course the key historical actors, like Nelson Mandela, Walter Sisulu and Oliver Tambo, did not have the benefit of historical hindsight and can scarcely be condemned for trying something different when non-violent resistance had obviously failed to move the regime and had become more and more difficult to undertake.

Although Martin Luther King Jr. had shown some awareness of the South African campaigns of the mid-1950s . . . he first indicated a deep and abiding interest in South African developments in 1959 when he wrote to Chief Lutuli to express his admiration for the latter's courage and dignity and to forward a copy of *Stride Toward Freedom*. The Sharpeville massacre in 1960 and the awarding of the Nobel Peace Prize to Lutuli in 1961 for his espousal of non-violent resistance heightened King's interest and prompted him to speak out vigorously against apartheid. In a 1962 address to the NAACP national convention, King exemplified his doctrine of non-violence by referring to Lutuli: "If I lived in South Africa today, I would join Chief Lithuli [*sic*] as he says to his people, 'Break this law. Don't take the unjust pass system where you must have passes. Take them and tear them up and throw them away.'"

King made his fullest statement about South Africa in a speech given in London on 7 December 1964, as he was on route to receiving his own Nobel Peace Prize in Oslo.

> In our struggle for freedom and justice in the U.S., which has also been so long and arduous, we feel a powerful sense of identification with those in the far more deadly struggle for freedom in South Africa. We know how Africans there, and their friends of other races, strove for half a century to win their freedom by non-violent methods, and we know how this non-violence was met by increasing violence from the state, increasing repression, culminating in the shootings of Sharpeville and all that has happened since. . . . [E]ven in Mississippi we can organize to register Negro voters, we can speak to the press, we can in short organize people in non-violent action. But in South Africa, even the mildest form of non-violent resistance meets with years of punishment, and leaders over many years have been silenced and imprisoned. We can understand how in that situation people felt so desperate that they turned to other methods, such as sabotage.

Like Mandela two decades later, King was sensitive to differences between the two contexts that would make non-violence more feasible and effective in the American case. But in the same speech he indicated a way that non-violence could be brought to bear against apartheid. "Our responsibility presents us with a unique opportunity," he told his British audience. "We can join in the one form of non-violent *action* that could bring freedom and justice to South Africa; the action which African leaders have appealed for in a massive movement for economic sanctions." Almost exactly one year after his London speech, King made another strong appeal for sanctions in an address on behalf of the American Committee on Africa. "The international potential of non-violence has never been employed," he said. "Non-violence has been practiced within national borders in India, the U.S. and in regions of Africa with spectacular success. The time has come fully to utilize non-violence through a massive international boycott. . . ."

King, who gave vigorous support to the sanctions movement for the remaining three years of his life, did not of course live to see the anti-apartheid movement come to the verge of success without unleashing the violent revolution that so many observers had believed would be necessary for the overthrow of white supremacy. It is now possible to argue that the breakthrough that came with the release of Nelson Mandela and the unbanning of the ANC was as much, if not more, the result of international non-violence as the fruit of a strategy of violent resistance inaugurated by the Congress in the 1960s. The apartheid regime was not in fact decisively defeated on the battlefield or driven from power by a domestic insurrection. The armed struggle of the ANC served to remind the world that blacks were determined to be liberated from white oppression, but it was the ethical disapproval of much of humanity that destroyed the morale and self-confidence of South Africa's ruling whites, and the increasingly effective economic sanctions that persuaded its business community and those in the government whom they influenced that apartheid had no future. Of course those sanctions would undoubtedly have been lighter and the disapprobation less sharp if the domestic resistance of the 1980s had not provoked the government into a final desperate effort to suppress dissent by force. But that domestic resistance was primarily a matter of withdrawing cooperation from the regime. Not entirely non-violent, it was predominantly so — a great domestic boycott to parallel the international one. The spirit of Gandhi, long since repudiated by the ANC in exile, was alive and well in the United Democratic Front, the domestic movement that rallied behind the ANC's goal of a non-racial democratic South Africa. In 1989, with the emergence of the Mass Democratic Movement, South Africa once again saw massive non-violent actions against segregation, led this time by clergymen like Allen Boesak and Desmond Tutu — both of whom had been greatly influenced by King and the church-based American Freedom Struggle — and featuring the singing of African-American freedom songs. Non-violence may not have been sufficient to liberate South Africa, but it is no longer possible to deny that it has played a major role in bringing that nation to democracy. It would not be beyond the power of historical analogy to describe the successful anti-apartheid movement as Birmingham and Selma on a world scale.

QUESTIONS TO CONSIDER

1. Compare the leadership and organization of the American and the South African racial protest movements of the 1950s and 1960s. How was Martin Luther King Jr. instrumental in making the Civil Rights movement a moral and religious crusade? Why were ANC leaders unable to give their movement this dimension? In what sense did African Americans build a local grass-roots movement, while South African blacks did not? Why?

2. Describe the philosophy of nonviolent resistance as practiced by the American Civil Rights movement and the South African Defiance Campaign. What was the influence of Mahatma Gandhi on the two movements? What forms did nonviolent black resistance take? Why does Fredrickson distinguish between "those who regarded non-violence simply as a tactic and those who viewed it as an ethic"?

3. Why were many white Americans receptive to Martin Luther King Jr.'s political aims and his nonviolent approach in the 1950s and 1960s? How did the Civil Rights movement's relationship to the white power structure differ from the situation faced by black activists in South Africa? Why did the ANC resort to violent resistance in the 1960s? Was this change of tactics a mistake?

4. Both the American and South African desegregation protests operated in an international context. How much mutual knowledge or influence existed between the two movements? How did the effects of the Cold War and decolonization in Africa help the American movement but hinder the South African campaign? In what way was the sanctions movement of the 1970s and 1980s an application of "Birmingham and Selma on a world scale"? Why did it succeed?

5. How relevant is the story of nonviolent change Fredrickson tells to today's struggle for racial equality and economic empowerment? Why has there been so much black-on-black violence in both the United States and South Africa in recent decades? Why has American black protest been less successful in improving education and employment than in ending segregation?

The New Feminism
in America and Great Britain

OLIVE BANKS

After a hiatus of more than a generation following the campaign for suffrage, organized feminism was reborn in the 1960s. Betty Friedan's book The Feminine Mystique *(1963) was the trigger, galvanizing millions of female readers. In it, Friedan indicted post–World War II American culture for reviving the old image of the happy housewife and attempting to brainwash women into believing that their fulfillment could come only through marriage and children. Friedan's book tapped a pool of resentment that had been growing as more and more middle-class women entered the paid work force and encountered prejudice on the job. By 1964, too, American women could use the Civil Rights Act to file federal complaints against discriminatory practices. In the following year, young women participating in the Civil Rights and New Left movements separated from patronizing male colleagues to begin "consciousness-raising" sessions where they shared stories of oppression and envisioned a world transformed by "women's liberation." The stage was set for a movement that would eventually challenge sexism in all the institutions of public and private life.*

In the following selection, British historian Olive Banks provides one of the clearest analyses available of the ideas and tactics of the new feminist movement. Banks distinguishes between two kinds of feminism at work during and after the 1960s. First, "equal-rights" feminism, a traditional version of women's agitation that concentrates upon removing legal and economic barriers to equality, was reborn in the struggle for equal pay and nondiscrimination. Then, emerging from the New Left, a new radical feminism ("women's liberation") sought revolution rather than reform and called for a transformation in traditional notions of womanhood, sexuality, and the family. Banks is particularly astute in sorting out the varieties of feminism and in showing how their different goals and strategies often hampered the movement's effectiveness. Note, too, how the two phases of the feminist movement mirrored the stages of protest in the Civil Rights movement of the 1960s. Both movements evolved from a liberal "integrationist" phase toward a more radical emphasis upon autonomy and revolution that challenged basic cultural and political norms — a process that brought important new ideas to light but also elicited greater opposition from the mainstream.

Another valuable feature of Banks's essay is its comparative dimension. Like Faces of
Feminism, *the larger study from which it is taken, this selection casts the story of the
women's movement as a transatlantic chronicle and it highlights parallels between American
and British feminism. "What was most striking," Banks concludes in her book, ". . . were
not the differences but the similarities between the two countries. Time and time again developments occurred at the same time in the two countries, in spite of very large differences
in the social and political context as well as in the style of leadership." British feminists had
stronger ties to male socialists and trade unions, while American feminists were quicker to
condemn male "patriarchy," rather than capitalism, as the enemy. But both national feminist
movements surged in the 1960s, both split into equal-rights and radical factions, and both
ended up concentrating on legal battles over economic discrimination and abortion. As you
analyze Banks's essay, try to determine why such striking transatlantic parallels occurred.*

*In the late 1970s, Banks points out, the feminist movement's momentum seemed to dis-
sipate as the Equal Rights Amendment faced popular resistance and right-to-life groups
opposed abortion. When the world economy dipped into recession and Anglo-American
politics swung to the right, many voters decided that the liberal social changes of the 1960s —
including social-welfare programs and racial "affirmative action" as well as women's rights —
had gone too far and should be halted or even reversed. By the 1990s, some feminists saw
a dangerous "backlash" against women's rights in the rise of a "men's movement," the resurgence of sexual stereotyping in the mass media, and the conservatives' promotion of "family
values." Nevertheless, within a generation the Anglo-American feminist movement had
brought tremendous progress in women's economic and social status, and had reshaped cultural notions of womanhood, equality, and sexuality in ways that would not be forgotten.
Indeed, as the International Women's Conference in Beijing (Peking) in 1995 made clear,
Western feminist ideas and aspirations were reaching women around the world and were beginning to mobilize them to protest the worst features of their own subordination.*

GLOSSARY

ANDROGYNY   The state of having both masculine and feminine characteristics.

CIVIL RIGHTS ACT OF 1964   An American law passed at the height of the Civil
Rights movement that prohibited discrimination in public accommodations, schools,
and employment on the basis of color, race, religion, sex, or national origin.

EQUAL EMPLOYMENT OPPORTUNITY COMMISSION (EEOC)   A U.S.
government agency established by Title VII of the Civil Rights Act of 1964 to hear
complaints and to order redress when discriminatory actions have been found. A similar government agency, the Equal Opportunities Commission, was set up in Great
Britain in 1975.

EQUAL RIGHTS AMENDMENT (ERA)   First proposed in 1923, an amendment
to the U.S. Constitution that would give women an explicit constitutional guarantee of
equal rights not afforded by the equal protection clause of the Fourteenth Amendment.
In the late 1960s, passing the ERA became a key goal of the National Organization for
Women and a focus of the revived women's rights movement. It was approved by Congress in 1971–1972, but then faced opposition from conservative groups defending traditional views of women and family. Despite national polls showing majority support,

the ERA failed to gain ratification by the 1982 deadline, falling three states short of the thirty-eight required.

FRIEDAN, BETTY (1921–)   A student of psychology and freelance writer who helped to launch the contemporary feminist movement with her book *The Feminine Mystique* (1963). In 1966 Friedan and others formed the National Organization for Women. Her later writings have emphasized the importance of family and, contrary to the position of some radical feminists, the necessity of including men in feminist movements.

GILMAN, CHARLOTTE PERKINS (1860–1935)   A prominent American feminist intellectual and reformer of the Progressive Era. She is celebrated for her short story "The Yellow Wallpaper" (1892), which criticized the stifling stereotypes of women; her utopian fantasy *Herland* (1915), which depicted a world without men; and her advocacy of women's economic independence.

MARRIAGE BAR   A law or practice that forbids married women from being hired for jobs. Its governing premises are that income is not necessary for married women, that their employment takes jobs away from men, and that married women's proper roles are childcare and housekeeping.

MARXIST   A follower of the economic and political philosophy of Karl Marx (1818–1883), the chief theorist of modern socialism and communism. An economic determinist, Marx interpreted the history of society as the working out of class struggle, which would eventually result in the proletarian (working-class) overthrow of bourgeois society.

NEW LEFT   The political wing of the international student movement of the 1960s. The New Left was born in the Civil Rights and students movements, opposed to the war in Vietnam, and committed to personal and political liberation in ways that ranged from pacifism to violent revolution. It took its name from its opposition to the "Old Left," the traditional socialist and communist parties, which it charged with complicity in the established order.

ONEIDA COMMUNITY (1848–1881)   A religiously inspired communal experiment located in western New York. The Oneida Perfectionists practiced "complex marriage," a controlled form of free love in which members rotated sexual partners and children were raised communally. In its later years, the community practiced eugenics, or selective breeding, which caused conflicts that hastened its dissolution.

PROTECTIVE LEGISLATION   Laws that protect women in their role as childbearers; for example, by limiting their hours or conditions of work or by providing wives' pensions. Although seen by many feminists as important reforms in the early twentieth century, such laws later came under attack for denying women equal economic opportunity or (in cases of wives' benefits) for discriminating against men.

ROE V. WADE (1973)   A landmark case in which the U.S. Supreme Court ruled, with some qualifications, that state laws prohibiting abortions were illegal. The constitutional right of privacy includes the right of a woman to terminate her pregnancy, but after the first trimester (three months of pregnancy) the states' interest in public welfare means they can regulate abortion, and after the second trimester they can prohibit it. The decision aroused a nationwide controversy that continues between "pro-life" and "pro-choice" advocates.

SUMMERSKILL, EDITH (1901–1980)   A British medical doctor and Labour Party politician who was a member of Parliament from 1938 until her death. An energetic equal-rights feminist, Summerskill promoted legislation dealing with clean food, abortion rights, preventive medicine, equal pay, and married women's rights. Among her legislative victories were the Clean Milk Act (1950), which mandated pasteurization, and the Married Woman's Property Act (1964), which entitled married women to half of the family's savings.

THALIDOMIDE SCARE   An outcry that occurred when Thalidomide, a sleep-inducing drug sold in Europe from 1957 to 1961 without the need for a prescription, was found in 1961 to produce skeletal defects in developing fetuses. It was recalled from use, but not until it had caused the malformation of eight thousand children around the world.

TRADES UNION CONGRESS (TUC)   Formed in 1869 by British workers, an organization that became an influential mouthpiece for organized labor and a powerful parliamentary pressure group. The congress admitted its first woman delegate in 1875, and after World War I it absorbed the Women's Trade Union League.

WOMEN'S ADVISORY COMMITTEE (NATIONAL LABOUR WOMEN'S ADVISORY COMMITTEE)   An organization created in Britain in 1931 to raise support for trade unionism among women workers. After 1945, it became increasingly militant, battling with male trade union leaders and pressing Parliament on equal pay and other issues.

WOMEN'S BUREAU   A U.S. government agency established in 1920 to gather information on American women and to support protective social welfare legislation such as mothers' pensions and maximum hours laws.

1. REBIRTH OF THE EQUAL RIGHTS TRADITION

[B]y the end of the 1950s pressure was building up both within Congress and outside it for legislation to end discrimination against women, particularly in the area of employment. Undoubtedly, a major factor here was the dramatic change in the pattern of the female labor force brought about partly by changes in demand and partly by demographic factors, such as the low birth rate of the 1930s and the early marriages of the 1950s, which had reduced the supply of women. The resulting increased demand for women's labor brought large numbers of married women into the labor market, not only into manual work but, more significantly for our present purpose, into clerical and service occupations. This influx of married women into non-manual work was not, however, accompanied by any real increase in the proportion of women in professional and higher administrative employment. Indeed, although the *number* of women in professional employment had increased, the *proportion* shows an actual, if small, decline between 1940 and 1964. Moreover, this decline was in spite of a dramatic increase in women's participation in higher education during the same period. It is not altogether surprising therefore if women, and especially middle-class women in professional and semi-professional careers, were becoming dissatisfied with their conditions of employment and ready to look sympathetically at the idea of legislation against discrimination in pay and employment opportunities.

There were other changes in the 1960s that were likely to predispose women towards an equal rights version of feminism and away from the emphasis on the maternal function that feminists and anti-feminists had come, in their different ways, to share. The decline in the American birth rate, after the years of the "baby boom," had started in 1957 and was to continue throughout the 1960s. Women were not only having fewer children, but they were also marrying later, and, in the middle classes, more of them were going on to graduate — as distinct from undergraduate — study. Moreover, as Jessie Bernard has pointed out, all these changes had started some years *before* Betty Friedan wrote her celebrated attack on the feminine mystique in 1963. This suggests that her critique, and especially its astonishing reception, was a consequence rather than a cause of a new mood amongst middle-class women. . . .

It was against this background . . . that in 1961 President Kennedy set up his Commission on the Status of Women. The motives of Kennedy himself are not altogether clear, although we know that the idea originated with Esther Peterson, who had been on Kennedy's campaign staff and had then been appointed to take charge of the Women's Bureau. Initiative also came from the Business and Professional Women's Clubs, whose leaders were active on the Commission and the several State Commissions that followed. . . .

The Report, when it appeared, was relatively modest in its proposals, although it documented many areas of discrimination, thus playing a significant role in reinforcing the consciousness of inequality in the minds of individual women, especially those already active in politics. . . . However, the Equal Rights Amendment itself was opposed, the Commission proposing instead that an end to discrimination in employment should be achieved by voluntary effort. Equal pay nevertheless was approved, and legislation to this effect [the Equal Pay Act of 1963] followed shortly after. The Report also came out in favor of an end to certain forms of legal discrimination, particularly in the area of marriage and property.

By 1964, however, the Civil Rights Act had already made the Commission's preference for voluntary effort out of date. Intended originally to deal with racial discrimination, the word sex was added by a Southern congressman in what appeared to be a last-minute attempt to kill the bill. In fact the amendment was accepted and the amended bill was passed, so that women were now included, almost by accident, in the brief of the Equal Employment Opportunities Commission set up to administer the Act. Even the Commissioners themselves were unenthusiastic about the inclusion of sexual discrimination in their brief, and the first Director sought to ignore the issue of sex, arguing that its inclusion was a fluke.

Perhaps the most immediate effect of the refusal of the Equal Employment Opportunities Commission to enforce the sexual provisions of the Act was the impetus it gave to the foundation of the National Organization [for] Women, or NOW as it is more usually called. The President's Commission, and later the State Commissions, had brought together a number of politically active women who became increasingly aware of the need for a new feminist pressure group. Eventually, action was taken at a National Conference of State Commissions in 1966 and the new organization began its work by trying to place pressure on the Equal Employment Opportunities Commission to implement the Civil Rights Act as it applied to women. . . . Indeed, without pressure from NOW it seems likely that the sex discrimination aspect of the Act would have remained virtually a dead letter.

The establishment of NOW was followed by a number of other equal rights groups, often with more specialist interests, some of which split off from NOW as its program widened and became more radical. The Women's Equity Action League, for example, founded in 1968, was a group of largely professional women who focused their action chiefly upon discrimination in education and employment, although they also campaigned against tax inequalities. The National Women's Political Caucus, founded in 1971, was formed to support the entry of more women in political office. In 1969, academic women began to organize themselves into professional associations, and by the end of 1971 there were women's groups in no less than thirty-three professional associations. . . .

In the meantime, attitudes towards the Equal Rights Amendment continued to change. The Women's Bureau, one of its most consistent and determined enemies since the 1920s, changed significantly in 1969 with the appointment of Elizabeth B. Koontz as its head. Under her guidance the Bureau was drawn into the women's rights movement and reversed its attitude completely. Changing attitudes were also reflected in President Nixon's Task Force on the Status of Women, which, in direct contradiction to President Kennedy's earlier Commission, came out in support of the Equal Rights Amendment in 1969.

At first the trade union leadership refused to follow the Women's Bureau in its change of mind and, indeed, chided it for abandoning its traditional attitude to protection. . . . By the 1960s some women's unions were beginning to challenge the accepted trade union line and to argue that protective legislation had in fact been used selectively to benefit men rather than women. The Equal Rights Act of 1964, by making protective legislation illegal, was also a significant factor in changing attitudes, especially when it began to be demonstrated that it was in fact working-class women who were involved in bringing cases to the attention of the EEOC. Eventually the AFL/CIO was forced to reassess its position under pressure from women trade unionists and abandoned its opposition in 1973.

NOW, after a brief internal struggle, was in support of the amendment from the start, and it was pressure from NOW, as well as from women within Congress like Martha Griffiths, that brought it before the Senate Judiciary Committee in 1970 and then on to the full House. Eventually, after a series of defeats, it was approved by [the] Senate in 1972 and started on the long process of ratification before it could finally become law. Its successful passage through Congress was a consequence of a period of intense political lobbying at both the national and grass-roots level in which even not overtly feminist organizations took part. This large measure of public support helped women in Congress to prove that there was a real demand for the amendment. . . .

The period 1970–1972, in fact, was a time when the unity of the women's movement was at its height and opposition even came to seem politically dangerous. In 1970 the number of women in Congress rose to fifteen and more of them than ever were committed to feminist issues. The 1972–74 Congress, in particular, passed a large batch of women's rights legislation at the instigation of individual women members. At this stage, too, opposition to the amendment was still largely unorganized. The feminist movement was not united in its support, and even the traditional trade union hostility was in the process of change. It was easy, therefore, for both friends and enemies to exaggerate the degree of consensus in its favor.

It can be argued, however, that all the equal rights legislation of this decade was, in a real sense, in advance of public opinion, as witnessed by the difficulties in its implementation. Neither the equal pay legislation nor the legislation on equal employment opportunities was able to do very much to break down the widespread and deeply rooted discrimination against women in employment. Moreover, if the tide seemed to be in favor of equal rights legislation for both Negroes and women during the 1960s, the 1970s were years of a growing conservatism in politics. Consequently, if at first the ratification of the Equal Rights Amendment appeared to go smoothly (with twenty-eight states ratifying in the first year), an organized opposition developed quickly and progress has in fact been slow, with some states actually attempting to rescind their original ratification. By 1979 the deadline had still not been met and Congress agreed to an extension until 1982 [at which time the ERA failed to be ratified]. . . .

The opposition to the amendment is largely conservative rather than from the left (although some left-wing groups remain opposed). . . . Conservative women's groups, too, are prominent, including the Daughters of the American Revolution, and there has been a determined effort to rouse women in particular against the amendment on the grounds that it will lose them a number of privileges including a husband's obligation to support his family and exemption from the draft. To a large extent, the STOP-ERA campaign has concentrated its efforts on the South and on rural areas, and has tried to appeal to those women who take a traditional view of their place in society. The stand taken by feminists on abortion and homosexuality has also brought into active opposition the National Council of Catholic Women and a number of anti-abortion groups like the National Right to Life campaign as well as those opposed to homosexual rights.

The feminists, meanwhile, have been unable to sustain either the intensive lobbying or the grass-roots support that characterized the campaign at the national level. This is partly because of the tendency, already indicated, to splinter into separate groups following specific and often narrow goals, and partly . . . , as we shall see, a move away from equal rights and towards the more radical implications in the concept of women's liberation. For these radical feminists the search for alternative life styles becomes more important than legislative reform.

Finally, the achievement of some measure of equal rights through legislation has co-incided with a change in the economy from boom to recession. If the equal rights movement started in a manpower crisis in which womanpower was an asset to be placated, its implementation has had to take place in an atmosphere of falling opportunities, which like the Depression of the 1930s turns women into rivals. It is not surprising, therefore, if recent years have seen such set-backs in the implementation of equal rights as the complaint of "reverse discrimination" on the part of white males.

In Britain, too, the 1960s saw a revival of the equal rights tradition of feminism, although . . . the prolongation of the suffrage fight until 1928 kept that tradition alive longer than in the United States. So did the women's groups in the labor movement who represented a radical tradition in feminism almost entirely absent from the American scene. Women politicians, like those in the United States, were few in number, but some of them were influential, and a few active feminists continued to keep the feminist point of view before Parliament. Within the trade union movement, the opposition to the marriage bar and the campaign for equal pay was pressed consistently, especially by the white-collar unions. . . .

In the 1960s the campaign for equal pay gained ground under increasing pressure from women trade union militants and encouraged in particular by the eventual achievement of equal pay in the public service in 1961. There was also a revival of male demands for equal pay, and the return of a Labour government in 1964, committed, in principle at least, to equal pay, also served to encourage the hopes of the campaigners. . . .

[E]qual pay as a feminist issue was kept alive by women activists within the trade union movement. During the 1920s and 1930s women trade unionists joined with feminist groups to protest at the imposition of marriage bars in the civil service and local authorities. . . .

The Women's Advisory Committee also frequently took up a feminist stance. . . . There were unsuccessful requests for a women's industrial charter in the 1930s, and in 1944 the Conference had criticized the lack of science teaching for girls. The pressure for an industrial charter was renewed after the war and in 1963 such a charter was approved by the TUC [Trades Union Congress]. Anticipating many of the demands of the new movement, it asked not only for equal pay, but also for better employment opportunities, better apprenticeships and training facilities, retraining for older women, and health and welfare facilities for women at work.

Within the Labour Party, itself, women's groups also supported the issue of equal pay, although with less insistence than the women trade unionists. During the 1960s the issue was revived and there were repeated resolutions at National Labour Women's Conferences. By the end of the 1960s Labour Party women were actively involved in the general issue of discrimination against women, which was part of the new women's movement and will be described in more detail later. Without their pressure, indeed, it is likely that the Labour Party as a whole would have been far less responsive to women's rights. . . .

Clearly, therefore, the active feminism that existed . . . in the . . . Labour Party . . . and in the women's trade union movement did not die out altogether with the coming of women's suffrage. It remained as a small but growing pressure within a labor movement that was largely indifferent to, if not at times even hostile to, feminist demands. Moreover, there are clear signs that this pressure from women activists was growing in intensity and significance even before the new women's movement reached Britain from the United States. . . .

In 1938, Edith Summerskill entered Parliament, and she was to prove to be the most active and forceful of the feminist politicians of the next two decades. An early advocate of birth control, she also campaigned on such issues as clean food and the power of the drug industry, but it is [as] an advocate of the rights of the housewife that her feminism is most clearly expressed. For some years she was president of the Married Women's Association, founded in 1938 to improve the economic position of the wife in the home. As early as 1943 she took up, unsuccessfully, the case of a housewife whose husband claimed her savings from her Co-op dividends — a case that demonstrated that legally the housekeeping money was the sole property of the husband. . . . In 1963, however, she successfully introduced a Married Woman's Savings Bill, which eventually became law and entitled a woman to half her savings. This meant that a married woman who had no earnings of her own could nevertheless claim to have contributed, by her work for the family, to the family income, a principle that was later to become an important plank in the new feminist program.

There were therefore, even during the unpromising 1950s, signs that equal rights feminism was not only alive but struggling to make itself heard. So far, it is true, it had achieved little success and even in the early 1960s there were few indications of the enormous change of mood that was to come. Edith Summerskill's bill . . . had been successful, and equal pay in the public service had finally been achieved, but equal pay in general had been blocked by the wage freeze and there seemed little real prospect of any immediate solution.

In 1968 it was both Human Rights Year and the fiftieth anniversary of the suffrage campaign, and these focused attention on equal rights as a political issue. The equal rights legislation in the United States provided a useful model, and so did race relations legislation in Britain. Rumors of an upsurge of feminism in the United States may also have added to the new mood. Most significant of all, however, was a quite new and apparently spontaneous outbreak of militancy on the part of women workers against discrimination. In June, for example, there was a strike of women at Ford's for equal pay that was given a lot of publicity and aroused considerable public sympathy. Also in that year there was a small but very militant revolt of bus conductresses against the trade union policy of not allowing them to be bus drivers. . . .

Trade union women activists were already disturbed by the failure of the Labour government to implement its election policy on equal pay, and organized a National Joint Action Committee for Women's Equal Rights that pressed hard for action on equal pay. Barbara Castle was eventually persuaded to lend her support and an Equal Pay Bill was introduced by her, and passed, with the united support of almost all the women MPs [Members of Parliament], by a Labour government in 1970.

It was at this time that the issue of discrimination against women became a major political issue. In 1967 Betty Lockwood had become the chief woman officer and Assistant National Agent of the Labour Party, and from this time the party began to take an increasing interest in sex equality. In 1968 the National Council of Labour Women considered a report, *Discrimination Against Women,* which led to a Green Paper published in 1972 when the Labour Party was in opposition. In the meantime the Labour MP Joyce Butler had introduced a Sex Discrimination Bill that was supported by women's organizations, like the Townswomen's Guilds, that were by no means overtly feminist. Pressure continued from the National Labour Women's Advisory Committee, and there was a period of intense discussion within the Labour Party. In 1974 a Labour government White

Paper, *Equality for Women,* superseded the earlier Green Paper and was followed in 1975 by the Sex Discrimination Act, which made such discrimination unlawful in education, advertising and the provision of public facilities. An Equal Opportunities Commission was also set up with wide powers of investigation and publicity to implement the Act.

As in the United States, however, the passage of equal rights legislation did not in itself guarantee that discrimination would cease. Indeed in both countries, in the short term at least, the effect has been very small. I have already noted the virtual failure of the Equal Pay Act in the United States to change the pattern of women's earnings, and this seems also to have been true in Britain. Not only does the Act not apply to those jobs that are clearly stratified by sex, but employers have been reluctant to implement the Act, and tribunals have tended to apply the law conservatively. The issue of protective legislation also creates problems, since equal pay is dependent on the elimination of different conditions of work as between men and women. Yet both the TUC and most women trade unionists are still basically in favor of the retention of protective laws for women, and efforts of employers to use equal pay to end restrictions on night-work, for example, have sometimes met with opposition from the women themselves.

The Equal Opportunities Commission, like its American counterpart, has been criticized for its unwillingness to take the vigorous action necessary as well as for limitations on its powers. This is not to suggest that the legislation itself has been valueless since it can be effective in individual cases, as indeed can the Equal Pay Act; it may also . . . have a part to play in educating public consciousness as well as the consciousness of women themselves. The results, however, have underlined the limitations of legislation as the main weapon in the battle for equal rights and, as in the United States, have emphasized the necessity for the equal rights movement to look elsewhere for an answer to the problem of discrimination.

The drive for the traditional equal rights claimed by feminists since the early days of the movement is, however, only one aspect of the new feminism and in many ways perhaps the least distinctive part. The movement known as Women's Liberation in fact had its own beginning in the United States independently of the equal rights movement and independently too of the whole tradition of feminism as it had developed in the past. Later, it is true, it was to search for, and discover, its founders, but initially at least it was a spontaneous response of a group of young women to their own experience of discrimination. Later, the liberation movement and the equal rights movement were to lose their distinctive identities, and in Britain at least they were never so far apart as they were in the United States. Nevertheless, if the division is at times an arbitrary one, it is useful as well as convenient. The following [section], therefore, will be concerned with those aspects of the new feminism that take us beyond equal rights, and, making use of a whole new vocabulary, turn from discrimination to oppression, and from equality to liberation.

2. RADICAL FEMINISM

The origins of radical feminism — or, in the more popular terminology, the women's liberation movement — have often been described. . . . Like the equal rights campaign it began early in the 1960s, when small groups of women activists in the civil rights movement, and later in the New Left, began to be conscious of the limited role assigned to women in the movement, and in particular their exclusion from decision-making and their relegation to domestic and other auxiliary chores. Such a role was of course typical of women's political involvement, but the women making the protest were not only themselves highly educated but part of a movement that stressed an equal rights ideology. It is no coincidence, therefore, that radical feminism in the 1960s and the first wave of nineteenth-century feminism in the 1830s arose within the context of natural rights and moved from a consideration of justice for the Negro to justice for women.

However, the attempt by these women to raise the issue of women's rights met not only with a refusal to listen to their arguments, but with a level of contempt and ridicule that did a great deal to stimulate the incipient feminism of the women involved. Hostility to their male colleagues led eventually to open revolt, and in 1967 women's groups were founded in New York and Chicago respectively and women's liberation as a movement was born. The next few years were filled with intense activity. Groups sprang up more or less spontaneously, some of them the result of a split within existing groups as a feminist ideology gradually developed. Journals and articles added to the intellectual excitement and to controversies between different sections of the new movement. Demonstrations of one kind and another gave publicity that, if not always favorable, spread knowledge of the new feminism and its ideas to women who had previously had little political involvement of any kind. Fundamental to these groups, however, was that they were not simply feminist, but female. The principle of male exclusion, which is still a characteristic of radical feminism, seems to have been initially at least a direct consequence of male rejection. The women had attempted, at first, to develop their feminism within the civil rights, New Left and other radical movements. It was only later that they moved out of these male-dominated organizations to form their own groups in which women, as women, could discuss their problems together. Later, male exclusion as a principle was to become a significant aspect of the developing ideology. . . .

In the next few years radical feminism continued as a very loose federation of independent groups. It did, however, develop certain characteristics that served to define it as a movement, if not as an organization. During these years, the radical feminists had to work out their relationship with the New Left and particularly that between feminism and socialism. The result was a feminism that differed considerably both in ideology and tactics from the equal rights feminism that was developing at the same time. Moreover, these differences sprang directly from the origins of the women's liberation movement in radical politics. Thus, whereas NOW began as a political pressure group with little grass-roots involvement, radical feminism was deliberately anti-elitist. There were attempts within it, not always successful, to break down traditional leadership roles and to create new kinds of structure with the emphasis on participation. There was a preference for direct action, as for example the demonstration in 1968 against the Miss America pageant, rather than the political lobbying that certainly characterized equal rights feminism at this time. A particular invention of the radical feminists was the consciousness-raising group, which spread rapidly as it seemed to meet the needs of many women to talk over their problems with other women and to discover shared experiences.

Ideologically, radical feminism has no single doctrine and no simple set of goals or aims. Indeed its opposition to organization, and its respect for spontaneity and self-expression, meant not only that each group developed its own program, but that there were constant splits as groups divided on issues of both ideology and strategy. On the whole, however, the movement is united in its opposition to what it sees as patriarchy or women's oppression by man — a concept that, in its implications, is far wider and more radical than the equal rights concept of feminism. Much of the energy of the feminists, and especially of the feminist intellectuals, has therefore gone not simply into action, or even propaganda, but into a search for the *source* of man's power over women; one of the main lines of division is to be found in the alternative answers that individuals and groups have provided to this crucial question.

The Marxist feminists, who represent one kind of answer, try to retain their loyalty to both socialism and feminism. Consequently they continue to give priority to issues of class, although they no longer see feminism, as do many orthodox socialists both male and female, as a necessary consequence of a socialist victory. They are agreed, however, that feminism without socialism is impossible and for this reason, if for no other, the struggle for socialism is given pride of place. . . .

Radical feminists, on the other hand, see sex as a form of oppression independent of social class. Indeed patriarchy, the oppression of women by men, is seen as not only predating capitalism but continuing after capitalism itself has been superseded. Consequently man himself becomes the exploiter and women the major oppressed class. For some radical feminists, indeed, socialism becomes quite irrelevant, since it will merely succeed in replacing one group of men by another. Nevertheless it is important to realize that even those radical feminists who seem to depart most widely from orthodox Marxism betray in countless ways their origin in the New Left. This is revealed most clearly not in the actual content of their ideology, which is often very un-Marxist, but in the kind of concepts they employ and the manner in which they employ them. [I]t is the particular style this gives to the movement that provides women's liberation with its special characteristics and serves to differentiate it quite sharply from other kinds of feminism. It is this, certainly, that marks it, potentially at least, as revolutionary rather than reformist in its orientation, and that indeed, because of the basic and also far-reaching implications of sex-role divisions in society, makes it even more radical than Marxism in the extent of the changes it proposes. At the same time, by emphasizing sexual rather than economic exploitation, radical feminist writers often treat men as an exploiting class as if they were completely analogous to the ruling class in Marxist orthodoxy, except that the class war becomes a war between the sexes. . . .

. . . The emphasis . . . on women's reproductive functions, and the part played by marriage and the family in the oppression of women, have been and to a large extent remain central to the women's liberation movement both in the United States and elsewhere. Radical feminists therefore, quite unlike the equal rights feminists, have tended, as Jo Freeman has pointed out, to concentrate on the "traditional female concerns of love, sex and children," even if they have been concerned about them in a very untraditional way.

To criticize marriage is not of course necessarily *new*, since nineteenth-century socialists, and indeed many feminists at that time and later, were opposed to marriage laws that denied women legal rights, just as they were opposed to an economic system that forced women into loveless marriages and kept them tied to cruel and perhaps dissolute men. The radical feminists go further however, alleging that marriage is at the very root of woman's subjection to the man because through it man controls both her reproduction and her person. Few aspects of marriage and the family remain unscathed in this attack, although perhaps it is the position of the wife as "unpaid domestic laborer" and the traditional sex roles within marriage and the family that come under the heaviest and most frequent fire. Romantic love is another favorite target since it is seen as a way of trapping women into accepting their own oppression.

The alternatives to marriage and the family put forward by the radical feminists are not necessarily new either. . . . The free love union that is sometimes advocated was, for example, a favorite remedy with some groups in the nineteenth century. Even the attack on individual love as possessive and the advocacy of group marriage have their counterpart in the nineteenth-century Oneida community and indeed elsewhere. There is also a renewal of the ideal of celibacy that attracted some of the most conservative of the early feminists, although the open advocacy of lesbianism, the final symbol of sisterhood, could not have occurred at any earlier time. What is new, however, is the way in which these ideas, attractive to isolated individuals or small groups, have now become the very core of radical feminism.

New, too, is the strong emphasis on alternatives to traditional patterns of child-rearing, whether through state-supported services or the self-help of some kind of commune. This was certainly a preoccupation of some nineteenth-century communitarian socialists, and later of a few feminists, of whom Charlotte Gilman is perhaps the most notable example, but most feminists paid little attention to such ideas. . . .

Radical feminism has also shown a deep concern with the issue of female sexuality. To some extent, . . . this concern has never been absent from the feminist movement; from its earliest days it has criticized the way in which women have been made the victims of male lust, both within and outside marriage. . . . The radical feminists too are deeply concerned with male violence towards women, expressed in such issues as rape, and see sexual violence in particular as a significant consequence of male domination and female oppression. What is new, however, is the serious exploration by the radical feminists of the nature of female sexuality and the conditions under which it can flourish. The argument that the sex act itself is defined in male terms, for male pleasure, and that female satisfaction requires different techniques and a different approach is a good example of the attempt of the radical feminists to come to terms with women's needs without either denying them altogether or subordinating them to male demands.

This attempt to redefine female sexuality is combined with a new look at the effect of sexual permissiveness on women. Increasingly, greater sexual freedom has come to be seen as a doubtful benefit, operating as it does in the interests of men rather than women. . . . Consequently, sexual permissiveness, *in itself,* is no longer seen as necessarily liberating but, like romantic love, part of the sexist trap into which women are led by men. Much feminist thinking has therefore gone into the problem of how to allow women sexual freedom without at the same time contributing to their domination, and it is in this context that we must understand the preoccupation with such issues as abortion law reform and, on a wider front, the attack on male-dominated medicine and the demand, central not only to radical feminism but . . . to feminists of almost every kind, that in political decisions and in personal relationships women are allowed to control their own bodies. The radical feminist attack on beauty contests and their dislike, in advertising and elsewhere, of the presentation of women as "sex objects" is another aspect of this campaign.

The separatism of the radical feminists, to which attention has already been drawn, and the emergence, after 1970 in particular, of radical lesbianism as an important force in the movement have exaggerated the tendency in some sections of the movement to advocate the replacement of heterosexual love either by celibacy or by lesbianism, an advocacy made more plausible by the acceptance of a view of female sexuality that not only sees it as different from that of men but argues that its satisfaction does not necessarily involve a heterosexual relationship. . . .

While it is easy to exaggerate the importance of lesbianism as an aspect of radical feminism, the association of the two was sufficiently close to make [some feminist leaders] feel the need to repudiate the claim that a radical feminist need necessarily be a lesbian. Moreover, the definition of man, and by implication all men, as the enemy — the repudiation of men as friends and allies and the exclusion of men not only from consciousness-raising sessions but from other activities — had given powerful "pro-woman" emphasis to some sections of the movement. Women are seen not only as innocent victims but also as "good," whereas men are not only oppressors but also "bad," a view that vividly recalls the ideal of female superiority that characterized much earlier feminist thinking. For some radical feminists the elimination of male domination, if not of men altogether, would free the world not only of the oppression of the female by the male but of oppression itself. Moreover, in their forms of organization, radical feminists often try to eradicate characteristics that they classify as male, which include hierarchy, competition and aggression. Consequently, the qualities that they perceive as female and wish to encourage and perpetuate include just those "soft" qualities of affection, cooperation and even tenderness that were part of the ideology of femininity in both the nineteenth and the early twentieth centuries. There is little discussion, however, of the source of what are perceived as these more desirable feminine qualities and the extent to which they are the result of societal processes rather than "nature" (of which perhaps the most important is the very oppression from which all the feminists want to free women). . . .

The presentation of what may be described as the ideology of radical feminism in this way makes it appear more systematic and certainly more unified than it really is, and it is necessary to stress once again that radical feminism is not a "movement" in any concrete sense of the term and that it in fact represents a wide variety of positions. . . . Even the issue of male exclusion, which has been a very dominant aspect of the ideology, can mean very different things to different people, and the argument that men should be excluded from the movement does not necessarily imply for all women that they must also be excluded from their lives. . . .

Most of those who have attempted to examine the development of radical feminism are agreed that it was seriously weakened by internal disputes, by its lack of formal structure and by the theoretical weaknesses that continued to plague it. The years just before 1970 were its heyday, and through the 1970s it has fallen into a decline, its most committed followers retreating into feminist communes where they could practice only a kind of personal redemption. Others have moved into political action at the level of feminist issues like rape and abortion, the significance of which is reformist rather than revolutionary in its implications.

If the 1970s saw the decline of radical feminism, they were also years in which equal rights feminism was increasingly radicalized as NOW moved into many of the positions originally occupied by the radical feminists. This had in fact started before 1970 with the adoption by NOW of abortion as a feminist issue. Introduced for the first time in 1967, it aroused considerable controversy and caused the more conservative elements in NOW to form the Women's Equity Action League, which concentrated on issues of employment, education and tax inequalities. By 1970, the strike organized by NOW centered upon three issues — abortion on demand, 24-hour child care centers, and equal opportunity in employment and education — that took the organization firmly beyond a narrow equal rights policy. Lesbianism was another highly controversial issue within NOW when lesbians tried to claim it as a feminist issue, but after 1970 lesbianism was acknowledged by NOW as a legitimate concern of feminism even if some leading feminists continued to be anxious about the effect of a lesbian image on the movement.

Thus, over time, NOW broadened its activities and began to explore issues of female sexuality and alternative life styles borrowed from the radical feminists. To some extent this arose from changes in the membership of NOW itself, as the publicity attracted initially by radical feminists drew much larger numbers of women into the organization. There was also within NOW a growing awareness of the inadequacy of a narrow equal rights feminism. Nevertheless, the net effect has been what [David] Bouchier has described as the de-radicalization of radical feminism. If the goals of NOW have extended beyond the concept of equal rights, the solutions they propose are often vastly different from those of the radical feminists, and the end result has been a "moderate" feminism with policies that, like those of equal rights, are essentially reformist in character. Bouchier has argued that this was brought about partly by a surrender from within radical feminism itself, weakened as it was by internal disputes and a lack of structure, partly by the media, which distorted and ridiculed the message of the radicals, and partly by what amounted to a takeover by the better-organized NOW, which enabled it to capture the new recruits who were being attracted into feminism at this time.

The practical effect of this de-radicalization has been an increasing limitation of feminism to specific feminist issues and a move away from a radical critique of society. These issues include attempts to change the laws on abortion, birth control, divorce and property, to improve child care facilities, to change the image of women in the media, and to end discrimination against women in education and employment, some of which do not go very far beyond the equal rights tradition. More radical perhaps are the attempts to provide help and support by women for women in such areas as abortion and rape, but even these are essentially reformist rather than revolutionary in aim, whatever their ultimate implications.

One of the most significant of the issues that has joined radical feminists and NOW has been the abortion campaign. . . . [H]istorically the movement for change in the abortion laws has been based on the health of the mother and the child. Public discussion during the 1960s was stimulated by both the thalidomide scare and the German measles epidemic; pressure for some degree of reform built up and some states made minor revisions in their abortion laws. It was left to the feminists to demand the right to abortion as a matter of justice, an aspect of a woman's right to control her own reproduction, and this became a part of NOW's campaign as well as of the radical feminists. There were, however, divisions on tactics, with NOW preferring the more traditional method of lobbying and the radical feminists more direct action, such as picketing, demonstrations and civil disobedience. There was also some disagreement on whether to work only for total repeal or whether to work within the abortion law reform movement for a limited measure of reform. Finally in 1973 a Supreme Court decision [*Roe* v. *Wade*] came near to allowing abortion on demand, although there were still restrictions on the timing of the abortion and it was still largely in the control of the medical profession, restrictions that feminists continue to oppose. There has also been the need to combat the attempts, since 1973, to overturn the Supreme Court decision, and anti-abortion groups, as we have seen, are important opponents of the feminist movement and the Equal Rights Amendment. As part of the right to abortion campaign, feminist groups have also set up abortion referral services to help women get around the inadequacies of the system.

Another consequence of the de-radicalization of feminism has been a move away from the sex war and the politics of confrontation between men and women to the position that the existing relationship between the sexes, and in particular the present sex-role stereotyping, oppresses both men and women. According to this version of feminism, the institutions of marriage and the family need to be changed, but by reform rather than abolition. The solution lies in what is frequently termed androgyny, or role-sharing, in which both personality and role behavior will cease to be sex-typed. Moreover, since it is the system, rather than men, that is seen as oppressive, change depends not upon a revolutionary struggle but upon the conversion of both men and women to a new system from which both will gain. This will require a change both in the system of child care and in life styles, so that the burden of child care does not fall solely on women, and in sex stereotyping, through changes in the educational system.

Such a position departs from the equal rights tradition by demanding radical change in the position of men and women in society, but it is very far indeed from the radical feminists who view man as the oppressor. It is also largely outside a Marxist perspective, although conceivably some version of androgyny could be combined with Marxism. Its appeal perhaps is particularly to those who, like Betty Friedan, dislike the sex-war analogy, which, she claims, "makes a woman apologize for loving her husband or children." She asks for a "two sex movement for human liberation" and an end to the "obsolete sex roles, the feminine and masculine mystiques, which torment us mutually."

The androgynous approach is by no means without serious weaknesses at the theoretical level and may represent no more than an attempt to avoid the revolutionary confrontation inevitable in both Marxist and radical feminism. At the same time, by accepting the need for quite large changes in male/female roles, it avoids some of the difficulties that have increasingly become apparent in equal rights feminism. For this reason it is likely to continue to be an important element in feminism, particularly in the United States where Marxist feminism has remained undeveloped. Indeed it is possible . . . that social and economic changes, irrespective of feminist pressures, are already pointing towards a more androgynous society. Before passing on to these more general issues, however, it is necessary to move on to a survey of radical feminism as it has developed in Britain and in particular to examine the ways in which it has differed from the movement in the United States.

As in the United States, radical feminism arose from within the revolutionary left, although it was, from the first, strongly influenced by the American movement, news of which came from American women in London and from the network of radical journals. Groups began to be formed in 1969, some associated with existing male revolutionary groups, others independent. An important landmark was the Oxford conference in 1970, which attracted some 600 participants; its success may be said to have started the movement in Britain. The policy that emerged from the conference centered upon equal pay, improved education, 24-hour nurseries, free contraception and abortion on demand, policies that indeed reflect the practical orientation of the British movement.

Perhaps the main difference between the United States and Britain, however, is the closer link in Britain between socialism or Marxism and feminism. Although by no means sympathetic to women's claims, there was never the deep rift between radical men and women that occurred, and indeed persisted, in the United States and kept the two groups not only apart but hostile to each other. Consequently Marxist feminism has continued to be much stronger in Britain than in the United States, and many of the most influential British feminists have tried to reconcile Marxism and feminism rather than to develop an independent feminist theory. The concern with Marxism at the theoretical level is, however, only one aspect of the relationship. There is more concern in Britain with the economic exploitation of women and closer ties between feminism and women in the trade union movement, so that issues like equal pay and child care provision have a more immediate and practical significance.

This is not to suggest that radical British feminists do not share, to some extent at least, the anti-male perspectives of their American counterparts. Within the British movement the practice of excluding men has been followed just as strongly in meetings, conferences and seminars, extending, at times, to a retreat from heterosexuality itself. Moreover, all the themes of radical feminism in the United States can be found within the writings of the British movement. It does seem, nevertheless, that the extreme version of the anti-male ideology has not taken root to such an extent in Britain as in the United States. Furthermore, radical feminists in Britain have been active in a large number of political campaigns that have tended to bring them into an alliance with both equal rights feminists and women in the labor and trade union movements. These issues, of which there are many, include the campaign against anti-abortion laws, better provision for battered wives, changes in the law on rape, better social security provision and improved child care facilities. Such work, because it involves political tactics of one kind or another, may well involve working with or through men. Women in the trade union movement, for example, forced their unions to back demands for day nurseries.

The campaign against the abortion laws is perhaps the most successful and the most impressive of the radical feminists' excursions into politics and is worth examining in a little more detail. . . . [T]he campaign initially had as its chief concern the health and well-being of the mother and child. As in the United States, it was the thalidomide scare that was perhaps the most powerful influence in turning public opinion towards the idea of reform, and this occurred before the emergence of the new feminism in the late 1960s. Even when, in 1963, a younger generation took over leadership of the Abortion Law Reform Association [ALRA] and there was a dramatic increase in its level of activity and in the size of its membership, this was not linked to any specifically feminist argument. Indeed at this time the argument that it was a woman's right to choose was rejected by the ALRA.

There was considerable support for some measure of reform from women's organizations, many of which were by no means specifically feminist in their orientation, although it may well have been considered by them as an issue of special relevance to women. On the other hand, support for a change in the law did not come only from women, and during the 1960s the campaign seems to have been part of a general movement to liberalize the legal system in the direction of more individual freedom especially, although not exclusively, with respect to sexual morality. During the early 1960s, for example, such issues as homosexuality, divorce and euthanasia, as well as abortion and contraception, became of increasing concern to groups that had previously ignored them. . . .

The [Abortion] Act, which came into operation in 1968, went a considerable way to liberalize the abortion law, although the restrictions that it imposed, and the difficulties of implementing the Act, meant that, in the final event, it was a long way from free abortion on request. Moreover, in the years since its passage, the energies of the reformers, as in the United States, have perforce been concentrated on maintaining the Act rather than on pressing for further reforms. What is interesting for our purpose, however, is that the case for abortion has come to be seen increasingly in feminist terms. Already by the early 1970s, as we have seen, abortion was a key issue in the women's liberation groups, and in 1971 a national woman's demonstration made free contraception and abortion on demand one of its main aims.

The feminist involvement in the abortion issue can be seen very clearly in the first serious threat to the 1967 Abortion Act in 1975. A Woman's Right to Choose campaign was organized that brought feminist arguments and feminists themselves into the very center of the battle. Even the Abortion Law Reform Association was won over; it not only adopted the feminist slogan "a woman's right to choose" but argued the feminist case for the right to abortion on request. By 1979 the labour and trade union movement was deeply involved in the controversy and in that year the TUC and the women's movement organized a joint protest march that brought the two groups together for the first time. In the case of abortion law reform, therefore, the radical feminists in Britain have played an important part in radicalizing not only feminism itself but also reform movements concerned with feminist issues. The same case could be made with respect to rape and to violence against wives, since it is largely the radical feminists who have raised these as significant legal and political issues rather than as personal and psychological problems.

As in the United States, however, the feminist movement in the late 1970s has had to meet both an ideological backlash, partly produced by its own earlier successes, and the challenge of an economic recession, which threatens the gains that women have actually won. The heady optimism of the early 1970s has indeed gone, and it is possible that we may be entering another period of decline such as that which characterized the Depression of the 1930s and, in that instance, lasted for a whole generation. Whether this will occur again is a matter, perhaps, for speculation rather than prediction. . . .

QUESTIONS TO CONSIDER

1. What social and economic trends supported the rebirth of feminism in the 1960s? What evidence does the author provide that on-the-job discrimination led to equal-rights agitation in England and America? What were the strengths and limitations of the legislative and equal-rights approach to improving women's status?

2. Describe the ideology and tactics of the radical feminists of the 1960s and 1970s. Where did radical feminism come from? In what ways did it differ from equal-rights feminism? How did radical feminists differ among themselves on issues such as economic versus sexual exploitation, sexuality and the family, and the role of men? How, according to Banks, is an androgynous approach a compromise between the equal-rights and radical positions?

3. Compare the history of the American Civil Rights and feminist movements in the 1960s and 1970s. What similarities do you see in their origins, ideas, tactics, and development? What differences? What common factors help to explain their rise and decline?

4. What parallels does the author find in the timing, content, and outcome of the modern women's movements in the United States and Britain? How do you account for these similarities? In what ways were the two movements different? Why?

5. Banks points out that an "ideological backlash" and the economic recession of the 1970s slowed down the progress of feminism in the United States and abroad. Why did the renewed prosperity of the Reagan and Clinton years fail to revive feminist organizations? Why did teen pregnancy and sexual harassment become prominent issues during those years? Have looser attitudes toward sexuality hindered or promoted feminism? Do you think women's progress is inevitable, or can it be reversed?

GLOBALIZATION
AND EMPIRE

When Americans considered their nation's status in the world as they entered the twenty-first century, they faced starkly opposed images from abroad, each a different reflection of America's power. "Why America Fascinates and Infuriates the World" was the subtitle of a best-selling report of 2002 on dozens of interviews with foreigners. On the one hand, there was the overwhelming presence of American popular culture on the world scene. Globalization — the rapid acceleration of the movement of goods, capital, and ideas across national boundaries — had been promoted by America's aggressive free-trade policies and dominated by its mass culture industry. Globalization created a worldwide consumer culture that spread American music, TV programs, clothing, and fast food everywhere. English relentlessly infiltrated native tongues, making it the true international language and the medium for 90 percent of transactions on the Internet, the "World Wide Web" that facilitated global exchange and came to symbolize it. It was only a slight exaggeration to say, as did a writer in the *New York Times,* that America's freewheeling democracy and its optimistic culture "fills the hearts and minds of an entire planet with its dreams and desires."

On the other hand, there was mounting evidence that much of the world resented America's predominance. America's European allies and Latin American friends felt bullied by U.S. trade practices, developing nations complained that the American-dominated World Bank chained them to economic colonialism, and the secularism of American culture alienated fundamentalist Muslims, who viewed the United States as "the Great Satan." When the Cold War ended and the Soviet Union splintered, the United States became the world's lone military superpower, able to flex its muscles at will. Gradually but unmistakably, American leaders moved from the nation's "multilateral" tradition of pursuing international alliances and agreements toward "unilateral" economic decisions and military interventions. The horrifying terrorist attacks of September 11, 2001, gave a huge push to this move. U.S. president George W. Bush declared a global "war on terrorism" and pressured other nations to go along. The United States invaded the terrorists' hideout in Afghanistan and, flaunting the United Nations and world opinion, waged war on Iraq to depose its ruler, Saddam Hussein, and install a new government. Critics at home and abroad began to speak of an "American empire," a phrase that was soon invoked with approval by those who believed that the United States must take on greater responsibilities in the new, hyperconnected world where local crises had immediate global repercussions and where terrorism threatened the rule of law.

As the essays by Niall Ferguson and Joseph S. Nye Jr. in this chapter show, each of these current trends, globalization and empire, has a history to explore and compare. Ferguson examines America's current "imperial moment" against the record of past empires, particularly the "liberal empire" that Great Britain tried to construct from the 1850s to the 1930s. Impressed by the British Empire's promotion of global commerce and democratic institutions, Ferguson shows that America today wields more power than Britain did and notes that its leaders voice similar ideals. He concludes that in order to defuse the threat of tyrants and terrorists around the world, the United States needs to put aside its "denial" and to take up the imperial "burden" of its British predecessor. Nye's historically informed look at globalization leaves him less enthusiastic than Ferguson about America's imperial turn. Tracing globalization to long-term trends in international technology and trade as well as recent breakthroughs, he argues that its economic and cultural features will be less and less dominated by the United States and, more important, that the planetary problems it creates cannot be solved by America's "going it alone."

Is the United States following the imperial model of Great Britain? *Should* it? Is globalization simply another name for American empire? To what extent has global connectedness been imposed by the United States the same way that free trade and the English language were promoted by Great Britain? As we look forward, will globalization undermine American influence by spreading economic competition and by generating nationalist or private opposition? Will the United States move toward greater unilateral action in order to control globalized chaos, or will some form of "world government" emerge to deal with transnational problems such as terrorism, pollution, and nuclear proliferation? It should become clear from your reading of Ferguson and Nye that their preferences and predictions differ. Each shows, however, that comparative and transnational approaches can place current trends in broader perspective and may also suggest "lessons" — both positive and negative — for us to consider as we debate America's future and that of the world to which it is inextricably tied.

Imperial
Denial

NIALL FERGUSON

In 1987 British historian Paul Kennedy's best-selling book The Rise and Fall of the
Great Powers *stirred controversy by linking the fate of the United States to the gloomy
precedent of Rome, the Hapsburgs, and Great Britain. Was the United States following
Hapsburg Spain, Napoleonic France, and, most recently, the British Empire into decline?
Kennedy forecast no inevitable doom for America, but he argued that the nation had recently
lost its clear economic and military preeminence. Faced with increased competition from
resurgent Germany and Japan, the United States had become a debtor nation whose share
of world production began to fall. Its disastrous war in Vietnam was evidence of imperial
"overreach," the situation where military commitments outrun economic resources, as had
happened with Britain and Rome. In response to those who predicted a "new world order"
with multiple centers of power, Kennedy argued that the United States was poorly prepared
by its history and culture for the "multipolar" diplomacy and lowered economic expectations
that this change would bring.*

    *Events have a way of embarrassing historians who take on the role of prophets. No
sooner did Kennedy's dismal prognosis appear than things began to look up for the United
States. In the later 1980s and through the 1990s, the American economy surged from gains
in productivity, the rise of the computer industry, and booms in banking and real estate, while
rivals such as Japan and Germany stagnated. As other western nations cut back on worker
benefits and welfare-state commitments in order to compete on the world market, the United
States showcased its free-market economy and limited national government as the model for
survival of the "fittest" global competitors.*

    *In the sphere of international relations, when the Berlin Wall came down in 1989 and
the Soviet Union disintegrated two years later, the United States became the world's only
superpower. It took a while for this "unipolar moment," as one columnist called it, to sink
in and for talk of a multipolar world order to subside. On the one hand, officials in the
George H.W. Bush and Bill Clinton administrations proclaimed America's "world responsibilities" to spread democracy and free-market economics abroad, and Clinton deployed
America's military against Serbia and Sudan as well as in America's traditional imperial*

"backyard," the Caribbean. On the other hand, Clinton committed the United States to a multilateral strategy of pursuing international alliances with "partners" and negotiating global protocols on the environment, chemical weapons, and nuclear testing.

Any lingering ambivalence about unilateralism seemed to disappear with the frightening terrorist attacks on the Pentagon and New York's World Trade Center on September 11, 2001. President George Bush, who had promised a "humbler" foreign policy and criticized "nation-building" during his campaign, immediately declared an unofficial "war" on terrorism, which the United States forced other nations to join. Ignoring international disapproval, Bush invaded Afghanistan to punish a regime that supported the al Qaeda terrorists, then waged war against Iraq to depose its despotic leader, Saddam Hussein, and impose a new government in his place. Meanwhile, American officials ridiculed the United Nations, alienated traditional European allies, and refused to sign international environmental agreements. By 2003, in short, it began to look as if the New World Order would be dictated by the United States.

America's aggressive unilateral turn opened a public debate over the prospect and the morality of an "American empire." In an influential article in the New York Times, *political scientist Michael Ignatieff noted that the United States had moved unmistakably toward a new version of empire not built on colonies and conquest but based on enforcing order in the world, promoting American values and interests, and exempting itself from international rules. Without taking sides, Ignatieff warned that this decision for empire implied large and lasting commitments abroad, risked a fierce backlash from its enemies, and threatened democratic freedoms at home. As other political commentators pitched in, it became clear that the escalating dispute between anti-imperialists and "neoimperialists" echoed the controversies of a century earlier, when Americans had argued over annexing the Philippines.*

British historian Niall Ferguson recently entered this debate by considering America's current situation against the record of previous empires in world history. In the face of Americans' denial that their nation is an empire, Ferguson points out that it broadly resembles prior imperial powers, and he argues that words such as "hegemony" and "superpower" are evasions that mask the many forms that imperial rule can take.

If the United States is an empire, what kind is it or should it be? Ferguson addresses this question by comparing today's America and the "liberal empire" that Great Britain tried to impose upon its colonies and dependents in the years between the 1850s and the 1930s. Although the United States controls less territory than Britain did at the height of its empire, Ferguson argues that America's military and economic power is even more dominant. More important, Ferguson sees a remarkable similarity between the two empires' ideals. When American presidents announce that they are intervening to support free trade, representative government, human rights, and international law around the world, they are promoting institutions that British officials successfully planted in their dominions, according to Ferguson. Ferguson does acknowledge differences between America's current world position and that of England a century ago. Still, given his positive assessment of Britain's legacy, he seems to suggest that its "liberal empire" can become the model for an American successor. Believing that "empire is more necessary in the twenty-first century than ever before," he urges Americans to accept the imperial "burden" and to move toward a more formal imperialism of unilateral intervention and direct overseas rule.

In what sense is today's United States an empire? Does a term like "hegemony," which implies persuasion and indirect rule, better describe America's role in the world? Is it possible or desirable for the United States to enforce international peace? Are the effects of America's power abroad as benign as Ferguson claims Britain's were, or are they fraught with injustices and dangers? If Great Britain failed to create an "empire to end all empires," how could America expect to succeed?

As you read Ferguson's essay, consider the similarities and differences between the current world role of the United States and that of Britain at its zenith. Also compare his characterization of American imperialism with the versions of American empire portrayed by other authors in this volume, especially Robin Winks and Vince Boudreau (Selections 9 and 10) on America's role in the Philippines and John Lewis Gaddis (Selection 19) on America's Cold War empire. Finally, it would make sense to return to Ferguson's essay after reading Joseph Nye's discussion of the limits of American power in the next selection of this chapter.

The fact that public discussion about America's place in the world shifted from Kennedy's empire in decline to Ferguson's empire in denial in a mere fifteen years should make us hesitate to predict the future. Whether the British Empire's high point or its fall tells us more about America's future remains unclear. In any case, comparing today's America to imperial Britain provides a globally and historically informed vision of the nation's future to debate, and it may help us to avoid mistakes of the past.

GLOSSARY

ABBASID CALIPHATE   The temporal and spiritual rule of Islam that was held by the Arabic family descended from Abbas, the uncle of Muhammad, for over five hundred years. Gaining power in 749 through an alliance with Shiites, the Abbasids established their capital at Baghdad and served as caliphs until they were overthrown in 1258 by the Mongols under Hulagu Khan.

AHMAD, MUHAMMAD "AL-MAHDI" (1844–1885)   The leader of an Islamic religious brotherhood (or dervish) whose swelling band of followers captured Khartoum in 1885 from British imperial forces and who then established a theocratic state in Sudan.

AL JAZEERA   An Arabic television news network founded in 1996 and based in Qatar but broadcast worldwide. Its programs cover international events from a pan-Arab and pro-Islamic perspective.

BRETTON WOODS   The common name for the United Nations Monetary and Financial Conference, held in July 1944 at Bretton Woods, New Hampshire. The conference drew up plans for the International Monetary Fund and the International Bank for Reconstruction and Development. These organizations were intended to promote international monetary cooperation and to stabilize exchange rates. Contrary to participants' hopes, however, most nations maintained restrictions on trade and currency exchange.

BYZANTIUM   Another name for the Byzantine Empire, the eastern part of the Roman Empire that became its successor. The Byzantine Empire was governed from the city of Constantinople, which had been founded by the Roman emperor Constantine in 330. After Rome fell in 476 to the Goths, the Byzantine Empire ruled the Balkan Peninsula and Asia Minor (present-day Turkey) until Constantinople was captured by the Ottoman Turks in 1453.

CRIMEAN WAR (1853–1856) A conflict between England, France, and Turkey, on one side, and Russia, on the other, over control of the Palestinian holy places and various territories bordering the Black Sea. Defeat of the Russian troops on the Crimean peninsula ended Russia's dominant role in southeastern Europe and restored Turkey's boundary in Asia.

DREADNOUGHT A turbine-driven British battleship launched in 1906 that featured heavy-caliber guns mounted in turrets. Ships modeled upon it became known as Dreadnoughts, and they dominated the world's navies until after World War II.

EUROPEAN UNION (EU) The organization for the political and economic integration of Europe that was established in 1993 as the successor to the Common Market (1958). Encompassing twenty-five nations, the EU includes a parliament and court system, a free- travel and -trade zone, and a common currency, the euro.

FREUD, SIGMUND (1856–1939) An influential Austrian psychiatrist whose theory of psychoanalysis traced the workings of unconscious drives in the forming of human personality and, by implication, of civilization.

GENERAL AGREEMENT ON TARIFFS AND TRADE (GATT) An agreement to phase out and to reduce tariffs that was negotiated by 23 nations in 1947. Enlarged to include 125 nations before it was replaced by the World Trade Organization in 1995, GATT played a major role in expanding world trade in the half-century after World War II.

GOLD STANDARD The use of gold or a currency that is convertible to gold at a fixed rate as the medium of payment for international trade. The gold standard was first employed by Britain in 1821, was adopted in the 1870s by most industrialized nations, and governed international trade until the outbreak of World War I. After the 1920s the gold standard was supplemented with the use of stable convertible currencies, mainly British pounds and U.S. dollars, but its reign ended in 1971 when the United States ceased converting dollars to gold. Since then the international monetary system has been based on dollars and other paper currencies.

GROSS DOMESTIC PRODUCT (GDP) An indicator of national economic health that measures the market value of the nation's total output of goods and services (excluding income from overseas investment) in a given period, usually one year. The GDP's three main components are consumer purchases, private investment, and government spending.

HOBSON, JOHN A. (1858–1940) An English economist and reformer who opposed imperialism, interpreting it as a product of the moral and economic excesses of capitalism.

INDIAN MUTINY (1857–1858) An unsuccessful rebellion against British rule that began among Indian troops employed by the British East India Company and spread through northern India. Although it was brutally suppressed, the rebellion led to the abolition of the East India Company and other imperial reforms.

INTERNATIONAL MONETARY FUND (IMF) An agency of the United Nations set up in 1944 that uses a fund collected from member nations to purchase foreign currencies, with the goal of assisting payment of international debts and stabilizing exchange rates. The IMF has been criticized for being dominated by the United States (its largest contributor), for bailing out incompetent or corrupt regimes, and for imposing rigid financial conditions upon the nations it assists.

IRISH FAMINE   The worst famine in nineteenth-century Europe. The Great Potato Famine (1845–1849) was caused by a blight that ruined Ireland's potato crop, its rural population's main source of food. Perhaps a million people perished from hunger and disease, and about a million and a half emigrated to British lands or to the United States. The British government's attempts to relieve the distress were grudging and ineffective, intensifying Irish resentment of British rule.

JODHPURS AND PITH HELMETS   The riding breeches and lightweight helmets that became the typical outfit worn by British explorers and imperial officials in Africa and Asia.

LENIN, VLADIMIR ILYICH (1870–1924)   The Bolshevik leader who seized power in the Russian Revolution of October 1917 and declared the world's first communist government. Lenin viewed imperialism as "the highest stage of capitalism," during which the relentless search for profits drove capitalist governments to take over foreign markets.

MACAULAY, THOMAS BABINGTON (1800–1859)   An English historian and politician who, as a member of the Supreme Council for India from 1834 to 1838, began a uniform system of education and drafted a legal code for the colony.

MAXIM GUN   A powerful machine gun invented by an American, Hiram Maxim, but first manufactured by the British in 1884. Employed by British colonial troops in Africa after 1892, the Maxim gun enabled small British armies to kill thousands of native warriors in Matabeleland (later called Rhodesia) and Sudan and to push into central Africa.

MING DYNASTY   The dynasty that ruled China from 1368 to 1644. The first Ming emperors expelled the Mongols and sent naval expeditions to southeast Asia and India. Later emperors established a vast government bureaucracy and extended the Chinese empire from Korea to Burma.

PAX BRITANNICA   "British peace": the peace imposed by Britain's military and naval supremacy upon its dominions and, by extension, upon the international scene from 1815 to the outbreak of World War I in 1914.

RWANDA   A land-locked republic in central Africa where fighting between the Hutu and Tutsi peoples broke out in 1990 when Tutsi-led rebels invaded from Uganda. During a wave of anarchy in 1994 an estimated half million civilians, mostly Tutsi, were slaughtered by roving militia and two million refugees fled to camps in nearby countries. A UN peacekeeping mission ended in March 1996.

SEIGNIORAGE   Government revenue gained from the coinage or provision of currency.

USEUCOM (U.S. European Command)   Established in 1952, the unified command of American troops stationed in Europe. By 1993 its area of operations was expanded to include Africa and the Middle East.

WORLD TRADE ORGANIZATION (WTO)   The successor to GATT, established in 1995 as an international body to monitor trade, ensure equal market access, reduce protectionism, and resolve international trade disputes. The WTO expanded GATT's domain to cover services and intellectual property as well as goods. Opponents of globalization have criticized the WTO for promoting the interests of multinational corporations and for excluding protections against environmental damage or exploitation of low-skilled workers.

✯ ✯ ✯ ✯ ✯ ✯

It used to be that only critics of American foreign policy referred to the "American Empire." During the Cold War, of course, both the Soviet Union and the People's Republic of China harped incessantly on the old Leninist theme of Yankee imperialism, as did many Western European, Middle Eastern and Asian writers, not all of them Marxists. But their claim that overseas expansion was inspired by sinister corporate interests was not so very different from the indigenous American critiques of late-nineteenth and early-twentieth-century overseas expansion, whether populist, progressive or socialist. In the 1960s these critiques fused to produce a new and influential historiography of American foreign policy usually referred to as revisionism. Historians like Gabriel and Joyce Kolko argued that the Cold War was the result not of Russian but of American aggression after 1945, an argument made all the more attractive to a generation of students by the contemporaneous war in Vietnam — proof, as it seemed, of the neocolonial thrust of American foreign policy. The reassertion of American military power under Ronald Reagan prompted fresh warnings against the "imperial temptation."

This tradition of radical criticism of American foreign policy shows no sign of fading away. Its distinctive, anguished tone continues to emanate from writers like Chalmers Johnson, William Blum and Michael Hudson, echoing the strictures of an earlier generation of anti-imperialists (some of whom are themselves still faintly audible). Yet criticism of American empire was never the exclusive preserve of the political Left. In the eyes of Gore Vidal, the tragedy of the Roman Republic is repeating itself as farce, with the "national-security state" relentlessly encroaching on the prerogatives of the patrician elite to which Vidal himself belongs. Meanwhile, far to the Right, Pat Buchanan continues to fulminate in the archaic isolationist idiom against East Coast internationalists intent on entangling the United States — against the express wishes of the Founding Fathers — in the quarrels and conflicts of the Old World. In Buchanan's eyes, America is following not the example of Rome but that of Britain, whose empire it once repudiated but now imitates. Other, more mainstream conservatives — notably Clyde Prestowitz — have also heaped scorn on "the imperial project of the so-called neoconservatives."

In the past three or four years, however, a growing number of commentators have begun to use the term *American empire* less pejoratively, if still ambivalently, and in some cases with genuine enthusiasm. Speaking at a conference in Atlanta in November 2000, Richard Haass, who went on to serve in the Bush administration as director of policy planning in the State Department, argued that Americans needed to "re-conceive their global role from one of traditional nation-state to an imperial power," calling openly for an "informal" American empire. This was, at the time, bold language; it is easy to forget that during the 2000 presidential election campaign it was George W. Bush who accused the Clinton–Gore administration of undertaking too many "open-ended deployments and unclear military missions." As Thomas Donnelly, deputy executive director of the Project for the New American Century, told the *Washington Post* in August 2001, "There's not all that many people who will talk about it [empire] openly. It's discomforting to a lot of Americans. So they use code phrases like 'America is the sole superpower.'"

Such inhibitions seemed to fall away in the aftermath of the terrorist attacks of September 11, 2001. In a trenchant article for the *Weekly Standard,* published just a month after the destruction of the World Trade Center, Max Boot explicitly made "The Case for an American Empire." "Afghanistan and other troubled lands today," Boot declared, "cry out for the sort of enlightened foreign administration once provided by self-confident Englishmen in jodhpurs and pith helmets." When his history of America's "small wars" appeared the following year, its title was taken from Rudyard Kipling's notorious poem "The White Man's Burden," written in 1899 as an exhortation to the United States to turn the Philippines into an American colony. The journalist Robert Kaplan also took up the imperial theme in his book *Warrior Politics,* arguing that "future historians will look back on 21st-century United States as an empire as well as a republic." "There's a positive side to empire," Kaplan argued in an interview. "It's in some ways the most benign form of order." Charles Krauthammer, another conservative columnist, detected the change of mood. "People," he told the *New York Times,* were "now coming out of the closet on the word 'empire.'" "America has become an empire," agreed Dinesh D'Souza in the *Christian Science Monitor,* but happily it is "the most magnanimous imperial power ever." His conclusion: "Let us have more of it." Writing in *Foreign Affairs* in 2002, the journalist Sebastian Mallaby proposed American "neo-imperialism" as the best remedy for the "chaos" engendered by "failed states" around the world. One reading of Michael Ignatieff's recent critique of American "nation building" efforts in Bosnia, Kosovo and Afghanistan is that these have not been *sufficiently* imperialistic to be effective.

While Mallaby and Ignatieff are perhaps best described as liberal interventionists — proponents of what Eric Hobsbawm has sneeringly dismissed as "the imperialism of human rights" — the majority of the new imperialists are neoconservatives, and it was their views that came to the fore during and after the invasion of Iraq in 2003. "Today there is only one empire," wrote James Kurth in a special "Empire" issue of the *National Interest,* "the global empire of the United States. The U.S. military. . . are the true heirs of the legendary civil officials, and not just the dedicated military officers, of the British Empire." Speaking on Fox News in April 2003, the editor of the *Weekly Standard,* William Kristol, declared: "We need to err on the side of being strong. And if people want to say we're an imperial power, fine." That same month the *Wall Street Journal* suggested that the British naval campaign against the slave trade in the mid-nineteenth century might provide a model for American policy against nuclear proliferation. Max Boot even called for the United States to establish a Colonial Office, the better to administer its new possessions in the Middle East and Asia.

Within the Pentagon the figure most frequently associated with the "new imperialism" is Deputy Secretary Paul Wolfowitz, who first won notoriety, as undersecretary of defense under the current president's father, by arguing that the aim of U.S. policy should be to "convince potential competitors that they need not aspire to a greater role or pursue a more aggressive posture to protect their legitimate interests." That line, so controversial when it was written back in 1992, now seems remarkably tame. Nine years later the Office of the Secretary of Defense organized a Summer Study at the Naval War College, Newport, to "explore strategic approaches to sustain [U.S. predominance] for the long term (~50 years)," which explicitly drew comparisons between the U.S. and the Roman, Chinese, Ottoman and British empires. Such parallels clearly do not seem outlandish to senior American military personnel. In 2000 General Anthony Zinni, then commander in chief of the U.S. Central Command, told the journalist Dana Priest that he "had become a modern-day proconsul, descendant of the warrior-statesman who ruled the Roman Empire's outlying territory, bringing order and ideals from a legalistic Rome." It is hard to be certain that this was irony.

Officially, to be sure, the United States remains an empire in denial. Most politicians would agree with the distinction drawn by the historian Charles Beard back in 1939: "America is not to be Rome or Britain. It is to be America." Richard Nixon insisted in his memoirs that the United States is "the only great power without a history of imperialistic claims on neighboring countries," a view echoed by policy makers throughout the past decade. In the words of Samuel R. "Sandy" Berger, President Clinton's national security adviser, "We are the first global power in history that is not an imperial power." A year later, while campaigning to succeed Clinton, George W. Bush echoed both Nixon and Berger: "America has never been an empire. We may be the only great power in history that had the chance, and refused — preferring greatness to power, and justice to glory." He has reverted to this theme on several occasions since entering the White House. In a speech he made at the American Enterprise Institute shortly before the invasion of Iraq, Bush stated: "The US has no intention of determining the precise form of Iraq's new government. That choice belongs to the Iraqi people. . . . We will remain in Iraq as long as necessary and not a day more. America has made and kept this kind of commitment before in the peace that followed a world war. After defeating enemies, we did not leave behind occupying armies, we left constitutions and parliaments." He reiterated this lack of imperial intent in a television address to the Iraqi people on April 10, when he declared: "We will help you build a peaceful and representative government that protects the rights of all citizens. And then our military forces will leave. Iraq will go forward as a unified, independent and sovereign nation." Speaking on board the *Abraham Lincoln* aircraft carrier on May 1, [2003] the president rammed the point home: "Other nations in history have fought in foreign lands and remained to occupy and exploit. Americans, following a battle, want nothing more than to return home." . . . Indeed, it appears to be one of the few issues about which all the principal figures in the Bush administration are agreed. Speaking at the George Washington University in September last year [2003], Secretary of State Colin Powell insisted: "The United States does not seek a territorial empire. We have never been imperialists. We seek a world in which liberty, prosperity and peace can become the heritage of all peoples, and not just the exclusive privilege of a few."

Few Americans would dissent from this. Revealingly, four out of five Americans polled by the Pew Global Attitudes survey last year agreed that it was "good that American ideas and customs were spreading around the world." But were the same people to be asked if they considered this a consequence of American imperialism, hardly any would concur.

Freud defined *denial* as a primitive psychological defense mechanism against trauma. Perhaps it was therefore inevitable that in the aftermath of the September 11 attacks, Americans would deny their country's imperial character more vehemently than ever. Yet as U.S. foreign policy has moved from the defense to the offense, the need for denial would seem to have diminished. It may thus be therapeutic to determine the precise nature of this empire — since empire it is, in all but name.

Hegemony and Empire

Julius Caesar called himself *imperator* [emperor] but never king. His adopted heir Augustus preferred *princeps.* Emperors can call themselves what they like, and so can empires. The kingdom of England was proclaimed an empire — by Henry VIII — before it became one. The United States by contrast has long been an empire, but eschews the appellation.

Define the term *empire* narrowly enough, of course, and the United States can easily be excluded from the category. Here is a typical example: "Real imperial power . . . means a *direct* monopoly control over the organization and use of armed might. It means *direct* control over the administration of justice and the definition thereof. It means control over what is bought and sold, the terms of trade and the permission to trade. . . . Let us stop talking of an American empire, for there is and there will be no such thing." For a generation of "realist" writers, eager to rebut Soviet charges of American imperialism, it became conventional to argue that the United States had only briefly flirted with this kind of formal empire, beginning with the annexation of the Philippines in 1898 and ending by the 1930s. What the United States did after the end of the Second World War was, however, fundamentally different in character. According to one recent formulation, it was "not an imperial state with a predatory intent"; it was "more concerned with enhancing regional stability and security and protecting international trade than enlarging its power at the expense of others."

If the United States was not an empire, then what was it? And what is it now that the empire it was avowedly striving to "contain" is no more? "The only superpower" — existing in a "unipolar" world — is one way of describing it. *Hyperpuissance* [hyperpower] was the (certainly ironical) coinage of the former French foreign minister Hubert Védrine. Some writers favor more anemic terms like global *leadership,* while Philip Bobbitt simply regards the United States as a particularly successful form of nation-state. A recent series of seminars at Harvard's Kennedy School opted for the inoffensive term *primacy.* But by far the most popular term among writers on international relations remains *hegemon.*

What is this thing called hegemony? Is it merely a euphemism for *empire,* or does it describe the role of the primus inter pares, the leader of an alliance, rather than a ruler over subject peoples? And what are the hegemon's motives? Does it exert power beyond its borders for its own self-interested purposes? Or is it engaged altruistically in the provision of international public goods?

The word was used originally to describe the relationship of Athens to the other Greek city-states when they leagued together to defend themselves against the Persian Empire; Athens led but did not rule over the others. In so-called world-system theory, by contrast, hegemony means more than mere leadership, but less than outright empire. In yet another, narrower definition, the hegemon's principal function in the twentieth century was to underwrite a liberal international commercial and financial system. In what became known, somewhat inelegantly, as hegemonic stability theory, the fundamental question of the postwar period was how far and for how long the United States would remain committed to free trade once other economies, benefiting from precisely the liberal economic order made possible by U.S. hegemony, began to catch up. Would Americans revert to protectionist policies in an effort to perpetuate their hegemony or stick with free trade at the risk of experiencing relative decline? This has been called the hegemon's dilemma, and it appeared to many writers to be essentially the same dilemma that Britain had faced before 1914.

Yet if the British Empire was America's precursor as the global hegemon, might not the United States equally well be Britain's successor as an Anglophone [English-speaking] empire? Most historians would agree that, if anything, American economic power after 1945 exceeded that of Britain after 1815, a comparable watershed of power following the final defeat of Napoleonic France. First, the extraordinary growth in productivity achieved between around 1890 and 1950 eclipsed anything previously achieved by Britain, even in the first flush of the Industrial Revolution. Secondly, the United States very deliberately used its power to advance multilateral and mutually balanced tariff reductions under the General Agreement on Tariffs and Trade (later the World Trade Organization). Thus the reductions of tariffs achieved in the Kennedy Round (1967) and in subsequent "rounds" of negotiation owed much to American pressures such as the "conditionality" attached to loans from the Washington-based International Monetary Fund. By contrast, the nineteenth-century spread of free trade and free navigation — the "public goods" most commonly attributed to the British Empire — were as much spontaneous phenomena as they were direct consequences of British power. Thirdly, successive U.S. governments allegedly took advantage of the dollar's role as a key currency before and after the breakdown of Bretton Woods. The U.S. government had access to a "gold mine of paper" and could therefore collect a subsidy from foreigners in the form of seigniorage (by selling foreigners dollars and dollar-denominated assets that then depreciated in value). The gold standard offered Britain no such advantages, and perhaps even some disadvantages. Finally, the Pax Britannica depended mainly on the Royal Navy and was less "penetrative" than the "full-spectrum dominance" aimed for today by the American military. For a century, with the sole exception of the Crimean War, Britain felt unable to undertake military interventions in Europe, the theater most vital to its own survival, and when it was forced to do so in 1914 and in 1939, it struggled to prevail. We arrive at the somewhat paradoxical conclusion that a hegemon can be more powerful than an empire.

The distinction between hegemony and empire would be legitimate if the term *empire* did simply mean, as so many American commentators seem to assume, direct rule over foreign territories without any political representation of their inhabitants. But students of imperial history have a more sophisticated conceptual framework than that. At the time, British colonial administrators like Frederick Lugard clearly understood the distinction between "direct" and "indirect" rule; large parts of the British Empire in Asia and Africa were ruled indirectly — that is, through the agency of local potentates rather than British governors. A further distinction was introduced by John Gallagher and Ronald Robinson in their seminal 1953 article on "the imperialism of free trade." This encapsulated the way the Victorians used their naval and financial power to open the markets of countries outside their colonial ambit. Equally illuminating is the now widely accepted distinction between "formal" and "informal empire." The British did not formally govern Argentina, for example, but the merchant banks of the City of London exerted such a powerful influence on its fiscal and monetary policy that Argentina's independence was heavily qualified. In the words of one of the few modern historians to attempt a genuinely comparative study of the subject, an empire is "first and foremost, a very great power that has left its mark on the international relations of an era . . . a polity that rules over wide territories and many peoples, since the management of space and multi-ethnicity is one of the great perennial dilemmas of empire. . . . An empire is by definition . . . not a polity ruled with the explicit consent of its peoples. [But] by a process of assimilation of peoples [and] of democratization of institutions empires can transform themselves into multinational federations or even nation states." It is possible to be still more precise than this. In table 1 below I have attempted a simple typology intended to capture the diversity of forms that can be subsumed under the category "empires." Note that the table should be read as a menu rather than as a grid. For example, an empire could be an oligarchy at home, aiming to acquire raw materials from abroad, thereby increasing international trade, using mainly military methods, imposing a market economy, in the interests of its ruling elite, with a hierarchical social character. Another empire might be a democracy at home, mainly interested in security, providing peace as a public good, ruling mainly through firms and NGOs [nongovernmental organizations], promoting a mixed economy, in the interests of all inhabitants, with an assimilative social character.

The first column reminds us that imperial power can be acquired by more than one type of political system. The self-interested objectives of imperial expansion (column two) range from the fundamental need to ensure the security of the metropolis by imposing order on enemies at its (initial) borders to the collection of rents and taxation from subject peoples, to say nothing of the perhaps more obvious prizes of new land for settlement, raw materials, treasure and manpower, all of which, it should be emphasized, would need to be available at lower prices than they would cost in free exchange with independent peoples if the cost of conquest and colonization were to be justified. At the same time, an empire may provide "public goods" — that is, intended or unintended benefits of imperial rule flowing not to the rulers but to the ruled and indeed beyond to third parties: less conflict, increased trade or investment, improved justice or governance, better education (which may or may not be associated with religious conversion, something we would not nowadays regard as a public good) or improved material conditions. The fourth column tells us that imperial rule can be implemented by more than one kind of functionary: soldiers, civil servants, settlers, voluntary associations,

TABLE 1

Metropolitan System	Self-interested Objectives	Public Goods	Methods of Rule	Economic System	Cui Bouo?	Social Character
Tyranny	Security	Peace	Military	Plantation	Ruling elite	Genocidal
Aristocracy	Communications	Trade	Bureaucracy	Feudal	Metropolitan populace	Hierarchical
Oligarchy	Land	Investment	Settlement	Mercantilist	Settlers	Converting
Democracy	Raw materials	Law	NGOs	Market	Local elites	Assimilative
	Treasure	Governance	Firms	Mixed	All inhabitants	
	Manpower	Education	Delegation to local elites	Planned		
	Rents	Conversion				
	Taxation	Health				

firms and local elites all can in different ways impose the will of the center on the periphery. There are almost as many varieties of imperial economic system, ranging from slavery to laissez-faire, from one form of serfdom (feudalism) to another (the planned economy). Nor is it by any means a given that the benefits of empire should flow simply to the metropolitan society. It may only be the elite of that society that reaps the benefits of empire (as Lance E. Davis and R. A. Huttenback claimed in the case of the British Empire); it may be colonists drawn from lower-income groups in the metropole; it may in some cases be subject peoples or the elites within subject societies. Finally, the social character of an empire — to be precise, the attitudes of the rulers toward the ruled — may vary. At one extreme lies the genocidal empire of National Socialist Germany, intent on the annihilation of specific ethnic groups and the deliberate degradation of others. At the other extreme lies the Roman model of empire, in which citizenship was obtainable under certain conditions regardless of ethnicity (a model with obvious applicability to the case of the United States). In the middle lies the Victorian model of complex racial and social hierarchy, in which inequalities of wealth and status were mitigated by a general (though certainly not unqualified) principle of equality before the law. The precise combination of all these variables determines, among other things, the geographical extent — and of course the duration — of an empire.

With a broader and more sophisticated definition of empire, it seems possible to dispense altogether with the term *hegemony*. Instead, it can be argued with some plausibility that the American empire has up until now, with a few exceptions, preferred indirect rule to direct rule and informal empire to formal empire. Indeed, its Cold War–era hegemony might better be understood as an "empire by invitation." The question is whether or not the recent, conspicuously uninvited invasions of Afghanistan and Iraq presage a transition to more direct and formal imperial structures. Adapting the terminology of table 1, the American empire can therefore be summed up as follows. It goes without saying that it is a liberal democracy and market economy, though its polity has some illiberal characteristics and its economy a surprisingly high level of state intervention ("mixed" might be more accurate than "market"). It is primarily concerned with its own security and maintaining international communications and, secondarily, with ensuring access to raw materials (principally, though not exclusively, oil). It is also in the business of providing a limited number of public goods: peace, by intervening against some bellicose regimes and in some civil wars; freedom of the seas and skies for trade; and a distinctive form of "conversion" usually called Americanization, which is carried out less by old-style Christian missionaries than by the exporters of American consumer goods and entertainment. Its methods of formal rule are primarily military in character; its methods of informal rule rely heavily on nongovernmental organizations and corporations and, in some cases, local elites.

Who benefits from this empire? Some would argue, with the economist Paul Krugman, that only its wealthy elite does — specifically, that part of its wealthy elite associated with the Republican Party and the oil industry. The conventional wisdom on the Left is that the United States uses its power to impoverish people in the developing world. Others would claim that many millions of people around the world have benefited in some way or another from the existence of America's empire — not least the West Europeans, Japanese and South Koreans who were able to prosper during the Cold War under the protection of the American nuclear "umbrella" — and that the economic losers of the post–Cold War era, particularly in sub-Saharan Africa, are victims not of American power but of its absence. For the American empire is limited in its extent. It conspicuously lacks the voracious appetite for territorial expansion overseas that characterized the empires of the West European seaboard. It prefers the idea that foreigners will Americanize themselves without the need for formal rule. Even when it conquers, it resists annexation — one reason why the duration of its offshore imperial undertakings has tended to be, and will in all probability continue to be, relatively short. Indeed, a peculiarity of American imperialism — perhaps its principal shortcoming — is its excessively short time horizon.

ANGLOPHONE EMPIRES

All told, there have been no more than seventy empires in history. If the *Times Atlas of World History* is to be believed, the American is, by my count, the sixty-eighth. (Communist China is the sixty-ninth; some would claim that the European Union is the seventieth.) How different is the American empire from previous empires? Like the ancient Egyptian, it erects towering edifices in its heartland, though these house the living rather than the dead. Like the Athenian Empire, it has proved itself adept at leading alliances against a rival power. Like the empire of Alexander, it has a staggering geographical range. Like the Chinese Empire that arose in the Ch'in era and reached its zenith under the Ming dynasty, it has united the lands and peoples of a vast territory and forged them into a true nation-state. Like the Roman Empire, it has a system of citizenship that is remarkably open: Purple Hearts and U.S. citizenship were conferred simultaneously on a number of the soldiers serving in Iraq last year, just as service in the legions was once a route to becoming a *civis romanus*. Indeed, with the classical architecture of its capital and the republican structure of its constitution, the United States is perhaps more like a "new Rome" than any previous empire — albeit a Rome in which the Senate has thus far retained its grip on would-be emperors. In its relationship with Western Europe too, the United States can sometimes seem like a second Rome, though it seems premature to hail Brussels as the new Byzantium.

The Roman parallel is in danger of becoming something of a cliché. Yet in its capacity for spreading its own language and culture — at once monotheistic and mathematical — the United States also shares features of the Abbasid caliphate erected by the heirs of Muhammad. Though it is often portrayed as the heir — as well as the rebellious product — of the western European empires that arose in the sixteenth century and persisted until the twentieth, in truth the United States has as much, if not more, in common with the great land empires of central and eastern Europe. In the nineteenth century the westward sweep of American settlers across the prairies had its mirror image in the eastward sweep of Russian settlers across the steppe. In practice, its political structures are sometimes more reminiscent of Vienna or Berlin than they are of The Hague, capital of the last great imperial republic, or London, hub of the first Anglophone empire. To those who would still insist on American "exceptionalism," the historian of empires can only retort: as exceptional as all the other sixty-nine empires.

Let us consider more precisely the similarities and differences between this American empire and the British Empire, against which the United States at first defined itself, but which it increasingly resembles, as rebellious sons grow to resemble the fathers they once despised. The relationship between the two Anglophone empires is one of the leitmotifs [themes] of this [essay] for the simple reason that no other empire in history has come so close to achieving the things that the United States wishes to achieve today. Britain's era of "liberal empire" — from around the 1850s until the 1930s — stands out as a time when the leading imperial power successfully underwrote economic globalization by exporting not just its goods, its people and its capital but also its social and political institutions. The two Anglophone empires have much in common. But they are also profoundly different.

As we have seen, the United States is considered by some historians to be a more effective "hegemon" than Great Britain. Yet in strictly territorial terms, the latter was far the more impressive empire. At its maximum extent between the world wars the British Empire covered more than 13 million square miles, approximately 23 percent of the world's land surface. Only a tiny fraction of that was accounted for by the United Kingdom itself: a mere 0.2 percent. Today, by contrast, the United States accounts for around 6.5 percent of the world's surface, whereas its fourteen formal dependencies — mostly Pacific islands acquired before the Second World War — amount to a mere 4,140 square miles of territory. Even if the United States had never relinquished the countries it at one time or another occupied in the Caribbean and Latin America between the Spanish-American War and the Second World War, the American empire today would amount to barely one-half of 1 percent of the world's land surface. In demographic terms, the formal American empire is even more minuscule. Today the United

States and its dependencies together account for barely 5 percent of the world's population, whereas the British ruled between a fifth and a quarter of humanity at the zenith of their empire.

On the other hand, the United States possesses a great many small areas of territory within notionally sovereign states that serve as bases for its armed services. Before the deployment of troops for the invasion of Iraq, the U.S. military had around 752 military installations in more than 130 countries. Significant numbers of American troops were stationed in 65 of these. Their locations significantly qualify President Bush's assertion in his speech of February 26, 2003, that "after defeating enemies [in 1945], we did not leave behind occupying armies." In the first year of his presidency, around 70,000 U.S. troops were stationed in Germany, and 40,000 in Japan. American troops have been in those countries continuously since 1945. Almost as many (36,500) were in South Korea, where the American presence has been uninterrupted since 1950. Moreover, new wars have meant new bases, like Camp Bondsteel in Kosovo, acquired during the 1999 war against Yugoslavia, or the Bishkek air base in Kyrgyzstan, an "asset" picked up during the war against the Taliban regime in Afghanistan. At the time of writing, about 10,000 American troops are still based in Afghanistan, and it seems certain that a substantial force of 100,000 will have to remain in Iraq for at least the next few years.

Nor should it be forgotten what formidable military technology can be unleashed from these bases. Commentators like to point out that "the Pentagon's budget is equal to the combined military budgets of the next 12 or 15 nations" and that "the US accounts for 40–45 per cent of all the defense spending of the world's 189 states." Such fiscal measures, impressive though they sound, nevertheless understate the lead currently enjoyed by American armed forces. On land the United States has 9,000 M1 Abrams tanks. The rest of the world has nothing that can compete. At sea the United States possesses nine "supercarrier" battle groups. The rest of the world has none. And in the air the United States has three different kinds of undetectable stealth aircraft. The rest of the world has none. The United States is also far ahead in the production of "smart" missiles and pilotless high-altitude "drones." The British Empire never enjoyed this kind of military lead over the competition. Granted, there was a time when its network of naval and military bases bore a superficial resemblance to America's today. The number of troops stationed abroad was also roughly the same. The British too relished their technological superiority, whether it took the form of the Maxim gun or the *Dreadnought*. But their empire never dominated the full spectrum of military capabilities the way the United States does today. Though the Royal Navy ruled the waves, the French and later the Germans — to say nothing of the Americans — were able to build fleets that posed credible threats to that maritime dominance, while the British army was generally much smaller and more widely dispersed than the armies of the continental empires.

If military power is the sine qua non [essential feature] of an empire, then it is hard to imagine how anyone could deny the imperial character of the United States today. Conventional maps of U.S. military deployments understate the extent of America's military reach. A Defense Department map of the world, which shows the areas of responsibility of the five major regional commands, suggests that America's sphere of military influence is now literally global. The regional combatant commanders — the "proconsuls" of this imperium — have responsibility for swaths of territory beyond the wildest imaginings of their Roman predecessors. USEUCOM extends from the westernmost shore of Greenland to the Bering Strait, from the Arctic Ocean to the Cape of Good Hope, from Iceland to Israel.

It is of course a truth universally acknowledged that large overseas military commitments cannot be sustained without even larger economic resources. Is America rich enough to play the part of Atlas, bearing the weight of the whole world on its shoulders? This was a question posed so frequently in the 1970s and 1980s that it became possible to speak of "declinism" as a school of thought. According to Paul Kennedy, military and fiscal "overstretch" doomed the United States — like all "great powers" before it — to lose its position of economic dominance. For a brief time after the fall of the Berlin Wall it was possible to rejoice that the Soviet Union had succumbed to overstretch first. The economic travails of Japan, once touted as a future geopolitical contender, added to the sense of national recuperation. While America savored a period of "relative ascent" unlike any since the 1920s, when an earlier peace dividend had fueled an earlier stock market bubble, declinism itself declined. By the end of the 1990s, however, commentators had found new rivals about which to worry. Some feared the European Union. Others looked with apprehension toward China. Samuel Huntington too saw "unipolarity" as only a transient phenomenon: as Europe united and China grew richer, so the world would revert to a "multipolarity" not seen since before the Second World War. In Emmanuel Todd's eyes, French fears about American "hyperpower" ignored the reality of an impending decline and fall.

If recent rates of growth of population and output were to continue for another twenty years, America could conceivably be overtaken as the largest economy in the world by China as early as 2018. Yet it is highly unlikely that growth rates in either country will be the same in the next two decades as in the previous two. All we can say with certainty is that in 2002 American gross domestic product, calculated in international dollars and adjusted on the basis of purchasing power parity, was nearly twice that of China and accounted for just over a fifth (21.4 percent) of total world output — more than the Japanese, German and British shares put together. That exceeds the highest share of global output ever achieved by Great Britain by a factor of more than two. Indeed, calculated in current U.S. dollars, the American share of the world's gross output was closer to a third (32.3 percent), double the size of the Chinese and Japanese economies combined. In terms of both production and consumption, the United States is already a vastly wealthier empire than Britain ever was.

Nor are these the only measures of American economic dominance. In Britain's imperial heyday, only a handful of corporations could really be described as "multinational," in the sense of having substantial proportions of their assets and workforce in overseas markets. Today the world economy is dominated by such firms, a substantial number of which — ranging from Exxon Mobil to General Motors, from McDonald's to Coca-Cola, from Microsoft to Time Warner — are American in origin and continue to have their headquarters in the United States. The recent history of McDonald's provides a vivid example of the way American corporations have expanded overseas in search of new markets, much as the old Hobson-Lenin theory of imperialism would have led one to expect. In 1967 McDonald's opened its first foreign outlets in Canada and Puerto Rico. Twenty years later it had nearly 10,000 restaurants in 47 countries and territories, and by 1997 no fewer than 23,000 restaurants in over 100 countries. In 1999, for the first time, the company's foreign sales exceeded its American sales. Today there are more than 30,000 McDonald's restaurants in over 120 countries; fewer than half, 12,800, are in the United States. Like Donald Rumsfeld, Ronald McDonald needs his map of the world, and it presents a striking alternative geography of American empire. In the words of the company's chief operating officer, "There are 6½ billion people on the Earth and only 270 million live in the US. . . . Who else is positioned around the globe to deal with that opportunity?" *Coca-colonization* is a hackneyed catchphrase of the antiglobalization "movement," but it conveys a certain truth when one considers the geographical range of the soft drink company's sales: 30 percent to North America, 24 percent to Latin America, 22 percent to Europe and the Middle East, 18 percent to Asia and 6 percent to Africa. Significantly, the Real Thing's fastest-growing market is the People's Republic of China.

The relatively rapid growth of the American economy in the 1980s and 1990s — at a time when the economy of its principal Cold War rival was imploding — explains how the United States has managed to achieve a unique revolution in military affairs while at the same time substantially reducing the share of defense expenditures as a proportion of gross domestic product. The Defense Department Green Paper published in March 2003 forecast total expenditure on national defense to remain constant at 3.5 percent of GDP for at least three years. That should be compared with an average figure during the Cold War of 7 percent. Given Paul Kennedy's "formula" that "if a particular nation is allocating *over the long term* more than 10 per cent . . . of GNP to armaments, that is likely to limit its growth rate," there seems little danger of imminent imperial overstretch. In short, in terms of economic resources as well as of military capability the United States not only resembles but in some respects exceeds the last great Anglophone empire.

GOING SOFT

One argument sometimes advanced to distinguish American hegemony from British empire is qualitative. American power, it is argued, consists not just of military and economic power but also of "soft" power. According to Joseph Nye, the dean of Harvard's Kennedy School, "A country may obtain the outcomes it wants in world politics because other countries want to follow it, admiring its values, emulating its example, aspiring to its level of prosperity and openness." Soft power, in other words, is getting what you want without "force or inducement," sticks or carrots: "It is the ability to entice and attract. Soft power arises in large part from our values." In America's case, "it comes from being a shining 'city upon a hill'" — an enticing new Jerusalem of economic and political liberty. Nye is not so naive as to assume that the American way is inherently attractive to everyone, everywhere. But he does believe that making it attractive matters more than in the past because of the global spread of information technology. To put it simply, soft power — or what other writers have called Americanization — can reach the parts that hard power cannot reach.

But does this make American power so very different from imperial power? On the contrary. If anything, it illustrates how very like the last Anglophone empire the United States has become. The British Empire too sought to make its values attractive to others, though initially — before the advent of modern communications technology — the job had to be done by "men on the spot." British missionaries, intent on spreading their islands' various brands of Christianity, fanned out across the globe. British businessmen too introduced their distinctive styles of accounting and management. British administrators applied their notions of law and order. And British schoolmasters drummed reading, writing and arithmetic into colonial elites. Together all of them contrived to spread British leisure pursuits like cricket and afternoon tea. The aim was without question to "entice and attract" people toward British values. Moreover, these footslogging efforts were eventually reinforced by new technology. After the advent of transoceanic telegraphs, London-based press agencies could supply newspapers around the world with Anglocentric content, but it was the advent of wireless radio — and specifically the creation of the British Broadcasting Corporation [BBC] — that really ushered in the age of soft power in Nye's sense of the term. On Christmas Day 1932 King George V was able to broadcast to the entire British Empire. Within six years the BBC had launched its first foreign-language service — in Arabic — and by the end of 1938 it was broadcasting in all the major languages of continental Europe. There is no question that the BBC played an important part in encouraging dissent in Axis-occupied territories during the war; why else did Joseph Goebbels [Nazi propaganda chief] so obsessively prosecute Germans caught listening to it? In some ways, the soft power that Britain could exert in the 1930s was greater than the soft power of the United States today. In a world of newspapers, radio receivers and cinemas, in which the number of content-supplying corporations (often national monopolies) was relatively small, the overseas broadcasts of the BBC could hope to reach a relatively large number of foreign ears. Yet whatever soft power Britain thereby wielded did little to halt the precipitous decline of British power after the 1930s.

This raises the question of how much America's soft power really matters today. If the term is to denote anything more than cultural background music to more traditional forms of dominance, it surely needs to be demonstrated that the United States can secure what it wants from other countries without coercing them or suborning them, but purely because its cultural exports are seductive. One reason for skepticism about the extent of American soft power today is the geographical reach of these cultural exports. True, thirty-nine of the world's eighty-one largest telecommunications corporations are American, and around half of all the world's countries rely principally on the United States to supply their cinemas with films. But a very large proportion of Hollywood's exports go to long-standing American allies within the Organization of Economic Co-operation and Development. Apart from Japan, Asian countries — particularly India — import very few American productions. Likewise, most translations of American books and foreign users of American Internet sites are to be found in Europe and Japan. The only other region where a major channel of communication may be said to be dominated by American culture is Latin America, where 75 percent of television programs are U.S.-made. It would be too much to conclude that American soft power is therefore abundant where it is least needed. It may well be that a high level of exposure to American cinema and television is one of the reasons why people in Western Europe, Japan and Latin America are still, on the whole, less hostile to the United States than their counterparts elsewhere. Still, the fact remains that the range of American soft power is more limited than is generally assumed. The Middle East, where the BBC began its foreign-language broadcasting, is now much more resistant to the charms of "Anglobalization" than it was then. The advent of Al Jazeera shows that the entry barrier into the soft power game is now quite low. Even in war-torn Somalia, American forces found their foes able to dominate the local air-waves with anti-American propaganda. Soft power could not avert genocide in Rwanda: when the United Nations Secretary-General Boutros Boutros-Ghali asked the Clinton administration to jam the murderous broadcasts of Radio Mille Collines, he was informed that such a step would be too expensive.

There is one exception, and that exception provides another example of what the British Empire and today's American empire have in common. Missionaries are as important a channel for cultural dissemination in the developing world today as they were a century and a half ago. Because of the multiplicity of Christian sects involved, it is not easy to find reliable figures for the total number of American missionaries working outside the United States today. Estimates (for Protestant missionaries only) suggest that there are between 40,000 and 64,000, a relatively small number compared with the 300,000 or so American missionaries working within the United States. Nevertheless, even small numbers of evangelical missionaries can achieve a good deal, furnished as they are with substantial funds from congregations at home. In April 1994 the Churches of Christ had a total of 223 missionaries in Latin America, with the largest number (81) in Brazil. Seven years later, although the number of missionaries in the region had fallen by nearly half, the total membership of Churches of Christ congregations had increased by 60 percent. One estimate (published in 1990) puts the proportion of Latin Americans who are now Protestant as high as 20 percent. The extraordinary display of evangelical faith by the victorious Brazilian team after the last soccer World Cup final lends credibility to that estimate. More recently, encouraged by evangelists like Luis Bush (himself born in Argentina), missionaries have turned their attention to the "unevangelized" millions who inhabit a so-called window of opportunity between the tenth and fortieth latitudes. According to the Center for the Study of Global Christianity at Gordon-Conwell Theological Seminary in South Hamilton, Massachusetts, the number of Christian missionaries to Islamic countries has almost doubled since 1982, from around 15,000 to 27,000; half of them are Americans.

But what of America's official, secular values and altruistic goals? Are these not fundamentally different from those of past empires, which were selfish and exploitative in their intentions? It is often argued that American policy makers since Woodrow Wilson have renounced imperialism, seeking instead to encourage the spread of Wilsonian principles: international law, democracy and the free market. Somehow — presumably because they are so self-evidently good — these ideas have "come to dominate international affairs." The most that the United States therefore needs to do is "act as the chief of the constabulary" to prevent any unenlightened forces from challenging this benign world order.

There is certainly no shortage of vintage Wilsonian rhetoric in President Bush's "National Security Strategy" published in September 2002, which explicitly states that it is a goal of American foreign policy "to extend the benefits of freedom across the globe." "We will actively work," the document declares, "to bring the hope of democracy, development, free markets, and free trade to every corner of the world . . . America must stand firmly for the nonnegotiable demands of human dignity: the rule of law; limits on the absolute power of the state; free speech; freedom of worship; equal justice; respect for women; religious and ethnic tolerance; and respect for private property." Yet this "strategy of openness" is not without its imperial precursors. From the second half of the nineteenth century until the Great Depression, the British Empire shared many of the same aspirations. The young Winston Churchill once defined the goals of British imperialism as being "[to reclaim] from barbarism fertile regions and large populations . . . to give peace to warring tribes, to administer justice where all was violence, to strike the chains off the slave, to draw the richness from the soil, to plant the earliest seeds of commerce and learning, to increase in whole peoples their capacities for pleasure and diminish their chances of pain. . . ." Is this so very different from the language of American idealism? As Senator J. William Fulbright observed in 1968, "The British called it the 'white man's burden.' The French called it their 'civilizing mission.' Nineteenth-century Americans called it 'manifest destiny.' It is now being called the 'responsibilities of power.'" The "promotion of freedom" or the "strategy of openness" is merely its latest incarnation. The fact is that liberal empires nearly always proclaim their own altruism. When he spoke of the United States as an "empire of liberty," Thomas Jefferson was merely purloining a hoary trope of British imperialism. Edmund Burke had identified "freedom" as a defining characteristic of the British Empire as early as 1766.

Like the British Empire, in any case, the United States reserves the right to use military force, as and when it sees its interests threatened — not merely reactively but on occasion preemptively. Thus President Bush's "National Security Strategy" asserts that the United States reserves the right to "act preemptively . . . to forestall or prevent . . . hostile acts by our adversaries . . . even if uncertainty remains as to the time and place of the enemy's attack." Soft power is merely the velvet glove concealing an iron hand.

A BRITISH MODEL?

Unlike the majority of European writers who have written on this subject, I am fundamentally in favor of empire. Indeed, I believe that empire is more necessary in the twenty-first century than ever before. The threats we face are not in themselves new ones. But advances in technology make them more dangerous than ever before. Thanks to the speed and regularity of modern air travel, infectious diseases can be transmitted to us with terrifying swiftness. And thanks to the relative cheapness and destructiveness of modern weaponry, tyrants and terrorists can realistically think of devastating our cities. The old, post-1945 system of sovereign states, bound loosely together by an evolving system of international law, cannot easily deal with these threats because there are too many nation-states where the writ of the "international community" simply does not run. What is required is an agency capable of intervening in the affairs of such states to contain epidemics, depose tyrants, end local wars and eradicate terrorist organizations. This is the self-interested argument for empire. But there is also a complementary altruistic argument. Even if they did not pose a direct threat to the security of the United States, the economic and social conditions in a number of countries in the world would justify some kind of intervention. The poverty of a country like Liberia is explicable not in terms of resource endowment; otherwise (for example) Botswana would be just as poor. The problem in Liberia, as in so many sub-Saharan African states, is simply misgovernment: corrupt and lawless dictators whose conduct makes economic development impossible and encourages political opposition to take the form of civil war. Countries in this condition will not correct themselves. They require the imposition of some kind of external authority.

There are those who would insist that an empire is by definition incapable of playing such a role; in their eyes, all empires are exploitative in character. Yet there can be — and has been — such a thing as a liberal empire, one that enhances its own security and prosperity precisely by providing the rest of the world with generally beneficial public goods: not only economic freedom but also the institutions necessary for markets to flourish. In this regard, Americans have more to learn than they are prepared to admit from their more self-confident British predecessors, who, after the mid-nineteenth-century calamities of the Irish Famine and the Indian Mutiny, recast their empire as an economically liberal project, concerned as much with the integration of global markets as with the security of the British Isles, predicated on the idea that British rule was conferring genuine benefits in the form of free trade, the rule of law, the safeguarding of private property rights and noncorrupt administration, as well as government-guaranteed investments in infrastructure, public health and (some) education. Arnold Toynbee's injunction to his Oxford tutorial pupils destined for the Indian Civil Service was clear: "If they went to India they were to go there for the good of her people on one of the noblest missions on which an Englishman could be engaged."

Let me emphasize that it is not my intention to suggest that Americans should somehow adopt the Victorians as role models. The British Empire was very far from an *ideal* liberal empire, and there is almost as much to be learned from its failures as from its successes. But the resemblances between what the British were attempting to do in 1904 and what the United States is trying to do in 2004 are nevertheless instructive. Like the United States today, Great Britain was very ready to use its naval and military superiority to fight numerous small wars against what we might now call failed states and rogue regimes. No one who has studied the history of the British campaign against the Sudanese dervishes, the followers of the charismatic Wahhabist leader known as the Mahdi, can fail to be struck by its intimations of present-day conflicts. Yet like the United States today, the Victorian imperialists did not act purely in the name of national or imperial security. Just as American presidents of recent decades have consistently propounded the benefits of economic globalization — even when they have deviated from free trade in practice — British statesmen a century ago regarded the spread of free trade and the liberalization of commodity, labor and capital markets as desirable for the general good. And just as most Americans today regard global democratization on the American model as self-evidently good, so the British in those days aspired to export their own institutions — not just the common law but ultimately also parliamentary monarchy — to the rest of the world.

Americans easily forget that after the blunders of the late eighteenth century, British governments learned that it was perfectly easy to grant "responsible government" to colonies that were clearly well advanced along the road to economic modernity and social stability. Canada, New Zealand, Australia and (albeit with a restricted franchise) South Africa all had executives accountable to elected parliaments by the early 1900s. Nor was this benefit intended to be the exclusive preserve of the colonies of white settlement. On the question of whether India should ultimately be capable of British-style parliamentary government, Thomas Babington Macaulay was quite explicit, if characteristically condescending: "Never will I attempt to avert or to retard it [Indian self-government]. Whenever it comes it will be the proudest day in English history. To have found a great people sunk in the lowest depths of slavery and superstition, to have ruled them as to have made them desirous and capable of all the privileges of citizens, would indeed be a title to glory all our own." Not dissimilar aspirations were being expressed in some quarters last year on the subject of democratizing the Arab world. Speaking at the United Nations in September of last year, President Bush himself made it clear that this was one of his objectives in invading Iraq.

QUESTIONS TO CONSIDER

1. Why, according to Ferguson, have many Americans been reluctant to refer to an "American Empire"? Why has this inhibition begun to fall away in recent years?

2. What are the different ways that "empire" can be defined? According to the author, how is empire similar or different from hegemony? How can imperialism include direct or indirect rule? Where does the present-day United States fit in Ferguson's typology of empires? Why does Ferguson call America "[only] as exceptional as all the other sixty-nine empires"?

3. How does Ferguson compare the present world position of the United States to that of Great Britain at the height of its empire (from the 1850s to the 1930s)? Consider issues of territorial expanse, military power, economic dominance, "soft power," globalization, foreign-policy goals, and attitudes toward imperial rule. What resemblances does Ferguson see between "what the British were attempting to do in 1904 and what the United States is trying to do in 2004"? What differences?

4. According to Ferguson, in what ways could the British Empire serve as a model for an American version of "liberal imperialism"? What lessons should the United States today draw from the British experience of empire? Why does Ferguson believe that "empire is more necessary in the twenty-first century than ever before"?

What should the United States do to take up the imperial burden it has inherited from Britain? Does Ferguson believe that Americans will embrace empire? Why or why not?

5. Many scholars assert that the United States is an empire, or has been one at some point in its history, but they use the term in different ways. Compare the nature of imperialism as described by Ferguson with the versions of American empire portrayed by Robin Winks (Selection 9) and John Lewis Gaddis (Selection 19). What similarities or differences do you see? How useful are the distinctions these authors make between "formal" and "informal" empire, territorial possession and hegemony, or "empire by imposition" and "empire by invitation"? Would Winks agree with Ferguson's generally positive assessment of British imperialism? How do these authors describe American empire? Would Winks and Gaddis agree with Ferguson that Americans have been "in denial" about their nation's imperial power?

24

Globalization and
American Power

JOSEPH S. NYE JR.

The social science wordsmiths are at it again. In earlier chapters that covered industrializa-
tion and urbanization in the nineteenth century, we noticed that scholars coin new words —
often large, impersonal ones ending in "ation" — to describe social processes bigger than the
nation that have changed the lives of people around the world. Today's new word is "global-
ization," which is being invoked by political leaders and pundits as the growing transnational
force that everyone must reckon with. To be sure, globalization means different things to dif-
ferent people. There is widespread agreement, however, that the concept refers to an intense
acceleration of the movement of capital, goods, people, and information around the world dur-
ing the past generation. Its most obvious elements are the instant communication of com-
puters, the creation of a worldwide entertainment industry, and the widening effects of local
financial crises, but they also include the ominous rise of global terrorism.

In some ways, as Joseph Nye points out in the following essay, globalization is an old
story. Its seeds were planted when separate human societies or tribes first made contact with
one another through war, trade, and disease. Such contact started to reach truly global pro-
portions when the expansion of Europe's trade and influence in the 1500s, along with its
colonization of the Americas, joined most of the world's people into an economic system
dominated by western Europe. When Nye points out that the spread of the English lan-
guage and British legal institutions spurred globalization before the twentieth century, he ac-
knowledges the role that the British Empire played in imposing global uniformity, as Niall
Ferguson suggested in the previous selection. But Nye shows that after World War II dra-
matic new developments were at work to make globalization "thicker and quicker," so that
its effects are complex and sometimes unpredictable.

The United States, not Britain, took the lead in this recent round of globalization.
America emerged from the destruction of World War II as the world's preeminent economic
power, and it oversaw the expansion of free trade through new international financial
institutions such as the World Bank. The United States pioneered advances in computer
technology and the "information revolution" that replaced industrial manufacturing as the
driver of economic growth. The demise of the Soviet Union left the United States the lone

military superpower. Just as important, America's "soft power" — the attractiveness of its values and success, as opposed to the "hard power" of military or economic coercion — made its way of life a model for much of the world's people. As Nye points out, America's ethnic diversity and its openness to innovation ensured that its market would be a microcosm of the world and helped prepare American-produced movies, TV programs, and music to go out and conquer the globe.

Is globalization, then, just another name for American empire? Not really, says Nye. The historian Alexander Motyl defines empire as "a hierarchically organized political system with a hublike structure — a rimless wheel — within which a core elite and state dominate peripheral elites and societies by serving as intermediaries for their significant interactions." Evaluating this concept of empire, Nye demonstrates some of its shortcomings for describing today's global system. First, he points out, there are different dimensions of power besides the political. Nye envisions the contest for global power as a three-level gameboard. On the top level of military power, America dominates; on the middle board of economic power, it is one key player among several; and on the bottom board of "transnational relations . . . outside government control," including bankers and terrorists, America exerts relatively little control. Second, according to Nye, the hub-and-spokes image of empire overstresses the role of the United States in developing and controlling globalization. Rather than a highway radiating from an American "core," globalization is a two-way street that leaves the United States vulnerable to global economic competition, to backlash against increasing economic inequality, or to damage from planetary problems such as pollution or terrorism. Because power is being dispersed by alternative connections between the spokes, the United States is neither the center nor even sometimes in the loop. The new global network, Nye concludes, is a lot more like the Internet than an empire, more a web than a wheel.

What this suggests is that rather than unilateral actions like America's economic bullying of developing nations or its "preemptive war" against Iraq, some form of international cooperation will be necessary to manage globalization's problems. Globalization points toward a diffusion of power among nations as well as a growing role for new international players such as multinational corporations, churches, labor and environmental groups, and — unfortunately — computer hackers and terrorists. This trajectory shows why economically the United States will not be able to continue its domination and why politically it can't "go it alone." What form the new "multilateralism" may take is the subject of Nye's conclusion. Somewhere between an "American empire" and a beefed-up United Nations, he believes, a new system of shared international power will have to be organized. "The paradox of American power" — the title of Nye's book from which this excerpt is taken — is that as we proceed into the twenty-first century, America's might is "too great to be challenged by any other state, yet not great enough to solve problems such as global terrorism and nuclear proliferation." In contrast to Niall Ferguson's enthusiasm for empire (Selection 23), Nye suggests that Americans must trade imperial delusions for the realities of international negotiation and compromise.

With a broad view of the past informing its preview of America's and the world's future, Nye's essay provides a fitting conclusion to this book. Notice, too, how it incorporates the "four c's" of comparative history that were mentioned in the book's Preface. Nye examines a concept — globalization — that attempts to describe a universal social process or international trend. He provides a broad context for it by discussing the roots of globalization in a millennium of exploration and contact between peoples. He details connections between nations and peoples that have brought worldwide economic and cultural transformations. And he offers comparisons that document persisting national differences, such as those between the United States and Japan, despite globalization. It is my hope that Nye's essay and the others in this book have given you a sense of the varieties of comparative history and have demonstrated the value, and even the necessity, of viewing American history in international perspective.

GLOSSARY

ASYMMETRICAL WARFARE   Combat in which the opponents have markedly different military capabilities and the weaker side uses unconventional tactics, such as guerrilla warfare, land mines, or attacks on civilians.

EUROPEAN UNION (EU)   The organization for the political and economic integration of Europe that was established in 1993 as the successor to the Common Market (1958). Encompassing twenty-five nations, the EU includes a parliament and court system, a free-travel and -trade zone, and a common currency, the euro.

GENERAL AGREEMENT ON TARIFFS AND TRADE (GATT)   An agreement to phase out import quotas and to reduce tariffs that was negotiated by 23 nations in 1947. Enlarged to include 125 nations before it was replaced by the World Trade Organization in 1995, GATT played a major role in expanding world trade in the half-century after World War II.

GROSS DOMESTIC PRODUCT (GDP)   An indicator of national economic health that measures the market value of the nation's total output of goods and services (excluding income from overseas investment) in a given period, usually one year. The GDP's three main components are consumer purchases, private investment, and government spending.

INTERNATIONAL MONETARY FUND (IMF)   An agency of the United Nations set up in 1944 that uses a fund collected from member nations to purchase foreign currencies, with the goal of assisting payment of international debts and stabilizing exchange rates. It has been criticized for being dominated by the United States (its largest contributor), for bailing out incompetent or corrupt regimes, and for imposing rigid terms of economic development upon the nations it assists.

MEIJI RESTORATION   The surrender of power in 1868 by the Japanese shogun, or military ruler, to the young emperor Meiji (1852–1912) after agitation demanding a new government and stronger resistance to foreign economic influence. The restoration brought the downfall of feudalism, the establishment of a centralized administration, and the rise of westernizing leaders determined to make Japan a modern industrial state.

NORTH AMERICAN FREE TRADE AGREEMENT (NAFTA)   A 1992 trade pact that gradually eliminates most tariffs, customs duties, and other trade barriers among the United States, Canada, and Mexico. Its impact upon the member economies, including the loss of U.S. manufacturing jobs and the decline of Mexican family farms, remains controversial.

PROTECTIONISM   The policy of protecting domestic industries from foreign competition through subsidies or the placing of tariffs, quotas, or other legal restrictions on imports.

SILICON VALLEY   A high-technology industrial region around the southern shores of San Francisco Bay in California, so called because after the 1950s it became a center for computer manufacturing and research.

TIANANMEN SQUARE   A huge public square in central Beijing (Peking) where a series of pro-democracy student demonstrations in June 1989 were suppressed by the Chinese government with the loss of hundreds of lives.

WELFARE STATE   The expansion of national governments in developed Western nations from the 1870s to the 1960s to promote citizens' well-being in the areas of health, employment, family life, and retirement, and more generally, to mitigate the worst effects of urban-industrial capitalism.

WORLD BANK   Established in 1946, an international organization affiliated with the United Nations that provides loans for debt relief and for projects that promote economic growth in developing countries. Like the WTO, its policies encourage free-market reforms that have not always helped poorer nations.

WORLD TRADE ORGANIZATION (WTO)   The successor to GATT, the WTO was established in 1995 as an international body to monitor trade, ensure equal market access, reduce protectionism, and resolve international trade disputes. It expanded GATT's domain to cover services and intellectual property as well as goods. Opponents of globalization have criticized the WTO for promoting the interests of multinational corporations and for excluding protections against environmental damage or exploitation of low-skilled workers.

Americans feel their lives affected more and more by events originating outside the country. Terrorists from halfway around the world wrought havoc in New York and Washington. Or to take an economic example, who would have thought that imprudent banking practices in a small economy such as Thailand in 1997 would lead to the collapse of the Russian ruble, massive loans to stave off crisis in Brazil, and the New York Federal Reserve Bank's intervention to prevent the collapse of a hedge fund from harming the American economy? In an ecological example, helicopters recently fumigated many American cities in an attempt to eradicate the potentially lethal West Nile virus, which might have arrived in the blood of a traveler, via a bird smuggled through customs, or in the gut of a mosquito that flitted into a jet. . . . And as the twenty-first century began, rioters protesting globalization filled the streets of Washington, Prague, Quebec, Genoa, and other cities where leaders met.

MADE IN AMERICA?

Globalization — the growth of worldwide networks of interdependence — is virtually as old as human history. What's new is that the networks are thicker and more complex, involving people from more regions and social classes. The ancient Silk Road that linked medieval Europe and Asia is an example of the "thin" globalization that involved small amounts of luxury goods and elite customers. . . . Economic globalization increased dramatically in the nineteenth century. In their 1848 *Communist Manifesto,* Karl Marx and Friedrich Engels argued that "all old-established national industries have been destroyed or are being destroyed. . . . In place of the old local and national seclusion and self-sufficiency, we have intercourse in every direction, universal interdependence of nations."

The idea that globalization equals Americanization is common but simplistic. The United States itself is the product of seventeenth- and eighteenth-century globalization. As Adam Smith wrote in 1776, "the discovery of America, and that of a passage to the East Indies by the Cape of Good Hope, are the two greatest and most important events recorded in the history of mankind . . . by uniting, in some measure, the most distant parts of the world." But it is also true that the United States is a giant in the contemporary phase of globalization. In the words of French foreign minister Hubert Vedrine, "The United States is a very big fish that swims easily and rules supreme in the waters of globalization. Americans get great benefits from this for a large number of reasons: because of their economic size; because globalization takes place in their language; because it is organized along neoliberal economic principles; because they impose their legal, accounting, and technical practices; and because they're advocates of individualism."

It is understandable, and probably inevitable, that those who resent American power and popular culture use nationalism to fight it. In the 1940s, French officials sought to ban Coca-Cola, and it was not finally approved for sale in France until 1953. In a well-publicized 1999 case, José Bové, a French sheep farmer . . . , became a French hero and earned global press coverage by protecting "culinary sovereignty" through destroying a McDonald's restaurant. No one forces the French public to enter the golden arches, but Bové's success with the media spoke to the cultural ambivalence toward things American. As Iran's president complained in 1999, "The new world order and globalization that certain powers are trying to make us accept, in which the culture of the entire world is ignored, looks like a kind of neocolonialism."

Several dimensions of globalization are indeed dominated today by activities based in Wall Street, Silicon Valley, and Hollywood. However, the intercontinental spread of Christianity preceded by many centuries Hollywood's discovery of how to market films about the Bible. And the global spread of Islam, continuing to this day, is not "made in USA." The English language, which is spoken by about 5 percent of the world's people, was originally spread by Britain, not the United States. Ties between Japan and its Latin American diaspora have nothing to do with the United States, nor do ties between French-, Spanish-, and Portuguese-speaking countries, respectively. Nor does the contemporary spread of AIDS in Africa and Asia. Nor European banks lending to emerging markets in Asia and Latin America. The most popular sports team in the

In 1950, Time *magazine commissioned this painting depicting the global spread of Coca-Cola. Its caption —* "WORLD & FRIEND: *Love that piaster, that lira, that tickey, and that American way of life" — merges corporate profit making with confident promotion of an American lifestyle in the booming years after World War II. (Getty Images.)*

Reaction to American-style globalization was not always positive. As American soft drink sales abroad soared, resentment against "Coca-colonization" arose among those who feared the loss of national autonomy and local customs. In 1950, while the French debated approving Coca-Cola for importation, this cartoon depicted the American beverage as a seductress luring France away from his legitimate Beaujolais wife. (Cartoonists & Writers Syndicate.)

world is not American: it is Manchester United [a British professional soccer club], with two hundred fan clubs in twenty-four countries. Three of the leading "American" music labels have British, German, and Japanese owners. Some of the most popular video games come from Japan and Britain. The rise of reality programming, which has enlivened or debased the standards of television entertainment in recent years, spread from Europe to the United States, not vice versa.

As British sociologist Anthony Giddens observes, "Globalization is not just the dominance of the West over the rest; it affects the United States as it does other countries." . . . Globalization is not intrinsically American, even if much of its current content is heavily influenced by what happens in the United States.

Several distinctive qualities of the United States make it uniquely adapted to serve as a center of globalization. American culture is produced by and geared toward a multiethnic society whose demographics are constantly altered by immigration. America has always had a syncretic culture, borrowing freely from a variety of traditions and continuously open to the rest of the world. And European concerns over American influence are not new. A number of books were published on the subject a century ago — for example, a British author, W. T. Stead, wrote *The Americanization of the World* in 1902. The United States is also a great laboratory for cultural experimentation, the largest marketplace to test whether a given film or song resonates with one subpopulation or another, or perhaps with people in general. Ideas flow into the United States freely and flow out with equal ease — often in commercialized form, backed by entrepreneurs drawing on deep pools of capital and talent. A Pizza Hut in Asia looks American, though the food, of course, is originally Italian. There seems to be an affinity between opportunities for globalization and these characteristics of American society.

American culture does not always flow into other societies unchanged, nor does it always have political effects. The ideas and information that enter global networks are "downloaded" in the context of national politics and local cultures, which act as selective filters and modifiers of what arrives. McDonald's menus are different in China, and American movies are dubbed in varying Chinese accents to reflect Chinese perceptions of the message being delivered. Political institutions are often more resistant to transnational transmission than popular culture. Although the Chinese students in Tiananmen Square in 1989 built a replica of the Statue of Liberty, China has emphatically not adopted American political institutions.

Globalization today is America-centric, in that much of the information revolution comes from the United States and a large part of the content of global information networks is currently created in the United States and enhances American "soft power." French culture minister Jack Lang warned that soft power "moved mostly in one direction because Americans were so closed-minded and provincial, if not grossly ignorant of other cultures." But Lang misses the openness of American society, which accepts and recycles culture from the rest of the world. Moreover, some U.S. practices are very attractive to other countries: honest regulation of drugs, as by the Food and Drug Administration (FDA); transparent securities laws and practices that limit fraudulent dealing, monitored by the Securities and Exchange Commission (SEC). U.S.-made standards are sometimes hard to avoid, as in the rules governing the Internet itself. But other U.S. standards and practices — from pounds and feet (rather than the metric system) to capital punishment and the right to bear arms — have encountered puzzlement or even outright hostility in other nations. Soft power is a reality, but it does not accrue to the United States in all areas of activity, nor is the United States the only country to possess it. Globalization is more than just Americanization.

THE NATURE OF THE BEAST

Globalization — worldwide networks of interdependence — does not imply universality. . . . [A]t the beginning of the twenty-first century almost one-half of the American population used the World Wide Web, compared to 0.01 percent of the population of South Asia. Most people in the world today do not have telephones; hundreds of millions of people live as peasants in remote villages with only slight connections to world markets or the global flow of ideas. Indeed, globalization is accompanied by increasing gaps, in many respects, between the rich and the poor. It does not imply either homogenization or equity.

Even among rich countries, there is a lot less globalization than meets the eye. A truly globalized world market would mean free flows of goods, people, and capital, and similar interest rates. In fact we have a long way to go. For example, even in the local NAFTA market, Toronto trades ten times as much with Vancouver as with Seattle, though the distance is the same and tariffs are minimal. Globalization has made national boundaries more porous but not irrelevant. Nor does globalization mean the creation of a universal community. In social terms, contacts among people with different religious beliefs and other deeply held values have often led to conflict: witness the great crusades of medieval times or the current notion of the United States as "the Great Satan," held by some Islamic fundamentalists. Clearly, in social as well as economic terms, homogenization does not follow necessarily from globalization.

Globalization has a number of dimensions, though all too often economists write as if it and the world economy were one and the same. But other forms of globalization have significant effects on our day-to-day lives. The oldest form of globalization is environmental interdependence. For example, the first smallpox epidemic is recorded in Egypt in 1350 B.C. The disease reached China in A.D. 49, Europe after 700, the Americas in 1520, and Australia in 1789. The plague or black death originated in Asia, but its spread killed a quarter to a third of the population of Europe in the fourteenth century. Europeans carried diseases to the Americas in the fifteenth and sixteenth centuries that destroyed up to 95 percent of the indigenous population. Since 1973, thirty previously unknown infectious diseases have emerged, and other familiar diseases have spread geographically in new drug-resistant forms. The spread of foreign species of flora and fauna to new areas has wiped out native species, and efforts to control them may cost several hundred billion dollars a year. On the other hand, not all effects of environmental globalization are adverse. For instance, nutrition and cuisine in both Europe and Asia benefited from the importation of such New World crops as potatoes, corn, and tomatoes, and the green revolution agricultural technology of the past few decades has helped poor farmers throughout the world.

Global climate change will affect not only Americans but the lives of people everywhere. Thousands of scientists from over a hundred countries recently reported that there is new and strong evidence that most of the warming observed over the last fifty years is attributable to human activities, and average global temperatures in the twenty-first century are projected to increase between 2.5 and 10 degrees Fahrenheit. The result could be increasingly severe variations in climate, with too much water in some regions and not enough in others. The effects in North America will include stronger storms, floods, droughts, and landslides. Rising temperatures have lengthened the freeze-free season in many regions and cut snow cover since the 1960s by 10 percent. The rate at which the sea level rose in the last century was ten times faster than the average rate over the last three millennia. . . . It does not matter whether carbon dioxide is placed in the atmosphere from China or the United States; it affects global warming in the same way. And the impact on American policy was clear in the reactions of other countries in the early days of George W. Bush's administration. After foreign protests and a National Academy of Sciences report, President Bush had to reverse his early position that there was inadequate evidence of human effects on global warming.

Military globalization consists of networks of interdependence in which force, or the threat of force, is employed. The world wars of the twentieth century are a case in point. During the Cold War, the global strategic interdependence between the United States and the Soviet Union was acute and well recognized. Not only did it produce world-straddling alliances, but either side could have used intercontinental missiles to destroy the other within the space of thirty minutes. Such interdependence was distinctive not because it was totally new, but because the scale and speed of the potential conflict were so enormous. Today, terrorist networks constitute a new form of military globalization.

Social globalization is the spread of peoples, cultures, images, and ideas. Migration is a concrete example. In the nineteenth century, some eighty million people crossed oceans to new homes — far more than in the twentieth century. But ideas are an equally important aspect of social globalization. Four great religions of the world — Buddhism, Judaism, Christianity, and Islam — have spread across great distances over the last two millennia, as has the scientific method and worldview over the past few centuries. Political globalization (a part of social globalization) is manifest in the spread of constitutional arrangements, the increase in the number of countries that have become democratic, and the development of international rules and institutions. Those who think it is meaningless to speak of an international community ignore the importance of the global spread of political ideas such as the antislavery movement in the nineteenth century, anticolonialism after World War II, and the environmental and feminist movements today.

Changes in the various dimensions of globalization can move in opposite directions at the same time. Economic globalization fell dramatically between 1914 and 1945, while military globalization increased to new heights during the two world wars, as did many aspects of social globalization. (War disrupts existing societies and spreads new ideas.) So did globalization increase or decrease between 1914 and 1945? The economic deglobalization that characterized the first half of the twentieth century was so deep that the world economy did not reach the 1914 levels of international trade and investment again until the 1970s. This was in part a reflection of the enormous disruption of World War I, but there was another problem as well. The industrial world had not come to terms with the inequalities created by rapid economic globalization. Markets outran politics in Europe, and the great political movements of communism and fascism stemmed in part from popular reactions to the inequalities that accompanied laissez-faire world markets.

Is such economic deglobalization and attendant political disruption likely in the years to come? It's possible, but less likely than it was a century ago. For one thing, after 1945 the creation of the welfare state put a safety net under poor people in most developed countries, which acted as a safety valve that made open economies and economic globalization more acceptable. There is a positive correlation between the strength of the welfare state and the openness of economies. Globalization is not destroying (as opposed to constraining) the welfare state in Europe and the postmodern societies. While political reactions to economic globalization have been growing in postindustrial societies, they are not like the mass movements that overturned the political systems in Europe in the first half of the twentieth century. At the same time, international inequality has increased in some regions, including countries such as China. In much of the less developed world, the absence of safety nets could become a cause of political reaction against economic globalization. International protest movements that include American citizens and organizations have increased and, as we shall see below, are raising difficult policy questions.

In short, globalization is the result of both technological progress and government policies that have reduced barriers to international exchange. The United States has been a major instigator and beneficiary of the contemporary phase of globalization, but we cannot control it. Moreover, if protests and government policies were to curtail the beneficial economic dimensions of globalization, we would still be left with the detrimental effects of military and environmental globalization. Globalization is a mixed blessing, but like it or not, it creates new challenges for American foreign policy.

TWENTY-FIRST-CENTURY GLOBALIZATION: WHAT'S NEW?

While globalization has been going on for centuries, its contemporary form has distinct characteristics. In a phrase, it is "thicker and quicker." Globalization today is different from how it was in the nineteenth century, when European imperialism provided much of its political structure, and higher transport and communications costs meant fewer people were involved directly with people and ideas from other cultures. But many of the most important differences are closely related to the information revolution. As Thomas Friedman argues, contemporary globalization goes "farther, faster, cheaper and deeper."

Economists use the term "network effects" to refer to situations where a product becomes more valuable once many other people also use it. . . . [O]ne telephone is useless, but its value increases as the network grows. This is why the Internet is causing such rapid change. A knowledge-based economy generates "powerful spillover effects, often spreading like fire and triggering further innovation and setting off chain reactions of new inventions. . . ." Moreover, as interdependence has become thicker and quicker, the relationships among different networks have become more important. There are more interconnections among the networks. As a result, system effects — where small perturbations in one area can spread throughout a whole system — become more important.

Financial markets are a good example of system effects. As mentioned above, the 1997 Asian financial crisis affected markets on several continents. The relative magnitude of foreign investment in 1997 was not unprecedented. The net outflow of capital from Britain in the four decades before 1914 averaged 5 percent of its gross domestic product, compared to 2 to 3 percent for rich countries today. The fact that the financial crisis of 1997 was global in scale also had precursors: Black Monday on Wall Street in 1929 and the collapse of Austria's Credit Anstalt bank in 1930 triggered a worldwide financial crisis and global depression.

But today's gross financial flows are much larger. Daily foreign exchange flows increased from $15 billion in 1973 to $1.5 trillion by 1995, and the 1997 crisis was sparked by a currency collapse in a small emerging market economy, not by Wall Street. Further, the 1997 crisis caught most economists, governments, and international financial institutions by surprise, and complex new financial instruments made it difficult to understand. In December 1998 Federal Reserve Board chairman Alan Greenspan said: "I have learned more about how this new international financial system works in the last twelve months than in the previous twenty years." Sheer magnitude, complexity, and speed distinguish contemporary economic globalization from earlier periods and increase the challenges it presents to American foreign policy.

Military globalization also became more complex. The end of the Cold War brought military deglobalization — that is, distant disputes between the superpowers became less relevant to the balance of power. But the increase in social globalization over the past several decades had the opposite effect and introduced new dimensions of military globalism: humanitarian intervention and terrorism. Humanitarian concerns interacting with global communications led to pressure for military interventions in places such as Somalia, Bosnia, and Kosovo. And fundamentalist reactions to modern culture interacted with technology to create new options for terrorism and for asymmetrical warfare. . . .

As American officials fashion foreign policies, they encounter the increasing thickness of globalism — the density of the networks of interdependence — which means that the effects of events in one geographical area or in the economic or ecological dimension can have profound effects in other geographical areas or on the military or social dimension. These international networks are increasingly complex, and their effects are therefore increasingly unpredictable. . . .

Quickness also adds to uncertainty and the difficulties of shaping policy responses. As mentioned at the outset, modern globalization operates at a much more rapid pace than its earlier forms. Smallpox took nearly three millennia to conquer all inhabited continents, finally reaching Australia in 1775. AIDS took little more than three decades to spread from Africa all around the world. And to switch to a metaphorical virus, in 2000 the Love Bug computer virus needed only three days to straddle the globe. From three millennia to three decades to three days: that is the measure of the quickening of globalization. . . .

Direct public participation in global affairs has also increased in rich countries. Ordinary people invest in foreign mutual funds, gamble on offshore Internet sites, travel, and sample exotic cuisine that used to be the preserve of the rich. Friedman termed this change the "democratization" of technology, finance, and information, because diminished costs have made what previously were luxuries available to a much broader range of society. *Democratization* is probably the wrong word, however, since in markets, money votes, and people start out with unequal stakes. There is no equality, for example, in capital markets, despite the new financial instruments that permit more people to participate. A million dollars or more is often the entry price for hedge fund investors. *Pluralization* might be more accurate, suggesting the vast increase in the number and variety of participants in global networks. In 1914, according to John Maynard Keynes, "the inhabitant of London could order by telephone, sipping his morning tea in bed, the various products of the whole earth, in such quantity as he might see fit, and reasonably expect their early delivery upon his doorstep." But Keynes's Englishman had to be wealthy to be a global consumer. Today virtually any American can do the same thing. Supermarkets and Internet retailers extend that capacity to the vast majority of the people in postindustrial societies. . . .

This vast expansion of transnational channels of contact at multicontinental distances, generated by the media and a profusion of nongovernmental organizations, means that more issues are up for grabs internationally, including regulations and practices (ranging from pharmaceutical testing to accounting and product standards to banking regulation) that were formerly regarded as the prerogatives of national governments. Large areas of the governance of transnational life are being handled by private actors, whether it be the creation of the code that governs the Internet or the establishment of safety standards in the chemical industry. . . .

What the information revolution has added to contemporary globalization is a quickness and thickness in the network of interconnections that make them more complex. But such "thick globalism" is not uniform: it varies by region and locality, and by issue. As we shape our foreign policy for this new century, we will have to respond to issues that involve greater complexity, more uncertainty, shorter response times, broader participation by groups and individuals, and an uneven shrinkage of distance. The world is more upon us, but in terms of our policy responses, one size will not fit all.

GLOBALIZATION AND AMERICAN POWER

With the end of the Cold War, the United States became more powerful than any state in recent history. Globalization contributed to that position, but it may not continue to do so throughout the century. Today globalization reinforces American power; over time it may dilute that power. Globalization is the child of both technology and policy. American policy deliberately promoted norms and institutions such as GATT, the World Bank, and the IMF that created an open international economic system after 1945. For forty-five years, the extent of economic globalization was limited by the autarkic policies of the communist governments. The end of the Cold War reduced such barriers, and American economic and soft power benefited both from the related ascendance of market ideology and the reduction of protectionism.

The United States plays a central role in all dimensions of contemporary globalization. Globalization at its core refers to worldwide networks of interdependence. A network is simply a series of connections of points in a system, but networks can take a surprising number of shapes and architectures. An airline hub and spokes, a spiderweb, an electricity grid, a metropolitan bus system, and the Internet are all networks, though they vary in terms of centralization and complexity of connections. Theorists of networks argue that under most conditions, centrality in networks conveys power — that is, the hub controls the spokes. Some see globalism as a network with an American hub and spokes reaching out to the rest of the world. There is some truth in this picture, as the United States is central to all four forms of globalization: economic (the United States has the largest capital market), military (it is the only country with global reach), social (it is the heart of pop culture), and environmental (the United States is the biggest polluter, and its political support is necessary for effective action on environmental issues). As argued above, the United States has played a central role in the current phase of globalization for a variety of reasons, including its syncretic culture, market size, the effectiveness of some of its institutions, and its military force. And this centrality has in turn benefited American hard and soft power. In this view, being the hub conveys hegemony.

Those who advocate a hegemonic [dominating] or unilateralist foreign policy are attracted to this image of global networks. Yet there are at least four reasons it would be a mistake to envisage contemporary networks of globalism simply in terms of the hub and spokes of an American empire that creates dependency for smaller countries. This metaphor is useful as one perspective on globalization, but it does not provide the whole picture.

First, the architecture of networks of interdependence varies according to the different dimensions of globalization. The hub-and-spokes metaphor fits military globalism more closely than economic, environmental, or social globalism because American dominance is so much greater in that domain. Even in the military area, most states are more concerned about threats from neighbors than from the United States, a fact that leads many to call in American global power to redress local balances. . . . That is, the hub-and-spokes metaphor fits power relations better than it portrays threat relations, and . . . balancing behavior is heavily influenced by perceptions of threat. If instead of the role of welcome balancer, the United States came to be seen as a threat, it would lose the influence that comes from providing military protection to balance others. At the same time, in economic networks a hub-and-spokes image is inaccurate. In trade, for example, Europe and Japan are significant alternative nodes in the global network. Environmental globalization — the future of endangered species in Africa or the Amazonian rain forest in Brazil — is also less centered around the United States. And where the United States is viewed as a major ecological threat, as in production of carbon dioxide, it is less welcome, and there is often resistance to American policies.

Second, the hub-and-spokes image may mislead us about . . . two-way vulnerability. Even militarily, the ability of the United States to strike any place in the world does not make it invulnerable, as we learned at high cost on September 11, 2001. Other states and groups and even individuals can employ unconventional uses of force or, in the long term, develop weapons of mass destruction with delivery systems that would enable them to threaten the United States. Terrorism is a real threat, and nuclear or mass biological attacks would be more lethal than hijacked aircraft. . . . [G]lobal economic and social transactions are making it increasingly difficult to control our borders. When we open ourselves to economic flows, we simultaneously open ourselves to a new type of military danger. And while the United States has the largest economy, it is both sensitive and potentially vulnerable to the spread of contagions in global capital markets, as we discovered in the 1997 "Asian" financial crisis. In the social dimension, the United States may export more popular culture than any other country, but it also imports more ideas and immigrants than most countries. Managing immigration turns out to be an extremely sensitive and important aspect of the response to globalism. Finally, the United States is environmentally sensitive and vulnerable to actions abroad that it cannot control. Even if the United States took costly measures to reduce emissions of carbon dioxide at home, it would still be vulnerable to climate change induced by coal-fired power plants in China.

A third problem with the simple hub-and-spokes dependency image that is popular with the hegemonists is that it fails to identify other important connections and nodes in global networks. New York is important in the flows of capital to emerging markets, but so are London, Frankfurt, and Tokyo. In terms of social and political globalization, Paris is more important to Gabon than Washington is; Moscow is more important in Central Asia. Our influence is often limited in such situations. The Maldive Islands, only a few feet above sea level in the Indian Ocean, are particularly sensitive to the potential effects of producing carbon dioxide in the rest of the world. They are also completely vulnerable, since their sensitivity has to do with geography, not policy. At some time in the future, China will become more relevant to the Maldives than the United States is, because they will eventually outstrip us in the production of greenhouse gases. For many countries, we will not be the center of the world.

Finally, as the prior example suggests, the hub-and-spokes model may blind us to changes that are taking place in the architecture of the global networks. Network theorists argue that central players gain power most when there are structural holes — gaps in communications — between other participants. When the spokes cannot communicate with each other without going through the hub, the central position of the hub provides power. When the spokes can communicate and coordinate directly with each other, the hub becomes less powerful. The growth of the Internet provides these inexpensive alternative connections that fill the gaps.

As the architecture of global networks evolves from a hub-and-spokes model to a widely distributed form like that of the Internet, the structural holes shrink and the structural power of the central state is reduced. It is true, for now, that Americans are central to the Internet; at the beginning of the twenty-first century, they comprise more than half of all Internet users. But by 2003, projections suggest, the United States will have 180 million Internet users, and there will be 240 million abroad. This will be even more pronounced two decades hence, as Internet usage continues to spread. English is the most prevalent language on the Internet today, but by 2010, Chinese Internet users are likely to outnumber American users. The fact that Chinese web sites will be read primarily by ethnic Chinese nationals and expatriates will not dethrone English as the web's lingua franca [common language], but it will increase Chinese power in Asia by allowing Beijing "to shape a Chinese political culture that stretches well beyond its physical boundaries." And China will not be alone. With the inevitable spread of technological capabilities, more-distributed network architectures will evolve. At some time in the future, when there are a billion Internet users in Asia and 250 million in the United States, more web sites, capital, entrepreneurs, and advertisers will be attracted to the Asian market.

The United States now seems to bestride the world like a colossus, to use *The Economist*'s phrase. Looking more closely, we see that American dominance varies across realms and that many relationships of interdependence go both ways. Large states such as the United States — or, to a lesser extent, China — have more freedom than do small states, but they are rarely exempt from the effects of globalization. And states are not alone. . . . [O]rganizations, groups, and even individuals are becoming players. For both better and worse, technology is putting capabilities within the reach of individuals that were solely the preserve of government in the past. Falling costs are increasing the thickness and complexity of global networks of interdependence. The United States promotes and benefits from economic globalization. But over the longer term, we can expect globalization itself to spread technological and economic capabilities and thus reduce the extent of American dominance.

GLOBALIZATION AND LOCAL CULTURES

Local culture and local politics also set significant limits on the extent to which globalization enhances American power. Contrary to conventional wisdom, globalization is not homogenizing the cultures of the world.

Although they are related, globalization and modernization are not the same. People sometimes attribute changes to globalization that are caused in large part simply by modernization. The modernity of the industrial revolution transformed British society and culture in the nineteenth century. The global spread of industrialization and the development of alternative centers of industrial power eventually undercut Britain's relative position. And while the modernity of the new industrial centers altered their local cultures so that in some ways they looked more like Britain than before, the cause was modernization, not Anglicization. Moreover, while modernity produced some common traits such as urbanization and factories, the residual local cultures were by no means erased. Convergence toward similar institutions to deal with similar problems is not surprising, but it does not lead to homogeneity. There were some similarities in the industrial societies of Britain, Germany, America, and Japan in the first half of the twentieth century, but there were also important differences. When China, India, and Brazil complete their current process of industrialization, we should not expect them to be replicas of Japan, Germany, or the United States.

In the same vein, though the United States is widely perceived as being at the forefront of the information revolution, and though the information revolution results in many similarities in social and cultural habits (such as television viewing or Internet use), it is incorrect to attribute those similarities to Americanization. Correlation is not causation. If one imagines a thought experiment in which a country introduces computers and communications at a rapid rate in a world in which the United States did not exist, one would expect major social and cultural changes to occur from the modernization. . . . Of course, since the United States exists and is at the forefront of the information revolution, there is a current degree of Americanization, but it is likely to diminish over the course of the century as technology spreads and local cultures modernize in their own ways.

Evidence of historical proof that globalization does not necessarily mean homogenization can be seen in the case of Japan, a country that deliberately isolated itself from an earlier wave of globalization carried by seventeenth-century European seafarers. In the middle of the nineteenth century it became the first Asian country to embrace globalization and to borrow successfully from the world without losing its uniqueness. During the Meiji Restoration Japan searched broadly for tools and innovations that would allow it to become a major power rather than a victim of Western imperialism. It sent young people to the West for education. Its delegations scoured the world for ideas in science, technology, and industry. In the political realm, Meiji reformers were well aware of Anglo-American ideas and institutions but deliberately turned to German models because they were deemed more suitable to a country with an emperor.

The lesson that Japan has to teach the rest of the world is not simply that an Asian country can compete in military and economic power, but rather that after a century and a half of globalization, it is possible to adapt while preserving a unique culture. Of course, there are American influences in contemporary Japan (and Japanese influences such as Pokémon in the United States). Thousands of Japanese youth are co-opting the music, dress, and style of urban black America. But some of the groups dress up like samurai warriors onstage. As one claims, "We're trying to make a whole new culture and mix the music." One can applaud or deplore or simply be amused by any particular cultural transfers, but one should not doubt the persistence of Japan's cultural uniqueness. . . .

. . . [T]here is some evidence that globalization and the information revolution may reinforce rather than reduce cultural diversity. In one British view, "globalization is the reason for the revival of local culture in different parts of the world. . . . Globalization not only pulls upwards, but also pushes downwards, creating new pressures for local autonomy." Some French commentators express fear that in a world of global Internet marketing, there will no longer be room for a culture that cherishes some 250 different types of cheese. But on the contrary, the Internet allows dispersed customers to come together in a way that encourages niche markets, including many sites dedicated only to cheese. The information revolution also allows people to establish a more diverse set of political communities. The use of the Welsh language in Britain and Gaelic in Ireland is greater today than fifty years ago. Britain, Belgium, and Spain, among others in Europe, have devolved more power to local regions. The global information age may strengthen rather than weaken many local cultures.

As technology spreads, less powerful actors become empowered. Terrorism is the recent dramatic example, but consider also the relations between transnational corporations and poor countries. In the early stages, the multinational company, with its access to the global resources of finance, technology, and markets, holds all the high cards and gets the best of the bargain with the poor country. With time, as the poor country develops skilled personnel, learns new technologies, and opens its own channels to global finance and markets, it successfully renegotiates the bargain and captures more of the benefits. When the multinational oil companies first went into Saudi Arabia, they claimed the lion's share of the gains from the oil; today the Saudis do. Of course, there has been some change in Saudi culture as engineers and financiers have been trained abroad, incomes have risen, and some degree of urbanization has occurred, but Saudi culture today certainly does not look like that of the United States. . . .

Economic and social globalization are not producing cultural homogeneity. The rest of the world will not someday look just like the United States. American culture is very prominent at this stage in global history, and it contributes to American soft power in many, but not all, areas. At the same time, immigrants as well as ideas and events outside our borders are changing our own culture, and that adds to our appeal. We have an interest in preserving that soft power. We should use it now to build a world congenial to our basic values in preparation for a time in the future when we may be less influential. As globalization spreads technical capabilities and information technology allows broader participation in global communications, American economic and cultural preponderance may diminish over the course of the century. This in turn has mixed results for American soft power. A little less dominance may mean a little less anxiety about Americanization, fewer complaints about American arrogance, and a little less intensity in the anti-American backlash. We may have less control in the future, but we may find ourselves living in a world somewhat more congenial to our basic values of democracy, free markets, and human rights. In any case, the political reactions to globalization will be far more diverse than a unified reaction against American cultural hegemony.

Political Reactions to Globalization

. . . Domestic institutions channel responses to change. Some countries imitate success, as exemplified by democratizing capitalist societies from South Korea to Eastern Europe. Some accommodate in distinctive and ingenious ways: for instance, small European states such as the Netherlands or Scandinavia have maintained relatively large governments and emphasized compensation for disadvantaged sectors, while the Anglo-American industrialized countries have, in general, emphasized markets, competition, and deregulation. Capitalism is far from monolithic, with significant differences between Europe, Japan, and the United States. There is more than one way to respond to global markets and to run a capitalist economy.

In other societies such as Iran, Afghanistan, and Sudan, conservative groups resist globalization strongly, even violently. Reactions to globalization help stimulate fundamentalism. In some ways, the Al Qaeda terrorists represent a civil war within Islam, which seeks to transform into a global clash of civilization. Global forces can reformulate ethnic and political identities in profound and often unanticipated ways. In Bosnia, political entrepreneurs appealed to traditional identities of people in rural areas in order to overwhelm and dissolve the cosmopolitan identities that had begun to develop in the cities with devastating results. And Iran has seen struggles between Islamic fundamentalists and their more liberal opponents — who are also Islamic but more sympathetic to Western ideas.

As mentioned earlier, rising inequality was a major cause of the political reactions that halted an earlier wave of economic globalization early in the twentieth century. The recent period of globalization, like the half century before World War I, has also been associated with increasing inequality among and within some countries. The ratio of incomes of the 20 percent of people in the world living in the richest countries to those of the 20 percent living in the poorest countries increased from 30:1 in 1960 to 74:1 in 1997. By comparison, it increased between 1870 and 1913 from 7:1 to 11:1. . . . As increasing flows of information make people more aware of inequality, it is not surprising that some choose to protest.

Whatever the facts of inequality, there is even less clarity concerning its causation or the most effective remedies to it. In part, increases in inequality by country are a straightforward result of rapid economic growth in some but not all parts of the world. They demonstrate that movement out of poverty is possible, although often hindered by political factors as well as resource constraints. Most of the poorest countries in the world — whether in Africa or the Middle East — have suffered from misrule, corruption, and inept macroeconomic policies. The weakness of their political systems can be blamed in part on colonialism and nineteenth-century globalization, but the sources of their recent poor performance are more complex. Several countries in East Asia that were equally poor in the 1950s used networks of globalization to greatly increase their wealth and status in the world economy. It is difficult to find any countries that have prospered while closing themselves off from globalization, but openness alone is not sufficient to overcome inequality.

Equally striking is the uneven distribution of the benefits of globalization among individuals within and across countries. For instance, in Brazil in 1995, the richest tenth of the population received almost half of the national income, and the richest fifth had 64 percent, while the poorest fifth had only 2.5 percent and the poorest tenth less than 1 percent. In the United States, the richest tenth received 28 percent of income, and the richest fifth had 45 percent, while the poorest fifth had almost 5 percent and the poorest tenth 1.5 percent. Across countries, inequalities are even more dramatic: the richest three billionaires in the world in 1998 had combined assets greater than the combined incomes of the six hundred million people in the world's least developed countries.

Consider also China, a poor country that has been growing very fast since its leaders decided to open their economy in the 1980s, thus exposing their society to the forces of globalization. China's "human development index" as calculated by the United

Nations — reflecting life expectancy, educational attainment, and GDP per capita — showed dramatic gains. Hundreds of millions of Chinese were made better off by market reforms and globalization, but hundreds of millions of others, particularly in the western parts of the country, saw little or no gain. And some will be made worse off, particularly as China exposes inefficient state-owned enterprises to international composition under the terms of its accession to the World Trade Organization (WTO). How China handles the resulting politics of inequality will be a key question in its future.

Will this inequality create problems for American foreign policy? In the late nineteenth century, inequality rose in rich countries and fell in poor countries; up to half of the rise in inequality could be attributed to the effects of globalization. Many of those changes were due to mass migration, which explained about 70 percent of the real wage convergence in the late nineteenth century. The political consequences of these shifts in inequality are complex, but the historian Karl Polanyi argued powerfully in his classic study *The Great Transformation* that the market forces unleashed by the industrial revolution and globalization in the nineteenth century produced not only great economic gains but also great social disruptions and political reactions. There is no *automatic* relationship between inequality and political reaction, but the former can give rise to the latter. Particularly when inequality is combined with instability, such as financial crises and recessions that throw people out of work, such reactions could eventually lead to restrictions on economic globalization.

The recent surge in protests against globalization is, in part, a reaction to the changes produced by economic integration. . . . Some protesters wanted more international regulation that would intrude on national sovereignty; others wanted less infringement of sovereignty. But whatever the incoherence of the coalitions, they were able to capture global attention from media and governments. Their concerns about corporate domination of "neoliberal" [free-market] globalization, about growing inequality, about cultural homogenization, and about absence of democratic accountability managed to touch responsive chords, if not to ignite a mass movement. To the extent that the United States wants to see economic globalization continue, it will have to think more clearly about the responses to such charges and about the governance of globalism. . . .

The Governance of Globalism

If laissez-faire economics has built-in instability, and networks of interdependence are stretching beyond the boundaries of the nation-state, how is globalism to be governed? A world government is not the answer. Some writers draw an analogy from American history, asking today's nation-states to join together as the thirteen colonies did. Just as the development of a national economy in the late nineteenth century led to the growth of federal government power in Washington, so the development of a global economy will require federal power at the global level. Some see the United Nations as the incipient core. But the American analogy is misleading. The thirteen original colonies shared far more in English language and culture than the more than two hundred nations of the world share today, and even the Americans did not avoid a bloody civil war. By the time a continental economy developed, the framework of the American federation was firmly in place. Rather than thinking of a hierarchical world government, we should think of networks of governance crisscrossing and coexisting with a world divided formally into sovereign states.

Many countries' first response to global forces is to take internal action to decrease their vulnerability to outside influences — they resort to protectionism when they can do so at reasonable cost. Sometimes they are limited by costly retaliation, as in recent trade cases between the United States and the European Union. In agriculture and textiles, however, the rich countries' protective responses impose costs on poor countries who are ill placed to retaliate. On the other hand, some unilateral responses can be positive. In the 1980s, United States firms reacted to Japanese and European competition in automobiles by implementing internal changes that increased their efficiency. In some instances, such as general accounting procedures or transparent regulation of security markets, companies and governments unilaterally adopted external standards to enhance their access to capital. Competition in standards need not lead to a race to the bottom, as countries may unilaterally decide to race to the top. For example, Israel decided to adopt the European Union's pesticide standards, and a number of Latin American countries have espoused U.S. standards.

These examples reinforce a relatively obvious point: for now, the key institution for global governance is going to remain the nation-state. In the face of globalization, however, even countries as strong as the United States will find that unilateral measures will often be insufficient, will fail, or will generate reactions. Countries facing increased globalization will become, therefore, increasingly willing to sacrifice some of their own legal freedom of action in order to constrain, and make more predictable, others' actions toward themselves. They will find, like Molière's character who discovered that he had been speaking prose all his life, that the world has long had cooperative institutions for managing common affairs. Hundreds of organizations and legal regimes exist to manage the global dimensions of trade, telecommunications, civil aviation, health, environment, meteorology, and many other issues.

To achieve what they want, most countries, including the United States, find that they have to coordinate their activities. Unilateral action simply cannot produce the right results on what are inherently multilateral issues. Cooperation may take the form of bilateral and multilateral treaties, informal agreements among bureaucracies, and delegation to formal intergovernmental institutions. Regulation of global flows will often grow by layers of accretion rather than by a single treaty and will long remain imperfect. Some cases are easier than others. For example, cooperation on prosecution of child pornography on the Internet is proving easier than regulation of hate mail, as there are more shared norms in the former case than in the latter.

Finally, some attempts at governance will not involve states as coherent units. . . . In the public sector, different components of governments have informal contact. Rare is the embassy of a large democratic country today in which foreign-service personnel form a majority of those stationed abroad. Instead, the majority of officers in American embassies come from agencies such as agriculture, transportation, commerce, energy, NASA, defense, intelligence, and the FBI.

On the private side, transnational corporations and offshore fund managers are playing a larger-than-ever role in creating rules and standards. Their practices often create de facto governance. International commercial arbitration is basically a private justice system and credit rating agencies are private gate-keeping systems. They have emerged as important governance mechanisms whose authority is not centered in the state. In the nonprofit sector . . . there has been an extraordinary growth of organizations — still largely Western, but increasingly transnational. . . . [T]hese organizations and the multiple channels of access across borders are able to put increasing leverage on states and intergovernmental organizations as well as transnational corporations.

The soft power of these organizations is frequently seen in the mobilization of shame to impose costs on national or corporate reputations. Transnational drug companies gave up lawsuits in South Africa over infringement of their patents on AIDS drugs because, in the words of the *Financial Times,* "demands for greater social responsibility from business are getting louder, better organised, and more popular. They cannot be ignored. . . ." Similar campaigns of naming and shaming have altered the investment and employment patterns of companies like Mattel and Nike in the toy and footwear industries. Some transnational corporations such as Shell have set up large staffs just to deal with NGOs [nongovernmental organizations]. Jean-François Rischard of the World Bank, for instance, advocates "global issues networks" that would issue ratings that measure how well countries and private businesses are doing in meeting norms on the environment and other issues that affect the welfare of the planet. The process would be quick and nonbureaucratic, and the sanctions would be through imposing damage on reputations. . . .

How should we react to these changes? Our democratic theory has not caught up with global practice. Financial crises, climate change, migration, terrorism, and drug smuggling ignore borders but profoundly affect American citizens' lives. British sociologist Anthony Giddens believes that because they escape control by sovereign democratic processes, they are one of the main reasons for "the declining appeal of democracy where it is best established." For some, such as undersecretary of state John Bolton, the solution is to strengthen U.S. democracy by pulling out of intrusive institutions and rejecting any constraints on sovereignty. But even the unilateralists and sovereigntists will find that international institutions are necessary because many of the issues raised by globalization are inherently multilateral. . . .

On balance, Americans have benefited from globalization. To the extent that we wish to continue to do so, we will need to deal with its discontents. This cannot be accomplished by resorting to slogans of sovereignty, unilateral policies, or drawing inward, as the unilateralists and sovereigntists suggest: "If we can't do it our way, then we just won't do it. But at least we the people, the American people, will remain masters of our ship." This prescription mistakes the abstractions of sovereignty for the realities of power. The result would be to undermine our soft power and America's ability to influence others' responses to globalization. Instead, the United States should use its current preeminence to help shape institutions that will benefit both Americans and the rest of the world as globalization evolves. . . .

. . . Under the influence of the information revolution and globalization, world politics is changing in a way that means Americans cannot achieve all their international goals acting alone. The United States lacks both the international and domestic prerequisites to resolve conflicts that are internal to other societies, and to monitor and control transnational transactions that threaten Americans at home. We must mobilize international coalitions to address shared threats and challenges. We will have to learn better how to share as well as lead. As a British observer has written, "The paradox of American power at the end of this millennium is that it is too great to be challenged by any other state, yet not great enough to solve problems such as global terrorism and nuclear proliferation. America needs the help and respect of other nations." We will be in trouble if we do not get it. . . .

QUESTIONS TO CONSIDER

1. How does Nye define globalization and chart its history? What levels or dimensions of globalization does he describe? To what extent would Nye agree with Niall Ferguson (Selection 23) that globalization prior to 1945 was a product of the British Empire? How does he think globalization since World War II differs from that of previous stages or eras?

2. Why does Nye call the idea that globalization equals Americanization "simplistic"? How has the United States been well situated to instigate and benefit from globalization? In what ways have other nations resisted or countered American cultural influence? Is Nye's analysis of the impact of American culture abroad consistent with Jeffrey Jackson's discussion of the reception of American jazz in 1920s France (Selection 14)?

3. To what extent, according to Nye, is today's globalization the product or reflection of American empire? Does the hub-and-spokes image of empire adequately describe the workings of globalization, or does Nye find a better metaphor? As globalization develops, will it increase or reduce American economic dominance? Why?

4. What impact will globalization have on the world's cultural diversity? Why, according to Nye, will the rest of the world "not . . . look just like the United States"? How will different national governments react to economic globalization? Why might globalization heighten economic inequality? What problems may increased economic instability and inequality raise for nations or for international organizations?

5. How, according to Nye, is globalization to be managed? Why does he believe that the U.S. federal-style government cannot be a model for a world government? What forms of international or "multilateral" cooperation does Nye propose instead? Why does Nye reject unilateralist or imperial responses by the United States? Would Niall Ferguson (Selection 23) agree?